CONTEMPORARY EDUCATION

Contemporary Education

A Comparative Study of National Systems

SECOND EDITION

JOHN FRANCIS CRAMER
Professor of Education,
Portland State College

GEORGE STEPHENSON BROWNE
Professor Emeritus of Education,
formerly Dean of the Faculty of Education,
University of Melbourne

Harcourt, Brace & World, Inc.

New York · Chicago · Burlingame

to

M. O. C.

S. M. B.

Contents

Part III

The Schools in Action:
The Operation of School Systems

Part IV

Educational Developments in Some Asian Countries

Preface

Teachers and school administrators have long been aware of the fact that they have much to learn from the practices of other lands. While problems appear to be much the same in other countries, the answers that are worked out in response to them often differ widely. Each country, of course, develops the type of educational system that will best meet its needs as it sees them. Because of differences in historical background, economic and social conditions, and points of view, no country could adopt the school system of any other. Nevertheless the struggles and successes of other school systems can teach educators much that will be helpful in the solution of their own problems.

It is the authors' hope, however, that this book will be read not only by teachers and school administrators but by all those interested in the problems of education. The study of the educational systems of other nations, and of their successes and failures, can point the way to a better understanding of one's own national system, its shortcomings and merits. Above all, the comparative study of education can bring the realization that educational dilemmas, wherever they occur, are not exclusively national. And as the study of these pages will reveal, no educational system is static. Taking into account the major changes and reforms attempted in several countries in the last ten years, this revised edition of a book published in 1956 attempts to bring the picture up to date. A disadvantage of any book on this subject is that educational statistics become out of date almost as soon as they appear in print. Education is constantly undergoing transformation, and while change does not necessarily mean progress, there can be no progress without change.

This book is divided into four parts. Part I introduces the subject by sketching some of the basic influences or background factors that determine the character of national systems of education. Part II, which will be of especial interest to school administrators, describes in detail the administration, control, and finance of school systems in seven major nations. Because of their interesting differences in administrative patterns, countries such as Australia and Canada, which seldom appear in similar texts, have been included. Part III describes the operation of the schools themselves, from preschool classes to universities and adult education, in the same seven nations. Part IV has been substantially changed for this edition. It draws attention to the school systems of three major Asian nations that are meeting some very special problems.

Many official departments and agencies have willingly supplied statistics and information on educational programs under their jurisdiction. Among these have been the Ministry of Education, London; the Scottish Education Department, Edinburgh; the Research Bureau of the International Cultural Relations Division of the Japanese Ministry of Education in Tokyo, and in particular Mr. Masaru Iwayama; also Professor Mamoru Oshiba of the Himeji University of Technology in Japan; the Ministry of Education, New Delhi; the Commonwealth Office of Education for Australia; the Australian Council for Educational Research; the Dominion Bureau of Statistics, Ottawa; and the Hochschule fur Internationale Padagogische Forschung, Frankfort on the Main.

Individuals who have been very helpful included, among others, M. Edouard Morot-Sir, Representative in the United States of French universities; S. M. S. Chari, First Secretary, Education, of the Indian Embassy; Sir Eric Ashby, Master of Clare College, Cambridge; Allen Gibb and Kenneth MacKirdy, for materials on Canadian education; Dr. K. T. Hu, Teachers College, Columbia University, and Professor K. T. Ley, Taiwan Normal University.

In acknowledging their gratitude and appreciation to all of these people, the authors accept full responsibility for all statements and conclusions within the book.

J. F. Cramer
G. S. Browne

Part I
Basic Factors

I

Influences Affecting the Character and Development of National Systems of Education

COMPARATIVE education must be much more than a descriptive catalogue of systems of education as they exist at present. It must try to discover why systems have developed along different lines, why some are progressive and others are inclined to lag behind, why some are dominated by restrictive political ideologies while others encourage freedom and variety within their framework.

To understand the school systems it is necessary to go behind the scenes and examine the social and political forces that are at work; for educational systems generally reflect the social and political philosophies of their countries, whether or not those philosophies are clearly stated.

Nor is there any sort of uniform pattern. Some systems are the expression of a long, slow evolution and can be understood only by a study of the history and traditions of the countries concerned. Others are the result of a sudden revolution and are then used by the revolutionary government to further the ideals of the new regime. Still others are imposed on, or suggested to, defeated nations with the idea of reestablishing these nations along lines acceptable to the victors. Disaster within a nation will sometimes bring about a vital educational revival, as in Prussia after Jena and in Denmark after the loss of Schleswig-Holstein.

Sometimes a sudden acceleration of social change within a nation will be reflected in changes in the educational system. Thus the Education Act of 1944 in England was one of a striking series of social reforms growing out of World War II. Recently, also, we have had the spectacle of young nations, with suddenly awakened national aspirations, seeking to develop systems of education along modern lines to combat illiteracy and to help achieve their national ambitions.

Educational systems are influenced by social and political forces, but the reader must be wary of assuming a correlation between types of educational administration and types of political systems. Table 1–1, which indicates some possible ways of organizing the control of education, illustrates this point. For example, columns 1 and 3 would seem to be the most suitable groups for democratic nations, yet we find France and Australia, both unmistakable democracies, listed in column 2, with an authoritarian type of centralized control over their educational systems. On the other hand, we find that Japan, which before World War II was a staunch member of the second grouping, has moved over into the first column as a result of political changes initiated by the Allied occupation; and it might be noted that the Argentine system, during the Peronista period in that country, was moving toward the second column. In the end, it is the spirit of an educational system that counts, rather than its form.

When I. L. Kandel completed his well-known pioneer study of comparative education, he described his task as "the discussion of the meaning of general education, elementary and secondary, in the light of the forces—political, social, and cultural—which determine the character of national systems of education. The problems and purposes of education have in general become somewhat similar in

TABLE 1–1
Some Types of Educational Control

1 *Strong local responsibility and decentralized control*	2 *Strong national or state control—centralization*	3 *Responsibility divided between national and local units*	4 *National control of policy, but decentralization of administrative details*
United States	France	England & Wales	U.S.S.R.
Canada	Irish Republic	Sweden	East Germany
Switzerland	Philippines	New Zealand	Argentina
Japan	Australian States	Denmark	Bulgaria
	West Germany	India	Communist China

most countries; the solutions are influenced by differences of tradition and culture peculiar to each." [1]

Kandel names the following countries as "the leading educational
laboratories of the world": England, France, Germany, Italy, Russia,
and the United States. He examines in detail the historical background and main features of each of the educational systems of
these six nations, with considerable emphasis on the forces of nationalism and national character as powerful influences in educational development.

Another author, Nicholas Hans, of the University of London,
makes a penetrating study of the educational factors and traditions
lying behind national systems of education, and illustrates these with
a brief but illuminating study of four countries—England, the United
States, France, and the U.S.S.R. Hans lists his factors as follows and
gives a chapter to each:

1. Natural factors: racial, linguistic, geographic, and economic
2. Religious factors: Catholic, Anglican, Puritan
3. Secular factors: humanism, socialism, nationalism, democracy [2]

Still another approach has been adopted in this chapter. The
authors feel that the major influences affecting the character of national systems of education today may be grouped under seven
headings:

1. Sense of national unity
2. General economic situation
3. Basic beliefs and traditions, including religious and cultural
   heritage
4. Status of progressive educational thought
5. Language problems
6. Political background: communism, fascism, democracy
7. Attitude toward international cooperation and understanding

It may be useful in this introductory chapter to examine these influences in some detail. Such an examination will also serve the purpose of introducing the student to some of the problems discussed
in the succeeding chapters. The student will undoubtedly discern
for himself, in the detailed country-by-country treatment in Parts II

[1] I. L. Kandel, *Comparative Education*, p. xi.
[2] Nicholas Hans, *Comparative Education* (London and New York), 1949.

and III, additional examples of the operation of the influences discussed here.

Sense of National Unity

MOST nations today are the result of admixtures of various ethnic groups, so that it is often a problem to secure national unity. Countries in which national unity is well developed recognize fewer problems in the organization of their educational systems than do those which contain strongly or bitterly opposed national groups. Sometimes the dominant group in the country will attempt to use education to enforce conformity upon the minority, and this attempt to reach a unified approach to educational problems will actually result in increasing the disunity inherent in the national situation.

Great Britain is a good example of a country whose educational system reflects a satisfactory solution to the problem of unity. The Celtic groups in Wales and Scotland live within her borders, but they live in harmony and cooperation with the English and consider themselves part of the national unit, even though the Welsh speak a different language. As a result, one educational system embraces England and Wales, to the satisfaction of both countries, and the Scottish system is closely akin. The 1944 Act applies to England and Wales and has its counterpart in the Scottish Education Act of 1945.

The United States has achieved great success in the assimilation of millions of foreign immigrants as loyal American citizens; the second generation of these have become almost aggressively nationalistic. The roll of an American military platoon or of a football team sometimes looks like a catalogue of widely differing European names, but they are all Americans. The strength of the educational system has contributed greatly to this Americanization. Moreover, although there are some 31,700 school districts in the United States, there is a sense of national educational purpose common to all.

Germany between 1870 and 1945 had developed an intense feeling of national unity and its educational system was closely linked to this attitude. Under the Nazis, feelings of nationalism reached a pitch of hysteria reflecting an almost pathological condition on the part of the people. In contrast with its former unity, Germany now presents the tragic spectacle of a nation divided into two bitterly opposed republics, each looking at the other with suspicion, and with two educational systems, each claiming to be a real expression of democracy.

Japan's rapid recovery after defeat in World War II was largely due to a well-developed sense of national unity. Before and during the war this took the form of a fanatical nationalism, inspired by the vision of Japan as the leader of East Asia and eventually of the world. After defeat and disillusionment, Japan listened to the Emperor's injunctions to follow the paths of democracy as directed by the occupying powers. Under American guidance the educational system was reorganized so effectively that it has persisted along democratic lines and will probably continue to do so. This could never have happened but for the feeling of the Japanese people that they would be able to continue as a unified nation with new hopes for the future.

France is an example of a self-contained nation with an intense pride in what she believes to be her cultural leadership of Western civilization. France was not completely successful in developing an educational program for her former colonies, perhaps because an attempt was made to extend French national unity to them with little regard for their own rising feelings of nationalism. A Western visitor reported seeing small black boys in an African colony school rise and repeat in chorus, "All our ancestors were Gauls." France attempted to make the colonies provinces of France and to confer on them the benefits of French culture, but in the North African states war and revolts were the result. The new national schools of these African states, however, still show a certain French influence.

In South Africa we find a situation where a white minority fears and oppresses the native majority and refuses it access to citizenship and education. This has resulted in dangerous hostility and hatred. The situation is further confused by the fact that the white minority is itself composed of two national groups, with a bilingual system of education and even of broadcasting. This is not the soil in which a progressive system of education can flourish.

New Zealand and Hawaii provide contrasts to this situation. New Zealand is proud of her Maoris, regarding them fully as New Zealanders and admitting them to equal educational and social privileges with the whites. There are Maori members of Parliament and a Maori bishop, and some years back the acting prime minister was half Maori. In Hawaii for many years the Hawaiians, Japanese, Chinese, Filipinos, and others have had the same opportunities as whites and have attended the same schools.

Fiji presents a problem of a different type. It is a British crown colony with a small nucleus of white inhabitants and a native population of 172,000 Fijians. The Fijians are a fine, intellectual Melanesian group; but they are now outnumbered in their small cluster of islands by 205,000 Indians, imported for work on the sugar plantations and in the mills, but now demanding a share in Fijian affairs. There are schools for Fijians, schools for Indians, and schools for whites; a unified school system seems difficult to attain.

In New Guinea another difficult situation appears. There is a native population of a little over a million, divided into small groups without any sense of national consciousness, broken up into hundreds of village communities, and speaking nearly a hundred different languages. The Australian government has launched a widespread system of schools, but the difficulties confronting the organizers of this system can be imagined.

The Soviet Union has apparently had considerable success with many of the national minorities within its vast expanse. The former division of Russian Turkestan affords an example. In czarist days these and other outlying provinces were oppressed and left in ignorance and superstition. After the Revolution the Soviet authorities set out to cultivate in the minorities a sense of national unity and loyalty to the Communist regime. This was accomplished partly by industrial drives and partly by encouraging local educational programs based on each group's own language and cultural background. In some cases there were only spoken languages, and alphabets had to be constructed. Russian was introduced as the general second language. The aim was to build up Communist republics, but there seems to be no doubt that great progress was made, both industrially and educationally. Provinces which in 1915 were very backward and had a high percentage of illiteracy now boast modern cities, a more prosperous economy, and less than 10 percent illiteracy. Apparently the improvement went hand in hand with an education program that inculcated, first of all, pride in the particular province or republic, and then pride in the whole Soviet structure. A sense of belonging or of national unity was deliberately cultivated.

General Economic Situation

THE ECONOMIC resources of a country affect greatly the level of educational opportunities that can be provided. It is obvious that a country which is compact, well populated, rich in natural resources, and which has good facilities for communication and transportation is in a position to spend generously on its educational system. Sparsely populated countries, largely agricultural in nature, find it much more difficult to provide the necessary financial support for a complete and highly developed program of education. Only a limited portion of any nation's total income can be expended on social and educational services, and poor countries find it difficult to support advanced school systems.

That a wealthy country will embark upon a progressive educational program is by no means certain. Many other factors can operate and interfere. When England was wealthy and powerful in the early part of the present century, there was an attitude of complacency about the "two-class" educational system; it was not until two world wars had crippled the economic position of the country that the famous Education Act of 1944 was produced. For a time England was hampered by lack of funds, but she retained her vision of educational achievement and, as her economy improved, began to translate the dream into practical accomplishment.

Japan represents a country where an intense mobilization during World War II impoverished the nation and left her educational system almost in ruins. But she recovered in a remarkably short period of time, aided by the United States, and produced a new plan of democratic education which retained many of the good features of the older system, but discarded the emphasis on militarism and authoritarianism. By 1964 her school buildings had been restored, and her school system ranked as one of the best and most liberal in the world.

It does not follow, however, that a country must be wealthy to have a good educational system. A great deal depends on the quality of the human material in the country concerned. The Netherlands has at present a sound and progressive system of education which gains the admiration of visiting educators. Yet, at the end of the war, 40 percent of the productive capacity of the country had been wiped out, several of its cities were in ruins, a tenth of the arable land had been destroyed by sea-flooding, and 60 percent of the railroads were gone, together with half of the merchant fleet. In addition, the Dutch faced a colonial revolt which lost them the great treasure house of Indonesia. But they were not dismayed: they built up their schools and their economic position side by side. The Dutch worked very hard,[3] and foreign capital flowed in to help them until today the country has been transformed into one of the most prosperous lands in Europe. The relevant point for this chapter is that even in their darkest hours the Dutch spent 20 percent of their national budget on schools and would consider no retrenchment.

There is another striking example. When in 1864 Denmark had Schleswig-Holstein torn from her and her general economic condition seemed desperate, the folk high school movement roused the nation. Denmark, in spite of poor soil and bad climate, became the "model dairy farm of Western Europe," and today is a contented and progressive country, which has earned the title "Kingdom of Reason." The folk high schools are still one of the highlights of educational achievement.

Australia presents a different aspect of the problem. Here we have a continent of about the same size as the United States but with only 11 million people within its borders. The task is to carry effective education to a widely scattered population, and thus the educational planning must be on a different basis from that in many other countries.

There are, of course, many countries where the economic position is so weak that any attempt at educational advancement, if it exists at all, has to be sponsored by some outside organization. The greatest achievement in this connection was UNESCO's program of Fundamental Education. It is a sobering thought for educators that UNESCO found more than half of the people in the world to be illiterate and thus unable to obtain ideas from newspapers or books. Fundamental Education aimed not merely at developing literacy, but included giving information about health, recreation, agriculture, and general citizenship. A beginning was made with Fundamental Education projects in India, Mexico, Ecuador, Haiti, Nigeria, Thailand, Egypt, and the Gold Coast, but in many of these countries the

---

[3] In 1951, the loss in man-days through industrial work-stoppages was:

United States	22,560,000	0.120 percent of total man-days
United Kingdom	1,694,000	0.024 percent of total man-days
Netherlands	67,000	0.005 percent of total man-days

Fundamental Education movement has been absorbed into a growing national education system.

Modern education is becoming increasingly expensive, and it seems inevitable that those countries in a strong economic position will have to help the weaker ones. Signs of this were revealed in the United States Point Four program and the Peace Corps, the Colombo Plan of the British Commonwealth, and many of UNESCO's activities.

Fundamental Beliefs and Traditions

IN MOST countries educational developments have been profoundly affected by fundamental beliefs and traditions in the culture of the people. Ralph Linton has analyzed the culture of a people into elements, which he suggests are:

1. *Universals*—those things which all people in a country do in the same way, such as eating the same food, wearing the same clothes, speaking the same language, and holding the same ideas of political and religious institutions and the same standards of polite conduct.

2. *Specialties*—the specialized vocational skills and training which make for division of labor in a society, and the accepted ideas about class and social position within the culture.

3. *Alternatives*—those things about which individuals exercise their own personal choices, such as making use of inventions and other new ways of doing things.[4]

These factors influence the development of a national culture and therefore affect the work of those who develop a curriculum for the schools of the country.

In Japan, for instance, Bushido—the Way of the Warrior—and Shinto—the Way of the Gods—permeated the whole educational framework for centuries. During the years before World War II these national traditions expressed themselves in militarism and ultranationalism, but both Bushido and Shinto, with their basic ideas of loyalty, obedience, courtesy, and reverence for elders, also produced a national charm of demeanor, particularly noticeable in Japanese children and women, which it is pleasing to note Japan has retained.

After the Revolution in Russia, when educational missionaries made their way into some of the Muslim minority groups in south-

---

[4] Ralph Linton, *The Study of Man*, Appleton-Century, New York, 1936.

west Asia to inaugurate campaigns against illiteracy, they preached emancipation of women and equality of educational opportunity for them. This was so contrary to the local belief that women were inferior beings without souls that strong hostility was aroused and many of the teachers were assassinated. In the far north of eastern Asia, when new schools were established, children came to them with strange symbols on their faces inscribed in blood, and could not be persuaded to wash them off because they had been placed there by shamen ("spirit doctors") to prevent the evil spirits of the West from harming the children.

Turning to western Europe, we find in France a tradition of select cultural leadership so strong that the educational system has aimed steadily at the production of an educational elite. When various liberalizing ideas, such as the *école unique* and the Langevin reforms, were suggested, with the idea of giving a more adequate education to all the children, they were opposed and delayed because of the fear that the traditional high standard of French scholarship would suffer.

Similarly, in Germany the belief that the universities should stand for a very thorough training in scholarship and research, often expressed in extreme specialization within narrow fields and dependent upon a high standard of work in the secondary schools, was very strong—so much so that for more than forty years the proposal of the *Einheitschule*, or uniform ladder of opportunity for all pupils, was discussed but never brought into being, for fear that the standard of work in the universities might be adversely affected. After World War II, in the reconstruction of German education in both West and East, the idea of the *Einheitschule* was incorporated in the program, but in the universities of the Federal Republic of West Germany there is still considerable opposition to the introduction of a *Studium generale* or general-culture course that aims at toning down the extreme specialization in university work.

Had the United States, after the American Revolution, remained a cluster of states along the eastern seaboard, American education might have remained conservative, with the Latin grammar school a prominent feature. It is difficult to assess the importance of the westward movement which forged the special characteristics of the American people and gave individual qualities to American education. Sturdy independence remained, and added to this was a certain adventurous spirit, combined with a desire to find something that would work quickly and well. There also developed a strong desire for equality of opportunity for all and an optimistic belief in the perfectibility of man. American education today reflects all these qualities. American schools look more to the future than to the past. The search for the glittering West still goes on, and it seems to be the will of the American always to be "seeking the end of the rainbow."

Among the fundamental beliefs that have influenced education none is stronger than religion. The pages of this book will reveal many instances where religion has affected the development of national systems. Even Communism seems to be a type of religion, with Marx and Lenin as its apostles. It is understandable that religion should wield an important determining influence, for many educational movements have had religious bases, and throughout the Middle Ages in Europe the church was the sole agency which supplied the schools and kept the flames of culture and civilization burning.

With the rise of national systems of education the church has lost much of its power over the schools. In the United States, France, Japan, and Australia the schools supported by the state are secular: religious teaching is not permitted in school hours by the regular staff. In England and Holland, however, schools built by religious sects, if efficient, may be aided financially and may become a definite part of the national system. In Newfoundland, education is administered by seven religious denominations, and in the province of Quebec, two educational systems, Catholic and Protestant, work side by side, providing state schools of their own faith.

The Catholics believe firmly that their religious beliefs and teachings must permeate the whole of school work and, in consequence, have built up widespread networks of Catholic schools in many predominantly Protestant countries. These extend, in some cases, from nursery schools to Catholic universities. As a part of the Counter Reformation the Catholic Church established certain orders which undertook, among other duties, the task of spreading education with a religious basis. The Jesuits and the Christian Brothers now have a worldwide influence. On the other hand, in Catholic countries where there was no Protestant Reformation to combat, such as Spain and Portugal, education is still backward and the percentage of illiteracy is high.

The Anglican tradition has worked in a different direction. Unlike the Catholics, who give careful attention to the education of all groups in their communities, irrespective of social status, the Anglicans, influenced perhaps by the unusual character of the English Reformation, gave most of their attention to grammar schools for the ruling classes and left education of the common people to charitable organizations. The late arrival of England in the field of national education is largely due to this influence. The "great public schools" of England, although originally established as schools for poor boys, later developed as aristocratic schools under the aegis of the Church of England and built up the so-called English tradition of education—culture, discipline, religion, service—which has spread to the county schools and all over the British Commonwealth. These public schools trained for England thousands of statesmen and leaders, but their former monopoly in this respect has now been challenged by the county or state secondary schools.

With the other Protestant sects, we find the early adoption of the idea of education for the masses. The Lutherans carried this through northern Germany and Scandinavia, and Prussia was one of the first countries to establish a national system of education. As early as the sixteenth century, Scotland was given a plan by John Knox for universal education. This was not put into effect at the time, but it was never forgotten and eventually became one of the mainsprings of the Scottish national system. In the United States the Calvinists were very strong in the early days of New England, their doctrines being expressed, sometimes in intolerant fashion, by the Congregational Church. Harvard and Yale were established by the Congregationalists. In Massachusetts in the seventeenth century only members of the Congregational Church in good standing could be citizens. Quakers and Catholics were not allowed to enter the colony. and several Quakers who came back after banishment were executed. Connecticut was more liberal and allowed freedom to members of other Protestant churches, while Pennsylvania and Rhode Island permitted freedom of conscience to all. However, out of this welter of warring religious opinions came one generally accepted principle, that there should be a system of universal education backed by the state and local communities. This began to operate as early as the middle of the seventeenth century. A hundred years later, church control of schools had become much weaker, and eventually the state took over the management of the schools on a nonsectarian basis.

In country after country, the state has taken over from the church the control of its schools. This does not mean the elimination of religious ideas, except in the U.S.S.R., where religion is banned from the schools as a "reactionary influence associated with capitalism." In many countries sectarian schools exist side by side with nonsectarian state schools, sometimes with state subsidies and sometimes not. The Education Act of 1944 in England actually made it compulsory that in all schools controlled by the state, each school day should commence with a ceremony of religious devotion and also that religious instruction should form a definite part of the curriculum in each school. However, this is on the basis of an agreed syllabus which is undenominational and provides full exemption for those pupils whose parents object to their attendance.

Status of Progressive Educational Thought

OLD FORMS of educational procedures are notoriously tenacious, but some countries are more receptive than others to new ideas. Most educational reforms seem to be the result of the inspired leadership of some individual or group: they rarely arise as a general demand of the people themselves. The Renaissance had all the qualities of an educational revolt, but its results for the schools were disappointing. Instead of using the splendid content of the New Learning, educators became enamored of the language forms of Latin and Greek, and schools were condemned to nearly four centuries of formal classical study, without any examination of its real results or influence. There were rebels against this—Bacon, Locke, Montaigne, Mulcaster, and Comenius—but their message did not receive serious attention at the time. It was Rousseau who first set in motion the reform movement that has grown into the progressive educational ideas of today. What he said with so much vehemence was translated into practical maxims of school method by Pestalozzi, Herbart, and Froebel, and from them there is a direct line to the modern ideas of John Dewey. Dewey's educational philosophy has had a profound effect in the United States, Germany, the Netherlands, Switzerland, and most of the English-speaking countries.

Other preachers of a new educational gospel were Bishop Grundtvig and Christen Kold in Denmark, who inaugurated the folk high school movement, and the philosopher Gentile in Italy, who accomplished wonders as Minister of Education in the early days of the Fascist regime, until the increasingly militaristic complexion of affairs drove him out of office. Perhaps all we can say is that countries which came under the influence of such reformers were fortunate, but at the same time conditions must have been favorable for the reception of their ideas.

It is notable that countries with centralized systems of educational administration seem to be less hospitable to new educational movements than those where the administration is decentralized. France, Japan, and the Australian states, all with sound and well-organized systems of education, contributed little to educational experiment and advancement prior to 1940. The old orthodoxies were too strongly entrenched. There were few school libraries, there was a great deal of oral teaching, and examinations tended to dominate school procedures. Such changes as were made were imposed from above, and the atmosphere of conformity to a set syllabus prevented the emergence of new ideas stemming from the constructive thinking and experience of the teachers themselves. Japan has now swung over to decentralization, and it is interesting to note that, in the short space of twenty years, much diversification in courses and considerable educational experimentation have taken place.

In the latter years of the nineteenth century, educational psychology began to grow in importance, and the emphasis in school work began to shift from the subject matter to the needs of the learners. Progress was slow with this new educational influence, but there was a marked acceleration after 1910. The United States, England, and Germany were prominent in applying psychological procedures to methods of teaching. Today there is hardly a country where the educational system is unaffected by the rapidly accumulating results of psychological research.

Language Problems

WHEN a country possesses a uniform and accepted language without intricate dialects, the organization of a national system of schools becomes much simpler. England, the United States, and France are obvious examples. If national unity is strong, it is possible to have two or even three languages without endangering the effectiveness of the educational system. Wales is bilingual; two languages are spoken in Belgium and three in Switzerland.

But in countries where different languages correspond to differences between national or semihostile groups, or where there are widely differing dialects, or where the language is so complicated that it takes a long time to learn, serious problems confront the organizers of a system of schools.

In India there are 14 main language systems and hundreds of dialects. The percentage of illiteracy is very high, approaching 88.2 percent among the women. The British were unable to deal with this problem. Since India gained its independence, Hindi is being emphasized as the basic language of India, and Urdu that of Pakistan. At the same time, some of the other languages, such as Tamil and Bengali, are dominant in certain districts; India will probably have to pass through a long "multiple language" stage before any sort of unity in language is achieved, if it ever is. The long period of English domination of India, and the use of English in the schools as a second language, did not succeed in establishing English as a unifying factor.

In Africa there is a maze of native languages and dialects and a high percentage of illiteracy. The French, true to their traditions, tried to solve the problem by making French, as far as they could, the compulsory language. The British, on the other hand, made a scientific study of native languages, reducing them to written alphabets where necessary and producing textbooks in the native tongues for use in schools. Recent years have seen the creation of 32 or more new independent states, all eager to develop mass educational systems and to reduce illiteracy. Because of the rising spirit of nationalism, they have stressed native languages. Some of these countries continue to teach European languages, especially in secondary schools and universities. Ambitious Africans still wish to learn a European language as an instrument of advancement for themselves.

In China the problem takes a different turn, in that the classical written language is different from the many spoken variations and is hard to learn and interpret. From 1919 onward the Nationalist movement gave a good deal of attention to language, advocating an assimilation between the spoken and written language in a form called *pai-hua* ("plain talk"). This reform made considerable headway, and before long, newspapers, novels, pamphlets, and plays were using this new style which was intelligible to so many more people. A second development was the order issued by the Nationalist government that *kuo-yu* (Mandarin) should be used in all schools and on the radio as the national language. This was essentially the same as *pai-hua*. Marked progress was made, and although illiteracy was still high, many more Chinese people in widely spread districts began to use *kuo-yu*. The People's Republic has carried forward this procedure, and by using Russian methods of posters, wall news-papers, and intensive instruction by special teams of teachers, is con-tinuing the campaign against illiteracy, using *kuo-yu* as the medium.

In Turkey, until 1928, the script in use was an Arabic type. To reduce illiteracy and to help Turkey to become a modern nation, Kemal Atatürk introduced the Latin alphabet. This was a drastic and apparently difficult step, but it was successful. Ten years later, throughout Turkey, newspapers, books, official notices, and school texts were all being published in Latin type.

Japan faces a problem in that the written language, derived cen-turies ago from Chinese characters, places a great burden on school children and even on university students. The original script was called *Kanji*, and a reformed phonetic script, used in part by the newspapers, is known as *Kana*. There are so many characters to learn in *Kanji* that a high percentage of illiteracy in this country might be expected, but such is not the case. It speaks well for the work of the prewar Japanese schools that in 1940 a percentage of literacy higher than 95 was claimed. At the same time the Japanese are worried about the complexity and intricacy of their written language, and efforts have been made by reformers to introduce *Romaji*, a form with a Latin script. There has been much debate about this. A sim-plification seems certain to be adopted eventually, and it is perhaps significant that a little *Romaji* is now being taught in all Japanese elementary schools.

It is not generally appreciated that in the widespread territories of the Soviet Union there are more than 150 national groups speaking languages other than Russian. From the time of the Revolution the Russians have encouraged all of their national minorities to de-velop their own cultures and languages and to use Russian as a sec-ond language. Many written alphabets have been constructed by linguistic teams to assist backward groups, and the use of Russian Cyrillic characters is being encouraged as a move toward national unity. In several different languages, and mainly for the use of schools for the national minorities, the State Publishing House of Moscow issues thousands of textbooks and readers, many of which are attractive in the quality of their printing and illustrations.

No real progress seems yet to have been made in the construction or adoption of an international language that would be acceptable to all nations and used by them as a means of communication with each other. Esperanto has won very little acceptance. Perhaps in the future UNESCO may be able to deal effectively with this difficult but interesting project.

Political Background

IT IS obvious that the political atmosphere surrounding an educational system must be one of the most powerful influences affecting its development. Education in itself cannot bring about a social change: it must follow the political and social trends of the country concerned. No government would allow an educational system to preach revolution or even to indulge in destructive criticism of the basic political theory of the country. Education, however, can create rebels through enlightenment. The numerous young Russians who, before the Revolution, made their way to universities in France and Switzerland are an example of this. Unfortunately they returned burning with revolutionary zeal, only to find themselves ground between two millstones after 1917 and discarded by both sides—the tragedy of the Russian intelligentsia.

As national systems of education were built up in the nineteenth and early twentieth centuries, they reflected the aspirations of their countries. A perusal of the history textbooks used in schools will show this. Some of the teaching was so nationalistic that it tended to make the countries susceptible to war propaganda; this was certainly true in Germany and Japan, and to a lesser extent even in the English-speaking countries. "My country, right or wrong" may not have been explicitly expressed, but the feeling was present in the teaching, and in times of extreme commercial rivalry or other crises national antipathies could easily be fanned into flame. Education was recognized as a valuable medium for maintaining national sentiment, sometimes in a beneficial manner, but on other occasions tending to be extreme and dangerous.

Dictators have regarded education in different ways. For some it has been an instrument for furthering the purposes of their regimes. Hitler utilized it for "the making of Nazis" and set up in Germany a Minister who controlled the whole of the educational system throughout the country, this being the only occasion when Germany has had a central Ministry of Education. Mussolini apparently started off with a genuine desire to give Italy a better system of education and commissioned the philosopher Gentile to devise and put into operation an ideal system. Gentile, with a free hand, worked wonders in the space of about two years, and it was only after his resignation that the new Italian education began to show signs of extreme national fervor and militarism. Kemal Atatürk created a new Turkey by issuing daring decrees which seemed to cut right across the older beliefs of the country, but these were successful, and the development of a modern system of education was one of his strong points. In Spain today, however, Franco and his regime seem not to be very much interested in national education; the percentage of illiteracy is high, with compulsory education ending at about 12 years of age. In 1948, out of a population of 28 million, there were only 212,000 pupils in secondary schools in Spain, while in Canada, with a population in the same year of 13 million, there were 410,000 pupils in secondary schools.

The Communist countries consider education to be of very great importance. The U.S.S.R. states as the aim of Russian education "the building of a new social order based on enlightenment." As a consequence of this, in the early stages a vigorous campaign was waged against illiteracy, which was estimated to be between 80 and 90 percent in 1917. Twenty years later it had fallen, according to Russian claims, as low as 12 percent, and some parts of the Soviet Union now claim complete literacy. There is no doubt of the strength and vitality of education in the U.S.S.R. and other Communist countries, but to the Western democracies it seems to be vitiated by its intense, one-sided propaganda. The textbooks for Russian schools, particularly in history and the social studies, represent the United States, Britain, and France as warmongers and the ruthless oppressors of their own people. Communist countries are depicted as the only lands where life is worth living, and capitalism is pictured as a tyranny which is showing definite signs of decadence and decay. This attitude is found also in the satellite countries of the Soviet Union. It also appears strongly in the East German Republic, nominally independent, but under rigorous Russian control.

In the democratic countries the educational systems are also used for the inculcation of democratic ideas and procedures, but without the fierce propaganda of the Communists. Perhaps this is because the democratic nations feel more secure and can trust their own people. The very essence of their educational beliefs is the encouragement of tolerance and freedom and variety. Many teachers would find it hard to say how democracy can be taught: it is a way of life rather than a political doctrine. When the Allied powers undertook the task of turning Japanese education in a democratic direction, they found themselves puzzled as to the best ways of presenting a picture of democracy to the Japanese, who had never known it. They began one of the most interesting experiments in the history of education, but the educators concerned found that they had first to make a careful analysis of democracy and how it might be taught. Perhaps the *Primer of Democracy*, which was eventually produced for Japan, and of which millions of copies were sold, would be useful in the schools of the democratic countries themselves. But the influence of democratic beliefs and procedures on our educational systems is not in any way lessened or weakened by the absence of the intense propaganda which permeates the schools in Communist countries: it is stronger for being less aggressive and more deep seated.

Attitude Toward International Cooperation

A COMPARATIVELY new influence that is beginning to affect educational work in many countries is the effort to promote understanding and friendliness between nations. The old attitude of "These people are different from us, so what they do must be queer and wrong," is being slowly replaced by "What are these people really like; what are their achievements and problems?" The inclusion of social studies as a broad field in the curriculum rather than as a series of separate subjects has made a contribution toward this point of view. But this influence is not without opposition. Extreme nationalists in many countries view with suspicion the development of any type of "international-mindedness." The study of the achievements of the United Nations and of UNESCO is opposed in some quarters as tending to lessen ideas of national sovereignty.

However, hundreds of exchanges of pupils, university students, and teachers are taking place between different countries each year, and many individuals are getting an opportunity to learn at first hand how other people live and work. Courses of study are carefully planned to show more sympathetically the life of people in different environments. Chauvinistic textbooks have been rewritten in the attempt to avoid giving offense to other peoples and to eliminate feelings of superiority over all other people. The great Scandinavian organization called Norden has succeeded, through a completely voluntary and unofficial program, in rewriting the history textbooks of the three northern nations.

In spite of formidable difficulties in its early stages of planning, UNESCO is beginning to make its influence felt. Certain difficulties remain to be overcome, but its publications and posters are now to be found in schools all over the world. The well-known sentence in UNESCO's preamble—"Since wars begin in the minds of men, it is in the minds of men that the defenses of peace must be constructed"—has issued a challenge to the schools of the world.

UNESCO's program of Fundamental Education found many nations willing to provide capital and personnel in an effort to raise the standards of living and of education among the more backward and underprivileged peoples of the earth. For some years the refusal of the Soviet Union to have anything to do with UNESCO seemed to handicap the general spread of the organization's activities. The decision of the U.S.S.R. in 1954 to join the other nations who are members of UNESCO may have heralded the beginning of an era of greater effectiveness.

The work of the United Nations, particularly of the less publicized subordinate organizations, has been effective in getting nations to work together. The Declaration of Human Rights, although not fully implemented, has had a great appeal for some of the smaller nations. The study, in the schools of the world, of the working of the international organizations has aroused hope that international cooperation may be achieved in wider areas. Some of the national programs, such as the Point Four Plan and later foreign-aid programs of the United States and the British Commonwealth's Colombo Plan, have also had widespread effects.

These, then, are some of the influences that affect the structure and development of national systems of education. Recognition of their existence and importance makes comparative education a fascinating and valuable study. It is hoped that the pages of this book will help readers to see education not merely as a matter of classrooms, textbooks, and organizations, but rather as a rapidly expanding system of social services, worldwide in its effects, moving toward greater cooperation in the task of the betterment and enlightenment of all people of all nations.

Part II

The Administration, Control, and Finance of Schools

2

The Control of Public Education

ACH NATION, out of its own historical, social, and cultural background, attempts to find answers that will solve its problems in its own way. The development of a national system of education, like that of all other social institutions, is limited and determined by such background factors in the life of the nation. Educational reforms and practices that are imported from one country to another tend to be modified to fit local traditions and practices, or else to die out entirely, or to become insulated from the everyday life around them. But imported practices may have some residual effect. This effect is greatest when the school system is organized so that it can receive ideas from any source and can adapt them to its own use.

Although the beliefs and prejudices of peoples may differ, the general problems that must be solved in establishing and operating school systems show a great deal of resemblance from country to country. The problems of the organization of the school system of a country, of who shall control the schools, of who shall pay for education, of how the control and finance shall be divided—all these vex governments in every part of the world. The answers that any country accepts are of interest to other countries and so form a basis for a comparative study of school systems.

Defining the aims and purposes of education is a difficult problem in many lands. This has been well stated by Leicester Webb:

The activity called education is distinguished by the importance and the uncertainty of its aims. Doctors, engineers, lawyers and mariners are not continually preoccupied with the problem of defining the result they are trying to bring about. The captain of a ship is not asked to choose between rival philosophies of navigation; the purposes of his activity change little according to time or place. But the question "What am I trying to do?" challenges the good teacher all the days of his teaching life; it demands of him a philosophy of education; and it demands, what is hardest of all, that he shall never accept his own answer as final. To say the task of the teacher is to equip the child with the systematized experience of the past is not to make even a partial escape into certainty, since the past is, for the purposes of education, a creation of the present. What is true of the teacher is even truer of those who control the administration of systems of education; for them, indeed, the avoidance of a static outlook is much more difficult than for the teacher. Systems thrive on finality; to change them is to incur inconvenience and expense and to arouse the antagonism which comes of habits disturbed. To agree that there can be no final agreement on the aims of education is to establish a proposition of which the importance is often neglected. For it follows that an education system is not judged by its aims alone. It should be judged also by its capacity to tolerate, at a given moment, differing philosophies of education. The construction of such a system is a problem of government, and a problem more susceptible of practical solution than most of the problems which beset the educationist.[1]

One of the early problems to be solved (and one related to the aims of education) is the relation of the individual to the units of government, to the religious forces of the nation, and to society as a whole. Depending upon the history and philosophy of a people, differing answers are given to the question of who shall control, administer, and pay for education. The relationships between parents and children, parents and the church, families and the local community, political parties and the state, local and central authorities— all of these determine in large measure the form of organization for education that will gradually evolve.

In the institutionalization of education, the social group attempts to shape the rising generation into the patterns that are accepted as desirable within the group. The control of education depends upon the decision as to which groups shall participate in control and how the division of authority shall be established. The various answers to these questions will be considered in this section.

[1] Webb, *The Control of Education in New Zealand*, pp. 1–2. Quoted by permission of the New Zealand Council for Educational Research. (Where only brief identifying data as to sources appears in footnotes, further bibliographic data will be found in the Bibliography on pages 578–87.)

Education has become so important in the life of every nation that it is essential that some administrative machinery be devised to control and operate it. The quotation from Sir Graham Balfour is often cited, that the purpose of educational administration in a democratic nation is to "enable the right pupils to receive the right education from the right teachers, at a cost within the means of the State, under conditions which will enable the pupils to profit by their training." [2] This sounds simpler than it really is, because practically every word in the statement may mean something different to different people in different countries. Here again the conflict in values, which has been mentioned above, determines what a particular country will consider the "right education."

It is certain that there is no single, simple blueprint for an educational system which will be "right" for every country. The type of educational program which will best fit the younger generation of a country to develop as the best interests of that country may require, and as the people of the country desire, seems to be best for that country. This permits a wide variation in types of organization and control, according to the historical and cultural ideas of the citizens.

Comparative studies have been made from time to time of the cost of education in various states and countries, showing how much is actually being spent on schools. No satisfactory study has ever been attempted to show how much should be spent by a nation, or what proportion of the national income a country could afford to spend on schools. It is probably true that no country in history has spent all that it could on education.

The development of the concept of democracy as a way of life, not merely as a political system, has influenced philosophies and practices of education in many parts of the world. Governments and peoples have become aware that, in a nation where all the citizens have civic responsibilities, it is necessary for all of the people to have an education for intelligent citizenship. This concept has stimulated the development of universal systems of education, without stratification on the basis of class or economic status or without the development of a special type of education for an intellectual elite. It is equally true, however, that universal systems of education have been developed in countries which have accepted a totalitarian philosophy, with purposes far different from those of the democratic states. In

[2] I. L. Kandel, *Educational Administration* (London, 1921), p. 38.

the succeeding chapters we will study some of the types of organization which have been developed by different nations.

Agencies of Direct Control

HISTORICALLY, four different forces have been influential in the organization of formal education: the church, the guild or occupational association, the local community organized for self-government, and the national government. In comparatively recent years, with the rise of totalitarian governments, a modern fifth force, that of the single dominant political party, has emerged as a factor in the organization of education. In studying the control of schools in any country, it is first necessary to determine which force or combination of forces has become the dominant factor in the administrative machinery of education.

CONTROL OF EDUCATION BY RELIGIOUS GROUPS

Some of the earliest schools were established, supported, and controlled by the church. In many instances the relationships between parents and the church have determined the provision of schooling. Different countries developed different attitudes toward this problem: in some countries the parent controlled his own children and decided how much education they were to receive in church-connected schools; in others the church controlled the children and made the decisions.

As governmental agencies have moved into the area of public support for schools, their approach to the problem has varied. In some Canadian provinces, all public schools are either Catholic or Protestant. In Ireland all schools are church schools, with public support but with very little public control. Some governments have moved reluctantly in the direction of providing state-supported education for children who are not served by existing church-connected schools. Some countries have attempted to achieve the ideal of universal education by subsidizing church-connected and private schools, as well as public schools, from public funds. Other nations have met the problem by providing a system of public education which is wholly secular in nature and lay in control.

One problem arising from church-connected schools was the difficulty in developing from them a universal public school system that could cover the entire country. In the early development of education in Australia, most of the schools were operated by one or another of the leading church groups in the country—Church of England, Roman Catholic, Presbyterian, or Methodist. It was generally found that all four groups provided complete (and competing) elementary and secondary programs in any city or large town, but that all of them neglected the rural areas. In a huge, sparsely populated country, this raised many problems. Eventually the Australians decided that only by setting up a state-controlled system could education for all be provided.

The educational history of Great Britain was similar. When the demand for broadening the old-style curriculum in the English schools began to be felt, in the reign of Charles II, it was found that the power of the ecclesiastical authorities was so great that the laws barred the introduction of new courses into the schools or the hiring of instructors to teach them. So important was the religious qualification for teaching that a law of 1662 required every teacher, public or private, in home or school, to subscribe to a declaration that he would "conform to the liturgy by law established" and to obtain a license from the archbishop, bishop, or ordinary of the diocese. Nonconformists were almost completely deprived of education, for in 1665 the Five-Mile Act imposed a fine of forty pounds or six months' imprisonment on any Nonconformist teacher who came within five miles of a town.

In France the struggle between clerical and lay forces to control the educational system has been hotly contested since the Revolution. The aim of the revolutionary leaders was to remove all education from the control of the church, because they considered the clerical attitude to be antirevolutionary and antirepublican. The public school system which eventually was established in France was planned to be universal, lay, and secular, but the controversy has not yet been completely settled.

One of the best examples of a straightforward solution of the problem, whereby the state provides the support for education through public taxes, and the church maintains its control over education, has been worked out in Canada in the province of Quebec, where the schools are at the same time public and sectarian.

CONTROL OF EDUCATION BY OCCUPATIONAL ASSOCIATIONS

Medieval schools, especially those originated by the church, were mainly interested in the preparation of young men for the clergy, or in training leaders to be loyal sons of the church. This type of education failed to reach a large proportion of the population. There grew up at this time a distinction that has persisted, to a certain extent, to the present time—a distinction between the scholar-clerks, the learned, intellectual class, trained in church schools, and the remainder of the population, which was assumed to be more interested in matters of practical, everyday life than in books. The development by the tradesmen's and artisans' guilds of a system of apprenticeship training was a logical outgrowth of this situation. A system of vocational education was established which has continued, although with major changes, down to the present. The idea of a division of education into general and intellectual on the one hand and practical and vocational on the other is not unknown today.

Many of the schools established by the guilds changed their nature completely as the years passed. Some of the most exclusive (and most academic) of the great public schools in England originated as charity schools for apprentices or for orphans.

In the United States, with the aid of federal subsidies, a system of apprenticeship has been developed in recent years which permits some participation in control by the crafts and the local school districts. Unfortunately, one of the effects of the great development of the trade-union movement in the United States has been to restrict the apprenticeship program. In France an apprenticeship program has been developing in the last few years which permits a greater degree of local participation than does the local school system. Both employers and unions participate in these programs. In general, the influence of the occupational associations has lessened in recent times.

CONTROL BY THE LOCAL COMMUNITY

Local communities have been quick to recognize the importance of providing educational opportunities for their children. In the United States local school legislation was passed early in the seventeenth century. At the same time the principle of taxation of all the citizens of a community to pay for the education of all the children was established. The early laws were permissive in nature; they allowed local taxpayers to levy taxes upon themselves and set up schools. Very soon laws began to be passed requiring the opening of schools and the provision of funds to pay for them.

The interest of parents and of local communities in the education of their children has always been great; the extent to which they are permitted to participate in decisions affecting the education of their children depends upon the machinery of national, state, and local government. In some countries, such as Great Britain and the United States, the tradition of local self-government is very strong, and local units of government are well developed. In others, such as Australia, local self-government has never been important, and machinery for community participation is almost totally lacking. In France, where all governmental functions are centralized, education, like most other public functions, is controlled and administered by the national government from Paris.

CONTROL OF EDUCATION BY THE NATION-STATE

The participation of states and nations in the provision of education is much more recent than that of the other groups which have been discussed. In many countries the entrance of government on the educational scene came very late and consisted of an attempt to correct deficiencies in existing school programs and to spread more widely the opportunities for education. This governmental intervention has varied from the one extreme of providing subsidies from public funds to existing church and private schools, leaving them quite independent, to the other extreme of establishing universal national school systems which parallel, and to some extent replace, the existing programs. A more recent development, seen in countries which have only lately developed a strong nationalistic sentiment, has been the complete national control of all education in order to serve a national purpose.

In nations that are organized under a federated form of government, such as Australia, Canada, and the United States, there exists an intermediate governmental agency between the local school unit and the nation—the state government. The relative authority and responsibility of national and state governments varies with the country concerned and gives rise to new patterns of control, administration, and finance.

CONTROL OF EDUCATION BY A POLITICAL PARTY

Since the end of World War I there has developed a new type of national control, which many regard as a perversion. Instead of operating an educational system to foster the best interests of all sections of the population, this type of control attempts to use the educational system in order to preserve the preeminent position of the political party in power. This type of regime makes no distinction between formal and informal education; all of the forces of mass communication, culture, and schooling are controlled by the party, in order to force every individual to conform to the pattern that the party sets for all to follow. This type of control was developed by the Fascists in Italy and the Nazis in Germany. In each case the purpose was only partially achieved, and the system was finally abandoned after the government was defeated in war. In the Soviet Union the Communist Party has adopted the idea of totalitarian control of education and culture, and has further refined and developed it. Today all cultural and educational activities throughout the Soviet Union are completely directed and controlled by the Party. This result has been achieved in spite of an apparent decentralization of school organization.

Indirect Control of Education

IN ADDITION to the machinery of government which any country may set up, there are various forces that, in effect, have control over the type of education which may be established. Some of these affect the operation of the schools and will be considered later in Part III. However, since they are controls, they deserve mention here.

VALUE SYSTEMS

One powerful control that helps to determine the type of education that is provided lies in the system of values generally accepted by the people. The general climate of opinion, or the philosophy of the people, determines how extensive the educational offerings shall be, how long the children will remain in school, what proportion of the youth of the country will receive more than a bare minimum of education, and what the accepted purpose of schooling may be. In some countries the aim of education is expressed in terms of high standards of scholarship, and these nations accept as desirable a system of rigid examinations which eliminates a large proportion of the school-age group from secondary education. Another country may hold that the purpose of the school is to prepare for intelligent citizenship; the parents of such a nation would be repelled by the idea of wholesale elimination by means of examinations in a few academic subjects.

Cultural lag is a worldwide problem, since not all features in any culture change at the same rate. All countries agree that one of the functions of the school is to pass on to the new generation the heritage of the past. If this is interpreted so that all attention is directed backward to the past, the schools not only do not help to overcome the cultural lag, but they may actually accentuate its effects. Study of classical literature may be retained in the school curriculum, not for its value in present-day living but because it has traditionally been included. The influence of parents may increase the cultural lag. A modern father who wants up-to-date equipment in his store or factory and a new car to drive may be shocked to learn that the school his son attends differs in any respect from the school he attended thirty years before.

In every country the voice of the traditionalist is heard. The classical curriculum of some present-day secondary schools in France and Germany, or of the classical colleges of Quebec, would seem very familiar to Vittorino da Feltre, who established a secondary school in 1423. Those who argue that the best possible curriculum would consist of a study of a selected list of "Great Books" chosen from the classics, uphold a tradition which is hundreds of years old and do not admit that new times can call for new educational procedures.

Sometimes it is a religious influence that tends to emphasize the backward look and to increase cultural lag. Church-connected schools may appear to be interested in eternal survival to the neglect of present-day living. There are countries where the schools are classical in type and controlled by sectarian influences, where little or nothing is done about the prevailing high rates of illiteracy, poverty, malnutrition, and ill health.

In many countries educational reformers have been active, some of them in the field of what is to be taught, others in the study of the child or of the learning process. Names like Froebel and Pestalozzi, Rousseau and Montessori, Dewey and Thorndike, and many others might be mentioned. New educational ideas have influenced schools in different ways and to varying extents. The reformers have taught that the child is not a miniature adult, but an individual who develops in a natural way. They have argued that education is not intended to prepare for life, but is life itself. They point out that a school system which continually looks backward is incapable of preparing young people to make adjustments to a constantly changing society.

In most countries there is no unanimity on the subject of the purposes of education, or what should be taught in the schools, or how it should be taught. School systems are caught in a struggle for power between competing groups in society who hold and fight for different sets of values. The school may find itself between the forces of classicism and modernism; between capitalism and socialism; between those who seek greater international cooperation and the narrow nationalists; between those who believe in complete secular control of the schools and those who want control in the church; between those who believe in wider educational opportunities for all and those who believe in education only for the intellectually elite. In large measure the type of school organization and curriculum which develops in any country is the resultant of these diverse forces within society.

THE TAXPAYERS

An important control in every system of education is the man who pays the bill. If the schools charge fees, they must produce results which the father of the pupil expects, or he will remove his child from school. If the schools are dependent on tax money, then the individual taxpayer exerts his influence, directly or indirectly. If he votes for local school board members who make the budget, his influence is direct and important. If the state or national budget pays most of the cost, the influence must be exerted through legislators or members of Parliament. The more democratic a state or nation may be, the more the professional administrators of the schools are affected by the ideas of the people who pay the taxes. This is undoubtedly a good thing, for the schools belong to the people, and even highly trained professional administrators should work closely in touch with the people.

PRESSURE GROUPS

Sometimes a democratic system runs the risk of falling a victim to small and highly organized minority pressure groups, which may exert an influence out of all proportion to their numbers. These groups may exert a powerful control over the administration of schools and the work of the teachers. In a small district this type of control may be felt quickly and drastically. In a centralized system, however, there is a possibility that the effect of such pressure groups may be felt simultaneously in every school in the country.

EXAMINATIONS

In many countries one of the most powerful controls is the examination system. External examinations, written by university authorities or by education departments (not by the teacher of the class), become an important part of the school program. They determine whether or not a pupil may proceed on to secondary or higher education and whether he may enter certain professions; they tend to fix, at an early age, the entire social and vocational future of the pupil. In some cases they determine minutely the content of every course taught in the school; they affect classroom procedure and methods; and they set limits on the amount of professional freedom allowed to every teacher in the system.

Examinations have been criticized in many countries; reforms and modifications have been frequently suggested and sometimes accepted. In many school systems, as an English educator, J. F. Wolfenden, has said, "It is evident that the examination tail is wagging the teaching dog." In some schools the principal or headmaster has no choice in the curriculum—he merely selects the particular series of required courses which will prepare a boy or girl to pass a specific examination. Under such a system teaching can become mere cramming, and the nervous strain on pupils becomes intense. To the extent that external examinations determine teaching procedures, courses of study, and the future of pupils, they become very potent controls over education.

Types of Organization and Control

THE FIRST country to be studied is the United States, a federal union, with powers distributed between the national government and the states, in which the national government exercises little control over education, but provides some financial and other assistance. The constituent states have legal responsibility for and control over schools, but they have, in most instances, delegated much of their authority to local school districts which they have created. The local school districts, representing the people in the communities, have strongly developed their participation in school administration, control, and support. Although there are wide variations in the methods of administration and support in the fifty states, in general the system can be said to typify strong local control.

The second country is England, which represents an interesting division of responsibility between the national government and local units. The balance between these participating authorities has been carefully worked out. The local education districts are larger than the average American school district, but smaller than the states, although in population some of them exceed many of the American states. A great deal of freedom is permitted to the local authorities in the administration of the programs, and the national government provides a large part of the financial support. This country offers an example of divided control.

The third example is France. Nearly all governmental functions in France are centralized in the national government. Local self-government is relatively unimportant and is largely dependent on the national authority. Little or no local participation in control or administration of schools is permitted, although some local taxes are levied to support the schools. France is an example of centralized national control.

The fourth type of organization is exemplified by Australia. Like the United States, Australia has a national government, state governments, and local community organizations. As in the United States, the national government has no responsibility for or control over education, although it makes some financial contributions. The constituent states, like the American states, are constitutionally responsible for education. The Australian states differ from the American states, however, in that they have not created local school districts or authorities to operate the schools. The educational system of an Australian state is a state system, as completely centralized within the state as the French system is within the nation, and with practically no local participation or support. Australia illustrates a centralized state system.

In the fifth example, Canada, may be found a variant of the pattern of a federated nation. Here, as in the other two, the national government has no authority over education and makes only minor financial contributions to it. The provinces (which are comparable to the Australian and American states) have constitutional responsibility for the control and support of schools. The provinces have set up systems of school districts very similar to the plan of organization in the United States. In most of the provinces there is no distinctive difference from the organization followed in the United States, but in two provinces the plan is so different that it deserves special consideration. In Newfoundland and Quebec all public schools are controlled by sectarian groups, and multiple school systems exist side by side. In these provinces may be found an example of sectarian control.

Another federated system of government may be found in the Union of Soviet Socialist Republics. In this case the federal government has wide powers and responsibilities in public education, but has delegated many of them to the constituent republics which make up the Union. A decentralized system of organization and control has been carefully planned, giving authority to the republics and to smaller local government units. Support of the schools is provided for in the budgets of the Union, the republics, and the local districts. In spite of this decentralized plan of organization, however, the entire system is completely controlled by the small minority of the population who are members of the Communist Party. Since the Party is not decentralized, and since it controls all republican and local government organizations, it controls every phase of educational activity throughout the Union. This is done with the purpose of maintaining its control of the government and securing the conformity of all citizens. This is an illustration of party control.

Before World War II the government of Germany was totalitarian in nature and philosophy. It controlled public education in the interests of the dominant political party. While there was some decentralization of educational administration, the actual control was in the hands of the National Socialist party. After the war, under Allied tutelage, the system was democratized and provided for major control by the states. Since the end of the Occupation the German schools have continued to make progress, and they form an interesting example of a reconstructed system of education.

The operation of schools in the same group of countries will be covered in Part III. A reader who is interested in getting a more complete picture of the educational system of a single country should read the corresponding chapter of Part III immediately after he has completed the Part II chapter on that country. In this manner, if Chapter 16 is read immediately after Chapter 8, one might concentrate on the schools of Communist Russia. The chapters in Part II are designed to illustrate different types of educational control.

3
Local Responsibility:
The United States

N O PEOPLE in the world have held the idea of educational
opportunity for all of the children of all of the people more
strongly than the Americans. This faith in education—as a
leaven to make one people of immigrant strains from many lands,
as a door for children to opportunities better than their parents enjoyed, as a preparation for participation in the difficult business of
citizenship in a democracy—has permeated American thinking since
colonial days. The establishment of the complete school system to
carry out this ideal has been a long and painful struggle. Americans
sometimes fail to realize that although their history is short in comparison with that of Old World nations, they have the oldest public
school system in the world.

The Historical Background

AS Commager has written,

No people ever demanded so much of education as the Americans.
None ever have been served so well by its schools and its educators.
From the very beginning education has had a very special, and a very
heavy, task to perform. The various states and regions could not achieve
unity without a sentiment of nationalism. The nation could not absorb
tens of millions of immigrants from all parts of the globe without rapid
and effective Americanization. Economic and social distinctions and
privileges, severe enough to corrode democracy itself, had to be fought.
To our schools went the momentous responsibility of inspiring a people

to pledge and hold allegiance to these historic principles of democracy, nationalism, Americanism, and egalitarianism.[1]

The development of education in the New World had its roots in the movements in Europe which developed during the Protestant Reformation and the associated political activities which took place at that time and later. The early settlers, particularly in New England, were mainly Protestants who were seeking religious freedom and were fleeing from authoritarian churches and authoritarian governments.

The colonists who came to America brought a tradition of local self-government with them from Europe, and this was strengthened by the relative isolation of the small settlements founded along the Atlantic coast. They were thrown upon their own resources and developed attitudes of independence and self-reliance. Depending upon the colony and its circumstances of establishment, the settlers organized their little community governments to operate as direct democracies. These conditions were instrumental in shaping the character of later generations. The American people came to believe in accomplishing things through democratic processes and in doing things for themselves rather than in leaving matters to the state.

As early as 1642 and 1647, Massachusetts Bay Colony passed laws requiring each town to provide schools to teach children reading, writing, and religion, and to pay for these schools out of town funds. Since the local towns were supported by taxation, this was in effect the first state action to require local communities to provide for publicly supported education. This action set the pattern, which later was followed almost universally throughout the country, of state legislation setting up local taxes for the support of local schools. By the time of the American Revolution this pattern had become general throughout New England and New York, and as settlers from that region moved west into the new territories that were opening up, they carried some form of local organization with them, all the way to the Pacific coast.

This early Massachusetts legislation was based on the principle that the education of youth was essential to the well-being of the state. Under this interpretation, it was conceived that the state had an obligation to provide such education at public expense.

[1] Henry Steele Commager, *Life*, October 16, 1950; copyright by Time, Inc.

Other colonies depended upon private or parochial schools, believing that it was an obligation of the parent to furnish education for his own children. Some of the colonies provided pauper schools for children whose parents were unable to meet this obligation. Even in these colonies, it was the local community or the local congregation which established the schools.

After 1820 the movement toward universal manhood suffrage gained such momentum that it affected attitudes toward education. This movement was a strong force in breaking the control of the churches over common schools. When the right to vote was no longer limited by religious or property qualifications, the realization developed that general education was not only a necessity for all citizens, but that the state would have to provide for and support it. The newly organized labor movement became active in demanding free education for all children as a natural right.

In the beginning, in most of the states, the state was merely a benevolent bystander. Early legislation was usually permissive; state laws enabled local communities to provide schooling for the children in their area and to levy taxes to support the program. By the middle of the nineteenth century the authority of the state governments was firmly established, and the attitude of legislatures changed. Instead of saying that the local community might provide and pay for schools, states began to pass compulsory-education laws, requiring each community to maintain schools and to compel all children within specified ages to be in attendance. The states moved into the provision and control of the training and certification of teachers and the supervision of schools. They began to prescribe curricula and to approve textbooks.

Throughout these developments, the importance of local participation in the control and support of local schools was recognized. Increased state interest in the education of all the children, in equalizing educational opportunities and in the burden of educational costs was accompanied by an unchanged belief in the importance of local administration and the desirability of keeping the schools close to the people. This local control of community schools has always been very important to the American people, and attempts to diminish it have always met with determined opposition. In many cases, the additional requirements placed on school districts by state legislation, without additional financial support, created serious problems for the local authorities, and this has been a continuing problem.

By 1850 the various states had provided for elementary or common schools, supported by taxes, and the movement to establish free public secondary schools had begun. In the famous Kalamazoo case of 1872, the Supreme Court of the state of Michigan declared that the voters of a school district were clearly within their rights if they decided to establish a high school and to raise the taxes to pay for it. This decision, which was followed by other state courts, established the right of the states to provide free public secondary education. Beginning with the founding of the University of Virginia in 1819, various states opened state universities, thus completing the public school system, open to all citizens and supported by public funds.

Federal Activities in Education

THE CONSTITUTION of the United States, adopted in 1789, was a compromise between advocates of a strong central government and those who favored a loose federal union. It provided that all powers not expressly delegated to the national government would be reserved to the states. Since at that time all of the schools in the country were operated by church or local groups, it is not surprising that education was not considered to be a responsibility of the new national government and was not mentioned in the Constitution. But the national government has moved consistently to encourage and to strengthen education in the states.

As new territories came into the Union, and later became states, the unoccupied lands became national territory and property. In the Northwest Territory Ordinances of 1785 and 1787, part of this national domain was set aside as an endowment for school purposes. While the earliest federal statutes gave control of these lands to the townships within the new states, a change in national policy in 1803 made the states the custodians of school lands, and thus the control of school endowments passed to the state governments. Of the 16 states in existence in 1800, eight had definitely provided for education in their state constitutions. Beginning with Ohio in 1802, every state admitted to the Union has received federal land grants in support of schools. Every state constitution has provided (in varying language) for free and general education in the state.

For the first few states, Congress appropriated one section of land in each township (one square mile in each thirty-six) for the support of schools. By 1830 the grant was increased to two sections in each township; later states received four sections. Between the admission of Ohio in 1802 and Arizona and New Mexico in 1912, the national government granted over 29 million acres to new states— an area larger than England and Wales. These school lands were sold or leased by the states and the proceeds placed in "Irreducible School Funds," with the interest earned used to help pay for the operation of the schools.

The federal government has continued to support public education in the states. The Morrill Act, passed during the Civil War, aided in the establishment of colleges of agricultural and mechanic arts in the states. Because grants of national lands were made under this act, these have since been called the "land-grant colleges," although they now receive annual grants in money. The Smith-Hughes Bill, passed during World War I, provided federal aid for high school programs in agriculture, homemaking, and trades and industries. These grants were increased by the George-Deen Bill in 1939, and the vocational fields receiving subsidies were expanded. In all of these grants, the federal government has entered into contractual relations with the state governments, acknowledging direct state responsibility for education. During World War II, however, the national government made some direct grants to local school districts to assist in meeting emergency increases in costs due to war activities and to unusual shifts in population caused by the war.

In 1867 Congress provided for a federal Department of Education. The name of this department has been changed several times, but since 1929 it has been known as the United States Office of Education. Its functions were originally stated as follows: the collection, publication, and interpretation of statistics and factual information concerning practices and procedures in different parts of the country; and the general promotion of education. It was not intended that the department should have any administrative responsibility for any schools or school systems. The apportionment and administration of federal funds to aid specific programs in the states has greatly increased the activities and influence of the Office of Education, however. Under the guise of maintaining standards, the Office of Education has assumed a measure of control over the land-grant colleges and vocational education. In 1939 this office was transferred from the Department of the Interior to the Federal Security Agency, which is now the Department of Health, Education, and Welfare.

The federal government, through Congress, has direct responsibility for the public school system of the District of Columbia. Efficient school systems, with various amounts of autonomous control, but under federal supervision, are operated in Guam, Samoa, and the Virgin Islands. The federal government also has responsibility for the education of children in the Canal Zone and for Indians living on reservations. There are federally operated schools for dependents of military personnel overseas. In 1963 the government took steps to establish schools on military bases within the United States wherever the nearby state schools refused to provide integrated programs. During times of emergency, such programs as the Works Progress Administration, the Public Works Administration, and the National Youth Administration have had an important impact on education. These programs have been financed by large federal appropriations and have operated within the states in many educational fields.

The Role of the State in Education

IN MOST of the states the educational system is headed by a state board of education. The method of selection of members of these boards varies widely. Miller and Spalding reported in 1952 that "three state boards are wholly ex officio, and twenty-one boards are partly ex officio. Three are elected by the people, two are elected by a state board convention, and one is elected by the state legislature. Thirty state boards are appointed in whole or in part by the governor. The range in size of the board is from three to nineteen members. Twenty boards have from seven to ten members." [2] Most of the states require that the state boards of education be composed of laymen; in a few cases professional school people may be members.

As executive officer of the state board or state department of education, every state has a chief school officer, usually called the "state superintendent of schools," "superintendent of public instruction," or "state commissioner of education." In 24 states this officer is appointed by the state board of education, in 16 he is appointed by the governor, and in 10 he is elected by the people. The professional staff of state departments of education varied in 1962 from 16 full-time members in Wyoming to 302 in New York.

[2] Miller and Spalding, The Public Administration of American Schools, p. 115.

The original function of the state department of education was mainly clerical, but increased assumption of educational responsibility by the state has greatly increased the importance of the department. The passage of the Smith-Hughes Act in 1917, which added many responsibilities in handling state and federal funds and the supervision of vocational education programs, was accompanied by a large increase in state department staffs.

The functions of the state department vary widely among the different states, depending upon the responsibilities assigned to them by the state legislatures. The most important of these functions (which are not exercised by every state department of education, nor considered of equal importance in different states) are as follows: distribution of state funds or of federal funds coming to the state; enforcement of state laws regarding education; determination of curricula and courses of study; adoption or recommendation of approved lists of textbooks; certification of teachers; approving or consulting on school-building standards; provision for library services; and operation of teachers' colleges.

One excellent study suggests lists of responsibilities that authorities have considered proper for state departments to assume in the fields of administration and of instruction. In the field of administration, the state has responsibilities in the area of financial aid; organization of administrative units and attendance areas; uniform methods of accounting and reporting; standards of budget preparation; provision of auditing services; debt-service administration; criteria for school plant; standards and specifications for transportation services; minimum specifications for school supplies; distribution of state-provided textbooks, library books, and audio-visual aids; improvement of the quality of noninstructional personnel; regulation of auxiliary services; setting of salary schedules or minimum salary standards; and supervision of attendance services. In the field of instruction, the state has responsibilities for teacher education and certification; for courses of study and curricula; for goals or standards of evaluation; for school libraries and instructional materials; for the provision of field services; for control over services financed fully or in part by federal funds; and for the in-service improvement of instructional personnel.[3]

Field services have become increasingly important. Many of these

[3] Southern States Work Conference, *State Responsibility for the Organization and Administration of Education* (Bulletin No. 1, 1942), Tallahassee, Florida.

were originally provided under state plans for administering federally aided vocational education programs. Under this group come state supervisors and specialists in vocational agriculture, homemaking, trades and industries, distributive education, guidance services, and rehabilitation programs. Others were added as the state departments expanded their services to the local school districts. This has resulted in the employment of supervisors and specialists in elementary and secondary education, in physical education and health, music, art, curriculum development, and in the education of physically handicapped and other atypical children. Many state departments also provide consultants on problems of school buildings, finance, transportation services, school lunches, and school libraries.

Because the multiplication of small, poorly financed local school districts was recognized to be an inefficient and uneconomical method of operating an educational program, an extensive campaign for the consolidation of small districts has been carried on. This has been accompanied in some states by a growing tendency to centralize more control in the state department of education, and has been emphasized by increased participation by the state in the financial support of local schools. The problem of getting a more efficient and economical method of operation and a wider tax base with accompanying equalization of the burdens of school support has gone hand in hand with the problem of retaining as much local control as possible in the administration of the schools.

The National Education Association recommended in a research bulletin issued in 1944,

The state department, in accordance with law and state board policies, should establish minimum standards and essential regulations for the teachers and schools of the state; supervise the distribution of state and federal funds among the schools; maintain a state-wide system of school records, reports and appraisal. Beyond the discharge of these important but limited duties the department should be a service agency, providing needed information, stimulation and guidance rather than comprehensive and detailed educational prescriptions for the schools of the state.[4]

[4] National Education Association, *Proposals for Public Education in Postwar America* (Research Bulletin No. 22, 1944), pp. 48–49.

Community Responsibility for Education

SINCE the United States is composed of fifty states, one must speak, not of the "American school system," but rather of fifty different school systems. Although all of the states are organized into some form of local school districts, these districts differ according to local conditions and the cultural and historical backgrounds of the states. State school laws list as many as sixty different names for school districts, and authorities have classified them under seventeen different headings.[5] Although there has been a constant decrease in the number of school districts in the country, due to consolidations, there were still approximately 31,700 separate school districts in the nation in 1962–63. This was a decrease from the 116,999 school districts listed in 1939–40.

A long list of court decisions has established that the responsibility for public education is a state function and that this responsibility cannot be escaped by the delegation of authority. Yet almost every American state has delegated the greater amount of its authority to local school district organizations. These are creations of the state legislatures, quasi-municipal corporations, and their powers are specifically listed in the statutes. All the powers of local districts may be increased, reduced, altered, or eliminated by action of the state legislatures. These powers usually include the right to employ and discharge school employees, purchase sites, build and equip buildings, purchase supplies and services, determine the curriculum, exercise control over students in the schools, and levy taxes to pay for carrying out these duties. All of these powers are subject to limitations in state laws and regulations. In the grant of specific powers, the right to make necessary rules and regulations and to take steps necessary to implement these responsibilities is generally assumed. However, unlike a person, a school district is not authorized to do anything which is not specifically prohibited by law.

Generally local school district organizations have been formed with the single purpose of operating the schools of the district. They are usually completely independent of other agencies of local government, which may have responsibilities for health, roads, police, fire protection, and other services. The historic unwillingness of the

[5] Walter S. Monroe, *Encyclopedia of Educational Research*, Macmillan, New York, 1950, p. 1083.

American people to place their schools under the direction of a municipal governing body is said to stem from the desire to keep education free from partisan politics. The 1962 annual *Census of Governments* of the Bureau of Census listed 34,678 school districts which were administratively and fiscally independent of any other government, and 2,341 districts which lacked sufficient autonomy to be classified as independent governmental units.

Educational authorities generally have disapproved of the fiscally dependent school district, and some evidence shows that it has not worked out well in practice. One argument against dependence has been that with education in a subordinate position, and responsibility for maintaining efficient school systems only one of a number of problems facing a local governing body, funds available are too often insufficient to provide an efficient and economical operation, and necessary funds are very difficult to obtain. Another reason for reluctance is the more frequent interference from local politics that may be expected, since city councils are much more sensitive to political pressures than are independent school boards. The extent to which local schools may be free from domination by municipal governments is a decision made by the people of the state through their law-making bodies. The most common plan is to have the schools controlled by a nonpartisan board of lay members, elected by the people and serving without pay. According to the National Education Association, in 1950 87 percent of the school districts studied elected members of the school board, and only 13 percent had appointed board members. In only 18 percent of the cases studied was the political affiliation of candidates for election to school boards indicated on the ballot.[6] In some cases where attempts have been made to absorb the schools into the municipal government there has been determined opposition.

Educational authorities have pointed out that education occupies a unique function in government and may be considered to be basic to all others. This claim has been established in court decisions and seems to be well established in practice. This does not mean that school districts are completely independent of the authority of other governmental agencies. The powers of a school district are definitely limited by the action of state legislatures. Schools and school districts are subject to court decisions and to the normal procedures

[6] National Education Association, *Fiscal Authority of City School Boards*, pp. 52–53.

for auditing the expenditure of public funds. It is in the field of local administration that the people seem to wish to keep the schools free from politics and close to the community.

FUNCTIONS OF THE BOARD OF EDUCATION

The usual officers of the school board are the president (or chairman) and the secretary (or clerk). In some states the clerk is chosen from outside the membership of the board, and in many schools the superintendent of schools is selected for this position. In such cases a clerical employee of the district keeps the minutes and records of the board, under the superintendent's direction. There has been a trend toward abolition of standing committees of the board, since matters coming before it are usually important enough to require the participation of all board members before reaching decisions.

One of the most important responsibilities of the school board is the selection of the professional staff. If the district is large enough, the executive officer is called the superintendent. The appointment of principals and teachers is generally made by the board upon the recommendation of the superintendent. School laws in most states require the board to employ professional staff members who hold valid teaching certificates in the state. In smaller districts the principal of the school has some of the responsibilities of a superintendent in larger school systems. In one-room rural school districts it is unusual for the board to consult with the teacher to any extent or to give him any responsibility other than teaching duties. In 94 percent of the districts studied by the National Education Association, the board has exclusive authority to employ nonteaching employees, without reference to any other governmental agency's civil service regulations. In general, all school boards have a free hand in the selection of teaching personnel.[7]

It is the school board which determines the educational policies of the district. In the exercise of this responsibility the board is limited by state laws and policies and by the wishes of the local community. In the development of policy the board is also influenced by the recommendations and leadership of the superintendent, who has been selected as a trained educational expert to advise them. The superintendent is also responsible for the establishment

[7] *Ibid.*, p. 70.

of channels of communication between the professional staff of the district and the board, which is composed of laymen.

It is generally agreed that the board should set the policies of the school district and that the superintendent should execute them. The boundary between policy-making and executive functions is not always clearly defined, and many possibilities for disagreement exist in this arrangement. Strong-minded board members sometimes try to interfere in routine matters of administration, and some superintendents attempt to impose their policies upon the board.

In addition to deciding upon general policy, it is the responsibility of the school board continuously to evaluate the success of the operation of the schools under the policies adopted. As a last resort, if the school board loses confidence in the advice of the superintendent or in his success in carrying out its wishes, it can, and does, make a change in executive officer. It may be, however, that some modification in policies will be indicated. Ideally, the policy of a local school district and the plan for putting it into operation should be a product of a full and complete interaction between the professional staff, the school board, and the community as a whole.

Another major responsibility of the school board is the preparation and approval of the district budget. Actually, the preliminary budget preparation is done by the superintendent and his staff; legally, the board accepts, rejects, or modifies the superintendent's recommendations and levies the taxes necessary to meet the budget. In 70 percent of the cases studied by the National Education Association the board levies its own taxes and determines the amount of these on the basis of the budget it has adopted. The budget is not subject to review by any other agency in 54 percent of the cases; in 40 percent of the cases the budget is reviewed by an outside agency, but in almost half of these the agency concerned must approve the budget as submitted. In only 6 percent of the cases is the district budget subject to review by more than one agency.[8]

Legal requirements usually say that the budget must be published before adoption, or presented at a public hearing. In 13 percent of the districts the budget must be approved by vote at a town meeting, and in 15 percent it must be approved by a school election.

The board has almost complete autonomy in spending the funds

[8] *Ibid.*, p. 56.

of the school budget, within the framework of state law. In 91 percent of the districts the board has exclusive responsibility for planning and building the school plant, and in 99 percent of the districts financial responsibility for the repair and maintenance of school buildings and equipment. The right to furnish and purchase supplies and equipment is universally a function of the local school board.

The Role of Voluntary Agencies and Private Schools

BECAUSE education is close to the heart of the average American citizen, it is not surprising that many organizations have taken an interest in what the schools are doing. Problems of increasing enrollments, shortage of teachers, needs for new buildings, and changes in curriculum arouse great interest among the lay public.

Local groups of interested parents have been formed in every part of the country to promote the welfare of local schools. These organizations were united in 1897 into a National Congress of Parents and Teachers. Each state has a State Congress, and local parent-teacher associations have increased widely throughout the country. These groups are interested in cooperation between the professional staff of the school and the people of the community, with a view to understanding each other's problems and interests in order to achieve the best possible education for their children. These associations have supported local school programs, have developed much helpful local interest and, in general, have not insisted on their own ideas as to what the schools should do. Parent-teacher associations have also served as excellent training schools for future school board members.

Not all of the organizations formed have been friendly and helpful. National and state and local groups have organized to present their own particular philosophies of education and to cause trouble for school administrators who did not agree with them. Some of these groups have been in favor of a traditional concept of education, wishing to return to methods and curricula that developed prior to the discoveries in scientific research and child psychology which have resulted in great curricular changes since the beginning of the century, and which were intended for a time when pupil populations were more selective and much more limited. Some are interested in popularizing their own particular economic ideas. Others are organizations of taxpayers, interested primarily in the reduction of local taxes and only secondarily in educational matters. All of the discussions and agitations arising out of these activities point up the need for a well-informed citizenry who have the final decisions about their own schools in their own hands.

Public education in the United States was preceded by church-related or private schools, and in spite of the tremendous growth in public schools and the great increases in public school enrollments, these nonpublic schools have retained great vitality and influence in the country. Most of the nonpublic schools in America today are church-connected. The right of a parent to select educational facilities of his own choice and at his own expense has been well established in the United States, in both practice and law. The existence of independent schools paralleling the public school system has been of real advantage to both. In general, nonpublic schools are licensed by the state or by the local school district but are quite independent of any controls except those of minimum state standards and regulations. Some of the states require nonpublic schools to meet the curricular standards of the public schools, and in some states they are required to employ teachers who hold valid state certificates.

Between 1840 and 1930 the proportion of children in public schools increased steadily, and the proportion enrolled in nonpublic schools correspondingly declined. Since 1930 the ratio of children attending nonpublic schools has remained at about 12 percent of the total national enrollment. In the main, church-connected schools follow the program of the local schools of the communities in which they are located, with the addition of religious instruction. In most states no public funds are available to support nonpublic schools, except that they are exempt from taxation. In some states certain benefits, such as free textbooks and supplies or transportation, are provided for public and nonpublic pupils alike.

About two-thirds of all the nonpublic schools in the elementary and secondary levels are operated by the Catholic Church. Most of the effort of the Protestant churches has been directed toward the establishment and support of church-connected institutions of higher learning. Nearly two-thirds of all the colleges and universities are independent or church-connected, but the public institutions enroll 61.2 percent of all the students. In 1962, of 2,043 higher educational institutions in the United States, 729 were tax-supported. Of the remainder 472 were independent, 481 Catholic, 334 Protestant, and 27 were Jewish, Latter Day Saints, or other sects.

Problems of Administration and Control

THE GREAT experiment in American education is the attempt to offer free public education to all, from the first grade through high school, in a democratically controlled system. All of the problems in administration and control of public education have not been solved, and many varied lines of attack and proposed solutions have been attempted or suggested. Some of the problems upon which the American people have been working are indicated below. It will be interesting to see, as this study proceeds, how many of the problems listed are common to school systems in many other parts of the world.

Need for Fewer and Larger School Districts

The movement for consolidation of small districts, reducing the number of one-teacher schools and weak administrative units, has progressed rapidly in the United States. In a way this is a move toward centralization, for it results in a reduction of the number of elected school boards. The problem of how to retain control by the voters of larger and more efficient units has received much attention.

The advantages of the larger unit of administration are obvious. The number of very small schools is reduced, and children can attend schools where each teacher teaches only one grade. Educational opportunities within a state can be more nearly equalized, and differences in ability to support local schools are evened out by a wider tax base. Larger schools can provide professional leadership and supervision; special facilities for, and trained teachers of, music, art, and physical education; health services; hot lunches; and better libraries. Better buildings can be provided, which become centers for the larger community.

But the movement toward consolidation is not universally accepted. Many rural people are strongly opposed to school consolidations, because they feel that they will lose their own small school and become submerged in the larger community. Many parents oppose having their children ride to school many miles in a school bus.

The question of just how large or how small an ideal school unit should be has not yet been settled to everyone's satisfaction.

Extent of State Participation in School Support

The local school district has depended almost entirely upon local land taxes for its revenues. If the area is wealthy, a comparatively small tax provides an excellent school. If the district is poor, even high taxes provide only a minimum program and meager facilities. Even the consolidation of a number of poor districts into one larger unit may not improve the financial position. Only the state, with its wider tax base and multiple sources of funds, is able to help in such cases. The problem of equalizing the burden of school support through state funds has been approached in various ways. State school funds have been used to pay grants to districts, rich and poor alike, on the basis of actual days of attendance. Other states have used state school funds to match local revenues on the basis of local effort to solve their problems. Sometimes state funds are used to equalize the burdens between poor and rich districts. In almost every state the amount of state support has increased in recent years. In 1960–61 the average of state support in the fifty states was 56.3 percent of the total cost, ranging from 4.0 percent in Nebraska to 79.6 percent in Delaware.

No state has yet achieved an ideal system of state support, but several of the states have developed excellent systems. The problem of the proper division of the burden of school costs between the state and the local districts, and of maintaining the proper relationship between the administrative responsibilities of the two agencies, remains to be completely solved.

Federal Aid for Education

School districts within a state are unequal in wealth and ability to support school services, and in the proportion of their population who are of school age, and similar disparities exist among the states of the union. Since mobility is high among the American people, poorly educated children from a needy state may become poorly educated adults in a wealthy state with fine schools. The experience of two wars showed the American people that rejections from the armed forces were greatest in states with low per capita wealth and minimum school standards. The demand for equalization from federal funds has developed throughout the nation.

It is generally agreed that the federal government should show an interest in the education of all the people. Disagreement arises when the question of how this concern should be made manifest is attacked in definite legislative proposals. It is recognized that federal funds appropriated to the schools will require some federal control of expenditures. If the money is made available for equalization, then the Congress will have to set up normal procedures to insure that the funds are spent for that purpose, in accordance with the provisions of the law. Fear of federal control in education coming with federal support arises mainly in the area of prescriptions of courses and standards of instruction and in the administration of state schools. Recent bills in Congress which have proposed federal aid to the states have contained specifically worded provisions that control, administration, and supervision of schools and educational programs are to be reserved to the states and are expressly forbidden to federal agencies. Even this definite wording has not entirely satisfied the critics who insist that when money comes, control follows.

The traditional separation of church and state in the United States also raises questions concerning the use of federal funds for education. Some insist that federal aid should be given to the children, not to the schools, and that grants should be made to public and nonpublic educational programs alike. Others feel strongly that public funds should be devoted only to public purposes, and that any federal aid to education should be allocated only to public schools in the states. The difficulty of finding any satisfactory formula that will meet with the approval of all concerned has delayed the passage of any aid-to-education bill by Congress. The problem of how to secure the aid of the broad taxing powers of the nation, and at the same time safeguard state and local control and meet the problems of the nonpublic schools, is still unsettled.

Relations of Local Districts to State and Municipal Authorities

When a school district has the right to levy taxes and to control its own budget, without the approval of some other state or municipal agency, it is said to be fiscally independent. If the board must secure the approval, in whole or in part, of a mayor, city council, or county commission in order to levy and spend taxes, it is fiscally dependent. In a large majority of the states school boards are fiscally independent, and the trend in favor of this situation seems to be increasing.

Educators and the public generally seem to have accepted the view that education is a state service and not a municipal one, and that school districts were established by the state to perform a specialized task. Political scientists who are interested in the coordination of public services frequently disagree with this point of view. They insist that municipalities as well as school districts are state creations, and that the state may, if it chooses, decide to combine them. They affirm that schools are only one of the many phases of local government and that they should not be financed or administered independently. School administrators argue that the schools are the most cherished public institutions and that to make them fiscally or otherwise dependent upon officials with many other interests and responsibilities would make them subordinate to less important functions and would do great harm. Studies have indicated that independent school districts show some superiority over dependent school districts, insofar as efficiency could be reflected in the distribution of the school dollar. But objective evidence bearing on this point is not complete or conclusive.

There appears to be no conclusive evidence that if education is a function of the state, local school systems must be independent of municipal authority. Many problems call for a coordinated attack by school or city authorities. One point of view is that expressed by DeYoung: "It seems not to be a question of fiscal independence or dependence, but the degree of voluntary interdependence." [9] On the other hand, Willard Givens, former secretary of the National Education Association, insisted that "control of the budget is an essential function of the local school board. A budget is a statement of educational policy in financial terms. Those who control the budget have the last word on educational policy. Everyone will agree that our schools can serve society best if kept free from partisan politics. Separation of education from other municipal functions is helpful in doing that. There is no other public service where partisan interference is more disastrous than in education.[10]

There are many areas, such as recreation, parks and playgrounds, health services, community planning, where the local school district and the local municipal authorities must work very closely together.

[9] Chris A. DeYoung, *Introduction to American Public Education*, 2nd ed., McGraw-Hill, New York, 1950, p. 666.

[10] Willard E. Givens, "Shall School Systems Be Independent of Other Government Agencies—The Affirmative," *School Life*, November, 1948, p. 48.

The problems of control and of budgetary relations have not been solved in every community or state. The trend seems to favor a greater degree of voluntary and legal cooperation between the school administration and city management, rather than the absorption of the school district by the municipal government.[11]

Education in the United States provides an interesting example of an interrelationship between national, state, and local governments. Although the major control rests with the people in the local communities, there has been a continual trend toward larger units of administration and greater financial support from the state. Through all of this, the principle of local control, with its corollary of intense local interest in schools, has been preserved.

[11] National Education Association, Educational Research Service, *Relationship of a Local School System to a Council-Manager Plan of Municipal Government*, April, 1939, p. 7.

4

Divided Responsibility: England and Wales

MARKED changes have taken place during the present century in English education. England was late and somewhat hesitant in entering the field of national education, and for many years a system of class stratification was reflected in the organization of the schools. It was difficult for a child of relatively poor parents to obtain the benefits of a good secondary education, and the higher positions in the professions and the civil service fell almost inevitably into the hands of graduates coming from the wealthier and more privileged classes.

At the present time, however, a reorganized system of English education aims to help establish a social democracy, and finds itself in the ranks of the world's most progressive educational systems. The change was gradual, but there was considerable acceleration during the reign of George V (1910–35), and the Education Act of 1944, passed while England was being assailed by such weapons as the V-2, must rank as one of the most farsighted pieces of educational legislation passed in any country. Scotland and Wales [1] shared in this

---

[1] In order that the reader may not be confused by the nomenclature, it should be noted that the official name of the country is "The United Kingdom of Great Britain and Northern Ireland." The term "Great Britain" includes England, Wales, and Scotland. The term "British" pertains to the British Commonwealth or dependencies. The populations of the constituent parts were (in the last census, 1961): England and Wales, 46,077,000 (of whom 2,640,000 lived in Wales); Scotland, 5,178,000; and Northern Ireland, 1,425,000.

This chapter deals primarily with educational developments in England and Wales, but in dealing with economic changes it is sometimes necessary to refer to all of Britain. Separate sections will deal with education in Scotland and Northern Ireland.

movement, but Scotland has had a different educational background and history and will be treated in a separate section at the end of this chapter.

The Historical Background

THIS book contends that drastic educational changes in any country stem from important social and economic changes. The first task of this chapter, therefore, will be to examine briefly the changes of this nature which have taken place in Britain.

ENGLAND IN THE NINETEENTH CENTURY

During the decades which followed the establishment of the American colonies, Britain, with its central geographic position and good ports, became the center of world trade. The developments in manufacturing during the Industrial Revolution turned her into the workshop of the world. Her ships were found in every sea and brought her great stores of raw materials which, with her high-grade coal supplies and abundant labor, enabled her to manufacture articles needed by the whole world. London became a very important banking center. Britain's colonies and dominions provided materials from all parts of the globe, and her prosperity was so great that she was able to make substantial foreign investments and establish credits in many countries. The biggest and strongest navy in the world guarded her trade lanes and guaranteed the safety of the home island.

Other salient characteristics of nineteenth-century England were nine hundred years of freedom from invasion, a strong tradition of individual liberty, a conservative established church, the economic doctrine of laissez faire, and relatively rigid social classes. The upper classes were powerful and influential. A strong middle class of businessmen, prosperous farmers, shopkeepers, and professional men was often referred to as "the backbone of the country."

The educational system in the nineteenth century followed this general organization of society. The great public schools, which were really wealthy and exclusive church and private schools, catered for the sons of the upper and middle classes. Their products had a virtual monopoly of places at Oxford and Cambridge universities and subsequently of positions in the civil service and the professions. The civil service had a fine tradition of efficiency and devotion to duty, well exemplified by a sentence taken from a civil service report issued in 1928: "The public expects a standard of integrity in conduct not only inflexible but fastidious." When Stanley Baldwin formed a Cabinet in the years preceding World War II, he made the statement, "I hope to form a government of which Harrow will be proud." Even in the Churchill government of 1951, a majority of the Cabinet members had been educated at Eton or Harrow. In 1963 Macmillan's Conservative government had a considerable number of former public school boys in its Cabinet.

A widespread network of county schools, under the aegis of the National Board of Education, provided a basic education for those boys who were destined to fill the humbler positions of life. There was slow but definite progress within the network of these county schools, and signs of a change were evident before World War I, but the whole educational system was representative of a prosperous and complacent England with very strong vested class interests.

WAR AND SOCIAL CHANGE

The twentieth century saw two world wars in which Britain spent her blood and treasure in desperate struggles to stem the tide of German aggression and maintain the ideals of democracy. She was well supported by the British Commonwealth and several powerful democratic allies, but in the early stages of each war she had to face a critical situation almost alone. In World War II, particularly, her imports stopped, her food supplies were low, and her war expenditures reached fantastic figures. She was forced to draw upon her overseas credits and foreign investments until they were expended. Victory in 1945 found her exhausted and in a difficult economic position.

Meanwhile in the years between the two wars other significant world changes had been taking place. Other nations had become important manufacturing centers, notably the United States, Germany, and Japan. The British Dominions and colonies had begun to set up their own factories. Britain's monopoly was gone, and she found herself in the position of having to fight for her economic existence. With the exception of coal, she was poor in natural resources, and incoming raw material and food had to be paid for.

Between 1945 and 1952 Britain made a gallant effort to reduce the alarming gap between the value of her exports and imports. She imposed heavy restrictions on a people that had already been severely tried during the war; she fought hard to increase her productivity and succeeded in raising the level of this figure to 70 percent higher than before the war. Then came another blow: Britain's expenditures were greatly increased by the need to rearm against possible aggression by Russia. Whether her economy would be able to stand the strain and whether she could continue to impose such heavy burdens on her own people were grave questions. The latter point was particularly important because great social changes had taken place and England had recognized the necessity of embarking on an ambitious program of social welfare.

Britain, in spite of the beauty of her countryside, has long been an urban and industrial country. The density of population in 1961 was about 564 to the square mile, compared with about 50 in the United States. Thirteen people work in mining, manufacturing, and building for every one in agriculture.[2] At the end of 1960 the total membership of British trade unions was about 9,803,000.[3] There were 650 trade unions, most of whose members support the Labor party. It is important to note that the British Labor party (influenced by the ideas of the well-known Fabian Society) discourages any idea of change by revolution or violence; it aims instead at gaining seats in Parliament and in local municipal councils by making a persuasive democratic appeal to the people.

The Labor party stands strongly for the principles of full employment, national ownership of public utilities, and an effective system of social security. Labor gained a signal victory at the polls after the war and formed a strong government which proceeded to enact legislation putting the party ideas into effect. The Conservative government which succeeded it, while upholding the necessity of retaining individual enterprise for the capitalist class, found itself obliged to continue a system which envisaged material prosperity for the whole people.

Class stratification in England still exists, but it is definitely being modified and lessened in importance. Clerical workers, shop assistants, and white-collar workers seem to be moving into the middle class, while the upper class is so heavily hit by taxation that in 1960 only 3,000 persons had an income, after paying taxes, of £6,000 or more a year. It is significant also that at Oxford and Cambridge many boys and girls from county secondary schools are now secur-

[2] *Britain: An Official Handbook*, 1963, p. 257.
[3] *Ibid.*, p. 471.

ing places and are also competing successfully in the examinations for admission to the civil service. It would seem that a "silent social revolution" is already well in progress.

In 1942 the Beveridge Report,[4] which met with general approval, declared the necessity of making war on "the giants of want, ignorance, idleness, squalor, and disease." This was to be done by means of a widespread program of social insurance and other measures aiming at freeing the people from the fears of dire poverty through unemployment, ill health, or desolate old age. In the years following the publication of this momentous report, the following measures appeared on the statute books:

1. The Education Act of 1944.
2. The system of Family Allowances (1946). (Five shillings a week until the age of 16 for each child in a family after the first. In 1962 this was raised to five shillings for the second child below the set age limits, and ten shillings for each subsequent child. The age limits are 15 for children who leave school at that age, and 18 for children who remain in school or are apprentices.)
3. National Insurance (not a dole system, but contributory insurance against sickness, unemployment, and industrial accidents).
4. National Health Service (involving free medical attention and hospital care and aimed at preventing illness as well as curing it).
5. The subsidizing of a planned system of housing.
6. The Town and Country Planning Act, whereby all developments were to be planned and supervised to prevent exploitation.
7. Welfare Services for the blind, the deaf, the disabled, and the old.
8. Welfare Services for children deprived of normal home life.

Thus we find Britain moving away from her older policy of laissez-faire and becoming a welfare state. Apparently one of the most important problems associated with this program is whether Britain can continue a policy of this sort, greatly increasing the controlling functions of the state and at the same time retaining her devotion to individual liberty. It may be that the answer lies partly in the provisions of the Education Act of 1944, which will be dealt with later in this chapter. If real equality of educational opportunity is attained,

[4] Sir William Beveridge, *Social Insurance and Allied Services*, H.M.S.O., London, and Macmillan, New York, 1942.

Britain will have moved a long way toward the ideal of a genuine social democracy.

What will all this provision for social security and general improvement of education cost? The cost is prodigious, although about half of the expense of social security measures is met by direct contributions. Putting the Education Act into operation meant the expenditure of nearly £300,000,000 per annum in the years immediately following the Act, but there was no road back. The expenditure on education for England and Wales (excluding university education) was estimated for 1962–63 at £1,017,000,000. Somehow the money was forthcoming, and the years 1945 to 1963 proved a time of great achievement in public education in England and Wales.

Landmarks in English Educational History

AN UNDERSTANDING of the present situation in English education is not possible unless the reader has some knowledge of the main happenings since 1700. Some of the most significant of these educational changes are mentioned below.

THE EIGHTEENTH-CENTURY BACKGROUND

In the early eighteenth century there were a number of grammar schools for boys, some of which were old foundations [5] going back to the fifteenth and sixteenth centuries. The most important and successful of these eventually came to be known as "public schools." Examples are Winchester (1387), Eton (1441), Rugby (1567), and Harrow (1571). There are two universities, Oxford and Cambridge, that date back to the thirteenth century. The only provision for education of the poorer classes was in dame schools and charity schools, the latter being established mainly by the Society for Promoting Christian Knowledge.

In the late eighteenth century Robert Raikes initiated a system of Sunday schools that was immediately successful and expanded rapidly under the influence of the Methodist Revival. The object was "to turn into respectable men and women the little heathen of the neighborhood." By 1800 these schools numbered more than 1,000. In the early nineteenth century, John Pounds, a cobbler, started "ragged schools" for destitute children, waifs, and strays.

---

[5] In England a "foundation" means an "endowed institution," the term often being applied to monasteries, schools, and hospitals.

They taught the three R's, together with some trade instruction, and gave one meal a day to the pupils. They were supported by gifts, and in 1870 there were 200 ragged schools in London.

In 1807 a Parochial Schools Bill aiming at two years' schooling for all children between the ages of 7 and 14 was passed by the House of Commons but was rejected by the House of Lords. In the early nineteenth century two religious societies, the National Society (Church of England) and the British and Foreign School Society established a number of elementary schools for both boys and girls. These schools used the monitorial system of Bell and Lancaster, whereby one teacher, aided by monitors, could handle about a hundred children. Finance was obtained from voluntary subscriptions and modest school fees.

THE BEGINNING OF STATE INTERVENTION

In 1833 the state made its first grant for education by allotting £20,000 to the two societies for building schoolhouses. In 1839, in spite of considerable opposition, this grant was increased to £30,000. In the same year an Education Department was established to supervise the distribution of grants and ensure efficiency in the schools. This was really the beginning of the present Ministry of Education.

With the aid of these grants, which were soon extended to cover more than buildings, and by collecting subscriptions and charging small fees, the two societies and others like them carried on, and gradually extended, their system of elementary education. It became obvious, however, that the situation was growing too complex for the voluntary societies to handle, and in 1870 an Elementary Education Act was passed in spite of strong opposition. School boards, locally elected, were required to provide elementary schools in areas untouched by the societies. As a result of the new act two types of elementary schools, "board schools" and "voluntary schools," began to exist side by side, both charging fees and both receiving state grants. The board schools, however, were supported by local taxes, while the voluntary schools still relied to a large extent upon philanthropic subscriptions. Education was still neither compulsory nor free. In 1880 elementary education was made compulsory, in 1891 it was made free in all but a few centers, and in 1899 the leaving age was raised to 12 years.

New universities were founded, London in 1836 and Durham in 1837. Later several university colleges, which prepared students for

London degrees, were established in the provinces. Most of these colleges subsequently acquired independent university status: for example, the university college in Birmingham became independent in 1900, Manchester in 1903, Liverpool in 1903, and Sheffield in 1905.

During the nineteenth century many more "public schools" came into existence, and there grew up a number of private preparatory schools which prepared boys for subsequent admission to public schools. These preparatory schools were expensive boarding schools. In the latter half of the century boarding schools for girls began to appear, organized on somewhat similar lines to the public schools for boys.

The turn of the century saw the replacement of the Education Department by the Board of Education, which supervised the development of English education until the 1944 Act changed it into the Ministry of Education.

TWENTIETH-CENTURY DEVELOPMENTS

In 1902 the Balfour Act made some significant changes. The school boards were abolished, and in their place the major local government bodies (the county or borough councils) were constituted as local education authorities (usually referred to as L.E.A.'s).[6] They were charged with the provision and support of elementary schools together with the supervision of instruction in these schools. This linked educational developments with the strong and effective system of local government in England and ensured local interest in the schools. The terms in use have changed little; the schools are now known as "council" or "county" or "provided" schools in contrast to the "voluntary" or "nonprovided" schools. The L.E.A.'s were also empowered to make arrangements for the establishment of county secondary or technical schools, to take over or grant financial assistance to existing grammar [7] schools, and to establish colleges for the training of teachers. Many of the voluntary schools agreed to accept this financial aid and to meet certain conditions laid down by the Board of Education.

In 1918 the Fisher Act cleared away the remaining fees in ele-

[6] The constitution and function of the L.E.A.'s is described fully later in this chapter (see pages 73–76).

[7] American readers should note that in England a "grammar school" is a secondary school and not a "grade" or "elementary" school.

mentary schools and made it compulsory for pupils to remain in school until the end of the term in which they reached their fourteenth birthday. At the same time it gave the L.E.A.'s the task of providing advanced practical instruction in senior or central schools for the older pupils. The 1918 Act also provided for the establishment of continuation schools, on the German pattern, for boys and girls 14 to 18 years of age who had left school. Attendance was to be compulsory for two half-days a week on the employer's time.

By this time the county secondary schools had increased in number and had become increasingly important in the community. In 1926 appeared the Hadow Report,[8] one of the most significant and influential documents ever issued by the Board of Education. This report pointed out that, in view of the imminence of secondary education for all pupils, there should be various types of secondary schools, particularly a "modern school," which would give a nonacademic type of secondary education for those pupils who did not wish to proceed along academic lines. Several of the L.E.A.'s experimented with this type of program, although not always using the name "modern school."

In 1936 another Education Act proposed that the upper limit of compulsory education should be raised to age 15, as of September 1, 1939, and also gave the L.E.A.'s the power to make grants to voluntary schools in order that there might be sufficient accommodation available for senior pupils when the leaving age was raised. The outbreak of World War II in 1939 unfortunately caused the suspension of many of the provisions of this act.

The twenty years prior to 1939 had seen a great expansion and improvement in both elementary and secondary education. The Spens Report (1938) had sketched plans and curricula for a technical type of secondary school and had also indicated that certain reforms in educational methods and procedure might with advantage be applied to the work of the grammar schools. There developed, however, such a diversity of types of school and so many anomalies that overseas observers were often puzzled to find any clear pattern in English education. Developments which had taken place seemed not to have been applied to the country as a whole, largely due to the English emphasis on the importance of local autonomy. It was ob-

[8] Board of Education, *The Education of the Adolescent*, H.M.S.O., London, 1926.

vious that there was need for coordination and consolidation. This was supplied by the Education Act of 1944, which was not so much a new departure as a measure based on the experience and experiment of previous years, presenting a coherent and comprehensive plan which would be applicable to the schools of the whole nation. The 1944 Act will be described later in this chapter.

THE ENGLISH TRADITION OF EDUCATION

Largely as a result of the ideals and work of the public schools, there had evolved an English tradition of education which placed great stress on the training of character. This tradition has been described by Sir Cyril Norwood as consisting of five elements: religion, culture, discipline, athletics, and service.[9] There is no doubt that this tradition passed over to, and influenced the work of, the county secondary schools. To it was added, however, a new outlook whereby the benefits of a good secondary education were to be made available to all children, and not merely a grammar school education at that. This position was well put by the Minister of Education at the time, Ellen Wilkinson, in her foreword to the pamphlet *The New Secondary Education:*

> As this pamphlet comes out, the British people are learning by the hard way to know how dependent is a civilized community on its farmers, transporters and miners, its manual and technical workers. Income and hours of work are now being adjusted accordingly. . . . The change in the public attitude to the craftsman and the technician is nothing less than revolutionary, and it has taken two world wars to teach the lesson. . . . Until education in the State secondary schools is as good as the best money can buy outside the State system, so long will inequalities remain. . . . No child must be forced into an academic education which bores it to rebellion, merely because that type of grammar education is considered more socially desirable by parents who can afford to pay for it. . . . The schools must have freedom to experiment, room to grow, variety for the sake of freshness, for the fun of it even. Laughter in the classroom, self-confidence growing every day, eager interest instead of bored conformity, this is the way to produce from our fine stock Britons who will have no need to fear the new scientific age, but will stride into it heads high, determined to master science and to serve mankind.[10]

[9] Cyril Norwood, *The English Tradition of Education.*

[10] Ministry of Education, *The New Secondary Education* (London), Pamphlet No. 9.

THE EDUCATION ACT, 1944

At this stage it might be well to give a summary of the main provisions of this important Act, still the basic framework of education in England and Wales. It set out to give every child and youth in the country an education suited to his individual abilities and aptitudes, irrespective of his social or financial position.

The Act simplified the whole system without giving up the variety and freedom which is so characteristic of English education. At the same time there is no doubt that it gave the national government an increase in power and control: whereas previously it was optional for a local authority to provide nursery schools, secondary schools, technical colleges, colleges of art, and Further Education, it now became *compulsory* for the authority to make this provision.

Administration

The Board of Education becomes the Ministry of Education, whose political head is the Minister of Education with a seat in the Cabinet. The number of local education authorities is reduced from about 300 to 146—62 counties and 83 county boroughs [11]—with the object of eliminating some of the weaker authorities and having larger units for increased efficiency.

Three Stages of Education

Primary. Primary education is divided into three stages: (a) nursery school and kindergarten—up to 5 years; (b) infant school—5 to 7 years; and (c) junior school—7 to 11 years. The term *elementary* disappears.

Secondary. Three kinds of secondary school are provided for: (a) secondary grammar school—with an academic type of curriculum leading toward university work; (b) secondary technical school—for those pupils with a distinct aptitude for and leanings toward technical work of a fairly high standard; and (c) secondary modern school—for those pupils whose needs are not met by either of the types of school mentioned above, but who would enjoy and profit by a balanced program of cultural and practical work, with a good deal of creative activities, physical education, and craft work.

The local education authorities have the right to combine all

---

[11] There is also one joint board for a county and a borough (Peterborough), raising the total number of L.E.A.'s to 146.

of these secondary programs into one "omnibus" school or to house them in separate school buildings on the same campus, but care must be taken that all three types have parity of esteem. Parents' wishes for the future of their children must be considered, but each local education authority has the final say in the allocation of pupils to schools.

Further Education. According to the Act, part-time and full-time vocational education is to be provided by the local education authorities up to the age of 18 years. Part-time courses are to be given, without fees, in county colleges and village colleges for one day or two half-days a week on the employer's time. The work is to be cultural as well as vocational, with emphasis on training for citizenship. For full-time vocational education, commercial colleges or colleges of art and music are to be provided by the local education authority. Fees may be charged in these, but no qualified student is to be debarred from taking a course through inability to pay these fees.

The Act sets the ages of compulsory education as from 5 to 15 years, with the Minister given the power to raise the upper limit to 16 years as soon as sufficient buildings and teachers become available.

Special Services and Social Welfare

Each local education authority is obliged to provide:

1. Special schools for children suffering from various kinds of physical handicaps.

2. Adequate medical service, including free medical and dental examination and treatment.

3. Boarding accommodation for those children who would otherwise be deprived of suitable education by the distance of schools from their homes. (When possible, parents are to help in defraying the expense involved.)

4. Clothing and footwear in case of necessity.

5. Free transport to school when a child under 8 years of age has to walk two miles, or a child over 8 years of age has to walk three miles. (In certain cases, where the additional distance is caused by the parent's desire to send his child to a particular school, the question of expense is to be discussed with the L.E.A. concerned.)

6. Facilities and equipment for recreational and physical training, including camps, playing areas, swimming pools, school journeys, and the like.

7. Free milk in the middle of the school morning.

8. A midday meal for all school pupils. (Funds for this are provided in a special grant from the Ministry of Education.)

Religious Education

The Act made the following provisions in the field of religious instruction:

1. In all schools, county or voluntary, the school day is to commence with an act of collective worship.

2. Similarly, in all county or voluntary schools, regular religious instruction must be given.

3. On the principle that religious liberty is an inalienable right of the British people, parents may ask for their children to be exempted from attendance at religious instruction or the daily religious assembly.

4. If a parent for valid religious reasons wishes to send his child to a particular school not in the immediate neighborhood of his home, this may be arranged with the L.E.A. concerned, provided unreasonable expenditure of funds is avoided. The L.E.A., however, must be satisfied that the general education in the school selected is suitable for the particular child.

5. No voluntary school is permitted to prevent any child from attending school for the reason that he does not attend any particular Sunday school or church.

6. In cases where voluntary schools have difficulty in maintaining the standard of buildings or curricula laid down by the Ministry of Education, they may elect to become "controlled schools." In that case the L.E.A. concerned will assume all responsibility for maintenance, building extensions, and repairs, but the school will be limited in any special type of denominational religious instruction to two days a week: on the other three days religious instruction must be given on the same lines as the "agreed syllabus" in county schools.

7. On the other hand, voluntary schools may elect to become "aided schools," in which case the L.E.A. concerned will only be responsible for maintenance, and the school managers will undertake all building alterations, extensions, and repairs. In these cases they may give the type of religious education which they desire.

8. In all schools supported entirely by public funds, the religious education will be according to an "agreed syllabus," quite apart from any particular creed or denomination.

Assistance Toward Higher Education

Provision is made for a generous system of state scholarships to assist able pupils to attend universities, technical schools, and other types of higher educational institutions. These scholarships provide not only the tuition fees but maintenance allowances based on the parental income, the allowances disappearing when the income of the parents reaches £1,500 per annum.

Private Schools

All private or church schools are registered and must submit to inspection to ensure that they meet the Ministry's standards of buildings, equipment, and qualifications of staff.

Schools which were formerly independent may apply for direct financial grants from the Ministry. In the event of grants being given, the schools may continue to charge fees, but the fee schedule must be approved by the Minister of Education. In addition they must offer 25 percent of their places to children from the primary schools and must agree to representation of the appropriate L.E.A. on their boards of governors.

It will be noted that although the government comes much more prominently into the educational picture than previously, the system of voluntary schools is retained side by side with the county schools. There are also numerous instances in the Act of tolerant provisions to prevent hardship and to avoid cutting off freedom of choice on the part of parents. The British desire for flexibility and freedom, with the strong belief that too much mechanization will kill a good plan, is evident in many of the provisions and in the way in which they have been applied. The Act, however, made a move toward an "ordered freedom," and there were many who felt that it contained a distinct danger of overemphasis on government authority and control. Nearly twenty years of experience, however, with the operation of the 1944 Act have shown that these fears were groundless; the same mixture of help, cooperation, and freedom was maintained.

The Role of the National Government

EDUCATION in England and Wales is administered by a mixture of centralized direction on broad policy matters and local autonomy in working out all the details. The Ministry of Education itself emphasizes that there are three essential characteristics of English education:

1. Although the final word on national policy remains with the Minister, great care is taken to ensure that the autonomy of the publicly elected local authorities is a reality. The Ministry of Education neither owns a school nor appoints a teacher.

2. A prominent part in educational affairs is played by voluntary agencies. In the past such an important share in the provision of educational facilities has fallen to religious societies and philanthropic bodies, at a time when the government was slow to act, that the tradition remains and is considered worthy of retention.

3. Head teachers are free to organize their schools as they wish, and there is no attempt on the part of the Ministry to dictate to teachers on such matters as curricula, syllabuses, teaching methods, or textbooks. The Ministry assists teachers by issuing many helpful pamphlets and circulars. One of the best known of these is the *Handbook of Suggestions for the Considerations of Teachers*. It will be noted, however, that the word *suggestions* was used, and not *directions*.[12]

The 1944 Act defines the duty of the Minister of Education as follows:

To promote the education of the people of England and Wales and the progressive development of institutions devoted to that purpose and to secure the effective execution by local authorities, under his control and direction, of the national policy for providing a varied and comprehensive educational service in every area.

The administrative system of the Ministry of Education, with its headquarters in London, can best be illustrated by the diagram in Figure 4-1.

The work of H.M.I. (Her Majesty's Inspectors) is so important that it needs to be described in some detail. The functions of the inspectorate can be briefly set out as follows:

1. To report to the Ministry on the efficiency of all educational institutions in their districts. (The inspectors are allotted districts and live in them.)

[12] Ministry of Education, *A Guide to the Educational System of England and Wales* (London), Pamphlet No. 2.

Fig. 4–1 Organization of the Ministry of Education in London

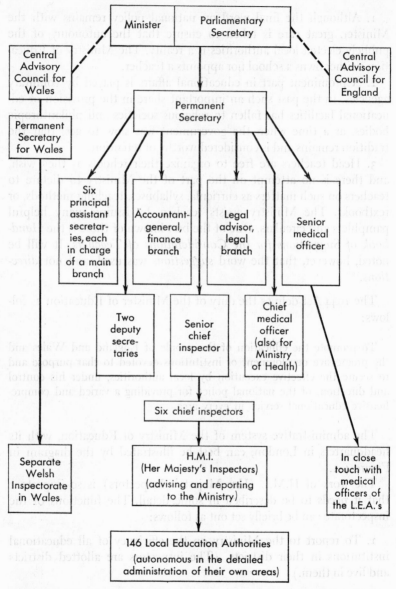

In 1964 the Ministry of Education was placed under a Secretary of State for education and science, with two Ministers under him.

2. To keep the Ministry informed on matters of educational procedure and teaching methods.

3. To advise the Ministry on general problems of organization and policy.

4. To assist the Ministry in the compilation of pamphlets and handbooks designed to be of help to administrators and teachers.

5. To advise the L.E.A.'s on matters of general educational policy, acting as representatives of the Ministry of Education.

6. To give help and guidance to schools and teachers in their districts.

7. To organize conferences and courses of instruction for teachers.

8. To keep in touch with professional associations, bodies conducting special examinations, and industrial and commercial organizations interested in education.

9. In certain cases to devote themselves for a period to study special aspects of educational work, for which they are qualified, such as educational broadcasts.

The inspectors do not rate individual teachers, as is the case in some centralized systems. It will be seen that H.M.I. need to be men of high professional qualifications, trained in administration and guidance, and should possess records of successful practical experience in schools. In order that they may keep themselves up to date they are given facilities, from time to time, for study, travel, and educational research.

The Role of the Local Community

THERE are no states in England and Wales, as in the United States and Australia: their place is taken to a certain extent by counties. Local government is strong, but it is becoming increasingly difficult to speak of any area of government which is entirely local and not affected by national policies and financial support. All local authority in Great Britain is delegated to local governing bodies by the national government. There are 62 administrative counties in England and Wales, and 83 county boroughs, which are the larger urban areas. County boroughs are independent, administratively, of the counties in which they are located. London has special administrative autonomy, but all of the other important cities in England and Wales are county boroughs. It should be pointed out that county boroughs are "one-tier" authorities, which exercise all local government powers within their areas. Administrative counties, on the other hand, are "two-tier" authorities, exercising some county-wide powers and sharing their powers and functions with other subdivisions, such as municipal districts or noncounty boroughs, urban districts, and rural districts. The rural districts are still further subdivided into parishes. For the purposes of local educational administration use is made of the 62 counties and 83 county boroughs.

The county and borough councils which are constituted as local educational authorities naturally have other important duties besides the supervision of education. They appoint Education Committees which do the educational work, while the ultimate financial responsibility remains with the council concerned. A majority of the members of the Education Committee must be members of the council; the others are usually prominent citizens interested in education and acquainted with the educational needs of the districts. The L.E.A., through its committee, appoints a Chief Education Officer or Director of Education who has much the same powers as a superintendent of schools in the United States. Under him is an administrative and clerical staff together with a team of specialists or organizers and possibly some school inspectors employed by the L.E.A. (not to be confused with H.M.I.).

To each L.E.A. is entrusted the work of ensuring that a full working system of primary and secondary education, together with units for further education, is in operation in its area. As some of the counties are large, with big population, certain of their educational functions may be delegated to "divisional executives." In a borough or urban district, for example, where the county authority would find it difficult to secure the specialized knowledge necessary for successful administration, such decentralization would occur.

Divisional executives consist of representatives of the county council, the various urban and rural councils within the division, the teachers in the county schools, and the managers and governors of voluntary schools. To these representatives may be added one or two persons in each division with special experience in educational affairs. The divisional executives work under the general supervision of, and keep closely in touch with, the county local education authority, which empowers each divisional executive to act for it in seeing that the provisions of the 1944 Education Act are put into operation in the district concerned.

Each secondary school has a board of governors. Some primary schools have boards of managers, although in many cases several primary schools are grouped together under the same board of managers. The powers of these bodies depend upon whether the school they govern is a voluntary school or one of the schools established by the L.E.A.

Teachers are appointed and employed by the L.E.A., after consideration of the recommendation of the boards of governors or managers concerned. There is security of tenure, and the salaries are laid down in a scale applicable to the whole of England and Wales, drawn up by a joint committee consisting of representatives of the L.E.A.'s and the teachers' association. A new appointee takes up his post at the salary indicated on the schedule for his qualifications and experience, irrespective of the L.E.A. for which he works.

Each L.E.A. was required by the 1944 Act to make a careful survey of the existing facilities for education in its area, together with what it considered to be the necessary expansions and developments. These "development plans," as they were called, were to be submitted to the Minister by April 1, 1946. Most of the L.E.A.'s went to great trouble in making these surveys and produced interesting and valuable plans for future development. If the Minister approved he issued an "education order" for the district, indicating the steps and timetable by which the improvements might be commenced: this was necessary as the Ministry would pay at least 50 percent of the cost.

In general it might be said that considerable interest is taken by each local community in the work and plans of its L.E.A. or divisional executive. Local municipal elections usually involve statements by the candidates about desirable educational projects and policies. Parents are interested in the election or nomination of managers and governors for schools and are keen to work with head teachers and staff members for the improvement of facilities in the schools. There is no doubt that the administrative system developed in England and Wales has managed to combine effectively a national education policy directed in helpful fashion by the Ministry of Education with retention of autonomy and keen public interest in each local education district.

A diagram of an actual county in England will help to show how the system of local education authorities works. The county is Lancashire.

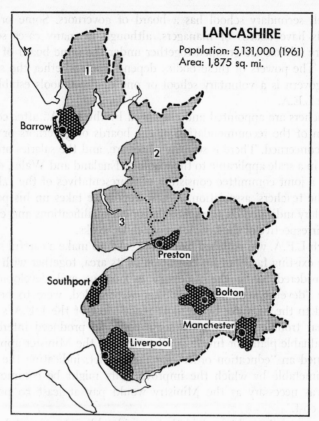

LANCASHIRE
Population: 5,131,000 (1961)
Area: 1,875 sq. mi.

Barrow

1

2

3

Preston

Southport

Bolton

Manchester

Liverpool

Educational Administration in Lancashire
(Showing the county, some of the county boroughs, and three
divisional executives.)

Preston is the county town, and the Chief Education Officer for Lancashire has his office
there. He is the executive officer for the county L.E.A., which supervises the whole of
Lancashire except the county boroughs. But Preston itself is a county borough, with its
own Education Officer.

There are 16 county boroughs which deal directly with the Ministry of Education: each of
these has its own Education Officer. Sample county boroughs shaded on the diagram
are Barrow, Preston, Southport, Bolton, Liverpool, Manchester.

There are 24 divisional executives of which Numbers 1, 2, and 3 are shown on the map:
each has a Divisional Education Officer who administers educational affairs for his divisional executive and also keeps closely in touch with the Chief Education Officer for
the county.

The Role of Voluntary Agencies

AT ALMOST every stage of educational activity in England and Wales there are voluntary organizations at work, in most cases in close relationship with the L.E.A.'s. This has resulted from the important part these bodies played in the eighteenth and nineteenth centuries before a government system of education was organized. It is characteristic of England, with her liking for variety and local autonomy, that participation by these groups has been retained and aided.

As a rule, schools and institutions organized by voluntary groups will be found in the fields of nursery school work, primary and secondary education, the training of teachers, youth activities, school journeys, and various forms of adult education. Most of the voluntary schools, more than 10,000 in number, are at the primary level and have been provided by religious denominations, particularly the Church of England and the Roman Catholic Church. As noted above, voluntary schools are given financial aid by the L.E.A.'s and in some cases directly by the Ministry, the extent of the control exerted over them varying according to the amount of financial help and the conditions under which it was given.

In addition there are independent schools, including many of the well-known public schools. Some of these schools have agreed to accept financial assistance from the Ministry on certain conditions, including the admission of a certain number of pupils nominated by the L.E.A.'s. The public schools are described in detail in Chapter 12.

Educational Finance

FUNDS for expenditure on education in England and Wales come from two sources. About 55 percent of the total educational expenditure is defrayed by the central Treasury. This is paid to the local education authorities in direct grants from the Ministry of Education. The remainder is provided by the local education authorities from local taxation ("rates").

The grants by the Ministry of Education to the local education authorities are based upon a percentage of their approved expenditure, not on their total costs. Each L.E.A. sends in a budget each year, and the amount of the grant is reassessed annually. Before World War II separate grants were made for elementary and higher education. For elementary education, the following formula was used: 60 percent of teachers' salaries; 50 percent of the expenditure on special services, such as school medical service, physical education, and hot meals; 40 percent of the cost of transportation of pupils; and 20 percent of the remaining net expenditure. An additional allotment was made, based on average daily attendance, and an equalization grant was given to help areas where taxation rates were already very high.

For education above the primary level, including secondary and technical and the training of teachers, 50 percent of the approved expenditure was paid by the Ministry. During World War II increased grants were paid to aid in such matters as the evacuation of children from danger areas and their accommodation in reception areas. This was actually a financial responsiblity of the Ministry of Health. A grant of 100 percent of cost was allowed for the provision of milk to school children, and a grant rising nearly to 100 percent was given in order that school meals might be extensively provided, involving also the building and equipping of new facilities for these meals.

After the Education Act of 1944 had been passed, the system was simplified. A detailed statement along the lines indicated above is still supplied, but the Ministry now makes a single combined grant to the L.E.A. for all educational expenditure, with special grants for school milk and the training of additional teachers in emergency training colleges. Additional amounts are still earmarked to assist poor and sparsely populated districts.

In 1948–49 the national expenditure on education in England and Wales from public funds (Ministry of Education and L.E.A.'s), exclusive of money for university education, was £215,000,000. In 1951–52 it was £291,000,000. In 1961–62 it was £928,000,000 and the estimate for 1962–63 was £1,017,000,000. The value of the pound sterling has been approximately $2.80.

Direct grants, that is, grants apart from those paid to local education authorities, are paid to certain grammar schools, voluntary training colleges, university departments of education, classes for adult education, and voluntary youth organizations. Grants are also given to individual students for scholarships at universities and senior technical schools. There are from 3,000 to 4,000 of these national scholarships, but the number is supplemented by about 8,000 similar scholarships offered by local education authorities.

The Ministry of Education has no control over the universities and university colleges in England and Wales, which are autonomous institutions. They receive government help, however, through direct grants from the Treasury. The Treasury is advised on these matters by a body, known as the University Grants Commission, which has no connection with the Ministry of Education. The total grant made by the Treasury to the universities and university colleges, including five in Scotland, amounted to £26,000,000 in 1951–52, and in 1962–63 exceeded £100,000,000.

Special Note on Wales

ALTHOUGH education in Wales has been generally considered as a division of the English system administered by the Ministry of Education in London, there are naturally some special problems peculiar to Wales which are worthy of notice. This was recognized in 1952 by the Ministry when a Welsh Education Office was opened in Cardiff: 80 percent of the general educational administration for Wales is now transacted from there. There are 17 Welsh local education authorities, each of which has worked out a scheme of development for its own district. The Central Advisory Council for Welsh Education still holds its meetings in London, and the Permanent Secretary for Welsh Education has his office in London. Welsh L.E.A.'s receive their grants of 55 percent from the Ministry of Education in the same way as the English L.E.A.'s. There is a separate team of Her Majesty's Inspectors with a special knowledge of the country operating in Wales.

The area of Wales is small—there are only three states in the United States which are smaller—and the population has never reached 3 million. About three-quarters of the Welsh people live in the industrial cities of the south, famed for their coal, iron, and tin. The rest of the country is predominantly rural, with small picturesque townships. About 10 percent of the people are farmers, often with small upland farms and sheep runs. Welsh is spoken in the rural areas and market towns, but not so much in the industrial cities.

Welsh education, in consequence, needs to provide for both industrial and rural areas. This is done effectively through the agency of the L.E.A.'s. The aim in the rural districts is not to pin the children to the soil, but to invigorate Welsh rural life and maintain its traditions, combining localized education with a knowledge of developments in the outside world.

A burning question is the extent to which Welsh should be the medium of instruction in the schools. Welsh is an attractive but difficult language, with much music and rhythm in its expression. Before the 1944 Act, the grammar schools, which were numerous, were English in atmosphere, and all instruction was given in English. It was a rare thing to find Welsh used in the schools of the industrial south. As long ago as 1846 a Commission declared itself as follows: "The Welsh language is a vast drawback to Wales and a manifold barrier to the moral progress and commercial prosperity of the people. It dissevers the people from intercourse which would greatly advance their civilization." But the Welsh language persisted. It is interesting today to go into a store in a northern town and listen to musical Welsh on all sides, until an attendant comes up smilingly and offers, in English, to be of help. The 1952 Report of the Central Advisory Council accepts a bilingual situation but wants Welsh taught to all Welsh children, with English as a first or second language according to the district. The districts where most school pupils speak Welsh are Merioneth, 88 percent; Anglesey, 84 percent; Cardigan, 80 percent. Those where relatively few pupils speak Welsh are Glamorgan, 7 percent; Radnor, 1.4 percent; and Monmouth, 0.4 percent. A survey in 1951 showed that in that year 29 percent of the people in the whole country spoke Welsh.

The developmental plans show that Wales was given educational facilities under the 1944 Act similar to those obtaining in England. In 1962 there were 442,000 pupils in schools maintained or assisted by the L.E.A.'s. Of these, in the secondary division, there were 91,-000 in modern schools, 62,000 in grammar schools, 1,737 in secondary technical schools, and 22,000 in comprehensive secondary schools. Continuation classes have existed for many years in the cities, but there is a great need for Further Education in many of the country districts. In order to provide the latter, it is proposed to establish residential colleges, with courses lasting two or three months, along lines somewhat similar to the folk high schools in Denmark.

There is a University of Wales, with constituent colleges in various parts of the country, and a Welsh Joint Education Committee which administers an examination for the General Certificate of Education, on lines similar to the English examination (see Chapter 12), but with a Welsh flavor. This certificate will admit the holder to either a Welsh or an English university.

Special Note on Northern Ireland

AS NORTHERN Ireland, with a 1962 population of 1,425,000, is part of the United Kingdom, a brief description of its educational administration will not be out of place. Northern Ireland was made a separate unit in 1920 and can now be described as a British enclave in the northern part of the Irish Republic. Education in the Irish Republic itself is largely controlled by the Roman Catholic Church. There are no local education authorities, but there is a Ministry of Education which subsidizes religious congregations or local managers of schools. A determined effort is being made to introduce Irish as the language of instruction, with the aim of making the Republic a Gaelic-speaking community; progress in this is difficult and slow, since there are so many trade and other connections with England and the United States.

The situation in Northern Ireland is very different. Here the English pattern is followed with certain local variations. Northern Ireland has a Parliament of its own and also has representatives in the House of Commons in London. There is a Ministry of Education in Northern Ireland, and education is administered under the terms of the Education Act of 1947, which follows the general lines of the English Act of 1944. The six counties and the two county boroughs form the eight local education authorities which work, as in England, through Education Committees.

There is a dual system of "county schools" and "voluntary schools." The expenses of county schools are defrayed entirely from public funds, while the voluntary schools receive generous grants. Most of the primary schools are voluntary schools, together with about one-third of the intermediate secondary schools and nearly all the grammar schools. There are no "modern" schools as in England, but the intermediate schools aim at giving a wide general education of junior secondary level; those pupils who are academically inclined move on to the grammar schools.

The local education authorities are required by the Ministry to organize a wide range of educational facilities, including the provision of hot meals, textbooks, and transportation of pupils. The three educational stages are called "Primary," "Secondary" (including technical), and "Further," along the lines of English nomenclature.

The grants given by the Ministry to various types of school can be set down as follows:

1. Sixty-five percent of the approved expenditure of Local Education Authorities; 100 percent of cost of milk and meals.

2. Sixty-five percent of the approved expenditure of voluntary-school managers on buildings, equipment, and maintenance of schools.

3. All of the cost of teachers' salaries in primary and intermediate schools. (A special formula is used for salaries in grammar schools.)

4. A per capita grant for pupils in effective attendance at voluntary grammar schools.

The two universities, Belfast and Magee University College, are autonomous but receive direct grants from government funds. There is a good health service provided for school children, involving free medical and dental treatment; this is organized by the Ministry of Health.

The Ministry of Education will pay grants up to 75 percent to recognized youth organizations for lecture courses, physical training, and recreational activities.

Further Education, the third stage in the Ministry's program, is as yet voluntary, but a wide variety of courses is available for both youth and adults; considerable success has been attained with these.

Administration of Education in Scotland

SCOTLAND is justly proud of her education. As long ago as the late seventeenth century the Scottish Parliament made it the duty of every parish to supply a school and a teacher. This was not carried out in full at the time, but many schools were established, and the Scottish people ever since have had an attitude toward education which could almost be described as reverence. The schools were originally controlled by the Presbyterian Church. However, when the Industrial Revolution caused the crowding of populations in towns and cities, it became necessary to make changes, and in 1872 the notable Scottish Education Act was passed, transferring the administration of schools from the church to the state. To administer the necessary grants the Scottish Education Department was established: this department has carried Scottish education through a number of pro-gressive developments to the sound situation of today.

The Act of 1872 set up about 1,000 local school boards, popularly elected, and with power to levy local taxes ("rates"). Attendance was made compulsory up to the age of 13, and voluntary evening schools were provided for older pupils.

In 1892 the provisions were extended to secondary education, and committees were set up in all the counties and in the five main cities. In 1908 the powers of the boards were increased to include medical examination of pupils, transportation to schools from remote areas, and the supply of food and clothing in needy cases. In 1918 an act simplified the organization by doing away with the 1,000 school boards and substituting 33 county education authorities and five urban authorities elected by the local voters. By the same act Scotland showed considerable foresight by arranging for all the voluntary or denominational schools to be taken over by the education authorities, thus putting an end to the "dual system" which was later to be such a problem in England.

In 1929 the elected committees were superseded by constituting the county and town councils as local education authorities, as in England, and empowering them to appoint Education Committees of which a majority were to be council members. This brings the account almost to the present day. In 1945 Scotland passed the counterpart of the English Education Act of 1944. The provisions were rather different, because of the absence of dual control and because of the fact that some of the reforms envisaged in the English Act had already been carried out in Scotland. Moreover, the organization of Scottish secondary education was different from that in England, and the Scots wished to retain their own system. Also there was no section in the Scottish Act comparable with the English section on religious education. The Scots are a religious people, but they believe strongly in religious freedom: in consequence there was nothing mandatory in their Act about religious observances or instruction in the schools—that was left to the local authorities to arrange if and as they saw fit.

Otherwise the provisions were the same as those of the English Act. The leaving age was raised to 15 on April 1, 1947, and will be raised again to 16 as soon as practicable. Further education is to be given on a part-time basis to all young people between 15 and 18 years of age who are not in school. This has not yet been put into operation. Fees were abolished at all stages and a generous system of bursaries and scholarships was expanded. Local education authorities were given the power to establish boarding schools and hostels, since this was considered essential for some of the sparsely settled districts in the Highlands. Independent schools, relatively few in Scotland, are to be registered and were made liable to inspection.

There are 35 educational areas in Scotland, varying from cities such as Edinburgh, Glasgow, Dundee, and Aberdeen to Highland rural areas, sparsely settled and consisting mainly of heath and moor, such as Argyll, Inverness, and Sutherland.

Of the amount spent each year on education, about one third is raised from local rates and the remaining two thirds comes from the Exchequer in the form of grants paid by the Scottish Education Department.

There are five universities, four being well-known ancient foundations established between 1411 and 1583; these are St. Andrews, Glasgow, Aberdeen, and Edinburgh. All receive grants from the University Grants Committee, which makes recommendations for Scottish as well as English universities. As in the case of their English counterparts, Scottish universities are autonomous.

The Scottish Education Department keeps all schools conversant with modern developments in educational organization and teaching methods by means of circulars and pamphlets. Some of these pamphlets, notably those issued in recent years by the Scottish Council for Educational Research, have proved to be of marked value and significance and have attracted attention throughout the whole British Commonwealth.

Summing Up

LOCAL self-government has deep historical roots in Great Britain. Parallel to this has been a reliance upon voluntary organizations and religious groups to furnish many services which are publicly provided in some other countries. These two forces have been faced with the developing concept of the welfare state, which requires much greater authority for the national government and gives to the state responsibility for many activities which were formerly matters of individual or local concern. With their usual genius for compromise, the British have worked out a system which provides for a broad national support and control of general policies, but which leaves much administrative authority in the hands of local units of self-government. At the same time they have preserved the contributions which have been made by voluntary agencies. The final pattern, as it is developing, is one of divided responsibility between the nation and the local groups, and a working partnership between all of the interested groups.

5

National Responsibility:
France

FRANCE is the largest western or central European country, although it is small in comparison with the Soviet Union or the United States. In an area smaller than the state of Texas but two and one-half times the size of Great Britain, there is a population of 46 million as compared with 52 million in Great Britain.

Although France is loyal to democratic principles and practices, it has developed a highly centralized form of government which, in education as in other governmental functions, keeps all real authority in the hands of the national administration in Paris and permits very little participation by the local people in any matters of real importance.

Historical Background

THE PRINCIPLE of centralization is very old in France, going back beyond the time of Louis XIV in the seventeenth century. The Bourbon monarchs insisted that the state, personified by the king, was the source of all power and of all benefits to citizens. Through various radical changes in the form of government, the basic principle of control of all governmental functions by the central government has persisted almost unchanged. Under the Revolution it was believed that the abolition of the historic provinces, and the elimination of any form of local autonomy, would make the state the protector of the rights of the individual. It was also believed that this would promote and develop a sense of national unity.

The Revolutionary Assembly did establish forms of local government, elected by the people in the departments and communes, by laws passed in 1789 and 1790, but these plans never got a chance to operate successfully. Napoleon established a highly centralized system of administration, with a hierarchy of appointed officials. With minor amendments, this system is still in operation. The new departments, which replaced the historic provinces, were headed by prefects appointed by the central government, and these administrative officials were "advised" by local councils which were also appointed.

There has been a continued effort in France to secure greater powers for the local government agencies. The departments and communes eventually won the right to elect their own councils, and the communal councils the privilege of electing the mayors, who are local officials of considerable influence and authority. When the Fourth Republic was established after World War II, there were suggestions for strengthening the authority of the departmental councils and transferring many functions from national to departmental control. None of these proposals have actually become effective, and the local governmental bodies are still supervised and controlled by an officer appointed by the national government, the prefect. The new Constitution established by the Fifth Republic greatly strengthened the powers of the President of France and correspondingly reduced the powers of Parliament.

Observers frequently have commented on the paradox of a nation which is democratic in outlook and belief, yet which operates its local governmental functions under a system as centralized as that of many totalitarian states. Lord Bryce remarked that the French government was constructed to trust the judgment of 40 million Frenchmen in national affairs, but did not trust the local people to handle their community affairs. A former President of France, Paul Deschanel, admitted that France was a republic at the top but an empire at the base.

In addition to the long historical precedent for centralized government, there appear to be two other explanations for the continuance of the system. One is the fact that centralized governmental machinery is a great advantage to the party, or coalition of parties, in power, and therefore no government is likely to change the system. It has been said that in France the opposition parties always attack centralization, while the parties in power always use and support it. The other explanation stems from the revolutionary heritage of the French people. Standing almost alone in a hostile Europe, and facing divisive influences within the country, France adopted the revolutionary slogan "France—one and indivisible." Any suggestion to lessen the authority of the national government seemed to move in the direction of greater disunity. All of the functions of government—political, educational, and economic—have been aimed at attaining a more complete unity of the French nation.

France thus resembles an authoritarian state in its administrative organization; but it differs sharply from such a state in its educational philosophy and objectives. As in other nations, the educational system is intended to produce patriotic citizens who will be loyal to the political ideals of their native land. France seeks to attain national solidarity, but it is not the political solidarity of the totalitarian state, which permits only one party and subordinates the individual to the state. The French have so many political parties that under the Fourth Republic it was difficult to secure a stable majority for longer than a few months. Under the Fifth Republic this danger has been minimized, because the President may rule almost without Parliament.

The French seek a cultural solidarity, a training of minds of new generations to think logically and clearly and to appreciate the cultural heritage of the nation. While the public schools of France, from one border to another, are uniform in a way that would be unbelievable to an American, private or church-connected schools are not discouraged or prohibited as they are in the Soviet Union.

The Development of Education in France

AS IN many countries, the first schools in France were developed by religious groups. Before the French Revolution practically all education in the country was church-connected, and almost entirely controlled by the clergy. In 1684 Jean Baptiste de la Salle founded the Brothers of the Christian Schools, which became a very influential teaching order, working especially in the elementary schools. During the Revolution the order was suppressed, but after the Revolution it was restored. It increased its service to the elementary schools, and also provided secondary, vocational, and teacher training schools. One of the first schools for training teachers in France was that established by the Christian Brothers at Rheims in 1684. Other religious orders were also active in education, particularly the

Jesuits, but because of its political activities this group was suppressed in France in 1764.

Revolutionary leaders suspected that the Catholic Church was
fundamentally hostile to the new Republic, and they feared that
children educated in church-connected schools would tend to support the clerical and antirepublican parties in the country. As in
Russia many years later, the struggle for control of the schools became a struggle for the minds of the children, who were to become
the new citizens. Basically the struggle was not anti-Catholic, for
most of the leaders on both sides were Catholics. It was a conflict
against clerical control of politics and education. The republican
government was committed to a system of elementary education
that would be "free, public, and lay"—one that would be firmly
republican in political philosophy and neutral in sectarian theology.
But the Catholic Church could not accept neutral schools; it called
them "godless" and fought them every step of the way. This attitude, in turn, strengthened the impression of the republican leaders
that the Church was antirepublican.

Because the Church maintained, at its own expense, a system of
sectarian schools paralleling and competing with the public school
system, the antagonism continued. The public school teachers came
to consider themselves the protectors of the Republic and of free
public education. They were inclined toward socialistic and paci-
fist ideas in politics, and became local leaders in these causes. The
priests, on the other hand, came to be identified with the more
conservative political groups and with opposition to the Republic
in the field of education. "In thousands of villages throughout France
the opposition between Left and Right, between the Republic and
the Church, came to be personified in the antagonism between
schoolmaster and priest." [1]

As the years went by, the differences began to seem less important
and the feelings became less intense. The Republic established itself
firmly, and the Church came to accept the government. Between
the two world wars the Christian Socialist movement among the
young priests lessened the extreme conservatism represented by the
Church. Unfortunately, a new development during World War II
opened the question again and added new vigor to the controversy.

[1] Gwendolen M. Carter and John H. Herz, *Major Foreign Powers,* 4th ed.,
p. 593.

The Vichy government of Marshal Pétain, in a desperate effort to win the support of the Church, provided financial assistance from state funds for church-connected schools. This seemed to prove to the opponents of Pétain that the Church was antidemocratic. After the war, when the Fourth Republic was established, there was a tremendous demand that these subsidies be withdrawn. The leaders of the Left parties were agreed on this, and they prevailed at the time, although Catholic resistance was stubborn. In 1951 the Pleven government, harassed by educational problems caused by a rising birth rate, provided for per capita payment from state funds for every pupil in the country. This aroused a great deal of opposition and controversy. The proponents of public funds for church schools complained that the subsidy was too small; liberal and Socialist leaders opposed the deviation from the historic principle of lay education.

The original 1951 law provided a subsidy of about 11 million dollars a year for all children attending state schools or church-connected schools, but the education authorities applied the law in such a manner that children under the age of 6 or those between the ages of 14 and 16 were not included. This hit the church schools harder than the public schools. In 1955 the Mendès-France ministry provided state subsidies for all children attending private and church-connected schools.

Under the Fifth Republic Premier Michel Debré provided emergency aid to Catholic schools in 1959, and later a more comprehensive plan was adopted, in spite of firm Socialist objections. This new plan offered a possibility of four relationships between the church schools and the state: (1) complete integration with the national school system; (2) a contract under which the state pays salaries of qualified teachers if the school meets certain national standards; (3) a "contract of association" which provides that all state regulations and curriculum will be adhered to, and that all teachers will be drawn from the public schools; or (4) complete independence of the church school without any national financial aid. Most of the Catholic schools have preferred the second of these choices. The Socialist party threatens to take over all church schools accepting state aid if it ever succeeds in forming a Socialist government.[2]

The problem of church schools is still one which stirs up deep ani-

[2] Carter and Herz, op. cit., pp. 593–94.

mosities in France; it is far from solved, and will indeed be difficult of solution. It is a natural issue for the Communists, who are strong in France, and who raise the anticlerical issue whenever they feel it will produce the greatest amount of disunity and discord. In spite of the fact that France has developed its rigidly centralized system to promote national unity, it is the schools that are used as issues in a great debate, with the anticlerical forces supporting the principle of "free, universal, and lay" education and the clerical forces using the slogan "freedom of instruction." This latter slogan does not mean freedom to instruct, but freedom for the parent to select the school that he wishes his children to attend, without additional cost.

In the eighteenth and nineteenth centuries a series of writers profoundly affected the development of education in France. The ideas of Rousseau not only shocked the thinkers of his own country, but they influenced educational thought in other parts of Europe and America as well. Condorcet in 1792 proposed a system of free and universal education that was far in advance of the thought of his time and resembled Thomas Jefferson's proposals for education in Virginia. Following a report made by Victor Cousin in 1831, the Minister of Education, Guizot, introduced legislation to establish the elementary system firmly and to provide for higher elementary schools and for teacher training.

The French Revolution was based on the ideals of "Liberty, Equality, Fraternity," and the equalitarian philosophy of those days is still influential. Its effect, however, is felt most strongly in respect to the rights of individuals; its influence on social institutions has been much less. The educational system and some of the social institutions of the French Republic seem to have been inconsistent with the ideas of equality. The secondary school system was built upon the principle of selecting an intellectual elite from the great mass of the people and training them for positions of authority and leadership. Still less democratic was the basis for entrance to secondary institutions. The secondary schools, which were the only pathway to higher education and to preferment in politics, industry, and the professions, were reserved largely to the children of the higher social classes and the wealthier people. The children of the working classes went to elementary schools and then continued on to higher elementary schools. Upper- and middle-class children began their education in preparatory classes attached to the secondary schools (*lycées* and *collèges*). Theoretically there was a unified and democratic school system, and a pupil of intellectual ability was entitled to move from one type of school to another. Actually, the transfer from elementary to secondary school was very difficult.

Until World War I the national school system thus operated to perpetuate class distinctions and to keep children with those of their own social and economic groups. Although it was intended to separate an elite based only upon ability and intelligence, actually the system operated to preserve the benefits of higher education for the children of the privileged classes. This separation into two distinct and parallel streams of education, elementary and secondary, and the difficult competitive examinations that acted as hurdles to be passed before children could transfer from one level to another were reflected in the low proportion of French children enrolled in secondary schools. In 1935 only 250,000 children (6 per 1,000 population) were enrolled in secondary schools in comparison with 11 per 1,000 in Great Britain and 36 per 1,000 in the United States. By 1948, after reforms had affected the whole program of secondary education, the total in French secondary schools had increased to 348,000. In 1961 the Ministry reported an enrollment of 1,245,000 in the secondary grades. In spite of its very selective nature, there is one aspect of secondary education that is more democratic than that of Great Britain: France has never developed the aristocratic and undemocratic "great public schools" of England.

REFORM MOVEMENTS

From the criticism of this double-track system of schooling in France arose many suggestions for reform. These came to be concentrated under proposals for a single or unified school system, the *école unique*. This proposal followed and was influenced by a similar movement for a unified school system in Germany called the *Einheitsschule*. The *école unique* was not intended to provide a single, uniform type of school but was thought of, instead, as a unified organization that would make possible a single educational ladder from preschool to university, with easy transfer from one school to another. It proposed, however, a rich and flexible variety of types of schools and school programs.

During World War I a group of young teachers, some of them serving in the trenches, formed an organization called *Les Com-*

pagnons de l'Université Nouvelle ("The Advocates of a New Educational System"). They proposed a complete reorganization of the school program to provide a common system that would eliminate class distinctions, facilitate transfer from one type of school to another, eliminate fees, and improve articulation between different types and levels of schools. The new school system would provide opportunities for development of talent and ability wherever they might be found. These reformers wrote articles for the newspapers and educational journals; they published a journal of their own and aroused a good deal of discussion and debate. The proposed *école unique* did not materialize, but the reformers attracted a great deal of attention to their ideas and to the problems of education, and they paved the way for eventual reforms.

In 1940 France surrendered to the Germans, and a Free French government was eventually set up in Algiers. In 1944, after four unhappy years of German occupation and national despondency, a Commission for Educational Reform was called together in Algiers by Capitan, the Commissioner for Education in the provisional government. In the autumn of 1944, after the Allied armies had liberated Paris, the report of the Algiers Commission was published. The Commission boldly recommended a number of reforms in secondary education and in the universities, and proposed that some of the ideas of the *école unique* be put into effect. The Commission charged:

The defeat and the tyranny would not have been what they have been but for the faintheartedness, the default or the treason of the controlling groups in the army and navy, in politics and finance, in industry and commerce. Those who could claim to have come from the summit of our educational system are those whose cowardice has been most scandalous.

The report recognized that the over-intellectualized cultural education given in the French secondary schools had been deficient in scientific and technical content, and that the very existence of the nation, in a scientific age, depended upon strengthening this weakness. Nothing was done to implement the recommendations of the Algiers Commission, but a new commission was appointed.[3]

[3] Both commissions bore the official title of *Commission d'Études de la Reform de l'Enseignement*. The Algiers report appeared in *Journal Officiel: Bulletin*

The new educational commission was headed by Paul Langevin, a distinguished physicist from the Collège de France. Langevin died before the report was complete, and Henri Wallon, an eminent child psychologist, succeeded him as chairman. The report, however, as published, has always been called the "Langevin Plan." It is a long-range plan for the development of education in France, and will be discussed in more detail below. The recommendations of the commission developed a great interest in education throughout the nation, and became the subject of acrimonious debates in Parliament. Some of the recommendations of the plan were enacted into law by the Delbos Act of 1949, which may be called the French equivalent of the 1944 Education Act of England.

It is not in education alone that French social institutions have been inconsistent with the ideals of equality. Labor and social security legislation in France lagged far behind developments in these fields in other European countries. The birth rate was constantly falling, and a generally pessimistic attitude prevailed. A postwar system of social security and family allowances (paid by employers) began to show some effects. Family allowances increase according to the number of children, and a father with four children may receive as much in allowances as in his regular pay check. Children's allowances are payable up to the age of 20 if the child continues in school. This system of subsidies has now been reflected in the birth rate, which is showing a steady increase each year. The population increase is not entirely a postwar phenomenon, such as many countries experienced, but a continuing condition which is mirrored in school enrollments. The system of allowances has also improved what the Americans would call the "holding power" of the schools.

The French believe that their standards of culture are preeminent in Europe and in the world. They believe that the state, through its national school system, is the guardian of what they call *"culture générale."* The concept of general culture is based first of all on a careful study of French language and literature as a bond that unites all Frenchmen and as the medium through which French culture is preserved and extended. Elementary schools treat the child as a miniature adult and teach him subject matter as an introduction to French culture. The child is taught to think clearly and logically, to

Officiel, November 16, 1944. The second commission's report (Langevin Plan) may be found in *Education Nationale*, Supplement, July 14, 1946; a final report was filed in 1949.

express himself well, and to appreciate the beautiful in his heritage. French secondary education is mainly general in nature, only recently somewhat vocational, and attempts to develop judgment, appreciation, and taste and to increase the ability to think clearly and logically and to write and speak well. The Russian secondary school intends to make a specialist of every pupil, to prepare him for a particular job; the French secondary school tries to develop an educated man or woman who can understand and use abstract ideas. Preparation for a vocation is more incidental, and specialized training comes later.

THE LANGEVIN PLAN

It was in an atmosphere of dissatisfaction with the existing system that the French Parliament decided to set up a commission to survey the entire educational system of the country. Langevin gathered a distinguished group of educators and others, representing all shades of public opinion. The report of his commission, which was first published in 1946, accepted many of the ideas of the Algiers Commission. It proposed a long-range plan for the future, of which only a portion has been enacted into law. Like the Algiers Commission, the Langevin Commission recommended full-time education up to the age of 18. Langevin's group accepted as basic premises the need to provide equality of educational opportunity for all, the need to expand and develop technical and scientific studies, and the importance of preserving the French ideal of general culture to educate the "whole man."

Like the *Compagnons,* the Algiers Commission, and other groups, the Langevin Commission sought to modify the general administrative structure of French education so that the parallel and overlapping systems of elementary, secondary, and technical education would be organized into a unified structure with the three stages of education comparable to the British system as provided by the Education Act of 1944. For the first time in France there was to be an educational ladder whereby all children might have an equal opportunity to pass from one level to another. The extent to which this reform has succeeded is discussed in Chapter 13.

It was recognized that all of these reforms could not be put into effect immediately. While the commission recommended compulsory education to the age of 18, it knew that this would be a long and costly process, requiring many new schools and additional teachers. It did recommend that the Assembly immediately raise the compulsory attendance age from 14 to 15, but this action was not taken for many years.

THE DE GAULLE REFORM OF 1959

On January 7, 1959, after 13 years of discussion and acrimonious debates, President de Gaulle issued a decree that attempted to put much of the school system into the Langevin framework, making use of the existing system and buildings. The school leaving age was raised to 16 for all children becoming six years old after January 1, 1959. This means that it will be many years before all will be required to remain in school until that age, but the principle has been established. The delay makes it possible to spread the demand for additional schoolrooms and teachers over several years. The school system is reorganized to provide a more complete educational ladder from preschool to university for all capable children, and some changes in terminology have been made to put the whole system more in line with Langevin ideas. These changes are discussed in Chapter 13.

The Role of the National Government in Education

AS HAS been pointed out, public education in France is a function of the state, like almost all governmental activities. It is under the supervision and control of a Ministry of National Education, headed by a cabinet minister, who is appointed by the Premier, approved by the President of France, and responsible to Parliament. The Ministry is a complex organization; the Minister is assisted by five directorates: one for general administration (including a section in charge of school buildings and the national center for educational documentation); and four other directorates, for elementary, secondary, technical, and higher education. There are numerous bureaus, sections, and subcommissions attached to the directorates and the Ministry. This ponderous and cumbersome piece of machinery does not provide for speedy handling of educational matters, especially since so many decisions affecting schools in remote parts of the country must be made in the central office.

Under the Fourth Republic, the Minister of Education, like the Premier and all other members of the Cabinet, was a member of Parliament. He held office as long as the government of which he was a member was able to command a majority of votes in Parliament. In the latter years of the Republic governments changed rapidly, and there were equally frequent changes in the head of the Ministry of Education. It is probable that the average tenure of a Minister of Education after World War II was about six months. Under the Fifth Republic, the Premier is authorized to appoint ministers who are not members of Parliament, and under the rule of incompatibility, a minister may not retain his seat as a deputy. This may provide greater continuity in the position of Minister of Education.[4]

The Minister is responsible to Parliament for the operation of the national educational system. He is responsible for the supervision of all educational institutions in the country, public and private. He must carry out the will of Parliament in executing educational laws passed by that body, but he has the power to draft decrees which have the authority of law if signed by the President. He has the power of nominating, for presidential appointment, the most important educational officers in the nation, and he also has the right to make many direct appointments on his own authority. With the advice of administrative officials and advisory councils provided by law, the Minister makes many important decisions. He prescribes curricula, courses of study, and methods of instruction for all public schools in the country. He approves examinations, the requirements for scholarships, and all administrative rules and regulations affecting every type of school. He has disciplinary power over all officials under his control, and hears appeals when conflicts arise. His actual power is very great and very far reaching.

This is particularly true in the area of prescribing regulations by ministerial decree. In the absence of legislation to the contrary, the Minister has wide legislative authority as well as administrative power. He can issue decrees which will have far-reaching effects; while Parliament can countermand these decrees, it may take a long time and much debate to do so, and in the meantime the ministerial decrees are in effect. It is French usage to call any change in the manner of handling educational matters a "reform." Many such reforms (some of which were definitely backward steps) have been put into effect by ministerial fiat.

Parliament, however, has direct control over all education in the country, for it must vote the annual budget, and this offers an op-

[4] Carter and Herz, *op. cit.*, p. 551.

portunity for a debate on educational questions. According to Kandel, who says that there is probably no country where the legislature devotes as much time to debating the problems of education as in France, the most heated debates are those which concern the preservation of the standards of French culture, rather than the amount of the budget.[5] Because differences between the Right and Left, between clericals and anticlericals, often come to a focus over educational matters, the debates on this subject frequently are heated and acrimonious.

Although the tenure of the Minister may be short, practically all other employees of the Ministry are permanent civil servants and are unaffected by changes in government. The Minister is assisted by rising young politicians who hold minor administrative posts under him and may change as the party control changes. The permanent staff of the Ministry carries on from year to year, and actually does the work of the department.

The Minister is also assisted by an advisory group called the Higher Council of Public Instruction, which is almost a miniature Parliament. It is made up of 56 appointed or elected members, each holding office for four years and subject to reelection or reappointment. Nine members are appointed by the President of France to represent private schools. The universities elect 27 members, secondary education elects 10, and elementary education elects 6. The council meets twice a year, although additional special meetings may be called. It acts as a court of appeal on disciplinary matters, and must be consulted by the Minister on questions of examinations, courses of study, methods of instruction, discipline, administrative regulations, and the supervision of private schools.

As links between the Ministry in Paris and the schools throughout the country there is a group of senior officials, the Inspectors-general of National Education. They are appointed by the President upon recommendation of the Minister. They have offices in the Ministry in Paris and make tours of inspection throughout the country according to assignments made. They visit schools and other educational programs, and make reports to the Minister and the directors. Each inspector-general is assigned to a particular level of education or to a particular field, and his reports cover his own specialty.

[5] Kandel, *Comparative Education*, p. 268.

At any time he may be assigned to make special studies or investigations for the Minister.

Probably no country in the world is more examination-ridden than France. Every step of the educational ladder is marked by examinations, and most of them are written by central authorities. A large proportion of the examinations are competitive, so that passing or failing is not necessarily determined by how well an individual does in the examination, but may depend on how many individuals the government has decided to permit to pass. Almost every examination carries with it a diploma or certificate or degree, and these are very important in French life. Although the Ministry writes encouraging paragraphs into the courses of study, urging the teachers to vary the courses and methods to meet local conditions and needs, these exhortations lack meaning as long as the examinations are uniform for the whole country. With the control of external examinations in the hands of a central Ministry, every phase of teaching in France can be effectively unified and coordinated.

It is interesting that France should provide us with an outstanding example of complete centralization of governmental functions in the national government. This situation has occurred in other countries, but has usually accompanied a political philosophy of authoritarian and autocratic nature, as in Nazi Germany. The French might attempt to explain the bureaucratic and centralized form of administration in several ways. They could point out that their frontiers have been crossed by invaders numerous times, and that national unity is very important to them. They might say that national administration protects their schools from monarchist influences and clerical interference. They could say that centralization has worked successfully in France for nearly three centuries, so why change it? It seems clear that centralization is the accepted method of government in France, and that there is little intention of changing it.

This does not mean that national control of education in France escapes criticism, or that any attempt is made to forbid criticism of the system. In this regard the French are very different from the Russians, who have as complete centralization, but do not permit any criticism to be voiced. There is a regionalist movement in France, which seeks to decentralize the country into homogeneous areas more logical than the artificial departmental divisions set up by the

Revolution. These groups would encourage regional tongues, such as Basque, Corsican, or Breton, and permit them to be used in the local schools. There has been much discussion of these proposals, which have been opposed as tending to break down the concept of France as indivisible.

The annual debates in Parliament provide a forum for much discussion of education, and the centralized administrative machinery does not escape notice. From time to time both houses of Parliament appoint investigating committees to study educational subjects, and the reports of these groups are widely debated. The Higher Council of Public Instruction includes lay members representing the public as well as representatives of the teaching groups, and this body debates and criticizes educational policies and regulations. The teaching profession is organized into a number of effective and active groups, which criticize administrative policies, draw up suggestions of their own, and bring educational matters to the attention of the general public. It was from this source that the movement for the *école unique* developed, and the efforts to educate the public are finally beginning to show some effects.

Centralization tends to magnify the importance of regulations and uniform standards and to minimize the importance of the individual. It tends to retard progress and to discourage educational experimentation and research. National requirements dominate all the schools; the same methods, curricula, courses of study, examinations, and competitions may be found from one end of the country to the other.

The Place of Regional Subdivisions in French Education

FOR PURPOSES of educational administration metropolitan France is divided into 16 regions or Academies, in each of which there is located a university. In January, 1963, it was announced that three new Academies would be established, at Nantes, Orleans, and Rheims. In addition there was discussion of a new Academy centered at Amiens. This would also mean the establishment of new universities in these areas. The huge Academy of Paris, which included one-fourth of the school pupulation of France, has been reduced in size by these changes.

The chief administrative official of the Academy is the rector, who is president of the university and chief representative of the

Ministry of National Education in the area. He is appointed from the university professors by the President, upon nomination by the Minister. He is responsible to the Ministry for all branches of education in his Academy and acts on behalf of all the directorates. The major portion of his time is devoted to secondary and higher education. The rector nominates candidates for appointment to administrative positions within his area, appoints members of examining commissions, supervises the conduct of examinations, selects the topics for essays to be included in the examinations, and presides over the Academic Council, which serves as a sort of cabinet to him.

The Academic Council is composed of the Academy inspectors, representatives of higher and secondary education and of the private schools, and elected representatives from the departmental and communal councils within its area. The council advises the rector on educational matters, largely in the field of secondary education. Academy inspectors are appointed by the President, upon nomination of the Minister. The educational qualifications for appointment as an Academy inspector are very high, usually a doctorate in letters or science or a similar high degree, and several years' experience as a teacher, principal, or an inspector. An Academy inspector is usually assigned to a department, where he has powers something like those of a superintendent of schools. He is charged with carrying out the policies of the Ministry, but has no authority to change the procedures or to initiate policies.

The Academies were organized by Napoleon, as a part of a grandiose plan for a system of national education in France that would be under his personal control. The organization has persisted practically unchanged and is the only type of administrative structure between the central government in Paris and the various local government bodies. The Academies cannot be compared in any way to American or Australian states, or to Russian republics. The Academy has no power or authority of its own; it operates administratively on authority delegated by the national Ministry. The existence of these regions cannot be construed as any decentralization of authority; it is merely the devolution of centralized power to regional offices.

The Place of Local Government in French Education

THE DEPARTMENTS

The largest units of local government in France are the 94 departments, of which 83 were established by the Constituent Assembly in 1790; others have been added as France expanded its territory. France has taken parts of its overseas empire into the government of the nation by making these possessions departments on the same basis as those in continental France. For many years four of the departments were in Algeria, and in 1946 French Guiana, Réunion, Martinique, and Guadeloupe became departments. This was an expression of the French desire to demonstrate the unity of France, to show that these areas are neither colonies nor possessions, but are completely assimilated into the French Republic. This policy was not successful in Algeria.

The Constituent Assembly deliberately planned to wipe out all traces of the old provinces of France, so that departments have no historical basis, as do the English counties. Most of the departments are not homogeneous units geographically, socially, economically, or ethnically. They are comparatively small geographical subdivisions, like the counties in most American states. The boundaries were determined by the ability of a citizen to make the trip by horse-drawn vehicle from his home to the seat of government in one day. Merely administrative subdivisions, the departments are governed by a prefect who is appointed in Paris.

The prefect, although appointed by the Ministry of the Interior, handles a variety of functions for a number of ministries. All local government subdivisions in France are charged with the local administration of national functions, as well as with handling matters which are left to the discretion of local authorities. The prefect is head of the elementary school system of the department, as the rector is head of the secondary school program for the Academy, which includes several departments. The prefect makes permanent appointments of teachers, supervises all financial accounts, supervises the award of certain scholarships, and is chairman of the departmental council for education.

The prefect is advised and to some extent supervised by an elected departmental council. In educational matters, he is advised by a separate departmental council for education made up of the prefect as chairman, the Academy inspector as vice-chairman, four members selected by the departmental general council, four elementary teachers elected by their fellow teachers, the principals of the normal schools for men and women in the department, two elementary inspectors appointed by the Minister, and representatives selected by the private schools in the department.

In some ways this council resembles a local education authority in England, but it has much less power. It does not represent the public, and is purely an advisory council to the prefect. Usually the council meets every three months, or at other times if called by the chairman. It gives advice on the number and location of schools, on the number of teachers required to staff the schools, and on the opening of private schools in the department. Members of the council may visit schools, but only to consider matters affecting sanitation and the school buildings. They have no authority whatever in matters of curriculum or methods of instruction. For expenses which the department voluntarily assumes, the general departmental council has responsibility.

Departments may levy taxes for education to be added to the direct national taxes; they are permitted to levy departmental taxes on land, buildings, and rentals, and to require licenses for trades and professions. They may levy an extraordinary or deficiency tax whose maximum is fixed by law. These sources provide about half of the departmental income for all purposes, including education; the remainder comes from national grants. The department is responsible for the repair and maintenance of normal school buildings; it must provide an office for the Academy inspector; must pay the cost of board and room for normal school students who do not live in dormitories; and may make additional salary grants to the elementary inspectors. The departmental council may, if it chooses, grant additions to the salaries of local teachers and may provide funds for prizes and scholarships for local schools.

THE COMMUNES

The unit of local administration which enjoys the greatest degree of local self-government is the commune. Unlike Great Britain and the United States, France organizes both rural and urban areas, regardless of area or population, into the same type of local government unit, the commune. Thus the city of Paris is a commune, as are all the other cities and towns, but so are very small rural areas with only a few square miles and less than fifty people. Of the 38,000 communes in France, many have fewer than 1,000 inhabitants.

Communal funds come from a variety of sources. The communes, like the departments, may levy taxes which are added to the national direct tax; they levy local taxes on dogs, animals for sale or slaughter, fees, licenses, and tools; and they may retain a share of certain indirect taxes levied by the national government. The communes also receive a variety of national grants.

The chief officer of the commune is the mayor, who is elected by the communal council and is responsible to the prefect and to the national government. The mayor has certain definite educational powers and responsibilities in the commune. He may propose new school buildings, approve the opening of private schools, supervise the school buildings, and promote attendance.

The mayor is assisted by a communal council and by delegates from the cantons, which are mainly judicial areas. The elementary inspector is an ex-officio member of all communal school boards in his district. The school board meets every three months, or oftener at the call of the president, the mayor. The school board is supposed to be responsible for the enforcement of the compulsory attendance law, and encourages attendance by awarding prizes. It has a small voluntary school fund, from which it may award prizes or grant aid to poor pupils. The communes pay sums allowed to teachers for rent, or pay for lodgings provided for teachers; they pay salaries of assistants in nursery schools; and in addition they provide sums for materials used in manual work and crafts. They may decide to maintain optional classes, under agreement with the national government, and to provide their own scholarships.

The duties and responsibilities of the local school boards are so unimportant and their authority is so minor that many communal councils have refused to appoint such boards, and members appointed sometimes refuse to serve. Some communal school boards, finding that their decisions may be overridden on any matter by the departmental council or the prefect, refuse to meet. The prefect may require a commune to buy a site, erect a building, or open or close a school, without regard to local school board or communal council action. If the school board or communal council fails to act, the prefect may select a site, plan and erect a building, and charge the cost to communal funds. School boards are told that they must not concern themselves with matters that have to do with curriculum or instruction, or with criticisms of teachers, methods, or equipment, since standards for these matters are prescribed by national authorities.

One other type of local participation appeared in recent years. Under the apprenticeship act, the local business firms were taxed to pay part of the cost of vocational education. Special councils were set up in every district, with some voice in the expenditure of this tax and the allocation of scholarships. The system allowed for a greater amount of local responsibility for vocational education than for the regular school program. Local industrial firms were permitted to set up their own training programs, and local people had some voice in their operation. Under the De Gaulle Reform of 1959 the nature of the apprenticeship centers has been changed, and it is not clear whether local participation has been continued to the same extent.

The Place of Voluntary Agencies and Private Schools

PARALLEL with the state system of public education is a system of private schools. These schools may be organized and supported by private individuals, by organizations such as trade unions, or by religious groups. The majority of them are under the control of the Catholic Church. The law recognizes the right of individuals and organizations to open schools at various educational levels, but rigid restrictions are enforced. A private school may not be opened without the approval of the local mayor, the public prosecutor, the departmental officials, the Academy inspector, and the Ministry of National Education.

The Ministry reserves the right to inspect all such schools, not as a measure of control over curriculum, but to ensure that instruction given is not contrary to French law and that provisions are made for adequate safety and sanitation. No qualifications for teachers in elementary schools or higher educational institutions are prescribed by law; secondary school teachers and principals must meet the national certification requirements.

Private schools grant their own certificates and diplomas, which have no official standing. In order to receive official certificates the student of an independent school must prepare to take the state examinations. This effectively keeps the curriculum of the private schools closely in line with the requirements of the national system.

Because of the uniformity within the public school system, very little experimentation with new methods is possible. In this situation, it would appear that private schools offer laboratories for new ideas not yet accepted or tried in the public schools. The *Ecole des Roches* is often cited as an example of a private school which has served as a stimulus to education throughout the country and has done interesting work with new methods and new materials. Some private technical schools have made contributions to educational theory and practice. In general, however, the contributions of private education to school practice have been minor and incidental. Most of the private and church-connected schools fail to take advantage of the independence they might enjoy. Their teachers are trained in the same system as the public school teachers. In addition, they find it necessary to prepare their pupils for public examinations. Since the private schools depend largely on fees collected from the parents, they are under social and financial pressures toward conformity. Church-connected schools incline toward conservatism in method and content, and show little interest in educational experimentation.

The Catholic schools stress the classics to an extent which reduces the amount of time devoted to sciences, and are more successful in the abstract than in the experimental sciences. The education in the church elementary schools is more dogmatic and formal than in the public elementary schools. The Catholic hierarchy has been unfriendly to the idea of the *école unique*, because it fears that this would mean a monopoly of education in the hands of the state. There are a few schools connected with Protestant churches and a few Jewish schools in France, but their influence is negligible.

The private schools situation has become even more complicated because of the lag in school building during the years of depression and war. The public school system has had great difficulty in attempting to provide for all the children who come to it. About 16 percent of the elementary pupils enrolled in the country, and 25 percent of the secondary school children, are enrolled in private schools. While most of these children are in church schools because their parents choose to place them under sectarian teaching, some of them attend Catholic schools because the public schools are overcrowded and the facilities inadequate. The parents who pay taxes to support the public school system and also pay tuition to private schools have been very loud in their demands for state grants to private education.

In 1951 the Pleven government, after a prolonged and heated debate, provided for some state assistance to church and private education. Because the question is very controversial in French politics, the government tried to find a solution which would help relieve overcrowding in the schools but would not arouse too much opposition. The result was embodied in two measures passed by the Assembly. The first provided for national scholarships, tenable in either public or private secondary schools, if the schools met national standards of buildings, teachers, hours of instruction, and standards of achievement. This law also provided funds to assist in building new schools and to employ new elementary teachers. The second act provided funds to be distributed on a per capita basis to all students between the ages of 6 and 14 attending elementary grades in either public or private schools. In the public schools these funds were allotted to the departmental councils for the upkeep of school buildings. For the private schools they were allotted to parents' associations to increase teachers' salaries. In 1953 the national government paid in grants to parents' associations of private and confessional schools a total of 3,112,000,000 old francs, which was calculated on the basis of 3,900 francs per pupil per year. The two laws were an attempt to alleviate the two worst problems facing French education, the lack of school facilities and the very low salaries paid to teachers in sectarian schools. It was hoped that indirectly the improvement in salaries would be accompanied by an improvement in the qualifications of teachers in private schools. As mentioned above, the De Gaulle Reform of 1959 increased the allocations for pupils in the private schools.

A number of voluntary organizations assist the schools in the field of health and school lunches. The medical inspection of the elementary schools has been completely reorganized since the end of the war. Organizations like the Higher Council of French Hygiene, the Higher Council for the Protection of Childhood, and the Higher Commission on Tuberculosis carry on programs in the field of health. A number of private organizations are concerned with infant welfare and health. Most of the maternal schools have private organizations as sponsors.

Parents' associations or committees of patrons are organized to assist the elementary schools. In the public schools these are usually appointed by the Academy inspector rather than organized by the parents themselves. In the private schools they may be elected or appointed by the school authorities. They raise funds for the benefit of the schools, assist poor children by supplying them with books and clothing, and help pupils find employment when they leave school. The funds of the committees are sometimes supplemented by grants from the local education councils. A parents' group interests itself in the physical facilities of the school, in cleanliness and sanitation, and in matters of attendance, but like all local groups, it is barred from interference in the educational program. Although they are not elected by the parents but appointed by officials in charge of national education, these groups serve as the only direct means of communication between the national schools and the public. There are no voluntary organizations in France like the parent-teacher associations in America.

Educational Finance

THE COST of public education is shared by the national government, departments, and communes. The increase in the percentage of the education budget coming from national funds is shown in Table 5-1. The budget of the Ministry of National Education is given in Table 5-2.

National funds are derived from income and direct taxes, from

TABLE 5-1
The Share of Education in the French National Budget

YEAR	PERCENTAGE OF TOTAL BUDGET	YEAR	PERCENTAGE OF TOTAL BUDGET
1875	1.64	1950	6.65
1900	6.54	1953	7.59
1914	7.12	1955	9.01
1926	4.36	1956	9.74
1939	6.38	1957	10.30
1945	8.42	1958	10.10

SOURCE : French Cultural Services, Documentation No. 2, New York: French Embassy (no date), p. 8.

TABLE 5–2

Budget of the Ministry of National Education in France *
(in millions of new francs) †

	1955	1957	1959	1960
Operating expenses, salaries, equipment	227,296	303,131	443,508	490,227
Adult education	22,890	27,392	37,290	47,290
Land and buildings for state schools	25,097	31,184	79,785	92,615
State subsidies for other schools (construction)	48,873	60,816	85,275	89,285
Totals	324,156	422,423	646,131	719,417

s o u r c e : French Cultural Services, Documentation No. 2, New York : French Embassy (no date), p. 8.

* In addition to the above amounts, certain other Ministries, using their own funds, are responsible for the support of many of the *grandes écoles.*

† There are five francs to the dollar.

luxury taxes and fees for services, from excise and turnover taxes, and from direct revenues from state monopolies and taxes on gambling. Expenditures on education are classified as ordinary and extraordinary. The national government pays salaries of all teachers in elementary, secondary, and normal schools, pays the cost of maintenance of buildings, and gives special aid to very poor communes. These are the ordinary expenditures. As extraordinary expenditures, the national government gives grants-in-aid to departments and communes to pay the interest on loans to build schoolhouses. (The departments provide sites and buildings for normal schools, and the communes provide sites and buildings for elementary schools.)

There are additional expenses which the national government may assume voluntarily, if requested to do so by departments or communes. These would include the cost of nursery schools or kindergartens, which are not required by law. If a local governing body wants to provide such services, they may be established, and the Ministry agrees to pay the same amounts as for schools required by law. However, in such a case the local subdivision must agree to maintain these schools, once established, for a period of time, usually for thirty years. National funds may also be used to aid local school funds, to provide instructional and laboratory equipment in special subjects, and to buy books for libraries.

In the field of secondary education, the national government assumes the entire cost of salaries and maintenance of buildings in the *lycées*. For the communal secondary schools, the *collèges*, the communes provide buildings, maintenance, materials, and equipment, and the national government pays the salaries.

The major part of the cost of public education is thus borne by the national budget, since the contributions made by the departments and the communes are comparatively minor. Inasmuch as a large part of the funds spent by departmental councils or communes come from national grants, it is very difficult to determine the proportion of school costs at each level. In elementary, secondary, technical, and agricultural schools, education is free, but fees are charged in higher education and in certain schools of the arts.

Problems of Organization and Control

PROBLEMS facing French education are not different from those which perplex educational authorities in other countries. In some ways the centralized system makes it easier for the Ministry of National Education to meet problems, for a single decree can be made effective in every school in the national system. On the other hand, the fact that so many things must be done on a nation-wide scale seems to make the problems larger.

Shortage of School Buildings

There is still a shortage of school facilities in France, as in many other countries. During the depression years very few schools were built; the depression was followed by invasion, occupation, and liberation, with the consequent destruction of many school buildings. The problem of coping with the increased birth rate and increased enrollments appears to be very great when faced as a national problem. It is the National Assembly that must vote funds to meet this situation in every part of the nation, in spite of the fact that a number of schools are built by local units of government. The government has recently been intensifying its efforts to meet this situation. France faces a very serious problem, complicated by the fact that many existing schools are very old and in poor condition.

Shortage of Teachers

The twin problem to the lack of schoolrooms is the shortage of teachers. Problems of the teaching profession will be discussed in Chapter 13, but the teaching situation in France, as in other countries, is made more difficult by the need of greater funds for salaries. It has been further complicated by raising the compulsory education age and keeping children in school longer. Although the economic condition of French teachers has been improving, it is still not attractive enough to bring as many young people into the profession as the country needs.

Shortcomings of Centralization

Although the centralized system of organization has been accepted in France for centuries, it is constantly being criticized. Some of the criticisms come from those who would like to have more regionalism, and desire to have education follow the patterns of the historical areas of France. Some criticisms have come from teachers' organizations, which would like to have more freedom for the teachers and less control from Paris. The system is criticized because of the inevitable delay and inefficiency which arises from the need to refer any question of importance to Paris for decision. It is criticized by local communities because by the time the bureaucrats in the Ministry, in the Academy, and in the department have worked out the details of every matter of administration, there is nothing left for the local school boards to do. Some of them refuse to go through the motions. But there is no strong demand for decentralization in the government of France, or for a really decentralized education program. It is probable that the answers to the criticisms will be found, if at all, within the framework of central control.

Some attempt has been made to offer a little adaptation of the work of the schools to local needs and conditions. Newer courses of study offer greater leeway to the teacher and encourage him to take advantage of the freedom which is available. But it is difficult to read much meaning into offers of freedom to the classroom teacher when such important factors as the course of study, the textbooks, the examinations, the preparation of teachers, and the inspection of schools are controlled centrally and operated in such a way as to secure uniformity throughout the nation. Again it seems probable that if an amelioration of this situation is achieved, it will be through less rigid requirements by the Ministry and greater discretion for the teacher. But it will have to be attained within the framework of the centralized system, with no real responsibility or control permitted to the local governments.

France provides an example of a democratic country which has deliberately chosen to have a highly centralized and bureaucratic government. The apparent paradox of a free people, loyal to the ideals of democracy, who permit themselves to be governed by a complex bureaucracy controlled in the capital city, has puzzled many observers. Russia has set up a system that appears to be decentralized but is in reality rigidly centralized in order to maintain a minority party in control of the state. France has the most completely centralized system of education in Europe, and yet it has not used this system to control the people, as the schools of Russia are used. The French have chosen to organize their government and their school system in this manner in order to secure unity among the people and to preserve something that is very important to them, the ideal of the "general culture" of France.

6

State Responsibility:
Australia

AUSTRALIA is approximately the same size as the conterminous United States. Most of the continent is a vast undulating plateau, with an eastern highland region running parallel to the coast. There are rich coastal lands and vast pastoral districts, but a large part of the interior has little or no rainfall and is arid country and sand-ridge desert unfit for any form of agriculture. It is thus a mistake to assume that the country could absorb an unlimited number of settlers. There is an active immigration policy, limited almost entirely to immigrants of the white race, but this policy must go hand in hand with the development of the country. The present population is nearly 11 million, and it is estimated that by the year 2000, unless there are unforeseen developments in water supply and soil fertility, the total population of the continent will not exceed 15 million.

The system of educational administration in Australia is unique in some respects. Australia provides the only example of a nation in which the component states each have highly centralized systems of educational control, with practically no local participation by the parents and citizens. The national government plays a relatively minor part, apart from education in the Australian Territories, in the armed forces, and at university level, where there has been a marked increase in financial provision by the Commonwealth in recent years. The Commonwealth government has no say in the way education is administered in any of the states.

Foreign observers have often criticized this system on the ground that it is too authoritarian in character and too restrictive and stereotyping in its influence. They wonder why a liberal democracy

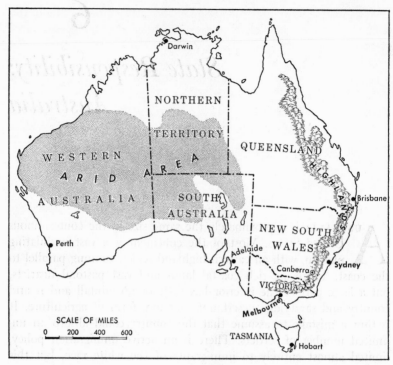

Australia
(Showing the states, their capitals, and the extent of the arid area.)

has adopted a system which seems more suited to an authoritarian regime. The most penetrating analysis by an overseas expert was made by Kandel in 1937.[1] He describes the Australian system, together with that of New Zealand (which has many similar features but is not so highly centralized), as "education for efficiency," by which he means a rather rigid type of scholastic efficiency without sufficient regard for the real spirit of education. More recently, Butts, of Teachers College, Columbia University, made a scholarly and thought-provoking examination of the administration of Australian education.[2]

[1] I. L. Kandel, *Types of Administration, with Particular Reference to the Educational Systems of New Zealand and Australia*, 1938. Quoted by permission of the Australian Council for Educational Research.

[2] R. F. Butts, *Assumptions Underlying Australian Education*.

Australian educational officials, on the other hand, defend the system by stating that it was not arbitrarily chosen, but grew out of certain historical circumstances. Centralization seemed to be the only remedy for a desperate situation. Moreover, they maintain that it is well suited to the geographic and economic characteristics of a large continent with many sparsely settled areas, ensuring a uniform standard of good education for all districts and avoiding the differentiation of educational treatment which is sometimes found in a decentralized system.

The Social and Political Background

THE FIRST settlements were made in the latter part of the eighteenth century, and six self-governing states gradually developed, all busily concerned with their own affairs and reluctant to lose any of their independence. Eventually it became obvious that joint action was necessary in matters that concerned Australia as a whole, such as defense, immigration, and trade with other countries. A federation movement grew steadily in strength, culminating in the establishment of the Commonwealth of Australia in 1901. However, under the federal Constitution the states retained the right to legislation in matters which were not considered to be the concern of the federal government. Education was one of the spheres of action retained by the states.

The six states still remain,[3] although there have been occasional suggestions to break them up into smaller units. Their areas, populations, and capital cities are shown in Table 6-1. It is difficult to compare them with American states, as most of the Australian states are so large. The reader may gain some impression from the information that New South Wales is about the size of Texas plus Virginia, and Victoria is about the size of Minnesota. The total population of Australia is about that of Illinois, although its area is more than fifty times as great.

A glance at Table 6-1 reveals the surprising fact that 56 percent of the Australian people live in the six capital cities, which have thus become natural centers of control in their respective states. This ex-

[3] Northern Territory and the Australian Capital Territory are not states but are territories under the control of the Commonwealth government, roughly comparable to the former status of Alaska and the present status of the District of Columbia.

TABLE 6–1
Area and Population of Australia and Its States

STATE OR TERRITORY	AREA IN SQUARE MILES	POPULATION DECEMBER 31, 1962	STATE CAPITAL	POPULATION OF STATE CAPITAL JUNE, 1962
New South Wales	309,433	4,016,635	Sydney	2,215,970
Victoria	87,884	3,013,447	Melbourne	1,956,400
Queensland	670,070	1,550,370	Brisbane	635,500
South Australia	380,070	999,693	Adelaide	593,500
Western Australia	975,920	765,715	Perth	431,000
Tasmania	26,215	369,403	Hobart	63,313
Australian Capital Territory	939	68,824	Canberra	63,313
Northern Territory	523,620	26,284	Darwin	12,700
Totals	2,974,581	10,810,371		6,027,211

SOURCE : *Australia in Facts and Figures*, Canberra: Department of the Interior, 1963.

plains to some extent how a centralized system of administration has fitted easily into the geographical situation.

The Commonwealth government early entered the field of legislation for social welfare in order to give Australian workers a sense of security. There are liberal schemes for hospital benefits; pharmaceutical benefits; pensions for widows, invalids, and elderly persons; maternity allowances; unemployment and sickness benefits; and child endowment. Child endowment has been in effect since 1941; it applies to all families irrespective of income and provides 55 cents a week for one child and $1.10 a week for each additional child under 16 years of age. In 1960 endowed children numbered 3,229,000.

It may be well to remember that it is not easy for 11 million people to finance the development of a continent as large as the United States or as large as all of Europe exclusive of Russia. The existence of such immense distances and vast open spaces, together with the fact that the population is widely dispersed, has had a definite influence on the evolution of the school system. To this influence may be added the congregation of somewhat more than half of the population in six coastal cities and the consequent tendency for the affairs of each state to be controlled from its capital.

Historical Background of Australian Education

AUSTRALIA was first settled in 1788. New South Wales was the first colony and Tasmania (1803) the second. The others came into existence during the early nineteenth century as promising locations were found at various points on the long coastline. The earliest settlements were peopled by convicts sent out from Britain, but before long, free settlers began to arrive in considerable numbers, and after a few decades the transportation of convicts to the Australian colonies ended.

British laws of those days included about 200 offenses which were punishable by transportation overseas; some of these would seem trivial today—for example, the theft of a loaf of bread by a starving person. Some of the convicts were hardened criminals, but many were political offenders who were reasonably well educated. The latter and the rapidly growing number of free settlers brought with them the cultural and educational traditions of Britain, and the development of schools in the new country followed the general trend of developments in England. This has been the case right up to the present day. Even now the main subjects and school procedures are modeled on those of England and Scotland, often with a time lag due to lack of realization that English education has made distinct advances during recent years. It is only recently that Australian schools have begun to experiment with subjects and activities appropriate to Australia's position as a democratic outpost in the South Pacific.

Thus, in accordance with English procedure at the time, the provision of educational facilities in the early days was left to religious societies and private enterprise. Suitable teachers were hard to find, and the establishment of schools was haphazard. As the settlements expanded, church control over most of the schools was the general rule and bitter sectarian rivalries developed. In New South Wales a National Board looked after the work of such publicly supported schools as were founded, while a Denominational Board distributed government subsidy to the church schools. The result in both New South Wales and Victoria was that schools were on a competitive basis in influential and thickly populated areas, while outlying districts in many cases had no schools at all.

In Victoria in 1862 a single Board of Education was set up to administer the affairs of all the schools. At this time about 60 national schools and 400 denominational schools were involved. The board consisted of five laymen, all of different religious denominations. It is interesting to note that this new arrangement contemplated a decentralized system with local committees to appoint teachers and collect fees. Local districts were also expected to bear half the cost of building and equipping the schools. But the squabbling went on, and in 1866 it was found that 100,000 Victorian children of school age were not in school. New South Wales had a somewhat similar experience.

The position in Victoria became so bad that in 1872 the state took the bull by the horns and passed an act instituting a national centralized system which was to be free, compulsory, and secular. A perusal of the documents and newspapers of the time reveals no clear reason for the adoption of centralization except that the authorities were in despair over the continual religious bickerings and the neglect of the rapidly growing rural districts. Local government has never been as strong in Australia as in England or the United States, and the framers of the act seemed to turn naturally to complete control from the capital city as the best way of remedying the situation.

The other states in turn followed Victoria's lead—South Australia and Queensland in 1875, New South Wales in 1880, Tasmania in 1885, and Western Australia in 1893. Church schools continued to exist, but they no longer received state subsidies. There was no unity of action in making education free; small fees were charged in New South Wales until 1906 and in Tasmania until 1908.

The new system was almost immediately successful. In Victoria school attendance doubled and applications for new schools poured in from all parts of the state. In all the states the rural areas began to be well served with small schools; the tradition was soon established, and has remained ever since, that the pupil in a small country district must receive as good an educational opportunity as a pupil in a city school.

In 1862 the system of "payment by results" was introduced in England and shortly afterwards found favor in Australia. By it a teacher was paid a small basic salary with an added bonus for every pupil who could make a reasonable showing in the three R's. This system lasted in some Australian states for nearly forty years. Australian education never recovered from its influence, for the belief remained that examination results were very important and that teachers had to be carefully watched by inspectors to ensure that their work was sound. Official scrutiny of examination results still plays a big part in all Australian schools.

After the basic Education Acts had been passed in each state, the administration of education came to be carried out by Education Departments under the control of a Minister of Education and with a Director of Education as the chief permanent officer. The Australian states were fortunate in some of the early directors, notably Peter Board in New South Wales, W. C. McCoy in Tasmania, Frank Tate in Victoria, and Cyril Jackson in Western Australia. These were men of vision and force of character who did not allow the procedures of centralization to neutralize the leadership of the chief education officer.

Although the states ceased to give subsidies to denominational schools, and even purchased some of the buildings, church schools have continued to flourish. Following the English precedent of great public schools, such as Eton, Harrow, and Rugby, with a long history and set of traditions behind them, a number of Australian church-connected schools developed along somewhat similar lines. Examples are The King's School (1840) in Sydney, St. Peter's (1847) in Adelaide, Geelong and Melbourne Grammar Schools (1858) in Victoria, and Hutchins School (1847) in Hobart. Schools such as these, together with many smaller grammar schools, were often under the general jurisdiction of a particular denomination but governed by councils of influential patrons and alumni. Later in the century similar schools for girls began to emerge. A Roman Catholic system, starting with ten schools in New South Wales in 1835, steadily developed in each state, with both elementary and secondary divisions.

The independent schools have grown in number until at present they educate, without any subsidy from public funds, about one-fourth of the total school population and form a powerful and important section of the general educational network in Australia. Although less exclusive than their English counterparts, these independent schools, with the exception of those organized by the Roman Catholic Church, provide for the wealthier sections of the community, including the more prosperous divisions of the middle class. Thus it may be said that each Australian state has produced three systems of education: the state schools, the Roman Catholic schools, and the independent (non-Catholic) church-connected schools, together with a few influential private schools not connected with any church.

There is provision in the legislation of all states that instruction in nonstate schools must be regular and efficient. Winners of scholarships or any allowances provided by state governments are only permitted to take these up in schools recognized as efficient. In 1905 Victoria passed a Registration of Teachers and Schools Act, whereby all nonstate schools had to meet certain requirements as to physical facilities and were allowed to employ only registered teachers who possessed certain required qualifications of training. This did not mean state interference in the actual management or procedures of the school but gave a guarantee to the public that certain essential standards would be met.

A certain amount of indirect control over independent schools is exercised through the public examinations, which most pupils, in state and nonstate schools, aim at taking. The course of study and methods of instruction are thus controlled by the examinations which every secondary school is preparing its pupils to pass.

About 1900 the state systems began to enter the field of secondary education, although not without protests from the church schools. Before many years had passed, each state possessed an expanding network of high schools and technical schools, which became increasingly successful. For a long time the upper limit of compulsory attendance in all states was 14 years, but in recent years it has been increased to 15 years in New South Wales and Victoria, and to 16 years in Tasmania. Legislation has been passed in South Australia and Western Australia whereby the school leaving age may be raised to 15 years; in South Australia the school leaving age is the end of the term in which the child reaches the age of 14 years, and in Western Australia he is now not permitted to leave until the end of the school year in which he turns 14, it being assumed that the year begins with the first school day.

Centralization in many ways has served Australia well. It has provided within each state a reasonable equality of educational opportunity for all districts and has established a good uniform standard of instruction and teacher training. Since each state tends to resemble the others in its educational organization and operating procedures, there is considerable uniformity throughout the nation. The system has given the teachers civil service status, security of tenure, and good pensions. The system of promotion of teachers in each state has practically eliminated any possibility of political influence in making appointments.

On the other hand, many critics feel that the Australian centralized system has produced too much uniformity and has tended to rob the schools of freedom and experimentation. There are signs that some changes may be made. In 1947 New South Wales experimented, in the Murrumbidgee area, with the establishment of a separate educational district, freed in some respects from central control and placed under the authority of an Area Director of Education. After the effects of this experiment had been observed for a few years, the state was divided into seven education areas of this type, including West Sydney and Sydney proper, the latter being administered by the central office. In 1949 Queensland divided its huge area into five divisions, each under an Area Director of Education. This movement is carefully watched by the other states, and the head office in each state still keeps a fairly tight hold on procedures. It may lead in the end to a judicious blending of centralization and decentralization in each state on something like the English pattern. At the present time it is not decentralization in the sense of giving more authority to the local people; it might better be described as a devolution of authority from the central office to regional administrators.

Moreover, during the last twenty years several ameliorating features have developed to lessen the rigidity of the system. There has been a definite slackening in the authoritarian attitude of the Education Departments, in that inspectors have been instructed to give less time to rating the skill of teachers and perusing examination results, and more attention to helping teachers and accelerating the movement for cross-fertilization of ideas.

Research divisions have been organized at each head office, curriculum-revision sections have been instituted, and teams of counselors and psychologists have been appointed. Teacher training has been greatly improved, teachers' salaries have risen, and opportunities for exchange teaching and overseas study have been provided. Designs for new school buildings are more modern in character, widespread systems of conveyance to secondary and consolidated schools have been arranged, and more variety has been introduced, both in subjects and in content of subject matter.

Centralization still means that improvements in the educational system of any state are imposed from above, and rarely grow from the thinking of the teachers themselves or from representatives of the people of a particular school district, but Parents' and Citizens' Associations are now playing a much larger part, even if indirectly, and both governments and Education Departments are becoming much more aware of the importance of local bodies.

The Role of the National Government

AS THE federal Constitution left education in the hands of the states, for 40 years after 1901, the Commonwealth government played very little part in educational activities. In recent years, however, the Commonwealth has undertaken certain educational tasks which appear to lie within its own sphere of action. Even then the federal authorities have been careful not to interfere with state administration: for instance, they have paid New South Wales to staff and manage the schools of the Australian Capital Territory, and South Australia to undertake similar responsibilities in the Northern Territory. Educational activities of the Commonwealth government have been as follows:

1. The establishment of a National University at Canberra.
2. The establishment of an Australian Universities Commission to examine the needs of Australian universities and make recommendations to the federal government.
3. The organization of native education in New Guinea and in the Trust Territories.
4. The development of a scheme of education and welfare for the aborigines in the Northern Territory. (This large area is under direct Commonwealth control, and there is no interference with state rights.)
5. The granting of assistance through 4,000 open entrance scholarships and 125 postgraduate scholarships for study at universities and other higher institutions.
6. The establishment of one model preschool center in each state capital.
7. The organization of a program of national fitness in all the states.
8. The establishment of technical assistance programs (e.g., the Colombo Plan and the scheme of Commonwealth Cooperation in Education). Under these programs fellowships and scholarships are

made available to students in other countries to study in Australia, and Australian experts can work in overseas countries.

9. The institution of a system of education for migrants in camps and holding centers (a program later handed over to the states).

The Commonwealth government is the sole taxing authority for the major taxes in Australia; it allocates amounts to the states in accordance with their needs and their annual budgets. There is no federal control over state spending, and the amounts are allocated on the basis of what the Commonwealth government thinks is a reasonable proportion of the total amount available. The constant complaint of the states is that they do not receive enough money and are consequently compelled to curtail their programs of public works and social services, including education. Several appeals have been made to the Commonwealth Treasurer, by such bodies as the Australian Teachers' Federation, which has asked for a special grant of £100,000,000 ($224,000,000) to place Australian schools on a sound footing. The reply to this has always been that educational expenditures are to be determined by the states themselves.

Although the Commonwealth government by the Constitution cannot interfere in the control of education in the states, it does give considerable assistance to, and even exercises some control over, university education in the states through the Australian Universities Commission and is constantly bombarded by suggestions that it make more federal money available to the states for the expansion of educational facilities. These requests imply, however, that the states wish to retain control of their own educational systems.

In 1945 an Education Act that set up the Commonwealth Office of Education was passed. Included in the Act was provision for the establishment of a Universities Commission, the main functions of which were to provide for the university training of discharged members of the Australian armed forces and for financial assistance to students. The Director of the Office of Education was to act as Chairman of the Universities Commission and its activities were closely integrated with those of the Office. In 1959 the Education Act of 1945–59 was passed. It is similar to the 1945 Act but established a Commonwealth Scholarships Board with a structure and responsibilities similar to the Universities Commission which it replaced. At the same time a new body was established, the Australian Universities Commission, described on page 373.

The functions of the Commonwealth Office of Education are defined in the following terms:

1. To advise the Minister on matters relating to education;
2. To establish and maintain a liaison, on matters relating to education, with other countries and the states;
3. To arrange consultation between Commonwealth authorities concerned with matters relating to education;
4. To undertake research relating to education;
5. To provide statistics and information relating to education required by any Commonwealth authority; and
6. To advise the Minister concerning the grant of financial assistance to the states and other authorities for educational purposes, and shall include such other functions in relation to education as are assigned to it by the Minister.

There is little doubt that the establishment of the Commonwealth Office of Education was in some measure inspired by the model of the United States Office of Education, and it represents an important acknowledgment by the federal government in Australia of its concern in a field that had been constitutionally regarded as a preserve of the states. It was probably not the intention of its originators that the Office of Education should be responsible for all the educational activities of the Commonwealth government, and it has certainly not proved to be so. The Department of Territories, for example, administers education in the Northern Territory and in external territories of the Commonwealth. There is no federal Ministry of Education and the office is included in the portfolio of the Prime Minister.

Since its establishment the Office's activities have fallen broadly into three major areas: research and information, student training schemes, and international relations in education. In the last two fields its role has been especially significant. The Australian government has given strong support to programs of assistance to less developed countries, such as the Colombo Plan, and the Office has had the increasing task of planning and supervising the training of students who come to attend Australian universities and similar institutions as part of these programs. The Scheme of Commonwealth Cooperation in Education, begun in 1959, increased Australia's relations with other countries of the British Commonwealth, and the development of activities under the Scheme has added greatly to the work of the Office. In addition, the Office prepares advice on Australian participation in UNESCO and a number of other international bodies and provides a secretariat for the Australian National Advisory Council for UNESCO. The Director of the Office is Chairman of the Committee.

Other activities in which the Office participates include the Commonwealth Scholarships Board. The Office provides a chairman and a secretariat for the Board and is responsible for the supervision of policy and for coordinating administration of the Commonwealth Scholarship Scheme and of Commonwealth Postgraduate Awards. As part of the Office's research program studies are undertaken of the success and failure of the students who hold awards. In the field of language teaching the Office carries on research and development work that is chiefly concerned with the problems of teaching English as a second language, not only to new settlers in Australia but to increasing numbers of sponsored visitors and students from overseas who are coming to Australia to study. As part of its information activities the Office prepares bulletins and statements on selected aspects of Australian education and publishes a journal, *Education News*. It also undertakes investigation in the field of comparative education.

When the Commonwealth Office of Education was first established there was apprehension in the state Education Departments that there might be interference with their activities. This did not happen. Relations between state Education Departments and the Commonwealth Office in areas where their interests converge have developed satisfactorily so that close liaison and cooperation now exist.

The Role of the State Government

A BRIEF account has been given of the origin of centralized systems of administration in the Australian states. As the population increases and larger cities and towns develop in the rural areas the system may be modified. At present, however, the fact that the population density progressively decreases as one leaves the capital cities and the prosperous coastal areas and moves into the interior means that control remains centered in the capitals. Local government outside the six large cities is limited in scope and lacks the financial resources to participate to any extent in support of schools. Centralization seems to be firmly entrenched.

In the six Australian states, except for minor local differences, the pattern is essentially the same. The head office of the Department of Education in the capital city is the powerhouse which controls and gives energy to the whole educational network within the state. But there are signs of change. Regional area directors have a number of responsible functions and can operate autonomously in some things. Also, in recent years much greater authority has been given to head teachers, school councils, and school committees. In addition school inspectors and regional officers of the Public Works Department have been allowed to initiate minor works and spend up to designated limits without reference to the head offices of Education Departments.

The political head of the Education Department is the Minister of Education. He is a member of the Cabinet and changes when the party in power changes. His duty is to develop an educational program for the state in accordance with the policy of the government in power. He has to approve the major decisions of the department and sanction principal items of expenditure. Matters of marked importance he carries to the Cabinet for its consideration and assent before putting them into operation. Much depends on the personality of the Minister of Education and his prestige within the Cabinet. A weak Minister sometimes gets scant attention from a government which has many other demands on its funds and energies.

The year's budget for educational expenditure is presented to the Treasurer and the Cabinet by the Minister. If there happens to be a period of financial stringency at the time, the budget is apt to be reduced and word goes out to all schools that strict economy must be practiced. In recent years, however, most of the state governments have treated education as generously as possible. There have been many strong Ministers of Education who, working under favorable conditions and backed by their Cabinets, have initiated and carried through progressive measures on the advice of their permanent officers. The whole system is buoyant or depressed according to the state government's current policy and financial position. There are no local authorities to hold the fort until better times come.

The chief permanent officer under the Minister is the Director or Director-General of Education. He is appointed by the Cabinet and in most cases is a successful departmental officer who has worked his way up through the system. Once appointed, he holds his position irrespective of any subsequent changes in the party in power. Sometimes criticism has been leveled at the average age of appointees to this important office, for many Directors have been well past fifty years of age on appointment, and in some cases have been over sixty, with only a few years to serve before retirement. Recent appointments in New South Wales, Victoria, and Western Australia have been younger men with good administrative records and at least twelve to fifteen years of professional service ahead of them. The appointment of a brilliant young man from outside the service is practically unknown. The position of Director of Education is a very important one, for he is adviser to the Minister and wields great power. What he says, subject to ministerial approval, goes for every school and every teacher in the whole state.

Under the Director is a team of permanent administrative officers in charge of various divisions within the department. This powerful hierarchy can best be shown by means of Figure 6-1. Years of experience in the running of this complex machine have resulted in building up a set of procedures well known to the teaching service, and the whole administrative system works effectively and smoothly. The basis of administration is the latest version of the State Education Act, amended from time to time, and the book of departmental regulations based on the act.

The total expenditure on schools comes from revenue derived from general taxation by state and Commonwealth governments. By agreement between the various governments the collection and subsequent allocation of income tax is reserved for the Commonwealth government. There is nothing in the nature of a local school tax to supplement these funds. No school makes up a budget for the year; all its expenses are attended to by the Education Department. There are no bond issues or special loans. Each year the Education Department prepares an estimate of educational expenditure for the next twelve months. This is submitted by the Minister to the Treasurer and to Parliament.

National loan funds, corresponding to proceeds from the sale of federal bonds in the United States, are allocated to each state through the use of a special formula. The state government, in turn, allocates its share among its various departments. Funds received by Education Departments are used to renovate old buildings and to build new ones. No control by the Commonwealth government is involved, except limitation of the amount which may be borrowed

Fig. 6–1 Organization of the Education Department of One Australian State (Victoria)

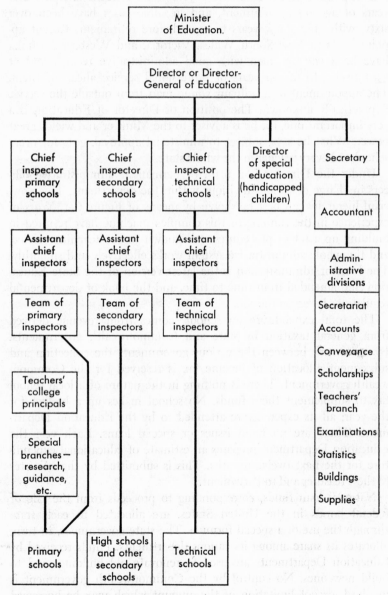

A Director of Teacher Training works in collaboration with all divisions.

TABLE 6-2
Educational Expenditure by Australian States, 1960–61

STATE	POPULATION JUNE, 1961	TOTAL EXPENDITURE ON EDUCATION (AUSTRALIAN POUNDS)	EXPENDITURE ON EDUCATION PER CAPITA IN EACH STATE £ s. d.
New South Wales	3,917,000	56,949,000	14.13.11.
Victoria	2,930,000	40,193,000	14.17.10.
Queensland	1,518,000	16,947,000	11. 5. 5.
South Australia	969,000	14,127,000	14.15. 2.
Western Australia	736,000	11,378,000	15.11.10.
Tasmania	350,000	5,756,000	16. 8.10.
All States	10,420,000	145,350,000	14. 1.11.

SOURCE: *1962 Report of the Commonwealth Grants Commission.*
Amounts are given in Australian pounds (£ = $2.23). The Australian expenditure in 1951 was £49,000,000.

each year. At the present time the states complain that their revenue does not permit them to provide for all the school construction needed. The difficulties are accentuated by the fact that educational expenditures are constantly rising as modern developments make heavier demands. Conveyance [4] of pupils in Victoria alone amounts to more than £2 million a year. Rather than establish state-owned bus services, the Education Departments let contracts for this service to local farmers and transport companies. For the whole of Australia the figure for transport now exceeds £8,000,000.

In each state the Department of Public Works, rather than the Education Department, undertakes the construction of new school buildings, but the officers of the Education Department have a large and often dominant say in the actual planning. This centralization of the building program has often led to long delays, with resulting protests from local school committees. Some moves have been made in several of the states to decentralize to some extent the activities of the Public Works Department. For some time after World War II money was available for buildings, but there was a shortage of labor

[4] The word "conveyance" is used in Australia rather than "transportation." The latter term was used in early days in connection with the transportation of convicts from England.

and materials. After 1952 there was plenty of labor and materials but funds were short. A local district may be asked to supply or suggest a site for a new building, but neither the headmaster nor the local parents are consulted about the design of the building or the courses to be offered. These decisions are made by the Department of Education, but there is a tendency to show the plans to the headmaster for comment. Some very effective buildings of modern design have been erected in some of the states since 1945, but there is a uniformity of design within a state which is typical of centralized control.

If a state is genuinely enthusiastic about education it can set aside a considerable amount of its grant from loan funds for school buildings. In 1960–61 the Victorian government allocated £10,570,000 for this purpose and five high schools and six junior technical schools, all badly needed, were established. By 1963–64 this particular amount had doubled.

Only a limited amount of school supplies are provided by the Education Departments. Each head teacher is given a small grant for maintenance and cleaning. In some states writing materials and readers are supplied in the elementary schools, but no textbooks are furnished in the secondary schools. Sometimes high school pupils may get their books at reduced prices through school bookstores. The standard of school furniture, equipment, and supplies does not compare favorably with that in the United States, Britain, or Canada. This is partly due to the fact that the Education Departments do not have enough money to be lavish and have to provide equally for all schools. On the other hand, no school is forgotten, and all receive equal treatment.

THE INSPECTORS

The inspectors' function is to ensure the effectiveness of the work done in the schools, to assess the abilities and achievements of the teachers, and to report on these matters to the Education Department. There are inspectors for each of the three divisions—elementary, secondary, and technical. As the inspectors of elementary schools have the longest historical record and the firmest tradition, it may be well to discuss their work in detail.

In Victoria, for example, where there are approximately 1,930 elementary schools and 11,530 teachers, there are 31 inspectors, 21 of whom work within the limits of the city of Melbourne. A rural inspectorate contains about 70 schools, many of them one-teacher schools. The inspector is expected to pay at least one annual visit to each of his schools, spending a day or possibly more, examining the pupils' work, consulting with the teacher, and watching him conduct the school's operations. Larger schools receive visits of from two to five days. If the work of the school is found to be weak, the inspector will give advice and return at a later date to give additional help. When a team of secondary inspectors visits a secondary school in his district, the elementary inspector also attends to give them any assistance necessary. He also visits regularly each nonstate school in his district, where his responsibility is not to rate the teachers' work but to determine whether the school is suitable for pupils who hold government scholarships.

The fact that the teacher's promotion depends very largely on the character of his inspector's report has tended to place undue emphasis on the part of the inspector's duties which deals with assessing [5] and has prevented teachers from appealing frankly to the inspector for help when they know their work is weak. There are few consultants or helping-teachers as in the United States, ready to help a teacher but never being called upon to report to the head office on the teacher's efficiency. A move has been made in this direction by the appointment of supervisors and group leaders. The main work of the supervisors, however, is administrative rather than supervisory, organizing groups of specialists in such fields as physical education, forestry, and school broadcasts. Group leaders, on the other hand, are often head teachers of schools in rural towns; they keep a friendly eye on inexperienced teachers in their area, occasionally visiting them to give advice and assistance. Group leaders are paid traveling expenses, but no additional remuneration for their work.

In the past the elementary inspectors were truly the watchdogs of the head office, giving each teacher a numerical rating of efficiency expressed as a percentage of complete success, or allotting a letter mark. In recent years, however, there has been a significant change in this procedure of assessing and the duty of helping the teachers and supplying them with new ideas has been stressed. New South Wales now has abolished "efficiency marks," and Victorian inspectors divide teachers into four broad groups—outstanding, very good, good, and unsatisfactory. This latter change, however, is only one of

[5] The corresponding American term for *assess* would be *rate*.

degree; the teacher still knows that what the inspector thinks about his work will be reported to the Education Department and will affect his chance of promotion.

Australian educators insist that it is difficult to operate a state-wide system of classification and promotion, with thousands of teachers on the same list, without individual reports on each teacher's efficiency. The inspector is faced with the unenviable task of attempting to make a just appraisal of a teacher he sees at work only one day a year.

In 1938 Kandel recommended that Australia change the inspectors into what he described as "educational leaders for their communities rather than watchdogs for their departments." [6] They would then have as their function the development of educational policy for their districts, and would be assisted by small committees, local councils, and parents' associations. This would require limiting the work of assessing teachers to simple reports on efficiency. The education officer would need to have a district headquarters and a small team of consultants and specialists to help the teachers in their work. Such a procedure might arouse local interest in the educational program for the district. The proposal has been discussed widely, and some moves have been made in this direction, but no state has adopted it fully. Several states have changed the title from inspector to superintendent.

The method of selecting inspectors tends to perpetuate the system. Inspectors are chosen with great care from teachers with outstanding academic and professional records. The average age at time of appointment is about 40 years. They are, in general, men and women with excellent personal qualities, but they have grown up and prospered in the system and they will not tend to alter it much. This is particularly so when their supervisory duties are so carefully delineated, although within certain limits they have a fairly free hand. The appointment of an inspector from outside the service, or one who has had any experience in another state, is a rare occurrence.

Inspectors of secondary and technical schools do not work as individuals, but as teams, dealing with all the schools in the state. They are subject-matter specialists, mainly academic, who have been successful teachers and organizers. They have the same task of

6 Kandel, op. cit., p. 86.

assessing teachers, but they are also expected to give expert advice on the way the subjects should be taught. It is difficult to avoid a certain tension in the schools when their visits take place, although individually the inspectors may be helpful and popular. The teachers cannot help feeling that they are on trial during the inspection and breathe a sigh of relief when the inspectors leave.

In Victoria the secondary inspectors serve two masters, the Education Department and the Schools Board. The latter body is in charge of the system of accrediting schools for some of the school-certificate examinations [7] and borrows the services of the secondary school inspectors to obtain reports every three years on those schools, state and nonstate, which are permitted to use the system of accrediting. Thus the secondary school inspectors visit the state schools every year, and in addition report to the Schools Board every three years on the general organization of all state and nonstate accredited schools. For these schools they report not so much on the work of individual teachers as on the general organization of the school, the qualifications and experience of the staff, and the maintenance of required standards in examinations.

In general the tendency is to work all of the inspectors too hard and to give them insufficient time for reading and keeping up to date on professional matters. In addition to inspecting schools they are expected to organize conferences and refresher schools (in-service training programs) and most of them serve on subject-matter committees. The failure to give them adequate clerical assistance in the field means that often, after inspecting schools and watching teachers at work all day, they have to spend their evenings writing lengthy reports in longhand, thus making them, for part of the time, very expensive clerks.

In recent years the various Education Departments have recognized the desirability of sending their inspectors to other Australian states, New Zealand, and occasionally to Britain, in order to see other schools at work and to compare notes with fellow workers in their own field.

Many Australian teachers and officials are beginning to believe that more consultants and specialists should be available for helping teachers, and that consultants should not be hampered by the requirement of making out efficiency reports.

[7] The system of accrediting schools is described on pages 367–68.

Curricula and courses of study for state schools are issued in printed booklets by the Education Departments. Originally there was little scope for initiative on the part of the practicing teacher, who was expected to adhere closely to the official course of study. In Victoria, for example, there was practically no change in the elementary school curriculum between 1902 and 1934. In the latter year the Education Department accepted the principle enunciated by the Melbourne University School of Education, that "no program of school work will function effectively which is not evolved to some extent out of the thinking of the teachers who are to apply it." In consequence, a revision was carried out in 1934 by appointing committees of teachers in all parts of the state to suggest changes. This was very successful, and the district meetings of teachers sent in many valuable suggestions, mainly in the direction of shifting the emphasis from subject matter to consideration for the pupils. Unrealistic and nonfunctional elements, such as formal grammar, were replaced and many educational activities were introduced. Projects, handicrafts, and outdoor excursions became popular.

At present there is in most states a Standing Curriculum Committee. This committee establishes principles of procedure for the numerous subject-matter committees, which consist of teachers, inspectors, and administrative officers. The Education Department prints and circulates the courses, with details of the material which it considers should be included. Local variations are permitted if the consent of the deparment is obtained. Even so, most of the teachers seem content to follow the prescribed courses rather than to experiment.

THE EXAMINATION SYSTEM

External examinations, that is, examinations prepared and corrected by some authority outside of the individual school, play a prominent part in Australia. They provide a powerful control by the state over the work done and in some of the states seem to dominate the educational procedures.

Originally all of the schools had examinations, sometimes called "Qualifying Examinations," to decide which pupils would be permitted to proceed to secondary school. It is now common practice in all states for pupils to proceed to secondary education without formal examination.

At present the examinations in secondary schools throughout

Australia vary in number and name in the different states, so that it is not possible to present a chart covering the whole country. New South Wales has an Intermediate Examination at the end of the third secondary year, and a Leaving Examination at the end of the fifth year.[8] These examinations are prepared and corrected by the Education Department. Entrance to the university, or matriculation, is based on the Leaving Examination, provided that certain subjects are taken and the grades are high enough.

In Victorian secondary schools, students face four successive external examinations in four successive years. The first is the Proficiency Examination, taken at the end of the third secondary year, which is prepared by the Education Department. The Intermediate Certificate, supervised by the Schools Board, is taken at the end of the fourth year. The Leaving Certificate, also supervised by the Schools Board, is at the end of the fifth year. Those who intend to try for university entrance remain in school for a sixth year and take the Matriculation Examination which is prepared by the university. Those students who intend to stay in school until the age of 17 or 18 may bypass the Proficiency and Intermediate Examinations, which are important only for those who drop out of school at the end of the third or fourth years. A student must have passed in five subjects in the Leaving Examination as well as in four subjects at the Matriculation Examination before he is eligible to matriculate at the university. Possession of the various certificates is important to boys and girls seeking employment, for employers seem to consider them essential. Since these examinations hold such an important position in the entire educational program, no curriculum revision can be very effective if it does not seek primarily to prepare pupils to pass examinations.

The Schools Board in Victoria is technically a university body, outside of the Education Department, appointed to draw up courses of study for secondary school subjects and to control the Intermediate and Leaving Examinations. The chairman is the dean of the School of Education in the university, and members are drawn from the Education Department, the state schools, the nonstate schools, the university, and business and commercial interests. It appoints standing committees for each of the secondary school sub-

---

[8] Changes are being made in New South Wales. See the reference to the implementation of the Wyndham Report, on page 366.

jects on the examination list. These committees include a number of successful teachers, and their function is to keep the course of study up to date, to recommend examiners, and to report to the Schools Board on the general progress of secondary school work. This board exercises a very important control on a state-wide basis.

EXPERIMENTS IN DECENTRALIZATION OF CONTROL

There have been some tentative moves toward decentralization of control in Australia. In 1947 New South Wales set up an educational district in the Murrumbidgee area, a rich farming area with four large towns, about 300 schools, and 15,000 pupils. The main responsibilities of the Area Director in charge of the district were as follows:

1. To make a survey of buildings and facilities and secure sites for future development.
2. To approve building repairs up to £350 on any single project.
3. To transfer teachers within the area in cases not involving promotion.
4. To approve variations in school routine.
5. To supervise and record assessments of teachers made by inspectors.
6. To encourage the development of libraries, young farmers' clubs, youth activities, and adult education.

All of these functions are carried out under the supervision of the head office in Sydney. The Area Director keeps in close touch with the Director-General of Education. The promotion of teachers, which is on a state-wide basis and often involves transfer to another area, is not a function of the Area Director. The secondary inspectors are still responsible to Sydney, and important appointments, such as heads of large schools, are still made by the head office.

After five years' experience with this initial experiment, six additional areas were established, covering all of New South Wales except the far western region. These new districts began operations under Area Directors in 1952. It is interesting to note that one of the new units is the western half of the large city of Sydney. The remainder of the city is still directly under the head office, which also keeps a general control over all the areas.

The second move was made in Queensland, a state of immense area (670,000 square miles, two and one-half times the size of

Texas). In 1949 the state was divided into five administrative areas under Regional Directors of Education. The Director-General in Brisbane retains control over such matters as the opening and closing of schools, the appointment of teachers to secondary and technical schools, the determination of the number of teachers allowed to schools of varying size, and the preparation and evaluation of examinations. Each Regional Director is asked to work out a policy for his district, appoint and transfer elementary teachers, organize school libraries and physical education programs, establish the centers where state examinations will be held, provide for repairs to be made locally, and supervise the inspection of elementary schools. One copy of the inspector's report in each case is sent to the head office with the Regional Director's comments.

It is important to note that in each state the changes originated in the head office and involve only decentralization of administration. The head offices in Sydney and Brisbane are relieved of much troublesome routine detail and many matters can be settled more quickly by an officer closer to the local situation. The change has been a good one, but it has not come about because of any demand from the local people for more decentralization. So far the local citizens are still outside of the system. Further developments in these two projects will be watched with interest in other states. They may lead to a true decentralization with some autonomy for the districts concerned and with some participation in school affairs by the people themselves, but up to this time the situation may more accurately be described as a devolution of centralized authority to smaller areas rather than true decentralization.

The Role of the Local Community

THE READER may wonder why the districts in which the schools are located do not provide financial aid to the schools. To a small extent they do. Each school has a school committee or school council, with some minor responsibilities prescribed by the Education Department. The members are made up of elected representatives of the parents and representatives appointed by the department. In addition, many schools have active and interested Mothers' Clubs, and others are linked with Parents' and Citizens' Associations. These organizations raise funds for radio sets, public-address systems, visual aids, and library books, and are often assisted by a subsidy from the government. The amount raised is not very large, and it is difficult to get any statistics on the total spent in any one state. Any substantial contribution by local districts to the building, maintenance, and equipment of schools would necessitate a revolution in the thinking of the people, who have long become accustomed to leaving everything to the states.

As has been mentioned previously, Mothers' Clubs and other local groups work hard to provide equipment which the Department does not furnish. But the members of the local community have nothing to say about who the teachers will be, what the curriculum will be, or whether they will get a new school building. If a new school is provided, they are not consulted in the planning. Under these circumstances, it is very difficult to arouse any real interest in local schools, since the people tend to believe that the schools belong to the state.

The Place of Voluntary Agencies and Private Schools

THE MAIN work carried on by voluntary agencies in Australia is in the organization of nursery schools and kindergartens in each state by organizations such as the Free Kindergarten Union. This association, composed mainly of women with ideals of social service, has gradually built up over the years a network of preschool centers in the industrial areas of the cities. World War II showed the need of an expansion of this work, when so many mothers were working. These Free Kindergarten Unions have established training colleges in Sydney and Melbourne to prepare teachers, but the financial burden has become very great. The state governments have made grants to assist the groups, which previously relied entirely on voluntary contributions. The Commonwealth government has assisted in the establishment of model kindergartens in each capital city. In Victoria and Tasmania the Education Departments require the registration of kindergarten teachers, based on their qualifications and training.

In New South Wales there are departmental infant schools; in Western Australia the superintendent of kindergarten work is an Education Department officer; and in Tasmania the Education Department is deeply involved with a number of preschools for which it is at least indirectly responsible. Thus the importance of nursery schools and kindergartens is becoming more widely recognized, and some sections of the people are asking that the states take them over. The Free Kindergarten Unions, in spite of their financial difficulties, are reluctant to have a government department take over the schools, because they fear that the spirit of preschool work would be hampered by government centralization. The Education Departments do not feel that they have the funds to enter this field.

The nonstate schools fall into three main groups: the Roman Catholic schools, the schools of other religious denominations, and the undenominational independent schools. These do not receive any state funds, except the indirect subsidization that comes through government scholarships in the secondary schools. They play an important part in the total educational program, since they educate about one-fourth of all the children in school. Table 6–3 shows the number of schools of each denomination, as compared with the number of government schools.

The word "control" at the head of one column in Table 6–3 is not entirely accurate. The Roman Catholic schools are organized and controlled by the Church as a separate system, but many of the

TABLE 6–3
Numbers of State and Nonstate Schools in Australia, 1960

CONTROL OR DENOMINATION	NEW SOUTH WALES	VIC- TORIA	QUEENS- LAND	SOUTH AUS- TRALIA	WEST- ERN AUS- TRALIA	TAS- MANIA	TOTAL
State schools	2,699	2,154	1,521	654	521	286	7,835
Roman Catholic	671	439	267	122	173	44	1,716
Church of England	35	36	16	13	9	5	114
Seventh Day Adventist	17	7	3	3	5	3	38
Presbyterian	13	14	3	2	2	1	35
Methodist	7	4	5	3	3	1	23
Lutheran	3	7	2	13	—	—	25
Other denominations	—	4	—	2	1	1	8
Undenominational	68	35	10	5	123	5	246
Total nonstate schools	814	546	306	163	316	60	2,205

source: *Official Year Book of the Commonwealth of Australia*, 1962.

other schools that come under the general supervision of their denominations are actually financed and controlled by school Councils upon which the denominations are represented.

The Roman Catholic Church set to work in the early days of Australia to build up a system of schools that would incorporate the belief of the Church that the education of its children must be permeated by Catholic religious teaching. From 31 primary schools in New South Wales in 1840, the system has expanded until Catholic elementary and secondary schools now enroll more than 417,000 children in every part of Australia. The relationship between the Catholic and the state schools is cordial and much cooperation takes place.

The general organization of Catholic education is on a diocesan basis, directed by the bishop of the diocese, who has a diocesan inspector to advise him. In each capital city there is a Catholic Director of Education who supervises the Catholic schools of the state and maintains liaison with the Education Department and with the university. Each diocese, however, manages its own affairs quite independently, so that in effect, the Catholic system is decentralized. The schools follow the courses prescribed by the state Education Department, with the addition of religious teaching.

The Catholic schools differ from other nonstate schools in that their fees are low, except in their large boarding schools. They are open to all, and are thus more nearly comparable, as far as the social and financial position of their pupils is concerned, with the state schools. Catholic authorities still press for state subsidies, but there has been little indication that any government would yield to this demand. In country districts, however, pupils attending the Catholic schools are permitted to travel to their schools in buses which are paid for by the state.

The schools organized under the jurisdiction of the Protestant churches and the smaller number of independent schools illustrate a very different aspect of Australian education. These schools have great social prestige in the community, and most parents who can afford to pay the fees prefer to send their children to these schools rather than state schools. The larger church schools resemble in many ways the public schools of England, on which they were modeled. Although associated with the various religious denominations, most of these schools are governed by councils composed of alumni and influential businessmen. Many of them date back to the middle of the nineteenth century and have, in consequence, accumulated a good deal of history and tradition.

Only a few of them are exclusively for boarders, such as Geelong Grammar School [9] in Victoria and Frensham Girls' School in New South Wales. Most of them have a limited number of boarders and a large group of day pupils. The larger and wealthier schools have attractive buildings and extensive playing fields. A number of boys and girls complete their elementary education in the state schools and then transfer to the larger church schools for secondary work. The fees are sometimes high, so that only the better-off families can afford these schools. The annual fee for a boarder at Geelong Grammar School is £600, or $1,350, for board and tuition.

The schools are independent of any state control, except that the Education Department inspects those eligible to take winners of government scholarships, and many of their students take the public examinations. As in England, there is a national Headmasters' Conference and a Headmistresses' Conference; these meet in different states annually to discuss problems common to all nonstate schools. Since the establishment of state high schools early in this century, there has been considerable competition between the two types of secondary school, and some of the weaker church and private schools have disappeared. Today, however, the big church schools stand very high in public esteem and have longer waiting lists than ever, in spite of increasingly heavy expenses and the necessity of charging higher fees.

Problems Facing the Administration of Australian Education

TEN YEARS ago very little criticism of Australian education came from within the systems themselves. As public servants the teachers were prohibited by law from voicing criticism, and they still are, but today the opinions of teachers on many educational subjects manage to get heard. The higher officials who were inclined to take the position that the Australian system was the best possible plan of educational organization, by visits to other countries have been made more flexible in their points of view. The ordinary citizen who rarely came into contact with any critical discussion about modern ideas on educational administration, and in many cases thought that

[9] Geelong Grammar School, one of the most famous of the Church of England schools, is largely a boarding school, but takes some day boys from Geelong.

all countries used a centralized system and followed the same procedures as Australia, now is beginning to be better informed.
Formerly there was not much opportunity for parents and citizens
to visit schools, observe school happenings, and confer with teachers,
except for one week during the year called Education Week, but
now the parents are beginning to play a more important part.

Some of the influences which have enabled sound educational
information and criticism to reach the public are as follows:

1. Most of the officials today possess university degrees in education and have studied the systems and problems of other countries.

2. Teachers have begun to voice criticisms and suggestions through
group meetings, education workshops during vacations, summer
schools, and union and association meetings.

3. The Schools of Education at the universities have done a good
deal to inform parents through newspaper articles, radio, and television.

4. The Institutes of Educational Research in the various states
have organized many public meetings about educational topics of
importance.

5. Educational journals of national circulation are beginning to
make themselves felt.

6. The establishment of the Australian College of Education, with
chapters in each state, provides a good channel for information and
criticism. Fellows and members of the College are drawn from all
types of educational institutions, public and private. The standard
of its discussions, reports, and publications is a high one.

The Problem of Excessive Centralizaton

Although centralization has served Australia well in the past, with
the rapid growth in population since World War II continuance of
the centralized system of educational administration is likely to result in a very cumbersome machine. The problem was described by
Leicester Webb, writing nearly thirty years ago about centralization
in New Zealand; his comments were even more applicable to Australia in the days when Australian educational administrators rushed
to the defense of centralization whenever it was criticized.

The numerical grading of primary teachers, the methods of inspection
associated with it, the domination of the teaching profession by the
inspectors, the rigid application of the seniority rule to promotions within

the department, these and other characteristic features of the system have no positive justification. Their purpose is the negative one of safeguarding the profession against such abuses as parochialism, nepotism, and extravagance. The safeguards are now so elaborate that they make constructive action almost impossible. Teachers, inspectors, and administrative officers present the spectacle of an army immobilized by its own defence works.[10]

The vivid figure of speech at the end of this quotation is too strong to be applied to the present situation, but centralization is still firmly enthroned. The position was also discussed by Kandel thirty years ago. He said:

> The efficiency attained by centralized control may be purchased at too great a price. A central authority tends to grow by the power it wields, and when such an authority exercises at once the right to legislate, as it does in both countries [Australia and New Zealand] by Orders-in-Council, to execute, and to judge, the result is inevitably rule by a bureaucracy which imposes its will and ultimately secures uniformity in aspects of the educational process where uniformity is least desirable. The progress of education is thus sacrificed at the altar of efficiency, and the final result is a feeling of complacency.[11]

The experiments which are being made in New South Wales and Queensland may offer some hope that the rigid control by the head office may be slightly relaxed. They do not indicate that any substantial amount of local participation is being considered, but the authoritarian attitude of the Education Departments is being somewhat reduced, and greater flexibility is being introduced into the courses of study, although the general framework is still prescriptive. The fact that the centralized system operates so efficiently and economically is the greatest deterrent to any major reorganization, but the problem is always there. The dominating position of the state capitals also seems to favor the continuance of centralization. For example, Victoria, the capital city of Melbourne, had a population in 1962 of 1,956,000, while the second city in the state, Geelong, had a population of only 94,000.

Centralization is also closely linked with the weakness of local government in Australia, compared with the situation in Great Britain or the United States. For more than a century the people

[10] Leicester Webb, *The Control of Education in New Zealand*, pp. 124–25.
[11] Kandel, *op. cit.*, p. 51.

have been accustomed to leaving everything to the state governments. This has worked very well in some matters, but in education it has meant that there is little participation in school affairs by the local people. The schools have tended to belong to the government rather than to the people. This has often been noted by observers from overseas. Kandel points out that "One of the chief weaknesses of centralization is the absence of agencies for the development of an alert and active public opinion on what constitutes a sound education." [12]

The Function of the Inspectors

Both local and foreign critics of Australian education have pointed out that the place of the inspector is the key position in the actual working of the centralized system. Kandel writes of the selection of inspectors:

In a system which is hierarchically organized, with promotion dependent on a satisfactory fulfillment of assigned duties, no opportunity is provided for acquiring the experience and insight necessary for successful administration. The Departments of Education are assisted by a corps of inspectors who are themselves promoted because of success of a type demanded by the system. Promotion to an inspectorship is not by seniority, but by a combination of qualities considered desirable in a system which is itself routinized and mechanized; promotion under such conditions is virtually a promise to perpetuate the system. [13]

Kandel then proposes, as has been mentioned before, that the inspectors should no longer be required to spend their time rating teachers, but they should become educational leaders in their communities and have increased authority and freedom. He goes on to say:

Such a proposal would not disturb the present system; it would simply mean a redefinition of the educational policy of the central authority and of the functions of the inspectors. The reform proposed would have nearly all the educational advantages claimed for decentralization; it would make possible that adaptation of education to the local environment which is the central principle of current theory; it would provide a method of coordinating the various branches of education which does not exist at present; it would make for experimentation; it would en-

[12] *Ibid.*, p. 53.
[13] *Ibid.*, p. 60.

courage variety within a common framework; it would capitalize the professional ability and responsibilities of teachers and inspectors; and it would provide opportunities for training and elevating public opinion. The cost of education—administration, maintenance and teachers' salaries—would continue to be borne by the central authority representing the State as a whole.[14]

Problems of Finance

Although the years 1950–60 were a period of great prosperity for Australia, and the state governments have had reasonable funds for social services and education, the states will need much additional help if they are to provide an effective educational service for a rapidly increasing population. Expenditures on education have been mounting faster than resources. In 1952 the total expenditure on education in South Australia was £4,327,000; in 1961 it was £14,-127,000. In Victoria the 1952 expenditure was £13,127,000; in 1964 it was £74,000,000.

As the Commonwealth government is the principal taxing authority, it seems clear that the Commonwealth must either enter the educational field or give larger grants to the states. The states, on the other hand, although desirous of larger grants, are jealous of their autonomy in educational affairs and are fearful of losing this, although no sign of direct interference by the Commonwealth in educational matters has yet appeared. In 1963 the Commonwealth granted £60,000,000 to the rapidly expanding Australian universities, conditional upon state grants and student fees amounting to at least £90,000,000.

In recent years many fine new schools have been built in all states. In 1950 there were 48 state high schools in Victoria; in 1960 there were 149 and the number in 1964 was nearly 200. But there is still an alarming shortage of accommodation. Classes, in the metropolitan areas particularly, are far too big. Education Departments are expanding their activities in accordance with modern educational developments, but the problem of sufficient finance is always present. The expenditure of £250,000,000 on school buildings, divided among the six states, would still leave a great deal to be done. The question of how best to finance adequately a modern educational program for this continent about as large as the United States but containing only 11 million people remains as yet unanswered.

[14] *Ibid.*, p. 87.

The Problem of Planning Ahead

Few if any of the Education Departments have publicized long-range plans of development for their systems. If there are any such plans they are unknown to the general public or to the teachers. There is nothing similar to the planning carried out by local education authorities in England under the encouragement of the Ministry of Education. It would seem that a centralized system of administration, with its wide view of necessary developments over the whole state, would be in an admirable position to produce a blueprint of an educational program for the ensuing ten years and to gain public support for it. This has not happened in Australia. The head office, in most cases, has been so busily taken up with the minute details of administration that not enough time has been available for long-range planning. An even more cogent reason is that such a blueprint could be issued only by the Minister of Education with the approval of the Cabinet, and state governments are reluctant to commit themselves or their successors for years ahead.

The reader might gain the impression, from the foregoing statement of problems and from the criticisms quoted, that Australian education lacks vigor and definiteness. The reverse is the case. The centralized system works so efficiently that there is little stimulus to change it. The question is whether centralization, which served Australia so well in the earlier and formative stages, has not served its purpose, and whether the time has not come to introduce more variety, freedom, and experiment into the system by adopting some measure of decentralization and thus providing a greater incentive for local authorities to assist in certain aspects of educational planning and management.

7
Sectarian Control:
Some Canadian Provinces

I N CANADA geographical characteristics and national development
have had very pronounced effects upon school organization.
Canada is the single largest area in the British Commonwealth.
It extends for 3,700 miles from east to west, and from the northern
border of the United States to the Arctic Ocean. Its area is greater
than that of the continental United States and is almost as large as
the entire continent of Europe. The population of over 18 million is
concentrated in a belt a few hundred miles wide along the southern
edge of the country, and most of its area is very sparsely settled.
About 5 million of the people are French-speaking; these are concentrated in the provinces of Ontario and Quebec. The distribution of the population has tended to encourage local control of
schools, even though constitutionally the responsibility has been
strongly centralized in the provinces. As in the United States, one
may not speak of a national school system. There are ten provinces;
if we count the dual system in Quebec and the seven systems in
Newfoundland, we may say that Canada has seventeen separate
school systems.

Historical Background

IN NO country do the effects of national origins, language, and re-
ligious differences upon public education show more clearly than in
Canada. The first settlements were French, and for more than one
hundred and fifty years parts of eastern Canada were completely
French in language, government, and culture, and homogeneously
Catholic in religion. In 1763 all of Canada was ceded to Great

Britain, and English-speaking Protestant settlers began to come into the country. The Maritime Provinces had already been settled by English-speaking people, and on the far Pacific coast, the colony of British Columbia had been established by the English.

The early settlements were developed in isolation and fostered great self-reliance. All local services, including education, had to be provided by local enterprise, so that communities came to regard their schools "with jealous and proprietary pride. This keen interest in local schools has had its disadvantages. It is the reason for the comparatively late development of the larger administrative units in Canada. It accounts for the fact that the provinces in which the municipalities are strongest and most self-conscious lag farthest behind in this development. In other respects, the jealous pride in schools, which is so noticeable in Canada, is an incalculable asset. It prevents the central administration from becoming bureaucratic. It forbids the imposition of inappropriate and exotic patterns. It is the best safeguard against regimentation which may open the way to totalitarianism." [1]

The Development of Education in Canada

IN FRENCH Canada, schools and education were from the beginning the responsibility of the Church. The early French settlers in Quebec had been accustomed to free elementary schools in France, conducted by the clergy, by teaching orders, or by private individuals, and were well prepared to retain their Catholic faith. When they found themselves without schools, they were anxious for their children to receive similar training from the Church. Various teaching orders in New France did all that they could to provide for the increasing number of children. Some parish schools were opened, and attempts were made to provide for the training of teachers in Quebec to supplement the number of teachers who would be brought from Europe. However, the development of a new country left little time, energy, or funds to devote to schools, although the efforts continued. According to Percival, "As the years passed, the efforts toward providing education became spasmodic. It must be admitted that, at the time of the Cession of Quebec, no regularly organized system of schools existed. Nevertheless, a good deal of education

[1] J. G. Althouse, *Structure and Aims of Canadian Education*, p. 24.

was carried on privately as well as through the Church and its organizations." [2]

As soon as the English arrived in Quebec, the problem of education for their children received attention. An army sergeant was detailed as the first teacher, and in 1801 the Royal Institution for the Advancement of Learning was established by law. The English hoped that the schools to be established would cause the "French and English to intermingle and outwear any racial difference that might exist." [3] This might have worked out satisfactorily but for the suspicions of the Roman Catholics, who absolutely refused to cooperate with these schools. As the years went by, various amendments were made to the basic law, each one trying to make the legislation less overwhelmingly English, Protestant, and Anglican. An act in 1826 allowed each *fabrique*, or church council, to establish its own elementary schools. Under the provisions of this law Catholic schools began to appear in almost every parish in Quebec. In 1846 a very important law was passed, providing for two completely separate school systems, Catholic and Protestant, operating under the same law. This basic system has been in effect in Quebec since that date.

Although the law has been changed from time to time by amendments, and the administrative machinery altered, the fundamental principle has been unchanged, that Catholics and Protestants would be permitted to set up and control separate public schools in the same area. The basic requirement for establishment of a school in a given area has been the presence of a group of residents, of either faith, large enough to elect a school board and to provide local finance for the school. As a result, two entirely separate school systems are maintained, and in almost every locality where there are children of the two faiths there are separate public schools. Peter White may pay taxes to a Protestant district and send his children to its school, while Pierre Blanc, who lives next door, pays his taxes to a Catholic district and sends his children to a Catholic school. For tax purposes, each school district is made up of a group of not necessarily contiguous pieces of property, rather than all of the property within a certain geographical area. The tax rates of the two districts may be different; one district may maintain a high school and the other may not; the boundaries of the two districts need not

[2] W. P. Percival, *Should We All Think Alike?* p. 29.
[3] *Ibid.*, p. 33.

coincide. Included in the Protestant schools are the Jews and all other non-Catholics. "Pupils of one faith have no rights whatever in the schools of the other, even in the same town or district, though they may be accepted by arrangement with the school board—usually on the payment of an 'outsider's fee,' which may be as low as a dollar or two a month per child or may be much higher, for no fee is set by law." [4]

In the United States, as great numbers of immigrants of different nationalities arrived in the country, they were gradually assimilated and Americanized. The single public school system was one of the strongest forces in attaining this result. English became the accepted language of all Americans, even in French-speaking Louisiana. The French-speaking and English-speaking school systems of Canada have similarly facilitated the assimilation of great numbers of immigrants, but into French-Canadian or English-Canadian communities. A bilingual school system might have brought about a greater amount of unity within the population, but the French-speaking Canadians and the English-speaking Canadians go to separate schools.

In Canada likewise there is multiplicity of thought because we have no common descent, no common language, no common religion. We have fundamental differences of customs and tradition, but we have one indispensable condition of a nationality, namely, an independent political entity with fixed political boundaries. . . . The problem of differences of thought is great in Quebec. It has been so since the English settled there in 1759. Then a great struggle started, a struggle of intellect and will that has not yet ceased and which may last for a long time. It is a struggle of two cultures, one of which had been deeply rooted there for a century and a half before the advent of the second.[5]

This historical background has resulted in a constitutional limitation which is embodied in the British North America Act of 1867, which is Canada's constitution. Where religious minorities enjoyed special rights in education before a province entered the Dominion, these rights could not be abrogated after federation. In case of disputes about these rights, provisions were made for appeals to the Governor-General-in-Council and to the Privy Council in Lon-

[4] *Ibid.*, p. 34.
[5] *Ibid.*, p. 26.

don. Beginning in 1871 a series of such appeals were taken, and the decisions depended largely upon the rights which had been established at the time of union. In general, the right to maintain separate Catholic or Protestant schools was affirmed, except in the newer provinces carved out of Dominion territories, where no such rights had previously been in existence. As a result of this provision there are separate schools in three provinces, Quebec has a dual system of public schools, and Newfoundland has been enabled to retain its multiple system of sectarian schools. Althouse says,

Few administrators would be likely to choose these complications if they were asked to devise a school system *de novo*. Yet these minority rights are a part of our heritage; they cannot be ignored. The improvement in the quality of the minority schools in every Canadian province in which they exist is clear evidence that they are not ignored.[6]

The Place of the National Government in Education

IN THE Constitution of the United States powers not specifically granted to the federal government were reserved to the states. When the representatives of the colonies met to bring about the formation of the Dominion of Canada, they had the advantage of having watched carefully the development of the American Union for a period of seventy-five years or more. The recently concluded Civil War in the United States had emphasized, in the Canadian view, the possibilities of disunion inherent in a system of strong states. They tried to attain greater national unity by granting only specified powers to the provinces, which did not become sovereign states. The Dominion Parliament was given powers to act in all matters not exclusively assigned to provincial legislatures, and was even given authority to overrule provincial legislation.

Separation of church and state is not as complete in Canada as in the United States and Australia. The limiting legal provisions are due to the problems of sectarian groups and to the division between French-speaking and English-speaking Canadians which were experienced between 1840 and 1870 under the Act of Union. This Act, uniting Upper Canada (Ontario) and Lower Canada (Quebec), was superseded by the British North America Act, which protects

[6] Althouse, *op. cit.*, p. 24.

the rights of religious minorities in the provinces to establish and operate sectarian schools.

Under this arrangement, the Canadian provinces have jurisdiction over education, except for the provisions of the British North America Act of 1867. But the Dominion government is not without authority in the educational field. It protects the rights of religious minorities, it has provided crown lands for the support of education, and it is responsible for the operation of schools in the territories. It has provided a limited amount of financial aid for vocational and higher education, and has supported research and statistical activities.

At the time of federation, crown lands belonged to the provinces, not to the Dominion. When Prince Rupert's Land Territory was taken over from the Hudson's Bay Company in 1870 and renamed the Northwest Territories, the federal government assumed title to public lands in this area. New provinces (Alberta, Saskatchewan, and Manitoba) established later from the Northwest Territories did not receive title to the crown lands, which were retained by the Dominion. In 1872 the federal government reserved sections 11 and 29 in every township in Manitoba for the support of the schools, and later the same sections were set aside as school endowments in Alberta and Saskatchewan.[7] The Common School Fund, which had been provided as a school endowment in the Province of Canada, was taken over by the Dominion in 1867, and the annual income divided between the provinces of Ontario and Quebec. In 1930 all rights to natural resources in the newer provinces were returned to the provinces, together with compensation for the period when they had been held by the Dominion government.

Although the national government has few educational powers, it has shown an interest in the development of education in the provinces. Legally it has authority over schools in the two territories not yet organized into provinces, the Northwest Territories and the Yukon Territory. (The textbooks and curricula of the province of Alberta are followed in the Northwest Territories, and those of British Columbia in the Yukon Territory.) The federal government also assumes responsiblity for the education of Indians (whose

[7] This arrangement is similar to the one followed in the division of public lands in the western United States—2 square miles of the 36 in each township being set aside for public school aid.

school population totals about 20,000), for Eskimos, and for training for national defense.[8]

The national government also provides subsidies for vocational education—about 8 percent of the total cost—and collects educational statistics. The amount provided for vocational education subsidies in 1961 by the national government was $27,293,000. There is no federal Department of Education, nor, as in Australia and the United States, a federal Office of Education. The Dominion Bureau of Statistics publishes an *Annual Survey of Education in Canada.* The Canadian Education Association collects and publishes research studies and provides educational authorities in the provinces with information about procedures and practices in other provinces. A National Research Council, in conjunction with the national research laboratories in Ottawa, maintains laboratories, offers scholarships to research students, and pays grants-in-aid for investigations conducted at the university level by provincial Departments of Education.[9]

In 1952, as a result of recommendations of a Royal Commission on Arts, Sciences, and Letters, a new form of federal participation developed in the provision of federal grants to be used to increase staff salaries in the universities. An indirect aid to education by the Dominion appears in the field of school broadcasts. In general the programs are prepared and produced by the provincial Education Departments, but they are paid for by federal funds through the Canadian Broadcasting Corporation.

The Role of the Province in Education

IN EACH of the provinces (except Quebec) the public school systems is headed by a Cabinet Minister, who is usually called the Minister of Education. He is a member of the provincial legislature and of the party in power at the moment. With other members of the Cabinet, he determines the broad educational policies of the government. He is responsible to the legislature, and through these elected representatives, to the people.

[8] F. K. Stewart, "Canada," *Year Book of Education*, 1952, Evans Bros. Ltd., London, pp. 252–74.

[9] J. G. Althouse, "Canada," *Educational Yearbook*, 1936, International Institute of Teachers College, Columbia University, New York, p. 130.

Directly under the Minister is the Deputy Minister of Education (called the Superintendent of Education in Quebec, Chief Director of Education in Ontario, and Chief Superintendent of Education in New Brunswick). He is the chief permanent employee of the Department of Education, and its executive officer. He advises the Minister on matters of policy. Since he retains his position when governments and ministers change, he ensures a measure of continuity in departmental policy. The Departments exercise control over courses of study, teacher training, examinations, textbooks, minimum requirements for school buildings, and legislative grants. In most provinces public libraries are under the jurisdiction of the Department of Education. Supervision of local authorities is maintained by elementary and secondary inspectors appointed by the provincial departments. In some provinces the Department grants city school systems the right to appoint a city superintendent of schools.

Support of public education is divided between the provinces and

TABLE 7–1
Financial Statistics of Canadian Schools, 1962

PROVINCE	TOTAL EXPENDITURES (DOLLARS)	PROVINCIAL GRANTS (DOLLARS)	PER-CENTAGE BORNE BY PROVINCE	COST PER PUPIL (DOLLARS)
Alberta	117,987,850	8,114,268	6.9	368.32
British Columbia	145,535,715	77,632,903	53.3	372.24
Manitoba	60,659,474	26,440,890	43.4	304.22
New Brunswick	34,750,651	12,925,015	37.2	225.60
Newfoundland	19,383,243	19,383,243	100.0	151.90
Nova Scotia	43,497,150	22,676,662	52.1	256.81
Ontario	547,001,212	201,146,687	36.7	293.65*
				622.75†
Prince Edward Is.	5,704,389	3,979,621	69.7	253.31
Quebec	518,960,000	200,479,000	34.7	359.00
Saskatchewan	105,357,895	31,385,295	29.7	354.00
Canada	1,598,837,759	604,163,584	37.8	——

sources: Annual Reports of the Departments of Education for each province, 1962.
* Elementary.
† Secondary.

TABLE 7-2
Comparison of Educational Costs in Canadian Provinces, 1958

PROVINCE	COST PER PUPIL (DOLLARS)	PERCENTAGE OF PERSONAL INCOME REQUIRED TO PAY GROSS COST
Prince Edward Is.	124.30	3.42
Newfoundland	136.10	4.30
New Brunswick	190.00	4.87
Nova Scotia	199.80	4.44
Quebec	223.10	3.75
Manitoba	264.10	3.65
Ontario	299.50	3.65
Saskatchewan	308.20	5.20
British Columbia	339.90	3.92
Alberta	383.40	5.25
National average	270.50	3.95

SOURCE: *Annual Report of the Department of Education, Province of Nova Scotia*, Halifax: Queen's Printer, 1962, p. xvii.

the local administrative units, with some minor financial aid for vocational education from the Dominion government. Provincial grants range from a high of 100 percent of the cost of education in Newfoundland down to 6.9 percent in Alberta. The sources of financial support in the various provinces are indicated in Table 7-1. These figures are for illustration only and are not directly comparable, since provincial Departments of Education do not follow a uniform style in their reports. Some of them list the total number of pupils in average attendance, and others give only the total number enrolled during the year. The financial figures are for 1962. Because of the close intermingling of public and private funds in Quebec, it is difficult to compare figures on costs and support with those of other provinces. A comparative study of costs per pupil in the various Canadian provinces, made in 1958, is shown in Table 7-2.

QUEBEC
When the question of sectarian differences becomes of paramount importance in a province, basic modifications in the provincial educational system and in the Department of Education become necessary. Operating under a common law, the Education Department

of Quebec controls two separate and distinct public school systems. A Council of Education, divided into a Catholic Committee and a Protestant Committee, sets the general policies. The council as a whole seldom if ever meets, but the committees meet separately four times a year, and are responsible for the organization, administration, and supervision of their respective school systems. Organized into separate sections, Catholic and Protestant, the dual system operates from kindergarten through university.

The Roman Catholic Committee of the council consists of the bishops of the various dioceses in the province, with an equal number of lay members, and four other members appointed by the government. The Protestant Committee consists of a number of members appointed by the Lieutenant-Governor-in-Council (which is really the Cabinet) equal in numbers to the lay members of the Catholic Committee, and seven associate members, one of whom represents the Protestant Teachers Association of Quebec.

Each committee makes regulations for the normal schools under its jurisdiction, for departmental examinations, for the course of study, for textbooks, and for the work of the inspectors. They make recommendations, which must be approved by the Lieutenant-Governor-in-Council, for the apportionment of provincial grants. The head of the Education Department is called the Superintendent of Education; he is assisted by a French Secretary and an English Secretary (who is also Director of Protestant Education). The French Secretary acts as secretary of the Catholic Committee, and the English Secretary as secretary of the Protestant Committee. The Superintendent of Education is chairman of both committees.

There is an Inspector-General of Catholic Schools, assisted by regional and local inspectors. There is also an Inspector-General of Protestant Schools, with a high school inspector and other assistants. Both English and French are official languages in Quebec. The Catholics, who outnumber the Protestants about seven to one, are mainly French-speaking, although there are English-speaking Catholics who have their own separate schools. The Protestants are mainly English-speaking, although there are a small number of Protestants of French extraction, who also have special schools. Whatever the primary language of the school may be, much time is given to the other language.

Both Catholic and Protestant Committees operate normal schools for the training of teachers for the schools under their jurisdiction.

All of the universities of Quebec are independently controlled, and all receive government grants. They are McGill University and Sir George Williams College (nonsectarian), Laval University and Montreal University (Catholic), and Bishops College University (Anglican).

NEWFOUNDLAND

Another example of separate schools controlled by sectarian groups occurs in the province of Newfoundland, where there are no less than seven distinct school systems. All of the schools in the province are sectarian, with minor exceptions to be noted later. They are under the jurisdiction of the Church of England, the Roman Catholic Church, the United Church of Canada, the Salvation Army, the Seventh Day Adventists, the Pentacostals, or the Moravians. School enrollment, following the general distribution of the population, is about as follows: 36 percent Catholic, 25 percent Church of England, 19 percent United Church, 6 percent Salvation Army, and very small percentages in other denominations. About 11 percent are amalgamated or community schools. The Department of Education is headed by a Deputy Minister, assisted by an administrative officer. There are five Superintendents of Education, one for each of the major denominations operating schools, and a Director of Amalgamated School Services.

Responsibility for educational policies rests with a Council of Education, with the Minister of Education as chairman, the Deputy Minister as vice-chairman, and the denominational representatives as members. The superintendents are senior civil servants (although at times some of them have been clergymen and the Salvation Army representative is a lieutenant-colonel in that organization). They act as delegates from their respective denominations to the Department. Within the Education Department the council sets policies and regulations which are applicable to all schools in the province. All of the sectarian school systems are supported by public funds.

The Department of Education makes grants to local districts for teachers' salaries and for maintaining and equipping buildings. The province pays approximately half the cost of new school buildings (sometimes more if the districts are extremely poor).

Local Responsibility for Schools

IN EASTERN Canada, three early influences affected the development of local schools. The French influence has always been strongly in the direction of complete control by the Roman Catholic Church, through its parishes. The English influence tended toward control by the Church of England, but with a great deal of local autonomy. The influx of loyalists from the New England colonies after the American Revolution strengthened the English tradition, but carried with it a renewed emphasis on strong local government. The western provinces were more affected by developments in education in the United States, and the educational systems in this part of the country resemble American state programs in many ways. In both groups of provinces, the tendency has been to develop a strong provincial Department of Education, which delegates part of its authority and responsibility to a multiplicity of local school boards.

QUEBEC

The province of Quebec is divided into school municipalities, each of which elects a Board of School Commissioners, except in larger cities, where the commissioners are appointed. Roman Catholic priests, ministers of other denominations, and male taxpayers 21 years of age and older (who can read and write) are eligible for election as members. If a layman is elected to a school board he must serve the full term of three years, unless he is over 60 years of age or has served within the last four years. Most Boards of School Commissioners are composed of five members, elected for three-year terms. However, in the cities of Montreal and Quebec a board is appointed. For the Catholic school board the Lieutenant-Governor-in-Council appoints four of the members, and the archbishop three others. For the Protestant school board three are appointed by the Lieutenant-Governor-in-Council and three by the city council.

School boards select teachers, choose school sites and erect buildings, decide the rate of taxation, and levy the local school taxes. They must make provision for the attendance of all children who live within the district and provide transportation for those who live too far from school to walk. However, the regulations do not require a school board to provide free transportation for pupils who live more than five miles from school. If a child lives more than five miles from the nearest school of his sectarian choice, his parents are relieved from the payment of school taxes if they do not send their child to school. Apparently there is no provision for enforcing compulsory attendance in such a case.[10]

The people of a school district, through their elected school board members, decide what type of school they want and how much they are willing to pay for it. If local pride is sufficient, the schools will have excellent buildings and equipment and well-paid teachers. If a community is satisfied with poor buildings and inadequate equipment and poorly paid teachers, there is nothing to prevent it from maintaining this type of school. Provincial inspectors inspect the school from time to time and report conditions to the Education Department, but the province has no final authority to compel the local community to meet high standards. Inspectors frequently have had to complain about the apathy and neglect of local school committees. One reason for inferior schools may lie in the inadequate tax base of small schools serving a minority population. The available taxable wealth of a community, if divided, may be insufficient to support two entirely separate school systems, even though it might be adequate to support one excellent program. Southern states in the United States have learned how expensive it is to attempt to support duplicating school programs for Negroes and whites.

Minorities in any community may withdraw from the majority and form their own school districts, if there are sufficient pupils to justify the opening of a school and a sufficient number of taxpayers to elect a school board and support a school. This process is called "dissent" and is carefully guaranteed by law. Individual taxpayers may choose to have their taxes go to the support of whichever school district they designate. Corporations pay their taxes to a "Neutral Panel"; these taxes are then allocated to the Catholic or Protestant districts involved on the basis of the school population in each.

The French-speaking school districts in Quebec are generally coterminous with the Catholic parishes, and therefore a Catholic school district may include several schools within its boundaries. The province has 1,620 school boards for 9,259 schools. Some of the

[10] W. P. Percival, *Life in School*, p. 17.

parishes, and hence the local schools, are very small. Because of the parish organization, there has been little interest in consolidating school districts into larger units of administration until very recently. One-teacher schools are very common in the Catholic parishes, and although there has been some resistance to the idea of unifying such schools within the same district, there was a reduction of 382 small schools in 1960–61.

Since the Protestants are a minority in Quebec communities, it has been to their advantage to consolidate small schools into larger units, thus securing better facilities and teachers as well as a broader tax base. A Protestant Central School Board was organized on the Island of Montreal, and this greatly improved the educational standards of the area as far as Protestant schools are concerned. By 1950 the Canadian Education Association reported 64 consolidations of small Protestant schools, and nine other central school boards covering large areas. In 1960–61, 42 Protestant school municipalities that did not operate schools were annexed or united with adjacent school districts, and the total number of Protestant school boards was reduced to 226.[11] Members of the central boards must be tax-payers within the area served by the board and are elected by members of the local district boards. Administrative economies and improvements in standards have followed these consolidations, particularly at the high school level.

NEWFOUNDLAND

Local education authorities in the province of Newfoundland are known as Education Districts, and the school boards are appointed by the Lieutenant-Governor-in-Council. The entire province is divided into Education Districts, which are administered by a single denomination except in the case of 23 which are called "Amalgamated Districts." There are 308 districts, of which 92 are Church of England, 80 Roman Catholic, 92 United Church, 17 Salvation Army, 23 amalgamated or interdenominational, 2 community, 1 Seventh Day Adventist, and 1 Pentecostal.

This division does not involve much actual overlapping, since the geographical distribution of the population is somewhat along denominational lines. A survey in 1944 showed that approximately

[11] *Quebec Annual Report*, 1960–61, p. 39.

15 percent of the settlements had a duplication of school services, and one-third of these were in the larger towns. In the city of St. John's and the larger communities, each of the four denominations has a board of education, and taxpayers pay to support the Education District of their choice. In industrial centers there has been a trend toward amalgamation of school services. In 1960, 23 communities were operating interdenominational schools for all children except the Roman Catholics, who insist on maintaining their own separate schools. Among these amalgamated schools are some of the largest and best in the province.

LOCAL ADMINISTRATION IN OTHER PROVINCES

Public opinion in Canada seems to be firmly attached to the small local unit of administration. This is known in most of the provinces as the school district or school section. Boards of school trustees are elected by the taxpayers of the district, and they have authority over the selection of teachers, maintenance of school buildings, erection of buildings, and purchase of supplies and equipment. Problems of the very small districts with inadequate tax bases have long vexed Canadian education, and demands for provincial equalization funds have frequently been voiced. Provincial grants for specific purposes have been increasing, and the proportion of total support which is derived from provincial sources has also been increased.

Out of the demand for equalization of educational opportunities and help for weaker districts has developed a widespread movement for larger units of administration. The greatest resistance to school consolidation appears in the eastern provinces. In the western provinces there has been a tendency to approach the establishment of large units of administration through broad provincial legislation. But strong opposition has developed even in the west. The people of Alberta voted down proposals to legislate small districts out of existence in 1932 and 1933, and similar proposals failed to win rural support in Ontario in 1926 and 1927.

East of Saskatchewan reorganization has been slower and more gradual, because of a number of factors: the traditional attitude toward the control of the small school by the local community; more highly developed municipal organization; local topography; and distribution of population. Where sudden sweeping changes have been made, it has been in the western part of the country. Many of the administrative plans provide for sub-unit boards to assist and advise the large unit boards. In the east the local school boards have retained more authority than in the west.

In Prince Edward Island an Advisory Reconstruction Committee reported in July, 1945, that there should be a "reorganization of the whole province as one unit for the purposes of finance and the gradual establishment of thirty areas or regions for high school purposes, each to be presided over by a Board." The high school board was to consist of seven members, of whom three were to be appointed by the government and four elected at a meeting of representatives of the elementary school districts in the area. It was recommended that the provincial government provide 50 percent of the cost of the site, building, and equipment, and 25 percent of the cost of maintenance and operation. Under this plan elementary schools would continue to function as before under their own boards. On May 30, 1963, the first large school unit for the administration of both elementary and secondary education was established. Fifteen new regional high school units were approved in the years 1960 to 1963.

Nova Scotia passed an act in 1942 which authorized the establishment of larger units, with the major share of the cost of education to be borne by the counties. By 1946 the entire province had been reorganized into 24 such county units. It was reported that local indebtedness had been reduced, financial and educational equalization achieved, and sound financial administration established. At the same time Nova Scotia established consolidated regional high schools of the comprehensive or "composite" type, as they are called in Canada. Between 1951 and 1961 the number of one-room schools declined from 1,088 to 491.

In 1943 New Brunswick had 1,350 school boards. In that year the County Schools Finance Act was passed, making possible the establishment of county units of finance and administration. All 15 of the counties have now taken advantage of the Act and regional high schools have been established. This has made it possible for people in the rural areas to enjoy some of the advantages of the urban school system.

Legislation passed in 1945 in Manitoba permitted the establishment of larger units of administration called "school areas." Since 1947 an experimental larger unit has been in successful operation.

In this province residents of the school districts involved must vote for the reorganization.

In 1945 Saskatchewan began establishing larger units without provision for a popular vote unless 20 percent or more of the local residents petitioned for an election. The entire province now operates with 66 school units, which include 4,849 districts.

Alberta passed a law in 1936 which made possible larger units. By 1948 the province had been reorganized into 57 school divisions by the consolidation of small districts. An average school division has an area of 2,000 square miles, employs 70 teachers, and enrolls 1,500 pupils.

British Columbia completely revised the school administrative areas in the province by legislative enactment in 1946. In place of the former 650 school districts, there are now 73 administrative areas and 26 small unattached rural districts. In this province there was no provision for vote by the electors of the districts involved; the reorganization took place all at one time by action of the provincial government.

In some American states various devices have been used to encourage consolidation of small districts. Among these are increasing state aid to consolidated districts, reducing aid to small districts that refuse to consolidate, and raising standards for accreditation to a point that very small districts find difficult to meet. Apparently none of these methods has been used in Canada. Where the provincial legislature has not stepped in and made the reorganization, the plans have provided for local action through elections. While the larger units have proved to be in better financial condition, it does not appear that provincial or federal funds have been used to expedite the reorganization. Althouse points out:

. . . Progress is achieved in a typically decentralized pattern. It does not take place on an unbroken front, or at an equal pace. It is irregular; sometimes it is very slow. At any moment it presents a patchwork appearance and calls for continuous compromises. At its worst, strong local control permits prejudice or complacency to defer too long the reforms that should be the children's right and the nation's hope. But local control in Canada seldom remains at this worst. It is becoming better informed and is always susceptible to appeals to local pride. No satisfactory substitute has been found for keen local interest in schools and pride in their efficiency. These give body and meaning to sound educational procedures; they identify the school and the community in an inimitable way. With the retention of local interest, educational progress may be slow and spotty; it is almost never temporary. Gains made are consolidated, for they are indigenous improvements.[12]

The Place of Voluntary Agencies and Private Schools

THE WORK of the Canadian Education Association as an agency to collect statistics and to carry on and publish research studies has already been mentioned. In the absence of a national Office of Education, this organization performs many of the functions of such a national agency. Provincial authorities and educational leaders in the various provinces are kept aware of developments in other parts of the country by the publications and studies of the association.

Provincial home-and-school (parent-teacher) organizations have grown in number and influence. Total membership of parent-teacher and home-and-school organizations is approximately 400,000. They maintain local groups which work closely with local school units. At both the national and provincial levels education committees have been set up by various business, women's, and labor organizations. Stewart says that these groups have stimulated educational thinking among lay and educational people and have served to keep public education in the minds of the leaders of the country.[13]

In addition to the public and "separate" schools (see pages 151–52) there are private schools throughout the provinces. These do not receive any public funds. The majority are boarding schools and are usually church-connected. In 1962 there were 1,055 private schools in Canada, which reported an enrollment of 182,109 pupils, about 4 percent of the total enrollment. They employed 10,929 teachers.[14] The provincial departments of education exercise some indirect control over private schools in two ways. Students in these schools either must take the departmental examinations, or else the schools must submit to inspection by departmental authorities in order to be "accredited," which exempts their students from the necessity of taking departmental examinations before transferring to a public school. Both of these situations work to ensure that the curriculum and

---

[12] Althouse, *Structure and Aims of Canadian Education,* pp. 28–29.

[13] Stewart, *op. cit.,* p. 272.

[14] Dominion Bureau of Statistics, *Some Statistics of Private Elementary and Secondary Schools—Canada,* 1962–63, pp. 2, 3, 8, 17.

course of study in the private schools do not differ in any marked degree from those in the provincial schools.

Problems of Administration, Finance, and Control

CANADA is in the same situation as the rest of the world, facing twin problems of an increasing birthrate and inadequate school funds to meet the demands of the growing school population. In 1945 a survey committee of the Canadian Education Association listed major problems facing Canadian education.[15] Some of these problems will be discussed in Chapter 15, but problems dealing with finance and organization will be considered here.

The Need for Increased Provincial Grants

There has been a substantial increase in the proportion of school support assumed by the provinces, but the amount is still small in some of them. The percentage of financial aid provided by the provinces varies from 6.9 percent in Alberta to 100 percent in Newfoundland. The inequalities in assessed valuation and wealth between school districts are so great in every province that Canadian educators are pressing for more assistance in equalization on a province-wide basis.

The Shortage of School Buildings

The increase in school population finds school districts with a pressing need for more buildings and with power to borrow funds practically exhausted. In such cases the only solution educators can see is provincial grants to aid in building new schools. Many Canadian schoolmen feel that the need for better-built and better-equipped schools can be met only if the meager local resources are supplemented by provincial grants.

Problems of Transportation

The existence of sparsely settled areas and the movement toward school consolidation has required extensive provision of transportation facilities. This has become very expensive in many districts, and demands a greater share of local revenues than the localities wish to divert from the teaching budget. The solution to this prob-

[15] Quoted in Stewart, op. cit., p. 254.

lem again seems to be provincial grants to subsidize transportation programs.

The Need for Increases in Teachers' Salaries

This problem will be discussed in detail in Chapter 15, but the requirement for increased funds to pay salaries is worth noting here. The provinces and the districts must find additional money to raise the low level of salaries paid to teachers in most provinces.

The Problem of Larger Units of Administration

This movement is progressing rapidly in the western provinces and in the Maritime Provinces. It is moving much more slowly in the central part of the country. Consolidation of small and inefficient school districts has resulted in both administrative and financial improvements, and the tendency in this direction will continue. However, Canadians hope to find a means of providing larger and more efficient units of organization and administration, while at the same time maintaining local interest in local schools, and local control within the larger unit.

The Problem of Federal Aid for Education

Canada has rich provinces and poor provinces, just as there are rich and poor states in the United States. Canadian educators realize that no matter how completely they reorganize small school districts into more efficient units, and provide adequate equalization programs on a provincial basis, there will be some provinces with wealth enough to provide only a minimum program. They see the only answer in aid to the provinces from a federal equalization fund. Althouse says:

There is among the provinces an ever more vocal demand for a federal subsidy for general education, on the ground that it is needed to equalize the educational opportunities available in the various provinces. This request is always coupled with the stipulation that the subsidy should not be accompanied by any federally-prescribed conditions beyond some sort of matching with provincial funds devoted to the same purpose. . . . I have never encountered active opposition to an equalizing subsidy; I have seen prompt opposition to anything which was construed as federal assumption of control over education.[16]

[16] Althouse, *Structure and Aims of Canadian Education*, p. 23.

Like the United States, Canada has chosen to have a decentralized form of public education. The Dominion government shows an interest in encouraging educational progress, but does not participate to any great extent in the educational program. The provinces, like the American states, have legal authority over school programs, but have delegated much of their authority to local units which they have established. The local communities, through administrative units of varying size, display a great interest in their own schools, and exercise control over them within wide limits. In some of the provinces, because of historical reasons, separate schools are provided for religious minorities, but supported from public funds. In two provinces, Quebec and Newfoundland, multiple school systems supported by public taxation are operated, and are controlled by sectarian religious groups. These variations are designed to provide for the citizens in the local communities the types of school that they want their children to have.

8
Party Control:
The Soviet Union

THE LARGEST continuous territory on earth under a common political authority is the Union of Soviet Socialist Republics. It covers an area of eight and one-half million square miles, or nearly three times that of the United States, and has a population of over 214 million people. The Union extends from the Baltic Sea in Europe to the Pacific Ocean in the East, and from the Black Sea and the Gobi Desert in the south to the Arctic Ocean. It runs from southern deserts through fertile temperate areas and barren steppes to ice-bound waters. The development of the frontier eastward has been as important a factor in Russian history as the westward development of the frontier has been in the history of the United States.

The Soviet Union is composed of more than 180 different nations and nationality groups, and about 150 different languages are spoken in the country. The population includes such different groups as peoples of aboriginal types similar to the American Eskimos in the far north, nomadic peoples in the deserts of the south, Finns, and Armenians. Approximately 60 percent of the population are Russians, or "Great Russians," as they are called. Another 20 percent of the population are Ukrainians, and the other one-fifth includes all the diverse minorities. Of the 180 nationality groups in the country, not more than a dozen include more than 1 percent of the total population, and some groups are very small. Religions are also various. There are Lutherans in the Baltic areas, Roman Catholics in the former Polish areas, Orthodox Catholics in most of the Russian areas, and Muslims in the Asian republics.

According to the 1960 census, the total population of the U.S.S.R. is 214,400,000. There are approximately twenty million more women than men, which is one indication of the heavy losses that the Russians suffered during World War II. Some twenty-five million of their people were killed. For 1959 the census listed 52 percent of the population as urban and 48 percent as rural.

Historical Background

IN 1905 imperial Russia was an absolute monarchy. Its supreme authority was a czar whose position was hereditary and who possessed all legislative, judicial, and executive powers. He was aided by governmental departments, whose officers he chose himself and who were responsible only to him, and by the Holy Synod of the Russian Orthodox Church. There were oases of scholarship and learning, of scientific achievement, and of great musical and theatrical culture, but as a whole the country was in a state of feudal backwardness and illiteracy. Very little was done for the common people, who lived in ignorance and poverty. Czarist governments were aggressively expansionist, adding to their empire large areas populated by peoples of varying races, religions, and political beliefs. Many of the minority groups remained fiercely hostile to all Russian influences and resisted attempts at "Russification." The czar's government discriminated against minority nationalities and attempted to prevent the use of native languages and native religions.

Education was provided for the children of nobles, the wealthy classes, and government officials, and was closely controlled by the state and the church. About 75 percent of the people were illiterate, and many of the national minorities were without a written language. Universities were carefully watched by the government, and the students were regarded as potential political revolutionaries. Many students did engage in political plots; numbers of them were arrested and sent to Siberia, or fled to other European countries.

The 1905 Revolution resulted in some theoretical limitation of the powers of the czar, but there was no material amelioration in the condition of the common people. One of the results of World War I was revolution in the war-weakened countries of Italy, Germany, and Russia. In each country the government was eventually seized by a single group, and all pretense of democratic government ended. The result was a dictatorship, either by an individual or by a dominant political faction. In Russia the imperial government was overthrown in March, 1917, by a revolutionary government headed by Alexander Kerensky, and in November, 1917, the Bolsheviks, a small minority led by Lenin and Trotsky, took control. The present Soviet government has maintained itself in power since that time, and every resource of government, culture, and propaganda has been mobilized to maintain the Communist Party of the Bolsheviks in power.

Partly as a result of the great diversity of languages and nationalities, the Soviet Union has been organized as a federal state. It consists of fifteen constituent republics, called "Union Republics," roughly corresponding to major national groups. Smaller national groups are organized into "autonomous republics" (of which there are sixteen), "autonomous regions" (of which there are nine), and ten "national areas." These units are progressively smaller in size and population, from the Union Republic down to the national area. The autonomous republics and autonomous regions are included within and subordinate to the Union Republics. The national areas consist largely of backward and less developed regions, and are governed as territories. The Russian Soviet Federated Socialist Republic (R.S.F.S.R.), with its capital at Moscow, is by far the largest Union Republic and includes within its boundaries more than one hundred nationality and linguistic groups.

Educational Background

THE NEW Bolshevist leaders, faced with the herculean task of trying to unify and control the huge area of the Russian Empire, inhabited by so many diverse national and linguistic groups, turned to education as one method of achieving their aims. First they attacked the widespread illiteracy problem. In many areas this meant creating an alphabet and a written language for people who had never had them. They compiled and published grammars, dictionaries, and textbooks in many languages and dialects. By 1940 they were able to claim that even the smallest nationality group in the Soviet Union had its own grammar and school textbooks in the vernacular. Throughout the Soviet Union elementary education was developed entirely in the native languages. Since the 1917 Revolution, dozens of language groups have developed their own literary language, and hundreds of thousands of books have been published in these languages. The vocabularies of most minority groups had to be expanded greatly, because of the addition of new words and concepts based on the rapidly developing industrialization of the country. Today, native languages that previously had comparatively meager vocabularies now have available to them a wide range of books translated from other languages.

The purpose of this attack on illiteracy was not entirely humanitarian. If the people were to be taught the ideas of Marx and Lenin, they had to be able to read political tracts. If they were to master the industrial and agricultural skills that the development of the nation required, they had to be able to read manuals and books of instructions. It was much simpler to teach backward peoples to read their own languages first than to attempt to teach them Russian and then to teach new ideas in this strange new language.

By 1930 the Soviet government announced that 70 different languages were being used in the elementary schools, and that even the most backward peoples were receiving education in their native tongues. This fact made it possible to promulgate, in that year, the first decree concerning compulsory education.

"RUSSIFICATION"

The history of czarist Russia had been a repetition of wars and invasions and conquest, by means of which Great Russia extended its power across Asia to the Pacific Ocean. The czars were as imperialistic as any of the great European powers, and although their conquests consisted of contiguous territories within the great Eurasian land mass, these extensions encompassed peoples of as many varied languages, colors, religions, and nationalities as any of the other great colonial empires. Following the 1917 Revolution the area of the empire was reduced, but the Communist government has shown itself to be as aggressively imperialistic and expansionist as its imperial predecessor, and has added territories to the Union which were never a part of czarist Russia. Under the czars the governmental policy was also strongly nationalistic, and a policy of "Russification" was ruthlessly carried out.

There is no reason to believe that the long-range aim of making the entire Soviet Union a completely Russian state has been forgotten, though it may have been postponed. The study of the Russian language in every republic is begun by the third grade (sometimes as early as the first grade) as a compulsory subject, even though the native tongue is used in the elementary school. Native languages are used in the early grades, but minority nationalism, in the political sphere, is discouraged and repressed. Minority peoples are taught to take pride in the history, arts, and language of their region, but against a total Russian background. History books are rewritten to show the greatness of the Russian people and the fortunate state of the minority groups in being permitted to enter into a younger-brother relationship with the superior Russian culture.

The use of Russian increases in the higher schools, and bright young people learn that proficiency in the major language opens up great opportunities for political and economic advancement. Great numbers of selected non-Russians are studying in Russian universities and higher institutes. Most higher education is conducted in Russian.

In Uzbekistan, for example, the first textbooks were printed in the Arabic alphabet. In 1928 a latinized alphabet was introduced for greater ease in teaching and learning. In 1940 the authorities ordered that all alphabets in the Union based on the "archaic" Latin had to be replaced by the Russian alphabet. This order made teaching more uniform throughout the Union, and facilitated the study of the Russian language and the use of Russian textbooks. Also, when the Arabic language was printed in Russian letters, it effectively cut the Asian Muslims off from reading religious books. Today the elementary textbooks used in Uzbekistan are in the Uzbek language but are printed in Cyrillic characters. Most of the textbooks used in vernacular schools throughout the Soviet Union are straight translations of Russian texts. Native groups whose languages have Persian, Turkic, or Arabic roots have been ordered to orient the development of their languages upon Russian, and thus break their connections with foreign "bourgeois" cultures, according to Magidoff. He also reports that the rule that Russians who live and work in a national minority republic must learn the native language is being increasingly ignored.[1]

COMMUNIST EDUCATIONAL PHILOSOPHY

The dominant factor in all educational development in the Soviet Union is the Communist ideology. The relationship between the individual and the state differs very little from the relations between individuals and government in Fascist Italy or Nazi Ger-

[1] Robert Magidoff, *The Kremlin Versus the People*, p. 123.

many. The aim of education in the Soviet Union is to advance and perpetuate the Communist philosophy, and to raise a new generation of inspired fighters for the Communist regime. It is an instrument of indoctrination and of propaganda that is not confined to formal instruction in the schools but permeates every aspect of the life of every individual for twenty-four hours a day. As Lenin stated: "Our task in the school world is to overthrow the bourgeoisie, and we openly declare that the school, apart from life, apart from politics, is a lie and a hypocrisy." [2]

All of the resources of mass communication, controlled by the relatively small Communist Party elite, are used to direct the total population. From newspapers, radio, television, theater, and moving pictures, from lectures and billboards, the same orthodox points of view are endlessly repeated. No dissident opinions are permitted or tolerated in any area of life—these are deviationist and must be ruthlessly suppressed. Not only are psychological and propagandistic influences utilized to ensure conformity, but the economic life of the country is also mobilized to destroy individuality. The citizen of the U.S.S.R. owns few private assets; he is always aware that his very physical existence and survival—his allotment of food, shelter, and employment—are dependent upon remaining in the good graces of the all-powerful Party and state. He is paid wages, but he knows that his job depends upon his conformity. This does not mean that there is no wealth, but wealth comes as a prerogative of official position or approval. The Communist elite live very comfortable lives, but lives of absolute adherence to the Party line. "Any anticommunist word or move is an act against the state," as Cross puts it. The secret-police mentality is not concerned with comparatives in crime and punishment. [3]

Soviet propaganda has been established on the idea of dictatorship of the proletariat; previously controlling interests are to be repressed until a classless society, based upon the workers and peasants, has been achieved. In recent years much less attention has been given to the concept of a classless society. A new Communist elite, composed of bureaucrats and intelligentsia, has arisen and is favored in every way over the workers and peasants. According to

[2] Quoted in Edgar W. Knight, *Twenty Centuries of Education*, Ginn, Boston, 1940, p. 539.

[3] James Eliot Cross, "Is Liberation Possible?" *Atlantic Monthly*, May, 1953, p. 65.

Kulski, every educated man in Russia is a bureaucrat. His livelihood depends upon the state, which is his employer, and upon the orders he receives from the professional politicians who are his masters. An elevated economic and social position, good housing and food, pleasant vacations and the guarantee of opportunities for his children—all these are available to the members of the elite classes who follow the correct line of action and thought.[4]

It is a common assumption that the goals and values of the Communists have been the same throughout their period of ascendancy. Actually there have been great changes in Soviet educational policy, derived from alterations in Party plans and philosophies. The educational goals which determined developments in Russian schools from 1917 to about 1932 were very different from those which are accepted today. Sudden and unexpected shifts in the Party line are a feature of the Russian scene, and the situation which is described as apparently accepted today may be very different from the official requirements of tomorrow.

The Russians believe that education is divided between *nurture*, which is bringing out the innate capacities of the individual, and *instruction*, which is giving him certain information and professional and technical training. Heredity is not considered as important a determinant as it is in other parts of the world. Communist orthodoxy required until recently the acceptance of the Lysenko theory of genetics, rather than the more usually accepted Mendelian concept. Lysenko believed that acquired characteristics could be inherited through a cumulative process from generation to generation. During the more than forty years in which the Communists have controlled the government, they have had to add a third factor to this picture, that of "self-training." Through this means they can lay the blame for deviations not on the environment under which an individual has been brought up but upon the man himself for having certain weaknesses of character. He who fails the state has failed in his own self-training. By controlling the environment and the instructional process, and by stressing self-discipline, the Party hopes to develop the "New Communist Man" it desires.

While the power of the Communist Party and the state is directed

4 W. W. Kulski, "Class Stratification in the Soviet Union," *Foreign Affairs*, October, 1953, p. 145.

toward forcing compliance on the part of adults, there is a somewhat different approach toward children. Originally teachers were considered leaders and directors of learning, rather than enforcers of discipline. Although there is no corporal punishment, discipline in the schools is quite rigid. The opinion of the group, the "collective," is mobilized to bring deviationists into line and children are taught to consider Communism as the best of all possible systems. At the same time they are carefully shielded from contact with any divergent points of view. Communist doctrines and the Communist society are made to appear as attractive as possible. The Communists await new generations that have grown up without knowledge of any other system—people who will believe in and support what the Soviet system stands for. They are, however, willing to use coercion on the adults who have had experience in other societies and have known life under different conditions.

The first Commissar of Public Instruction for the Soviet Government, Lunacharsky, announced in 1927 that the educational system would be based on nature, labor, and society as centers of interest. The tremendous need for trained industrial workers led the government in the early years to subordinate everything else to labor as the principal theme of education. Vocational training took precedence over general education, and the theoretical and practical study of the part played by labor in society became the central theme of Bolshevist education. From the beginning it has been difficult to define any separation between vocational and general education in Russia. The life of every worker, in school and out, is raised to its highest potential in the development of the country, and community interests are brought into the schools. All adult life is permeated by education in the form of indoctrination.

THE CAMPAIGN AGAINST ILLITERACY

Many of the minority nationalities, especially in central Asia and the far north, were almost completely illiterate at the time of the Revolution, and many of the linguistic groups were without an alphabet or a written language. In order to provide written materials and to begin an education program in the vernacular it was therefore necessary to invent an alphabet first. Complete and accurate statistics on literacy or education in the Soviet Union have always been difficult to obtain, and published figures are often heavily loaded

TABLE 8–1
Literacy Rates in U.S.S.R., Ages 8 to 49 (percentage of population)

GROUP AND DATE	MEN	WOMEN	BOTH SEXES
Urban population			
1897	65.5	43.1	55.6
1926	88.0	73.9	80.9
1939	97.6	91.0	94.2
1959	99.5	98.1	98.7
Rural population			
1897	34.3	9.6	21.7
1926	67.3	35.4	50.6
1939	93.7	79.2	86.3
1959	99.1	97.5	98.2
Urban and rural			
1897	39.1	13.7	26.3
1926	71.5	42.7	56.6
1939	95.1	83.4	89.1
1959	99.3	97.8	98.5

SOURCE: *Narodnoe Obrazovanie*, No. 4, 1960, quoted in *Soviet Education*, Vol. II, No. 8, p. 62. Reprinted by permission of the International Arts & Sciences Press.

with propaganda.[5] From Russian sources of information, it appears that great changes have been achieved among the so-called backward peoples. The first All-Union census, taken in 1939, indicated that for the total population of the U.S.S.R. between the ages of 9 and 49 years the literacy rate (which had been announced officially as 56.6 percent in 1926) had risen to 89.1 percent. The 1959 census reported 98.5 percent of the population between these ages as literate. The results of these census tabulations are shown in Table 8–1.

According to the 1959 census, 99.3 percent of the men and 97.8

[5] It is essential for the reader to understand that official statements from Russian authors may not be as reliable as similar material quoted from other countries. Soviet writers decry "bourgeois objectivity" as an evidence of weakness, and many descriptive accounts seem to be heavily tinged with propaganda. Statistics on illiteracy, school enrollments, and population cannot be accepted uncritically, although the 1959 census provided some up-to-date figures. Statistics are sometimes not directly comparable with those of other countries. This means that this chapter, as well as Chapter 16, makes greater use of secondary sources than do other chapters.

percent of the women were literate. However, of the population which was reported "literate" in 1939, 82.8 percent were listed as having had four years or less of education. No figures are reported on the percentage of the population with less than four years of education in 1959, but it was reported that 58,708,000 had completed at least seven grades of schooling. During World War II the United States Army rejected several hundred thousand inductees as "functionally illiterate" because they had had four years of education or less. This seems to indicate that the Russian definition of literacy simply means some ability to read and write. It must be recognized that some of the improvement shown in statistics can be attributed to the death of older illiterates. Recent Soviet publications give less prominence to a discussion of the literacy problem in the Soviet Union.

The elimination of illiteracy among women in the U.S.S.R. is said to have progressed even more rapidly than in the population as a whole, because a larger proportion of the women were illiterate in 1917. In the Muslim central Asian republics, where illiteracy among women was nearly 100 percent in 1917, the change was especially great.

By 1959 it was claimed that illiteracy had been completely eliminated in many of the republics. Ten years earlier Kuprianov had stated that the 10 percent illiteracy rate remaining in the Soviet Union could be accounted for almost entirely by the addition of territories annexed to the Union after World War II.[6] It is interesting to note that he insisted that the areas obtained from prewar Poland, Rumania, East Prussia, Finland, and the Baltic states were more illiterate than the average of the Soviet Union. The 1959 census reported that the literacy rate in the areas added to the Soviet Union after the war was 93.5 percent for the men and 81.6 percent for the women.[7]

With the increase in the number of potential readers, there has been a corresponding expansion in the amount of printed material available. In 1913 czarist Russia had 859 newspapers, with a total daily circulation of 2.7 million copies. All except 84 of the papers were printed in Russian, and these were distributed among 24 other languages. In 1938, of 8,550 newspapers reported in the U.S.S.R., 2,188 were in non-Russian languages. With the increased interest

[6] Trofim I. Kuprianov, *Year Book of Education, 1949*, p. 383.
[7] *Narodnoe Obrazovanie, op. cit.*, p. 63.

in reading, the demand for books has also become greater. Libraries have been established widely in areas where books were formerly very rare.

The republic of Kazakhstan, the second largest in the Union in area, has been cited as an example of changes made in literacy and reading. This republic is said to have had less than 2 percent literacy in 1917, and this literacy was confined to the clergy, landlords, merchants, and officials. The figure was reported to have risen to 22.8 percent in 1926, and to 76.3 percent in 1939. In czarist times no newspapers were published in the Kazakh tongue; in 1939 Kazakhstan claimed 262 newspapers, of which 128 were in the Kazakh language, and the remainder in the languages of minority peoples in the republic. Since that time, because of the migration of Russian-speaking people to the Kazakh area, there are many more newspapers, many of them in Russian. The Kazakh S.S.R. operates a large State Publishing House, which reports the issuance of millions of volumes other than textbooks, and which operates 10,500 local libraries, with over 10 million volumes.[8]

THE TWO MAJOR PURPOSES OF SOVIET EDUCATION

It is evident that present-day Soviet schools have two major purposes. In the first place, the school is an instrument of indoctrination in the principles of Communism. According to Kandel, "The aim of education is thus defined, not in terms of an abstract philosophy, but in accordance with the paramount claims of the social order." [9] Russian educators have explained that the major aim of instruction is an understanding of the world and the cultural heritage of the present time. They describe these matters in terms of class struggle and admit that the Marxian interpretation of history will differ widely from that of the "bourgeoisie." Since the impact of this Communist ideology cannot be complete unless all are literate, literacy has been the primary objective in the educational campaign.

The second major aim of Soviet education has been the training of people to be able to participate in the industrial development of the nation. Lenin recognized that it would be impossible to build a modern industrialized state that could hold its own against a potentially hostile world unless the people were educated to modern

[8] Abdykhami Sembayev, *Year Book of Education*, 1949, p. 411.
[9] I. L. Kandel, *Comparative Education*, p. 478.

procedures. So the place of labor in society, the requirement that each individual have some specialized skill, is stressed at every level in Soviet schools. Together the ideas of communization and industrialization dominate the educational programs.

The Place of the National Government in Education

THERE are two types of government departments, the All-Union Ministries, the authority of which extends over the entire nation, and the republic ministries, the authority of which is confined to one republic. In the last analysis, almost all fields of activity in the Soviet Union are supervised by a national authority; the difference lies in whether this authority is exercised through a ministry within each republic or is directly exercised on a national scale.

Educational policies originate in the Presidium and the Central Committee of the Communist Party. After approval by the Supreme Soviet and the Council of Ministers of the Union (which is largely pro forma), the policies are implemented by the fifteen republic Ministries of Education. There is no All-Union Ministry of Education over all elementary and secondary schools, but in periodic conferences of the republic Ministers of Education uniform policies are agreed upon. This arrangement gives the appearance of a decentralized system but ensures conformity to national policies and national planning.

Up until the last few years higher education and specialized secondary schools were under an All-Union Ministry of Higher Education. Now each of the fifteen republics has a Ministry of Higher Education, but the All-Union Ministry of Culture coordinates the work of the universities and specialized secondary schools throughout the country. Formerly there was an All-Union Ministry of Labor Reserves which controlled certain factory and vocational schools, but did not contribute to their support. The young people formerly assigned to the Labor Reserve are now being sent to regular schools of various types.

Before the Revolution the greatest part of the financial support of schools was borne by the imperial government. Under the Soviet regime, a large part of the cost of education falls upon the republics and the local communities. The unified budget of the Soviet Union, however, includes the budget of the federal government, of the constituent republics, and of the various local government bodies.

Local and republic budgets are drawn up locally, but they must be checked and approved by the central authorities and deficits are made up from federal sources. Some grants are made to the republics for specific purposes.

As will be explained later, higher education in the Soviet Union is specialized according to fields. An institution which includes several schools or faculties is called a "university." A single-faculty institution, which trains specialists for one narrow field, is called a "higher institute." Some polytechnic higher institutes may have several faculties in closely related fields. On the secondary level there are specialized vocational schools which are called *tekhniki*; lower level teacher-training schools are called "teachers' institutes," and there is an increasing number of pedagogical institutes on the university level.

Many of the higher technical institutes are organized under the supervision of a particular ministry in a republic; for example, the aviation institutes which train specialists for that industry come under the Ministry of Aviation. All of the regulations governing higher institutions, and those governing the curricula and methods of specialized secondary schools, come under the Ministry of Culture.

Article 121 of the 1936 Constitution of the U.S.S.R. provides that all citizens have the right of education. Federal decrees implementing this provision have the following basic principles:

1. The state has complete monopoly of education. There are no private schools. Some nursery schools, kindergartens, and adult education programs are supported financially by cooperatives, trade unions, and collective farms, but these are supervised and controlled by the public authorities.

2. All instruction is secular, and there is complete separation of church and state.

3. Education is to be universal, free, secular, and compulsory between the ages of 7 and 15.

4. Absolute equality is guaranteed for all national, religious, or linguistic groups throughout the country, and all nationality groups have the right to elementary education in their own language. In all non-Russian schools Russian is the compulsory second language after the fourth grade (often earlier).

5. Equal opportunities for boys and girls in secondary and higher education are guaranteed.

Soviet educational literature says that decentralization of educational responsibility and control has been established in order to permit each republic to work out its own system of education, giving due consideration to its own national and other peculiarities. Nevertheless, there is almost complete uniformity. Although responsibility has been decentralized, authority is in fact highly centralized. This effect is attained in two different ways.

In the first place, in spite of the many local and regional organizations set up to operate schools, no decisions of any moment are made at a level lower than the republic Ministry of Education. In order that these ministries may work closely together, periodic congresses are held, at which uniform policies are established. Policies that have been approved at the national level become directives that must be followed by all republics. As a result of this procedure, the system of public schools is substantially the same, even though there are fifteen separate ministries of education. Even such details as the amount of time to be spent on each part of the course of study, and the time when reviewing should begin, are determined by decrees issued by the ministries, after agreement among themselves.

In the second place, education in the Soviet Union is under a dual control exercised by the ministries of education and by the Communist Party. While the machinery for control may appear to be decentralized, the Party is completely centralized and monolithic, and this force acts to ensure uniform educational policies throughout the Union, no matter how much independence appears to have been given to the local authorities.

The Place of the Constituent Republics in Education

IN SOME respects the Union Republics of the U.S.S.R. might be regarded as parallels of the states in the United States or Australia, or the provinces in Canada. The Soviet of Nationalities is somewhat analogous to the United States Senate in its place in government. Each Union Republic has 25 deputies in this body, each autonomous republic has eleven, each autonomous area has five, and each national area has one. However, the differences between the relationships of the Union Republics to the Union and of the states to the federal government in the United States are very great. One major difference is the overwhelming dominance of one of the Union Republics, the Russian (R.S.F.S.R.), in comparison with the other constituents. The R.S.F.S.R. covers three-quarters of the area of the Soviet Union and contains more than half of the total population of the country. The federal organization of the U.S.S.R. is much more complex than that of the United States, for a constituent republic may include within it various regional divisions, such as autonomous republics and regions.

According to the Soviet Constitution, Union Republics have the right to maintain their own armies, to conduct their own foreign policies, to maintain their own diplomatic and consular representatives abroad, and even to secede from the Union. No republic has dared attempt to do any of these things, except that these theoretical powers have been cited to justify seats in the United Nations for the Union Republics of the Ukraine and Byelorussia. Some regional areas with less than Union Republic status have been advanced or reduced in status; for example, the assumption has been made that some of the backward areas might eventually become Union Republics, and the former Union Republic of Karelia, once part of Finland, has been absorbed into the R.S.F.S.R.

Although the Constitution seems to say that Union Republics have greater powers than American or Australian states, in actual practice they have far less authority. This is true, in the first place, because each of them is controlled by the Communisty Party, which, as has been pointed out, is completely centralized in its control machinery. In the second place, in a planned economy, all plans are made by national control bodies, and the economy of any part of the country must be coordinated with the plans for the country as a whole. In the third place, since the federal government controls the finances and economy of the country, it is in a position to control every activity of the component parts of the Union. It is evident that the autonomy of the Union Republics is more apparent than real.[10]

FEDERALISM IN EDUCATIONAL CONTROL

Decentralization of educational control among the small divisions of the nation is also more a matter of appearance than of fact. Each Union Republic has its own Ministry of Education, which controls

[10] Carter and Herz, *Major Foreign Powers*, 4th ed., p. 255. The authors are particularly indebted to this source for much of the material in this chapter.

preschool institutions, elementary and secondary schools, and adult education within the republic. The republic ministries also finance the vocational schools, although some of these are established by industrial ministries. Each of the fifteen autonomous republics has its own Ministry of Education, but these are subordinate to the ministries of the Union Republics. For example, the Yakhutsk Autonomous Republic is within the R.S.F.S.R. and receives instructions and directives from the ministry of that republic. In accordance with the Communist habit of public criticism of officials, one may read in the press reprimands and criticisms of the educational system of a regional area by the republic Minister of Education. If no higher directive exists, the local Ministry of Education may have some freedom of action. The Georgian S.S.R. found that the compulsory study of Russian cut so deeply into the time allotted to other subjects that it reorganized its schools to provide an additional year of study beyond the primary level, thus anticipating the 11-year school in other areas.[11]

A Ministry of Education has a complex organization of departments, sections, commissions, and committees. It is headed by the Minister of Education (formerly called the "Commissar of Education"), who is a member of the Union Republic Council of Ministers. The Union Republic Planning Commission is attached to this council, and since everything must be a part of the overall state plan of development, education must fit into the total planning situation. The responsibilities of the ministry are much broader than those of the departments of education in many countries, because of the many activities outside of formal schooling that are included. A listing of some of the departments within the ministry shows the varied activities which are covered.

A Department of Organization and Administration works with local authorities, handling problems of teacher training, buildings, finance, and methods, for both elementary and secondary schools. There are sections within the department for each of these activities, and a director for each section. A Department of Vocational Education supervises the training of specialists in agriculture, industry, and other fields. A Department of Adult Education is responsible for work among adults and for various types of adult activities. A

[11] Department of State, *The Current Status of Soviet Education* (mimeographed report), Washington, D.C., March 31, 1953, p. 4.

Department of Social and Polytechnic Education is in charge of social welfare, work with delinquent children, and preschool education. A Department of Literature and Publications controls all publications within the republic—books, magazines, newspapers, as well as moving pictures and theatrical performances. A Department of Scientific and Arts Institutes is in charge of scientific societies, research institutes, biological and meteorological stations, musical institutes, museums, art galleries, historical monuments, state theaters, and circuses. The State Scientific Council, under the Ministry of Education, is a research agency, charged with the preparation of curricular materials and courses of study for all educational institutions within the republic, and for educational research, especially into methods of teaching and examinations. In the R.S.F.S.R. this is called the Academy of Pedagogical Sciences. Three commercial concerns or "trusts" are controlled by the Ministry of Education: the State Publishing House, the Board of Management for State Motion Picture Enterprises, and the State Supply Board, which manufactures and supplies school furniture and equipment.

Kandel showed the multifarious activities of a Ministry of Education:

Through its boards and departments the Ministry defines, but does not directly prescribe, the scope of general and social education throughout the country in accordance with the ideology of the new social order; it performs the same function for vocational and professional education; and through an occupational census determines the number of students to be trained in every field of activity which requires such preparation; it has undertaken the responsibility for the liquidation of illiteracy and for developing a program of political education; it stimulates and encourages the development of the fine arts, music, and drama; it plans, controls, and censors publications of every kind, whether newspapers, periodicals, pamphlets or books; it promotes the establishment of scientific institutions to make them readily accessible in all parts of the country for study, research, and the dissemination of scientific knowledge; and finally, it collects information of a financial and statistical nature in all matters affecting education.[12]

The ministry is allocated certain funds from the budget of the republic and it distributes these funds to the local agencies of administration. Each republic makes its own budget, and this must

[12] Kandel, *op. cit.*, p. 310.

be approved by the national government. Between the ministry and the local authorities and local schools, the connecting links are the inspectors, who are appointed by the ministry. An inspector is appointed after at least five years of successful teaching experience, and special training courses are provided to prepare him for his duties. His major responsibility is to improve the standard of teaching. He visits a school and works very closely with the principal, gives information on the activities and policies of the Ministry of Education, takes part in local conferences, brings material on recent developments in educational theory and method, and gives advice to individual teachers. In order to keep informed on modern methods, he is attached to a local educational-research institute. He may give suggestions to teachers, criticize their work, or offer to teach demonstration lessons himself. His criticisms are not used to rate teachers, although, in cooperation with the principal, he may recommend a teacher for an award or honor. The ministry's instructions to inspectors are that criticisms should always be constructive.

The Role of the Local Authorities in Education

EACH of the Union Republics is divided into provinces or regions (*oblastny*). There are some 160 of these and each has its own Education Administration, which is held responsible to the ministry for general school and out-of-school programs and facilities within its boundaries. Regions are further divided into districts (*raiony*), which are units composed of urban and rural areas. Districts are further divided into cities and large towns, small towns, and villages. (Small towns and villages are usually parts of collective or state farms.) Small towns and villages come under the District Education Department, which is in turn responsible to the *oblast'* Education Department, and through it to the Ministry of Education for the republic. Cities and large towns may have their own Education Departments.

The Soviet Constitution guarantees the vote to everyone except criminals or insane persons. Before 1936 elections were indirect; the individual voter cast his ballot only once, to elect a deputy to his village, town, or rural government council (soviet). District, regional, and republic congresses of soviets, and finally the All-Union Congress of Soviets, were elected by the unit immediately below. Since 1936, all elections to all representative bodies, from the village soviet to the Supreme Soviet of the U.S.S.R., have been direct. In theory, the soviet of a local unit of government possesses the legislative and executive power in its area, but in practice the working power resides in an executive committee elected by the soviet under the guidance of the Communist Party.

In each area (rural division, city, district, and region), the executive committee of the soviet appoints an education committee from its members, giving precedence to individuals with educational experience. The executive committee also appoints a Director of Education for the area. The local education committee is responsible, on the one hand, to the executive committee of its own soviet, which appointed it, and on the other to the Education Department of the next larger territorial division, and so on up to the Minister of Education. There is thus a complex overlapping of authorities to which the local departments are responsible, which is characteristic of the Soviet system. The voters, through their elected representatives, and the higher educational authorities are thus theoretically in a position to influence the development of the educational system. But the possibility is more apparent than real. Carter says:

When it comes to effective influence, however, the element of democracy fades. There is a striking difference between the appearance of popular control and the way in which local affairs are run. Constitutionally the soviets are vested with power, but in practice they do not exercise it. The enthusiastic fervor of the elected deputies and "activists," to which observers testify, makes a strange contrast, to pragmatic Western people, with the obvious centralization of authority in administrative and Party hands. The most difficult question to answer is: Why has the Soviet government erected such a vast system for popular participation in local affairs if it intends indefinitely to withhold power from the populace? Lenin popularized the slogan "Every cook must learn to govern." What will happen when all have learned? [13]

The Education Department of a local area appoints the principal of a school, and he in turn appoints the teachers, subject to the approval of the education committee. The educational authority is concerned with matters of school buildings and equipment, it must approve the school budget, and it is responsible for all general education within its area except for higher education and the training of teachers. The education committee must be consulted on any

[13] Carter and others, *Major Foreign Powers*, 2nd ed., p. 534.

important decision that is made by the principal. It must provide adequate living facilities for the teachers and must assume responsibility for the program and facilities for out-of-school educational and leisure activities within the area. The announced aim of Soviet education is to make all the schools for the common people, no matter how remote these schools are from the cities, of equal standards and facilities. They have not yet been able to achieve their goal, but they are attempting to do so by placing responsibilities upon the local authorities.

Each school has a local school council, which includes the teachers, principal, school physician, and representatives of the school clerks, janitors, Communist Party organization, workers' unions, and Komsomols (the Young Communist youth organizations). Matters affecting the internal operation of the school and the health and comfort of the children, as well as matters affecting the welfare and convenience of teachers, are considered by this body.

In addition to public funds made available through the Education Departments, there are always contributions made by local citizens and organizations. During the difficult times of World War II, when many schools were destroyed or disrupted, parents became accustomed to aiding in the repair and improvement of school buildings. This attitude of parental participation was encouraged, and it has been extended since the war. The parents, the local trade union, or the management of the collective farm or local factory may make contributions for the enlargement or improvement of the school building, or for the provision of special equipment or facilities. The habit of parents assisting in the cleaning or redecorating of local schoolrooms before the opening of a new term is said to have become general. Parents also make contributions of money or food to improve the type of meals offered in school lunchrooms.

Every Soviet administrative unit has its own budget, and the education budget forms a part of the total. The proportion allocated to education by the area executive committee is distributed to the individual schools, and the local principal buys directly the items of school supplies and textbooks that are needed. These are all purchased from the State Publishing House or the State School Supply Trust. Salaries of teachers and other employees are set by official decrees, and funds are provided in the budget to pay these costs. All expenditures are audited, and while the principal has authority to spend money within the budget for any authorized items, he may be called to account for any lack of judgment or for unauthorized spending.

In addition to the inspectors of the central authority, who represent the Minister of Education, there are local inspectors, appointed by the local education authorities. These are chosen from teachers with at least three years of experience, and they are expected to assist the teachers in every way possible. The local inspectors have less authority than the central office inspectors.

Every school has a school parents' association, which elects a parents' committee for every class, and a school parents' committee, with the principal as a member, for the whole school. These committees have been asked to help in enforcing compulsory attendance and in popularizing educational ideas among parents. They are asked to assume responsibility for needy pupils, for orphans, and for the children of men in the armed forces. They help to raise funds for school equipment and materials, and assist in the leisure-time activities of the children. They help the teachers on school excursions and field trips, prepare food for special occasions, and sometimes help in sewing or woodworking classes.

The Role of the Communist Party in Education

THE RULING force behind the government of the Soviet Union, and the governments of all its subdivisions, is the Communist Party, for it controls all elections. Only Party members or Party-approved candidates may be elected or appointed to office, whether in local areas, the republics, or the federal Union. Every collective farm, every factor, every locality, every industry, has its Communist cell or cells; there are thousands of such units. They make sure that Communist policies are carried out in every aspect of Soviet life. Party members obey orders unquestioningly, and infractions of the rules are severely punished, sometimes by the highly publicized "purges." The leaders of the Communist Party are all-powerful in the Soviet Union, and under Stalin the General Secretary of the Party was the real ruler of all Russia.

Admission to membership in the Party is a coveted privilege, not a right, and only a small minority of Soviet citizens ever attain membership. There were not more than 23,000 members in March, 1917; this number grew to 200,000 in November, 1917, and to over 6 million in 1947. There have been repeated purges of a large proportion of the membership, and of the 6 million members in 1947, more than half had joined during or after the war. After the war complaints were heard that the Party had grown too large and that further purges were needed. It is estimated that there were 9.7 million members in 1961, in a nation of 214 million people.

All citizens of the Soviet state must be so conditioned by the environment and by the constant indoctrination of the formal and informal educative process that they will accept without question the point of view of the Communist elite. In addition it is necessary to train leaders who will dominate the masses and to provide a novitiate through which candidates for Party membership can pass. For this purpose the Party has established a hierarchy of youth organizations alongside the regular school system. These organizations select future Party members and leaders by means of a process of rigid screening and rigorous training. The Young Communist organizations are discussed further in Chapter 16.

Although the educational system of the Soviet Union has all the machinery of a decentralized system, it is, because of the dual nature of the controls, a rigidly centralized organization. Parallel with the formal and nominal governmental machinery for administration and control, which is decentralized in form, there stands the Communist Party. It functions at every level, and is not decentralized in any degree. Party representatives dominate every soviet from the rural village to the Presidium of the Supreme Soviet. The doctrine of the Party is proclaimed by the Central Committee, and there can be no disagreement in any particular. The Party line may change from time to time, but the change is always made by the official Party machinery at the top, and the word is sent down to the lowest Communist cell. No matter what language is taught in the lower schools, or what formal organizations are held responsible for them, the control remains always in the same place, the central organization of the Party. Since the Party line cannot vary from one end of the country to the other, the actual result is complete centralization within the forms of a decentralized system.

Finance

STATISTICS on education within the Soviet Union are difficult to secure, and are rarely comparable with figures given in other countries. Cost figures are especially difficult to compare with those of

Western democracies. Since there is practically no private ownership in the U.S.S.R., governmental budgets include much of the cost of agriculture, industry, trade, and transportation, as well as governmental expenditures normally included in other national budgets. The unified budget of the Soviet Union, which includes the budget of the federal government and also those of the Union Republics and the local subdivisions, amounts to approximately 75 percent of the national income. At least 50 percent of the Soviet budget is used for capital outlays in the building of new industrial plants, for providing working capital in industrial and commercial enterprises, and for financing reconstruction and repairs.

Government revenue comes from two sources: taxation and earnings of state-owned enterprises. About 90 percent of the profits of state farms, industries, commercial organizations, and transportation facilities go into government funds—either through direct or indirect taxes. The remaining 10 percent is used for extra incentive payments to labor or as working capital. The bulk of the income from taxation comes from the trade-turnover (general sales) tax. This tax is levied on every transaction from the original producer to the consumer, so that the tax is pyramided to tremendous rates. On basic commodities such as food the tax may be high enough to cause the consumer to pay three times the original cost of the item. In 1962, in order to provide greater incentives to agriculture, retail prices on meat were increased about 35 percent; this was in addition to a sales tax which ranged from 55 to 82 percent. On luxury items such as tobacco and cosmetics the sales taxes are even higher.

Because a sales tax is regressive, with greater impact on the poor than on the rich, it is frequently criticized in Western countries as unjust and undemocratic; under the Soviet system an extremely high sales tax is levied on necessities and luxuries alike, with the heaviest burden falling on the workers and peasants who support the regime. Income taxes are low, with a maximum of 13 percent. When the Communists say that they will soon be able to eliminate taxes entirely, they refer to the obvious direct income tax; they can do without this since they rely so much upon hidden taxes.

The *World Handbook of Educational Organizations and Statistics,* published by UNESCO, gave prewar figures on educational expenditures at various levels. These are shown in Table 8-2. Since a major part of the income of Union Republics and local subdivisions

TABLE 8–2
Expenditures for Education in U.S.S.R., 1939

AUTHORITY	TOTAL SUM IN MILLION RUBLES	PERCENTAGE OF ANNUAL EDUCATIONAL EXPENDITURE	PERCENTAGE OF TOTAL BUDGET OF THE AUTHORITY
Union (Federal)	4,828	23	4.1
Union Republics	3,600	17	30.8
Local authorities	12,641	60	46.8
Total	21,069	100	13.6*

SOURCE: UNESCO *World Handbook*, 1951, p. 389. Reprinted by permission of UNESCO.
* Percentage of national budget.

comes from federal funds (because the Union government controls major forms of taxation), it is probable that this table showed which authorities spent the money, not the source of funds expended.

The Chief Economist of the U.S.S.R. Ministry of Finance reported that the budget for 1961 planned to spend a total of 4.8 billion new rubles on education. (Prior to 1961 the official value of the ruble was about 25 cents; since revaluation it is given as equal to $1.11.) Of this amount it was planned to spend 2.8 billion on compulsory education schools, 768 million on kindergartens, 525 million on boarding schools, and 185 million on schools for young workers and young farmers.[14]

The Communist Party and the Soviet government have accomplished a great deal of the task they laid out for themselves in 1917. The struggle against illiteracy has been a remarkable achievement. The insistence on every teacher becoming a propagandist for the regime, as well as the severe ideological restrictions on all intellectual activity, have hampered the development of the educational program. Two- and even three-shift schools have been common, because of the great shortage of buildings, a condition that is just now being improved. In spite of strenuous efforts to produce more trained teachers, the problem of supplying the schools with teachers is still a difficult one. The way in which the goals have been achieved in the operation of schools will be discussed in a later chapter.

[14] V. Basov, "Education and National Economy," *Soviet Education*, Vol. III, No. 2 (September, 1961), p. 56 (from *Narodnoe Obrazovanie*, 1961, No. 3).

9

Reorganized Education: West Germany

G ERMANY is the land of Goethe and Schiller, of innumerable masterpieces in the realm of music, now numbered among the world's artistic treasures, and of a celebration of Christmas that is perhaps the most beautiful devised in any land. There is no doubt that the Germans are an extremely capable and industrious people, with a capacity for thoroughness and attention to detail. They have made many outstanding contributions to literature, philosophy, medicine, art, and scientific research. During the last century their universities were the model on which many American graduate schools were patterned and were thronged with foreign students anxious to share the benefits of German learning.

But there has been another Germany—a land of Junkers and the General Staff, of Hegel, Bismarck, Krupp, and Hitler. This was a nation disciplined, highly organized, acquiescent of authority, and obsessed with a policy of "blood and iron"—a nation which, in the pursuit of a dream of national grandeur, plunged the world into the disaster of two terrible global wars.

Now a new, reconstructed Germany is emerging. It is a land that seems to be dedicated to democratic principles, that has made a remarkable recovery from the ravages and destruction of war, and that has again become a great power in western Europe. It appears to have renounced the doctrines of the Nazis, and is developing its schools on democratic principles. Having passed through a period of guidance by occupying powers, it has rebuilt its educational system on modern lines that are still basically and traditionally German.

Prewar German Education

THROUGHOUT its development German education has been characterized by efficiency and thoroughness. The Germans have always believed in the power of efficiency and have been quick to use it in furthering the national aim of the time. The history of the past century of German education may be divided into four phases or periods: (a) education under the Empire, 1870–1918; (b) liberalization under the Weimar Republic, 1918–33; (c) Nazification, 1933–45; and (d) postwar reconstruction, after 1945. These may seem to be separate stages, but the keen observer can see some of the same beliefs and traditional influences at work in all four periods.

GERMAN EDUCATION UNDER THE EMPIRE, 1870–1918

The very idea of a national school system controlled by the state may be said to have originated in Germany. Signs of this appeared as early as the sixteenth century, when several German states began to establish state-church school systems, but it was left to Prussia to be the first modern state to institute a true national system without any church control. Frederick William I (king, 1713–40) had built a number of new schools, improved the status of teachers, and made a move toward compulsory attendance. In the reign of Frederick the Great (1740–86) a School Code was enacted which became the basis of the Prussian school system. In 1794 a General Code definitely made Prussian schools state institutions.

This century of educational progress seemed to have gone for nought when Prussia was crushed and humiliated by Napoleon at Jena in 1806, losing half her territory and population. The situation was desperate; then Prussian pride and hope were revived by a concerted effort in which education played a prominent part. The campaign was led by Stein, Fichte, Scharnhorst, and Humboldt, and its educational side was so successful that it was long afterwards referred to by the Germans as "the example never to be forgotten." Prussia was set upon her feet, and shared in the victories over Napoleon at Leipzig and Waterloo.

For a time it appeared that there would be a continuation of social and educational reforms working side by side, with a democratic system of education providing equal opportunity for all, but

9-1	German Schools Under the Empire, 1870–1918

YEARS IN SCHOOL				YEARS OF AGE
17				22
16			Universities and other Hochschulen	21
15		Technische Hochschule		20
14	Fachschule (Advanced technical school)			19
13				18
12				17
11	Fortbildungsschule (Part-time continuation school)		Gymnasium	16
10			Real-gymnasium	15
9				14
8		Mittelschule (Intermediate school)	Oberreal-schule	13
7	Volksschule (Elementary school)			12
6			Lyzeum	11
5			(Secondary schools)	10
4				9
3				8
2	(Transfer point to secondary education)		Vorschule (Preparatory school)	7
1				6

this was not to be. A period of reaction set in during the reign of Frederick William IV (1840–61), and a return was made to the religious and autocratic control of education in order that a well-disciplined military state might be organized. Before long the two-class school system shown in Figure 9–1 was well established.

Through the defeat of Austria at Sadowa in 1866, Prussia became the leader of the movement to unify the German states. Prussia's ability as a leader was demonstrated by victories over Denmark and

France, and the final triumph came with the Proclamation at Versailles in 1871 of a German Empire of 25 constituent states.

There followed forty years of economic progress and steady growth of national power. Germany built up a strong army and navy, expanded the merchant marine, and obtained a number of overseas colonies. Prussia's struggles for freedom in the early nineteenth century had been defensive rather than offensive, but after 1870 Germany's attitude changed to a strong feeling of militaristic nationalism. Schools and universities openly taught that Germany's rivals were encircling her with a girdle of steel, and that she must break through this ring in order to achieve her proper destiny in the world and to spread German culture. Other nations became alarmed as they watched Germany's growing military and naval strength. German army officers drank toasts to *Der Tag*—the day when German armies would march to their triumph. This path led directly to World War I, but the outcome for Germany was defeat and not triumph.

Let us examine briefly the German school system during this imperial era, as illustrated in Figure 9–1. The system was definitely "two-class." The objective was to produce on the one hand a body of highly trained and intelligent experts, leaders, and officers, and on the other hand a vast array of capable, obedient, and well-disciplined followers. Students began in either the elementary or the special preparatory schools, and after the age of 9 there was little further chance of admission to the privileged system of secondary schools. A few bright pupils were permitted to transfer from one type of school to a higher type, but the individual concerned was placed in a class below his age level, and had considerable difficulty in catching up with the curriculum. Children of wealthier parents began their schooling in the *Vorschule*, which was a private preparatory school.

On the secondary level each type of school was distinctive and played its own significant part. The *Mittelschule* represented a sort of halfway house and gave a humanistic secondary education with one foreign language. It was popular but was a junior division and carried no special privileges, nor did it lead to the university.

The *Gymnasium* was the secondary school of high prestige. Every ambitious boy aimed at entering a *Gymnasium* and worked hard to secure entry at the age of 9 years. The curriculum was classical, with nine years of Latin, seven of French, and six of Greek as the main subjects. Every German scholar of note was trained in the *Gym-*

nasium, where the disinterested pursuit of knowledge and culture was the principal objective. Admission to the *Gymnasium* had a social aspect, in that a highly valued privilege awaited the boy who completed successfully all stages to the upper second class. This was *Das Einjahrige,* which limited his compulsory military training to one year and allowed him, within limits, to select the regiment in which he would serve. This privilege was so highly prized that parents urged their sons on to severe study to attain the reward which reflected credit on the whole family. Moreover, the *Abitur* or Maturity Certificate at the end of the upper first class opened up the prospect of an immediate medium-class civil service position or entrance to the university. Higher civil service careers were reserved for university graduates.

The *Realgymnasium* represented a trend in German educational thought in the direction of modern languages and science rather than emphasis on the classics, although Latin continued to be stressed. The *Oberrealschule,* a third type, gave three to six years of Latin in the final classes on an optional basis, but its main subjects were modern languages, science, and mathematics. In addition to its major subjects, each type of school included some time in its curriculum for German literature, religion, history, music, and gymnastics. The relative importance of these schools can be gathered from the fact that in 1910 there were 304 *Gymnasien,* 122 *Realgymnasien,* and 75 *Oberrealschulen* in Germany. The universities drew their students mainly but not entirely from the *Gymnasien.*

Girls did not have as many educational opportunities as boys, but there were reasonably good facilities for them, and some capable young women were able to secure admission to universities. Conservative opinion, however, held that the course at the *Mittelschule,* with emphasis on domestic economy and infant welfare, was sufficient for a girl. The *Lyzeum* was the girls' secondary school. There was very little coeducation in Germany except in small elementary schools in country districts. Girls' schools were staffed about 50 percent by men teachers.

On the other side of the two-class system, after a sound education in the *Volksschule,* many boys and girls passed on to a continuation school (*Fortbildungsschule*); these, though not compulsory in all parts of Germany, were rapidly gaining in favor. They originated in Munich under a famous educator, Kerschensteiner. The principle behind them was that a liberal education might be gained in connection with the student's vocation. (It is interesting to note that the idea of the continuation school was incorporated into the English Education Acts of 1918 and 1944, and in the future will probably become more important in English education than it is now.)

After being apprenticed in a recognized trade, the German student attended continuation school connected with this trade for three or four years—generally from ages 14 to 18—two half-days a week on his employer's time. The work was both liberal (including German literature and history, music, and religion) and vocational. The best tradesmen in each trade were employed as teachers in the vocational classes and the schools achieved high educational standards. Some of the continuation schools admitted girls, especially those schools which had courses in tailoring, lithography, household arts, and other vocations open to women.

In addition there were numerous full-time technical schools training students in agriculture, forestry, skilled trades, commercial work, and other important phases of the extensive economic life of the country. The higher divisions of technical work were given by a technical high school (*Technische Hochschule*); these schools were of university rank and similar to the institutes of technology in some other countries.

The German universities at this period attracted students from all over the world because of the high quality of their work in all fields of learning. Fees were low. There was no system of residential colleges as in England, and the students lived in private homes. Most courses culminated in the doctorate (the only university degree conferred in Germany), but state examinations had to be passed in order to gain entrance to the professions. After the rather rigid regime of the *Gymnasium*, students sometimes found the sudden transition to the freedom of the universities a heady draught and squandered themselves in drinking and dueling.

The nationalistic ideas of the time were prominent in the universities and there was much discussion of Germany's future in world affairs, but there is no doubt about the high quality of the scholarship and scientific research. While the whole system tended to train leaders and followers of the state, the universities also attached great importance to pure learning and to the development of individual talents for their own sake. The contributions of German universities at this period to philosophy and science, and to German culture generally, were so marked that their interruption and partial cessation during World War I was a disaster to the world as well as to Germany itself.

GERMAN EDUCATION UNDER THE WEIMAR REPUBLIC, 1919-33

After Germany's defeat and disillusionment, the new Constitution of Weimar in 1919 raised hopes that militarism might be put aside and that Germany might join the ranks of the democracies. For the next fourteen years the Republic struggled on, but finally collapsed because the middle classes were so hard hit by inflation and other economic disabilities, and the political changes were not accompanied by the necessary social reorganization of the country. The upper classes, which were never in sympathy with the new regime, remained resentfully in the background.

The Weimar authorities were enthusiastic and resourceful. They believed that some marked educational changes were necessary and they proceeded to carry these out. As a result there followed a period of liberal influences in education which at first seemed very promising. Included in a new statement of objectives for the schools was a clause urging the cultivation of a spirit of reconciliation and friendship with former enemy nations. To further the principles of democracy, the exclusive preparatory school, the *Vorschule*, was abolished and the *Volksschule* became the *Grundschule*, or common basic elementary school for all pupils. The age of transition from elementary schools to secondary schools was raised to 10 years, and opportunities for transfers were provided at an even later age.

The school was definitely separated from the church and inspections by ministers of religion were no longer permitted. Much freedom was given to teachers. State Ministries issued fewer prescriptions than previously, and allowed the schools to experiment with subjects and activities. There had long been much discussion about an *Einheitsschule*, or uniform type of comprehensive school for all pupils (similar to the French idea of an *école unique*). This idea again came into prominence. No final decision was reached, but two new types of secondary school were introduced, the *Aufbauschule*, which allowed "late bloomers" to complete a secondary course in six years, between the ages of 12 and 19, and the *Deutsche Oberschule*, which was a cultural type of secondary school with a curriculum based on the finest achievements of German literature, art, and science, as contrasted with domination by the classics. Continuation schools and people's high schools were extended and encouraged. In short, the new government sought to lessen the rigidity of the two-class system and to provide opportunites at various levels for all talented pupils. In the universities a measure of self-government was introduced and an attempt made to stop dueling and drinking.

Encouragement was given to progressive methods of teaching, such as class activities, school journeys, and individual guidance. Some excellent adaptations of the Dalton Plan were worked out by German schools during this period. Schools began to experiment with self-government, particularly in Saxony, and parent-teacher associations were formed. Corporal punishment was abolished. New textbooks were published, incorporating many progressive ideas.

The Youth Movement was at its best during the Weimar Republic. This movement originated before World War I as a protest of youth against severe intellectualism and domination by adults. It was of a romantic character, with walking tours during weekends and holidays to places of historic and literary interest. The young people wore simple costumes and tramped to the music of guitars and banjos. Eventually there were 3,000 hostels associated with the Youth Movement, and members of accredited youth associations from other countries were invited to join in their use. The Weimar government encouraged this movement, and urged each school to have a *Wandertag* each month, a day on which the whole school went out of doors on some planned excursion.

Here, then, was the genesis of a democratic school system. Had the Weimar Republic been successful in maintaining its national and educational policy, the whole subsequent history of the world might have been different. But the Republic was apparently doomed from the beginning. It was too democratic for many disgruntled German groups smarting under the Treaty of Versailles. It was a gallant attempt, but it was born out of defeat and had to struggle constantly against a pressure of antidemocratic forces. From 1924 to 1929 the Weimar government was reasonably successful, but an economic crisis in 1931 plunged it into great difficulties. The reactionary groups were still there, and no marked change had taken place in the social organization of the country. The Junkers, the army, and the powerful industrialists were implacably hostile and were waiting for their chance. The Weimar government was never sufficiently sure of itself and never seemed to inspire confidence. As the economic situation grew worse, the National Socialists seized the opportunity to place before the thwarted and discontented elements a picture of a newer Germany. There were to be jobs for all and a steady march toward the reestablishment of Germany as a powerful nation. This tempting prospect was difficult to resist, and the Weimar Republic fell.

THE NAZI PERIOD, 1933–45

In order for the Nazis to achieve their objective of a totalitarian state which would enable Germany to break out of its encirclement and assume a position of dominant leadership in the world, it was important for all educational agencies to preach the Nazi doctrines vigorously. The liberal tendencies of the Weimar period had to be checked and German children led to a spirit of devotion to the new regime.

Public welfare was set above that of the individual; democracy was regarded with contempt; only one political party was permitted; and freedom of the press and of speech were radically curtailed. Some of the groups which supported the rise of National Socialism had not anticipated that Hitler would make "The Party" supreme in everything.

Mein Kampf showed clearly the spirit that was to pervade German education during the next ten years. Hitler asserted that nature's law was that evolution produced stronger and stronger races, attracting like to like, while the weaker races deteriorated and disappeared. The stronger must dominate the weaker races and refrain from mixing with them lest nature's labor of thousands of years in improving the breed fail. Declaring that the supreme achievement of nature was the Aryan race, he threatened that if the Aryan race were conquered, the dark veils of an uncultured age would descend once more. The Jew was depicted as the greatest possible contrast to the Aryan, a parasite within the body of other nations. Germany was fighting, he said, a battle for the survival of the heroic virtues and the uplifting of all mankind.

The educational corollaries of ideas like these were that all individuals must be trained to be willing, submissive, and uncritical servants of the will of the state. They must revere the Nazi doctrines with something like religious fervor. History, literature, art, music, and even science must be patriotic and must incite to national endeavor. All teachers must be Nazis and must believe in and teach the doctrines of racial purity and German leadership. Pupils must be taught to admire the armed forces and to see in them the emblem of Germany's future might and greatness.

In the early days of their regime, it was the spirit rather than the structure of education that the Nazis changed. The major reorganization did not come until 1938, and even then much of the original framework remained intact.

There were, however, some changes made at the beginning of the Nazi period. For the first time in German history there was federal control. A National Ministry of Education and Youth Welfare was established, which issued instructions about courses, textbooks, and general procedure. Teachers were officials of the Reich; they were not at first required to be members of the Nazi party, but it was quietly intimated to them that it would be wise for them to join. Physical training, including endurance marches, obstacle races, and the elementary study of topography, was emphasized. Coeducation was discouraged, and a return was made to much sterner discipline, which a boy was expected to take without any sign of flinching.

The intellectual side of the school program began to suffer severely. The details of administration were decentralized, with considerable authority wielded by a local leader (*Leiter*). School committees and parents' councils were restricted and weakened. The modern ideas of the Weimar period were not entirely discarded, but were given a Nazi twist. For example, school libraries were encouraged, but they were required to contain a basic set of 120 books nominated by the *Leiter*. Visual education and school broadcasts were widely used, but they were carefully supervised to make certain that they were of the right political color. Life outside of the school was given special emphasis, particularly through the Hitler Youth (*Hitlerjugend*), and schools were allotted a prominent part in Nazi parades and festivals. A picture or bust of Hitler was to be found in every schoolroom. New textbooks were published, which stressed Nazi principles and made a special feature of the so-called racial purity and the attractive future which awaited Germany if there were wholehearted support of the Nazi program.

In 1938 a plan of reorganization was approved which made the schools definite instruments of the Nazi regime. It was very thorough in its conception and at the same time avoided too much interference with the existing system. The number of preschool centers was increased in order to help working mothers. The *Grundschule* was retained and continuation schools were extended and strength-ened. All city pupils whose education was limited to the *Grund-schule* were required to undertake a Rural Year (*Landjahr*), which they spent on farms or in special camps in order to learn something of rural life and its problems.

So much for the "followers." It was in the selection and education of "leaders," however, that the Nazis made their most important changes. Secondary education was remolded to meet this end. The actual enrollments in secondary education were reduced, for "Secondary Education for All" did not appeal to the Nazi leaders. Fewer girls were admitted than previously, for the Nazis believed that the keynote of girls' education should be the "three K's"—*Kirche, Küche, Kinder* (sometimes irreverently translated by English-speaking students as "Kirk, Kitchen, and Kids").

The remodeled system of secondary education can be briefly described as follows. The *Mittelschule* remained a junior secondary school, with commercial subjects, practical courses, and one foreign language prominent in its curriculum. The *Deutsche Oberschule,* stressing German literature and history, became the main type of secondary school, attended by three-fourths of the pupils who were admitted to the secondary level. The Nazis approved strongly of the *Aufbauschule,* which continued to give opportunity for pupils who showed talent later than the age of 10. Many of these schools were in country towns and corresponded to what are called "consolidated schools" or "union high schools" elsewhere. On the other hand, the Nazis did not like the *Gymnasium,* of which they were suspicious, thinking that it stood for non-German culture and for independence of thought. Enrollments in this type of school were severely cut, but these schools were permitted to train a certain number of students for university work and other specialized positions.

For the training of officers and party officials a new type of secondary boarding school was established—the National Political Education Institute, often known as the Napoli School. Included in its course was a considerable amount of National Socialist politics, together with hard military training. Fees were charged. There were 37 of these schools in 1943, and three of them were for girls.

The secondary school which really excited the ambitions of every Nazi youth, however, was the *Adolf Hitler Schule,* a boarding school with a course extending over six years, for boys from the age of 12 to the age of 18. Selection for this school was very rigorous. Each candidate had to show excellent physical health, and his family had to have a record of loyalty to the Party. There were ten of these schools in 1943. No fees were charged. The regime was Spartan in character; the boys wore uniforms and lived in barracks. The aim of the program was to produce skilled leaders for high party posts and superior officers for the armed services.

The *Adolf Hitler Schule* was only the first stage in an ambitious plan for the training of Nazi leaders which was never put into full operation because of the Nazi defeat. Under this plan, students who had completed the course in the *Adolf Hitler Schule* were to be sent out for several years into the ordinary life of the community, taking up what occupations they could, as well as meeting the conditions of labor service and military service. During this period they were to be secretly watched; those who showed strength of character and powers of leadership were to be brought back for a nine-year course in one of the "Castles of the Nazi Order." At the end of this time, when they were 30 years of age or older, the majority were to be given Party positions of some importance, but the carefully selected minority were to proceed for three further years in the Party University, which was to have been established on the shores of Chiemsee, the beautiful lake in Bavaria. This scheme was to have sifted the young male population of Germany in such a way that the strongest in character, loyalty, and intelligence, after many searching tests, were to become the potential leaders of the National Socialist Party and the future rulers of Germany.

Side by side with the system of education was the powerful organization known as the Hitler Youth. This appealed more to young Nazis than had the former German Youth Movement, attractive and beneficial in character as the latter had been. The new organization combined political indoctrination and participation with the development of physical fitness. There were several divisions of the Hitler Youth, according to age. Boys between 10 and 14 years of age were members of the *Jungvolk*; between 14 and 18 they belonged to the *Hitlerjugend*. Girls between 10 and 14 were in the *Jungmädel*; between 14 and 18 they were in the *Bund Deutscher Mädchen*.

By 1942 there were 5 million members of the Hitler Youth. There was a great deal of marching and physical training, as well as social service projects for the units to carry out. For instance, when there had to be a large-scale evacuation of children from bombed cities, its organization was left largely to the Hitler Youth. Spectacular rallies were held from time to time. There is no doubt that the glamorous aspects of this movement caught up many boys and girls in the Nazi net. The schools were asked to allow their pupils a certain amount of time off to attend Hitler Youth activities, and the quality of the academic work fell away in consequence. The intolerant and even brutal side of the movement was vividly portrayed in Erika Mann's *School for Barbarians,* and in Walt Disney's short color film *Education for Death.*

In the realm of higher education there were eight main institutes for advanced study, of which the university was one type. The others provided training in such fields as agriculture, commerce, art and music, teacher training, and political science.

This account of an educational system designed to produce loyal members of the Nazi party has been given in some detail in order to emphasize the difficulties which confronted any attempt, after Germany's collapse in 1945, to give a new spirit and a different set of objectives to German education. It must be remembered that a whole generation had grown up between 1933 and 1945 knowing nothing else but the Nazi system of propagandist education.

Postwar Reorganization of German Education

THE ALLIES entered Germany in the autumn of 1944, and Germany surrendered unconditionally in May, 1945. The Potsdam Agreement of 1945 provided for separate administration of the several zones by the occupying powers and for the handling of matters affecting the whole of the country through a Control Council representing these powers. It provided for the trial of war criminals and the removal of all Nazis from public and semipublic offices. Clause 7 called for a redirection of German education in order to eliminate Nazi and militarist doctrines and to make possible the successful development of democratic ideas.

No provision was made, for the time being, for a central German government, but it was hoped that there would presently emerge a united German democracy on the federal level. This hope was spoiled by the steadily growing hostility between the former allies of East and West.

Following the German surrender, Alsace-Lorraine was returned to France, Austria became an independent republic under occupation, and Poland was given the eastern portion of Germany up to the Oder and Neisse rivers in return for the eastern Polish territory handed over to Russia. In this way the size of Germany was reduced from the 184,000 square miles of 1939 to 138,000 square miles (20,000 square miles less than California), but the population was not greatly reduced, since millions of Germans were moved westward out of the surrendered territories. Prussia in effect disappeared, part going to Poland, part to Russia, and the remainder being divided among four zones.

When Germany surrendered, education was in a chaotic state. Thousands of schools had been destroyed or badly damaged by bombing—in Cologne 90 percent—and in the evacuation many of the pupils had been dispersed throughout districts far from their homes. There was a great shortage of teachers, and equipment and textbooks seemed to have disappeared. Most of the pupils over 15 had been drawn into some type of war service. Housing conditions were appalling, and the general difficulties were increased by thousands of refugee children pouring in from the East.

The first step for the Allies was to get the schools in operation again, often in borrowed and ramshackle buildings, with classes of 60, 70, and even 80, and often in two or three shifts. Each zone did what it could and gradually the situation began to improve.

The Nazi-instituted position of *Reichsminister* of Education was abolished. The Control Council set up an Education Committee, and at first it was hoped that the committee would arrive at something like a uniform system for the whole of Germany, but this did not happen. Ideas varied considerably in the different zones, with a distinct contrast between the West and East. Development in the early stages might be set down briefly as follows:

In the American Zone the occupying forces tended to leave measures of education reconstruction largely to the Germans, subject to the objectives laid down in the Potsdam Agreement. Each of the states (*Länder*) was given administrative responsibilities for education in its area. The schools were opened more or less on traditional German lines, although Bavaria was inclined to be conservative and influenced by the opinion of the Catholic Church.

Continuation schools and adult education were encouraged. Textbooks of the Weimar days were reprinted, and the Americans arranged, as a temporary measure, for the rewriting in German of many suitable American or English textbooks, with good illustrations. Five million copies of these books were distributed. United States military authorities made a marked contribution toward good will in the situation by directing their attention toward measures to interest German youth; they organized sports, musical clubs, and youth groups.

In the French Zone a tighter control was kept. Many teachers and students were brought in from France to help in the schools, and it was inevitable that French educational ideas should be introduced. Moral and religious instruction was stressed. The question of textbooks gave a great deal of trouble. Technical and agricultural schools were encouraged because they could help in economic reconstruction. The French were successful in getting most of the refugee and homeless children off the streets, and attendance at school began to rise. They reopened the University of Mainz, which had been closed since 1797, feeling that here was an opportunity for a fresh start untrammeled by any Nazi or militaristic influences.

The authorities of the British Zone had much the same idea as the Americans of giving responsibilities to the Germans, with the *Länder* as administrative units. The destruction in the British Zone had been very severe, and there was a considerable shortage of food. Schools, often in halls and cellars, were organized in shifts, and a hot meal was given each day to pupils and teachers. The British used broadcasting to supplement the work, and Radio Hamburg sent out a daily program of lessons. More attention was given to the education of girls than under the Nazis. There was much discussion about the question of denominational versus mixed-denomination schools, but no decision was reached.

With great difficulty six universities were set in operation again, for most of the libraries had been destroyed and there was a great shortage of equipment. The life of the students was hard, for they were ill clad and ill fed. The percentage of young women in the universities soon rose from the Nazi figure of 10 percent to about 25 percent.

In the Russian Zone action was direct and positive. The Russians instituted strong central control, with administrative details left to the *Länder*. All measures were administered through the agency of German officials known to be favorable to Russian ideas. The Russian Zone included part of the city of Berlin and the entire district surrounding the city; in this area, where destruction had been especially severe, debris had to be carried away, and living conditions were extremely bad. Schools in Berlin, beset by the scarcity of buildings and the extreme shortage of teachers, operated on a basis of three and even four shifts a day.

The Russians decreed that education was solely the responsibility of the state, and must be divorced from any kind of religious interference. They declared that German education had never been democratic, and that it must be made so. The main feature of their reorganization was the old idea of the *Einheitsschule*, which they put into operation by the stroke of a pen, although Germany had been debating the question, without action, for sixty years. The textbook difficulty was a problem in the Russian Zone too; it was overcome temporarily by printing in German those Russian texts which were suitable. Since the facilities of the country districts were inadequate, a policy of consolidation of small schools was adopted, under which many rural children were transported to convenient centers. Dormitories were built for orphans and children from remote areas.

THE ALLIED CONTROL COUNCIL'S DIRECTIVE OF 1947

Sufficient progress had been made in all zones to warrant the Allied Control Council issuing Directive No. 54, which attempted to consolidate the educational situation, to reemphasize the principles involved, and to indicate directions of future advances. Its most important sections were as follows:

1. Care must be taken to ensure equality of educational opportunity for all.
2. The elementary and secondary stages in schools should not overlap or be competitive; one should follow from the other.
3. The democratic way of organizing government and civil life must be stressed in schools.
4. Compulsory attendance to the age of 15 should be aimed at, followed by part-time attendance to 18.
5. Teachers should be given training of university status.
6. There should be free textbooks and free tuition to all, with maintenance grants in needy areas.

Although this was one of the rare instances in which the four members of the Control Council actually reached agreement, the directive was inevitably interpreted in different ways in the West and in the East.

THE NEW REPUBLICS

In May, 1949, the German Federal Republic, consisting of the Western zones, was established. It had a population of 45 million and the capital was located at Bonn. The Russians were not slow in following suit, and in October, 1949, they established in the East the German Democratic Republic, with a population of 15 million and the capital in East Berlin. This really meant a partition of the country, with independent development of educational policies in East and West.

It is clear that education for democracy cannot be effective unless social changes in the community favor democratic ideas. It is impossible to implant democratic points of view in a society which is suspicious of them. The West German republic has made steady progress toward evolving a truly German democracy; the East German republic has followed the concepts of Communist countries.

West Germany has made a phenomenal economic recovery, as a result of American aid; it has brought about a drastic currency reform, and has seen a growing demand for German products. East Germany appears to be in constant economic difficulties. The partition of Germany seems to be an accomplished fact, although hope of reunification remains strong among the Germans. Meanwhile educational developments in the Western and Eastern republics follow separate lines. We shall continue the discussion of education in the German Federal Republic (West Germany).

The Role of the Federal Government in Education

THROUGHOUT German history public education was the responsibility of the many state or city governments. Only during the thirteen years of the Nazi regime was a National Ministry of Education set up to control all education. After the war the Germans reverted to the system of state control which had been provided under the Weimar Republic. The basic law of the German Federal Republic provides that the entire educational system shall be under the supervision of the states. Each of the 10 *Länder* (and West Berlin, which is often referred to as the eleventh *Land*) is responsible for its own cultural and educational programs. Some responsibility is delegated

From *Major Foreign Powers*, 4th edition, by Gwendolen M. Carter and John H. Herz, copyright, 1949, 1952, © 1957, 1962, by Harcourt, Brace & World, Inc., and reproduced with their permission.

in most of the states to subdivisions of governments. Some federal interest, but not control, in education is exercised through the federal Ministry of the Interior.

The federal government plays no part in educational administration or supervision but lays down certain general principles. The basic law includes the following provisions:

1. Every school shall be under the supervision of a state.

2. The right to establish private schools is to be respected, but such schools must not indicate social position or wealth. They are not to differ socially from the public schools, and they must reach the same standard of work as the public schools.

3. Religious instruction is to be part of the normal program of the schools, but no teacher is to be compelled to give it, and parents may withdraw their children from religious instruction if they wish.

The Role of the States in Education

EACH of the *Länder* has enacted a basic educational law or School Code. Bremen and Hamburg, for example, did so in 1949, and West Berlin in 1948 (revised in 1951). Although West Berlin is not a part of the Federal Republic, its procedures are based on the same principles, and there are frequent conferences between educational authorities in West Berlin and those of the *Länder* of the Federal Republic. The cost of supporting schools is shared by the states and the local subdivisions. The proportions contributed vary, but some of the states have allocated as much as 16 percent of their total budgets to education. To this is added the amounts raised by local subdivisions.

There are thus eleven different systems of education in West Germany, with diversity in many respects. The map on page 209 shows the division of the country into the two republics, the subdivision into states, and the isolated position of the western sectors which comprise West Berlin. The Occupation Powers did not succeed in building up a modern democratic system of schools, and the states have reverted to the traditional German patterns existing in the states before the Nazi regime.[1]

The individual states maintain their autonomy jealously, and dif-

[1] Walter Schultze, "Recent Changes in Secondary Schools, Federal Republic of West Germany," *Phi Delta Kappan* (November, 1961), p. 64.

ferences exist in curricula, educational methods, textbooks, and religious background. A Conference of State Ministers of Education,
established in 1948, meets regularly several times a year and maintains a small permanent secretariat at Bonn. At these conferences
discussion takes place on common educational problems such as
reciprocity of teaching certificates. Unanimous decisions of the Ministers are referred to the state legislatures for adoption. Usually the
legislatures accept such recommendations, but the Conference has
no authority to enforce its decisions.

The work of the Conference of Ministers has shown considerable
results. More agreements have been reached by the Ministers and
adopted by the states than was ever achieved during the period of
the Weimar Republic.[2] Among the unanimous agreements may be
listed the following:

1. To open the school year in the spring. (Only Bavaria starts its
school year in the autumn.)

2. To establish uniformity in the length and duration of summer
vacations.

3. To adopt grades of equal value for use in school reports and
certificates.

4. To introduce a foreign language as an elective in the elementary schools.

5. To require that students in the intermediate and secondary
schools begin a foreign language in the fifth year and start a second
language in the seventh year. The choice of languages may vary.

6. To promote uniform principles of spelling.

7. To establish an agreement on the principles of political education to be taught in the schools.

8. To grant mutual recognition to certificates of maturity required
for university entrance.

9. To practice reciprocity between the states on examination
certificates of elementary teachers.

10. To standardize the professional training to be required of
secondary teachers.

The goal of these agreements has been to protect the diversity
in German cultural life that contributes to the richness of German

---

[2] *Education in Germany*, Frankfort on the Main: Hochschule fur Internationale Pädagogische Forschung, 1954, p. 10.

culture, and at the same time achieve enough uniformity in procedures to facilitate transfers from one state to another.

A difficulty has arisen from the fact that West Germany has had to absorb millions of displaced persons, bombed out from their original homes or expelled from former German territories in the East. Some of them are former city dwellers who have had to find new homes in rural districts, and many have located in areas where the predominant religion was different from their own. This has meant that no state is now as religiously homogeneous as it was before the war.[3]

In most of the states there are three levels of administration: (a) the State Ministry of Education and Culture; (b) the Government District level; and (c) the local level, rural or urban. General school policies, curriculum planning, examinations, certification and appointment of teachers are the responsibilities of the state level. Supervision of elementary schools is a responsibility of the local level, and supervision of secondary schools is handled by the Government District. Intermediate and local units receive instructions from the Ministry, and must secure permission to deviate from the prescribed procedures, even in experimental programs.

State administration brings the schools closer to the people than did the National Ministry, and therefore has some democratizing effect. It does, however, permit the perpetuation of local practices which do not lead to the unifying of German culture or to an overall unity in the German school system. In some degree the Conference of State Ministers tends to counterbalance this tendency.

School finance is complicated in Germany, because practices are not uniform among the states. The states, the local subdivisions, and some private organizations (usually in the case of vocational schools) contribute to the support of education in varying proportions. In 1959 the total expenditure on general education was about 5,300 million DM, with an additional 700 million DM spent on vocational schools. Some schools are permitted to charge fees. Usually the state pays teachers' salaries and pensions, and under certain circumstances contributes to the cost of buildings and maintenance. The general practice is for the local districts to erect and maintain buildings. In some cases the state will make grants to private schools

[3] Reller and Morphet, *Comparative Educational Administration*, p. 44; *Education in Germany, op. cit.*, p. 9.

which agree to eliminate tuition charges, to make up for loss in income. No specific taxes are earmarked for schools.

The curricula issued by the Ministry are detailed and prescriptive. Supervision over the academic program is exercised by the state, and the local subdivisions are mainly concerned with matters of physical plant and detailed administration. The states approve lists of textbooks, and the local schools may choose from these. The comprehensive examinations for the secondary schools are prepared at the state level, and the Ministry is represented on the examining committees.

The Role of the Local Community in Education

AS STATED above, the local subdivisions are largely concerned with matters of physical administration, and major academic decisions are left to the state. Because there are no special local school taxes, the people have no direct influence on school decisions. Parent-teacher associations are organized, but they have very little to say about school policies and offer little opportunity for the expression of opinion. The ingrained habit of acceptance of authority keeps the citizens from attempting to exert influence on their own local schools.

The Place of Private Schools

THE BASIC law of the Republic guarantees the right to establish private schools within the framework of laws of the respective states under which they will be organized. These schools are affected by state supervision and regulation, and may under some circumstances receive state subsidies. They are supposed to be operated on an equalitarian principle; that is, if they promote segregation on the basis of economic status, they are not approved. If the children are permitted to satisfy the requirements of the compulsory education law by attendance in a private school, the school must be inspected and approved by state authorities.

In some of the *Länder* there are confessional schools, operated by religious groups. In areas such as Bavaria and the Rhineland, which are predominantly Roman Catholic, there are many Catholic schools. In states that are predominantly Lutheran there are schools operated by this denomination. As has been mentioned, the absorption of millions of refugees has materially changed the religious composition of the states, and the question of confessional or nonsectarian schools is hotly debated in many places.

West Germany learned much from the Occupation, but in general the states have reverted to the traditional patterns developed during the days of the Weimar Republic. The federal government has no constitutional authority over schools, except for the broad guidelines established by the basic law. The eleven states have developed their own school systems, with some minor decentralization to governmental subdivisions in administration. Some overall conformity, but not uniformity, has been achieved through the work of the voluntary Conference of State Ministers of Education and Culture.

Part III

The Schools in Action:
The Operation of
School Systems

10

The Operation
of School Systems

I N PART II we have seen how national systems of education are organized, controlled, and financed. In Part III we turn to a detailed investigation of the schools in action. Each chapter in this Part examines the various levels of a national school system, including preschool, elementary, secondary, vocational, higher, and adult education. Variations in curriculum within the various levels are described. Each chapter also discusses the training, status, and salaries of teachers and concludes with a statement of current problems in the operation of schools.

The Historical Development of School Systems

IN THE discussion of systems of education, we have become accustomed to beginning with the nursery school or kindergarten, and extending the study on up the educational ladder through the elementary, secondary, and higher schools. This logical approach to a comparison of school systems will be followed in Part III. But it is well to keep in mind that this is not the way that school systems actually developed. Universities emerged in an organized form before the preparatory schools that are now listed before them. Early teaching programs on the elementary level were more or less unorganized, and the earliest secondary schools developed to prepare boys for universities already in existence.

The formal organization of elementary, secondary, and university education has now become well established in most countries. There have been reorganizations, but the main outline is fixed. In recent years the greatest developments in many countries have been at the extreme upper and lower ends of the educational ladder, in the areas of kindergartens and nursery schools and of adult education.

The first universities were established about eight hundred years ago. They were communities of scholars, gathered together in a loose association. They had no established physical location or permanent plant—no classrooms or halls, no libraries or laboratories, no offices. The scholars gathered a group of students around themselves and taught in their homes or in hired rooms. At one time the University of Paris, in an argument with the government of the time, voted to move to London. This could easily have been done, since it would have required only the removal of the professors, with their personal belongings, to the latter city.

The courses of lectures, and such organization as existed in the groupings of teachers and students, were not called "university" at all, but "studium." The first use of the term *university* was at Bologna, where it applied to guilds of foreign students, who organized to protect their own interests against those of the professors and the townspeople. These student guilds hired the professors and fined them if they lectured too long or arrived late for class. In spite of the fact that some of these medieval teaching communities were very large (Padua had 35,000 students in the fifteenth century), there was no administrative structure and there were no administrative officials as we know them today.

It was in Paris that the term *university* first came to be applied to the company of masters, rather than to the company of students. The modern university has followed the pattern of Paris rather than that of Bologna. The first universities were either controlled by the Church or were closely related to it; they were primarily concerned with the preparation of the clergy. Before long they were also preparing students for other professions, such as law and medicine, and, of course, from the very beginning they were preparing the brightest students to become teachers of other students. At this time elementary education was carried on in an unorganized fashion in monasteries and in the courts of princes, where bright boys were taught to read and write.

It was the development of the universities that brought about the organization of secondary schools. What was probably the first true secondary school was established at Mantua in 1423. Vittorino da Feltre, whose training had been in medicine, organized the school, after experience in teaching in the court schools of Venice and Padua. He made a careful selection of passages from the classics, chosen for their moral content and influence, and based his curriculum on these. Up to this time the reading of Greek and Latin writers had been frowned upon, because they were considered to be pagan and anti-Christian. The problem of the Renaissance educator was to harmonize the newly rediscovered classical literature with Christian teachings. In his school, Vittorino tried to combine the study of the classics with the chivalric education of the courts and the Christian teaching of the monasteries. He also took a great interest in athletics and physical training and stressed these for his boys.

The aim of the Renaissance school was to educate boys to be Christian gentlemen, who would understand the classical languages and literatures and who would be loyal sons of the Church. This first school, and others like it, soon came to emphasize preparation for university work.

Vittorino's school was a very successful preparatory school. It demonstrated so clearly the place that secondary education could play that it became the model for secondary schools in Europe and for the earlier types of American secondary schools. A French secondary school, the *Collège de Guyenne*, founded in the sixteenth century, reached the height of its influence under the direction of Elie Vinet, between the years 1556 and 1570. Vinet's school offered a ten-year program, for boys between the ages of 6 and 16. It was a rigorous education, made up of recitations, reading, and study of Latin and Greek, with French as a minor supplementary subject. The boys rose at four o'clock in the morning and spent the whole day in supervised study and recitations. A large proportion of its students continued on into the university.

The public schools that were established in England in the fourteenth to sixteenth centuries were originally intended to give free instruction to poor children in order to teach them "the good Christian life and manner." Since they were very successful in preparing boys to pass the entrance examinations for Oxford and Cambridge, they soon became exclusive preparatory schools for the children of the gentry. They became secondary schools in the sense of keeping boys in school until they were ready to enter the university.

The French *lycée* and German *Gymnasium* followed the same pattern of classical curriculum and preparation for university work. In all of the European countries, courses which were later to be considered elementary were added to the secondary schools. Boys entered the secondary schools at the age of 6 or 7 and remained until they were ready for university examinations. When a demand for wider educational opportunities resulted in the foundation of real elementary schools, these were kept entirely separate from the secondary program. Thus it came about that a boy who wished to enter the university had to start his secondary-school training at the beginning of his school course. Parallel systems of education developed, one for the common people, ending at the close of the elementary-school period, and the other for the children of the gentry or a few of the more gifted poor boys, who entered a different type of school. This parallel system of education has persisted in some countries down to the present time.

The "grammar school" of the American colonies was a transplanted English public school. Very early, however, many of these schools were controlled and supported by the colonial or town governments. Rarely did these schools receive endowments, and they were seldom founded by religious or private associations. In curriculum, methods, and philosophy they were nearly identical with the English secondary schools of the period. This type of school was founded in all of the colonies except Georgia and North Carolina.

The grammar schools were most numerous in New England, although only in Massachusetts did any considerable number of them exist. The first one founded in America was the Boston Latin School, which opened in 1635 and has continued to the present time. Since the social and educational traditions which developed in America soon differed from those in Europe, the nature of secondary schools changed. The Latin schools came to be replaced by the academy, which had a much more liberal curriculum.

Even the Latin grammar schools came to broaden their offerings to make some provision for the practical everyday needs of the people. Courses in practical mathematics, especially in navigation and surveying, were added as early as the middle of the eighteenth century. The first academy was opened in Philadelphia in 1751, and included three types of courses, Latin, English, and mathematics. Benjamin Franklin had suggested such a school as early as 1743, and his writings had much influence on its development. This institution was very close in philosophy and curriculum to the *Realschule* in Germany, which arose as a protest against the rigorous and non-functional curriculum of the *Gymnasium*. The academies flourished and became the typical secondary educational institutions in the United States after the Revolution.

The *Realschulen* of Germany started in 1747. Hecker established such a school at Berlin, and included in its curriculum German, French, Latin, writing, drawing, history, geography, geometry, arithmetic, mechanics, architecture, religion, and ethics. Within fifty years these schools had been accepted as a part of the German school system and were established in all of the important cities.

In comparing the development of secondary education in the various countries, it is important to notice how closely each has kept to the original classical and university-preparatory concept, or how widely it has varied from such ideas. The French *lycées* and the classical colleges in Quebec still follow quite closely the original pattern set by Vittorino da Feltre. The same is somewhat true of the English public schools, and the grammar schools in England have not deviated far from the pattern. The American high school and the public high schools of Canada have moved farthest in the opposite direction. The problem of whether a high school should be a school for all the children of all the people, or should be a selective institution which sifts out a few of the best students for further work, has been answered in a variety of ways in different countries.

In studying the educational programs of different countries it soon becomes evident that each does not accept the same definition of the term *secondary education*. In some systems secondary education refers to a certain number of years of work, following an elementary-school course. In the United States it has meant traditionally the ninth to twelfth grades, although it now means, in many places, the seventh to twelfth grades. In England it is now defined as the period of education after the age of "eleven-plus," which means that the elementary stage ends at approximately age 11. In France secondary education was, until after World War II, a completely separate system, which might begin at 5 and continue until university entrance. Thus, as Moehlman has pointed out, some countries operate under a "one-track" plan, while others have a "two-track" system.

The term *elementary school* was first used in England, where it referred to a school organized to give the "elements" of education to the children of the poor. It was designed to give them enough education to enable them to get along in the world, but not enough to make them discontented with their position in society. As democratic ideals developed and spread, and as education became more universal, this term fell into disrepute in England and was discarded. The British now prefer to use the term *primary education*. The British meaning of elementary education has never been current in the United States, and the first level of the public schools has continued to be so designated.

Changes in the Curriculum

IN MANY parts of the world it is generally accepted that the formal education of the great majority of the citizens will end with the completion of the elementary school; frequently the period of compulsory education is the same as the length of the elementary school program. Until recently, the greater proportion of French school children who stayed in school until age 14 spent their last two years in a "higher elementary school" which was not considered to be a part of the secondary school system. Until the end of the nineteenth century the bulk of American children ended their formal education with graduation from the elementary grades. The tremendous growth of the public high school system in the United States since 1901, and the raising of the compulsory-attendance age in most states, has changed this situation completely. But it is important to realize that the idea of the high school as a school for all youth is an exception to the general practice around the world.

Early primary schools in most countries provided only a few months of training for a few years for most of the children. With the general adoption of a system of grades and the passage of compulsory-attendance laws, the elementary school has gradually lengthened. It is generally six to eight years now in most countries. With more time available, the curriculum also has been increased. To the rudiments of the three R's have been added new subjects, such as geography, civics, history, music, art, nature study, physical education, and health.

If elementary school is the only education that the majority of the citizens of a country will receive, the responsibility of the curriculum makers is very great. Within a few years the children must be taught all that they are expected to know and that they can be taught through a school program. This has resulted in heavy subject-matter requirements for young children in many countries. Much of the material covered is very difficult for immature minds and is taught in the hope that it will have some functional value when the children are old enough to make use of it. Much of it is learned in verbalization that enables a child to get through examinations but really lacks meaning to him.

All over the world there has been an increasing interest in child psychology and in the meaning of the learning process. Psychologists have become aware of the principle of maturation and of what "readiness" means in a school. Among other things, readiness means that while some children are ready to learn to read at age 5, others will learn more easily if they wait till they are nearly 7. Proper procedures by the teacher and proper experiences for the child may produce much greater readiness at an earlier age than otherwise. Although these facts are known in most countries, some school systems still insist on teaching all 5-year-olds alike and begin formal reading and arithmetic at an early age.

With the lengthening of the school-life expectancy of the average American pupil to include junior or even senior high school education, curriculum-makers in the United States have been able to make important changes in the grade placement of subject matter. Reading instruction does not begin until the child is psychologically ready for it, and the introduction of formal arithmetic may be delayed until the second or even the third grade. It has been possible to add a great deal more science and social studies to the course of study and to give increased attention to preparation for citizenship. But it is important to realize that this too is an exception to general worldwide practice.

Philosophies of Education

THE ACTUAL practice in any school depends upon the philosophy of education held by the educators and by the people who support the school. American educators have been much interested in the formulation of statements of educational philosophy. Every country has its own philosophy of education, but not every system has given thought to expressing it in words. It is in the operation of the school system, more often than in published statements of policy, that the educational philosophy may be discerned.

The principal aim of the public school system in the United States is preparation for citizenship. This is not the main objective of schools in many other countries. In most western European countries and in many others, the purpose of the school is to achieve high standards of scholarship in the mastery of a specified body of subject matter. In pursuance of this aim, the schools become more and more selective in the upper grades, so that the proportion of the school-age population is much smaller in the secondary grades than it is in American schools. In a comparative study of school systems, it is important to remember that most of the world does not accept the American ideal of preparation for citizenship as the main goal of public education.

This difference in the concept of the purpose of education is also important in the area of higher education. A much greater proportion of young Americans between the ages of 18 and 22 are in colleges and universities than is the same age group in any other country. This situation is due only partly to the high standard of living of the American people and the disinclination of employers to hire immature or half-educated people. It also stems from the belief of the American people that it is a good thing to have as high a proportion of college-trained citizens as possible. Here again the concept of education for citizenship comes strongly into the picture.

There is also the fact that the American university, particularly the publicly supported state university, has a strong sense of responsibility to provide services for the people who pay for it. To the traditional functions of the university, instruction and research, has been added the function of service to the community. This service has found expression in many ways, in general extension and cooperative agricultural extension programs, in the addition of new types of courses to meet the needs expressed in the community, in the development of many services to the local areas within the state.

A great university president has said:

The value of the university has been under discussion since the days of Alfred and Charlemagne and each nation has formed its own answer. Its value to a monarchy is not the same as its worth to a republic. Its value to the all embracing church is not the same as its use to the individual man and woman. The church looks to the university for its defender and apologist; the individual for his own enlightenment and strength. The king looks to the university for agents and advisers; democracy for the antidote to the demagogue and the spoilsman. . . . Rightly or wrongly, sooner or later, the American college must give what the students want. The supply must meet the demand or there will be no demand. No doubt, we professors know better what is good for the student than the student himself; but unless we convince him of that, we must let him have, to a great extent, his own way as to what his studies shall be.[1]

The theory that the university exists only to separate out the comparatively few first-rate minds and to give them a highly specialized education in a narrow range of subject matter is more common in the world than the concept mentioned above. Most countries have very difficult entrance examinations for their universities and screen out all but a few students. Scholarship is the first and most important aim of university training. This point of view is well expressed by Ashby. He says:

Here is the criterion for determining what subject or parts of a subject should be taught by a university. If the subject lends itself to disinterested thinking; if, in brief, it breeds ideas in the mind, then the subject is appropriate for the university. If, on the other hand, it borrows all its principles from an older subject (as journalism does from literature, or salesmanship from psychology, or massage from anatomy and physiology), and it does not lead to generalization, then the subject is not a proper one for a university. Let it be taught somewhere by all means. It is important that there should be opportunities for training in it. But it is a technique, not an exercise for maintaining intellectual health, and the place for a technique is in a technical college. That is why universities will not introduce lectures in journalism, advertising, typewriting and salesmanship. . . . If universities consented to teach these subjects a real public demand would be satisfied. This too, no one denies. But satisfying public demands is not the university's business: it is not a state-subsidized intellectual department store, to satisfy this or that demand for skilled labor. . . . The university must at times give society, as Flexner has said, not what society wants, but what society needs.[2]

So it appears that in different countries the development of university education has varied with the historical and social backgrounds of the people and with the educational beliefs which were dominant. Some universities follow the principle expressed by President Van Hise, of the University of Wisconsin, in 1915: "If a uni-

[1] David Starr Jordan, *The Trend of the American University*, Stanford University Press, Stanford, Calif., 1929, pp. 11–12.

[2] Eric Ashby, *Universities in Australia* (Future of Education Series, No. 5), Australian Council for Educational Research, Melbourne, 1944, pp. 14–15.

versity is to have as its ideal, service on the broadest basis, it cannot escape taking on the function of carrying knowledge to the people." [3]

Other universities feel that they have no responsibility outside of their lecture halls and beyond their full-time students. It is significant that the University of Sydney, where Professor Ashby was teaching when he wrote the statement quoted above, does not engage in any type of university extension. As in so many questions concerning educational philosophy, the right answer is the one which more nearly meets the needs and demands and conforms with the beliefs of the people of that country.

The influence of the philosophy of higher education that is accepted in any nation upon the elementary and secondary education programs of that nation cannot be underestimated. If the educational leaders look upon the university as a training ground for a select few who are to be leaders, the secondary schools are generally restricted to the function of selecting these leaders and preparing them for entrance to the university. If the university is considered a part of the overall educational ladder for a much larger proportion of the population, then the concept of secondary education for all finds greater acceptance. These differences in philosophy also have their effects upon the elementary curriculum of the country and upon its provision of adult-education opportunities for those who are not enrolled in formal school programs.

The Status of Teachers

IN EACH of the countries covered in this Part, consideration is given to the recruitment, training, status, and salaries of teachers. There is a general similarity running through these descriptions, in that all countries face a similar problem of shortage of qualified teachers. The methods which are adopted to meet these problems vary according to national psychology and national economic conditions. In no country are the educational authorities satisfied with the amount of funds available for teachers' salaries, and in no country are the teachers entirely satisfied with prevailing pay schedules. This is true in spite of recent increases in salary levels in many countries. In most countries, the salaries of teachers are roughly comparable to the earnings of semiskilled workers.

[3] Quoted in *Universities in Adult Education*, UNESCO, Paris, 1952, p. 131.

It has been said before that that system of education is best for a particular country which gives to the people of that country what they desire from their schools. This will not be the same for any two countries studied. A system that is good for one country would not fit the needs of another. In any comparative study, it is of value to note what the different nations are doing and, as far as possible, why they are doing the things they do. A study of comparative education should not attempt to show that other nations are wrong because they operate their schools in a manner different from that to which the student is accustomed.

I I

The Operation of Schools
in the United States

EDUCATION in the United States is very complex. It was mentioned in Chapter 3 that the nation is a union of states, each of which has complete control of its own school system. In most of the states, control of education has been delegated to local communities by the state, and there is a wide variety of programs and procedures. This makes it inaccurate to speak of "the American school system" in the same way one might describe "the French school system." This fact has not always been clear to visitors from other countries.

There are, however, certain features common to all the state systems. American education provides a program for all children, beginning at age 6 and continuing to age 16 in some of the states, and to 18 in the remainder. Secondary education for all is a part of the program, and the percentage of the school population which remains in school for 12 years has been constantly rising. About 90 percent of the children between the ages of 5 and 17 are in school, which is a much higher proportion than in any other country. The proportion of young Americans who continue on to a university is also higher than in other parts of the world, and this group has also been increasing.

Historical Background

COMPULSORY education was a comparatively early development in the American states, but universal secondary education has developed upward from the elementary schools as a result of demand from local communities and through the establishment of public high schools by local school districts. Extension by the states of the period of compulsory education from age 14 to 16 or 18 came after the great increase in secondary school attendance.

The educational level of the American people has been consistently higher in each decennial census. The census of 1960 indicated that the median number of years of school completed by persons 25 years of age and over in the continental United States was 10.6 years. This has been accomplished in spite of continued immigration, requiring the assimilation of large numbers of new citizens from areas with lower educational requirements. The figure would be even higher if it were not for the lower level of educational attainments of Negroes in some of the Southern states and of Mexicans in the Southwest.

Expenditures on public education have been constantly rising throughout the nation. Total expenditures for public elementary and secondary education on a per capita basis increased from $4.10 in 1910 to $87.07 in 1960. In the same period the annual expenditures per pupil in average daily attendance increased from $33.23 to $375.42.

The general pattern of education is an eight-year elementary school, followed by a four-year high school. This has been called the 8-4 plan of organization. It is preceded, in many localities, by nursery schools and kindergartens. It is followed by a four-year college and by graduate and professional schools. This traditional pattern, however, has been varied in many different ways. The 6-3-3 plan consists of a six-year elementary school, a three-year junior high school, and a three-year senior high school. Another variation is a 6-6 plan of organization, with a six-year elementary school followed by a six-year secondary school. In higher education the pattern has been varied by the phenomenal growth of two-year junior colleges. Other variations have also been developed in some school programs. Figure 11–1 illustrates the general patterns that are followed.

The tremendous size of the educational undertakings of the American people is indicated in Table 11–1, which shows the enrollments by school levels in both public and private schools. About 12 percent of the total enrollment of elementary pupils is in private schools, and over nine-tenths of this number are in church-connected schools; a slightly lower proportion of the secondary students are registered in private schools. The influence of these independent-school pro-

11-1 Diagram of Education in the United States

YEARS IN SCHOOL					YEARS OF AGE
20					25
19					24
18	Graduate and professional schools			Adult education	23
17					22
16					21
15	Four-year colleges				20
14			Junior colleges	Technical institutes, Community colleges	19
13					18
12			Senior high schools		17
11	Four-year high schools			Six-year or junior-senior high schools	16
10					15
9			Junior high schools		14
8					13
7					12
6					11
5					10
4	Elementary schools				9
3					8
2					7
1					6
				Kindergartens	5
					4
				Nursery schools	3
					2

TABLE 11–1

Enrollment in Public and Nonpublic Education in the United States, 1962–63

	PUBLIC SCHOOLS	NONPUBLIC SCHOOLS	TOTAL
Kindergartens	2,131,473	*	2,131,473
Elementary schools	27,222,573	5,300,000†	32,522,573
Secondary schools	10,863,169	1,200,000†	12,063,169
Colleges and universities	2,596,904	1,609,768	4,206,672
Totals	42,814,119	8,109,768	50,923,887

SOURCE: *Digest of Educational Statistics*, U.S. Office of Education, 1963.
* Kindergarten figures included in elementary total.
† 1961–62 figures.

grams has been considerable. About half of the students in colleges and universities are enrolled in nonpublic institutions.

The philosophy of education that is generally accepted in the United States views education as a preparation for citizenship. In contrast to systems which emphasize academic achievement, allowing each student to advance as far as he has the ability to go and eliminating those who show less capacity for book learning, the

---

Note to Figure 11–1

In interpreting the school-system organization charts in this book, the student should be aware of three limitations inherent in their construction.

In the first place, the charts do not attempt to indicate all the alternative choices open to a student after he has completed one level of education. Where strict lines of progression have existed, as in prewar France or Germany, the location of various types of schools on the chart has been planned to indicate this progression; but where cross-mobility is frequent, no such progression can be assumed. Thus the American student may receive high school training in any of the types of schools indicated in Figure 11–1, and may then go on to a technical institute, a junior college, or a four-year college. On the other hand, in Imperial Germany (see Figure 9–1 on page 194) students entering the *Vorschule* were expected to advance to the *Gymnasium* and ultimately to the university. The reader should rely on the text treatment in each chapter to determine the degree of choice open to the student.

In the second place, the amount of horizontal space allocated to the various schools within a given age level is not intended to indicate the relative numbers of students attending such schools. The United States chart, for example, does not imply that many more students attend four-year high schools than attend senior high schools under the 6-3-3 plan.

A third consideration is that the charts cannot indicate every type of special school. They are intended to show the general or prevailing system.

American system of education tries to provide an educational program that will meet the needs of all citizens and that will keep them in school.

The basic conception of citizenship in a democracy vests every citizen with equal rights and equal responsibilities. Since each will have a vote with as much impact on government as the vote of any other citizen, each must be given as much preparation for intelligent citizenship as society can provide and is willing to pay for. This concept rejects the philosophy that aims to give all children an elementary education but to keep secondary education as a very selective program, restricted to the few who show unusual academic abilities. Rather than send out the majority of the future citizens into the community at the age of 14, with citizenship training incomplete, the American school tries to keep them for several more years, and to stress human relationships and adaptation to society as well as subject matter. This point of view has raised interesting questions of differentiation of school offerings and maintenance of educational standards.

Preschool Education

UNTIL 1933 the only nursery schools organized in the United States were those planned to serve children from homes in the high and the low economic groups. These schools were organized by voluntary agencies or by neighborhood groups. A few charitable organizations maintained nursery schools to care for children from poor homes while their mothers were employed. As a part of the general relief and employment activities of the federal government in 1933, the Federal Emergency Relief Administration authorized the organization of nursery schools. This program was intended to serve the needs of underprivileged children and also to provide employment for qualified teachers. Such schools usually were organized by local school agencies and supported by federal funds. During the first year the program was begun in 37 states, and 2,979 nursery schools enrolled 64,491 children between the ages of 2 and 5. By 1939 there were over 75,000 children enrolled in 3,000 schools.

During World War II it seemed desirable to provide nursery schools in shipyards and industrial plants, in addition to those in existing school-sponsored programs, in order to increase the number of mothers who could work in war industries. These schools frequently provided extended child care for longer periods of the day, as well as nursery school education. By 1945, 51,229 children were enrolled in extended-care centers. In 1946, at the close of the war, federal funds were withdrawn, and the majority of the nursery schools and child-care centers closed. However, the federally sub-sidized nursery schools had stimulated interest in the local commu-nities, and many localities found it possible to establish nursery schools and find local support for them. This development, however, has been very slow, and the proportion of children between the ages of 2 and 5 in school is still very small.

There has been a greater development in kindergarten education, which is usually given to children between the ages of 5 and 6, al-though some kindergartens have admitted 4-year-olds. Since 6 years is the normal age for beginning the first grade in American schools, there has been much interest in providing an educational experi-ence for the 5-year-olds. Both public and private kindergartens have been established.

By 1950 all of the states except one had authorized local school districts to establish public kindergartens and to expend local tax funds for their support, and 29 states had authorized the use of state funds for this purpose. In no state has it been made mandatory for the local districts to establish and operate kindergartens, and usu-ally the school board is required to submit the question to the tax-payers of the school district in a local election to receive authority to operate a kindergarten program.

Kindergartens usually operate on a half-day basis, and frequently on two shifts, morning and afternoon. The program is based on the psychological principle of readiness. Recent studies have indicated that many children should be at least 6 years old before they attempt to learn to read. This does not mean that every 6-year-old is ready to begin formal reading; the indications are that chronological age is an unreliable criterion, and that mental age is a much better basis for educational planning. Some first-grade programs find it necessary to continue the pre-reading methods of the kindergarten for some of the children for several months before beginning formal reading lessons.

But the kindergarten, while it does not teach reading, does place a great deal of emphasis on the preparation of the child for the more formalized work of the first grade. Instead of the busy work and occupations common in former years, the curriculum of the modern kindergarten emphasizes the development of vocabulary and interest in books and stories. Speech training through careful enunciation is an important part of the program, and preparation for later work in numbers is accomplished through counting objects and seeing numbers on calendars and in books. Eye-and-hand co-ordination is developed through finger painting, cutting and pasting activities, drawing, and work with blocks and other objects. Much attention is given to the development of proper health habits, and school lunches and mid-session snacks are carefully planned.

Training for citizenship must begin in the kindergarten. The treatment of each child as an individual is combined with the development of a respect for the rights and individuality of others. Imagination is developed through observation and storytelling, and interest in books is created by keeping the children surrounded by a great many books suited to the age and interests of the child. Educators feel strongly that the kindergarten should be closely integrated with the work of the first two grades of the elementary school, and that a great many advantages would be gained by having all children attend a kindergarten program which was a part of the elementary school organization. Studies tend to show that the child with kindergarten experience makes a quicker and better adjustment to the first grade and possibly makes better progress in later school life.

Elementary Education

THE ELEMENTARY school in the United States is generally considered to include the first six or eight grades of the common-school system, depending upon the organization that has been accepted for the secondary school. It has been called the "grade school" (tracing back to the time when the original ungraded schools were organized into yearly grades) or the "grammar school," not in the sense of the secondary grammar schools in England, but as the school where the basic fundamentals of the three R's and grammar are taught. When the British term "primary school" is used in the United States, it refers to the first two or three grades of the elementary school, which the British call "infants' classes."

Where elementary schools are free and compulsory, enrollment depends upon the number of children at each age level within the country. In the United States over 98 percent of the children between the ages of 6 and 13 are enrolled in school. Increases or decreases in the birth rate are reflected in school enrollments within six years. The lowered birth rates of the thirties were soon accompanied by reduced enrollments; the great increase in births after World War II flooded the elementary grades with additional pupils. Because of the increased life expectancy of the American people, however, the proportion of the total population attending school has decreased. In 1890, 22.5 percent of the total population were enrolled in elementary schools. By 1950, in spite of stricter enforcement of compulsory-education laws, improved educational facilities, and widespread transportation services, only 16.6 percent of the population were in the elementary schools. It is clear that annual birth-rate figures are more reliable than total-population statistics in predicting school enrollments.

Consolidation of small schools has continued throughout the country, and more children are being transported to school at public expense each year. The number of children riding in school buses increased from 1,902,826 in 1929–30 to 13,687,547 in 1961–62. During the same period, the number of one-room schools decreased markedly.

The central theme of the program of the elementary schools is education for American citizenship. The basic skills in the language arts—reading, writing, speaking, and listening—are taught, as well as the mastery of arithmetic that is basic for all citizens. The fundamental habits, ideals, and attitudes, as well as the skills and general knowledge, that every citizen needs are of equal importance. The purpose of the public school thus becomes one of integrating each individual into the life of the community and nation, and of making him a self-controlled and self-directed citizen.

The elementary school has evolved gradually from the traditional school of one hundred years ago to the more complex and progressive school of today. Since education in the United States is based on local autonomy, there is always a great deal of experimentation going on in all parts of the country. Different types of organization and of curriculum are tried out. In spite of the fact that there is no single governmental agency to prescribe for the American school system, there are always more points of likeness than of difference between any two American schools.

The average length of the school year in the United States in 1962 was 179.1 days. The length of school term varies among the states, ranging from an average of 152.5 days in Mississippi to 186.6 days in Illinois. Wide variations exist also in the length of the school day. A common practice is to have school in session from 9:00 to 12:00 in the morning and from 1:00 to 3:30 in the afternoon, Monday through Friday. The school day for the lower grades is often from 30 minutes to an hour shorter.

There is less tendency in the United States than in some other countries to prescribe "timetables" which allocate the number of minutes per day or per week to be spent on each subject. The integration or fusion of subjects into larger areas of instruction makes such a procedure difficult to administer. Activity programs tend to make prescribed time allotments obsolete. The trend has been to increase the amount of time spent on social studies and science, and to decrease the proportion of school time (although not necessarily the number of hours per year, because of the lengthened school terms) devoted to the three R's.

Most schools require some homework to be done by elementary pupils. However, the trend since the beginning of this century has been to reduce or even eliminate the assignment of homework. Studies have shown that there is very little correlation between pupil progress in school and the amount of time spent in home study. There has been a tendency to encourage voluntary homework of a recreational or related type, thus capitalizing on student interests aroused in the schoolroom and stimulating a wise use of leisure time.

Up to the end of the nineteenth century it was generally expected that the bulk of young Americans would end their formal schooling with the completion of the elementary school. Since 1900 the period of compulsory education has been lengthened and the proportion of the school population that continues into the secondary school has increased rapidly. This change in status of elementary education, from a terminal-education program to a stage in a much longer educational experience, has had its effect upon the philosophy, organization, and curriculum of the elementary school. No longer must elementary teachers feel compelled to cram into an eight-year course everything that the student needs to learn from school. It has been possible to shift the emphasis on particular subjects and to defer the introduction of difficult topics until later in the school life of the individual.

Much that was formerly taught in the traditional elementary school is now recognized as being too difficult for the average pupil, and much of it also was started too early in his school life. A great deal of the learning that was achieved under these circumstances was purely verbal and failed to become a functional part of the child's life. The acceptance of the principle of readiness has not been confined to reading alone. Most elementary schools have deferred the introduction of formal arithmetic for a year or two rather than begin it in the first grade. Social studies have been introduced throughout the elementary course, but much of the study of the former separate subjects of geography, history, and civics has been deferred until junior high school years or later.

Because of these changes in educational thinking, the development of the curriculum as a twelve-year program, running continuously from the first grade through the high school, has been generally accepted. This trend may also work to lessen the inclination of teachers to regard themselves as "elementary" or as "secondary" teachers and to make them more aware of what the rest of the school program is trying to accomplish.

Secondary Education

BECAUSE of the decentralization of American education, it is difficult to show that a "system" of secondary education exists in the United States. The traditional four-year high school enrolls about 18 percent of all the secondary pupils, the divided junior-senior high school about 50 percent, and most of the remainder are in undivided junior-senior six-year schools. The educational philosophy of the local school district determines the type of organization that has been selected. Approximately 90 percent of all 14- to 17-year-olds are enrolled in some type of secondary school.

The earliest secondary schools in the United States were established to prepare boys and girls for college. The course of study was narrow and classical and usually offered no choice of subjects. Preparation for life or for citizenship was a by-product and not an avowed purpose of the school. Less than 10 percent of the 14- to 18-year-old group were enrolled, and this was usually a highly select minority. They were either extremely bright children or the children of families in the higher economic levels.

Some time after the beginning of the twentieth century the attitude toward secondary education began to change radically. This change was in part due to the fact that public high schools were being established everywhere and that no tuition was charged. Whereas the children of the upper and upper-middle classes had attended private academies that charged fees, all the children were now able to attend a free, public high school. The growth of the high school movement was phenomenal. In the state of Oregon the proportion of 14- to 18-year-olds enrolled in school increased over 2,000 percent between 1900 and 1940, and the situation in other states was similar. As the new free public high schools developed, many of the older private secondary schools closed.

In 1900, 500,000 students attended American secondary schools, or less than 0.7 percent of a total population of 76 million. By 1940, six and one-half million students were enrolled, or almost 5 percent of the 132 million population. It has been estimated that this means that for forty years the American people built at the rate of three new high schools per day for five days a week during the school year, in order to provide for an increase of 900 new students per day. Today high school attendance is almost universal; in California, for example, 89.7 percent of the eligible students were enrolled in school in 1960.

Present-day American thought conceives of secondary education as a program concerned with all adolescent youth. Secondary education is understood to encompass the period of life beginning with the onset of adolescence and continuing through the post-adolescent period—an age range from about 12 to 20. Educationally, this means from the beginning of the seventh grade through the junior college or through the sophomore year in the university. Thus junior colleges are frequently discussed as essentially secondary in nature, although they cover the first two years of university work.

THE HIGH SCHOOL

High schools are organized on a departmental plan, in which each teacher handles one subject, or several related subjects, and meets five or six different classes each day. The class day is divided into periods of 45 to 60 minutes. A typical school day begins at 8:30 A.M. and closes at 3:30 P.M. Most schools provide a daily activity period, during which school clubs and activity groups meet. The usual activity period is 35 minutes long. There seems to be a tendency to shorten the lunch period and to close the school day at an earlier hour. There is also a definite trend toward lengthening the class periods from 45 to 55 or 60 minutes.

Because high schools are organized by local school districts, they are widely distributed throughout the country, even in the smallest towns. There are also union high schools that provide for high school pupils from several rural elementary districts. Because high school opportunities are made available to all pupils and usually at a convenient distance from their homes, the typical high school in the United States is small. In 1938 the median high school enrolled 138 pupils, and 40 percent of the high schools had enrollments of fewer than 100 pupils. There has been a tendency to close very small high schools and consolidate them into larger units. Consolidated or union high schools are larger on the average than the traditional four-year type. Most of the reorganized high school systems, that is, the combined six-year schools or those divided into junior and senior high schools, are found in cities and towns. American high schools very seldom provide boarding facilities, as is common in European secondary schools.

Although the proportion of 14- to 17-year-olds who continue in secondary school is higher than in any other country, administrators of secondary schools have been concerned with the "holding power" of the high school, the ability of the secondary school to adapt its offerings to the needs of a heterogeneous student group and to retain as many as possible until the end of the twelfth grade. Table 11-2 shows the number of students remaining in school, per 1,000

TABLE 11-2

Holding Power of Secondary Schools in the United States

GRADE	NUMBER RETAINED IN SCHOOLS	YEAR ENROLLED
5	1,000	1954-55
6	980	1955-56
7	979	1956-57
8	948	1957-58
9	919	1958-59
10	855	1959-60
11	764	1960-61
12	684	1961-62
Graduated	636	1962
Entered college	336	1962

SOURCE: *Digest of Educational Statistics*, U.S. Office of Education, 1963, p. 12.

fifth-graders. With the country facing problems of unemployment, the future of the high school "dropout" has received increasing attention. The question arose as to whether the traditional American high school was meeting the needs of nonacademic pupils and preparing them adequately for employment. This problem has been complicated by the increasing attention given to academic subjects and rising standards of achievement since the time of Sputnik.

The high school admits any pupil who has completed the elementary grades, without the entrance examinations required in many countries. Promotion is by individual subject; the classroom teacher is responsible for giving a mark in the subject and determining promotion or failure in the class. There are no school-wide examinations to determine promotion or graduation from the school.

Secondary School Curricula

The average high school student takes four or five subjects each year, and usually physical education or health in addition. Subjects are usually listed as "constants" or "solids," which are required of all students, and "electives," which are chosen by the individual student. The list of required subjects varies from state to state and from school to school, but it usually includes English and at least two years of social studies. Sometimes mathematics, science, or foreign languages are added to the list.

With the development of the elective system in the early years of the twentieth century, it became necessary to define the amount of work that would be required in one subject in comparison with others. The Carnegie Foundation for the Advancement of Teaching suggested a definition in 1906 which has been generally accepted. This has come to be called the "Carnegie unit," and is defined as the work represented in a class meeting for 45 minutes five times a week throughout the academic year of the secondary school. Requirements for graduation from a high school and for entrance to a university are usually expressed in Carnegie units. The general practice is to require fifteen or sixteen units for graduation, without any additional "leaving" examinations. Some universities require entrance examinations, and many use the College Entrance Examination Board, which was established in 1899 to administer entrance examinations for certain Eastern colleges, largely private schools.

The majority of the colleges and universities in the country use specified patterns of units of work as their basis for admission. They accept a transcript of work done from any accredited high school. Accreditation of high schools is accomplished in a number of ways. The most important is through regional associations of colleges and secondary schools, which set standards for training of teachers, library and laboratory facilities, buildings and equipment, and academic achievement. In some states the state department of education acts as an accrediting agency, listing the standard high schools within the state. State universities also act as accrediting agencies in some instances. The usual practice is for the universities in one state to accept the standardization or accreditation lists of another state or of a regional association in another part of the country. Since 1932 more than 40 percent of the colleges and universities of the country have liberalized their entrance requirements.

Not only has secondary education shown a tremendous growth in number of schools and enrollments (with a corresponding decline in student mortality during the high school years), but there has been a remarkable horizontal expansion in subject-matter offerings. The number of elective courses in the larger high schools has increased greatly. In some of the larger cities, a number of types of specialized secondary schools have developed. Technical high schools, commercial high schools, home economics high schools, agricultural schools, and other types of specialized secondary schools have been established. To a much greater extent the so-called "comprehensive" high school (called a "multilateral" or "omnibus" or "composite" high school in some other countries) has grown up. There has also been a marked tendency for the specialized high schools to become increasingly comprehensive in nature.

The comprehensive high school is a distinctive feature of American secondary education. It includes in its offerings all types of special education, combined in the same school. All students take the required core courses, such as English, social studies, science, and mathematics; as electives they choose the courses required to meet the needs of commercial, technical, agricultural, or home economics training. There has been a growing belief that it advances the democratic ideal to include all secondary students in the same high schools. This approach has gone far to solve the problem of parity of esteem for the various courses, which is of concern to secondary educators in England.

The tendency of the traditional high school to compartmentalize subject matter is gradually being modified. Most of the high schools offer a social studies course, which combines the offerings formerly given as separate courses in American and world history, American government, geography, and social and economic problems. General mathematics courses, combining arithmetic, algebra, geometry, consumer mathematics, and possibly the elements of trigonometry, have been established. General science, combining biological and physical sciences, is the usual ninth-grade science course. Some experimenting with advanced general science courses, combining physics and chemistry, has begun.

Student Activities

Since the major purpose of the high school is preparation for citizenship in a democracy, secondary schools have developed a wide variety of activities that provide opportunities to practice the procedures and functions of a citizen. Student government is highly developed, and student organizations elect their own officers and handle many of their own affairs. Student-body officers wield as much influence in a high school as do the prefects in an English secondary school, but they are elected by the students themselves instead of being appointed by the principal or faculty.

Student activities have been a part of secondary schools from the earliest times. Vittorino da Feltre's school at Mantua stressed sports and games. The earliest English public schools developed extensive sports programs, and a prefect form of student government was outlined in the statutes of Westminster College in 1383. Golf, cricket, rowing, and football were mentioned as activities in the English public schools in the eighteenth century, and a student publication began at Eton in 1786. Social clubs, natural history societies, and musical organizations appeared in the nineteenth century. The earliest American secondary schools showed a similar development of student activities.

The most common types of secondary school activities in the United States are student-government organizations, athletic activities, musical, dramatic, debating, and special-interest clubs (such as science clubs, photography clubs, and others), student publications, honor societies, service clubs, and homeroom organizations. From two-thirds to three-fourths of the teachers in any high school have assignments as faculty advisers to student organizations and activities. Physical education, music, English, science, and social studies teachers usually have the heaviest assignments to extracurricular loads. These are usually considered by the administration in making out the teachers' schedules, and in the selection of new teachers, principals and superintendents are much interested in an applicant's interest and abilities in extracurricular fields.

Student activities are financed from membership fees paid to an overall student organization, club dues, receipts from athletic contests, plays, concerts and operettas, and other money-raising activities. In some rare instances the board of education provides part of the funds to support athletic and other activities. Student managers and treasurers are responsible for funds, but there is a growing tendency to provide a central office or "bank" for the deposit and payment of funds, with student officers depositing all funds and drawing on them. Most schools provide for a regular audit of student funds, whether in a central treasury or in separate accounts.

There has been much discussion of the term "extracurricular." Many feel that all activities carried on under the direction of the school are part of the curriculum and equally important in the educational development of the students. These authorities prefer a term like "co-curricular activities." There is no essential difference between the basic objectives of a program of guided student activities and the objectives of the regular class program, although the activity program places greater emphasis on the aspects of health, wise use of leisure time, ethical character, and the development of citizenship.

THE JUNIOR HIGH SCHOOL

The 8-4 plan had been accepted as the desirable division of elementary and secondary schooling in most of the states by 1890. This arrangement was criticized by President Eliot of Harvard, who proposed a shortening of the elementary period. Several well-known committees studying secondary education recommended beginning secondary studies in the seventh grade. The first formally organized junior high schools were established in Columbus, Ohio, in 1909, and in Berkeley, California, in 1910.

The junior high school is planned as an institution to provide a suitable educational program for youth in early adolescence, that is, for the group between the ages of 12 and 14. It usually includes the seventh, eighth, and ninth grades and is housed in a separate building under its own administration. However, all writers on the junior high school emphasize that it should be regarded as an instructional program carrying out a particular educational and psychological point of view, rather than a special arrangement of grades or a matter of housing or of administrative practices.

The curriculum of the typical junior high school is more liberal and extensive than that of the former seventh and eighth grades in the elementary school or than that of the ninth grade in the four-year high school. Fusion courses are extensively used; the most common of these are combinations of English and social studies, social studies and science, or English, social studies, and science. These combined courses are taught in longer periods, usually by the same teacher. There has also been some tendency to use the large-unit method of teaching, correlating subjects such as science, social studies, and English with art, music, home economics, and industrial arts.

Subjects that are still taught as separate courses are usually more generalized than formerly. English, or language arts, is a combination of literature, grammar, writing, spelling, and speech. Social studies includes history, geography, government, social problems, citizenship training, and orientation. General science, which covers units from the earth sciences, biology, physical sciences, and astronomy, is an almost universal junior high school offering. Mathematics is usually taught as arithmetic in the seventh and eighth grades, and as general mathematics in the ninth. Since many students will not be required to take mathematics in senior high school, some consumer mathematics is included in this terminal course. General shop courses, which include woodworking, crafts, metalwork, and practical applications of science, have become usual. A general homemaking course combines work formerly taught in separate classes in foods and clothing.

Authorities in the field of junior high school education have listed a number of specific functions for this level of education. Among those most frequently mentioned are: (a) exploration of the interests, abilities, and aptitudes of pupils; (b) opportunity for pupils to explore the major fields of learning, and thus to make more intelligent selection of elective courses in the senior high school; (c) integration of learning experiences; (d) educational and vocational guidance; (e) improved articulation of elementary with secondary education; (f) individualization of instruction; and (g) socialization.

Some junior high schools provide a course of study which is common for all students throughout the three grades, but most offer electives in the ninth grade. Mathematics, general science, foreign language, art, music, homemaking, and general shop are frequently ninth-grade electives. Most schools require English and social studies throughout the three years.

Teaching procedures are usually adapted to individualized instruction practices. There have been widespread experiments in such practices as long-unit assignments, contract and project methods, maximum and minimum assignments, the use of a variety of textbooks for different levels of ability, and a wide use of library materials. Courses of study frequently suggest the minimum content of a course and permit wide freedom to teachers in adding enrichment materials and experiences.

Extracurricular activities are very important in the junior high school. These not only help in the exploratory functions of the school, but they offer opportunities for leadership and citizenship training that would be deferred if these pupils were submerged in a four-year or six-year high school, where the upperclassmen have an opportunity to monopolize the positions of leadership.

THE JUNIOR COLLEGE

As has been mentioned previously, there has been some difference of opinion as to whether the junior college should be classified with secondary or with higher education. Insofar as the junior college offers the first two years of university work, on a basis equivalent to work done in the four-year colleges and universities, it is definitely a higher educational institution. However, many junior colleges have been organized as an upward extension of the high school and have been administered as a part of the local school system. Much of the philosophy and practice of the American junior college would justify including it as a part of the secondary school system. The thirteenth and fourteenth grades, included in the junior college in the United States, are more directly comparable with the last years of a German *Gymnasium* or a French *lycée* than with the first years of a European university.

The junior college movement developed rapidly in the twenties, and by 1930 there were public junior colleges in 29 states. Private junior colleges had been in existence for a longer period, and have continued to play an important role. By 1960, 199 private junior colleges enrolled 54,986 students, and 310 public junior colleges reported an enrollment of 348,538 students.

The state of California has assumed the lead in this movement and the universities of that state have encouraged its development in view of the increased enrollments and crowded conditions on their campuses. During the depression of the thirties, enrollments in junior colleges increased because many students could not afford to go away from home to attend college. Students who did not plan to complete a full four-year course, or who could not finance a college education away from home, took advantage of the opportunities offered in local junior colleges.

The terminal function of the junior college has become very important. Since so many students do not intend to transfer to another institution, courses have been modified and liberalized to meet their needs. Many vocational courses of a semiprofessional or highly skilled nature have been developed. The junior colleges have found that they also have an adult education function to perform and have enrolled many part-time students in evening classes, generally of a terminal type. The function of preparing students to transfer into the junior year of a four-year institution has not been neglected, and studies have shown that junior college transfers have done acceptable work in the major institutions. Public junior colleges tend to stress the vocational and terminal types of courses more than the smaller private colleges. The development of terminal, vocational, and adult education classes has led many of the colleges to accept a broader responsibility for the post-high school needs of the locality they serve, and some of them have taken the name of "community college."

Vocational Education

A VERY large proportion of the program described as vocational or technical education in other countries is a part of the regular high school course in the United States. There are extensive vocational programs included in the secondary courses of the public schools, there are vocational classes in the junior colleges, and there are also public or private trade schools that specialize in technical work.

Around 1850 public interest in education centered on two aspects of the program: free public schools for all children, and technical training for farmers and workers. This agitation had its effect on the passage of the Morrill Act in 1862, which provided for federal subsidy for land-grant colleges of agriculture and mechanic arts. This development provided a high standard of technical education on the college level, but the interest in better programs for younger students continued. Some of the public schools provided technical courses, and some specialized high schools were established in the larger cities. Corporations and large industrial plants began to operate their own training schools, and privately organized technical institutes began training programs. The privately owned "business college" that gave short, intensive courses in typewriting, stenography, and bookkeeeping became a familiar phenomenon in American towns and cities. However, it was not until the passage of the Smith-Hughes Act in 1917 that a more comprehensive program was evolved.

The Smith-Hughes Act provided federal funds to match state and local appropriations for the support of high school courses in agriculture, home economics, and trades and industries. In the beginning funds were available to pay approximately half of the salary of a vocational teacher in any one of these fields, leaving only half of the salary cost to be paid by the local school district. This greatly stimulated the establishment of vocational education departments in high schools in all the states. State departments of education, or separate divisions of vocational education, allocated the funds and standardized and supervised the vocational programs throughout a state. These departments exercised more control over local educational programs in vocational fields than the state attempted in any other part of the curriculum. The federal government, which legally had no control over education, entered into contractual relations with the states to provide grants-in-aid, and indirectly set up controls by demanding that certain federal standards be met by all.

Programs subsidized by the Smith-Hughes Act became very popular and spread widely. Demands for funds increased, and Congress from time to time—by the George-Reed Act (1929), the George-Elzey Act (1934), the George-Dean Act (1936), and the George-Barden Act (1946)—increased the federal appropriations and also added to the fields covered in the original law. To the three original vocational areas was added that of distributive occupations. Table 11–3 shows the increase in enrollments in federally aided vocational classes throughout the country. In 1963, 4,286,000 were enrolled in federally aided vocational classes. The federal government provided $51,438,000 to aid vocational education, and the states and local school districts expended an additional $232,510,000.

These vocational courses became a part of the regular curriculum

TABLE 11-3
Enrollment in Federally Aided Vocational Classes
in the United States

YEAR	AGRI-CULTURE	HOME ECONOMICS	TRADES AND INDUSTRIES	DISTRIBUTIVE OCCUPATIONS	TOTAL*
1930	235,143	220,248	592,275		1,047,676
1940	596,033	871,891	804,515	156,615	2,429,054
1950	764,975	1,430,366	804,602	364,670	3,364,623
1960	796,237	1,588,109	938,490	303,784	3,768,149
1963	847,000	1,803,000	1,056,000	339,000	4,286,000

SOURCE: *Digest of Educational Statistics*, 1963, p. 19.
* Totals include enrollments in practical nursing, which began in 1956, and in technical education, which began in 1958.

of the high school and were selected as elective subjects by interested students. The principle of "learning by doing" became central in all of these programs. Vocational agriculture students were required to have practical projects, which might be productive programs on their fathers' farms, or individual ownership projects, which were carried on as part of the in-school course. Thus a boy might own and be responsible for a cow and calf, or a flock of chickens, or an acre of potatoes. Careful accounting of time, expense, and income was required, and the project was as important in the overall program as the theoretical class work in the school. Subjects selected in high school, in addition to the required core, were usually related to the student's vocational objectives.

Home economics education has been assisted by several federal laws. In the land-grant colleges and the federal cooperative extension service it is made available to college girls and to adult women. Through the Smith-Hughes Act a high quality vocational home economics program is given to high school girls. A large proportion of the high schools in the United States offer home economics, although they do not all qualify for federal subsidy. Many high schools require at least one year of homemaking for all girls, often in the junior high school grades, but in others all of the courses are elective.

Trades and industries, or vocational-industrial, education is intended to train workers for industrial vocations. American industry has been increasingly reluctant to employ boys and girls under 18 years of age. This fact has accompanied, but has not necessarily caused, the extended period of compulsory education. Employers feel that it is much easier to train an 18-year-old worker than one several years younger, and they prefer to have the boys and girls stay in school and continue their general education. Industrial education is becoming pre-vocational in type, teaching general shop subjects and related science and mathematics and leaving detailed operations to be taught on the job.

Many of the earlier forms of vocational education began in the ninth grade, but the trend has been to delay the beginning of regular vocational courses, particularly in trades and industries, until grades 11 and 12. More recently there has been some tendency to place specialized vocational programs in grades 12 and 13, or in grades 13 and 14. This puts these courses in the junior college years, or, as in the state of New York, in post-high school programs called technical institutes. There has been a growing acceptance of the idea of continuing general education for all through the regular high school years, and of delaying the introduction of technical courses until at least age 17. Most of the American states have laws which prohibit the employment of children under the age of 16, so that preparation of younger children to take jobs (as in Australia, where many go to work at 14) has not been a problem in America.

Vocational educators in the United States seem to accept the following principles as basic to any program of training for occupations: (a) since each individual is primarily a citizen, it is desirable to continue his general education while vocational training is going on; (b) training in vocational skills can best be given in practical, on-the-job situations; and (c) because of constant changes and improvements in industry and technology, retraining is often necessary.

Apprenticeship training has dropped in importance in the country in the last fifty years. Some of the trade unions have not encouraged the training of new workers in the skilled trades. Federal and state governments have developed a system of cooperative apprenticeship which has been operating successfully in most of the states. Apprenticeship councils, on which the local trade unions, the employers, and public school officials are represented, plan the courses, approve the teachers and employers with whom apprentices are placed, approve part-time courses in related subjects in school and plans for supervision of the on-the-job training, and determine the amount of credit in apprenticeship hours to be given each student.

Distributive education, which is much broader than just "retail selling," covers pre-service training for those who plan to enter the fields of marketing and merchandising. Some 5 million people are engaged in occupations which might be listed under the heading of "selling." The program operates like the industrial education courses; related subjects and general education are taken in the high school, and the boys and girls are placed in cooperative programs in business so that they have practical experience on the job.

There has been a development, in recent years, of area or regional vocational schools. These are planned to serve a larger area than the average school district and may be supported by a group of counties or by the state. These schools maintain flexible programs to serve the varied types of students who attend: day classes for full-time students, evening classes for employed workers, part-time day classes, and full-time classes in slack seasons for employed people. These programs may include courses in English, mathematics, and science and social studies as related to vocations. They may cover the last two years of high school or may be set up on a post-high school basis.

Much preparation for semiprofessional and highly skilled occupations is carried on in the colleges and universities, in courses of less than four years. (Professional education is discussed in this chapter under university education.) Junior colleges have been playing a part in the general program of post-high school, semiprofessional education, and trade training.

The picture of vocational education in the United States is not complete when the activities of the federal government, states, and local school districts have been listed. Private trade schools and institutions have done excellent work. Many industrial plants operate their own training courses and require all new employees to go through a training period. Some of these courses are short on-the-job courses, some are pre-induction training, but others, like the Ford Training School in Detroit, are operated very much like the public vocational schools.

There has grown up in the United States, as in many other countries, a tendency to treat academic education and vocational education as entirely different programs. The division between the two areas has been accentuated by the fact that the federal government subsidizes certain subjects in the high school curriculum and no others. On the other hand, much has been written on the interdependence of general and vocational education. Many authorities seek to show that education is an organic whole and cannot be divided into compartments. Much of the difficulty seems to arise from the definition of vocational education. For a prospective teacher of Latin, the study of the classics may be as vocational as blacksmithing is to a prospective metalworker. The most hopeful sign seems to be that in the comprehensive high schools, in spite of federal subsidies, there is a disinclination to segregate "vocational" students from "college preparatory" students.

University Education

HARVARD College was established in 1636, with the principal purpose of providing a literate ministry for colonial churches. It was a small institution, enrolling only 20 students in 1642 and 60 in 1660. It soon became more than a theological training school and established itself as a liberal arts college. The next institution of higher learning established in the American colonies was the College of William and Mary, which opened in 1693 at Williamsburg, Virginia. Other colleges were founded in the next century, but all of them remained small schools for long periods. Students entered at about the age of 14 and remained until they were 18, and the curriculum, while rigidly academic and classical, was by modern standards largely secondary in nature. The young students were governed by very strict regulations.

Private colleges and universities were established in the various states, usually by charter granted by the legislature, and were incorporated as nonprofit, charitable institutions. Since 1850 most of the new institutions have been chartered by state education departments or under the general laws of incorporation. Most of the private institutions began as colleges which offered only liberal arts instruction, and many of them have retained this character. Others added professional and graduate courses and schools, and so became universities.

The first state university was the University of Virginia, founded in 1819. Other states followed this example, and today every state includes a state-supported university in its public school system.

The Morrill Act, in 1862, provided grants of public lands to support in the states colleges of agricultural and mechanic arts. From time to time Congress has increased its subsidies for these schools, which are called the "land-grant colleges." Some of the states designated the state university as the land-grant college; others established separate institutions.

State universities derive a large part of their support from legislative appropriations; the proportion varies in the different states, but it is generally larger in the Western states. Some state universities, like the independent institutions, have large endowment funds which provide a substantial portion of their support. Other sources of income are student fees, gifts, and endowments. In all parts of the country, state normal schools and state teachers colleges are supported almost entirely from state funds.

The states exercise a good deal of control over all institutions of higher learning, public and private. State universities in the early days were given charters which made them fairly independent of state government; in recent years the trend has been toward increasing control by the executive branch of the state. This has accompanied the great increase in enrollments, which has called for increased state appropriations. Private institutions also feel a measure of state control. They must meet certain requirements in order to obtain a charter which permits them to issue degrees; they must meet state standards if they train students to become teachers or for some other occupations. In 22 states the state government exercises some supervision over an independent institution after issuing a charter.

According to the Office of Education, there were 2,100 institutions of higher education in the United States in 1962–63; 743 of these were publicly controlled, and 1,357 were private or church-connected institutions. The 1962 enrollment was 4,206,672, and the colleges and universities employed 334,000 staff members. The growth of university enrollments is indicated in Table 11–4. The decrease in 1953 enrollment compared to the 1949–50 peak reflects the departure of the veteran students who crowded the colleges after World War II.

There are many types of higher educational institutions in the country. The liberal arts college, which was the first type established, is still flourishing. Most of these are church-connected or independent institutions. There are independent universities which offer

TABLE 11–4

Enrollment in Higher Education in the United States

YEAR	ENROLLMENT	YEAR	ENROLLMENT
1889–90	156,756	1943–44	1,155,272
1899–1900	237,592	1945–46	1,676,851
1909–10	355,213	1949–50	2,659,021
1919–20	597,880	1953–54	2,510,968
1929–30	1,100,787	1955–56	2,839,000
1939–40	1,494,203	1960–61	3,610,000
1941–42	1,403,990	1962–63	4,206,672

SOURCES : John R. Morton, *University Extension in the United States*, Tuscaloosa: University of Alabama Press, 1953, p. 7 (for years 1889 to 1950); *Statistical Abstract of the United States, 1962*, p. 132 (for years 1953 to 1961); *School Life*, October, 1963, p. 27 (for 1962–63).

a wide variety of academic and professional work. The state universities have been growing in size and influence, and offer many types of educational programs. The land-grant colleges specialize in professional work in agriculture, engineering, home economics, forestry, and similar fields. Beginning as two-year normal schools, then developing into three- and four-year colleges of education, the teacher-training institutions now exist as separate colleges in every state. Many of them now grant bachelor's degrees, and some offer a great deal of graduate work. Municipal colleges and universities, locally financed and controlled, offer both day and night courses in academic and professional fields. The locally controlled junior colleges have been discussed above.

In general, higher education in the United States may be divided into two broad fields, liberal arts and professional. Each of these fields may be further subdivided into undergraduate and graduate levels. The liberal arts program, on the undergraduate level, may be a two-year junior college course (which may offer a degree of associate in arts or science), or a four-year course leading to a degree of bachelor of arts or bachelor of science. The four-year course is usually subdivided into a lower division (which may be called the junior college), consisting of the two first years, and an upper division, which is the last two years. The first two years continue the general education program, and usually specialization or choice of a major field is deferred until the beginning of the third year.

It has become common for the college program to be divided into broad fields, such as languages and literature, the social sciences, the sciences and mathematics, and the fine arts. Many colleges require all freshman and sophomore students to take one or two full-year courses in each of three fields. Certain courses, such as English or history, may be required of all, with some election permitted in the other fields. This plan has been developed in the hope that too early specialization may be avoided, and that each student will get some acquaintance with the major fields of learning, followed in the upper division by a certain amount of mastery of one major field. The program attempts to attain some breadth through the lower-division requirements, and some depth in the upper division, without sacrificing either.

Professional education in fields such as agriculture, dentistry, law, engineering, medicine, pharmacy, teaching, and theology is pursued in professional schools which may be part of a university or may be separate institutions which confine their instruction to a single profession. Often two, three, or four years of pre-professional liberal arts education is required before admission to a professional school. Three to five years of specialized training leads to professional degrees, such as doctor of medicine, bachelor of laws, or bachelor of engineering.

Graduate work requires the completion of the course for a bachelor's degree as a prerequisite. In the liberal arts fields, a minimum of one year of graduate study, and usually the submission of a written thesis, may lead to a degree of master of arts or science. In the professional fields a variety of master's degree programs are also provided, such as master of education or master of engineering. The doctor's degree may be earned in either a liberal arts or a professional field, usually after a minimum of two years of graduate study following the attainment of the master's degree and by the preparation of a doctoral dissertation.

Higher educational institutions usually are governed by a board of regents or board of trustees. In the case of state institutions the members of these boards are appointed by the governor or elected by the people. In some states interesting modifications of the plan have been adopted by placing control of all state-supported higher education under a single board. Private and independent institutions may be controlled by self-perpetuating boards or by the religious denomination which maintains the schools.

The executive head of a college or university is usually called the president. The various colleges or schools which make up a university are headed by deans. Within a school or college there may be departments according to subject-matter fields, each of which may be headed by a professor who is designated as department head or chairman. Other members of the faculty hold academic ranks, such as instructor, assistant professor, associate professor, and professor. Graduate students who give some part-time service may be designated as graduate assistants or fellows.

American universities conceive of their functions as being instruction, research, and service. In the case of the state institutions the responsibility of service to the state has been taken very seriously. Summer sessions, which started largely as an extension activity, have become a distinctive feature of higher education. Hundreds of thousands of students, young and old, attend university and college summer sessions for periods of four to ten weeks during the summer vacations. The usual summer-session program runs for six or eight weeks. A large proportion of the summer-session students are teachers who are working for advanced degrees or who are securing in-service training to keep them up to date in methods and materials.

Adult Education

THE EARLIEST form of educational program for adults was the public lecture. In the early years of the last century a variety of lecture programs developed, under the auspices of church organizations, of historical and philosophical societies, or of mechanics' institutes. These finally found their accepted form in the lyceum movement, which began in 1826. From that date until the outbreak of the Civil War the lyceums spread all over the country, and a national organization was formed to promote them. At one time over 3,000 local groups held weekly meetings, in which lectures, debates, and general discussions were featured.

From the lyceum developed the Chautauqua Institution. Starting from a summer camp at Chautauqua, New York, the institution developed into a nation-wide system of lectures, discussion groups and seminars, correspondence courses, directed home-reading courses, classes in college subjects, concerts, entertainments, and exhibitions. The annual Chautauqua program, held in a tent in the city park during the summer months, with lecturers and musical entertainers traveling on a circuit from one town to another, became a familiar part of the life of American cities and towns. These programs began to disappear after World War I.

As early as 1892 the University of Chicago started a program of university lectures for adults, and other large universities followed the same pattern, based largely on British experience. After many vicissitudes, the university extension movement became firmly established and has made a significant contribution to adult education in the country.

Public school systems have increased their services to adults in recent years. In California, which has one of the most extensive programs, about one-tenth of the people of the state take part in some type of adult education program sponsored by the local school system.

It is very difficult to ascertain the total number of adults who take part in some form of adult education activity in the United States. This is partly due to the fact that there is no provision for central collection and publication of statistics of the various programs, and only estimates are available. However, surveys have indicated that between 30 and 40 million adults participate in some type of continuing education. Paul Essert has developed, for the year 1950, a compilation of available statistics and estimates to show the magnitude of the program in the United States in that year: [1]

Cooperative agricultural and home economics extension	7,000,000
Commercial, college, and school radio and television	6,000,000
Public school adult education programs	3,000,000
University and college extension services	500,000
Private correspondence schools	1,000,000
Armed Forces educational program	250,000
Library adult education programs	1,500,000
Others	10,000,000
Total	29,250,000

Under the classification "Others" Essert lists such programs as alumni education, parent education, prison education, lyceums and chautauquas, leadership-training courses, vocational rehabilitation,

[1] Paul L. Essert, *Creative Leadership in Adult Education* (copyright, 1951, by Prentice-Hall, Inc., New York), p. 37. Reprinted by permission of the publisher.

programs of federal, state, and local governments, vocational education programs for adults, adult-guidance services, workers' education, community councils, citizenship classes for foreign-born, men's and women's clubs, religious groups, museum programs, settlements, and corporations. It must be noted that much of the educational activity carried on in England under the heading of "Further Education" is included in American high school programs, and that only a portion of the English program would be reported as adult education in the United States.

After the close of World War II there was a great expansion of adult education in the country. This came about partly as a result of the veterans' benefits under the various "G.I. Bills of Rights," which provided educational opportunities for former service men and women. Many of these used their rights to receive on-the-job training or to attend a college or university full time. Others took advantage of part-time programs also subsidized by government funds. During the war, the educational activities of the armed forces were carried on vigorously, and many veterans returned with a realization that it would be necessary to be better educated if they were to keep up with the increasing tempo of the times. In the course of World War II, millions of civilians had also been engaged in training programs and educational activities designed to prepare them to serve better in ways suited to the country's needs. Many of these individuals continued to seek out some type of educational program after the war ended.

The program for adults is much broader in the United States than ever before. Organizations like the parent-teacher associations have been active in the field of parent education. The League of Women Voters and similar groups carry on extremely effective citizenship-training activities, both formal and informal. A number of organizations and institutions have begun work in the field of the problems of elder citizens. New types of reading programs, such as the American Heritage series and the Great Books discussion groups, have become increasingly popular in the last few years. Television stations, often in cooperation with universities or colleges, offer formally organized lecture courses which approximate university classes, and in which individual work is done by correspondence lessons.

The discoveries of modern psychology have shown that it is certainly possible to "teach an old dog new tricks." The current goal of American adult education programs is to broaden the range of offerings in order to provide something that will be of interest and of service to nearly everyone, and to find the most effective ways of presenting materials and of helping adults to learn. The slogan "Lifelong Learning," which has been popularized by the University of California Extension Division, is coming to have nation-wide significance.

Education and Status of Teachers

THE FIRST teachers in the American colonies and states were not trained professionally, but were people selected because they met minimum requirements of education, character, and willingness to accept the low pay which the positions paid. The first state normal school was established at Lexington, Massachusetts, in 1839. It provided a one-year course of training; in 1860 this was increased to two years. Other states followed the example of Massachusetts and founded normal schools to train teachers for the elementary schools. The development of special schools for teacher training was a result of a great need for more teachers and for better prepared teachers. The four-year colleges and universities of the time were uninterested in this form of education, and in the beginning, at least, entrance requirements to the teacher-training programs were lower than college-entrance standards.

The normal schools gradually raised their standards and their requirements. In 1857 the Illinois State Normal University was founded (before there was a state university) with the avowed purpose of preparing well-trained teachers for both the elementary and secondary schools, thereby raising the entire program to the university level. As the years went on, most of the states passed through a series of developments that changed the normal schools from one-year courses to two and then three; then the schools became teachers' colleges or colleges of education and offered a four-year course leading to a bachelor's degree. Finally, in a few states, the name was changed from "state college of education" to "state college." Many of these colleges now offer work leading to a master's degree in education.

The need for professional training for secondary teachers resulted in the establishment of education departments in the colleges and universities. The first part-time chair of education was established at the University of Iowa in 1873, and the University of Michigan created a full-time education professorship in 1879. In 1887 Nicholas Murray Butler, then professor of philosophy and later president of Columbia University in New York, established Teachers College in that institution. This college has had great influence on the education of teachers and administrators in the United States and abroad.

Leaders in the United States gradually came to realize that it was desirable to think and speak of the "education" rather than the "training" of teachers. Teachers' colleges and schools of education in the universities have increasingly emphasized the general education of teachers, and the professional courses in subjects to be taught and in methodology have decreased proportionately in the curriculum. Most of the programs now give the same sort of general education courses in the first two years as are required in the lower division of the liberal arts colleges. Professional courses and supervised teaching experience have been delayed until the third and fourth years, or even until the fifth year.

Requirements for teachers' certificates vary among the 50 states. Usually the state department of education, or a state certification board, issues certificates which permit teachers to be employed within the state. Forty-four of the 50 states require at least the completion of a four-year course, with the bachelor's degree, as the minimum for high school teaching; the tendency to require a fifth year of work beyond the bachelor's degree is increasing. Graduation from a two-year normal school or at least two years of college education is the minimum requirement for elementary teaching in 36 states; others demand the completion of a four-year course and the bachelor's degree. Additional requirements are sometimes provided for special administrative or supervisory credentials, or for special certificates in certain fields, such as kindergarten or special education.

Because of the decentralization of school control in the United States, teachers are employed by local school districts, rather than by the national government, as in France, or the state government, as in Australia. When the prospective teacher has met the state's certification requirements, he applies for various positions within the state. This application may be made directly to the superintendent of schools of the local school district, or the applicant may work through teacher-placement agencies. These agencies may be operated by teacher-training institutions, by a teachers' association, by the state department of education, or by a private individual or company. The professional record of the teacher is compiled by the placement agency, including transcripts or brief descriptions of collegiate training, descriptions of various types of experience which the applicant has had, and letters of recommendation from professors or former employers. The local school board appoints the teachers, usually on the recommendation of the superintendent.

The American teacher does not have the absolute security of tenure which the French or Australian teacher enjoys. His tenure is usually with the school district in which he is employed. All states, however, have some type of legislation affecting and protecting teacher welfare. Thirty-eight states provide for permanent tenure, at least in the larger school districts; legal provisions covering conditions under which a teacher may be dismissed are found in 35 states; 34 states have minimum-salary schedules; and all states provide for teacher retirement. Sick-leave benefits, on a state-wide basis, are reported by 44 states.

There is much more mobility of teachers in the United States than occurs in some other countries. A typical state will include a large proportion of teachers who have had training or experience in other states. This is a situation which does not occur in Australia, for example, where all teachers are state public servants, and the only satisfactory way to achieve status in the state service is to be trained within the state and start at the bottom of the state's teaching force. A certain amount of interchange of ideas and enrichment results from having teachers in a school staff who have had experiences in other parts of the country.

In salary schedules there may be a considerable variation within a single state, since, within the limitations set by state laws, the local school districts establish their own salary scales. These are usually based upon training and experience, and the larger cities and wealthier school districts pay higher salaries. Unlike the salary schedules in countries where school inspectors follow a complicated system of assigning "efficiency marks" affecting the promotion and salary levels of teachers, American salary schedules seldom include an assessment of merit. Many authorities have held that this should be included. Since it is a very subjective factor, school districts have been reluctant to include it in salary scales which are completely objective in nature. Since the proportion of school support from state sources has been steadily increasing, and since a certain amount of state funds are usually earmarked for salaries, intrastate differ-

TABLE 11–5
Average Salaries of Teachers in the United States

YEAR	SALARY (DOLLARS)
1910	485
1920	871
1930	1,420
1940	1,441
1950	3,010
1963	5,797

SOURCES: *Statistical Abstract of the United States, 1953*, p. 121 (for 1910 to 1950); *National Education Association, Research Division, 1964* (for 1963–64).

ences may gradually tend to disappear. State minimum-salary laws have had their effect on the elimination of very low salaries.

The variation between the states is even more marked than between districts within a state, since the salary level depends largely upon the per capita wealth of the state and to a certain extent upon the proportion of children of school age in the population. Improvement in average salaries throughout the nation is indicated in Table 11–5. The 1960 average for the country as a whole, which was reported as $4,995, was based on averages in the various states which ranged from a low of $3,295 in Arkansas to a high of $6,859 in Alaska. The number of teachers employed in the public schools of the country increased from 523,210 in 1910 to 1,576,000 in 1963–64. In addition there were nearly 200,000 teachers employed in private schools.[2]

The National Education Association is an organization of teachers in elementary, secondary, and higher education, representing both public and private schools in all of the states. About one-half of the teachers in the country are members of the national association. A higher proportion of the teachers in the country belong to the various state teachers' associations and to local groups. These organizations are professional in nature and in philosophy, rather than teachers' unions. The American Federation of Teachers is affiliated with the trade-union movement and has branches in various states and districts. It does not publish membership statistics,

[2] *Statistical Abstract of the United States*, 1962, pp. 127–28.

but the number involved is much smaller than that of the professional associations.

A higher proportion of the teaching force are women than in some of the other countries considered in this book. In 1960 there were 402,000 men and 985,000 women employed in public elementary and secondary schools. Unlike some other countries, however, in most of the states women are paid on the same basis as men, with "equal pay for equal work" laws prohibiting lower salary scales for women.

An interesting and distinctive feature of teaching in the United States is the emphasis placed on in-service education. Previously it has been mentioned that a high proportion of American teachers attend summer schools. The long summer vacation period makes it possible for a teacher to spend six or eight weeks in professional improvement and still have some vacation time left. The extension programs of the colleges and universities, with their correspondence-study courses and evening classes throughout the year also enroll a high proportion of teachers. In-service training workshops for short periods are organized by school districts, and the resources of nearby teacher training institutions are utilized. Salary schedules are usually constructed in such a way that they stimulate further professional study, since the salary base, to which increments are added for experience, is higher for teachers with a master's degree and higher qualifications.

The marked increase in national birth rates, with consequent increased enrollments, and the lengthened period that the average pupil remains in school have accentuated the need for more teachers in every state. The teacher-training institutions have not been able to provide sufficient numbers of fully trained teachers to replace those retiring and dropping out of the profession and at the same time to meet the requirements for new classes each year. Emergency certificates have been issued, bringing into the schools partially trained people, or bringing back to teaching married women and others who have been away from the schools for some years. One advantage of the system of in-service education, and the availability of extension courses and summer sessions, has been to bring numbers of these emergency teachers up to regular certification standards each year. The problem of recruitment and supply of teachers remains a serious one.

In general the problem of shortage of teachers has not been met by lowering certification standards. Emergency certificates are usually issued for one year, and those holding them are required to attend summer session or take other additional training in order to have the temporary certificates reissued. The status of teachers in the United States has risen constantly during this century. Improved standards and higher salaries have been accompanied by increased public respect. It is interesting, also, that higher requirements for certificates and increased length of teacher-education courses have increased the number of young people who choose to enter teaching as a career.

Problems in the Operation of American Schools

SCHOOL administrators and school boards in the United States, like those charged with the responsibility for education in other countries, face certain problems, the answers to which are not accepted unanimously in the country. Some of these, growing out of the system of administration and control in the nation, have been suggested in Chapter 3, but may be mentioned again at this time.

The Shortage of Qualified Teachers

The lack of fully trained teachers began to become acute in 1948, and the problem has increased in importance since that time. As in other parts of the world, increased birth rates have brought floods of new children into the schools. Teacher-training institutions have increased the output of graduates (158,357 graduates in 1963), but these have not been sufficient to meet normal attrition rates and care for the increased enrollments. According to the National Education Association, the 1963 shortage was 118,000.[3] It has been estimated that there will be nearly twice as many children in school in 1965 as in 1948, and these children will have to find teachers waiting for them.

Increases in teachers' salaries, higher standards of preparation, and intensified recruitment campaigns have shown some success in increasing the number of teachers in training and in retaining teachers in the profession. Each of the 50 states has been concerned with this problem and has been attempting to find a solution.

[3] *Teacher Supply and Demand in Public Schools, 1963*, Research Division, National Education Association, 1963, pp. 5, 20.

The Shortage of School Buildings

During the years of depression and of war relatively few school buildings were erected, and the shortage of adequate schoolrooms would have been acute even if the enrollment had not increased. School building has been going on at a tremendous rate all over the country, and much progress has been made in modernizing the school plant and in getting ready for increased loads. Much of the problem is one of finance, since school buildings are paid for from local funds, usually from bond issues voted by the local taxpayers. Some districts have voted special building levies and are erecting new schools from current income, thus saving on interest costs. In spite of increased space made available in the postwar years, there are still children who attend only half a day, in double-shift schools. Every effort is being made to eliminate these and to provide for future growth.

The Responsibility of Public Schools for Kindergartens

The question of the age at which free, compulsory public education should begin has been a center of discussion. Educators are convinced that it would be better for the children if kindergartens could be made a part of the regular school program and integrated with the lower grades. Here again the problem is often one of finance. With the school districts straining every resource to add sufficient teachers and classrooms to provide for increase enrollments, it has been difficult to pay for public kindergartens for all children. While the number of 5-year-olds who attend public kindergartens has increased every year, the problem is still far from a satisfactory solution.

The Gifted Child

Thoughtful critics of public education have pointed out that schools in a system of universal education tend to provide a form of mass instruction, directed largely toward the average child. In countries where the education system is more selective, the gifted children are sifted out and given special opportunities. Many educators feel that progress has been made in meeting these criticisms. Even in large classes a great deal of individualized instruction is possible. Good teachers vary the requirements and the opportunities to meet the abilities and the needs of different types of children in the one class. The absence of a system of uniform, external examinations permits much variation in teaching methods and procedures. Some interesting experiments have been attempted, with excellent results, in providing challenging opportunities for the more gifted children in the public schools. Probably even more has been done to provide those children who are physically or emotionally handicapped with special classes and carefully planned programs to meet their needs. However, no American educator believes that the problem of the child who differs from the average of the class has been finally or satisfactorily solved.

Content and Methods

Since the first Sputnik roared into space, there has been increased interest among parents and educators in higher academic standards, especially in the fields of science and mathematics. Greater emphasis has been placed on these subjects and upon better teaching of foreign languages. New approaches to biology, chemistry, mathematics, and physics have been devised, and are in use in many places. In the newer approaches to mathematics, instruction begins in some cases as early as the first grade. Much of this work is experimental, and in some fields two or more different approaches are being tried out. School children are working harder than at any time in American educational history. Some authorities see problems of overemphasis on science and of corresponding neglect of the humanities and social studies. Increased stress on academic subjects may tend to increase the problem of dropouts.

The post-Sputnik era has been one of exciting experiments in new types of organization, such as team teaching projects and ungraded classrooms. It has been a time of experimenting with programed learning, both in new types of textbooks and in a number of teaching machines, and a time that has seen increased use of television in the classroom. Doubts have been expressed about the place of the teacher in a mechanized situation. The problem is one of making use of new devices, within the limits of financial practicability, in order to strengthen rather than to replace the classroom teacher.

The Universal Secondary School

The United States has come to accept quite completely the idea of secondary education for everyone. In spite of this, there is always criticism in some quarters that the high schools are not sufficiently selective. In some European countries the accepted answer has been that only those may go on to secondary education who can pass extremely difficult academic examinations or whose parents can afford to pay high fees in private schools. This answer has not met with much favor in the United States. It seems to go counter to the general philosophy that the first purpose of the school is to prepare for intelligent citizenship. The answer that has been worked out in the comprehensive high schools seems to be in the direction of providing a wide range of different types of courses to meet the needs and interests of those who cannot profit from, or who lack interest in, the academic curriculum. It is becoming more generally accepted that standards in education are not necessarily confined to standards in a restricted range of subject matter. This topic will probably continue to be debated.

The Junior College

Whether the junior college is secondary in nature or is a part of higher education seems to attract some attention. The fact that the public junior colleges are connected with the local school districts, and have developed as an upward extension of the high schools, seems to emphasize their role as a part of secondary education. The high proportion of students who find that the junior college is their last formal educational experience has led administrators to seek curricula which would have greater value for them than a course planned for transfers to a university. On the other hand, the excellent work that junior colleges have done in preparing students for further university education has added to their stature and general acceptance. It seems likely that the junior college will work out a place for itself, somewhat independent of the four-year college and of usefulness to the community.

Vocational and General Education

The question of bridging the gap between general education and vocational education is frequently discussed. The fact that the federal government has subsidized vocational courses in the high schools but not general education courses tends to emphasize the difference. In some states the administration of vocational education is somewhat separated from the regular high schools of the state, and this has caused an unnecessary division. Here again, the best answer seems to be the comprehensive high school, where all students are together in general education classes and select particular fields of specialization through choice of electives. Much of the division between theoretical and practical education, or general and specific, is artificial. The problem of bringing the entire secondary program into an organic whole is important.

Integration

The problem of the integration of racial minorities within the public schools is a severe one, but the concern with which many Americans have viewed the situation, and their intent to conform to the law, indicates that the problem may yet be solved. Segregation by race was at one time authorized or practiced in seventeen of the fifty states. In 1954 the Supreme Court held that in the schools segregation by race was a violation of the Constitution and directed that it be ended "with all deliberate speed." Recent federal court decisions have directed integration of local school systems in most of the cases coming before them, and the Supreme Court has upheld these decisions.

By 1963 at least token desegregation had been achieved in every state except Mississippi, and in the same year 161 new districts started some form of desegregation. This change has not been easily accomplished. In Little Rock, Arkansas, and in places in Alabama and Louisiana, there have been demonstrations and violence.

In the North the problem of "de facto segregation" has arisen from the concentration of Negroes and Puerto Ricans in certain housing areas, so that district schools have become predominately made up of one group. The accepted American principle of the neighborhood school is coming under attack. Opponents have stated that some proposed remedies (such as busing children to schools in another part of the city) might seriously discriminate against white children.

The United States faces a serious problem, and a maximum of intelligence and good will is required in order to find a solution.

Regionalism in Education

One attempt to solve the financial problem of providing specialized education that is faced by most small colleges and professional schools has been the pooling of resources by some states grouped in regional organizations. In the South, prior to the 1954 Supreme Court decision, such an attempt was made in order to provide "equal facilities" for Negro candidates for higher degrees. A more lasting contribution was the organization of Western states into an inter-state commission that drew up a plan covering specialized study in certain professional fields. The plan was based on the principle that it is expensive and uneconomic for each state to attempt to provide a complete program of higher education in every professional field. In expensive courses like medicine, dentistry, veterinary medicine, graduate social work, and mining engineering, it has been possible to work out compacts between the states so that the states without these professional schools could contract for places for their citizens in the schools of other states, and pay a share of the cost. This program offers possibilities for further development, in that a university may aim at achieving stature in a few fields of specialization without feeling required to provide for every possible profession. This is a special problem of finance in higher education, but it is also a field of cooperative relationships on a regional basis. It should make it more nearly possible for a single state to provide for its citizens within the limits of its ability to support specialized schools.

12

English Schools in Action

I N CHAPTER 4 the administrative machinery for education in England and Wales was described. The national Ministry of Education provides a substantial portion of the financial support and assures itself that the provisions of the 1944 Education Act are carried out, but leaves to the local education authorities (L.E.A.'s) the administrative details. The system is based on three important principles: (a) retention of as much authority as possible by the local authorities, backed by a considerable amount of national support; (b) allocation of an important share in educational activities to voluntary organizations; and (c) absence of any dictation to headmasters and teachers on details of school organization, curricula, and teaching methods.

Figure 12–1 illustrates the general organization of schools in England and Wales. In studying this diagram it should be borne in mind that the universities draw their students mainly from the secondary grammar schools, the public schools, and independent schools.

As we have pointed out in Chapter 4, it is possible to distinguish three divisions of English schools on the basis of the source and extent of their financial support. Enrollment and other figures for these schools are presented in Table 12–1. The totals reported for all schools in England and Wales in 1951–52 were 30,694 schools, 6,367,198 pupils, and 247,197 teachers; ten years later, in 1961–62, the totals were 34,537 schools, 7,663,246 pupils, and 322,661 teachers.

Preschool Education

DURING World War II, when so many British mothers were working, nursery schools were established by many voluntary organiza-

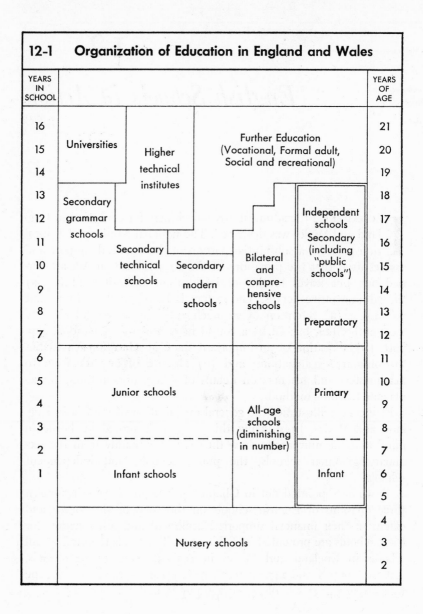

12-1 Organization of Education in England and Wales

YEARS IN SCHOOL						YEARS OF AGE
16	Universities	Higher technical institutes	Further Education (Vocational, Formal adult, Social and recreational)			21
15						20
14						19
13	Secondary grammar schools				Independent schools Secondary (including "public schools")	18
12						17
11		Secondary technical schools	Secondary modern schools	Bilateral and comprehensive schools		16
10						15
9						14
8					Preparatory	13
7						12
6	Junior schools		All-age schools (diminishing in number)		Primary	11
5						10
4						9
3						8
2	Infant schools				Infant	7
1						6
						5
	Nursery schools					4
						3
						2

TABLE 12–1

Statistics of Schools in England and Wales, January, 1962

	SCHOOLS OR DEPARTMENTS	PUPILS TOTAL	FULL-TIME TEACHERS Men	Women	Total
Schools Maintained by Local Education Authorities					
Primary	5,502	962,319	44	31,727	31,771
Junior with infants	12,095	1,647,917	14,934	43,845	58,779
Junior without infants	4,819	1,348,877	17,518	26,544	44,062
All-age	775	170,465	2,379	4,035	6,404
All primary schools	23,191	4,129,578	34,875	106,141	141,016
Secondary					
Modern	3,899	1,675,957	42,612	34,675	77,287
Grammar	1,287	708,343	22,196	15,741	37,937
Technical	220	97,411	3,705	1,504	5,209
Bilateral and multilateral	63	45,258	1,281	976	2,257
Comprehensive	152	157,477	4,701	3,201	7,902
Other secondary	269	151,266	3,914	3,262	7,176
All secondary schools	5,890	2,835,712	78,409	59,359	137,768
Junior	—	4,064,484	33,529	104,397	137,926
Senior	—	2,900,806	79,755	61,103	140,858
All primary and secondary	29,081	6,965,290	113,284	165,500	278,784
Nursery schools	455	20,881	—	946	946
Special	624	55,356	1,927	2,381	4,308
Hospital schools	86	3,440	49	350	399
ALL MAINTAINED SCHOOLS	30,246	7,044,977	115,260	169,177	284,437
Direct Grant Schools					
Nursery	20	701	—	39	39
Grammar	179	111,634	3,007	3,091	6,098
Special	114	8,460	364	479	843
Hospital	13	920	16	75	91
Institution	2	766	39	4	43
Technical	5	829	66	—	66
ALL DIRECT GRANT SCHOOLS	333	123,310	3,492	3,688	7,180
Independent Schools Recognized as Efficient					
Nursery	10	369	—	25	25
Primary	771	88,551	3,286	2,895	6,181
Secondary	284	73,840	3,619	2,171	5,790
Primary and secondary	438	141,467	2,905	5,623	8,528
ALL RECOGNIZED SCHOOLS	1,503	304,227	9,810	10,714	20,524
Other Independent Schools					
Nursery	205	5,380	3	317	320
Primary	1,418	88,481	727	4,102	4,829
Secondary	191	19,917	743	412	1,155
Primary and Secondary	641	76,954	1,237	2,979	4,216
ALL OTHER INDEPENDENT	2,455	190,732	2,710	7,810	10,520
Total All Schools	34,537	7,663,246	131,272	191,389	322,661

SOURCE: *Education in 1962, Report of the Ministry of Education for England and Wales*, London: H.M.S.O., 1963, p. 120.

tions and by some of the L.E.A.'s. The law permitted the L.E.A.'s to build and operate nursery schools if they wished.

The success of these schools showed preschool classes to be desirable for all children, not only for those in crowded industrial centers. The Education Act of 1944 required the local authorities to supply this need. Preference was given to nursery schools enrolling not more than 40 children, but nursery classes might be attached to primary schools if the L.E.A.'s thought this expedient. In some cases the 5- to 7-year-olds were enrolled in a special infant school, and many of these had a nursery school attached. (The normal usage in Great Britain is to call the lower grades, which are called "primary" in the United States, "infant classes"; and to call the elementary school the "primary school." The term *elementary* has not been used in England since 1945.)

The procedure in nursery and infant schools had, by 1944, already been laid down on modern lines. A report issued by the Board of Education in 1933 gives an idea of the objectives and atmosphere of these schools:

Between the ages of two and five the child is gaining knowledge of the world about him through his senses, and is learning to exercise these senses in themselves, and more especially sight, hearing and touch. The child's constant desire to look at things and handle them should be restricted as little as possible, and in school the child should be surrounded with objects and materials which will afford scope for experimentation and exploration.

In the ordinary urban environment there is little to satisfy the child's natural impulses; it is important, therefore, to provide an environment which will do so by keeping the children in the open air surrounded by trees, plants, animals, places that they can explore, pools in which they can paddle and sand pits in which they can dig.[1]

In spite of the soundness and attractiveness of the program for the nursery schools, there has been a failure to establish them in the numbers anticipated. In 1962 there were 475 nursery schools in maintained and grant-aided schools and these enrolled 21,581 children, a smaller number than in 1952. The main reason for the failure to establish additional nursery schools has been lack of funds. In a postwar period of abnormal growth of the school population, the local education authorities have had to use all their available

[1] Board of Education, *Infant and Nursery Schools*, H.M.S.O., London, 1933.

funds to provide for the children within the limits of compulsory education. It is a pity that finances have been so limited, for the nursery school is one of the brightest and happiest features of English education, an admirable link between life at home and the wider world of the primary school.

Primary Education

THE INFANT SCHOOL

Attendance at the nursery school is voluntary; compulsory education begins at age 5 in the primary school. The time between 5 years and 11-plus is divided into two periods, the infant school up to 7-plus and the junior school between 7- and 11-plus.

The 1933 Board of Education report just quoted goes on to discuss the function and activities of the infant school:

It is the function of the infant school to supply children between the ages of five and seven with what is essential for their healthy growth, physical, intellectual, spiritual, and moral. The first place in the training will still be given to the physical well-being of the child. Speech training should be continued. Since it is natural in children to express their sense of rhythm in movement, they should be encouraged to do so in various ways.

Constructive work of various kinds should occupy an important place in the activities of the infant school. In general, manual and aesthetic development are better secured when the child is left to make what he likes, how he likes, and, within reason, when he likes, rather than by any set of lessons.

The child should begin to learn the three R's when he wants to do so, whether he is three or six years old. Only in this way will the acquisition of the three R's come about incidentally as a part of widening interests and experiences. The principle underlying the procedure of the infant school should be that, as far as possible, the child should be put in a position to teach himself, and the knowledge that he is to acquire should come, not so much from the instructor as from an instructive environment.[2]

It is also the work of the infant school to introduce children to the disciplines of formal learning, but still with an atmosphere of exploration and enjoyment. Perhaps its most difficult task is to find

[2] Ibid.

out when each child is ready and anxious to learn to read and to form concepts of number. To begin these two skills too early or too late, or to force the child and make him reluctant to continue is to court disaster for him. Many procedures have been devised which help both teacher and child, and all teachers should be conversant with them.

In the infant school there should also be plenty of building and making things with different sorts of material, a constant acquaintanceship with music, good posture, and rhythmic movement, development of good health habits, and social training.

THE JUNIOR SCHOOL

Even before World War II the junior schools had, wherever possible, become "child-centered" schools, characterized by activity programs and special work in art and music. Encouragement in this direction had been given by the Board of Education in a report published in 1931, which pictured an almost ideal primary school. Two paragraphs from this report have been quoted again and again. They read as follows:

We are of the opinion that the curriculum of the primary school is to be thought of in terms of activity and experience, rather than of knowledge to be acquired and facts to be stored.

The traditional practice of dividing the matter of primary instruction into separate "subjects," taught in distinct lessons, should be reconsidered. The treatment of a series of central topics which have relations with many subjects, may be a useful alternative. It is, however, essential that provision be made for an adequate amount of "drill" in reading, writing, and arithmetic.[3]

The junior schools were thus in a position to make themselves almost ideal educational units. Under many gifted and discerning teachers admirable work was done, but two big problems prevented the schools in general from achieving the objectives set out for them by the Board of Education.

The first was that many teachers interpreted the statement about "activity and experience" as meaning that the acquisition of knowledge was not to be emphasized as long as the pupils were busily engaged in activity programs and projects. For some years in many schools the necessity of laying a basis of sound knowledge was for-

[3] Board of Education, *The Primary School*, H.M.S.O., London, 1931.

gotten. Fortunately the teaching profession realized the danger of this, and nowadays there is a happy balance between activity, reality, interest, and sound knowledge.

The second problem has not yet been solved. When the 1944 Act made secondary education available to all pupils in three kinds of school—grammar, technical, and modern—it was not long before parents realized that the grammar school was the one with the highest prestige; it led on to university courses and entry to the professions. The result was that there were more applicants for admission to grammar schools than that particular type of school could handle. If a child was relegated to a modern school, which had a general and practical program, both parents and children considered this something of a disgrace. Entry to the grammar schools was determined by the applicant's results in what was called the "11-plus examination." This examination tests in formal English and arithmetic and also uses a standardized objective test of intelligence. The tendency soon developed for the junior school, in its pupils' last two years, to coach all likely prospects, with methods akin to cramming, for the 11-plus examination. This meant that the fine ideals set down by the Ministry for the junior schools were thrown to the four winds. Strong pressure that the schools should undertake this special cramming was exerted by parents. *Punch* summed up the situation in a cartoon that depicted the mother of a newborn son saying to the doctor, "Doctor, do you think that he'll be able to gain a good result in the 11-plus?"

As the other types of secondary school secure recognition from the public for their very attractive courses, and even prepare some pupils for the General Certificate Examination at the end of secondary courses, public pressure is beginning to diminish a little, but the concern is still there. Perhaps nothing in education in England and Wales during the last twenty years has caused so much anguish and disappointment to parents and pupils or so much dislocation of good school courses as the 11-plus examination for entrance to secondary schools.

Secondary Education

IT IS in the secondary schools that the most significant changes have taken place in English education. Secondary education is no longer the privilege of a few select pupils: it has been made avail-

able to all. A good account of the changes which the Ministry of
Education and the Local Education Authorities have brought about
is given in the Ministry's booklet *The New Secondary Education*.
Here are some paragraphs from the introductory section of this
pamphlet:

In future there will be various types of secondary schools and various
courses within secondary schools, which will offer children an education specially suited to their particular needs. All these schools will have
the advantages and amenities hitherto exclusively associated with the
limited number of schools called secondary schools up to 1944. They
will have equally good buildings. They will enjoy the same holidays
and play the same games. There will eventually be boarding facilities for
all types of secondary schools. In all these schools the studies will be
related to the abilities and aptitudes of the pupils. The maximum size
of classes will be the same for all.

As a mere matter of finance it will, broadly speaking, cost as much to
build and equip and staff one type of secondary school as another, and
the jibe that the new types of secondary school have been advocated
because they are cheap should be heard no more.[4]

TYPES OF SECONDARY SCHOOLS

By the time of the 1944 Act a great many types of secondary and
post-primary schools had developed. These included grammar
schools, senior schools, higher elementary schools, central schools,
junior technical schools, commercial schools, and schools specializing
in art. Notable service had been rendered by many of them, but
the time had come for some kind of simplification. This simplification was achieved by the 1944 Act, which provided for only three
types: secondary grammar schools, secondary modern schools, and
secondary technical schools. It was expected that there would be
four pupils in the secondary modern schools for one in each of the
other two types. The figures for 1959 and 1962 for secondary schools
maintained by the L.E.A.'s and direct-grant schools are shown in
Table 12–2. The allocation to the different types of schools is by
means of the 11-plus examination, which consists largely of standardized tests of intelligence and attainment in basic subjects, together with reports from head teachers and scrutiny of junior school
records of candidates. The examination is administered by the local
education authorities, and corrected by the teachers according to

[4] Ministry of Education, Pamphlet No. 9, pp. 7–8.

TABLE 12–2
Numbers of Different Types of Secondary Schools, England and Wales

YEAR	SECONDARY MODERN SCHOOLS	SECONDARY TECHNICAL SCHOOLS	SECONDARY GRAMMAR SCHOOLS
1959	1,426	269	3,808
1962	1,466	225	3,899

SOURCE: Ministry of Education Annual Reports.

instructions which allow for no personal opinion by teachers on the correctness of answers. From the scripts and lists of marks in all schools, the local education authorities compile a single order of merit for the total area of the authority. An Examination Board then calculates how far down this list the allotment to grammar schools may go, and how far up the list the assignment to modern schools may commence.

The Secondary Grammar School

This type of school has existed for many years in England and is well known. Its curriculum corresponds to that of the "college preparatory" courses in American high schools. Its pupils stay in school for six or seven years and expect to enter the university or to take positions in banks or commercial establishments. The course of study includes English language and literature, foreign and classical languages, science, mathematics, history, geography, art, and music—all studied over a period of years in an academic manner, with marked stress on scholarly treatment and intellectual discipline. Most of the pupils take an examination, at the end of the course, for the "General Certificate of Education" (G.C.E.). The sixth form (for 17- to 18-year-olds) caps the work of the school and gives the senior pupils a special training in initiative and responsibility. Many of the grammar schools add such subjects as engineering, architecture, economics, commercial subjects, and technical drawing to their lists. There is a great range of voluntary clubs and societies, the schools are often organized in houses, and there is a prefect system of student government.

Grammar-school pupils sit for the General Certificate of Education between the ages of 15 and 18 years, but special permission must be obtained to sit before 16. The examination is held at two levels, ordinary and advanced, with a third division called "scholarship." Passes are given for single subjects, not groups of subjects. Entrance to the universities requires, as a minimum, a pass in English language and in four or five other subjects, of which at least two must be passed at the advanced level. There are eight university examining boards, examples of which are the Southern Universities Joint Board, the Cambridge Local Examinations Syndicate, and the Welsh Joint Education Committee.

The Secondary Technical School

This type of school is not entirely new either: it has developed from the junior technical schools that began to appear in 1905. They were good schools but suffered from certain disadvantages. They were regarded by many people as schools for artisans and domestic helpers, although most of the schools soon rose above this concept. They admitted pupils at the age of 13 years, and were often housed in senior technical school buildings, with a tendency toward being overshadowed by the senior schools. In some cases the general education aspect of their work was subordinated to trade training.

In 1938 the Board of Education issued the Spens Report which, among other matters, drew attention to the possibility of a new type of school to be called a "technical high school." [5] This school was to have the dignity and status of a good secondary school, with emphasis on science and mathematics in its curriculum, and was to admit only those pupils who had marked aptitude for technical work of a high caliber. Nothing much came of this report, although a few of these schools were established, until the 1944 Act, which gave full recognition to this type of school called "secondary technical school."

This school admits pupils at the age of "11-plus," although there are pupils admitted at the age of 13, which is regarded as a temporary measure. Those attending are boys and girls of high intelligence and natural aptitude for technical work, who wish to become skilled technicians in such fields as engineering, electricity, navigation, aeronautics, building trades, agriculture, applied art, and

[5] Board of Education, *Report of the Consultative Committee on Secondary Education, with Special Reference to Grammar Schools and Technical High Schools,* H.M.S.O., London, 1938.

the many divisions of home science. The schools have the same type of buildings, equipment, and grounds as other secondary schools, and they insist on a sound basis of general education for their pupils. Pupils remain in the secondary technical schools until they are 16 or 17 years of age. Some specialization in occupational training begins in the fourth year. Most of these schools have been developed in urban centers, although plans have been made in some country areas for schools specializing in agriculture, horticulture, homemaking, and building construction.

For some reason or other this type of secondary school has not met with public approbation. With the growth of science in industry it might have been expected that secondary technical schools would increase by large numbers each year, with both boys and girls clamoring for entrance. Actually there are fewer of these schools in existence than in 1945.

Apparently pupils prefer to make their way to possible scientific and technical positions of importance through the grammar school, which has a higher social prestige and which teaches sciences and mathematics very well. In the very beginning the Ministry declared that the secondary technical schools were intended to draw their pupils from the same levels of capacity as the grammar schools, but the parents and pupils continued to regard it as a possible second chance, somewhat inferior, for those who did not succeed in qualifying for the grammar school. For some years many secondary technical schools were housed in old buildings and employed teachers who gave only part-time service while they taught in technical colleges.

The secondary technical schools have built up a fine record and some educational authorities think they have a very successful future ahead of them. They present pupils for the G.C.E., and a number of these go on to universities, but something appears to prevent the secondary technical schools at present from fulfilling their destiny.

The Secondary Modern School

The most discussed type of English secondary school is the modern school. It would not be too much to say that the success of the whole tripartite plan depends upon the effectiveness of this type of school. The boys and girls who enter it, totaling more than all the pupils in attendance at all the other types of secondary schools, are expected to become members of the large group of workers in mills, factories, stores, shops, industrial plants, business offices, transportation services, farms, personal service, and in homes.

It is necessary to discover the special abilities possessed by these boys and girls, to develop their skills, and to train them in citizenship and responsibility. It is necessary to awaken their interest in school subjects and in books and in worth-while leisure-time activities. This requires a broad and interesting secondary education, lasting at least until the age of 15. It includes such subjects as English expression, social studies, health and physical education, games and sports, general science, general mathematics, workshop practice, homemaking, bookkeeping and other commercial subjects, arts and crafts, nature study, biology, history, geography, music, horticulture, film appreciation, and an elective language.

No attempt has been made by the Ministry to prescribe courses or subjects—this is left to the cooperative efforts of the L.E.A.'s, the headmasters and headmistresses, and the members of the school staffs. The watchwords of the modern school have been Reality, Interest, and Activity. From the standpoint of the pupil, the purposes of the courses he takes must be made clear. Assemblies, discussions, film programs, school orchestras and bands, school plays, field trips, local district surveys, and individual and cooperative projects are emphasized. In this way the modern school attempts to fit in with John Dewey's insistence that education can best prepare for life by giving participation in life itself.

Modern schools in country areas have special problems and interesting opportunities. Both the schools and the teaching staffs are smaller in these areas than in the city. Many pupils travel to and from school by bus, which cuts into the time available for school clubs and out-of-school activities. These schools tie their offerings to the special nature of their surrounding districts, emphasizing rural problems and rural activities. They are in a position to provide a great service in England if they foster a pride in, and a respect for, rural life.

The modern schools are urged not to consider the academic examinations (which play such an important part in the work of the grammar schools) as an essential part of their program. To do this would make them pale shadows of the grammar schools and thus lessen their usefulness. They are encouraged to issue their own cer-

tificates, showing the achievement of their pupils and their participation in activities.

The idea of the modern school is a fine educational concept, but
the difficulty remains of convincing the general public, as well as
many of the teachers, that this type of school is equivalent in status
and prestige to the more academic and traditional schools.

From the beginning of the 1944 Act's attempt to simplify and
reorganize the secondary schools it was evident that one of the main
difficulties was to achieve what the English call "parity of esteem"
for the three types of school. The grammar school, from its history
and traditions, and from the fact that it prepared for the university,
is regarded by parents and teachers as the superior school. It has
often been said that the cream of the pupils go to the grammar
school, the milk to the technical school, and the skim milk to the
modern school. Parents have been greatly disappointed when they
were advised that their child would be better suited to a modern
school. As a former headmaster of Eton, the Rev. C. A. Alington,
once remarked in an address, "The trouble is that no two parents
have ever given birth to an average boy."

This viewpoint about the modern school has to be overcome, and
the Ministry of Education in its publications has stressed the fact
that all three types of school should have the same material advantages. Some of the points made are as follows:

1. Every secondary school, no matter what type, should have, in
addition to classrooms and laboratories, an assembly hall, a properly
equipped gymnasium and showers, craft rooms, workshops, and a
dining room. It is emphasized that each should have a good library
with a trained librarian. It has been recommended that every school
make wide use of visual aids.

2. There should be no differentiation between salaries paid to
teachers in the three types of school.

3. All secondary schools should give definite attention to the teaching of citizenship, both directly and indirectly. Whether this is to be
done in social studies or in other ways, secondary schools should
provide information on the workings of national and local government and the work of UNESCO. The older pupils, in particular,
should be given a definite share in the planning and organizing of
the social and recreational side of the school's work.

4. Creative activities should be encouraged in all three types of school. No pupil should be deprived, because of choice of school, of opportunities to express and to discipline his feelings by participation in art, music, crafts, dramatics, and dancing.

5. Physical education and games, combined with health instruction, should play an important part in school life, with the aim of general participation rather than the development of "crack" teams. Medical and dental inspection and treatment are to be continued and expanded.

6. Milk and a midday meal should be available for all pupils, and the organization of meals should be made the occasion for unobtrusive instruction in good manners and social graces.

7. Religion, as specified in the 1944 Act, is required as a part of life and instruction in every school. The Act states specifically: "The school day in every county and voluntary school shall begin with an act of collective worship on the part of all pupils in attendance. . . . Religious instruction shall be given in every county and voluntary school." It was also suggested that spiritual values permeate all the work of the schools, apart from specific periods of religious instruction.

8. The Act urged that all secondary schoolwork be purposive as the pupil sees it. The purpose and value of school subjects should be carefully explained to pupils and discussed with them, and the resultant interest should be used to encourage hard, solid work and achievement.

9. Vocational guidance is considered to be essential to the success of all secondary schools. The special aptitudes of each pupil should be discovered and competent advice given about choice of occupation. In this regard, close contact should be maintained with parents and prospective employers.[6]

An unforeseen complication arose in that many pupils wanted to stay on in the modern schools and take extended or advanced courses. In 1960, 1,050 of these schools presented about 20,000 candidates for the G.C.E. Most of them tried for four subjects at the ordinary level. But more than 50 percent of them passed, which gave the authorities something to think about, for these children were supposed to be "nonacademic" types. It must not be thought, however, that all modern school children were yearning to follow

[6] See *The New Secondary Education*, Ministry of Education Pamphlet No. 9, 1947, IV.

this example; thousands of them presented themselves for commercial or technical certificates, for examinations qualifying them to enter the armed forces and H.M. Footguards, or for leaving-certificate examinations designed and administered by their own local education authorities to take place at the end of the fourth year.

Bilateral and Comprehensive Schools

In some cases schools have developed along bilateral lines, offering two courses instead of one. Combined modern and grammar, modern and technical, and technical and grammar schools all exist and are called "bilateral schools." Any school that attempts all three courses is called a "comprehensive school"; these have been the subject of much criticism because they are difficult to equip and staff, and some have abandoned one course and became bilateral schools.

London, in 1944–45, did not like the idea of separate schools and began to build comprehensive schools, where all three types were housed in one set of buildings, with 1,500 to 1,750 pupils mixing together for many school activities and community functions but separating for instruction in the subjects suited to each group. London's comprehensive schools in some ways resemble the larger comprehensive high schools in the United States, except that the pupils are not kept separate as much in the latter. In certain parts of London, in the dockside areas, for example, secondary modern schools are to be found.

WELFARE SERVICES AND THE SCHOOLS

A vast network of social-welfare services affects all the pupils in the statutory system of public education in England and Wales. These were developed some years ago on a voluntary basis, but the Education Act of 1944 and the National Health Service Act of 1946 made it compulsory for the L.E.A.'s to provide the necessary facilities and services. The School Health Service is a cooperative program between the Ministry of Health and the Ministry of Education, and the L.E.A.'s are required to maintain a School Health Service and a School Dental Service. L.E.A.'s are also empowered to make agreements with the authorities of independent schools for medical inspection and treatment of pupils in these schools.

The magnitude of the School Health Service in December, 1961 is shown in Table 12–3. L.E.A.'s are authorized to make arrangements with suitable hospitals for admissions and specialized treat-

TABLE 12–3
School Health Services in England and Wales, 1961

| | MEDICAL | | | DENTAL | | |
	Pupils given routine inspection	Special inspections	Treated or under treatment	Given dental inspection	Treatment required	Treated or under treatment
England	2,056,000	1,660,000	1,479,000	3,777,000	2,394,000	1,227,000
Wales	105,000	74,000	65,000	192,000	149,000	85,000

MEDICAL AND DENTAL PERSONNEL (ENGLAND AND WALES)		
Type of officer	Number	Full-time equivalent
Doctors	2,457	954
Dentists	1,675	1,069
Dental assistants	1,440	1,201
School nurses	7,326	2,660
Nursing assistants	502	255

SOURCE: "School Health Services," *Statistics of Education, Part 2, 1962*, London: H.M.S.O., 1962.

ment. The Health Service also includes the establishment of special schools for handicapped children. In January, 1962, there were 837 of these special schools with 5,641 full-time teachers and 68,186 pupils. The main handicaps of the pupils were defective vision, defects of ear and throat, deafness and partial deafness, defective speech, postural defects, orthopedic troubles, behavioral maladjustments, educational subnormality, and various types of delicate health.

Meals and Milk Service

For some years before World War II local authorities provided hot meals and milk, almost exclusively for undernourished children from poor homes. With the establishment of rationing during the war it was felt that all school children should be given a nourishing meal in the middle of the day, particularly as many of the mothers were engaged in war work and were not at home at noon. This program has been continued since the war, and in 1962, out of a total of 34,000 schools in England and Wales, only 300 were without facilities for hot meals. Parents are expected to pay if they can, the cost of the meal being about one shilling (or about 15 cents). The expense of providing building space, equipment, and staff for this gigantic venture has been borne by the Ministry of Education and not by the local authorities. On a selected day in October, 1962, a midday meal was served to 3,652,000 pupils. The meal usually consists of hot meat or fish and vegetables, followed by a dessert.

All new schools are designed with an attractive dining hall. The tables have gay table cloths and vases of bright flowers, and the serving is done by relays of pupils. In many schools, however, the children still take their meals on desks in the classrooms, but ingenious teachers find many ways of brightening up the scene. The fee of one shilling represents only the cost of the materials for the meal. The L.E.A.'s will, unostentatiously, pay for the meals of children whose parents are unable to meet the expense.

Milk was first provided to school children more than thirty years ago by voluntary effort, and children whose parents desired were given one-third of a pint of milk a day for a half-penny. In 1946, after the Family Allowances Act had been passed, milk for school children was made free. In 1962, 82.3 percent of school children in England were getting free milk each day, and in Wales 81.5 percent of the children were supplied. The Ministry of Education pays for the milk, and, as with school meals, L.E.A.'s may arrange for milk to be supplied to independent schools. In 1962, 408,000 or 82.9 percent of the pupils in independent schools took milk.

The 1944 Education Act gives local education authorities the power to provide suitable school clothing for children whose parents are not in a position to purchase it. The grant includes articles of clothing necessary for sports and physical training. This helps to place underprivileged children on a level with their fellows, and most schools are careful not to draw attention to the fact that some pupils have their needs supplied in this way.

THE INDEPENDENT SCHOOLS

The independent schools are those which are financially self-supporting, receiving no grants from public funds. They are not entirely independent in that they must be registered with the Ministry of Education, and the Minister can close any school which has inadequate accommodation or is not being conducted efficiently. There are many different varieties of independent schools, but the simplest classification is two-fold: "public schools," and "others."

The Public Schools

No description of English education would be complete without some account of the "public schools," which are said to be the "envy and despair of their critics." They have been largely responsible for the evolution of the English tradition of education. There is no doubt about the quality of the training they give in character building and liberal studies, although this training has been available only to a limited and somewhat exclusive group of pupils.

The public schools have been assailed by critics on all sides, mainly for their exclusiveness and their generally conservative attitude toward education. It has often been said that they have no place in a democracy. On the other hand, there is no doubt that the English people like the products of these schools and approve of the ideal of the English gentleman which is upheld by them. It was prophesied that after World War II the public schools would suffer a decline, but in 1952 and on through 1962 applications for admission were as numerous as ever. The prestige and glamour of the "old school tie," in spite of press cartoons and music-hall jokes, is as high as it was earlier in the century. To many Americans and others overseas the tail coat and tall hat of the Etonians and the shallow straw hat of the Harrovians are a source of mirth, but to the English patrons of these schools they are symbols of a long and interesting tradition.

A public school is defined as one represented on the Governing Bodies' Association or the Headmasters' Conference. In general, to qualify for membership a school must either be independent of any public grant or receive a direct grant from the Ministry of Education. It must also supply evidence of the freedom of the school and of the headmaster. At the time of the Fleming Report [7] in 1944 there were in the Governing Bodies' Association 87 independent schools and 65 schools receiving direct grants [8] from the Ministry. The Headmasters' Conference listed 83 independent schools and 98 receiving direct grants. In 1942 an Association of Governing Bodies of Girls' Schools was founded, with 78 independent schools and 35 receiving direct grants as members. There were also 23 girls' schools connected

[7] Ministry of Education, *The Public Schools and the General Education System*, H.M.S.O., London, 1944.

[8] Direct grants go directly to the schools concerned, without passing through the L.E.A.'s. In general they are given to schools only for some reason of tradition.

with the Public Day School Trust which affiliated with the Association. The majority of the boys' and girls' schools appear on both lists. The numbers involved have not changed materially since 1944.

The "great public schools" are Winchester (founded in 1387), Eton (1441), Shrewsbury (1552), Westminster (1560), Rugby (1567), Harrow (1571), Charterhouse (1611), and two London day schools: St. Paul's (1509), and Merchant Taylor's (1561). These schools have high prestige in the community. To have attended one of these schools gives a boy a hallmark that will last him all his life.

Eton, founded by Henry VI, is an outstanding example of the English public school. Its Tudor-Gothic buildings are surrounded by attractive grounds and playing fields near Windsor Castle. The school was originally intended for poor boys, called the King's Scholars, whose expenses were defrayed from the Privy Purse. A little later, wealthy paying pupils were admitted. At present the school has about 1,100 pupils, all in residence in "houses" of about 40 boys each. The house system, with boys of graded ages under the control of a housemaster, gives training in followership and leadership. For schoolwork there are classes, but the boys are also divided into small tutorial groups where they receive individual guidance. The masters are nearly all Oxford and Cambridge honors graduates, often with outstanding records in athletics as well.

Some of the older classrooms at Eton would horrify those used to the bright, functional rooms of an American high school, but the dingy walls and gnarled desks inscribed with scores of names are dear to the hearts of Etonians. In addition there are many modern classrooms and good laboratories. The curriculum still emphasizes classical and humanistic studies, but science and mathematics now receive adequate attention. The libraries are extremely good.

For formal dress the senior boys wear tall hats, tail coats, and white ties; the juniors wear Eton jackets, broad collars, and tall hats. Eton has given England ten prime ministers, including Wellington, Gladstone, Pitt, and Walpole; 22 governors-general of India, and a host of other famous men, such as Shelley, Sir Humphrey Gilbert, and Lord Roberts.

The girls' schools, organized on much the same plan, but later in date of foundation, include such well-known names as Cheltenham, Wycombe Abbey, Roedean, St. Paul's, St. Leonard's (Scotland), and Lowther (Wales).

The public schools are not controlled by the churches, but 75 of the independent schools of England and Wales have connections with a particular denomination. The Church of England has links with 63 and the Roman Catholic Church with six. In the nineteenth century many of the masters and practically all of the headmasters were in religious orders, but in 1944 only 24 of the headmasters were clergymen. All of the schools have chapels, and religion plays a prominent part in school life. The governing bodies vary in composition, but most of them are made up of representatives of the universities, the professions, and special local interests, as well as members of the associated church. The schools are supported by fees and income from endowments.

The main characteristics of the English public schools are the provision for a boarding-school education, the prefect system whereby the older boys have a definite share in the discipline and tone of the school, the house system which attaches the boys for residence to one of the houses under a housemaster, the emphasis on games and athletics, the attention given to religion, and the importance attached to participation by the boys in the corporate activities of the school.

Many critics state vehemently that there is something wrong with the whole public school system, that it has no place in a democratic society since it maintains the lines of division between social classes. Until comparatively recently the great majority of important positions in church and state went to persons educated in the public schools. With the steady growth of the county secondary schools, however, this situation has been changing, although gradually.

In 1942 the Board of Education appointed a special committee, under the chairmanship of Lord Fleming, to advise on means whereby the association between the public schools and the general educational system of the country might be developed and extended. This committee's report, published in 1944, is known as the Fleming Report. It made some interesting recommendations. The major one was that opportunities be provided for the enrollment of boys and girls who were considered capable of profiting by attending the public schools, regardless of the income of their parents. This was to be accomplished by giving the local education authorities the right to nominate a certain number of boys or girls for places, both day and boarding, in the public schools. In these cases the fees were to be paid by the local authorities. If the students were boarders, the parents were expected to pay part of the boarding fee if they were financially able. The committee also recommended that tuition and boarding fees in the public schools be set on a sliding scale according to the parents' income. In return for this concession, with the approval of the Board of Education, the L.E.A.'s might make contributions toward improvements and alterations in the schools. The L.E.A.'s were to have substantial representation on the governing bodies of schools to which they sent pupils.

This plan was never put into full operation, but many of the local education authorities were offered places in the public schools, and some of these were filled by pupils who had been educated in the county primary schools. Some of these pupils have been markedly successful. In recent years, however, the practice has seemed to die away, partly because the L.E.A.'s found it difficult to meet the expense, and partly because parents felt that their children might find difficulty in adjusting themselves to the public schools. There was little evidence to show that the latter assumption was correct, but many local education authorities preferred to keep their pupils in their own schools and even to establish boarding schools of their own.

The fact remains that the independent public schools, especially the large boarding schools, are as popular as ever. They continue to provide for a small but influential group of pupils, but they have lost their monopoly of positions in the civil service and at Oxford and Cambridge. They are also feeling financial strain; some of them have been forced to apply for substantial grants from the Ministry of Education and thus to become "aided" schools. In this case they are no longer independent schools, and they are asked to open at least 25 percent of the available places in their schools to pupils nominated by the local education authorities. The larger and more famous ones, however, are still completely independent, and will probably continue so. Whether they can withstand the social changes taking place in England and the steady growth of efficiency of the county secondary schools is yet to be seen.

The Preparatory Schools

There are about 480 preparatory schools. Although they begin in the primary years, they are so closely allied with the public schools that they are mentioned here. Preparatory schools take boys at the age of 8 or 9 years and prepare them to pass the examination for admission to the public schools at about the age of 13 years. They are expensive boarding schools, some being nearly as expensive as the public schools linked with them. Their curriculum and general school procedures are a preparation for the studies and the corporate life of the public schools. The tone and atmosphere is such that the boy will make a relatively easy transition to his senior school. Sir Cyril Norwood in *The English Tradition of Education* describes the process as that of a boy of 9 finding himself a "small minnow in a large pond," and after four years becoming a "large minnow in a small pond." This process is then repeated when he transfers to his public school. When he enters there he is again a "small minnow," and eventually, when he reaches the age of 17, he is once again a "large minnow," with the possibility of being a member of the cricket eleven and the football fifteen, and with considerable responsibility in the affairs of his "house" and of the school. The theory is that on entering the outside world similar experiences will face him, but his training will have fitted him for them. An example of a well-known preparatory school is Hildersham House at Broadstairs in Kent, with an enrollment of 65 to 70 boys. This school has a special connection with Rugby.

COEDUCATION

There have been very few coeducational schools on the secondary level in England. The public school tradition has been strongly against it; coeducation has been regarded as too much of a departure from the qualities thought necessary for a boys' school. This is in part due to a monastic tradition stretching back for centuries and in part to the relatively late educational emancipation of English girls and women. The girls' schools are mostly of recent origin, and it was only after World War I, and then with considerable misgiving and reluctance, that women were admitted to degrees at Oxford and Cambridge. The reorganized secondary education retains, in the main, the system of separate schools for boys and girls, although some coeducational modern schools have been established. Coeducation is common in Scotland; it will be interesting to see if it makes any headway in England during the next ten or twenty years.

THE EXAMINATION SYSTEM

To an American reader familiar with the frequent classroom tests given in high schools and the system of accrediting secondary schools so that colleges will accept their graduates, the English system of mass examinations conducted by external authorities may seem formal and rigid. No university in England accepts the certificate of a secondary school for entrance. Pupils who wish to enroll in a university course must qualify through an examination for the General Certificate of Education, and must make high enough marks in certain required courses to guarantee that they can do university work.

This examination system has existed for years, but it has undergone some liberalization. In 1951 the Ministry, believing that examinations were pressing too heavily on the schools, made some radical changes in procedure. The former School Certificate and Higher Certificate examinations were abolished, and the General Certificate of Education took their place. The G.C.E., as it is familiarly called, provides for different types of pupils and includes subjects suitable for many more courses than those in the old examinations.

A boy or girl entering the grammar school at age 11-plus is given a college-preparatory course until the age of 16 or 17. At the end of his fifth or sixth year he takes the examination for the General Certificate. There are eight examining bodies in England, each dealing with a fairly large area. For example, the Northern Universities Joint Matriculation Board covers the northern section, and the University of London Examining Board the metropolitan area. The eight boards prepare and correct their examinations independently, with some coordination through the Secondary Schools Examination Council, appointed by the Ministry of Education. The examinations are held twice a year, normally in June and December.

There are three levels of the examination: ordinary, advanced, and advanced with scholarship. The third level is the basis for the award of more than 12,000 scholarships, which provide free tuition at a British university and a maintenance grant. The three levels are intended to provide opportunities for different types of students, some of whom leave school and go to work, while others continue for university study. A certificate may be given for only one subject passed, although most pupils receive certificates showing four or more subjects. The certificates are issued by the Ministry of Education.

In 1962 there were, at the ordinary level, 43 subjects in which the pupils might be examined. The subjects which attracted the most candidates, with the percentages of those passing, were as follows: in English language, 293,154 presented themselves and 54.1 percent passed; in mathematics, out of 200,135, 57.2 percent passed; 56 percent of 300,753 who took science subjects passed; and in seven different modern languages 57.9 percent passed of 186,000 taking the test. The total number of entries for all subjects was 1,832,949 and the percentage of passes was 57.3. Girls, with 59.6 percent, did a little better than boys, with 55.5 percent.

At the advanced level in the same year there were 35 subjects for which pupils might sit. The subjects which attracted most candidates are shown in Table 12–4. Girls were still slightly ahead of boys in results of advanced-level examinations (70.1 percent as compared with 66.9 percent), were behind boys in percentage of distinctions obtained (3.9 percent against 4.8 percent), and were well behind in candidates for scholarships (10,104 compared with 30,953). In science subjects and mathematics the percent passing were almost equal: in mathematics: girls 67.0 and boys 67.4; in science: girls 67.4 and boys 67.2.

For the purpose of entrance standards universities require passes in five subjects, and at least two of these must be at the advanced level. If there is competition for places open in the university, those with the highest marks are accepted. Oxford University asks that the five subjects include English, a branch of mathematics or science, Latin or Greek, and a foreign language; two of the languages must be passed at the advanced level.

There is reciprocity between the eight examining bodies. A boy may pass the examination of the Welsh Joint Examining Board and be admitted to the University of Manchester or Bristol. Subjects

TABLE 12–4

Results of Advanced-Level Examinations, 1962

SUBJECT	TOTAL ENTRIES	PERCENT-AGE PASSED	PERCENTAGE GRANTED DISTINC-TION	ENTERED FOR SCHOLARSHIP
Physics	36,665	68.2	4.7	5,766
Chemistry	28,288	68.3	5.0	5,532
English literature	26,414	71.5	4.5	3,856
Pure and applied mathematics	21,161	69.3	5.1	3,840

SOURCE: "The General Certificate of Education Examinations," *Statistics of Education, Part 2, 1962*, London: H.M.S.O., 1962.

not on the official lists may be submitted to any of the eight examining bodies for approval at the ordinary level.

Professional or semiprofessional organizations sometimes require applicants to have the G.C.E. for entrance. For example, the Chartered Society of Physiotherapy asks applicants for its courses to have passed four subjects at the ordinary level, including English.

The reader will have noticed that some ambitious modern schools have been presenting candidates for the General Certificate of Education. The Ministry, however, feels that this is dangerous and may result in the schools in question putting their main effort into academic work for a few pupils, which is not the school's real objective. It would be better, according to the Ministry, for the schools to pass on these special pupils to the grammar schools and concentrate on the large number of nonacademic pupils in their charge.

In 1961 the Secondary School Examinations Council reported favorably to the Minister of Education on a proposal to retain the G.C.E. for academically minded pupils and devise a new School Leaving Certificate which would provide recognition and prestige for various courses and subjects in the modern schools. This proposal was still under consideration in 1962–63, since there was a considerable body of opinion that the new certificate would be considered inferior in status and that a better procedure would be to enlarge the scope of the General Certificate of Education.

Further Education

THE EDUCATION ACT of 1944 provided for a "Further Education" stage beyond the secondary, and separate from higher education in the universities. This includes much of the vocational work done in other countries in continuation schools and other part-time programs, and much of the work done in adult education programs. It was planned, however, to make extension courses readily available to boys and girls after the age of 15 years.

Prior to the 1944 Act local authorities were permitted and encouraged to provide various types of further education, with grants to assist them, but the Act made this provision compulsory. Section 41 of the 1944 Act states that local education authorities "are to secure the provision for their areas of adequate facilities for further education, that is to say: (a) full-time and part-time education for persons over compulsory school age; and (b) leisure-time occupation, in such organized cultural training and recreational activities as are suited to their requirements, for any persons over compulsory school age who are willing and able to profit by the facilities provided for that purpose." That the local authorities have given attention to this is evidenced by the increase in the number of institutions offering programs and the number of people participating.

The Ministry of Education regards "Further Education" as one of the most important divisions of English education, for it concerns the whole nation. Several points about this program should be considered:

1. The Ministry works out general policy and provides 55 percent of the cost. Local education authorities carry out the detailed organization with special regard for the needs of their own areas. Help from voluntary organizations is welcomed and utilized.

2. The Act says that this stage of education shall be compulsory up to the age of 18, but this section of the Act has not yet been brought into operation, nor does this seem to be probable in the near future.

3. Flexibility at all stages is the goal. A student may enter the program at any level, and remain within it as far as his capacity and wishes may carry him.

4. L.E.A.'s are bound by statute to provide adequate facilities for Further Education.

5. University education and the training of teachers are provided for separately and are not included in Further Education.

6. By far the greatest number of students are taking vocational courses.

TABLE 12–5
Further Education in England and Wales, November, 1962

NUMBER OF ESTABLISHMENTS		FULL-TIME STUDENTS	SANDWICH* STUDENTS	PART-TIME STUDENTS	EVENING STUDENTS	FULL-TIME TEACHERS	TOTAL STUDENTS
8,520	Men	84,751	15,550	475,440	874,554	21,791	1,390,295
	Women	68,192	429	129,292	1,042,395	3,683	1,240,308
	Total	152,943	15,979	604,732	1,856,949	25,474	2,630,603

SOURCE: Ministry of Education, *Statistics in Education, 1962*, London: H.M.S.O., 1962.
* A "sandwich" course is the name given to one in which periods of industrial training are sandwiched between periods of study in college.

7. There is a strong tendency for students to transfer vocational training in evening classes to day courses held on the employer's time.

Statistics on the Further Education program are given in Table 12–5. To provide for this army of students there are 7 National Colleges, 10 Colleges of Advanced Technology, 25 Regional Colleges, 166 Art Establishments, 38 Agricultural Institutes, 7,687 Evening Institutes (some are recreational but most are vocational), and 488 Technical Colleges and Colleges of Commerce.

VOCATIONAL COURSES

Most of the vocational courses, including technical, art, and commercial programs, are provided by the L.E.A.'s. More than a million students attend evening courses in such subjects as dressmaking, radio engineering, commercial art, journalism, and other fields. This program is very helpful to industrial employers, and in recognition of this fact the Ministry of Education has established National Certificates. These certificates are given at the conclusion of well-organized courses, extending over three to five years, in fields such as electrical engineering, chemistry, commerce, building trades, metallurgy, and textiles. Many evening students take courses in accounting and business administration. Some employers send apprentices to part-time day courses at technical schools, and large industrial firms sometimes set up their own schools. There are more than 30,000 students taking full-time courses in technical colleges and art schools.

NONVOCATIONAL COURSES

Local education authorities provide formal education for adults in 29 residential colleges or Centers of Adult Education, together with numerous short courses, conferences, and special gatherings in different parts of the country. All the universities in England and Wales have Departments of Extramural Studies or Departments of Adult Education.

The Workers' Educational Association is a federation of about 3,000 organizations with about 50,000 members. It is organized in 21 districts and works closely with the universities. The W.E.A. offers single lectures, short courses of ten lectures, courses lasting a year, three-year tutorial courses provided by a university, and vocational courses, generally residential. Sometimes the W.E.A. organizes courses abroad. Most of its offerings are open to the general public, as well as to members.

The Admiralty, the War Office, and the R.A.F. provide adult education for members of their services, often in collaboration with the L.E.A.'s, the W.E.A., and the universities. A wide network of correspondence courses is open to members of the armed forces who are at distant posts or who for other reasons cannot attend classes.

COUNTY COLLEGES

Another requirement of the 1944 Act was that all local education authorities, within three years after the leaving age had been raised to 15, should establish County Colleges. These colleges were to be attended by young people up to the age of 18 who were not attending school full-time. Part-time attendance, on the basis of one day a week on the employer's time, was to be provided. A similar plan had been proposed in the Fisher Act of 1918, when the new schools had been called "continuation schools." These had been suggested by the marked success of the German continuation schools originated in Munich by Kerschensteiner. Financial difficulties caused the abandonment of the 1918 plan. The County Colleges met with a similar fate, for England's war sacrifices made it impossible to finance a program which practically amounted to raising the leaving age to 18.

An anticipation of the move to establish County Colleges was made in Cambridgeshire a few years before World War II, as a result of the vision and energy of Henry Morris, Secretary for Education of the County Council. His objective, a slightly different one from that of the 1944 Act, was to revive interest in the rural countryside. He planned to establish Village Colleges, each of which, placed in a central position, would serve nine or ten villages by providing a post-primary school in the daytime and an educational center for youth and adults in the evenings and on weekends. His ideas received considerable support, and in 1937 the first college was opened at Sawston. Three others followed, the last of these at Impington, opened in 1939 just as war broke out. Impington was famous because of its beautiful buildings, designed by two distinguished architects, Gropius and Fry. In 1942, during the war, over 1,400 persons between the ages of 14 and 70 attended. In addition to the day school for boys and girls aged 11 to 15, it provided 18 clubs or societies for adults and eight for young people 14 to 20 years of age.

The subjects varied from folk dancing, dramatics, and music to rural science, child welfare, and modern languages. The "countrymen's colleges," as they were often called, attracted much interest and drew educators from many parts of the world.

YOUTH SERVICES

The organization of social, recreational, and educational facilities for youth during their leisure hours was until 1939 carried out by voluntary societies. The British government, alarmed at the possible disappearance of these facilities during World War II, established a National Youth Committee and made arrangements for the payment of grants from the Board of Education.

By the 1944 Education Act, service of youth was made, by statute, a part of Further Education. The L.E.A.'s all have Youth Committees and Youth Officers and voluntary organizations are encouraged to continue and to expand their efforts. Some of the most prominent of these voluntary organizations are: Boy Scouts, Girl Guides, Boys' Brigade, Federation of Young Farmers' Clubs, Junior Section of the British Red Cross, Y.M.C.A., Y.W.C.A., and the Welsh League of Youth. All are represented on the Standing Conference of National Voluntary Youth Organizations.

But the service of youth is a branch of English national educational activity which has not prospered. There has been much critical comment in recent years. The movement seems to have lost much of its original enthusiasm and drive. Causes of this appear to be lack of sufficient support from public funds, the growing appeal of many new fields of vocational training, and the lack of well-qualified leaders with inspirational force. A Committee of Enquiry in 1960 suggested the initiation by the Ministry of Education of a ten-year development plan aimed at bringing new life into the Youth Services of England and Wales.

Universities

IN 1962 there were 24 universities in the United Kingdom: 18 in England, four in Scotland, and one each in Wales and Northern Ireland. The list of these, with dates of foundation, is given in Table 12–6.

Oxford and Cambridge were the only universities in England for 600 years and have had a very powerful influence on the policies and

TABLE 12–6
British Universities and Dates of Establishment

UNIVERSITY	DATE OF FOUNDING
Oxford	Twelfth century
Cambridge	Thirteenth century
St. Andrews	
Glasgow*	Fifteenth and
Aberdeen	sixteenth centuries
Edinburgh	
Durham	1832
London	1836
Manchester (Victoria)*	1880
University of Wales	1893
Birmingham	1900
Liverpool	1903
Leeds	1904
Sheffield	1905
Bristol	1909
Queen's University, Belfast	1909
Reading	1926
Nottingham	1948
Southampton	1952
Hull	1954
Exeter	1955
Leicester	1957
Sussex	1961
Keele†	1962

SOURCES: H. C. Dent, *The Educational System of England and Wales,* University of London Press, 1961, p. 182; *Britain: an Official Handbook,* London: Central Office of Information, 1963, p. 169.

* There are two colleges of technology, one in Manchester and the other in Glasgow, which have practically the status of universities.

† Keele University is the new name that was given to the University College of North Staffordshire when in 1962 it became an independent university.

procedures of their nineteenth- and twentieth-century successors. They are world famous and students from many countries seek admission. Each of these two universities is made up of a number of colleges in which students reside; it is necessary to be admitted to a college in order to become a member of the university. There is a small minority of noncollegiate students, but one of the special features of Oxford and Cambridge is the benefit obtained from residential life. There are more than twenty colleges at each, most of them with famous names and histories. Examples at Cambridge are Clare (founded 1326), King's (1441), Jesus (1496), and Trinity (1546). At Oxford examples are Balliol (1264), New College (1379), Magdalen (1458), and Christ Church (1546). The colleges are autonomous, with endowments of their own. Students attend lectures in various colleges and in university halls, but they are also members of small tutorial groups in their own colleges, where they receive expert guidance in their studies from the tutors in charge. At Oxford and Cambridge it is advisable to have between £700 and £800 a year to meet all expenses, including maintenance and some travel during the vacations.

Athletic activities are prominent in university life, and the students are encouraged to take part in the numerous clubs associated with debating and drama. A degree with first-class honors from Oxford or Cambridge is regarded as a very high achievement. Most applicants for places in British universities put Oxford and Cambridge first in their list of preference, but only a limited number can be admitted to the colleges. At Oxford there are about 8,000 students, of whom 1,150 are women. At Cambridge there are about 8,500 students, with 760 women. In 1962 there were about 115,000 full-time students at universities in the United Kingdom, the percentage of women being higher at universities other than Oxford and Cambridge.

The four Scottish universities, St. Andrews, Glasgow, Aberdeen, and Edinburgh, were established in the fifteenth and sixteenth centuries. All have high academic standing. Scottish universities do not have residential colleges and in that respect are unlike Oxford and Cambridge. For centuries Scottish students have been noted for their devotion to education, and many of them have undergone considerable hardship in order to pay their way at a university. Fortunately the generous system of university scholarships now offered in Scotland, involving maintenance allowances and free tuition, makes these sacrifices no longer necessary.

The universities of Durham and London were established early in the nineteenth century. Durham is picturesquely situated in the north of England in the ancient buildings of Durham Castle, with the cathedral close nearby. Its students come from all parts of the country and reside in colleges. It has a modern adjunct, King's College, at Newcastle, where engineering and scientific courses are offered. London, by way of contrast, is a nonresidential university, the largest in Great Britain, with 40 constituent colleges spread all over the city. It has more full-time students than either Oxford or Cambridge. In addition, it has thousands of "external" students in Britain and overseas. These students take the matriculation examinations, receive lecture notes and course materials, and finally take the examinations for degrees without, in some cases, ever attending classes or lectures in London. Many of them are part-time students who take some course work. Some of its most famous units are the London School of Economics, the Imperial College of Science and Technology, the Institute of Education (which draws students from all over the world for advanced courses), and the group of postgraduate medical institutions which, in similar fashion, attract students from all parts of the British Commonwealth.

London University has rendered a great service to the British Empire and Commonwealth by developing a structure with an "external" as well as an "internal" degree. Students in any part of the world may present for university entrance and then for degree courses at London without attendance at the university. What they have to do is to pass the necessary examinations at a center approved by the university. This has given a start to several university colleges in England and Wales and also overseas by enabling them to establish a standard of work under the guidance and helpful criticism of the University of London.

The University of Wales was established in 1893 as a result of a strong demand by the Welsh people for a university of their own. The geography of Wales, with its rugged mountains and long valleys, made it necessary, because of transportation difficulties, to have a federal university, with four constituent colleges at Cardiff, Swansea, Bangor, and Aberystwith.

The two colleges of technology, at Manchester and Glasgow, are well known throughout the British Commonwealth for the high standing of their work. Their teaching in technological subjects qualifies some of their students for degrees at the universities in the two cities.

GOVERNMENT AND FINANCE

The universities are independent and self-governing bodies. They are organized with such bodies as the Council and Convocation, with a Chancellor as the nominal head and the Vice-Chancellor as the executive head. Universities receive direct grants from the Treasury on the advice of the University Grants Committee, whose members are appointed by the Chancellor of the Exchequer from persons with wide experience in education or administration. Some of the universities also receive grants from local education authorities and nearly all receive payments from the Ministry of Education for services in the field of adult education. Some have large endowment and all receive revenue from tuition and examination fees.

The University Grants Committee has been very helpful. It arranges for the Treasury to pay "recurrent grants," which form a stable contribution each year, and "nonrecurrent grants," which are made for special developments and emergencies, such as the necessity of revising staff salaries when a change in the cost of living makes this necessary. The committee has safeguarded the autonomy of the universities by opposing any detailed approval by the Treasury of university expenditures. It believes that the universities should be free to spend their grants as they themselves see fit. The Committee visits each university from time to time and discusses developmental and financial projects; the relations between the universities and the Grants Committee have been uniformly cordial.

The proportion of income provided for the universities from the Exchequer is increasing, and in 1961 it was 72.7 percent of the total cost from the national government. Another 2 percent came from L.E.A.'s, 9.4 percent from fees, and the balance from endowments, gifts, and other sources.

ADMISSION OF STUDENTS

Universities have absolute control over the admission, suspension, and expulsion of their students, and also over the appointment and dismissal of staff. Students who apply for admission to a university must, in the examinations for the General Certificate of Education: (a) have obtained a pass in English language and in either four or five other subjects; (b) include among the subjects passed a language other than English and either mathematics or an approved science; (c) pass at least two of the subjects at the advanced level; and (d) pass at the same sitting in two subjects at the advanced level and in one other subject not related to the two subjects taken at the advanced level, if only four subjects in addition to English language are offered.

Admission to the universities is by examination and selection; there is no religious or color bar. But the universities limit the number of undergraduates accepted, for, despite recent programs of expansion, applications from qualified students far exceed the number of places available. Students have been in the habit of lodging applications with at least six universities. In 1952 details were announced for a "clearing house" plan that will come into operation in 1964 after a trial period in 1963. Applications will then be sent to the Universities Central Council on Admissions instead of to individual universities, and the clearing house will then pass on rejected applications to the next university of the candidate's choice. Oxford and Cambridge, the medical schools of London University, and the universities of Scotland and Northern Ireland will not participate and will continue to use their own methods of admitting students. It must be remembered also that the universities render a valuable service to students of Commonwealth and other countries by accommodating 13,000 overseas students. Many of these, however, are in advanced or special courses.

SCHOLARSHIPS AND GRANTS TO STUDENTS

About 80 percent of university students in Great Britain are now aided from private or public funds. The development of this trend is illustrated by Table 12–7. In 1962 an Education Act put into

TABLE 12–7
Development of University Scholarships

	PERCENTAGE OF STUDENTS HOLDING SCHOLARSHIPS	
	1939	*1952*
England		
Cambridge University	39.0	67.8
Oxford University	55.2	71.7
London University	26.0	67.7
Other universities	44.4	79.5
Wales	61.4	88.3
Scotland	45.1	61.6

SOURCE: *Britain: An Official Handbook, 1963*, pp. 170–71.

operation the recommendations of the Anderson Committeee on Grants to Students that awards should be granted to all student-applicants who have two G.C.E. passes at the advanced level. There were 26,050 awards in all for 1963. Most L.E.A.'s had adopted the principle of automatic awards in 1960 and 1961.

One of the most interesting undergraduate awards is the Mature State Scholarship. These scholarships are awarded for full-time courses in liberal studies to students over the age of 25 who, for some reason or other, were unable to take a university course at the normal age. Among those receiving such awards have been two bricklayers, a plasterer, a fitter, a Falkland Islands surveyor, a Merchant Navy officer, two newspaper subeditors, a housewife, and a warehouse stock-keeper. Since the scheme began in 1947, 422 Mature State Scholarships have been awarded. Those who thought that this was a rash and even foolish plan are advised to consider that at the end of 1962, 319 of the 422 had completed degree courses, 286 of them gaining honors degrees, including 35 "firsts" in their honors courses.

A PROGRAM OF EXPANSION

British universities are expanding rapidly in order to meet the growing demand for tertiary education and the special need for scientists and technologists. In 1959 the total number of university students was 100,000. It is estimated that this will have increased by 1966 to 150,000, and to 170,000 by 1974.

This means the planning of an extensive building program for which the Exchequer, through the University Grants Committee, has authorized £104,000,000, with an additional £30,000,000 for buildings commencing in each of the years 1960 and 1965. To these Exchequer funds must be added money raised by the universities themselves.

To give Britain 30 universities by 1965, the University Grants Committee first of all authorized a new university in Sussex, at Brighton. This opened in 1961 and was only able to admit one student for every twenty who applied. It will eventually be able to take 6,000 students, and early in its career has broken with tradition by enrolling twice as many girls as young men. Six other centers were selected—Norwich and York, which opened in 1963, and Lancaster, Canterbury, Colchester, and Warwick which are all expected to be in operation by 1965. They are all filled with enthusiasm and declare that the "sheltered superiority" of Oxford and Cambridge is now over.

The Education and Status of Teachers

RECRUITMENT

The Ministry of Education is responsible for seeing that there is a sufficient number of trained teachers to staff the system of public education. The responsibility for the standard and content of teacher training lies with the universities, each university being responsible for the training within a given area.

The most recent report (1962) of the National Advisory Council on the Training and Supply of Teachers states that, with the present leaving age of 15, the school population will increase from nearly 7,000,000 in 1960 to 7,700,000 in 1970 and 8,900,000 in 1980. The Council reported to the Ministry that according to present plans the number of qualified teachers in service will be insufficient by a considerable margin to eliminate over-large classes (secondary classes of more than 30 and junior classes of over 40). By 1970 the total number of teachers will be 50,000 fewer than the number required to fulfill this aim. By 1980 there will be a gap of 40,000 full-time teachers.

There are two outstanding problems: (a) if the school-leaving age is raised to 16 in 1970, 20,000 additional teachers will be required to meet this increase alone, and (b) the wastage of young married women teachers is a matter for concern. The trend in recent years toward earlier marriage and earlier family building has greatly increased this wastage. In 1962 women represented nearly 70 percent of recruitment, but they built up only 33 percent of the net increase in the teaching force. In that year 19,000 women were recruited, but 17,000 left the service.

Emergency measures—publicity about teaching as a national service, and casting the net wider to bring in recruits—have helped but have not seriously reduced the deficit. Some other measures used have been: (a) employment of temporary and part-time teachers; (b) pressure on the training colleges to take in more students; (c) retention of some teachers beyond retirement age; (d) revision of regulations to make it easier for qualified women teachers to return after marriage; and (e) use of television and radio for the teaching of mathematics and science.

TRAINING

There were 186 teacher-training colleges in England and Wales in 1962–63; in that year about 51,000 students were enrolled. This number is expected to rise to 70,000 in 1966–67 and to 80,000 by 1970. Many of the colleges are being extended, and new ones are being built. Until recently the usual training course lasted for two years, but this was extended to three years in September 1960 and the first class of third-year students began their extended year's work in 1962.

The courses are generally residential, but recently eight colleges have been opened for day students only, with the idea of attracting students older than the average, whose domestic responsibilities would preclude them from living in college.

In 1963, 110 of the colleges were maintained by local education authorities, 49 by voluntary bodies such as the Church of England, the Roman Catholic Church, and various nondenominational groups; 27 were Education Departments of universities. There were 16,991 men in training, including 2,158 in universities, and 34,852 women enrolled, with 1,478 in universities.

There are seventeen areas in England and Wales where a responsible university has established an Institute of Education to coordinate and promote the training of teachers within the area. In the London area there are more than 30 training institutions, but in the area supervised by Exeter University there are only three. All the training institutions within any area are members of the Institute. A typical group would be:

1. The Education Department of a university. This department gives a one-year course devoted to professional training. The students are all graduates and most of them will teach in grammar schools. In many cases the courses lead to a Diploma of Education, or to a pass in the first year of a Bachelor of Education degree.

2. One or more General Training Colleges giving a three-year course of professional and cultural education. Some of these colleges may be maintained by a local education authority, others by the Roman Catholic Church or by the Church of England.

3. Several Specialist Training Colleges giving courses of training in the teaching of physical education, housecraft, or technical subjects. Courses last from one to three years.

The Institute guarantees the standard of work and supervises the general procedure of the colleges without undue interference in their management or the details of their work. The governing body of the Institute is the Vice-Chancellor of the university as ex-officio chairman, with representatives of the training colleges, the L.E.A.'s, and the Ministry of Education. L.E.A.'s, voluntary organizations, and universities doing this important work of training teachers are aided with grants from the Ministry of Education and given a good deal of help in their building programs. Students receive grants covering tuition and boarding fees.

After a student has completed his training and takes up an appointment in the schools, he is given opportunities of attending refresher schools, short courses, and special conferences. After he has had some experience he may apply for a year's exchange teaching in one of the Commonwealth countries, in Europe, or in the United States. It is the aim of the Ministry of Education that eventually all teachers in Britain should hold a degree and a course in professional training of university standard.

TEACHERS' SALARIES

With 146 separate employing authorities in England and Wales it might be expected that salaries would differ widely according to counties and districts, but this is not the case. Salaries of teachers in all schools maintained or aided from public funds are fixed in scales established by a joint committee representing the local authorities and the teachers' associations. This is known as the "Burnham Scale," since the original committee was formed under the chairmanship of Lord Burnham. The Minister of Education must approve the scale set by the committee: he cannot amend it, although he can reject it, if he finds this necessary. The Minister can make the scale compulsory for all L.E.A.'s and other employing groups. The scale is revised from time to time by the committee; negotiations for the latest revision were in progress at the end of 1962.

A basic salary is paid to all qualified assistant teachers. The basic salary increases by annual increments of £12 to £50. Teachers who are graduates receive an additional amount for that qualification. Extra payments are paid for positions of special responsibility. Head teachers are paid additional amounts. For many years the scales provided that women teachers receive four-fifths of the salaries of men in the same positions. The National Union of Teachers waged a long campaign for equal pay for men and women, and a movement to eliminate the differential was begun in 1955. It was completed, after seven stages, in 1961.

The Ministry of Education has organized a system of superannuation for all teachers, based on salary and years of service. The teacher and the employing authority each contribute 5 percent of his salary. The contributions are paid into the Treasury, which then pays all retirements and gratuities under the scheme. Absence of any provision for widows' and dependents' pensions has long been recognized as a serious shortcoming on this teachers' superannuation scheme. Negotiations were carried on about this during 1962 and it appears that a successful plan will be worked out, to be paid for by additional contributions but avoiding any reductions in the teachers' own benefits.

TEACHERS' ASSOCIATIONS

There are several teachers' associations in England and Wales that draw their members from the schools maintained and aided by the L.E.A.'s. The six main associations are the National Union of Teachers, the Incorporated Association of Assistant Masters in Secondary Schools, the Incorporated Association of Assistant Mistresses in Secondary Schools, the Incorporated Association of Headmasters of Secondary Schools, the Incorporated Association of Headmistresses of Secondary Schools, and the Association of Teachers in Technical Institutions. The independent schools have their own associations, both for heads of schools and assistant members of the staff.

Of the associations connected with government-aided schools, by far the largest and most powerful is the National Union of Teachers, often known as the N.U.T. Membership is open to any qualified teacher from nursery school to training college or university. There are more than 200,000 members. The N.U.T. has headquarters in London, but there are branches all over England and Wales. It publishes a widely read journal called *The Schoolmaster and Woman Teacher's Chronicle*. The N.U.T. carefully watches all matters connected with teacher welfare, remuneration, and status, but it also takes a lively interest in modern developments in methods of teaching and in the organization of schools. It has no political affiliations with any party, but at the same time it exerts a powerful influence in Parliament.

In most general elections, ten or more members of the N.U.T.

are elected to the House of Commons, not representing the N.U.T. but as members for various constituencies. At the general election of 1951, 18 were elected. The N.U.T. is prepared to sponsor certain candidates, paying all the expenses of their election campaigns, and to support others by giving them some financial assistance. This sponsorship and support will be given to a candidate from any political party—Conservative, Liberal, or Labor—provided the N.U.T. feels that national education and the welfare of the teachers will receive positive support from the member if elected. The N.U.T. is represented on many official committees; for example, it has 16 members on the Teachers' Panel of the Burnham Scale Committee. It has ample funds and in general exercises a strong and useful influence on the educational opinion of the country.

Schools in Scotland

IN 1945 the Education (Scotland) Act was passed, applying to Scotland the same progressive ideas which had been incorporated in the English Act of 1944. The two Acts were not identical, for Scotland had already put into operation some of the changes which were proposed in the English Act. There were also a number of provisions which applied to Scotland alone. The pattern of the two systems is similar in many respects, but there are some marked differences:

1. In Scotland there is no dual system, as in England, of county schools and voluntary schools. In 1918 the voluntary schools were handed over to the management of the local authorities.

2. A "public school" does not mean, as in England, a large independent school but is the term given to any school under the management of an education authority. Independent schools in Scotland are neither as numerous nor as prominent as in England. There are some important ones, such as Fettes and Loretto for boys, and St. Leonard's for girls, but most of the pupils in Scotland attend government schools.

3. The organization for secondary education is very different. The Scottish people do not believe in the English tripartite system but prefer comprehensive or "omnibus" schools, where all types of pupils are provided for in the same school.

4. Religious education is not mandatory in Scottish schools as in English; this is left to local authorities to arrange if they wish.

On the other hand, the 1945 Scottish Act reveals many similarities between the two systems, some of the chief ones being:

1. Local authorities in Scotland are now required to make provision for nursery schools and nursery classes if the demand exists. Previously this had been optional.

2. The leaving age was raised to 15 in 1947, and will be raised to 16 when staffing and buildings permit.

3. The local authorities must make provision for all types of handicapped children.

4. Further education must be organized for all young people between the leaving age and 18 years, in junior colleges, in various forms of adult programs, and in voluntary courses. As in England, the opening of junior colleges has been suspended for the time being because of financial reasons.

5. Local authorities must provide milk and hot meals for school children.

6. Local authorities are empowered to build hostels and establish boarding schools where necessary. This is especially applicable to some of the remote and sparsely settled districts in the Highlands.

7. Educational authorities must make adequate provision for physical education and recreational training throughout their areas.

8. Teachers' salaries are fixed for all education authorities according to a standard scale issued by the Secretary of State for Scotland after advice from a special committee representative of the teachers and of the L.E.A.'s.

The total population of Scotland in June, 1962, was 5,196,600, of whom 846,000 were of school age. There were 3,289 public or grant-aided schools in the country in 1962, divided as follows: nursery schools, 89; primary, 2,323; secondary, 752; and special schools, 125. Pupils enrolled in school in January, 1962, totalled 889,344. The numbers varied greatly in different education areas; for example, in the cities there were 183,339 in Glasgow, 71,545 in Edinburgh, 32,570 in Dundee, and 32,322 in Aberdeen. Some of the industrial areas also had heavy enrollments, such as 104,235 in Lanark, 57,646 in Renfrew, and 33,899 in Dumbarton. On the other hand some of the education areas were sparsely settled and made up mainly of heath and moor, such as Inverness, with 14,461 enrolled; Argyll with 8,818; Ross and Cromarty, 10,262; Caithness, 4,971; Shetland, 2,931; Sutherland, 2,290; and Peebles with only 2,007.

Instruction in the primary schools in Scotland, though sound, used to be rather formal. This thoroughness has been retained, but activity programs, excursions, projects, practical work, oral expression, improvement of reading rates and comprehension, and visual aids are all being used now. Head teachers and senior teachers can take special courses in the Colleges of Education on modern teaching methods. One of the results has been a greater eagerness to continue on in school to secondary and Further Education.

The primary schools have seven classes, from ages 5- to 12-plus, one year longer than in England. Certain subjects are prescribed as essential by the Scottish Education Department, but, subject to this one condition, head teachers may work out the courses of study best suited to the circumstances and environment of their schools. Promotion to secondary schools is based on a combination of an intelligence test, the school record, and achievement tests in English and arithmetic. This procedure is used to direct pupils to the most suitable courses, but the parents' wishes are given careful consideration. The tense situation caused in England by the "11-plus" examination seems to be absent in Scotland.

Junior secondary schools offer three-year courses of general education; senior secondary schools retain their pupils for five or six years and in many cases prepare them for higher education. Courses in secondary schools include literary, commercial, technical, homemaking, and rural divisions, the number of these offered in any particular school depending on the location of the school and the probable vocational future of the pupils. In the junior secondary school much more realism has been introduced into the work, with an increased recognition of the importance of learning by doing; probably as a result of this there has been a marked increase in the number of favorable reports sent in by employers of junior secondary school pupils.

The culmination of the secondary course in Scottish schools used to be marked by an examination known as the Scottish Leaving Certificate. It had the reputation of being a very sound examination, and was accepted as part of the qualification for entrance to any British university. It gave three guarantees:

1. That the pupil had had a sound general secondary course spread over five years.

2. That the school certified his proficiency in the subjects named in the certificate.

3. That he had passed a written examination in these subjects.

If a pupil failed in his written examination, but was highly regarded by his school, an inspector visited the school and investigated the discrepancy, passing the pupil if he decided that such a course was justified.

The Scottish authorities, however, did not want their main certificate to be a purely academic one. In order to provide for early leavers and different types of courses, they changed to the Scottish Certificate of Education, which is awarded at both the ordinary and advanced levels. The new certificate is similar in many ways to the G.C.E. in England but extends to fields beyond the educational field of the grammar school.

In 1962, candidates from all over Scotland presented for the first time at the ordinary level of the Scottish Certificate of Education. The results were most encouraging, and headmasters reported the good influence on the less able pupils of this more attainable goal. There were many comments on an eagerness and greater sense of purpose in classes where no such spirit had been evident two years earlier. Pupils normally presented at the ordinary grade at the end of their fourth secondary year and at the higher grade at the end of their sixth year. Table 12–8 gives some sample items from the long list of 54 subjects covered by the Scottish Certificate of Education.

Technical education is effectively organized in Scotland. There are four large technical colleges at Glasgow, Edinburgh, Dundee, and Aberdeen, each serving a large geographical area. They offer a variety of courses, such as engineering, building trades, art, commerce, agriculture, textiles, and navigation. In addition to day courses there are many evening courses that last from three to five years and lead to national certificates in engineering, building trades, chemistry, and naval architecture. Many of the chief engineers on ships in the British Mercantile Marine seem to have received their training in Scotland.

During the last few years there has been a big expansion of technical education in Scotland. Plans were approved for projects estimated to cost £1.3 million. These included a new College of Nauti-

TABLE 12–8

Examination Results for Scottish Certificate of Education, 1962

SUBJECT	ORDINARY GRADE		HIGHER GRADE	
	Presentations	*Passes*	*Presentations*	*Passes*
English	22,060	18,542	11,237	8,731
Arithmetic	31,665	26,417		
Mathematics	19,095	14,786	6,824	5,434
Spanish	369	281	154	112
Physics	11,359	8,816		
Chemistry and physics			4,691	3,621
Technical drawing	3,584	2,423		
Navigation	52	42		
Home management	1,235	1,012	508	394
Principles of accounting	2,165	1,454		

SOURCE: *Education in Scotland in 1962* (report of the Secretary of State for Scotland), Edinburgh: H.M.S.O., 1962, p. 122.

cal Studies in Glasgow, a new Scottish Woollen Technical College in Galashiels, and extensions to the David Dale College, Glasgow, to Esk Valley College, Midlothian, to Robert Gordon's College, Aberdeen, and to W. M. Ramsay Technical College and the College of Art, both in Edinburgh. These projects included Napier Technical College, Edinburgh, a new School of Architecture at Edinburgh, a new technical college at Clydebank, the new Anniesland Further Education Center, Glasgow, the second phase of Kirkcaldy Technical College, and extensions to Thurso Technical College and to the Scottish College of Commerce, Glasgow. Others valued at £765,000 were completed, including a new technical college at Arbroath, and the first phase of the extensions to Kirkcaldy Technical College, to Glasgow School of Art, and to the Reid Kerr College, Paisley.

In 1962 there were 14,391 students taking full-time courses, and 20,259 others were part-time students released from employment for various amounts of time per week. Other part-time students totaled 225,899.

Scotland provides a remarkably varied series of classes and lectures to meet the needs of adults. In 1962, 124,668 adults attended courses, studying such subjects as archeology, practical art, politics, sciences, Gaelic, Spanish, Russian, and philosophy.

In 1962 a number of voluntary youth organizations were in operation; 14,100 of these listed 38,000 unpaid leaders and 512,000 members. Local education authorities lent school buildings to 350 different organizations. Holiday camps, 1,800 in number, were organized by local units for visiting youth groups. Types of attractive educational ventures offered to youth organizations were the following: an exploration course in the Cairngorm area, a weather station maintained 4,000 feet above sea level, a course of practical exercises in boat maintenance, 4,600 entries in the Duke of Edinburgh's Award Scheme, an Outdoor Pursuits Training Center in the Highlands, and filming and sketching in the Western Isles.

Scotland is in an almost unique position in regard to the qualifications of its teachers. Of a total of nearly 32,000 teachers in 1952, all but 900 held regular certificates. Thirty-one percent of the primary teachers and 67 percent of the secondary teachers were university graduates. Women made up 83 percent of the primary school staff and 43 percent of the secondary school group. The figures for 1962 were almost the same: 30.5 percent of the primary teachers and 64.4 percent of the secondary teachers were university graduates, while women made up 83 percent of the primary school staff and 41.2 percent of the secondary staff. In 1961 there were 39,043 teachers employed full time in Scotland of whom 36,774 were certificated. The Colleges of Education, which are the teachers' training colleges of Scotland, give excellent courses, and special attention is given to in-service training of teachers in the field. In 1962, 5,700 teachers attended these special courses. More than 2,000 primary teachers took courses in the Cuisenaire method of teaching arithmetic. A further 1,050 primary teachers attended courses and conferences on recent developments in the teaching of science, geography, history, and other subjects in the primary school. Special conferences were held for infant mistresses. Many of the various courses and conferences were held locally in such centers as Kirkcaldy, Perth, Alloa, Forfar, Dumfries, and Galashiels with the full cooperation and assistance of the education authorities.

Conferences and courses for secondary teachers attracted a total enrollment of nearly 2,200. The seventh annual conference for teachers of history was attended by 187 principal teachers, and other conferences, some residential, were held for teachers of English, classics, commercial subjects, and science. A residential course on the use of the library in secondary schools, provided jointly by the Ministry of Education and the Jordanhill College of Education, was attended by 68 Scottish and English teachers. Other courses were held in statistics, economics, recreational mathematics, biology, physics, inorganic chemistry, outdoor physical education, music, Shakespearean drama, and technical subjects.

In addition, the colleges of education provided refresher courses for married women teachers returning to service, for music specialists, and for teachers of young children. They also provided courses and other educational gatherings of various groups connected with the educational services, e.g., naval officers and instructors at Rosyth, the staffs of approved schools, instructors in occupational centers, youth workers, and school chaplains.

Four Scottish teachers of Russian attended a four-week summer school in the U.S.S.R., and a reciprocal course for Soviet teachers of English was provided in Britain.

Teachers in Scotland have a respected status in the community, salaries are regulated by a special committee on which teachers are represented, and there is a good superannuation scheme. Students from many overseas countries such as Ghana, Cyprus, Kenya, and Egypt attend courses at Scottish colleges of education, and Scottish exchange teachers are to be found in Australia, Canada, New Zealand, and other Commonwealth countries.

Problems of the Operation of Schools in England and Wales

The Eleven-plus Examination

The restrictive nature of the 11-plus examination, at the end of what might otherwise be a more varied and more enjoyable period of work in the primary school, gives much concern to British educators and parents. The solution most frequently under discussion is to increase the weight given to the pupils' school records and to the opinions of teachers and headmasters concerning the proper placement of pupils in secondary schools. The examination, however, is administratively convenient and there is much inertia toward changing it.

Secondary Technical Schools

The secondary technical school has not been as successful as was hoped. In an age of electronics, space travel, supersonic jets, and atomic power stations, this type of school would seem to warrant both prestige and a large enrollment. The solution may be in the growth of bilateral secondary schools or the expansion of comprehensive schools.

The General Certificate of Education

The changes made in the Scottish Certificate of Education in widening its field to include more than 50 subjects for examination seem to have met with general approval. This move has tended to give equality to a number of different secondary courses and seems to have created a much greater sense of purpose in Scottish secondary schools. Discussion has been taking place in England and Wales about a somewhat similar widening of the G.C.E., to bring under its wing the secondary modern schools and the secondary technical schools.

School Buildings and Facilities

The problem of accommodation is nearing solution; many new schools have been built and the situation is steadily improving. There are still over-large classes, but this must also be attributed to a teacher shortage.

Shortage of Teachers

This remains the most serious problem of all. More recruits are coming in, courses of training are longer and better, but still there are not enough qualified teachers. New developments in teaching procedures use up some of the increase in numbers. All of this slows down the elimination of over-large classes and makes it difficult to contemplate raising the school-leaving age to 16.

There is a great deal of vitality in education in England and Wales. Important research is going on, many interesting conferences are being held, and in the community there is much discussion about education and its problems. National and local authorities are striving to furnish a national system of education that will provide the best possible opportunities for each child and will exemplify the accepted concepts of what is best for the whole nation. The 1944 Act, although it was the result of an evolutionary development of ideas over many years, was practically a revolution in education. The next few years should see sound consolidation and steady advance in the English school system.

13
French Schools in Action

REWAR education in France has been described in Chapter 5. The program was developed from French ideas of general culture and reflected the political system of centralization of authority in the national government. Within the Ministry of National Education separate organizations, or directorates, supervised and controlled separate systems of elementary, secondary, and technical education. Secondary education was a highly selective system that was intended to preserve the superiority of French culture. The Langevin Plan proposed extensive modifications of this program, and the recommendations of the plan and some of the results have been discussed in the previous chapter on French schools. In 1949 the Delbos Act put some of the Langevin recommendations into effect, and in 1959 President de Gaulle by a stroke of the pen made other changes.

National schools in France are organized on the principle of lay control with complete neutrality in religion. Religious instruction is considered to be the responsibility of parents and churches, not of the public schools. In order to facilitate instruction in religious principles outside of school, the state schools are closed on Thursdays, which are set aside for religious instruction in the churches. There are schools operated by private individuals and by sectarian bodies, and these parallel the national system.

Between the ages of 6 and 14, education has been compulsory by law, although enforcement has not been complete. Under the 1959 decree the upper age limit has been raised to 16 for all who begin school after January 1, 1959. Authorities report that about 65 percent of all French children now remain in school after the 14-year age limit.

While the coordination and articulation of the various school

13-1 Diagram of French School System, 1950

YEARS IN SCHOOL														YEARS OF AGE

Universities

Institutes attached to universities

Law · Arts · Sciences · Medicine · Pharmacy

Higher professional schools

Higher technical schools

Adult education

18 — 23
17 — 22
16 — 21
15 — 20
14 — 19

Preparatory year | Prep. course — 13 — 18

Final or terminal year — 12 — 17

Lycées and collèges

Cycle de détermination — 11 / 10 — 16 / 15

Cycle d'orientation — 9 / 8 / 7 / 6 — 14 / 13 / 12 / 11

Collèges modernes

Normal schools

Vocational schools · Collèges techniques · Apprentice centers

Complementary classes

Preparatory schools

Elementary schools — 5 / 4 / 3 / 2 / 1 — 10 / 9 / 8 / 7 / 6

5

Preschool education)
(Maternal schools, Crèches) — 4 / 3 / 2

13-2   Diagram of French School System, 1959

YEARS IN SCHOOL		YEARS OF AGE
18	Universities	23
17	Institutes attached to universities · Higher professional education · Higher normal schools · Adult education	22
16	Law · Arts · Sciences · Medicine · Pharmacy · Theology	21
15	Higher technical schools	20
14		19
13	Preparatory year · Normal schools	18
12	Terminal year	17
11	Classical · Modern · Technical · Collèges d'enseignement technique	16
10		15
9	Classical section · Modern section · Enseignement général · Fin d'études	14
8	Lycées and collèges · Preparatory year	13
7	Cycle d'observation	12
6	Classical · Modern · Post-primary	11
5		10
4		9
3	Elementary schools (Cycle élémentaire)	8
2		7
1		6
		5
	Preschool education (Maternal schools, Crèches)	4
		3
		2

programs has not been entirely complete and effective, the general pattern is changing materially. Much of the vertical separation between the various types of schools, as illustrated in Figure 13–1, has been eliminated, and a new program has been established that is based on three stages, or levels, of education.

The 1959 decree established the following program. All children between the ages of 6 and 11 are to attend elementary schools. For all children between the ages of 11 to 13 there will be an observation or orientation period. According to the aptitudes demonstrated in the observation period, the pupils will be assigned to one of several programs: the full secondary course at a *lycée*, a four-year professional course at a *lycée* or technical college, a three-year general education course in new general colleges, or a course in a specialized technical school. The third stage of public education is higher education, including the universities and the higher professional schools. The general organization of public education in France after 1959 is shown in Figure 13–2. Table 13–1 gives enrollments at each level in 1963.

Preschool Education

THE FIRST preschool programs were established as early as 1837, "to provide maternal care and the early stage of education suitable to the ages of the pupils." They were charitable institutions, and were originally called "*salles d'asile*" (literally, rooms of sanctuary). In 1881 the name was changed to *écoles maternelles* (maternal schools). In the smaller communes a different type of program developed, called *classes enfantines* (infant classes). These were attached to the elementary schools, often occupying rooms in the elementary school building, and they admitted children between the ages of 3 and 6. These schools were supervised by the principal of the elementary school.

Preschools have always been voluntary institutions in France. A commune may choose to open such a school but has not been required to do so. Once a school is established, the commune can apply for state grants to help support it, but that school must be maintained for at least ten years if the national government assists the program. The Ministry of National Education does not accept responsibility for the support of preschool education, but it

TABLE 13-1

Enrollment in French Schools, 1963 (in thousands)

	PUBLIC SCHOOLS	PRIVATE SCHOOLS	TOTALS
Maternal schools	1,356	209	1,565
Elementary schools	4,935	903	5,838
TOTAL ELEMENTARY	6,291	1,112	7,403
Collèges d'enseignement général	810	158	968
Collèges d'enseignement technique	292	150	442
Lycées (classical and modern)	954	360	1,314
Lycées techniques	246	63	309
Correspondence classes	75		75
TOTAL SECONDARY	2,377	731	3,108
Normal schools	32		32
Universities	292	8	300
Grandes écoles	23	11	34
TOTAL HIGHER EDUCATION	347	19	366
Total enrollment	9,015	1,862	10,877

SOURCE: Cultural Services of the French Embassy.

has assisted whenever agreements were made. Some of the maternal schools are operated by private organizations or by church groups and do not receive aid from public funds. Whether the maternal school is publicly or privately supported, the Ministry insists on the right of inspection and supervision and offers advice and guidance.

The maternal school is an independent institution with its own principal, and national regulations define in detail the specifications for the building and equipment. Qualifications of teachers are also specified, although an uncertified assistant may be employed. Class size is limited to 25 pupils, and the school to a total of 150. All children must have a medical examination upon entrance, and a medical officer visits the school from time to time. Absences are carefully checked, in order to keep in touch with the health of the children.

The curriculum consists of physical exercises, games, songs, drawing and manual work, exercises in observing and describing familiar objects, and instruction in moral habits. In the last year some reading, writing, and arithmetic may be introduced. Recent tendency has been to lessen the attention given to the three R's for the little ones, but French parents are so steeped in the scholastic tradition that they wish their children to be taught to read and write as soon as possible. These institutions are strongly influenced by the ideas of Decroly and Montessori, and have been free to experiment with modern educational methods.

Enrollment has been increasing in the *écoles maternelles* and the *classes enfantines*, although attendance is not compulsory. "An elite corps of *inspectrices* and teachers has given new life to this level of education." [1]

Elementary Education

THE FIRST cycle of general education is for children 6 to 11, and is common to all. Elementary education includes three stages: the preparatory course, for 6- to 7-year-olds; the elementary course, for 7- to 9-year-olds; and the intermediate course, for the 9- to 11-year-olds. Emphasis in the curriculum is upon the teaching of French, moral and civic instruction, reading and writing, arithmetic and the metric system, history and geography of France, object lessons and basic scientific ideas, elements of drawing, singing and handicrafts (with needlework for girls), and physical education.

On the elementary level the government has provided for various types of special schools and programs. Special classes in regular schools or special schools are provided for the mentally retarded, with the purpose of "readaptation." There are also special schools or classes to meet the needs of physically handicapped children. For pupils with delicate health there are some fresh air schools. In some places boarding schools have been established for those whose parents are transients, such as the children of boatmen and nomadic families. [2]

The general character of the French elementary school is rooted in the nation's belief in the principle of general culture. Frenchmen

---

[1] *Education in France: French System of Education,* Special Issue, Cultural Services of the French Embassy, New York (no date), p. 9. Material in this publication has been used extensively in this chapter.

[2] *Education in France, op. cit.,* p. 10.

believe that the elementary school must preserve national solidarity by giving all children the common heritage of the French nation. They stress the use of the common language as a unifying factor, develop faith in and reverence for the contributions the country has made to the world, and inspire belief in the preeminent place of France as a cultural leader. "French is always the medium of instruction even where Flemish, German or its Alsatian dialect, Basque or Breton happens to be the language of the home." [3] The French elementary school does not attempt to teach children everything that may be learned in the basic subjects. Instead, each child is to learn well in the elementary subjects "that of which we cannot be permitted to be ignorant."

Because elementary education in France expresses the ideals held by the adult citizens, the schools have not traveled very far in the direction of modern progressive-education theories, which speak of "child-centered schools" or of seeking to find and satisfy "children's own felt needs." Child psychology has not developed in France to the extent that it has in some other parts of the world and has had much less effect on course content and classroom methods. The French educator is interested in the development of personality, but of a personality attuned to the national ideal of the ethical man, one who is in harmony with the national ideal of an educated and cultured citizen. This attitude is also reflected in French ideas of discipline, which are based entirely on adult authority. Where the American educator speaks of helping to develop self-discipline on the part of the pupils and giving them a share in responsibility, the French teacher is very doubtful about this point of view.

Enforcement of the compulsory attendance law has not been very strict. The mayor of the commune, assisted by the school committee, is charged with taking a school census each year. A notice is sent to the parents of all children between the ages of 6 and 14, stating that they are responsible for the attendance of their children. The provisions of the law are met if the children attend either public or private schools, or if individual instruction is provided. Children who are not enrolled in a regular school must be presented for an annual examination conducted by the elementary inspector and a committee. If no maternal school is available, in some cases children may enter the first grade at the age of 5 years. If the children are continuously absent from school, the school committee posts

[3] Anthony Kerr, *Schools of Europe*, p. 145.

their names in a prominent place; parents of truants may be fined or imprisoned.

Parents who certify that their children are required to help work on the farm may have their children excused from attendance for three months a year by the school committee, with the approval of the elementary inspector. If the departmental council approves, children may be excused for two days a week throughout the year to work for their parents or other employers. Efforts have been made by the national government to improve the rate of attendance, particularly in the rural areas, but without great success. This situation was reflected in an increased illiteracy rate in rural areas in the period between the two world wars. Since the 1959 reform increased attention is being paid to this problem, and it is the intention of the authorities to enforce the new compulsory age limit of 16 years when it becomes applicable.

Schools are in session five days a week, including Saturday but not Thursday, and the elementary course is based on 30 classroom hours a week. The course of study is prescribed in minute detail by ministerial regulations. Some freedom is permitted to adapt the course to local needs and conditions, but this does not extend far enough to affect the uniform type of examinations which all must pass.

Pupils are promoted annually on the basis of their daily records and the recommendations of their teachers to the principal. To be admitted to the *cycle d'observation* pupils must be at least 11 years old and no older than 12. Admission is based on the school records and recommendations of teachers and principal. A written examination is given in each department for pupils whose records seem to be inadequate, or for those from private schools. The examining committee includes a representative from the public schools, a guidance specialist, a school doctor, and representatives of the parents.

Physical education is compulsory for all children in the elementary schools for at least two and one-half hours a week. Special training courses in the normal schools are provided to prepare teachers to handle physical education in the elementary grades. Some organized recreation, such as excursions, is included in the program. Most of the elementary schools are without adequate playgrounds or space for physical education activities, and organized sports are not an important part of the program.

Secondary Education

THE AIM of French secondary education is to provide the pupils with a general education that will not only prepare them for further study but will also give them an opportunity to acquire specialized knowledge and skills. Substantial emphasis is placed on the development of logical and critical thinking and of speaking and writing well. French educators believe strongly in the theories of mental discipline and the transfer of training, which are being followed less and less in other countries.

THE "CYCLE D'OBSERVATION"

Children between the ages of 11 and 13 are in the orientation or observation stage, during which their aptitudes are appraised. Following the French custom of naming the grades above the common elementary school in reverse order, the lowest grade is called the sixth class (*classes de sixième*), and the 12-year-olds are in the fifth class. The sixth and fifth classes are an integral part of the schools to which they are assigned (either elementary or secondary), and the program is as uniform as possible all over the country. However, pupils who intend to enter the classical sections of the *lycées* begin the study of Latin after three months in the sixth class.

At the end of the *cycle d'observation*, an Orientation Council, composed of the teachers of the orientation classes, studies the performance of each child and recommends the type of further education for him to pursue. Parents have two choices: they may accept the recommendation of the Council, or they may ask that the child be given a special aptitude test to see if he may enter another type of school which they may prefer. The observation and orientation of the child does not end with the completion of the fifth class. Possibilities for transfer from one type of program to another are provided at every level, especially for children who may develop later than others. Transfer is facilitated by the organization of special reorientation sections.

After the *cycle d'orientation* a French pupil has a choice of several different forms of secondary education. "But, in fact, they are already involved in certain forms, since the *cycle d'orientation* is part of the normal progression of studies." [4]

---

[4] *Education in France, op. cit.*, p. 11.

TERMINAL EDUCATION

A three-year program of studies (which will carry the average boy or girl to the end of his sixteenth year or the end of compulsory attendance) has been organized for the least intellectual group of children. The purpose of this program is to provide a rounding out of general education, and students are instructed in practical work to prepare for making a living. Different types of programs may be chosen, such as agriculture (for boys), agriculture and homemaking (for girls), rural crafts, or urban crafts. Much of the vocational training (which is reminiscent of the productive training in the U.S.S.R.) is carried on through contracts with private enterprises. Upon completion of the program, a certificate may be granted. The certificate is endorsed with the vocational specialization chosen and is called diploma of completion of studies (*diplôme de fin d'études*). Between now and 1967, when the new compulsory age will be effective, those who leave school at age 14 will receive a certificate of primary elementary studies (*certificat d'études primaires élémentaires*).

SHORT GENERAL EDUCATION

For the next highest group, a short course in general education, *l'enseignement général court*, is provided. Pupils are admitted after age 11, having taken the aptitude test. The course includes the two years of the *cycle d'observation* and three additional years. These schools are now called *collèges d'enseignement général*. They replace and absorb the former apprenticeship centers. A wide choice of different crafts may be selected, such as agriculture, building trades, winemaking, and industrial skills. Especially in the first two observation years the programs are essentially the same as the long general education programs. Graduates of these schools, who receive the *brevet d'enseignement général*, can enter nontechnical occupations or may be admitted to the normal schools for training as elementary school teachers.

LONG GENERAL EDUCATION

For the more intellectually gifted boys and girls, there is a longer program of general education, *l'enseignement général long*, which will continue for four or five years after the two-year observation period. All of the schools in the general program are now to be called *lycées,* instead of the old differentiation into *lycées* and *collèges,* since reforms have tended to erase the differences in training required for teachers in the two types of schools. There will be classical, modern, and technical *lycées,* or combinations of these types into one school.

After the observation cycle, there are several other cycles in the long program. The first, which is two years, offers three sections, two classical and one modern; one stressing Greek, Latin, and one modern language (the old classical *lycée* program); one emphasizing Latin and two modern languages; and the third concentrating on French and two modern languages. In the third two-year cycle, there is a choice of seven sections or fields of specialization. Three are classical, two modern, and two technical: the first continues Greek, Latin, and one modern language, but allows some study of the sciences; the second teaches Latin, two modern languages and a general orientation toward the social sciences; the third consists of Latin, one modern language and natural sciences; the fourth is characterized by the study of two modern languages and science; the fifth stresses experimental science and one modern language; the sixth stresses one modern language and fundamental industrial techniques; and the seventh is based on two modern languages and economics. For the final one-year cycle there is a choice of five specialties: philosophy, experimental sciences, mathematics, mathematics and technology, or economics and social sciences.

At the end of this program a student may receive the first university degree, the *baccalaureat.* The examinations for this degree are divided into two parts, one of which is taken at the end of the sixth year and the other at the end of the seventh, when the candidates are usually 17 to 18 years old. Due to the great increase in the number of candidates, the first part of the *baccalaureat* examination, now called the *examen probatoire,* has been decentralized, and is now given on the *arrondissement* level (an administrative subdivision of the department). The Academy inspectors are responsible for this examination, which will gain for successful candidates the *certificat de probation.* This is a small movement toward decentralization. The second part of the examination, which is still a national examination, offers for each of the seven sections mentioned above in the third cycle a separate *baccalaureat* examination and degree.

TECHNICAL COLLEGES

For students who show high intellectual ability in the preceding years, but whose interests are along technical lines, two programs are available, to prepare them for professional and specialized fields. The short course is given in *collèges d'enseignement technique*, and provides three years of study above the age of 14. This type of college continues general education, and prepares the students for specialized occupations. At the end of the third year the students take an examination to receive the *certificat d'aptitude professionelle* (C.A.P.).

The long course is usually given in *lycées techniques*, and is directed toward the training of specialists for middle-grade or semi-professional occupations. After the two-year observation period, the student may spend four additional years and receive a certificate of *agent technique*. If he continues a fifth year and specializes further, he may receive the *technicien breveté* title. A few of the brighter may remain in school for a sixth year and take the examination for the title *technicien supérieur*, which may be considered the equivalent of the *baccalaureat*, and which may admit the holder to engineering schools.

More attention is being paid to technical subjects in the new *lycées*, with some of them being called *lycées techniques*. The *baccalaureat technique* which graduates may receive stresses mathematics and theoretical science, and is not exactly "technical in the sense that this word is used in other countries." [5]

CURRICULUM AND METHODS

The original curriculum of the *lycées*, established by law in 1809 and extended to the *collèges* in 1812, was composed of subjects required for entrance to the universities—Greek, Latin, history, mythology, geography, metaphysics, ethics, optics, and astronomy. In 1814 a seventh year, with emphasis on the study of philosophy, was added. Various reforms over the years reduced the amount of time allotted to the study of the classical languages, and introduced modern foreign languages. French authorities insisted that the cultural and disciplinary values of subjects, not the usefulness of the subjects in later life, should determine their place in the curriculum.

[5] Charles H. Dobinson, "French Educational Reform," *Comparative Education Review*, Vol. 3, No. 1 (June, 1959), p. 11.

Eventually a program was worked out for a common cycle of four years, with a separation into "classical" and "modern" courses in the last three years.

The *baccalaureat* degree, which caps the secondary education program, is distinctively French. It is the first university degree and is a requirement for entrance to higher education. It is a part of university matriculation and must not be confused with the bachelor's degree that is given in American and British universities upon completion of a course in university studies.

Above the terminal year many secondary schools also provide special preparatory classes for the competitive examinations for entrance to the *grandes écoles*, or great higher schools, which are on the university level and lead to higher positions in the civil service and the professions. These preparatory classes are called the upper first class, or special class, in mathematics or rhetoric. The *baccalaureat* is thus one step toward admission to these higher schools.

With minor exceptions, none of the French secondary schools are coeducational. This means that any town of considerable size finds it necessary to provide one of each type of secondary school for boys and another for girls. Under some circumstances, if no other facilities exist, girls may be admitted to boys' schools, but never in equal numbers. If insufficient numbers of secondary students are available, secondary courses may be set up which include both sexes. These are transitional programs, and are closed when separate schools become practical. Younger boys may be admitted to the lower classes of girls' schools under some circumstances: if the school is very close to their homes or if they have older sisters in the school.

Secondary courses for girls have been extended since 1949. Not only are the girls educated in separate schools, but the curriculum is different. Secondary education for girls is of more recent origin in France than is secondary education for boys. Formerly most girls' schools provided a five- or six-year course, and girls who wished to take the second part of the *baccalaureat* examination were required to take the final one or two years in a boys' school. Now most of the girls' *lycées* offer the complete seven-year course. The curriculum includes courses in household management, handwork, music, and foreign literature in translation.

SCHOOL LIFE

A feature of French secondary schools that is very different from the American high school is the number of subjects studied every year by French students. When an American student would be taking four or five subjects a year, usually each for five days a week, the French student takes many more subjects throughout the seven-year course, and most of these subjects meet only two or three periods a week. It is not unusual for a student to carry twelve or more subjects throughout the secondary school course.

The classroom atmosphere of a French secondary school is stiff and formal, with much time devoted to formal lectures by the teachers, and with much note-taking by the students. Each student keeps exercise books (*cahiers*), which are an important part of the program. Comparatively few textbooks are used, reference books and other materials are not readily available, and there are practically no school libraries. Under these conditions the copying of material dictated by the teacher becomes the central part of the student's work. Little opportunity is given to learn the use of supplementary materials or to search out original sources. Since the examinations are of supreme importance in the educational career of every student, the materials dictated must be the type of work which might be called for in an examination. No matter how free the teacher might be to select materials, he will be circumscribed by the necessity of preparing his class to pass an examination which he did not write. This procedure illustrates once more the uniformity which exists under a centralized system, although in recent years an increased amount of attention has been given to development of independence and active participation on the part of the student.

The secondary school student in France spends more time in school than does his American counterpart. The school year is normally 42 weeks, and classes are in session six hours a day, five days a week. As in the elementary schools, Thursday rather than Saturday is the day off, although in some cases classes are held on Thursday mornings and Saturday afternoons are free. Outdoor activities are sometimes scheduled for Saturday afternoons.

Organized sports do not have the same position in French secondary schools as in British or American schools. Since the last war, a greater interest has been shown in physical fitness, and an expanded program of sports and games has been started. Previously physical education had been almost entirely neglected in French schools: most of them have no space for games or exercise other than a small paved court. Municipalities are urged to make available open spaces near schools for sports, but this is not required. Many secondary schools have boarders as well as day students, and excursions (*promenades*) are arranged on Thursdays and Saturdays, particularly for boarders. In recent years provision has been made for training physical education teachers, and more stress is placed on fitness in all of the secondary schools.

Self-government in any form is lacking in French secondary schools. The teachers do not concern themselves with student discipline, except of course in the classrooms; outside of the classroom deportment is the responsibility of a special proctor or usher (*surveillant*). Often this is a student who is paid a small salary and given board and room for taking charge of student discipline in dormitories and out-of-school hours. Regulations do not permit the formation of any student clubs or organizations with officers or rules; there are no student-body organizations. There is no official athletic group sponsoring school teams, and in sports one secondary school seldom competes with another. Some attempts have been made in a few schools to copy the attitude of English secondary schools toward sports, but this has not been successful or widespread. The interest of the French parent is exclusively devoted to his child's intellectual progress, not to activities which are intended to advance personality development or athletic achievement. Although there has been some discussion of the desirability of developing minor forms of student self-government as a preparation for citizenship, very little has been accomplished.

About half of the secondary students are boarders, who live under a semimilitary regime in dormitories. These are barracklike buildings, with as many as fifty beds to a room. In the dormitories the students are under the supervision of the *surveillant* and may not leave the school grounds except under unusual circumstances; even then they walk two by two, under constant supervision. They seldom have any contact with the world outside of the school, and only infrequently may they attend concerts, lectures, or motion pictures away from school. Under this closely regimented supervision the students spend all of their school lives. Since very little attention is given in the curriculum to the type of program called "general social studies" in the American high school, with its emphasis on social problems, government, and current events, and since there is little or no student organization or self-government, the students live in an almost monastic life with very little preparation for participation in the responsibilities of citizenship.

ORGANIZATION OF THE SECONDARY SCHOOL

The title of the head of a secondary school varies according to the school. In the *lycées* for boys he is the *proviseur;* in the boys' *collèges* he is the *principal;* in the girls' schools the head is the *directrice*. The academic teachers are called *professeurs,* and there are various grades of lesser functionaries who assist in special subjects. For administrative purposes France is divided into regions called *Academies*. In each Academy there is a university, which is headed by a rector. The head of a *lycée* is responsible to an administrative board composed of the rector of the Academy, the Academy inspector, the principal, the prefect, and representatives of the parents, the pupils, and the alumni. This board supervises the finances and the building facilities of the school and appoints members to visit the school. The administrative board meets every three months.

Many secondary schools have alumni associations, which provide funds for scholarships and prizes, and help students find employment when they leave school.

Within the faculty there are two councils. The class councils consist of all the teachers within a single class, who meet to coordinate the work of the class and to attempt to avoid putting too much work on pupils when making homework assignments. The instructional council is made up of all the teachers in a single subject-matter field. It attempts to promote articulation between the different classes in the seven-year course, to prevent overlapping in subject matter, and to develop a certain amount of harmony in teaching methods.

The French secondary student at age 18 has achieved a higher level of subject-matter mastery and intellectual grasp, within the limits of the curriculum prescribed, than the American high school senior. This results from a number of factors. The French secondary school is much more selective, and only the intellectually superior students are permitted to complete the course. The longer school year and longer school day means that the student in a French *lycée* has spent more hours in class than his American counterpart. The rigid examinations and the concentration of time and attention on subject matter, with very little opportunity for extracurricular activities, tend to increase the intellectual achievement.

An American educator might criticize the ascetic life provided in the secondary school as a poor preparation for life out in the adult world. He would also criticize the lack of provision for citizenship training and well-rounded activities, and the absence of opportunities to develop qualities of leadership. But most French educators and French parents appear to be well satisfied with the intellectualized education of their children. They would probably be equally critical of American education. Under the 1959 reform, proposals have been made to reduce the amount of study time prescribed for *lycée* students and to compensate for this by shortening the long vacation. In theory this would mean a little less pressure but more weeks of study. Dobinson, who is a keen observer of French schools, is skeptical of this. He feels that it will eventually mean more weeks of the same tremendous intellectual pressure on the students.[6]

Vocational and Technical Education

TECHNICAL education as an organized program is comparatively recent in France. It was not until 1892 that a special organization was provided and vocational sections introduced into the higher elementary schools. The industrial and commercial interests of the country, anxious to recruit more skilled and semiskilled workers, have always shown a great interest in this type of training. They succeeded for a time in getting the whole program out of the Ministry of Public Instruction's hands, and into the Ministry of Commerce and Industry, where they could control it. Even when it was returned to the Education Ministry, it was under a separate General Division.

Under the separate General Division for Technical Education, the program had its own budget, personnel, administrative machinery, examinations, and certificates. At the top of this system were a Higher Council for Technical Education, a normal school, and an inspectorate entirely independent of the other divisions of the Ministry. Because of the representation of employers on the Higher Council

[6] Dobinson, *op. cit.*, p. 11.

and certain fiscal arrangements concerning the apprenticeship tax, the large employers exercised a great deal of influence on the program. Representatives of the workers' unions were also on the Higher Council.

A variety of institutions grew up under the supervision of the General Division for Technical Education—trade schools; practical schools of commerce and industry; national, departmental, and communal vocational schools; the National Conservatory of Arts and Crafts; vocational courses in higher elementary schools; and others. Side by side with secondary schools concerned with general culture there developed narrowly specialized schools which were highly utilitarian. Some conflict has always existed between the two types of education, and there was even competition between the narrowly specialized schools and the vocational sections of the higher elementary schools, which included some general education in their curriculum. The whole system was constantly under criticism, and attempts were made to work out a closer coordination between secondary and technical education.

Great changes have been made since the end of World War II. Under the Ministry of National Education, technical education has become one of the teaching directorates of the national program, under the supervision of the rectors and the Academy inspectors, aided by technical advisers. Vocational guidance services have been put under technical education, and a guidance center is expected to be provided in every department.

The 1959 reform took further steps in the direction of closer integration. The apprenticeship centers have been absorbed into the *collèges d'enseignement général*. The seven-year *lycées techniques* have achieved a status nearer to that of the regular *lycées*, although the classical *lycée* will continue to be first in public estimation. Many *lycées* have added technical sections. In all of these programs there is a continuation of general education. The attempt of the vocational educators to achieve status in comparison with the general education program has led to the use of the term "technical humanities" in the program of the *lycées techniques*, and to the establishment of a technical *baccalaureat*.

In general, the Ministry of National Education retains control of all technical schools, although a number of other ministries (Agriculture, Public Works, National Defense, Interior, Health, Labor) are concerned with the programs and with the operation of some of the schools.

The Langevin Plan stressed the importance of developing a national feeling of pride in work and respect for the dignity of labor. (The French emphasis on intellectual development had always tended to depreciate the importance of manual labor in the national economy.) There is a parallel here with the emphasis on labor in the Soviet Union. However, the newer French program gives much more place to general education in all vocational courses than has ever been done in the U.S.S.R. It was because some conservative educators in France saw too much similarity between the Langevin recommendations and Russian practices that they vigorously opposed the report.

Universities and Higher Professional Education

HIGHER education in France includes the universities and their associated higher institutes, a wide range of specialized higher schools, and the *grandes écoles*. Each of the Academies has a university. The constituent schools of a university are called "faculties." Each university has a faculty of arts and one of sciences (one university has two of each), and all but one include a faculty of law. There are a number of faculties of medicine and of pharmacy, and the University of Strasbourg has two faculties of theology, Catholic and Protestant. Enrollment by faculties is shown in Table 13–2. The University of Paris, enrolling over 72,000 students, is the largest.

In addition to the faculties, each university includes a variety of research centers or institutes, and there are over 150 of these, connected with the 16 universities. These institutes train engineers for mining, electricity, or chemical industries, and metallurgy; they offer specialized work in biochemistry, meteorology, psychology, physiology, and in almost every other specialized field of research. There are a number of private universities, each with its attached specialized institutes; all of these are Catholic except for one Protestant school of theology.

The rector of the Academy is the administrative head of the university, and each faculty is headed by a dean. The University Council, with the rector as chairman, is made up of the deans of faculties, and is the policy-making body of the institution. Although the rec-

TABLE 13-2

Student Enrollment in French Universities, 1960–61 (by faculties)

UNIVERSITY	LAW	SCIENCE	LETTERS	MEDI-CINE	PHAR-MACY	TOTAL
Aix	2,109	5,482	4,034	2,133	721	14,479
Besançon		1,031	955	143	88	2,217
Bordeaux	2,159	3,628	3,564	2,269	452	12,072
Caen	945	2,295	2,298	452	159	6,149
Clermont	490	2,034	1,505	359	343	4,731
Dijon	838	1,211	1,436	152	70	3,706
Grenoble	1,407	4,191	3,122	295	160	9,175
Lille	1,845	3,907	3,023	1,677	685	11,137
Lyon	1,723	4,528	3,253	2,183	457	12,144
Montpellier	1,474	3,509	2,932	1,743	795	10,451
Nancy	1,027	2,697	2,165	1,138	401	7,428
Paris	14,358	19,319	22,825	13,169	2,778	72,449
Poitiers	1,142	2,207	2,484	622	276	6,731
Rennes	1,297	4,092	3,211	1,652	489	10,736
Strasbourg	1,453	2,735	2,328	1,183	378	8,077
Toulouse	1,372	5,196	3,261	1,417	447	11,693
Totals	33,634	68,062	62,395	30,587	8,697	203,375

SOURCE: Personal correspondence with M. Édouard Morot-Sir, Cultural Counselor, Representative in the United States of French Universities, December 14, 1962.

tor is appointed, and the universities are under the general direction of the Ministry, the faculties are comparatively autonomous. The school year is approximately 32 weeks, from November to June.

There is little coordination between the various faculties and institutes in the same university. Courses in economics, for example, are given separately in the faculties of law, science, arts, and in the specialized institutes of economics and commerce. Similar dispersion is the rule in every subject-matter field. Each faculty and institute has its own library, laboratories, and special facilities. The University of Paris has some 100 specialized libraries located in different buildings. Methods of teaching and research have become stereotyped and verbalized, even more than in the *lycées*. French professors show little interest in developments and research in foreign universities. Laboratories are often small, poorly equipped, and overcrowded. Laugier cited a physiological laboratory in the Sorbonne

(University of Paris) which had been established over 50 years previously to accommodate a maximum of 20 researchers and 20 students, and which had to handle 200 students in 1940 without any change in facilities.[7]

DEGREES

French degrees are diversified and difficult to compare with university degrees in other countries. In addition to degrees awarded by universities, and university titles and diplomas, there are state certificates and degrees which add to the complexity of the situation. University degrees are awarded by the faculty in which the work is completed, and may differ from faculty to faculty in the same institution. There are thus variations in degrees depending upon the length of the course of study and the major field of specialization University degrees begin with the *baccalaureat*, which is really university matriculation. Then comes the *licence*, based upon four semesters of work in the university, two of which may be spent in a foreign university. The *diplôme d'études supérieures* (diploma of higher studies), based on one year after the *licence*, and finally the *doctorat*, based on several years of research and the preparation of two theses, are higher degrees. Foreign students may earn university degrees. A new doctorate has been established, which is of greater interest to foreigners, requires less time to be spent on a wide area of cultural subjects and permits individual research in a narrow field of specialization. It is more nearly comparable to the Ph.D. in the United States or the D. Phil. in Great Britain. Degrees in law, medicine, and pharmacy are different from those in arts and sciences.

State competitive examinations also permit the state to award certificates and degrees: the *licence*, the *diplôme d'études supérieures*, the *agrégation*, and the *doctorat d'état*. The *agrégation* is a very difficult competitive examination, and the holders of this degree, called *agrégés*, are eligible for the most attractive positions in the secondary schools.

Formerly the possession of the *baccalaureat* admitted a student to a university; this is no longer the case. Students are now expected to spend an additional preparatory (*propadeutique*) year or two in preparing for a competitive entrance examination. This extra preparation is supposed to provide more general education, as recommended by the Algiers Commission and the Langevin Plan.

[7] Henri Laugier, "France," *Education Yearbook 1944*, p. 147.

THE UNIVERSITY COLLEGES

As a result of decrees promulgated in the fall of 1959, new institutions at university level were established, called university colleges. Some of these were transformations of existing institutes. They were established in large cities which did not have universities. Most of them are scientific in nature, in recognition of the demand for more advanced training in this field. By October, 1960, there were 12 of these colleges in operation. They offer only one or two years of work, and are not authorized, except in a few cases, to grant the *licence*. This movement is hailed in France as a move toward democratization of French university education. It is expected that in future years some of them may be raised to the status of university.[8]

THE "GRANDES ÉCOLES"

The national higher professional schools, the *grandes écoles*, are institutions established to provide executive and supervisory staff members for the administrative branches of government, the technical services, education, and the military services. They are established by the various ministries to educate their own senior staff members and to provide highly qualified specialists. Some of these schools, such as the higher normal schools at Saint-Cloud and Fontenay-aux-Roses, are operated by the Ministry of National Education. Other higher schools, such as the Polytechnic School, the Special School for Public Works, the Colonial School, the Agronomic Institute, and the various military colleges, such as Saint-Cyr, are run by the ministries directly concerned.

Students are admitted to these schools after very difficult competitive examinations, and the number who pass is determined partly by the standard of the examination but mainly by the number of places to be filled. Usually one or two years of preparatory courses beyond the *baccalaureat* are necessary to get ready for the examinations. As a rule students are at least 20 years of age when they succeed in obtaining admission to one of the *grandes écoles*. At the end of the course students may take an examination given by the school, and receive a diploma from the school, or they may take a more general state examination to receive a certificate which permits the holder to be appointed to certain specialized positions in the national service.

[8] *Education in France, op. cit.*, pp. 10–11.

The exclusive nature of the *grandes écoles* may be shown by a few 1950–51 statistics. The 120 great national schools listed a total enrollment of 18,987 students, or an average of 158 per school. The largest of these was the *École Nationale Supérieure des Beaux Arts*, which enrolled 3,049 students. But there were 52 of these special schools enrolling fewer than 100 students each, and six enrolled fewer than 20 students. In 1950–51, of 23,278 candidates who took the competitive entrance examinations, 4,024 were admitted, and 3,666 were graduated in the same year.[9]

These special schools have held a very important position in the preparation of an elite of leadership in government and the professions. They have kept themselves aloof from the universities and from each other, and have been criticized as being equally detached from the main currents of French life. They have had a complete monopoly of training for all important positions in government and the civil service. Reforms have been suggested: that the work of the higher schools be integrated with the universities; that recruitment to them be on a much wider base; that the courses be made more liberal and less specialized. It has been charged that the *grandes écoles* constitute a stronghold for the development of a special class or caste feeling, and that because of their monopoly of influential positions in government and education, they constitute a "state within a state." These criticisms became very strong in France during the Occupation, when Frenchmen in France as well as in Algiers were trying to discover the reasons for the humiliating defeat of their country and the apparent failure of its top leadership. Up to this time none of the reforms have been made effective, and the great higher schools still retain their important position in French life. Since most of the leaders in government—premiers, cabinet ministers, and top civil servants—are graduates of these schools, there is very little interest in changing them.

Adult Education

WHILE the national government has maintained its centralized control over elementary, secondary, technical, and higher education, it has been very slow to accept any responsibility for the education of adults. Much of the adult education work done in France is the

[9] *Recueil de Statistiques*, 1949–50–51, pp. 150–55.

responsibility of private organizations. Although the Langevin Report stressed the need for a new type of education for those who had ended their formal schooling, there has been nothing comparable to the provisions for "Further Education" in the English Education Act of 1944. In larger cities and towns, the government has provided centers for "popular education" (this term is used by the French in preference to "adult education") and these are placed at the disposal of voluntary organizations.

The trade unions operate labor colleges, which are similar in some ways to the workers' institutes in Great Britain. These offer popular lectures, provide radio services, and offer guidance in leisure-time and vacation activities. The most important organization in the field is the French League for Education, which works closely with the Ministry of National Education, but without financial subsidy. It operates programs in many of the centers for popular education.

One result of the predominantly formal type of education in the public schools has been that young Frenchmen, when they complete their education in school, dislike any type of formalized educational program. The government, in supporting such programs, stresses the possibility for "everyone to add to the general knowledge acquired during compulsory schooling and to avail him more readily of all the sources of culture and all the means of personal development." [10] Local schools, particularly in the rural areas, meet this problem by offering voluntary programs in nonacademic fields, such as art, dressmaking, and agriculture. Depending upon the interest and ability of the local schoolmaster, the local school often becomes the cultural center for rural areas.

Some work is done which resembles the extension services provided by the land-grant colleges in the United States. Much of this is performed by traveling agriculture and home economics experts who offer informal services, lectures, and advice. Seasonal schools of agriculture are provided for farmers, offering services similar to those given by county agricultural agents in America.

The Langevin Report recommended that adult educators should be specially trained and that the methods and subject matter of adult education should be different from those in the formal schools. It emphasized the need to discover and serve the immediate interests and needs of adults, without reference to intellectual and scholarly

[10] *Education in France, op. cit.,* p. 19.

methods and philosophies, in order to attract young people into the program. The government has encouraged these ideas by the appropriation of some funds, but very little that is practical has been accomplished.

Education and Status of Teachers

HISTORICALLY the training of teachers for elementary, secondary, and technical schools has been completely separate. The normal schools, established by the departments, were supervised and controlled by the departmental councils and the elementary education branch of the Ministry. Secondary teachers were trained in special higher normal schools or in the universities, and their education was under the direction of the secondary education branch of the Ministry and of the Academy inspectorate. Teachers were prepared for vocational education schools in special normal schools established and controlled by the Division of Technical Education. Because the training of secondary school teachers was longer and the competitive examinations more difficult, the status of teachers in the *lycées* and *collèges* was much higher, both socially and economically, than that of their colleagues in the elementary and technical schools. Even the titles were different: teachers in the *lycées* were called *professeurs*; in the elementary schools they were called *instituteurs* or *institutrices*.

THE NORMAL SCHOOLS

Each department has been required to establish two normal schools, one for men and one for women. Although they were established and controlled by the departments, most of their financial support now comes from national funds. All of the normal schools are boarding schools, and most of the students receive government grants to pay for tuition and living costs. The students are required to sign an agreement that they will teach for ten years after completion of the course; if they fail to do so they are required to reimburse the government for its investment in their education.

One result of the reforms following the Langevin Report is that all elementary teachers must now earn the *baccalaureat*. This may be done during the normal school course and is followed by two years of professional training. This increase in the academic standing of elementary school teachers is intended to raise the prestige of teachers in these schools and to lessen the gap between them and the secondary teachers. The normal schools give a certificate, the *brevet supérieure*, upon completion of the course, but students must pass a state examination and qualify for the certificate of teaching proficiency before they are accepted as regular teachers in the national service.

Normal schools operate under a semimonastic type of organization and discipline. The school day is rigidly scheduled; almost every hour from the time of rising at 5:45 in the morning until bedtime at 9:30 is planned. A heavy class schedule, amounting to about 30 hours a week in class, is divided between 15 to 18 different subjects, all of which are carried through each year of the course. Normally class work and supervised study account for about 10 hours a day, except for Thursday afternoons and Sundays. Even recreation time is scheduled and supervised. Male students may receive permission to leave the school grounds only on Sundays and holidays; female students may not leave the school except when written permission from the parents is presented. Parents must list the persons from whom students may receive letters while they are in residence at the normal school. It is evident that the students are thus carefully shielded from any contact with life outside of the school, and that the French system does not concern itself with the development of initiative, leadership, or training for citizenship. Since the war there has been some national interest in the development of a sports program, but this has been difficult to include in the normal school program because of lack of time and of physical facilities, and also because of the lack of any type of student organization or self-government.

In addition to the subjects which are included in the elementary curriculum and which the students are preparing to teach, the curriculum provides courses in general and professional ethics, educational psychology, and theory of education. Each teacher-training institution has a practice school attached to it. Observation and practice teaching take up about 50 half-days a year throughout the course. In order to provide a greater variety of experiences, students may be assigned for several weeks at a time to schools away from the normal school. They may also be assigned to take part in activities in the local schools outside of the regular school day, or to participate in the adult education activities in the community.

THE HIGHER NORMAL SCHOOLS

An interesting part of the elementary-teacher training program has been the provision for advanced training in the higher normal schools. There are two famous higher schools, one at Saint-Cloud for men and one at Fontenay-aux-Roses for women. Entrance to these institutions is by competitive examination, and fewer than 10 percent of the applicants are successful in securing admission. The normal entrance age is 20, and students are required to hold the *baccalaureat*. They may enter directly from secondary schools, but most of them are graduates of normal schools. The course is three years in length, and is made up of a common core in education and psychology, and two elective majors, one in letters and one in science. Graduates of these higher normal schools may become teachers in normal schools or may secure one of the better positions in the elementary schools. These *écoles normales supérieures* have very high prestige in the French educational system, and their graduates have a preferred status in the civil service.

THE TRAINING OF SECONDARY TEACHERS

Secondary school teachers are usually trained in the universities and may or may not have received special pedagogical training. Some graduate work in education is now available in most universities, and students who take the degree of *licence* may now take special courses to prepare them for examinations for teaching certificates. The *agrégation* is the certificate of great distinction; its holders may become *professeurs* in *lycées* and hold secure positions in the civil service. Recent reforms require *agrégés* (who hold a state certificate, not a university degree) to meet new government requirements for secondary teaching.

There are also special higher normal schools for secondary teachers (*grandes écoles normales supérieures*)—at the Rue d'Ulm in Paris for men and at Sevres for women. These institutions are famous for the high caliber of their graduates, and competition for entrance is very severe. A state competitive examination selects only as many candidates as there are vacancies in the special higher normal schools, and successful candidates receive grants which pay all of their expenses while in training. The course is four years, and students begin their training at the age of 20. At the end of the second year the *licence* is granted, at the close of the third year the diploma of higher studies. Some students leave school at this stage and begin their teaching; the remainder stay in school for a fourth year and take the state examinations for the *agrégation*. The number of *agrégés* is limited to the number of available positions, so that a teacher who secures this coveted certificate is assured of a position for life in French secondary schools. The standards of instruction are very high, the classes small, and there is a good deal of individual supervision. Although the curriculum is traditional and bookish, as in all of the great higher schools, there is some experimentation.

THE C.A.P.E.S.

A recent development has been the establishment of a new certificate, *certificat d'aptitude au professorat de l'enseignement du second degré*, usually referred to as "C.A.P.E.S." Candidates for this certificate must hold the *licence*. Preparation for this certificate may be done at a university, or at special regional centers which prepare students for the *licence* and the C.A.P.E.S. examination. These are called *instituts préparatoires à l'enseignement du second degré*. The competitive examination for the certificate is divided into two parts, theory and practice. The theoretical examination includes both written and oral tests—students in the higher normal schools who hold the *licence* are excused from the written tests.

Students who have passed the first part of the C.A.P.E.S. examination go to a regional pedagogical center (C.P.R.) before they take the practical part of the examination. The training at the center stresses active participation in teaching, under close supervision of educational advisers. Students who pass the examinations and receive the certificate may be assigned to positions as *professeurs* in secondary schools.

About 25 percent of the teachers on the secondary level are *agrégés,* and this certificate entitles them to increased salary and a reduction in course hours. *Agrégés* teach 15 class hours per week; those with the C.A.P.E.S. teach 18 hours. In either case, if they teach more hours they are paid an extra amount.

THE STATUS OF TEACHERS

All public school teachers in France are national employees and civil servants. Entrance to the profession is achieved only by passing national examinations, and all teachers are paid by the state on the basis of nation-wide salary schedules. Legislation covering the rights

TABLE 13-3

Range of Teachers' Salaries in French Public Schools, 1962-63 *
(in new francs)

CATEGORY	BASIC SALARY RANGE	HOUSING ALLOWANCE (20 PERCENT MAXIMUM OF BASIC SALARY)
Elementary teachers	7,505-16,316	901-3,625
Teaching assistants	7,775-16,316	1,555-3,263
Principals of elementary schools	7,928-21,448	1,585-4,289
Teachers and principals of technical schools	7,775-17,618	1,555-3,523
Lycées:		
Professors (licence or certificate)	7,775-22,865	1,555-4,573
Professors (agrégé)	9,728-29,108	1,945-5,821
University professors	22,865-30,640	4,573-6,128

SOURCE: M. Édouard Morot-Sir, Cultural Counselor, Representative in the United States of French Universities, December 6, 1962.

* In addition, new teachers of all ranks receive the following annual family allowances: 698 francs for two children in the family; 1,745 for three children; 4,887 for six children; and 1,407 for each additional child.

and benefits of teachers is voluminous and complex. Provisions for appointment, transfer, leaves, salaries, pensions, and disability allowances are uniform throughout the nation. Table 13-3 shows ranges in teachers' salaries and benefits paid in 1962-63. Special allowances are paid to teachers according to the number of children in their families, and special increments may be added by departmental or communal councils. Teachers hold positions of absolute security and have a satisfactory social position in the community.

French teachers are very active in a wide variety of professional organizations. There are teachers' organizations of every variety of political belief and affiliation, from the extreme Rightists to the Communists. There are also separate organizations of elementary, secondary, and technical teachers. These organizations are exclusive and restricted in membership, more or less suspicious of each other, and have tended to keep teachers of various educational levels and political beliefs apart. An overall organization, the *Fédération Générale de l'Enseignement,* has been formed, which is trying to band together the various organizations into one federation. Most of the elementary, normal school, and technical school teachers participate in this movement, as do some of the secondary school teachers. The federation is affiliated with the trade union movement, and has represented the teaching force as civil service employees in negotiations with the national government. In November, 1953, teachers throughout the country staged a twenty-four-hour strike, protesting that increases for military and judicial employees had left the teachers far behind in the general pay scale of government employees. The Laniel government negotiated with representatives of the strikers, who demanded an immediate 10 percent across-the-board increase and a complete study of the entire salary situation, with an idea of a much greater increase later. The government agreed to study the situation.[11] There has been a marked increase in teachers' salaries and allowances since that time.

Problems in the Operation of French Schools

TODAY education in France is in a state of activity and ferment. One might question, however, whether the traditional educational program of the nation, intended to provide the elements of education for the great mass of the population and a highly intellectualized and cultural type of education for an elite, has been sufficient to maintain the position of France as a great power and a leading industrial nation. Criticism has been seen in the proposal of the *école unique*, in the criticisms made by the Algiers Commission, in the recommendations of the Langevin Report, and in the broadening of opportunities for secondary education provided by the De Gaulle decrees. While this ferment did not result in a thorough-going reorganization of the system comparable to the 1944 Education Act in Great Britain, it has brought about changes at every level of the school system, and has aroused intense discussion and debate. However, most of the "reforms" run squarely up against the underlying French reliance on cultural education to produce an elite class. Most of the problems which concern the government and the educators of France are based on this unresolved conflict. As in many countries, many of these eventually come to the matter of budget, and some of these have been discussed in a previous chapter. Some of the difficulties, however, involve problems of basic educational phi-

[11] Associated Press report, *Portland Oregonian*, November 3, 1953.

losophies as well as financial resources, and these need to be discussed again.

The Exclusive Character of Secondary Education

The long fight to secure acceptance of the modern courses on an equal basis with classical studies seems to have been won, and the attempt to give the "technical humanities" an equivalent status is well under way. The fees which were formerly charged in secondary schools have been abolished, and children of poorer parents now have an equal opportunity for secondary education. Elementary schools have achieved a higher status, and the transfer from elementary to secondary education has been made less difficult. But the ideal of the *école unique* has not yet been completely realized. There is still a grave danger of compartmentalization of the elementary and secondary sections of the Ministry.

The essentially bookish nature of secondary education has been little changed. Dobinson stated very well the criticism of the traditional program:

> In French secondary and higher education booklore has been the dominant, almost the only, feature. Physical education of any form has played an insignificant part for the majority: to assist the students of secondary school or university in the development of their character was no part of the work of the *professeur*. Even self-government of any form in the *lycée* or *collège* did not exist. Discipline was (and in the majority of the *lycées* still is) the task of the ill-paid *surveillant*, often a student who acts as an usher in return for board and lodging and a small salary. In this hot-house of excessive cerebration the future leaders of France became strangers to action, excessively burdened with information, much of which was dead wood, and out of touch with the full-bodied life where body, as well as brain, had a part to play.[12]

In addition, there was the problem of separation between education and labor, between mental work and manual work, which has so concerned the Soviet Union.

French education, as it was conceived until now, actually created an antagonism between the pursuit of learning and the need for certain young people to enter a profession rapidly. Moreover, it encouraged too many young people on the secondary level to choose literary or legal

[12] C. H. Dobinson, "France—the Reform Movement," *Year Book of Education,* 1952, Evans Bros. Ltd., London, pp. 336–37.

careers to the detriment of technical or scientific ones. The shortage in France of high level technicians, researchers, and science and mathematics professors, proves this point rather convincingly.[13]

The French problem is to adapt the offerings and methods of secondary education to modern demands and modern ideas, and yet to hold fast to the traditional values in general education. Deeply rooted in the French mind is the idea that the only real culture comes from classical studies. For many years the best students were given classical training, and the prejudice has grown up that any other type of program involves work of lesser standard and less prestige. Many Frenchmen still hold this attitude toward modern scientific and technical training. Most of the teachers have been trained in traditional methods and show little interest in change. Added to this is the ever-present examination system, with the idea that high standards can be judged by the number of students failed in any examination.

The answer has seemed to be the extension and modernization of a system of secondary education which includes great stress on technical studies and a greater effort to orient young people toward scientific and technical careers. The *cycle d'observation*, with continued observation of pupils in later years and improved opportunities for transfer from one type of school to another, has been introduced in order to increase the flexibility of the system.

Although there has been a great increase in the number of students in secondary schools, there has not been a corresponding increase in the number of schools available, and existing schools are overcrowded. The De Gaulle government is trying to remedy this situation by allocating increased funds for school construction. The shortage is particularly true of schools for girls. Though there are many more *lycées* available for boys than for girls, practically the same number of applicants from each sex seek places.

Higher Education

The position of the *grandes écoles* in the preparation of future leaders in professional education, the diplomatic service, and government positions has been discussed. Reformers have suggested that these schools should be absorbed into the universities and that their work be coordinated with university education. Radical think-

---

[13] *Education in France, op. cit.,* p. 27.

ers have said that these schools should be closed and their work taken over by the universities. However, there seems to be little danger that these institutions will lose their preeminent position in France, if only because their graduates hold positions of importance in every branch of public life. Some way should be found to preserve the high standards of work which these schools have maintained, and yet to bring them more into line with modern trends of life and education. Some type of affiliation with the universities might be worked out which would be beneficial to both.

The universities were virtually unchanged by the De Gaulle reforms, although there is a movement to increase the number of universities and thus provide for more students at this level. The French universities need to find some way of coordinating the work among different faculties, in order to eliminate the overlapping and duplication between the many parallel programs in the same subjects. Recommendations looking toward this type of reorganization have been made, and will continue to be made, but little has been accomplished. As in some other countries, the universities are citadels of conservative and traditional patterns of educational thinking.

The slowness with which French universities have adapted themselves to modern developments in science and technology has been reflected in the enrollments and the distribution among faculties. Recent enrollment figures, however, show some change in this situation. In 1948, 29.8 percent of all university students were enrolled in the faculty of law; by 1961 this had dropped to 16.5 percent. In the same period the proportion of the students selecting the faculty of science increased: 17.1 percent in 1948 and 33.4 percent in 1961. The tendency to choose the faculties of law and arts is said to be due to the fact that a high percentage of the students enrolled in the universities are the children of public officials and professional people. Less than 7 percent of the students enrolled in French universities come from families engaged in industry or agriculture.

The Delbos Act which followed the Langevin Report contained a number of proposals for higher education, but few of them have been put into effect. The commission recommended better articulation between secondary and higher education, and better preparation in the secondary schools for specialized fields. They recommended a great expansion in the faculties of science and technology, and more attention to current research and experimentation in every field of university work. They proposed that more time be given to research and that research facilities be expanded. Finally, they suggested that facilities be provided for students and faculty members to travel and study in foreign countries. Many of these reforms depended upon additional funds being made available for new buildings, new equipment, and increased staff. Some of these things are now being initiated under the De Gaulle regime.

The Teaching Staff

In spite of the comparatively satisfactory and secure status of French public school teachers, there has been a great deal of unrest. Teachers have felt that they were falling farther behind other national employees in matters of salary and other benefits, and that education was being neglected. Since all teachers work for the same employer, the national government, any improvement that comes must be made available to every teacher. This financial problem has been reflected, as in other countries, in difficulties in recruiting sufficient numbers of teachers, especially for the technical schools.

The attempt to gather all of the teachers of France into a single professional organization has been part of the struggle to bring the schools closer to the people. Since, in a centralized system, the schools seem to belong to the national government rather than to the people, it is difficult for the citizens of a local community to make their wishes known or to affect in any way the development of their local schools. If the widely separated teachers' associations can come together into an effective force to speak for education, and if, as has been the case, this organization is affiliated with the General Federation of Labor, the working classes may be drawn a little more closely into the great debates on educational policy. The whole motivation of the reform movement has been toward increasing the opportunities of the common man in education and breaking down the exclusively elite nature of secondary and higher education in France.

The teachers' associations seem at times to be critical of the 1959 reform or, at least, of the way it is being implemented. They say that funds are not adequate to permit the various types of schools to perform the missions which are assigned to them. They feel that the subject matter taught during the observation period is not rigorous enough, and that the regulations governing this cycle need to be more precisely defined. They insist that the population increase has imposed poor working conditions on the teachers and that budget increases have been too little and too late to remedy this situation.[14]

An Expanding Education

All of the reforms looking toward breaking down the traditional separation between elementary, secondary, and technical education have had results in widening the educational opportunities and increasing the number of individuals who seek more than the minimum education. This results in demands for more buildings, more teachers, and better facilities. This finally comes down to the question of what proportion of the national budget may be devoted to education. The problem of private schools and their demands for state support has been discussed elsewhere, but these demands inevitably add to the financial problems of the national government.

A very large proportion of French school buildings are old and inadequate. The increasing birth rate is already posing problems for the existing buildings. The De Gaulle government has applied itself to this problem, and more than 150 new elementary schools and 60 lycées have been built. More would be done if the money were available. The application of new ideas for increased articulation between the different school levels, for improved and democratized elementary and secondary education, and for greater opportunity for the children of workers and farmers will inevitably be circumscribed by the amount of space and the number of teachers that can be provided.

It is evident that France is undergoing a difficult period of adjustment to conditions of new programs at a time of increasing enrollments and insufficient budgets.

[14] Denis Forestier, "Educational Reform in France," *Panorama*, Vol. 1, No. 3 (Autumn, 1959), pp. 6–7.

14

Australian Schools in Action

A DESCRIPTION of the administration, control, and finance of a centralized school system was given in Chapter 6. This chapter deals with the actual working of the schools under such a system. It should be remembered that the centralized administration offers less opportunity for freedom and initiative on the part of schools and teachers than exists under a decentralized system. There is a definite flavor of authoritarianism, and all schools tend to conform to a set pattern. Nevertheless the Australian system is a very thorough one, with the interests of poorer and remote districts carefully safeguarded. It must also be remembered that there are three types of schools in each Australian state: the state schools, publicly supported; the Roman Catholic schools; and the other nonstate schools.

Just as the schools in the United States are different among the different states, so are there differences among the state systems in Australia. The procedures show a great deal of similarity, but the names given to the schools and to the examinations may vary from state to state. Most of the descriptions given here will apply to the whole country, but from time to time examples will be taken from a particular state. The general organization of schools is outlined in Figure 14–1, which is for the state of Victoria. The leaving age (which marks the end of compulsory attendance) is 14 in all states except New South Wales and Victoria, where it is now 15, and in Tasmania, where it has been raised to 16. The transfer to secondary schools takes place generally at about the age of 12 to 13 years.

The total number of primary schools, the number of teachers, and the total enrollment by states are given in Table 14–1. Many of

14-1 The Organization of Schools in Victoria

YEARS IN SCHOOL		YEARS OF AGE

Chart content (columns from left to right):

- YEARS IN SCHOOL: 16, 15, 14, 13, 12, 11, 10, 9, 8, 7, 6, 5, 4, 3, 2, 1
- YEARS OF AGE: 21, 20, 19, 18, 17, 16, 15, 14, 13, 12, 11, 10, 9, 8, 7, 6, 5, 4, 3

Universities

Teachers' colleges

Royal Melbourne Institute of Technology

Adult education

Agri-cultural colleges

High schools

Junior technical schools

Higher elementary and central schools

Girls' second-ary schools

Consolidated schools

Correspondence instruction

Primary schools

Nursery schools and Kindergartens
(controlled by voluntary organizations)

NOTE: Except for nursery schools and kindergartens, this diagram reflects the general types of the 2,154 state schools. The 546 private schools (including 439 Roman Catholic schools) and some special state institutions are not indicated.

TABLE 14–1
Statistics of State Primary Schools in Australia, 1960

	NEW SOUTH WALES	VICTORIA	QUEENS- LAND	SOUTH AUSTRALIA	WESTERN AUSTRALIA	TAS- MANIA	TOTAL
Number of primary schools	2,498	1,908	1,469	591	494	261	7,221
Number of pupils enrolled	435,348	294,544	210,512	132,859	92,236	46,750	1,212,249
Number of teachers	12,601	10,904	6,432	4,023	2,375	1,719	38,054

SOURCE: Tables compiled by the Commonwealth Office of Education.

these schools are very small, particularly in the rural areas. There is more variety among the states in secondary education; some states have types of schools which others do not possess, and the names given to schools may vary from state to state. Table 14–2 indicates the number of secondary schools in each state and their enrollments.

TABLE 14–2
Statistics of State Secondary Schools in Australia, 1960

	NEW SOUTH WALES	VICTORIA	QUEENS- LAND	SOUTH AUSTRALIA	WESTERN AUSTRALIA	TAS- MANIA	TOTAL
Enrollment							
High schools	92,052	77,965	23,123	33,827	24,551	12,089	263,607
Junior technical schools		34,130					34,130
Home science or girls' schools		6,410					6,410
Central and higher elementary schools	18,190	9,198	3,298	1,159	497	724	33,066
Area schools				1,886		3,206	5,092
Total enrollment	110,242	127,703	26,421	36,872	25,048	16,019	342,305
Number of Schools							
High schools	147	149	51	70	62	18	497
Junior techical schools		65					65
Home science schools		16					16
Central and higher elementary schools	130	51	49	18		20	268
Area schools				19		42	61
Total schools	277	281	100	107	62	80	907

SOURCE: Tables compiled by the Commonwealth Office of Education.

Preschool Education

THE CHIEF development and expansion in preschool education has taken place since World War II. The Commonwealth Department of Health has established in each of the capital cities a model center, known as the Lady Gowrie Center, as an incentive to expansion and to encourage experimental work. Two of the states have made a small start in this field as a part of public education. New South Wales now operates 10 nursery schools, and Tasmania aids in the support of 52 centers. The other states are as yet reluctant to enter this field because of the feeling that other educational activities should be given priority in the allocation of limited financial resources.

Most of the preschool work in Australia is supported by voluntary organizations such as the Free Kindergarten Union, which raises funds from contributions and receives some state grants. In Victoria the Department of Health allots a per capita amount for each child and assists in building programs. The Melbourne Kindergarten Training College also receives some state assistance from the same source.

An organization called the Australian Preschool Association has been formed to promote the continuous expansion of preschool education throughout the country. It has appointed a Federal Officer and holds biennial conferences in the various states in turn. In 1962 there were some 900 centers affiliated with the Association, enrolling 41,000 children.

Primary Education

PRIMARY schools in Australia may be divided into four groups: schools in metropolitan and urban areas, small rural schools, consolidated or area schools, and schools providing instruction through correspondence. Each of these may be considered separately.

URBAN SCHOOLS

In the metropolitan and urban areas, primary schools in Australia do not differ greatly from those found in other English-speaking countries. The main difference stems from the fact that the course of study in each state is prescribed by a central authority (the state Education Department) and is imposed on all the schools in the state.

In the past, long periods of years used to elapse without any change in the established courses of study. The Education Departments have established curriculum-revision divisions on which experienced teachers and inspectors serve. Most of the states are interested in making substantial changes in their courses of study, and subjects are constantly being reviewed. Changes occur, however, much less frequently than in a decentralized system. In most states social studies courses have been introduced tending to break down the divisions between history, geography, and civics, courses which have also helped in introducing more pupil activities and in giving the teachers more freedom in the choice of topics.

The metropolitan schools often suffered from two disabilities, the inheritance of old and unsuitable buildings and the prevalence of over-large classes. The older buildings are gradually being replaced by new and functional buildings, and there has been quite a dramatic drop in the number of classes of more than 50 pupils in the last few years. As a result, the schools are able to use activity methods to a reasonable extent, to organize field trips, and to give training in swimming and outdoor sports.

SMALL RURAL SCHOOLS

The situation is interesting in the small rural schools. Since the earliest days of the state systems Australia has striven to give the rural districts equal opportunities with those of the cities. The one-teacher school, when well organized under an enthusiastic and well-trained teacher, can be a happy little democratic community where each pupil receives individual attention. From the teachers' colleges most young teachers go first into the rural areas and must win their spurs before qualifying for an urban position. The technique of handling a small one-teacher school receives a great deal of attention in the teachers' colleges. Many of these small schools have attractive grounds and gardens, radio sets, visual aids, playground equipment, workbenches, and small libraries. Some of them own and manage forestry plantations and are members of the state-wide Young Farmers' Clubs. A few schools include grades seven and eight as remnants of the old primary system.

CONSOLIDATED AND AREA SCHOOLS

The effectiveness of the small rural schools has delayed consolidation in many of the states. In at least one state, consolidation cannot take place unless the local people vote for it. However, the load placed on the teacher in a small school has become increasingly heavy, and there is a growing recognition that consolidation of these schools can provide advantages over the present system. As a result, in districts where distances for conveyance are not too great, consolidated schools are beginning to appear, and the number of small one-teacher schools is diminishing in every state.

In the United States consolidation means the merging of several schools into a larger one that more nearly approximates a city graded school. In one Australian state, consolidation resulted in a new type of school, which had characteristics different from those of any other school. Tasmania was a pioneer in this program. In 1936 the first "area schools" were established. These were formed by closing a number of small primary schools and developing a central school which was intended to increase the attractiveness of rural life. Area schools extended from the first grade through the primary grades, and included two or three years of secondary work. The original idea was copied from the area schools of East Suffolk, in England, but Tasmania has added many original features. The term "area school" is used in Tasmania and South Australia, but Victoria refers to "consolidated schools" and the other states use more conventional names such as "junior high school."

Most of the Tasmanian area schools have good groups of modern buildings, consisting of a home school for the regular school subjects, supplemented by craft rooms, carpenter shops, forges, metalworking shops, and leathercraft and extensive homecraft units. The main feature, however, is the school estate, which comprises a number of acres. On this estate are carried out many activities, such as bee-farming, horticulture, hop-growing, and the raising, on modern lines, of sheep, cattle, pigs, and poultry. None of these activities are large in extent, and each school undertakes only activities which link up with the interests and occupations of its immediate district. Local advisory councils of farmers, orchardists, or graziers take a great interest in these schools. They make gifts of pedigreed stock and supervise experiments such as pasture plots and flax-growing. The school subjects are carefully linked with the practical activities. The boys who make a concrete path learn something of the history of concrete and its modern uses. The schools are a delight to visit, because of the obvious interest of the boys and girls in their work. Care is taken that the pupils are not "pinned to the soil," so to speak; those with obvious academic abilities are urged to transfer to high schools.

The children are transported to the area schools by bus, and even this is made an occasion for lessons in deportment and social responsibility. Each school has an extensive landscaping plan for its own estate, and each year the school grounds grow more attractive.

The Tasmanian area schools provide an interesting exception to the general rule in a centralized system, in that the headmasters are allowed considerable freedom in planning the courses, and most of the children are not required to take state-wide examinations. Up to the age of 12 the children take the regular primary school course; after that they spend two or two and one-half days a week in practical activities on the estate. Student self-government is encouraged, and the children take a part in the planning and organization of the many activities involved in the operation of the unit. In the first years of the program, when the area schools were elementary schools only, many children showed a desire to stay on in school after the legal leaving age of 14. The success of this program is one reason why Tasmania later raised the leaving age to 16.

There are still area schools in Tasmania, but the idea at present is to develop them into comprehensive high schools with a rural section but giving a much wider selection of courses to the pupils. The Tasmanian Education Department has also been trying to devise a type of modern school that would provide similar advantages to children in the industrial areas of the cities.

Consolidation of rural schools has also taken place in some parts of Western Australia, South Australia, and Victoria. In these states the rural emphasis is not so marked in the course of study. In Tasmania one in every 11 of the male population is engaged in agriculture, while in Victoria the figure is one in 25. In the mainland states the courses in consolidated schools are more general in nature, without the estates which are a striking feature of the Tasmanian system. The schools are asked to adapt their courses to local conditions wherever possible. In Queensland the distances are so great that very little has been done in the way of consolidation; instead, the school is sometimes carried to the pupil, as in the case of homemaking laboratories built into railway cars. These are routed through the rural districts, and stop for a day or two in one place while lessons and demonstrations are given to all rural children within miles of the spot.

CORRESPONDENCE INSTRUCTION

In a continent as vast as Australia there are many children in the "outback" areas who are far away from any organized school. For them a system of correspondence instruction was established, which has now grown to include secondary and technical courses. Correspondence study—"School Through the Mailbox"—does not sound very exciting, but it has become a rather romantic feature of Australian education.

It began in 1914 when a settler in the Otway forest region of Victoria wrote to the Melbourne Teachers College, saying that his children were out of reach of any school and might grow up illiterate. He asked if anything could be done to help them. The students of the college undertook to supply lessons by correspondence. As soon as this became known, other applicants wrote in, and the students were unable to cope with the situation. The Education Department then assigned regular teachers to the work and started a state correspondence school. New South Wales immediately followed suit, and by 1922 each of the states had a primary correspondence school in operation. As the system grew, a special school building in each capital city was set aside as the headquarters, and a special staff was gathered from experienced teachers who were interested in this type of work. The program offered an excellent opportunity to use otherwise capable teachers who, through deafness or some other disability, were handicapped in classroom work.

Subjects are divided into one- or two-week units, with assignments to be carried out in each unit after the necessary reading and study has been completed. Each assignment includes new material, illustrations, practice examples, and finally, a test to be sent to the school. Each pupil has three workbooks, one at home, one at the correspondence school for correction, and one in transit. From this small beginning the system has grown until today thousands of pupils in each state pursue their studies without ever being in a classroom or seeing a teacher.

The plan has been very successful. Its pupils in many cases have done as well as children in the regular schools—in some instances much better. Perhaps the inaccessibility of education makes the opportunity more highly prized. One of the reasons for success is the personal way in which the teaching is carried out. The children are encouraged to write personal letters with their assignments, and the teachers reply. Cards are sent to the pupils on their birthdays and special leaflets on special occasions, such as those telling the children how to conduct their own ceremony of remembrance on Anzac Day or Armistice Day. Packets of seeds are sent for making small gardens, a special magazine is published containing pupils' work, and books may be borrowed from a special library.

The assistance of parents is obtained for the work of the youngest children, and instructions are sent to them about procedure. If there is anyone in the home who can read and who will help the child, any 6-year-old may start his schooling and learn to read. In the beginning only the basic subjects were available, but now all subjects, including crafts and nature study, are offered by the correspondence schools. The radio gives considerable help, through its regular program of school broadcasts and also through special programs for correspondence pupils. The Royal Melbourne Institute of Technology operates a shortwave system through which a correspondence teacher may talk to a student at a particular time and explain some work about which difficulty is being experienced.

In some states promotion is flexible, taking place not at the end of the school year but on the successful completion of the assignments for a particular grade. No fees are charged. Lesson assignments are carried to and from the pupils by railway, motor truck, horse transport, and even on the backs of camels.

There have been many interesting incidents in the history of the correspondence schools. On one occasion a farmhand wrote to the Education Department in New South Wales, saying that a few years before he had been illiterate but that he had done all the assignments of the three children of his employer. He had corrected them himself from the sets returned to the children by the correspondence school and had obtained the elements of an education. He felt that he owed a great debt to the correspondence school and offered to pay any fees that might be due.

The success of the system at the primary level led to its extension to secondary work in all states. Where possible, secondary students are asked to attend the nearest primary school, or at least to keep in touch with the nearest teacher for assistance. Otherwise the work is done entirely at home. Many of these students have done very well, and a number of them have later entered the universities. An example of the difficulties to be overcome is provided by the case of a boy who had completed the secondary course and wished to take the state Leaving Certificate Examination. In order to reach a center where this examination was to be given, he had to journey 20 miles by camel, 30 miles by mail truck, and the remainder by train.

Correspondence work was extended to the Technical Division as a result of the wartime demand of members of the armed forces for instruction in technical subjects. This was continued after the war in the rehabilitation service for ex-service men and women. Now each state has a system of technical instruction by mail, supplemented in some states by practical workshops in railways cars, which remain for a week or two on a siding in a fairly central location in remote districts. Some technical correspondence schools ask their students to come to the cities for short intensive courses in practical work in the technical schools. An interesting recent development in technical correspondence education is the organization of a scheme of correspondence scholarships operating under the Colombo Plan. Through this scheme, South and Southeast Asian students may take correspondence courses from the Australian technical colleges and the external division of the University of Queensland. Practical training is undertaken by the student in his own country.

Crippled children or those kept at home by periods of illness may keep up their work through correspondence. Nothing, perhaps, can entirely eliminate the social disadvantages of isolation, but correspondence teaching has at least removed the disadvantage of inadequate education for children in the remote areas. Australians believe that the availability of "School Through the Mailbox" has had an important effect on the settling of the outback. The num-

TABLE 14–3

Enrollment in Correspondence Education in Australia, 1961

STATE	PRIMARY	SECONDARY	TECHNICAL
New South Wales	3,400	1,718	11,137
Victoria	853	2,813	4,674
Queensland	4,377	2,377	7,434
South Australia	889	351	5,947
Western Australia	466	344	11,475*
Tasmania	91	243	201
Total Australia	10,076	7,846	40,868

SOURCE: Figures supplied by the Commonwealth Office of Education.
* The figures for Western Australia in this column give the number of courses in which students are enrolled, not the number of individual students.

ber of pupils who took advantage of this system of education in 1961 is shown in Table 14–3.

Another important and almost revolutionary development in correspondence education has been the appearance of the two-way "School of the Air." This enables the pupil to work at his correspondence assignments and ask questions or discuss the work with his teacher hundreds of miles away. Two-way radios provide this facility. It is found in New South Wales, South Australia, Northern Territory, Western Australia, and Queensland.

EDUCATION OF THE HANDICAPPED

In recent years there has been a marked increase in facilities for the education and welfare of handicapped children. All of the state Education Departments have shown great interest in this work, and have trained special teachers for handling various kinds of disabilities. There are special schools for crippled children, with provision both for boarders and for day pupils, and with conveyance arranged for the latter. Trained teachers are assigned to children's hospitals where there are groups of crippled patients. Sydney has a spastic center where methods of teaching devised to develop muscular control are used. Crippled children who must remain in their homes are enrolled in correspondence classes (see above).

There are six residential schools for the deaf, supported by public subscriptions, and several of the Education Departments have organized schools for the deaf. Teachers are sent abroad to learn the latest methods of teaching hard-of-hearing children. In addition to special residential schools for the blind, there are sight-saving classes for children with partial sight. A sight-saving classroom was built at Hobart about 25 years ago, with automatic light control and unusual blackboards designed to give a high visibility. Similar classes have been started in other states.

Speech clinics have been established in each state, and trained speech therapists are assigned to these. Wherever possible, specialists in this and other aspects of work for handicapped children tour the country districts to give advice and help. Delicate and undernourished children are assigned to open-air schools and camps, which are also used for periodic visits by children from crowded industrial areas. In several of the Australian states children from the far interior are on occasion brought down to seaside camps or to the capital cities.

Each state provides extensive educational services for backward and mentally handicapped children. There are ten residential schools and a number of special day schools throughout Australia for these children. There are remedial or opportunity classes for backward children, where physical education, art, music, and crafts are emphasized. Special training programs in the teachers' colleges prepare teachers for these classes. A commencement has been made in remedial classes for children with reading disabilities. The psychological branches of the Education Departments have been giving much attention to these classes, and it is expected that they will be increased in number.

FORESTRY AND HORTICULTURE

In 1923 the Victorian Education Department inaugurated a forestry scheme for primary schools. The objectives were to give pupils an intelligent appreciation of the beauty and value of trees, to help in the cause of conservation, and to provide a source of revenue for the schools. The Forest Commission cooperated with enthusiasm, supplied seeds and small trees, and paid 80 percent of the cost of fencing. Schools undertook to establish and look after plantations, mainly of pines, with the aim of cutting the first trees after twenty years and replanting continuously. In 1952 there were 363 such plantations, and the total production amounted to more than 6 million board feet of pine logs, bringing in a revenue to the participating schools of about £18,000. The money is used to purchase film projectors, radio sets, library books, and playground equipment. Many sections of poor land have been planted with trees. These are carefully tended by pupils who realize that they are building for the future, since no monetary return can be expected until 15 or 20 years have elapsed.

Victoria has also developed horticulture, or gardening, as an elementary school subject. For years teachers tried to beautify small rural schools by planting flower gardens, but they found that they were not expert gardeners and that they could not get a regular supply of plants. They solved this problem in 1913 by establishing a cooperative State Schools Nursery. The Education Department eventually helped in this program, and today over 2,000 schools are participating in it. Thousands of plants, seedlings, shrubs, bulbs, trees, and packets of seeds are distributed each year to the schools, particularly in rural districts and to correspondence pupils.

Secondary Education

FIGURE 14–1 shows that the Australian states possess a variety of secondary schools. It is difficult to work out a simple classification, as in England and the United States. The different types of schools have developed historically to meet the differing needs of particular groups. The major types of secondary school and their functions are listed below.

High schools offer a five- or six-year university preparatory course, although only a small but steadily increasing percentage of their pupils actually enter the university. There is a marked tendency to broaden the course offerings in these schools, and in consequence of this the Australians tend to describe a single high school with a variety of courses as a "comprehensive" or "multi-purpose" high school. Many Australian high schools are becoming less like the English grammar school and more multi-purpose in nature.

Higher elementary, central, and intermediate schools provide the first two or three years of secondary education and act as feeders for the high schools. In the country districts there is a tendency for pupils to drop out of school at 14 or 15 and go to work. Where two or three years of secondary work are added to a primary school, the Australians say that it has a secondary "top"; schools of this nature are now becoming rare.

Home science schools, or girls' secondary schools, offer two- or three-year courses for girls who will go into dressmaking, homemaking, or commercial work. They have been successful and popular, partly because the girls are not required to take the academic examinations. These schools have tended to develop four- or five-year college-preparatory courses in addition to the practical work, because of the higher prestige which the community gives to an academic type of secondary education.

Commercial high schools and agricultural high schools, which are not found in all states, combine a general cultural course with specialized commercial or agricultural courses. The area schools, mainly found in Tasmania, must be mentioned again here because they provide a secondary "top" to the primary courses, and appear to be developing into comprehensive high schools with rural sections.

In general, secondary education in Australia in the past has been dominated by the objective of preparation for the university. The main subjects in the curriculum are English, a modern language (generally French), physics, chemistry, mathematics, history, geography, biology, art, and Latin. The fact that school certificates are granted on the basis of examinations, sometimes internal but usually external, in these subjects, and that the examinations in some cases are prepared and supervised by the universities, has given these subjects great prestige in the community. As a result, the interests of the pupil who will not continue to the university have been subordinated to those of the college-preparatory students.

Nevertheless, there has been a marked expansion of secondary education since World War II, and this expansion has been accompanied by moves to broaden the scope of the curriculum. Comprehensive high schools are found in gradually increasing numbers, or in the case of many centers, the same purpose is achieved by building a technical school within the area.

Perhaps the outstanding development in Australian education since World War II has been the growing tendency of secondary school pupils to remain in school beyond the leaving age. This is apparently due, in the first place, to an increase in the attractiveness of offerings in subjects and courses of study, and secondly to the recognition by the community that in the years ahead an individual without a sound educational background of modern type will be seriously handicapped. This change is taking place in all six states, with Tasmania having a good start with its leaving age of 16.

When New South Wales raised the leaving age to 15, an opportunity was provided to expand and increase the courses offered to pupils in the secondary schools. The types of schools which included pupils to the age of 15 were to a certain extent set free from the restricting effects of university-entrance examinations. Secondary education in New South Wales is now in a state of vigorous expansion and reorganization. All high schools, except in the cities of Sydney and Newcastle, are comprehensive in character, and the junior technical schools correspond closely to the junior technical schools in England. In recent years New South Wales has increased the number of classrooms in operation each year, the biggest addition being 1,092 in 1960. In 1954 a commission of educational experts was appointed to make a survey of secondary education in the state, and to advise the Education Department on the best methods of future expansion and organization.

The report of this commission (known as the Wyndham Report)

has now been made public. It provided for the reorganization of secondary education in New South Wales, and its implementation commenced in 1962. There is to be a secondary course of six years with an examination at the end of four years (the School Certificate Examination) and another (the Higher School Certificate Examination) at the end of six years. This latter examination will be the university entrance examination. In the first year of secondary school studies, pupils will take a general course designed to ascertain abilities and interests. In later years there will be provision for different courses in the same subjects, and the course chosen will be selected on the basis of the student's record in earlier years. Although not recommended in the report, New South Wales retains the Intermediate Certificate Examination at the end of three years of secondary schooling, which for many pupils coincides with the school leaving age.

In Victoria many new high schools are being established, with university-preparatory, technical, domestic science, and general courses running side by side. The Victorian Education Department, however, is beginning to favor a closer approach to the comprehensive high school idea, offering a wide range of elective subjects rather than pinning the pupils down to labeled courses; most people now call these comprehensive schools simply "high schools." Vocational guidance is being introduced into the secondary schools in all states; the outstanding progress in this movement has been made in New South Wales.

The holding power of the Australian state secondary school does not yet compare with that of similar schools in the United States. On the average the leaving age is lower and many pupils go to work as soon as possible. The proportion of the school population continuing in secondary school is well illustrated in Table 14–4. A higher proportion of the pupils in nonstate schools stay in secondary school, since the economic factor is not so important in these schools.

The high schools and junior technical schools in all states are providing many pupils with an excellent education, particularly those who stay on for higher years in the courses. The teaching is very thorough, and extracurricular and athletic activities are growing in importance. The achievement of the pupils in academic class work is probably about a year ahead of that in most American high schools, although the many-sided interests and activities available in

TABLE 14-4

Holding Power of Australian State Secondary Schools (percentages)

	NEW SOUTH WALES	VIC- TORIA	QUEENS- LAND	SOUTH AUS- TRALIA	WESTERN AUS- TRALIA	TAS- MANIA
1st year in 1956	100.0	100.0	100.0	100.0	100.0	100.0
2nd year in 1957	85.0	91.3	87.1	77.7	80.6	92.0
3rd year in 1958	61.2	73.9	51.1	61.6	53.2	74.0
4th year in 1959	20.8	51.4	40.2	26.8	15.6	23.4
5th year in 1960	16.6	22.9	10.3	8.7	13.0	9.1

SOURCE: Annual Reports of the Ministers of Education for the six states. Figures for four of the states were not yet available for 1961.

NOTE: The number of pupils in each successive school year has been expressed as a percentage of the number commencing the first year of secondary schooling in 1956. In Queensland, where the transfer from primary to secondary schools occurs later than in other states, many pupils have reached the school-leaving age by the time this transfer occurs, and for this reason the number of pupils in each subsequent year has been shown as a percentage of primary Grade VII enrollments in 1956. In Victoria, of the first year class in 1957, 45 percent stayed on for the fifth year.

high schools in the United States are far greater and more varied than their counterparts in Australia.

The system of accrediting schools for examination passes is not as widespread as in the United States, but it exists in four of the six Australian states and is extending. There are marked differences, however, from the American pattern. Australian schools have more certificate examinations than American schools, taking place at definite stages during the pupil's secondary career. In two of the states, and for some schools in all the states, these examinations are still devised and corrected by an external authority, but internal examinations for these certificates are used in varying degrees in Victoria, New South Wales, Tasmania, and Western Australia.

For example, as far back as 1917 Victoria inaugurated a system of accrediting schools and this has steadily expanded. The controls are somewhat tighter than those used in similar systems in the United States. Schools that wish to be included in the "accredited" list must lodge an application with the Schools Board of the University of Melbourne. They are then visited by a team of inspectors which makes a survey of the facilities, school records, quality, and experience of the staff, and the standard of teaching being carried out. If the school measures up to the requirements it may then be accredited for the Intermediate Certificate Examination which takes place at the end of the fourth secondary year. This means that the school may conduct its own internal tests, and the Schools Board at the end of the year will accept the headmaster's certificate that certain pupils may be awarded the Intermediate Certificate. After a trial period with the Intermediate Certificate the school may be accredited, if its work is good enough and its staff sufficiently qualified, for the Leaving Certificate which is given at a higher stage. The inspection is repeated every three years and the character of the school's work is carefully reexamined. Most of the state high schools and a number of the nonstate secondary schools are accredited for these two examinations.

The matriculation examination, for entrance to the university, is given at the end of the sixth secondary year in Victoria. It is an external examination set by the university. No schools are accredited for this examination, as scholarships and honors are involved, and it is felt that all pupils competing should be on an even footing.

New South Wales has made its Intermediate Certificate Examination almost entirely internal, but returns to the external system for its Higher School Certificate since entrance to the university is decided on the basis of the latter examination. Tasmania has an internal Schools Board Certificate or Leaving Certificate and an external matriculation examination, but also issues special certificates for the pupils of its area schools according to an internal plan. Western Australia has made a start with accrediting, trying it cautiously at first with practical subjects such as art and various crafts. The other states, Queensland and South Australia, still adhere to external examinations, but there are signs that the system of accrediting schools for internal examinations will eventually spread throughout the whole of Australia.

The Education Departments of Australia, facing a rapidly expanding secondary education program, are concerned with the problem of organizing schools to provide for the interests of the varied types of pupils. Tasmania was inclined to believe that the tripartite system was a solution to the problem, but it is now moving toward the comprehensive type of secondary school. In other states experiments are being attempted which point more in the direction of the comprehensive high school. No fixed plan has been developed yet in any of the states, and there is much discussion and examination of each other's ideas.

Vocational Education

THE EARLIEST stages of vocational training are found in many of the secondary schools in all states. Victoria is the only state that uses the name "junior technical school." In this type of school the ages of the pupils, both boys and girls, range from 12 to 15. Senior technical schools or technical colleges carry on this work, and offer a wide variety of courses.

Technical education in Australia expanded greatly during the war, particularly during the period when the American forces in the Pacific made Australia their initial headquarters and an invasion by the Japanese seemed a possibility. The armed forces realized their need for thousands of trained technicians and munitions workers, more than they could hope to train themselves. The Commonwealth government initiated a nation-wide technical training program, using the existing technical schools and colleges for the purpose. Additional equipment was brought in from abroad, buildings were extended, and before long the technical colleges were beehives of industry, some of them working in shifts right around the clock. The armed forces sent detachments of servicemen for training, and thousands of civilians were trained for aircraft production, transport, munition works, and auxiliary services. Correspondence courses were organized for the benefit of servicemen in distant theaters of war. In all, 119,000 men and women were given technical training in 60 training centers.

When the war was over, it was realized that these expanded facilities were ideally suited for the training of returning ex-service men and women who had to be placed in civil employment. For this purpose a Commonwealth Reconstruction Training Plan was instituted, similar in some respects to the program carried on under the G.I. Bill of Rights in the United States. It actually went into operation a year or two before the war ended, and for several years a large number of young men and women were given training. The cost was defrayed by Commonwealth grants, and the trainees were paid a living allowance. Most of the courses were taken in technical schools, but many students were enrolled in secondary schools, universities, and agricultural colleges. The total number who have undertaken training under this program, full-time and part-time, is about 275,000.

The technical schools have now settled down to their regular programs, under the management of the states, but the great increase in their activities and the much added interest in the community in technical education that the war stimulated have been maintained.

A variety of courses are available in the higher technical schools and technical colleges. There are trade and certificate courses, mainly for part-time employed students. Apprentices take advantage of these courses, in many cases attending a full day a week on the employer's time and one evening a week on their own time. More than 50 such courses are available: examples are courses for printers, plumbers, railways mechanics, hairdressers, and dental technicians. The courses run from three to five years. In Western Australia special arrangements are made for country apprentices to attend short intensive courses in the cities.

There are diploma courses which require four years' full-time attendance. These are on the professional level, and credit is given for some of the work if the students transfer to a university. Besides courses in engineering and architecture, work is done at this level in commerce, home science, many divisions of art and applied art, radio mechanics and electronics, agriculture, food technology, applied physics and chemistry, personnel management, interior decoration, aeronautics, and navigation. One or two of these technical colleges were originally Schools of Mines. They continue to give instruction in various branches of geology and mining, but have broadened their offerings to include many other courses. Technical correspondence courses are very popular.

For some years there has been agitation for the establishment of higher institutes of technology, which would carry technical education to a much higher level. A first step in this direction was the opening of the New South Wales University of Technology in Sydney in 1949. Subsequently, the name of this institution was changed to the University of New South Wales; it now offers a range of courses comparable with that of other Australian universities.

AGRICULTURAL EDUCATION

In a country which depends so much on primary industries, one would expect to find a network of facilities for agricultural education. There is a reasonable coverage of this field, but not in any distinctive fashion. All of the Australian states have organized Young Farmers' Clubs, which are more comparable to the 4-H Clubs in the United States than to the Future Farmers of America. Boys and girls from elementary as well as secondary schools are members. Some of the rural high schools have courses in agriculture and arrange visits to neighboring farms and plant experimental plots. The Tasmanian area schools have done most in this direction.

All of the states, with the exception of Tasmania, have established agricultural colleges which give more advanced work in scientific farming. These are boarding schools with experimental farms as part of their campus. Most of them are administered by the Department of Agriculture rather than by the Education Department. They are not comparable with American agricultural colleges, which are on the university level. Most of the Australian agricultural colleges take students after three or four years of secondary work, at about the age of 15, and give a three- or four-year course in theoretical and practical agriculture leading to a diploma.

Many of the technical colleges in rural towns offer short courses in agriculture, as well as two- or three-year full-time courses. Subjects which are offered include animal husbandry, farm mechanics, sheep and wool, carpentry, horticulture, agricultural chemistry, and bookkeeping. One of these colleges, the Gordon Institute of Technology in Geelong, has established a worldwide reputation in subjects associated with wool and textiles; it attracts students from Asian and Pacific countries as well as from all over Australia.

Seven of the Australian universities offer full degree courses in agricultural science. Many of the graduates are employed as specialists by government departments of agriculture and by primary industries generally. With so many scientific developments in irrigation, wheat-breeding, dry farming, and the treatment of former semidesert areas with chemicals to render them suitable for cultivation, it is obvious that the Australian farmer needs a sound general education, a training in the basic sciences, and professional training in the techniques of modern farming. This training is steadily becoming more widespread.

Nongovernment Schools

THE NONSTATE schools in Australia play an important part in the educational network, providing for about 25 percent of the total enrollment. They divide themselves into three groups—Protestant schools of various denominations, Roman Catholic schools, and private schools. In 1960, as against 7,867 government schools in Australia, there were 2,228 nonstate schools. Of the latter the Protestant schools numbered 238, the Roman Catholic 1,727, and the private or undenominational schools 254. They receive no state subsidies, but certain small allowances are made in Canberra and in New South Wales.

The Roman Catholic schools are for the most part inexpensive as far as fees are concerned and provide opportunities for all classes in the community. The other schools charge fees varying from moderate to high, some reaching $1,350 a year. Only a few restrict themselves entirely to boarders; many have a limited number of boarders and a large number of day pupils. The larger and wealthier of these schools have attractive buildings and extensive playing fields. The general amenities in these schools are good, and school life is made interesting and pleasant, with many-sided interests encouraged and numerous activities provided for the pupils. A number of boys and girls take their elementary education in the state schools, and transfer to the larger church schools for the secondary stage.

The nonstate schools are independent of any form of control by the Education Departments, except that they must be approved by departmental inspectors before they can accept government scholarship winners. This independence is salutary where the state system is highly centralized, in that these schools are free to carry out experiments and variations of their own. Only some of them do this, the others being content to follow more or less conventional lines, modeled to a certain extent upon procedures in the public schools of England.

Only a few of the nonstate schools are organized on a coeducational basis. In the state schools practically all primary schools are coeducational and the same applies to high schools in the rural districts; in the cities there are some coeducational high schools, but the bigger ones are boys' schools or girls' schools. Australia seems to have followed English traditions in this regard, but coeducational secondary schools, in the state systems at any rate, are steadily growing in favor.

University Education

THE UNIVERSITIES of Australia are either state or national. There are no private or church-connected universities. Each state maintains one or more universities in its capital city, established by an act of the state parliament. A university college was established at Armidale, in the northeastern part of New South Wales, in 1938. In 1953 Parliament granted this college a charter which made it the independent University of New England.[1]

The same state has established the University of New South Wales in Sydney. At Canberra, the national capital, is situated the Australian National University, established as a research institute by the federal government. The University College of Canberra, which for some years was affiliated with the University of Melbourne, has now become the School of General Studies of the National University.

A second university, Monash, has been established in Melbourne and plans are under way for another university institution in Adelaide, South Australia. In 1961 a university college was established at Townsville as a part of the University of Queensland. At the present time in Sydney consideration is being given to the establishment of a third university and a Victorian committee is investigating ways of extending tertiary education in that state, either by the opening of another university or by some other means.

Reference here should be made to the Australian Universities Commission that was set up by the Commonwealth government in 1959, following an examination of the needs of tertiary education in Australia by a special committee, of which the chairman was Sir Keith Murray, chairman of the United Kingdom University Grants Committee. The Australian Universities Commission consists of a full-time chairman, chosen on the basis of his distinction as a professor at an Australian university, and six part-time members. This Commission examines the financial needs of universities and recommends to the Australian government the amount of grants necessary for universities to meet their commitments. These grants are made on a triennial basis. As the universities are, with the exception of the National University, state institutions, a considerable part of the funds necessary for these schools is provided by the state.

[1] New England is the name given to a group of northeastern counties in New South Wales.

In 1961 the Prime Minister announced the appointment of a committee to consider the pattern of tertiary education in relation to the needs and resources of Australia and to make recommendations to the Australian Universities Commission on the future development of tertiary education in the country.

During the past decade there has been a marked increase in enrollments at Australian universities, as shown in Table 14–5. In 1961 the total enrollments were 57,672. In 1951 the comparable figure was 31,671. The prediction of the professor of demography at the Australian National University is that university population in Australia will reach 88,500 in 1965 and 113,900 in 1970.

There are no liberal arts colleges in the American sense. Specialization begins much earlier, and students who intend to become doctors, lawyers, and engineers commence their professional training early in their courses. A medical student is expected to have a good grounding in physics, chemistry, and mathematics in the high schools. He does preliminary science courses in his first year in the

TABLE 14–5

Enrollment in Australian Universities, 1961

UNIVERSITY	DATE OF FOUND-ING	STUDENT ENROLLMENT			
		Full-time	Part-time	Exter-nal	Total
Sydney	1850	9,428	3,106	—	12,534
Melbourne	1853	7,226	3,720	505	11,451
Adelaide	1874	3,562	2,270	418	6,250
Tasmania	1890	766	544	150	1,460
Queensland	1909	3,854	3,058	2,613	9,525
Western Australia	1911	1,988	1,183	366	3,573
Australian National University*	1946	488	690	—	1,178
New England†	1954	694	142	1,700	2,536
New South Wales‡	1958	2,471	6,329	38	8,838
Monash	1958	334	29	—	363
Totals		30,811	21,071	5,790	57,672

SOURCE: Bureau of Census and Statistics, *University Statistics, 1961.*
* Now incorporates Canberra University College.
† Formerly New England University College.
‡ Formerly New South Wales University of Technology.

university, and in his second year, at the age of 19 or 20, begins the remaining five years of the medical course.

The American system of units or credits does not operate in Australia. To gain entrance to a university the student must pass in a stipulated four of five subjects in the university matriculation. In some states the failures run as high as 35 percent in a very highly selected group of applicants. If the student takes an arts course, he selects one or more major subjects, which involves taking parts I, II, and III in each subject in successive years. He secures approval for a course which involves some ten subjects or parts of subjects. A science course takes four years and may involve 12 or 13 subjects or parts. At the end of each year he takes an examination in three or possibly four subjects. If he chooses to work for a pass degree, he may select a fairly wide range of cultural subjects. If he elects a course for an honors degree, he specializes in one group, such as Germanic languages or history. He will then take courses closely allied to his major, with the possiblity of one or two elective subjects. Students in the honors course are a selected group to begin with, and they must reach a very high level of scholastic achievement to pass the examinations. Australian degrees are recognized at Oxford, Cambridge, and London, and also by American universities for graduate work.

All Australian universities are autonomous. Although they are supported by state and Commonwealth grants, no attempt is made to dictate policy or how the funds shall be spent. Each university is governed by a Council or Senate, composed of representatives of the state parliament, the teaching faculty, the graduates of the university, the undergraduate students, and prominent citizens of the community. The chancellor is an honorary official who is selected from the distinguished citizens of the state. The vice-chancellor is the full-time administrative head, comparable to the president of an American university. In cooperation with the Council, he directs the development of university policy. All academic matters are discussed by the Professorial Board, made up of the full professors of the institution. This board advises the Council on action to be taken, after consultation with the appropriate departments or faculties.

During World War II the Commonwealth government instituted a Universities Commission to advise the Manpower Commission on matters concerning university students. A few years later the Universities Commission began to take an active part in the provision of courses for ex-servicemen in universities under the Commonwealth Reconstruction Training Scheme. Later, it was charged with the responsibility of administering the Commonwealth Scholarship Scheme through which the federal government provides 5,000 scholarships each year to students undertaking courses in the universities, technical colleges, and other tertiary institutions. In addition, provision now exists for a scheme of postgraduate awards at Australian universities whereby some 125 scholarships are available for allocation to postgraduate students of high caliber who wish to proceed to advanced studies. The Universities Commission of World War II is now designated the Commonwealth Scholarships Board. A new Universities Commission was established in 1959.

Australian universities are financed by state grants and by a Commonwealth subsidy which is approximately one-third of the total amount collected from student fees. The cost of university courses may be gathered from the total fees charged for the following courses at the University of Melbourne: (a) a three-year course for the Bachelor of Arts degree, £285 ($600); (b) a four-year course for a science degree, £360 ($800); (c) a six-year course for a medical degree, £845 ($1,885).

Approximately half of the students are receiving scholarships from the Commonwealth or state governments, from private endowments, or from the Education Departments. Western Australia was originally a free university but it now charges fees.

None of the Australian universities are residential like Oxford, nor do they provide extensive dormitory accommodations like some American colleges. All, however, have residential colleges associated with them, usually built adjacent to the campus by religious denominations. These are not teaching colleges in the American sense of the word, but rather groups who live together. There may be some tutors associated with these colleges who assist in the teaching. Overall, some 14 percent of university students in Australia are resident in university colleges and halls of residence; an exception is found in the case of New England which is the closest approach in Australia to a residential university. It has four residential colleges on its campus, and other students live in a number of large houses in Armidale.

At the University of Western Australia a hall of residence, previously known as University Hostel, has now become Currie Hall and is an undenominational college with a council appointed by the university. It is proud of a pattern of self-government which has developed over the years.

The University of Melbourne has built, with funds raised by public subscription, an International House, principally to house students from the countries of Southeast Asia who attend the university. In some of the other states, committees are working with the object of raising funds to establish International Houses on their campuses.

Each university has a student union building, organized by the student body, which is the center of student activities. These buildings provide reading rooms, cafeteria and dining rooms, music room, theaters, locker rooms and showers, meeting rooms and offices for student body organizations, and meeting places for scores of clubs. Each year the universities hold a drama festival in each capital in turn. Interfaculty and intervarsity sports contests are held throughout the year. All students are members of the National Union of Australian University Students. This organization coordinates student body activities in the various states, sponsors student exchanges during vacation, holds All-Australian conferences, and arranges for Australian students going abroad to receive hospitality and aid from student organizations in other countries.

Adult Education

IT IS difficult to define adult education, since it is hard to distinguish between a young woman taking a course in needlework at a technical college in order to increase her professional efficiency and a young man who takes a course in the application of art to home decoration at a W.E.A. class for his own personal interest. In this section adult education is interpreted to mean community education carried on by a variety of agencies for students of all ages who take courses because of awakening cultural interests without intending to pass an examination or to obtain a certificate.

There is nothing in Australia to compare with the extension courses in the United States where thousands of students take courses for which they receive university credit. The Australian work is patterned after that of England, where the extension program is divided between university extension divisions and the Workers' Educational Association. In some of the states these efforts are unified under Adult Education Boards or Councils. The objective is to arouse the cultural interests of the community and to maintain them by suitable offerings and activities. For many years these adult groups were composed largely of teachers, bank clerks, and housewives, but recently a greater variety of courses and other offerings has made an appeal to a more varied constituency.

In New South Wales the state government in 1960 gave a grant of about £62,500 divided between the Department of Tutorial Classes of the University of Sydney, the Adult Education Section of the Public Library, and the Department of Adult Education of the University of New England. Many classes, discussion groups, film groups, and lectures are organized in all parts of the state. The Department of Tutorial Studies of the University of Sydney issues a fortnightly *Current Affairs Bulletin,* having taken this over several years ago from the Commonwealth Office of Education. This publication is very popular, over 20,000 copies being distributed every two weeks to subscribers all over Australia and overseas.

The former Documentary Films Council is now known as the New South Wales Film Council. During the year ending June 1962 it distributed some 37,000 films to various organizations in the metropolitan area and country districts.

Forty-four evening colleges, enrolling more than 33,000 students, offer courses in drama, physical education, oral and written expression, music, and arts and crafts. The amount expended on evening colleges in 1960 was £242,785.

In Victoria various activities of long standing were coordinated in 1946 by the establishment of a Council of Adult Education. It received a state grant of £68,000 for 1960–61. The council also charges fees for some of its courses. The council sponsors documentary film showings, ballet programs, and music recitals by prominent artists; it provides a traveling theater which visits country towns, and supplies discussion groups throughout the state with boxes of books and reference materials. Many regular classes are held in city and country centers. Each year a residential summer school is held by the council, with a leading theme for discussion. These summer schools have become very popular and it has been difficult to accommodate all the applicants for attendance.

Queensland established a Board of Adult Education in 1944, to coordinate activities throughout this large state. Classes in a variety of subjects are offered, both in Brisbane and in other centers. In

1961 some 6,500 lectures and class meetings were attended by 130,000 persons in 210 different locations in Queensland.

Western Australia is even larger than Queensland, but adult education in this state is vigorous and progressive. The Adult Education Board holds an annual summer school at Perth in the attractive university buildings on the banks of the Swan River. This session draws students from all parts of the state, and even from other parts of Australia. The mornings are devoted to a special theme for discussion, such as "Australia's Northern Neighbors," the afternoons to a variety of courses and recreational activities, and the evenings to concerts and plays in an open-air auditorium. Regular classes are organized in city and country centers, and a circulating library sends collections of books all over the state. Collections of records of symphonic music are also available for circulation.

Education and Status of Teachers

IN ALL Australian states, the teachers in government schools are civil servants. They enjoy the rights which go with this status, but they must also obey the public service regulations. The main privilege is security of tenure. Once accepted by the Education Department and placed on the classified roll, the teacher may look forward to continuous service, without fear of dismissal, until he is retired with a pension at the age of 60 or 65; in one state at least (New South Wales) women can retire at 55. It is difficult to dismiss a classified teacher, for the Public Service Board requires that the Education Department prove that he has been guilty of gross misconduct or some criminal act, or that he is hopelessly incompetent.

Public service regulations forbid the teacher to criticize the government, and the provision is taken to include criticism of the Education Department. This situation renders teachers and even higher administrators mute, and all pronouncements are made by the Minister and the Director. Only the teachers' unions seem to be permitted to voice criticisms and opinions. Teachers are not, however, denied the right to speak on any issue not concerned with their own Education Department.

Each state Education Department takes active steps to recruit for its own teaching services. In some states this is done largely through visits by departmental officers to secondary schools. A potential applicant is offered inducements in the last two years of his secondary course, in the form of financial grants to keep him in school. Under these circumstances the boy or girl agrees to enter the teachers' college, or the university, and to prepare for teaching.

All of the teachers' colleges preparing teachers for schools operated by the state governments are controlled and administered by the Education Departments; they offer two-year courses for elementary school teachers and longer programs for specialists such as teachers of infant grades or of handicapped children. Teaching orders of the Catholic Church have their own colleges for teachers and there is one college operating in Victoria which trains teachers for the independent schools of the state. State secondary teachers are trained in the universities and do their professional work in the Schools of Education. All fees and expenses, including substantial living allowances, in both teachers' colleges and universities are paid by the Education Departments for their own students. In return, the students sign a bond that they will serve the department for a specified number of years. Although the traditional method of training state secondary teachers was that they should do their first degree as well as their professional work at the university, circumstances have compelled some of the state departments to undertake both the academic and professional training of some of their prospective teachers for secondary schools in secondary teachers' colleges under their own control. The special circumstances are the necessity of training those who, though qualified for admission, are excluded by university quotas or have failed by narrow margins in university grades. The shortage of secondary teachers makes it essential that these should be trained and used.

Critics have pointed out that it is not the best procedure to have the employing authority entirely in control of the training of teachers, for there tends to be a certain amount of inbreeding of ideas. Lecturers in the teachers' colleges are often chosen from the departmental service and have been successful teachers under the system as it exists. The university Schools of Education are more independent, and are thus in a position to be critical on occasion, particularly since they train teachers for nonstate schools as well as state schools.

On completing a course of training the young departmental

teacher may be required to serve in any part of the state. Usually his early years of teaching are spent outside the metropolitan area, and then he may be transferred to a town or city. Later, to obtain promotion, he will probably have to go to the country again. This procedure, in a state-wide service, insures that the schools in rural districts receive young and enthusiastic teachers as well trained as those in the city schools.

All Victorian teachers are classified on one of three rolls—elementary, secondary, or technical—the procedure is similar but not identical in all states. The classes in one state are IV, III, II, and I. The classification is primarily one of teachers and not of schools, but schools are classified in the same groups, and a Class II teacher is found in a Class II school. The classification of schools is based on attendance, Class I schools being the largest ones. The classification of assistant teachers is not always the same as that of the schools, although the same four classes are used. Promotion lists are issued each year, giving the names of teachers in each class who are considered worthy of promotion to the next higher class. Those named on the promotion list are then free to apply for advertised vacancies in the next class. All vacancies are advertised in the official *Education Gazette*. Applicants must be on the Education Department's roll and eligible for a school of the class of the advertised vacancy. Applications are sent to the head office.

Promotion depends on teaching records certified by the inspector's reports, on the academic achievements of the teacher, and on seniority in the service. The senior qualified applicant is usually appointed. If he is not, he may appeal to an independent committee that will hear his case and, if it thinks proper, will displace the original nominee in favor of the appellant. This means that seniority plays a very important part in promotion and that older teachers get most of the higher positions. Some states have made provision for overcoming the factor of seniority by providing for special appointment in certain cases whereby a percentage of promotions may be made on the basis of ability irrespective of seniority. This procedure is used conservatively. In former years a young teacher had to wait long years before he could reach any of the higher classes, but recently promotion has come more quickly in the expanding service. This is especially true for women, and many more opportunities in special branches and positions have opened up for well-qualified men and women. Senior positions for headmasters, inspectors, and administrative officers are advertised within the service and it is almost unknown for an outsider to obtain one of these places. Women are not eligible for many of the higher positions. They can become senior teachers or heads of departments, and a few become headmistresses.

TEACHERS' SALARIES

Salaries of teachers in most of the states are determined by an independent body outside the jurisdiction of the Education Department. In four states teachers have access to the Arbitration Court. In Victoria an independent Teachers' Tribunal has been set up. One member represents the teachers, one the state government, the third member being an independent chairman. This body's decisions on salaries cannot be overruled by the government, which must pay the salaries set by the Tribunal. Teachers' salaries have risen considerably in all states in recent years, and teachers' pension systems are on the whole satisfactory.

Salary awards for primary and secondary teachers in Victoria which were in effect in July 1962 are shown in Table 14–6. Within any class the salary increments are automatic, but a teacher who has reached the maximum salary for a class must wait for any increase until he has gained promotion. A teacher beginning in the lowest subdivision of Class IV, with good reports and the necessary training, may expect to reach Class I between the ages of 45 and 50, and possibly one of the coveted "Special" places (headships of the largest schools) sometime after 50.

The headmaster of a moderate-sized high school would receive £2,400–£2,500, and of a large high school £3,100. An inspector of secondary schools would range in salary from £2,800 to £3,300. The chief inspector would receive £3,975. By comparison, the salary of a professor at a university, determined by the university council, would be £4,250. A reasonably successful businessman would be dissatisfied if his income were less than £5,000.

The system of classification, transfer, and promotion works effectively but the machine is so huge and impersonal that it tends to move teachers as units rather than as people. An example of this is the case of a headmaster of a secondary school in a rural district who developed such a successful school that its attendance rose

TABLE 14–6
Teachers' Salaries in Victoria, 1962 (in Australian pounds)

CLASS	SUBDIVISIONS									
	1	2	3	4	5	6	7	8	9	10
Primary Schools Division										
MEN										
Class IV	1,050	1,100	1,150	1,200	1,300	1,400	1,450	1,500	1,550	1,600
Class III	1,700	1,750	1,800	1,850	—	—	—	—	—	—
Class II	2,050	2,100	—	—	—	—	—	—	—	—
Class I	2,300	2,350	2,400	—	—	—	—	—	—	—
Special	2,650	—	—	—	—	—	—	—	—	—
WOMEN										
Class IV	840	880	920	960	1,040	1,120	1,160	1,200	1,240	1,280
Class III	1,360	1,400	1,440	1,480	—	—	—	—	—	—
Class II	1,742	1,760	1,785	—	—	—	—	—	—	—
Class I	2,114	2,164	2,214	—	—	—	—	—	—	—
Special	2,464	—	—	—	—	—	—	—	—	—
Secondary Schools Division										
MEN										
Class IV	1,080	1,130	1,200	1,320	1,440	1,550	1,630	—	—	—
Class III	1,730	1,780	1,830	1,880	—	—	—	—	—	—
Class II	2,080	2,130	—	—	—	—	—	—	—	—
Class I	2,330	2,380	2,430	—	—	—	—	—	—	—
Special	2,680	—	—	—	—	—	—	—	—	—
WOMEN										
Class IV	864	904	960	1,056	1,152	1,240	1,304	—	—	—
Class III	1,384	1,424	1,464	1,504	—	—	—	—	—	—
Class II	1,766	1,784	1,809	—	—	—	—	—	—	—
Class I	2,138	2,188	2,238	—	—	—	—	—	—	—
Special	2,488	—	—	—	—	—	—	—	—	—

SOURCE: Regulations made under the Teaching Service Act of 1958 which took effect on the 1st day of July, 1962. Previous cost of living allowances have been incorporated in these salaries.

above the figure for his particular class on the roll; this required that the headmastership be advertised again, and, to the consternation of the parents, their energetic headmaster was displaced by an older man in a higher class who appeared to lack the personal qualities and popular appeal of the original holder of the position. On the other hand, the system is, in a way, fair to all teachers in that it safeguards their right to compete for any position, but it gives mediocre teachers almost as much opportunity as outstanding ones. There is no possibility of political influence being used to obtain a desirable appointment, but there is no chance for a local community to express its desire for a particular person.

In contrast with some other countries, there is much movement from school to school within a state, so much so that it is difficult for any school to build up a special character dependent upon the personality of a headmaster and a group of teachers who will remain for a considerable period of time.

The teachers' unions are strong supporters of the system, which they feel not only gives security and equality of opportunity to all teachers, but also prevents the mediocre but reasonably capable teacher with a record of satisfactory service from being deprived of access to higher positions in the larger schools.

The professional organizations of teachers have a history which stretches back into the last century, but it is only within the last thirty years that they have become powerful. There is a teachers' union in every state, and an Australian Teachers' Federation, founded in 1921. The national federation attempts to develop policies affecting all the state teachers in Australia. In New South Wales the Teachers' Federation, which is the name used by the local state teachers' union, has affiliated with the trade-union movement and has become a forceful organization. In general teachers' unions have fought hard and successfully for better salaries and better working conditions. They have given some attention to matters of educational policy, and they present resolutions to their respective Education Departments. Their annual conferences provide an opportunity for much plain speaking, which the public service regulations do not permit to individuals. The Australian teachers' unions do not compare in professional prestige and influence with the National Education Association in the United States or the National Union of Teachers in England, but they have done a good deal for the general advancement of the teaching profession in Australia.

Teaching in Australia might be best described as a "near-profession." There are too many variations in requirements for teachers' certificates, too many temporary teachers, and too little control of their working conditions by the teachers themselves to warrant comparison with the professional status of doctors and lawyers. But the required qualifications are steadily improving, and the remuneration is becoming more adequate. The status of teachers in Australia has risen considerably in recent years; with signs of awakening public interest in education, it may rise much higher in the near future.

Problems of the Operation of Schools in Australia

SOME of the problems relating to the effective operation of schools in Australia have their roots in inadequate finance and lack of foresight in the past. Some state governments at the time of the depression before World War II cut educational expenditures severely over several years, with the result that the building programs fell far behind, teachers left the service, and classes became much too large. The resultant lag was very difficult to make up. Since World War II, however, grants for education became more and more adequate until we find a dramatic change in the total amounts spent each year, even allowing for changes in the value of money. For example, in Victoria the total expenditure on education in 1951–52 was £13,-127,000, or £5.14.1 per head of population; in 1960–61 it was £40,193,000, or £14.17.10 per head, and recently it has exceeded £50,000,000. But even this is not enough, and all six states are clamoring for more money as their populations increase, and pupils tend to stay on longer in the secondary education stage.

The other big cause of current problems is the tendency towards inflexibility of the centralized system. Changes take longer to initiate and longer to set in operation than they would under decentralization. The big machine tends to resist change, and prefers to continue working along older and well-tried lines.

Problems of Accommodation

When, in the 1950's, the increase in the postwar birthrate began to pour thousands of additional pupils into the schools, the problems of shortage of buildings and classrooms became acute in all states. Hundreds of prefabricated classrooms were imported from England and hundreds more were manufactured in Australia, but this was only a temporary expedient. These classrooms helped to stave off disaster, but the situation was still very serious, in spite of many good buildings erected in 1953, 1954, and 1955. Tasmania had been wiser in carrying on her building program in the earlier years and was even able to raise her leaving age to 16 without overcrowding her schools. Some of the states, however, saw little chance of raising the leaving age above 14 for years to come, not because of the lack of desire to do so but because there was simply not room enough for the additional pupils. Victoria, for example, did not raise her leaving age to 15 until the beginning of 1964. Building programs in all the states are now going ahead vigorously because the construction of new schools has been given high priority in all public works programs. The problems are those of the availability of money rather than any delay in spending.

The Problem of Over-large Classes

This is not a new problem. For many years there have been numerous instances of over-large classes in the metropolitan schools, particularly in the primary grades. Fifty has been a common number and classes of 60 and 70 have not been unknown. But when a postwar population explosion hit the schools, first the primary, and in later years many of the secondary, classes were close to bursting. This was where the time lag in building new schools and renovating old ones showed its calamitous results, and local authorities, although very much aware of the problem and extremely anxious about it, were powerless, in a centralized system, to take any action. In the early 1960s the severity of the problem began to lessen, as the wave of postwar children moved higher along the age scale. Now the universities are facing it, and have had to establish quotas, partly through not foreseeing the need for an increased number of places, and partly because of the growth in popularity of secondary and higher education.

The Problem of Shortage of Teachers

As in many other countries there was for some years a distinct shortage of teachers in Australia. This was originally due to inadequate salaries, indifferent working conditions, and dislike by many young people of the regimentation associated with centralization. Recently, however, salaries of teachers have been markedly increased, the status of teachers in the community raised, working conditions have improved, and the former rigidity of centralization has been considerably modified. Recruiting and training procedures have been made much more effective and many more recruits are coming forward, and of good type, but the swelling school population has absorbed the increased numbers of young teachers, leaving little or no surplus to cope with new developments in a rapidly expanding system.

The Education Departments have made strenuous efforts to attract young and promising recruits. Bonuses were paid to them in the secondary schools until they had good preliminary qualifications. In Victoria, as an example, the number of teachers' colleges was increased from the original one to eleven. In 1963 there were more than 1,000 in Victoria training to be secondary teachers. Every one of these was badly needed, for the numbers of pupils grew and grew, more schools were being opened, and many new branches of educational work were being commenced. The best that can be said is that the situation in 1963 was much better than it had been. It has proved difficult to secure and train specialists in psychology, guidance, visual education, physical education, and music, when so many were needed for the old established subjects. Teachers of mathematics and science have been tempted away to industrial and scientific positions. The fact that the well-qualified teacher is gaining the respect of the community and a much higher social rating is helping gradually in the campaign of recruiting, training, and keeping good teachers. It is interesting to note that because of the very rapid expansion in the number of schools and teachers, the balance between old and young teachers has changed considerably over the last decade in favor of the latter.

The Problem of Sensitivity to Current Opinion on Education

There are two sides to this problem. There are definite advantages in a school system that is sensitive to local needs and local thinking. Things get done more quickly, there is much greater pride in the schools, parent-teacher associations flourish, and in case of a crisis the local people quickly rally round.

On the other hand local thinking may be somewhat unbalanced and even badly informed. It can be responsive to pressures and propaganda which are not always healthy. This is the point made by a centralized administration, which in the past was not infrequently found defending itself fiercely against local opinion. Fortunately there is now the beginning of a much better understanding. A sign of this is the observance of Education Week, when the parents visit the schools and are very interested in the procedures. Perhaps every week in the whole school year should be an "Education Week."

The Problems of Curricula and Examinations

When the curricula for schools are laid down by a central authority it is unlikely that many variations or experiments will come into existence, even though approval may be gained for these. Actually the curricula in Australia are drawn up by expert teachers and administrative officers, and the courses are both sound and thorough in subject content. But when these courses of study, particularly in the secondary and technical stages, are linked with a system of comprehensive external examinations, freedom for teachers tends to become a nebulous ideal. The rather mechanical system of promotion of teachers intensifies this problem, for teachers are loath to embark upon experiments which may be only partially successful and thus may affect their chances of promotion. Of recent years the administrative authorities have tried to encourage variety and experiment, especially in those secondary schools which are working under the system of accrediting, but most teachers have elected to stand by the prescribed courses of study.

Several critics have drawn attention to this tendency towards rigidity. Kandel said, "The prescribed curriculum should be abandoned in favor of suggestions to teachers; the examination systems can be reformed; the system of rating teachers has no justification or validity as compared with opportunities for developing alertness by opportunities for continued study." [2]

Dr. K. S. Cunningham, formerly Director of the Australian Council for Educational Research, in 1937 suggested the major needs of Australian education:

More autonomy, greater flexibility, more exploration and experiment, the building up of a strong and well-informed public opinion on education, continuous study of the education problem as a whole, especially in its relation to social and industrial changes, . . . greater rapidity and thoroughness in putting new developments into operation, better material conditions and aids, higher professional standards and better status for the teacher, less formalism in school work, and more attention to the task of cultivating intelligent citizenship. [3]

H. C. Dent, former editor of the *Times Educational Supplement*, one of the best informed commentators in the British Commonwealth, visited Australia in 1952 and made a brief survey of Australian education. His subsequent comments, given in a letter to the Director of the Australian Council for Educational Research, included the following:

[2] Kandel, *Types of Administration*, p. 85.
[3] K. S. Cunningham, "A Critical Account of Australian Education," *Year Book of Education, 1937*, Evans Bros. Ltd., London, pp. 186–200.

The effects of the examination system upon teaching methods in all subjects, but especially practical and craft subjects, seemed to be most baneful. . . . About the procedures for appointing and promoting teachers I find it difficult to write with moderation. How can there be "exploration and experiment" with new subjects and teaching techniques unless heads of schools are selected for their imagination, initiative, enterprise, drive and courage? And if by chance such a head does get appointed, how can he possibly realize his aims and ideals unless he has some say in selecting his staff?

I came to the conclusion during my visit that three major reforms are essential to the salvation of Australian primary and secondary education, especially the latter. Promotion of teachers by merit must supplant promotion by seniority. Teachers must become convinced that they are not only free to experiment, but be actively encouraged to do so—which may mean the abandonment of departmentally prepared curricula. The stranglehold of examinations on the schools must be broken. Only when these reforms have been effected will it be possible to tackle with any hope of success the problems presented by the rapid increase and the changing character of the Australian population.[4]

The Problem of the Training of Administrators

Much remains to be done in Australia in regard to this important matter. There is no training school for educational administrators nor even a suitable training course. The Schools of Education in the universities try to give a wide picture of educational problems throughout the world and of different procedures in administration, but there is no practical training or opportunity of working temporarily under a system other than centralization. Teachers and administrators are sent abroad, as a reward for good work they have done, to make observations, but not to study at an approved School of Administration, as is the case with members of the Army, Navy, or Air Force. Australian administrators of education simply grow up in their own system and become imbued with the alleged superiority of its special features. A course in educational administration at the National University in Canberra, followed by twelve months' duty as an administrator in Britain, the United States, Canada, or Japan would result in much greater flexibility in the outlook of administration in Australian education.

---

[4] Letter to Dr. K. S. Cunningham, 1952, circulated privately to a number of officials and other Australians interested in educational developments.

The Need for a Clear Statement of Educational Objectives

No system can work effectively unless it knows its real objectives. Australia has need for the formulation or evolution of an educational philosophy of its own which will embody the characteristics of its own mode of life, its cultural ideas, and national aims. This is particularly the case since Australia has begun to realize that, although her cultural heritage came from western Europe, geographically she is part of Southeast Asia. This philosophy should not be something hard and fast, but a flexible statement which would give the community, including the teachers and the pupils, some idea of what the schools are trying to do.

There have been several attempts to make useful statements of educational objectives, as, for example, the one used by the committee which revised the primary curriculum in New South Wales in recent years. This particular statement has also been used jointly by the Australian Council for Educational Research and the New South Wales Education Department in preparing tests of basic skills. Other statements have been evolved in the Report of the Ramsay Committee on State Education in Victoria, in the Wyndham Report on Secondary Education in New South Wales, and in the new approach to the secondary curriculum prepared and issued in Western Australia. Add to these the excellent work of the College of Education, which is a kind of Royal Society concerned with all aspects of education in Australia, the continuous efforts of the Australian Council for Educational Research and, in each state, the State Institutes of Educational Research, and it will be seen that there is plenty of constructive thought in Australia directed toward the successes and the problems of education in this large continent.

15

Canadian Schools in Action

THE TYPICAL pattern of schools in a Canadian province is an educational ladder that provides for a continuous progression from kindergarten to university. The majority of children enter tax-supported schools at the age of 6 and may remain in school for eleven or twelve years. In most Canadian provinces the school-leaving age is 14 in the rural districts and 16 in the urban areas. At the secondary level a comprehensive high school, called the "composite high school" in Canada, is becoming popular, but there are a variety of secondary paths available in many places—commercial, agricultural, home economics, or vocational high schools. Small high schools have generally been restricted to a fairly narrow academic course, with few electives. There is, however, a trend toward making the traditional high schools less academic and the vocational schools a little more general in their offerings, so that composite high schools with wider opportunities for electives are becoming more common.

The organization of a typical school program in the English-speaking parts of Canada is shown in Figure 15-1. This has been made general, because details vary in the different provinces. Figure 15-2 shows a somewhat different type of organization in French-speaking schools, particularly in the province of Quebec. These two figures will illustrate the discussion to follow.

During recent decades, the average educational level of the Canadian people has increased from about eighth grade to nearly eleventh grade. For the adult population above 20 years of age, the average number of years spent in school increased from 7.5 years in 1901 to 10.5 years in 1951. A similar figure was not given for the 1961 census, but in that year of the total population not attending school, aged

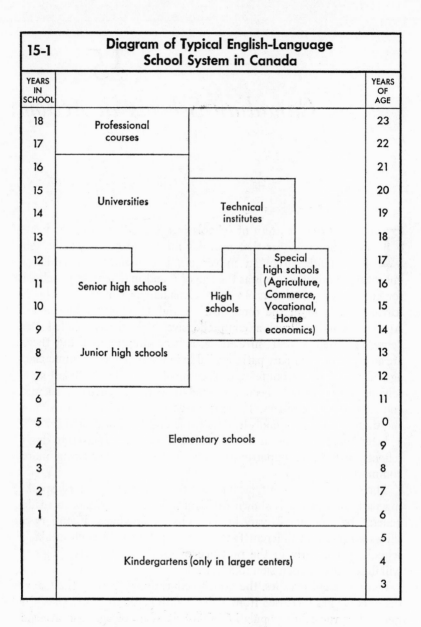

15-1 Diagram of Typical English-Language School System in Canada

YEARS IN SCHOOL					YEARS OF AGE
18	Professional courses				23
17					22
16	Universities				21
15		Technical institutes			20
14					19
13					18
12	Senior high schools		Special high schools (Agriculture, Commerce, Vocational, Home economics)		17
11		High schools			16
10					15
9	Junior high schools				14
8					13
7					12
6	Elementary schools				11
5					0
4					9
3					8
2					7
1					6
	Kindergartens (only in larger centers)				5
					4
					3

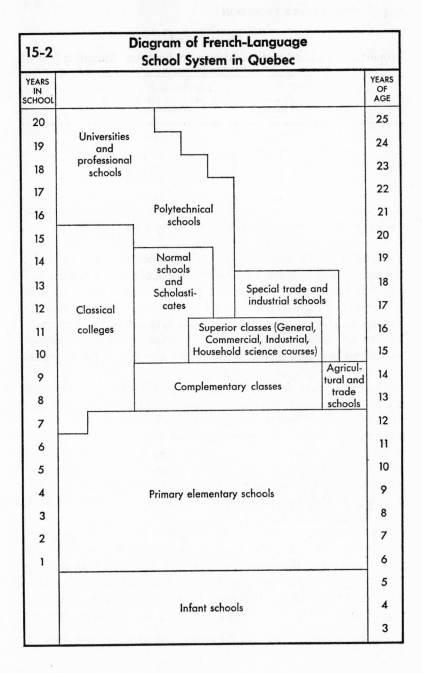

15-2

Diagram of French-Language School System in Quebec

YEARS IN SCHOOL		YEARS OF AGE

Universities and professional schools

Polytechnical schools

Classical colleges

Normal schools and Scholasticates

Special trade and industrial schools

Superior classes (General, Commercial, Industrial, Household science courses)

Complementary classes

Agricultural and trade schools

Primary elementary schools

Infant schools

Years in school: 20, 19, 18, 17, 16, 15, 14, 13, 12, 11, 10, 9, 8, 7, 6, 5, 4, 3, 2, 1

Years of age: 25, 24, 23, 22, 21, 20, 19, 18, 17, 16, 15, 14, 13, 12, 11, 10, 9, 8, 7, 6, 5, 4, 3

TABLE 15-1
Proportion of Canadian Population of School Age Attending School

DECENNIAL CENSUS	PERCENTAGE OF POPULATION BETWEEN AGES 5 AND 19 ATTENDING SCHOOL
1901	52.2
1911	52.9
1921	61.4
1931	61.7
1941	65.3

SOURCE: Dominion Bureau of Statistics, Reference Paper #31, p. 6.

5 and older (which includes 5-year-olds who have not started school), 7.7 percent had completed four years of schooling; 35.9 percent had completed elementary school; 24.2 percent had completed at least three years of high school; and 3 percent had had some university education. There were 2.8 percent who held university degrees. Illiteracy has decreased in Canada to a point where it is not now considered necessary to include questions about it in the decennial census.[1]

The census data shows some other interesting facts. The average age of the population has been increasing as a result of an increased life expectancy. While the population of school age, between 5 and 19 years, has decreased as a percentage of the total population, the proportion of those of school age who are actually in school, as shown in Table 15-1, has increased in every census. The number of pupils actually in school increased from 1,404,729 in 1901 to 3,266,-732 in 1941. Table 15-2 shows the enrollment in Canadian schools in 1961-62 by provinces.

The Canadian birthrate seems to follow the demographic pattern of other Western countries. It reached a low of 22 per thousand in 1937, increased during the last war, and showed a sharp upswing in 1945. It reached a high of 29.6 in 1947 and then fell off slightly. In 1962 it was 25.3 per thousand. By United States standards the Canadian birthrate has always been high, and the high rates in

[1] Dominion Bureau of Statistics, *Preliminary Statistics of Education, 1962–63*, p. 50.

Quebec, Newfoundland, and New Brunswick have tended to hold up the national average.

A study made in Nova Scotia compared costs per pupil and percentage of gross income devoted to education. This is given in Table 15–3.

Elementary Education

QUEBEC

Public schools in the province of Quebec, especially the Catholic schools, have little interest in "progressive education." The 1949–50 report of the Inspector-General of Catholic schools says:

> A school whose mission it is to instruct and train three-quarters of a million children cannot submit at once to the radical and quick changes which are extolled in certain quarters under a pretext of adaptation to new needs. Its first aim is to secure the general welfare by safe and tried methods, and such an attitude does not constitute a refusal to go ahead and make the necessary changes. The direction given by an inspector in a school district seeks to obtain the entire application of the unchanging principles which have already proved their worth.[2]

Wherever numbers permit, boys and girls are segregated in separate classrooms or separate schools, even before the seventh grade, and all of the superior primary schools, high schools, classical colleges, and normal schools are separate institutions for boys and girls. Most of the schools in other Canadian provinces are coeducational.

Because of the religious homogeneity of the French-speaking people of Quebec, the Roman Catholic religion permeates every bit of the life and work of the schools. Religion is a required subject throughout the school life of a boy or a girl, and takes up a good deal of time in the daily schedule. Outward manifestations of the religious atmosphere of the schools are the symbols, pictures, and posters that are very much in evidence in the schoolrooms, and the fact that a large proportion of the teachers are in clerical dress. The proportion of teachers in religious orders to lay teachers is about even in the Catholic schools of Quebec. Considered as a whole, the ratio is

[2] Michel Savard, Inspector-General of Catholic Schools, in *Report of the Superintendent of Education for the Year 1949–50, Province of Quebec*, Quebec, 1952, p. 4.

School Enrollment by Grades

GRADE	ALBERTA	BRITISH COLUMBIA	MANITOBA	NEW BRUNSWICK	NEW-FOUNDLAND	NOVA SCOTIA
Kindergarten		7,031	*		*	17,647
I	35,555	36,184	26,685	17,719	20,835	17,559
II	33,765	34,243	20,045	16,768	14,226	17,755
III	31,160	32,779	19,218	16,345	14,112	17,598
IV	29,864	30,831	18,539	16,157	13,624	16,698
V	27,960	29,388	18,410	16,027	13,153	16,544
VI	26,355	28,419	17,200	14,975	12,134	16,807
VII	26,371	29,389	17,960	14,960	11,488	16,775
VIII	25,310	29,114	16,046	13,061	10,058	14,988
IX	24,492	27,931	16,461	10,553	9,147	12,847
X	18,204	22,371	12,201	7,877	5,772	9,606
XI	14,506	16,909	10,160	5,052	3,772	6,806
XII	14,160	13,689	6,223	3,877	162	3,252
XIII		2,012		47		
Special				616	434	1,174
Total	307,702	340,290	199,121	154,034	128,917	186,056

SOURCE : Annual Reports of the Provincial Departments of Education, 1962.
* Kindergarten or pre-Grade I included in Grade I.

about one to five in the elementary schools, two to one in the intermediate grades, three to one in the higher grades in nonacademic schools, and more than nine to one in the higher academic schools and in the teacher-training institutions. The French-speaking school system in Quebec is European in attitudes, influences, discipline, and selection of subject matter. It is unique in North America and is practically untouched by any of the developments or practices in the English-speaking parts of Canada or in the United States.

The English-speaking elementary schools of Quebec are very much like those of the other Canadian provinces as shown in Figure 15-1.

In the elementary schools of Quebec there are differences between the curriculum in the Protestant and the Catholic schools. One example that may be cited is Canadian history, in which the French course of study pays little attention to the history of Canada after 1759, and the English course stresses history after that date.

15-2

in Canadian Provinces, 1961-62

ONTARIO	PRINCE EDWARD IS.	QUEBEC (CATHOLIC)	QUEBEC (PROTESTANT)	SAS- KATCHEWAN	CANADA
93,225	164	2,496	5,333	2,813	128,709
149,084	2,964	123,932	11,299	23,878	465,694
137,784	2,749	124,370	11,249	22,873	435,827
129,822	2,664	123,715	11,275	21,353	420,041
123,266	2,525	123,336	11,195	20,270	406,305
120,356	2,550	113,896	10,957	20,019	389,260
116,895	2,643	111,153	10,297	18,595	375,473
113,834	2,413	94,371	10,616	19,330	357,507
107,168	2,407	76,649	11,112	17,874	323,787
84,812	2,073	56,082	9,392	18,794	272,584
67,233	1,668	42,526	7,236	14,370	209,064
44,582	843	26,790	5,187	11,738	146,345
36,828	644	4,798	345	10,745	94,723
17,609					19,668
24,733	80	4,645	693	1,764	32,274
1,367,231	26,387	1,028,759	116,186	224,416	4,079,099

These curricular differences also appear between French-speaking and English-speaking schools in other provinces.

NEWFOUNDLAND

The elementary schools of Newfoundland are very similar to those of the English-speaking provinces to the west of them. The provincial Education Department sets the curriculum and courses of study that are to be followed by all of the sectarian schools, and all of these schools from time to time take the same provincial examinations. Only in the required classes in religion are the separate school programs significantly different.

Because the population of the province is scattered along the coasts in small settlements, the number of one-teacher schools is very high in Newfoundland. Of a total of 128,917 pupils enrolled in 1961, 8,767 pupils attended 398 one-room schools. Of these, 57 schools included six grades, 74 seven grades, 88 eight grades, 65 nine grades, 40 ten grades, and 10 had all eleven grades taught by one

TABLE 15–3
Costs of Education in the Canadian Provinces, 1958

PROVINCE	COST PER PUPIL (DOLLARS)	PERCENTAGE OF PERSONAL INCOME REQUIRED TO PAY GROSS COST
Prince Edward Island	124.30	3.42
Newfoundland	136.10	4.30
New Brunswick	190.00	4.87
Nova Scotia	199.80	4.44
Quebec	223.10	3.75
Manitoba	264.10	3.65
Ontario	299.50	3.65
Saskatchewan	308.20	5.20
British Columbia	339.90	3.92
Alberta	383.40	5.25
Total, all provinces	270.50	3.95

SOURCE : *Annual Report of the Department of Education, Province of Nova Scotia,* Halifax: Queen's Printer, 1962, p. xvii.

teacher. Of the one-room schools, 8 had between 41 and 50 pupils, and 58 had between 31 and 40.

The great increase in the number of first-graders each year has been a real source of concern to the Newfoundland authorities. They have been trying to provide sufficient teachers and classrooms so that children would not have to start their school life in badly overcrowded rooms. Although the law does not prohibit the acceptance of children under the age of 6 years, the Department has discouraged the admission of younger children. In spite of this, in 1960–61, 4,648 first-graders were reported as under 6 years of age. The total school enrollment in Newfoundland has increased from the 1949–50 total of 79,328 to 128,917 in the 1961–62 school year.

OTHER PROVINCES

Throughout the ten provinces, the average Canadian child enters a tax-supported school at the age of 6. Very few kindergartens and nursery schools are provided, except in the larger cities. In 1962 there were 128,709 children enrolled in nursery schools and kindergartens in the public schools. In the typical Canadian province, the first eight grades are included in the elementary school, although in some provinces only the first seven grades are considered elementary. In Alberta, where the junior high school is an integral part of the school system, the first six grades make up the elementary school.

The curriculum of the Canadian elementary school includes the basic language and arithmetic skills, social studies, health, literature, arts and crafts, music, nature study, and group activities. Because of the importance of the provincial examinations, stress is placed on mastery of subject matter and the learning of factual material that may be measured by examinations. However, the Dominion Bureau of Statistics reports:

> Slogans such as the "child-centered school," "activity program," "enterprise education," etc. serve to indicate a move away from concentration on subject matter, examinations, and grade standards. Others such as "the lighted schoolhouse," "Citizens' Forum," "National Farm Radio Program," "Antigonish Movement" point to a move toward community centers or other organizations which have in part resulted in more opportunities for social and athletic activities for school children, as well as for adults.[3]

Increased attention has been given to the education of handicapped children in recent years. Residential schools for the blind, the deaf, and for mentally deficient children are provided by provincial Departments of Education. Most of the provinces provide free textbooks for pupils in the elementary grades. School health services have been expanding, and traveling dental clinics are provided. For children who live too far away from any school to attend even if transportation were provided, the provincial Departments have organized correspondence schools, which give courses for children from the first grade to university entrance. In 1960 there were 42,158 pupils who received lessons by mail from the Departments of Education.

Secondary Education

QUEBEC

The high school system of Quebec is very different from that of the other provinces. The factor that determines whether a program

---

[3] Dominion Bureau of Statistics, *The Organization and Administration of Public Schools in Canada*, p. 7.

shall be administered by the French-speaking Catholic section of the Department of Education, rather than by the English-speaking Protestant section, is religion, not language. However, both language and sectarian differences have been important divisive factors in Canadian education. French has no legal status outside of the province of Quebec, except in the federal law courts. But in practice French-speaking schools usually are established in other provinces where a sufficiently large number of French people live in one area. In Ontario a controversy over bilingual schools, which resulted in a school regulation banning the use of French as a basic language of instruction in the province, was started by English-speaking Catholics, not by Protestants. The British Privy Council has ruled that the provisions of the British North America Act, which safeguard denominational rights, do not apply to language rights. In Quebec the secondary schools for the non-Catholic portion of the population, directed by the English-speaking Protestant section, are very similar to those in other provinces and to the secondary schools in other parts of the English-speaking world. The secondary schools of the Catholic section trace their formative influences to continental Europe and are very different from Anglo-Saxon schools. The Catholic Committee operates two separate high school programs, one for French-speaking Catholics and one for English-speaking Catholics.

The program of the French Catholic high schools is divided into two sections. The first, consisting of grades eight and nine, is similar in some ways to the junior high school in English-speaking programs, and is known as the "complementary classes." Since the purpose of these years is stated to be the strengthening and deepening of the knowledge of the subjects studied in the first seven years, the course is much more limited in scope than that of the English-speaking junior high schools and high schools. The pupil studies religion (a compulsory subject, 30 to 40 minutes a day), French, English, science, arithmetic, and an introduction to algebra. Since the school-leaving age in Quebec is 14 years, many of the children in the complementary classes will leave school upon completing them; but although this is a terminal program for a large proportion of the pupils, no social science is included in the list of subjects taken. These complementary classes are located in the parish in which the children live, and may be attached to a seven-year elementary school.[4]

---

[4] J. T. McIlhone, "Catholic High School Education in Quebec," p. 38.

The second section, which is made up of grades ten and eleven, and sometimes grade twelve, is known as "superior classes," and is roughly the equivalent of the senior high school in English-speaking programs. Generally the classes are consolidated into larger units serving several parishes, like an American union high school district.

Because it was not the intention of the Department of Education, when it established these high schools, to compete with the classical colleges as the traditional training ground for university candidates, but rather to give a more advanced education to the bulk of the children who would not enter university, these schools, except in very special courses, have not aimed to provide training leading to all the faculties of the university.[5]

When the student has completed the complementary classes he selects one of several alternative courses that are available in the superior classes. A boy must choose in the tenth grade whether to take a commercial course, which leads to employment in business or industry, or a general course, which is heavily scientific and may lead to some of the faculties of the university (agriculture, education, engineering, or forestry). A girl has a choice of three courses in the tenth grade: a commercial course similar to that of the boys; a general course, also similar to the boys'; or a "Special" or home science course, which drops the science courses and adds the study of Latin. General or "Special" courses will admit girls to the Faculty of Letters and to some of the professional schools (household science, nursing, education, or physiotherapy). Depending upon the electives chosen, the graduating student receives a commercial or general high school leaving certificate at the end of the eleventh grade. In some schools he may continue for an additional year of study. He can then, upon passing an examination, enter the sophomore class of some universities.

NEWFOUNDLAND

According to the Department of Education, secondary education in Newfoundland is a continuation of elementary education. This means that the ninth, tenth, and eleventh grades are academic, without vocational courses. A special commercial eleventh grade is provided in a few schools. The secondary grades usually form a post-

[5] Loc. cit.

elementary "top" to an elementary school, and pupils stay on in the same school, sometimes a one-teacher school. The Department recognizes that there are too few high school graduates to fill the needs of the province.[6] In 1960–61 the total secondary enrollment was 19,287, which was an increase of 11 percent over the year before.

OTHER PROVINCES

Except in very large cities, the preferred type of Canadian secondary school is the comprehensive or "composite" high school, offering some choice of academic, general, and vocational courses. In the larger cities, separate commercial or vocational high schools are established. Coeducational secondary schools are the rule in all provinces except Quebec, where the Catholic Committee provides separate schools above the seventh grade. In some cases girls may be admitted to technical or commercial schools with boys in Quebec.

The usual high school pattern is represented by grades eight to eleven or nine to eleven, with a twelfth grade added in many schools. Except in Ontario and British Columbia, where the twelfth grade high school leaving, the Junior Matriculation or high-school–leaving level is represented by the end of the eleventh grade. Only about 27 percent of Canadian high school pupils remain in school for the twelfth grade (see Table 15–4). In Alberta the junior high school is a part of the provincial school system, and some junior high schools are found in the larger towns of other provinces. Some provinces offer thirteenth-grade work in a few high schools or collegiate institutes. The thirteenth grade offered in British Columbia is equivalent to the twelfth grade in some other provinces; that is, it is called Senior Matriculation and permits students who finish it and pass the examinations to enter most universities at the sophomore level. The collegiate institute is a Canadian secondary school with specialized teachers and an academic university preparatory course.

In Prince Edward Island very few schools offer work above the tenth grade, and most of the eleventh and twelfth graders go to Prince of Wales College. This has been a four-year junior-college type of institution, including grades eleven to fourteen. This college also provides the provincial teacher-training program and has recently extended its offerings to the bachelor's degree. Most secondary education in Canada is free, although Prince Edward Island charges

[6] *Statistical Summary to the Annual Report of the Department of Education,* St. Johns, 1960, p. 9.

TABLE 15-4
Proportion of Seventh-Graders Remaining in Canadian Schools
(Number per 1,000 seventh-graders)

PROVINCE	VII	VIII	IX	X	XI	XII
Alberta	1,000	959	928	690	550	536
British Columbia	1,000	990	950	761	575	465
Manitoba	1,000	893	901	609	566	346
New Brunswick	1,000	939	705	526	337	259
Newfoundland	1,000	875	796	502	328	14
Nova Scotia	1,000	893	765	572	405	193
Ontario	1,000	941	745	590	394	326
Prince Edward Island	1,000	997	857	691	307	266
Quebec (Catholic)	1,000	812	594	451	284	50
Quebec (Protestant)	1,000	1,047	884	681	488	32
Saskatchewan	1,000	924	970	743	560	556

SOURCE: Annual Reports of the Provincial Departments of Education, 1962.

fees for the eleventh and twelfth grades. Some of the provinces have continuation or superior schools, which are elementary schools with secondary "tops" extending to about the tenth grade.

A study made by the Canadian Teachers' Federation indicates that the economic and social status of the family determines very largely how long children will remain in secondary school. A study of the high school population in one large Canadian city in 1943 revealed that for children of various vocational groups, the numbers enrolled in high school classes were not proportional to the total number of children of high school age in these groups. The more favored social and economic levels send a larger proportion of their children to high school than do those less favored. Relative probabilities of attendance from various groups, expressed in terms of 100 (the figure used as a base for the most favored groups), are: professional families, 100; bankers and business managers, 85; civil service and clerical, 65; skilled labor and public service, 59; unskilled labor, 15.[7]

Although there has been a widespread development of vocational education in the larger cities, the proportion of young Canadians remaining in school drops sharply after the seventh grade. This is

[7] M. E. LaZerte, *Teacher Education in Canada*, pp. 32–33.

shown in the comparative figures in Table 15–4. Much of this is due to the fact that so many of the Canadian people live in sparsely settled areas, where it is difficult to maintain high schools. Students are not eager to leave home and attend boarding schools. Nova Scotia has been establishing rural high schools with composite courses to encourage rural youth to finish their secondary school programs. In New Brunswick regional high schools have been established, so that no pupil lives farther than 20 miles from a secondary school. The poorest record of attendance in secondary schools in all Canada is in Catholic Quebec, where the authorities of the Catholic Committee have shown some concern about the small percentage of students who attend school above the seventh grade. Protestant schools in Quebec compare very well with national averages.

Vocational Education

QUEBEC

A wide variety of technical and vocational schools are provided in Quebec, and the control of these programs is diffused through many different government departments. Since there is no Minister of Education, at least nine Cabinet Ministers have something to do with education. This makes it very difficult, if not impossible, to get statistics on enrollment or costs that are comparable with other provinces. The Provincial Secretary is in charge of the Department of Education, and he is also responsible for the direction of schools of fine arts and advanced commercial schools. The Minister of Social Welfare and Youth controls most of the technical-education programs, providing about 50 schools in specialized trades and technologies, such as furniture-making, graphic arts, paper and textile trades, and correspondence courses in trades. Four-year technical schools in five cities offer day and night classes, and trade schools in 32 other centers offer two- or three-year courses. The Minister of Agriculture is responsible for intermediate, regional, and superior schools of agriculture. The Minister of Labor also conducts agricultural schools, agricultural orphanages, dairy schools, and apprenticeship programs. The Minister of Lands and Forests conducts schools for forest rangers, forest protection, and sawmill operation. The Minister of Mines operates schools for prospectors. The Minister of Hunting and Fishing runs schools of fisheries. The Minister of Industry and Commerce is responsible for a course for hotelkeepers, and the Minister of Health provides courses in hygiene. These technical schools are in addition to and separate from the universities, affiliated colleges, convents, commercial schools, and others.

NEWFOUNDLAND

Under the Department of Education there is a Division of Vocational Education, which maintains a provincial vocational institute in St. John's. This was established to give vocational training to ex-servicemen. The province also operates a School of Navigation. The famous missionary to Labrador, Dr. Wilfred Grenfell, organized institutes to offer work in arts and crafts, manual training, and cattle and hog raising, and these have been extended to Newfoundland as well as to Labrador. They now receive government support. In order to train voluntary leaders for work in handicrafts in organizations throughout the country, a National Handicrafts Center was opened in 1946. This program encouraged the use of native materials, but it was closed in 1950. Memorial University offers a three-year course in engineering, a two-year household-science course, and work in pre-agriculture.

OTHER PROVINCES

There is a wide variation among the provinces in the matter of provision for vocational and technical education. In the agricultural provinces there are vocational courses or divisions in the high schools, and sometimes a provincial technical institute. Larger cities provide separate vocational, commercial, or home economics high schools. A few separate agricultural high schools have been established. In the industrialized provinces there is a variety of special schools, as in Quebec. The federal government provides funds to subsidize vocational education in the high schools and in the specialized schools.

University Education

QUEBEC

There are five independent universities in Quebec which receive government grants. These are McGill University and Sir George Williams College (nonsectarian), Laval and Montreal universities (Roman Catholic), and Bishop's College University (Anglican). There are a number of small colleges in Quebec, and in some of the other provinces, which affiliate with one of the larger universities for the purpose of accreditation and granting degrees. In such a situation the lectures and class work are all done in the small school, but the work is accredited by the university, which writes and supervises the final degree examinations and awards the degrees. This is similar to the relationship which the University of London bears to a number of affiliated institutions.

One way in which the educational system of Quebec is unique in North America is in the system of classical colleges. These are small, highly academic eight-year schools which cover the work of four years of high school and four years of college. They are more like the classical *lycées* or *collèges* in France than like any other educational institutions in the Americas. These schools are planned to prepare young men and women for the advanced, specialized courses in the universities. The French-Canadian has always believed that a basic classical education was desirable for gifted young men and women, and that specialization on the university level should wait until the students have gained greater maturity. As a part of the Catholic school system of Quebec, independent and privately controlled yet receiving public funds, there are 41 classical colleges for boys and 17 for girls. A boy enters the classical college near his home after completing the seventh grade in the parish school; he remains for eight years and leaves with a bachelor's degree. He is now prepared to enter the professional schools of divinity, engineering, law, medicine, or science. J. T. McIlhone says:

In the classical college is to be found the realization of Quebec's philosophy of education: solid subject matter (humanities, sciences, social sciences) for a general education, and time as an ally for assimilation and maturity. Thus a classical college offers a thoroughly good high school and college course spaced over a period of eight years. Because the classical course is considered as a whole (it has not so far been thought of in any other way) and because educators are planning for eight years and not four, the subjects included in the course are naturally spaced differently than they would be if the planners were preparing for a shorter period, and the planning itself has a certain psychological soundness about it which cannot easily be disputed.[8]

Instead of the usual familiar names for the years in school (freshman, sophomore, junior, and senior), the names given to the various years in the classical college give an indication of the content and

[8] McIlhone, *op. cit.*, p. 40.

procedure followed. The first year, which would be the eighth grade, is called "Elements." In this year, besides religion, French, English, arithmetic, history, geography, and art, the elements of Latin and algebra are begun. The second year is called "Syntax"; it adds to the courses in Elements the study of Greek and geometry. The third year is called "Method"; here the study of Greek and Latin authors is introduced. The fourth year is named "Versification"; the previous studies are continued, with European history given emphasis. Thus, in the first four years, everything in the usual Canadian classical high school course has been offered, with the exception of chemistry and physics. In an English-speaking Catholic classical college, chemistry and physics may be elected in place of Greek. Because the course is planned as an eight-year complete unit, the completion of the fourth year in a classical college is not considered the equivalent of the eleventh grade and university entrance as in other provinces.

The fifth year in the classical college (which would be the freshman year in a university) is called "Belles-Lettres." Senior algebra and trigonometry are added to the other courses carried. The sixth year is named "Rhetoric," and adds mechanics as the science subject. In the seventh year, "Junior Philosophy," chemistry and analytical geometry are included in the curriculum, and in the eighth year, which is called "Senior Philosophy," physics and calculus are added. As in the English-speaking Canadian high schools, students carry all of the subjects throughout all the years of the course, and take final examinations at the end over the entire curriculum.

English-speaking Catholics in Quebec, given a measure of educational autonomy about fifteen years ago, have a secondary education system very similar to that of the English-speaking high schools throughout Canada; but they have one classical college in Montreal, and accept graduates of four-year high school courses into the fifth year of the college.

Chamberlin points out that the classical colleges epitomize the French-Canadian philosophy of education:

The educational contrast between English Canada and French Canada is almost as sharp as the contrast between the United States, on the one hand, and Argentina and Brazil on the other. It is the contrast between an Anglo-Saxon and a Latin conception of culture and way of life—the former more practical, the latter more theoretical. There is no question of one type being superior or inferior to the other; the two types are simply different, based on different values, on different psychological dispositions.[9]

The same author points out that the education of the French-Canadian was a handicap in modern war, and continues to be so in modern industrial and business life. Insofar as the classical-clerical type of education has been stressed at the expense of the sciences, the French-Canadian who tried to qualify as an aviator or an artilleryman was at a disadvantage, because he knew so little about science and mathematics. Science and mathematics are taught in the French-speaking schools, but receive much less attention than in the English-speaking schools. The same type of criticism was voiced in France during World War II, pointing out that the French classical and cultural education had not produced the type of leaders and citizens that the nation required.[10]

The rector of Laval University, Monsignor Camille Roy, conceded that the French universities in Canada had engaged too long in the training only of lawyers, doctors, and notaries, and have allowed English-speaking graduates from other provinces to monopolize the positions which call for technological training.[11]

NEWFOUNDLAND

A provincial junior college, called Memorial University College, was established in St. John's in 1925. In 1949 it was given the right to confer degrees, and the name was changed to Memorial University. There are several colleges operated by the churches, and some of these have affiliated with the university for degrees. Memorial University trains teachers and operates a large and successful summer school.

OTHER PROVINCES

In every province there is at least one university or college which receives a substantial portion of its financial support from provincial funds. In the western provinces the universities are provincial institutions, somewhat parallel to the state universities in the United States. The universities are not under the direct control of provincial Departments of Education, although they may receive grants through

[9] William Henry Chamberlin, *Canada Today and Tomorrow*, p. 216.
[10] *Ibid.*, p. 99.
[11] *Ibid.*, p. 181.

the budget of the Department. In the older provinces some of the independent institutions receive provincial funds.

University enrollments rose from a level of about 36,000 in 1940–41 to a high of 141,398 in 1962–63. About 2.8 percent of the Canadian people are university graduates.

Adult Education

EVERY Canadian province has expanded programs of education for adults. The Departments of Education, university extension programs, and voluntary organizations have been active in this field. In the rural communities the program has been built around the concept of the school as the community center, "the lighted schoolhouse." An active and effective Adult Education Association has helped to coordinate and popularize the work throughout the country. In Quebec one of the duties of the Superintendent of Education is to establish schools for adults and for the instruction of the laboring classes. This has been done largely through part-time courses in the specialized technical schools which have been discussed above. Evening classes are offered in the Schools of Fine Arts in Quebec and Montreal. Sir George Williams College is noted for its evening classes. The Protestant Committee reports the operation of six night schools for adults, and the Roman Catholic Committee operates 125 such schools. In Newfoundland, Memorial University has no organized extension department, but it offers adult courses in navigation, and for nurses in training.

Education and Status of Teachers

THE PATTERN of teacher preparation which is advocated throughout Canada is a general education through high school for elementary teachers, and through university for secondary teachers, followed in each case by a year of professional training before certification.[12] The actual practice varies widely among the ten provinces. In Catholic Quebec, girls who have completed the ninth grade may qualify in two years for the elementary diploma, which permits them to teach the first seven grades.

[12] *Recommendations Concerning the Status of the Teaching Profession,* Canadian Education Association, Ottawa, 1949, p. 12.

QUEBEC

Normal schools in Quebec are very small institutions. The 1961–62 Report of the Superintendent of Education lists 83 normal schools, with a total enrollment of 10,506, or an average of 126 pupils each. These institutions ranged in enrollment from 2 to 476 students. In addition there are scholasticates for the training of nuns and brothers. The 22 scholasticates for nuns show a total enrollment of 385, or an average enrollment of over 18 students in each, and they reported enrollments from 4 to 84. Scholasticates training brothers are slightly larger: the 12 listed show enrollments from 37 to 80 men, with an average enrollment of 59. The Institute of Education of MacDonald College (affiliated with McGill University), which trains teachers for the Protestant schools, reported a total enrollment of 866 in the School of Pedagogy in 1961–62.[13]

Admission to Catholic normal schools and scholasticates for boys is granted after the completion of the eleventh grade; these schools require a two-year course of study to qualify for the complementary diploma, and a third year to receive the superior diploma. Normal schools for girls and scholasticates for nuns accept students upon completion of the ninth grade, and require a two-year course for the elementary diploma. Completion of a third year earns the complementary diploma, and a fourth year is required for the superior diploma. The early age of admissions explains the fact that official reports from Quebec speak of normal schools for boys and girls.

Salaries paid to Quebec teachers are very low, even by Canadian standards. Although the Protestant schools in Quebec pay higher salaries than do the Catholics, in both systems rural teachers receive lower pay than in the urban schools. Reports of Protestant school inspectors have in past years indicated that low salaries were responsible for the employment of many unqualified persons as teachers.

These conditions exist, as Chamberlin points out, in spite of the fact that the Protestants, being better off financially than the Catholics in Quebec, are able to pay higher salaries and equip their schools better. In his view, the dual system promotes inequality of educational opportunity.[14]

Reports of inspectors of Catholic schools have referred in previous years to the problem of untrained teachers. The 1961–62 report of

[13] Annual Report of the Superintendent of Education, Province of Quebec, 1961–62, pp. 125, 347–55.

[14] Chamberlin, op. cit., p. 202.

the Superintendent of Education says that 2,925 teachers in the schools were "not legally qualified." [15] Members of the Catholic teaching orders are not required to hold official certificates to teach in Quebec. However, nearly 90 percent of the men and 93 percent of the women have teaching diplomas or other equivalents.[16] Members of Catholic teaching orders in other provinces are required to meet the same certification requirements as other teachers.

The tremendous burden which falls upon the taxpayers of a community when two separate school systems must be supported is more evident in the teaching force and in teaching salaries than in any other aspect of education. In the cities, where there is a large population and adequate property valuation upon which to levy taxes, teachers' salaries compare favorably with those in other provinces. But in the rural schools, where property values are low, the teachers carry the burden of the dual system, which results in extremely low salaries and poorly trained or untrained teachers.

NEWFOUNDLAND

The first teachers for Newfoundland were trained in Great Britain, and by 1851 the Wesleyans had opened a normal day school. The Church of England followed this example in 1855, and later other sectarian normal schools were established. In 1921 the first nonsectarian normal school was provided, but this closed in 1932, due to depression conditions. In 1934 teacher training became the responsibility of Memorial University, which now offers a four-year course leading to a degree of B.A. in Education. Summer sessions for teachers are an important part of the program of the university. The Department of Education of the province also conducts a summer school for beginning teachers.

Each denomination has a Board of Examiners, appointed by the Crown, which conducts examinations and grants certificates and licenses under general regulations established by the Council of Education. Licenses to teach may be issued to beginning teachers after the completion of one or more summer sessions. A provincial retirement act covers all teachers who are paid by the Department of Education. Economic conditions in the province and the cost of maintaining multiple school systems are reflected in the com-

15 *Report of the Superintendent of Education*, Province of Quebec, 1961–62, p. 200.

16 *Ibid.*

TABLE 15-5
Average Salaries of Teachers in Canada, 1962 (dollars)

PROVINCE	AVERAGE SALARY
Alberta	5,354
British Columbia	5,543
Manitoba	4,543
New Brunswick	3,249
Newfoundland	2,557
Nova Scotia	4,437
Ontario (elementary)	4,912*
(secondary)	7,548*
Prince Edward Island	2,598
Quebec, Catholic	
Lay teachers (men)	5,427
Religious teachers (men)	3,784
Lay teachers (women)	2,993
Religious teachers (women)	2,096
Quebec, Protestant	
Men	6,332
Women	4,273
Saskatchewan	4,528

SOURCE: Annual Reports of the Provincial Departments of Education, 1962.
* Ontario averages include salaries of principals.

paratively low salaries paid to Newfoundland teachers, as shown in Table 15-5.

OTHER PROVINCES
In the older Canadian provinces there was a shortage of schools and a shortage of teachers from very early days. Wherever possible the churches and the missionary societies provided teachers, but the demand was always in excess of the supply. Untrained and partially trained itinerant teachers found it easy to obtain employment anywhere. When it was first proposed in Ontario that normal schools be established, a letter addressed to certain opponents of the plan said:

Nor do your memorialists hope to provide qualified teachers by any other means, under present circumstances in this country, than by securing, as heretofore, the services of those whose physical disabilities, from age, render this mode of obtaining a livelihood the only one suited to their decaying energies, or by employing such newly-arrived immigrants as are qualified for common school teachers, year by year, as they come among us, as who will adopt this means of temporary support until their character and abilities are known and turned to better account for themselves.[17]

In discussing this early situation, LaZerte says: "May it not be that teaching is denied its deserved prestige today partly because of the unfavorable public attitude created towards it when persons of this type just described served as Canada's first teachers?" [18]

Although many teachers were untrained, almost from the beginning they were required to hold some sort of teaching certificates or licenses. Very seldom in the early days did formal education or teaching ability count for much in securing the license. Generally the requirements were good character, loyalty to the government of the day, and zeal for the doctrine of the particular sect which operated the schools. Certificates were granted by bishops or by local officials. The first state-supported normal school in North America was opened at Montreal in 1836, three years before the first state training school for teachers in the United States was founded in Massachusetts. The Montreal school closed in 1842 and made little impression on Canadian education. However, between 1847 and 1905 normal schools were established in all of the provinces.

In 1947-48 the Canadian Education Association made a study on "The Status of the Teaching Profession in Canada," which indicated the sources from which teachers were recruited:

The general social and economic status of the parents determines largely which high school students will select teaching as a vocation. The children from homes in the higher economic brackets seldom enter the teaching profession. Six times as many children from farm houses as from homes of all professional groups combined enter teaching; unskilled labor and personal service groups provide 50 percent more teachers than the professional groups. More teachers come from the homes of skilled labor workers than from the families of all the bankers, brokers, business and industrial managers, teachers, doctors, clergymen, lawyers, and accountants combined.[19]

[17] Quoted in J. G. Hodgins, *The Documentary History of Upper Canada*, VII, 115.

[18] LaZerte, *op. cit.*, p. 18.

[19] Quoted on p. 33.

Speaking of certification requirements, McIntyre says:

One wonders if there are such extremes in qualifications in any other profession. Perhaps the low esteem in which the teaching profession is held by the general public is a result of realization, by the public, of the low qualifications required for membership in the profession. Teachers holding certificates requiring six years beyond Junior Matriculation are surely on a level with other professional people. The same cannot be said of teachers holding the lowest certificates. The public apparently judges the profession by the lowest rather than the highest qualifications required.[20]

According to the Canadian Education Association in 1964,

In most of Canada, the shortage of elementary teachers is a problem of the past. Instead of worry about getting enough teachers, the problem now seems to be one of improving the qualifications of teachers presently employed, and of up-grading the quality of teaching. Due to the rapid development of secondary education and the increase in pupils of high school age, there is still a shortage of secondary teachers. The shortage of qualified secondary teachers is expected to continue for some time. On the university level the deficiency in numbers of teaching personnel is critically acute.[21]

Problems in the Operation of Canadian Schools

AS IN many countries, most of the pressing problems of education in Canada could be solved if more money were made available to the schools. Some of these problems were discussed in Chapter 7. In 1945 a survey committee of the Canadian Education Association listed fifteen problems facing Canadian schools.[22] In the twenty years since that time the list has changed drastically, both in the nature of the problems mentioned and their relative importance. The Canadian Education Association now lists the following as the fifteen problems facing education in the country.[23]

[20] G. F. McIntyre, *Teacher Education and Certification in Canada*, Canadian Education Association, Toronto, 1949, p. 87.

[21] Letter from C. B. Routley, Acting Executive Secretary, Canadian Education Association, May 22, 1964.

[22] Stewart, *op. cit.*, p. 254.

[23] Routley, *op. cit.*

1. Provision of education suitable for the potential school "drop-out."

2. Retraining of unemployed adults to meet the demands of the technological era.

3. Equal educational opportunities for all children regardless of family financial status, geographical location, etc.

4. Extension of technical-vocational education.

5. Meeting the cost of an expanded program in elementary and secondary schools.

6. Teacher supply at the secondary level, especially in science and mathematics.

7. The financing of higher education.

8. Growth and expansion of junior colleges.

9. Provision of guidance and counseling services for all pupils.

10. Extension of special education programs into rural areas.

11. The training of teachers for technical-vocational schools.

12. An improved program in adult education.

13. Extension of the program in the esthetic subjects.

14. The organization of larger units of school administration.

15. The more adequate preparation of teachers, both preservice and inservice.

16

The Schools of the Soviet Union

THE SYSTEMS of control of education that were discussed in Chapter 8 make uniformity of education in the Soviet Union inevitable. The decentralization through local governing bodies is only apparent, and the inflexible centralization of the dominant Communist Party ensures that throughout the nation the program is always basically the same.

All education is public, locally operated (but largely financed from state sources), and centrally controlled. No private schools of any type are tolerated. All schools are entirely secular, with religious education of any kind forbidden. (The Soviet Constitution guarantees both freedom of religious worship and freedom to teach anti-religious doctrines but does not permit religious teaching.) Coeducation was general throughout the country until 1943, when some separation of the sexes was introduced. Coeducation has again become the general practice.

For children 7 to 15 years of age attendance is compulsory by law, although this requirement is generally enforced only for those between 7 (or 8) and 12 years. UNESCO reported that in 1951 about one-third of the children between the ages of 12 and 15 were not in school, although that was mainly in rural areas.[1] Khrushchev has said that only about 80 percent of the children finish the seventh grade, and this figure includes repeaters. Recent efforts have been intensified to provide sufficient school buildings and teachers so that the law might be effective in all parts of the Union.

[1] UNESCO, *World Handbook*, 1951, p. 390.

The Pre-Reform Soviet School

THE FIRST stage of public education was preschool, which covered approximately ages 3 to 7. Nursery schools and kindergartens were provided in some areas, although most preschools were in the cities or connected with some industrial or agricultural activity. Attendance was voluntary, and in 1951 UNESCO reported that about 6 percent of the 3- to 6-year old group were in school.

The second stage was the elementary school, for pupils of 7 to 11 years. This was a four-year school, and compulsory education was universally enforced. At this stage the native language was used in every nationality area; the government announced that seventy different languages were used in elementary schools. In many rural areas the four-year school was the only school available. Figure 16–1 illustrates the organization of the various stages and schools before the 1958 Reform.

The third stage was the junior secondary school, with grades five to seven for the 11- to 13-year-olds. Wherever possible the first seven grades were housed in the same building, and the school was then called a junior secondary school, or an incomplete secondary school, or, more often, the seven-year school. In rural areas which maintained only elementary schools, the children had to attend a junior secondary school in the nearest center.

Beyond the junior secondary was the senior secondary stage, covering grades eight, nine, and ten and taking children to the age of 17. A school giving instruction in these grades as well as the earlier ones was called a senior secondary school, or a complete secondary school, or a ten-year school. In cities, industrial areas, and larger rural areas the three stages were included in the same building, taking pupils from 7 to 17 years.

At the end of the compulsory education period the boys and girls were divided into three groups, or "streams," depending largely on their vocational objectives and on their academic achievement. One large group was drafted into the Labor Reserve, put to work in factories or on collective farms, and attended a type of school connected with their work for one or two years on a part-time basis. These were the pupils who had shown the least academic aptitude in the final examinations. A second group entered technical or

16-1	Outline of Education in U.S.S.R. Before 1958	

YEARS IN SCHOOL		YEARS OF AGE
17	Research institutes and postgraduate courses	23
16		22
15	Universities and higher institutes	21
14		20
13		19
12		18
11		17
10	Senior secondary stage / Teachers' institutes / Tekhnikumi	16
9		15
8	Factory schools	14
7		13
6	Junior secondary stage	12
5		11
4		10
3	Four-year elementary stage	9
2		8
1		7
	Kindergartens	6
		5
	Nursery schools	4
		3

semiprofessional schools, for the training of what the Russians call "middle-grade" technicians. The third group, made up of the academically gifted, who had passed well in their examinations, either remained in the same school for three more years or transferred to the nearest senior secondary school, from which they might proceed to a university or higher institute.

Before the 1958 Reform there were 110,000 elementary schools, about 60,000 seven-year schools, and 25,000 ten-year schools. In addition there were 7,000 special and part-time schools, 3,750 specialized technical schools (*tekhnikumi*), 39 universities, and 730 higher institutes.

The Khrushchev Reform of 1958

IN OCTOBER, 1958, Nikita Khrushchev made a celebrated speech before the 20th Congress of the Communist Party, criticizing and condemning much of the practice of the existing school system. He put forward 48 propositions "On Strengthening the Relationship of the School with Life and the Further Development of the System of Public Education in the Country." On November 12, 1958, these theses were approved by the Central Committee of the Communist Party. The fact that these propositions were later officially approved by the Council of Ministers of the Soviet Union does not conceal the fact that the real power in the country and in the school system is the Party.[2]

Khrushchev criticized the ten-year school for producing lily-white-handed graduates who had never known manual labor and who wished to get into universities or higher schools in order to avoid it. He charged that teachers had held the threat of manual labor over the heads of pupils who were not studying hard enough. He claimed that the schools, as constituted, had helped to prejudice the pupils against the sort of occupations that most of them would have to follow. He contended that existing courses were an accumulation of facts and theories unrelated to the actual life of the community.

All Soviet theoreticians have emphasized the importance of labor, and the fact that labor and education should be closely interrelated. As the higher schools became more theoretical and divorced from manual labor, the development of classes of intelligentsia and work-

[2] George S. Counts, *Khrushchev and the Central Committee Speak on Education*, University of Pittsburgh Press, Pittsburgh, 1959, p. 1.

ers became more apparent in the Communist "classless" society. Marx defined classes in terms of those who used private property for private gain, as opposed to those who owned no property and were exploited by private operators.[3] The Communists never use the word class in connection with their country, but they do recognize that there is a definite amount of social stratification based on wide differences in incomes. Khrushchev was worried lest the upper strata of society lose contact with work and the workers. There seems to be no doubt that parents in the upper strata of Soviet life had used every effort and influence they could bring to bear in order to get their children into higher schools.

Khrushchev demanded a more practical type of curriculum, one that would strengthen the relationships between school and everyday life. This demand is in contrast to recent tendencies in the United States, where many people have been strongly advocating a return to more academic and abstract educational policies.

Policy Reversal in 1964

THE SOVIET UNION was in the process of changing its schools, particularly its secondary schools, from the traditional type of ten-year education that has been described above to an eleven-year plan when criticism of the eleven-year school began to develop early in 1964. This was carried on as a debate in the press and through letters to the editor. The old argument of lowered academic standards was raised anew, and shortages in the labor force were reflected in charges that young people were kept in school an additional year when they might have been out on the job. The length of the university course was also attacked, and early in the year the government proposed that higher education courses be reduced by one year.

On August 11, 1964, the press reported a decree of the Communist Party and the government reverting to the ten-year program. The adjustments in the curriculum that are planned will be largely in production training and productive labor. According to the 1958 Reform, schools were supposed to emphasize production training and productive labor. Now, productive labor for students has been criticized as being meaningless and time-consuming, with students standing around watching others at work. (Factory managers had

[3] Bereday and others, The Changing Soviet School, p. 248.

complained for years about the inefficiency of the young workers who were assigned to work only a few hours a week.) According to a dispatch from Moscow by Theodore Shabad in the New York *Times* of August 13, 1964, the transition is expected to be complete by 1966.

The discussion that follows describes the educational system patterned by the 1958 Reform and indicates the changes that are expected to result from the recent criticism. It may be some time before the full implications of this policy change in curriculum, in teacher education, and in university entrance requirements are known.

Preschool Education

SOCIAL or general education begins for the child in the nursery schools, for those who are fortunate enough to be admitted to one of them. These schools are under the supervision of the Ministry of Health. Attendance is voluntary, and only a small percentage of the 3- to 6-year-old group are enrolled. The schools may be day schools or, in some cases, residential. The primary reason for the establishment of these school programs has been to provide care for the child so that the mother may be free to work in a factory or on a farm. As long as it is necessary for most mothers to work, it is believed that in many cases the homes cannot provide as satisfactory an environment—social, physical, and psychological—as a well-organized nursery school or kindergarten. There seems to be a tendency to eliminate the distinction between these two types of schools.

The Russians believe that until the time comes in the industrial development of the Soviet Union when mothers no longer must work outside the home, the state has a responsibility for young children. It has also been said that nursery schools will be needed until every mother has been trained in the art and science of bringing up children. The great shortage of housing in the cities, which forces families to live in cramped and unsatisfactory quarters, also influences this policy. This belief has also been illustrated in the establishment of boarding schools. Decrees of the Council of Ministers have frequently emphasized the responsibility of factories, collective farms, and other enterprises to establish nursery schools and kindergartens for the children of their workers. These schools are organized and supported by the farm or factory management but are directly controlled and supervised by the ministries.

16-2 **Outline of Education in U.S.S.R.**
After Reform of 1958

YEARS IN SCHOOL				YEARS OF AGE
18	Research institutes and postgraduate courses			24
17				23
16	Universities and higher institutes			22
15				21
14				20
13				19
12				18
11	Senior secondary stage	Tekhnikumi	Evening and part-time secondary schools	17
10				16
9				15
8	Four-year junior secondary stage			14
7				13
6				12
5				11
4	Four-year elementary schools			10
3				9
2				8
1				7
	Kindergartens			6
				5
				4
				3

The health of the child is the first consideration of the nursery school. The children are under careful medical supervision, and physical activities are planned scientifically to ensure proper growth. These schools also serve an important purpose in the education of mothers: they are centers of information on child health and development, they provide consultative services for mothers, and they are centers for the distribution of milk. Statistics on declining infant mortality rates give evidence to Soviet statisticians that these programs are having some effect. The authorities acknowledge that the number of kindergartens is not adequate to meet the need, but they are giving attention to the problem of increasing them. In rural areas summer kindergartens are established, to free mothers at the time they are needed in the fields and to provide some services in areas where permanent programs have not been established.

Any organized group may set up a nursery school. In a large apartment block the housing committee may provide a nursery for the children of tenants; new apartments are built with special nursery and kindergarten rooms provided. Factories provide buildings and equipment for kindergartens for the children of their workers and pay the costs out of their own funds. Final financial responsibility then rests with the particular ministry that operates the factory. Larger collective and state farms provide nursery schools and kindergartens out of their own funds. Parents pay for the children's food, although no payment is required from large families. No matter who establishes such a school, the state supervises and controls the program.

In accordance with the Soviet belief in the importance of environment and that all education consists of "conditioning" the learner in a specific direction, as Kandel has pointed out, the training in proper attitudes and habits may begin as early as 18 months. (Some of the newer boarding schools are considering accepting children at six months.) Babies as young as four months are given physical exercises under the direction of a school physician, with the idea that nature can be directed from the earliest age in the development of growth and physique.[4] Nursery schools and kindergartens are usually well equipped, with nothing overlooked that might contribute to the growth and psychological development of the child. The "collectivist" point of view is developed with much stress on

[4] Kandel, *Comparative Education*, p. 176.

good-neighborliness, and even some toys are designed in such a way that children must play together. Large, light building blocks, which no one child can handle by himself, are sometimes provided.

The transition from nursery school into the more formally organized kindergarten is facilitated in an interesting manner. The kindergarten teacher visits the nursery school before the transfer is made, and is encouraged to visit the homes and become acquainted with the children and parents before they enter her school. Then the nursery school teacher takes her children to the kindergarten and stays with them for two or three days, or even for the first week.

The kindergartens, like the nursery schools, are organized for the convenience of working mothers, and the length of the school day depends upon the mothers' working hours. When necessary the children may be left at school all week, to return home only when the mother is not at work. Like the nursery schools, the kindergartens are organized as centers of parental education. Teachers are expected to know the children's home conditions and relationships between parents and children. Whenever possible, behavior problems which arise in preschool years are worked out between parents and teachers. Soviet educators insist that an atmosphere of affection and happiness should be the prevailing tone of a nursery school or kindergarten, since for so many hours a day the teacher must take the place of the mother. The teacher is instructed to treat each child as an individual and to make his school day a happy experience. On the other hand, it is considered most important that children should learn to live together cooperatively, and the games, the activities, and the special toys and equipment are planned to teach children to live and play happily together.

Although compulsory education does not begin until the age of 7, children are expected to know something of the three R's when they arrive at the elementary school. The rudiments of arithmetic and beginning reading and writing are taught in the kindergarten. When no kindergarten is available, parents are encouraged to teach some reading and writing before the children enter the first grade. However, many children come to the four-year school with no previous preparation whatever.

The last Seven-Year Plan made provision for nearly doubling the number of kindergartens, in the hope that by 1965 preschool facilities would be available for all who needed them. Because of criticisms that the articulation between nursery school and kindergarten is poor, there is a noticeable trend to combine them into one unified school. Preschools started in 1960 and later are all to be unified, and the others merged when possible.[5]

Elementary Education

ALTHOUGH the ideal of compulsory education had been one of the primary objectives of the Bolshevist Revolution, it was not until 1930, when the Central Committee of the Communist Party, acting on instructions from the Sixteenth Party Congress, issued decrees to the Commissariats of Education in the republics, that steps were taken to put it into effect. The first Five-Year Plan set definite objectives in the matter of availability of elementary education throughout the nation. Vigorous methods were utilized to establish schools and to provide teachers, and statistics of school enrollment rose rapidly. At that time compulsory education decrees included all children between the ages of 8 and 12 years. Later the upper limit was increased to 15 years; and then the lower age was set at 7 years. The four-year elementary school remains the basic school that practically all young Soviet citizens attend.

There are still many one-room, four-grade schools in the Soviet Union, but efforts are being made to eliminate all schools smaller than those with two teachers. In instances where the native peoples are still nomadic, the school may be in a tent, so that schools may move when the people follow their flocks. Efforts are made to ensure that these tent schools are as sanitary as conditions will permit, and to equip them with libraries and textbooks. Schools with less than 30 pupils generally have one teacher. In these schools the teacher works six hours a day, instead of the usual four-hour day, and is paid an extra allowance for the additional time worked. When there are two teachers, one is designated as head teacher. In such a school it is customary for one teacher to take grades one and three, and the other to be responsible for grades two and four. A teacher progresses with his class, so that in the next year the order is reversed.

The school day begins at 8:30 or 9:00 according to local conditions. Younger pupils are dismissed at 12:30 or 1:00, and the older ones at 2:00 or 2:30. Periods last 45 minutes with a 10- or 15-min-

[5] Gerald H. Read, "Trends and Problems in Soviet Education," *Phi Delta Kappan*, Vol. XLII, No. 2 (November, 1960), p. 49.

ute intermission. Bells ring at the beginning and end of classes. The schedule of classes is fixed by ministerial regulations, but this is not inflexible. Classroom atmosphere is very formal; the children rise when the teacher enters and leaves the room, and when they recite. They sit in a prescribed position and may not speak without raising a hand in the proper form and receiving the teacher's permission. There are definite homework assignments, and these are carefully checked in the first half of the next recitation period to see that they have been done properly.

Classrooms are bare and uninteresting, painted in a light color, frequently a light blue. There are several rows of wooden double desks with lids that lift up to provide storage for books or, in some higher schools, with shelves below the desks. Children's work is not displayed in the classroom but is sometimes on display in the corridors. On the wall behind the teacher's desk is a small blackboard, painted a chocolate brown. For the first two classes it is lined both horizontally and vertically, for the last two it is lined horizontally. Usually on the front wall are large colored pictures of Communist heroes.

There are between 30 and 40 pupils in an elementary classroom. Most of them wear school uniforms. The girls wear brown or blue dresses with black pinafores on school days and white pinafores on special days. Boys wear military-style uniforms with visored caps.

Emphasis in class methods is upon thorough teaching by the teacher, rather than on pupil activity and individual learning situations. Classes are formal, sometimes consisting of repetition of whole pages memorized from the textbook. Language teaching is detailed, based on drill, and stresses obscure rules of grammar and style rather than reading for enjoyment. These very formal elementary grades are in marked contrast to the free and spontaneous atmosphere of the kindergartens.

ELEMENTARY CURRICULUM

The curriculum is set by regulations of the Ministry of Education. It is uniform for all schools of each republic, and because of the regular meetings of the Ministers of Education to discuss such matters, it varies little from one republic to another. For the first three grades, reading forms the core of the curriculum. Regulations say that the pupils are not only to read the words but are also to understand the connections between the things they read and the actual life around them. Reading lessons are supplemented by demonstrations, field trips, and experiments. Dramatization of stories begins in the early grades; children are also taken to see plays performed by amateur groups and to the professional theater or to puppet shows.

Geography begins with learning about the home district and develops later into a study of the region, the republic, and the Soviet Union. Geographic information is never considered without associating it with the economic implications of each fact, in order to develop an understanding of the economic life of the Soviet Union. History begins with stories of the nationality group to which the children belong and develops, as the pupil progresses, into a study of the history of Russia and of the ancient and modern world. Great care is taken to make sure that the children understand the relations between historical events, as interpreted from the Communist point of view, and current events in the modern world. Maps, charts, pictures, and films are used to illustrate geographical and historical material.

In the elementary school one teacher teaches all subjects and progresses with the class from the first grade to the fourth. In addition to native language (reading, writing, and elementary grammar), history and geography, the course includes arithmetic, nature study, art, music, and physical education. Schools operate six days a week, and ministerial regulations provide for 24 lessons a week in the first and second grades, 25 for the third grade, and 27 for fourth graders. Table 16–1 shows the number of hours per year in grades one through four.

The basic textbooks used throughout the Soviet Union are the same, although they are published by different state publishing houses in the republics in many different languages. Teachers are permitted to supplement the basic texts with other materials collected locally. The use of Russian basic textbooks, translated into other languages, preserves the appearance of decentralization, and yet does not affect the uniformity of teaching throughout the Union.

One of the aims of all education in the U.S.S.R. is to teach children to live, study, and work "collectively." This teaching is done through the organization of student self-government, and through many school clubs. Each grade selects a class committee, and a general all-school committee is chosen from the members of the class committees. The pupils' committee has three major tasks to perform: it works with the School Council in the operation of the school and

TABLE 16–1
Curriculum and Time Allotment in Elementary Schools, U.S.S.R.

	HOURS PER YEAR IN EACH GRADE			
SUBJECTS	I	II	III	IV
Russian language and reading*	456	456	489	262
Arithmetic	229	229	196	229
Natural science				97
History				81
Geography				81
Physical education	33	33	66	66
Drawing	33	33	33	33
Singing	33	33	33	33
Hours per week	24	24	25	27
Hours per year	784	784	817	882

SOURCE : Kairov, *Pedagogika*, Moscow, 1948, p. 109.
* In grades I, II, and III, from the number of hours devoted to Russian language two hours a week are allotted to handwriting.

in the maintenance of order and discipline; it has certain house-keeping responsibilities, such as working with the school physician in matters of health and sanitation, propaganda in the community for proper health habits, and care of school property; and finally it helps in the program of political education in the school. In this third assignment committees are directed by the Young Communist organizations. The work of these organizations is described on page 465. Soviet educators believe that they can best achieve their educational aims by securing the wholehearted assistance of pupils who participate in their own government.

EXAMINATIONS
At the end of the fourth grade there is a transfer examination to determine which pupils will be permitted to enter the fifth grade, which is the beginning of secondary education. The Ministry issues examination cards, which list broad topics to be covered. Each card includes three such general themes in a single school subject. For example, in geography the subjects might be the wheat belt, the water transportation system, and the grazing lands. Each teacher develops lists of specific questions based on the general topics. As

soon as the examination topics are received from the Ministry, the teachers are notified, so that they may include the topics in the general review for the year. Sets of examination cards, each listing three specific questions or problems, are prepared for the actual examination.

Examinations, which are very important in the Soviet Union, are usually oral. The examining body is made up of the principal, the class teacher, two other teachers, and a representative of the Regional Education Authority, possibly an inspector. While examinations become even more important at the end of the eighth and eleventh grades, they take up much more time and are more formal for fourth graders than in other countries. Every pupil is required to recite in his own words something he has learned in school, a poem or a story. Examination cards for language, which includes reading and grammar, contain questions on sentence analysis and grammatical constructions. In arithmetic a pupil is given three problems to solve, one of which involves mental arithmetic. He must not only have the correct answer but he must be able to explain his method of solution. Marking is on a numerical scale, with grades ranging from five down to one. Much research has been reported on methods of conducting oral examinations. Reports on it stress the importance of establishing a friendly attitude between the pupil and the examiner, and on voice and phrasing of questions in examination success.

After the 1958 Reform Soviet schools were supposed to emphasize production training and productive labor. The first four grades are too young to attempt productive labor, but they have been given some production training. Visitors to Soviet schools seem to agree that in the first four grades this training has been very much like the handicrafts taught in American primary grades—coloring, paper cutting, clay modeling, and the like.

Soviet schools do not believe in individual differences in mental ability; they forbid the use of intelligence tests, or any discussion of an I.Q. All children are treated alike and all are expected to reach the same standards. The fact that some of them do not or cannot reach these standards is always blamed on the pupils' lack of concentration or on laziness. Failure may also be blamed on the lack of proper supervision in the home. It appears that most children get marks of three or higher; marks of one or two are seldom given. Teachers do not seem to be too rigorous in applying the lower marks, since they may feel that many low marks reflects on the quality of their teaching.[6]

DISCIPLINE

Since 1943 Soviet educational writings have given great attention to the subject of discipline. In the early days of the revolutionary regime education was based on extremely progressive methods, with much activity by the children and little repression and control. The Russians soon swung completely away from these "foreign" theories and practices and back toward stricter disciplinary methods, not too different from those of czarist times. Soviet leaders declared that school children had not had sufficient experience or knowledge of life to make decisions for themselves, and that these decisions must be made for them by adults. There has been some lessening of the rigidity in recent years, although the classroom atmosphere is still very formal.

The Communists believe that if children grow up in a well-ordered community, home, and school, they will soon accept the pattern of order and will develop into the type of citizen who will accept the regulation of his conduct by the state. As Eric Ashby pointed out, the Russians maintain that "authority and freedom, discipline and independence, obedience and self-respect, are incompatible." [7] They believe that the full development of personality can only come through discipline and conscious obedience.

In 1943 twenty rules for behavior in school and out were issued, covering matters of personal cleanliness, deference to teachers, posture in the schoolroom, and thoughtfulness toward older people and small children. Children under the age of 16 are not supposed to be on the street after 10:00 P.M. and are not allowed to attend theaters or moving pictures on school days without permission and without being accompanied by an adult. The rules are dictated during the language lesson and memorized in some schools.

When an elementary pupil becomes a behavior problem in class and the teacher needs help, he first calls on the school physician to determine whether there is a physical cause for the trouble. There are no child guidance clinics or psychological or psychiatric services available, but the teacher, principal, and doctor talk the matter over with the School Council. An effort is made to discover whether

[6] Bereday and others, *The Changing Soviet School*, p. 179.
[7] Ashby, *Scientist in Russia*, p. 45.

the problem is in the home conditions of the child. The greatest influence brought to bear on children who deviate from acceptable conduct is the public opinion of the class, through the class committee or the Pioneer organization. Such behavior is frowned upon as being against the good of the collective, rather than against the teacher.

SCHOOL LUNCHES

School lunches, which became general during World War II, have been continued and extended. Most schools provide a hot meal about noon or a little earlier for all children in the school. Soviet children get their main meal at home, between three and five in the afternoon. School meals are paid for by parents, although children of pensioners and disabled veterans, and those from large families are not required to pay. Parents' committees often help in preparing food and in providing meals for special occasions. During the war and later, because of the large proportion of working mothers, school lunches assumed great importance, and many schools provided dinners also.

In some apartment areas, where nearly all mothers are working, the schools may be operated on a prolonged day basis, and children may stay at school into the evening. They may have two or three meals at school, do all their homework, have their club or circle activities, and take walks and field trips under the direction of teachers. The younger ones take naps. Upper-grade children may do much of their productive labor in workshops attached to the schools.

Secondary Education

SECONDARY education in the U.S.S.R. is divided into two stages. The first, covering the years 11 up to 15, is almost invariably attached to a four-year school, and this combined school is called the eight-year school. The second stage is also in the same building with the preceding grades. When the 1958 Reform was passed, the second stage was to cover three years, for pupils 15 to 18, so that there would be an eleven-year school. The aim of the reform was to change all of the older ten-year schools into complete eleven-year schools, with all groups from 7 up to 18 in the same building. Now that policy has been reversed, and secondary education will end at age 17.

It is easier to find points of likeness between the elementary schools of other countries and the Russian elementary schools than it is to find similarities in secondary education. In many Western countries secondary education has been general in type, concerned with the transmission of learning for its own sake. In the United States it has been a blend of liberal education and training for a vocation. In some countries, if a pupil continues his schooling into the secondary stage, he has definitely decided to seek a "white collar" job and not one in manual labor or agriculture. In much of the world very few pupils complete secondary school unless they intend to proceed to the university. The danger of great numbers of pupils seeking secondary education in order to avoid manual labor was one of the major causes of the Khrushchev Reform of 1958, and subsequently the place of labor in the development of the nation was increasingly emphasized in Russian secondary schools for all pupils. It is true that, as in Great Britain, a variety of types of secondary schools have been provided, depending upon the vocational objectives of the students and the needs of the nation for trained workers in various fields. In some of these training in production and experience in productive labor has been more important than in others.

In the elementary schools one teacher teaches all subjects within a given grade; beginning with the fifth grade all subjects are in the hands of specialist teachers. All children follow the same curriculum, and all are expected to cover the same amount of work a year. Grading is usually according to age, but the recurring transfer examinations, at the ages of 11, 15, and 17 or 18, result in some retardation. Teachers are expected to give individual help to pupils who are not able to keep up with the class. Table 16–2 shows the curriculum in the junior secondary school with production training in grades five through eight, and the amount of time devoted to each subject.

In grades five, six, and seven, pupils study Russian or their own native language as the major subject. If the school is in a non-Russian area, the study of Russian language usually begins in the third grade; in Russian-speaking schools, the study of another European language is begun in the fifth grade. Other subjects are mathematics (arithmetic, algebra, geometry, and trigonometry), history, geography, biology, physics, chemistry, and the history and Constitution of the U.S.S.R. All pupils take physical education. The aim of the curriculum is to give all pupils a solid preparation in science and mathematics, and in the Communist interpretation of the social studies and modern politics.

TABLE 16–2
Curriculum of the Junior Secondary School, U.S.S.R.

SUBJECTS	HOURS PER WEEK IN EACH GRADE				
	V	VI	VII	VIII	Total
Russian	6	5	3	2	16
Literature	2	3	2	3	10
Mathematics	6	6	6	5	23
History and Constitution of the U.S.S.R.	2	2	2	3	9
Geography	2	2	2	2	8
Biology	2	2	2	2	8
Physics		2	2	3	7
Chemistry			2	2	4
Technical drawing			1	1	2
Foreign language	4	3	3	3	13
TOTAL	24	25	25	26	100
Drawing	1	1	1		3
Music; singing	1	1	1	1	4
Physical culture	2	2	2	2	8
TOTAL	4	4	4	3	15
Production training	3	3	3	3	12
Socially useful work	2	2	2	2	8
Socially productive training in classes	(180 total hours in eight-year school)				
TOTAL	5	5	5	5	20
Total	33	34	34	34	135

SOURCE: *Soviet Education*, Vol. II, No. 3 (January, 1960), p. 30 (from *Narodnoe Obrazovanye*, No. 11, 1959). Reprinted by permission of the International Arts and Sciences Press.

While production training is listed for the lower grades, it has consisted mainly of crafts and manual training of the simplest type—such as beginning needlework for girls and the use of simple tools.

Polytechnic workshop courses usually begin in the fifth grade. Elementary carpentry and turning, and sometimes elementary metalwork and machine shop, are given. Sometimes the boys and girls take the same workshop courses; more often the girls are in needlework classes. In rural areas gardening is required for all. Usually the type of workshop skills taught has some relation to the type of factory or agricultural employment available in the neighborhood. Thus, if a school is near an electrical factory, usable skills for this type of employment will be stressed. School courses taught as a part of the regular curriculum are called production training.

In some schools the students begin productive labor as early as the fifth grade, and in any case not later than the ninth grade. In most Moscow schools children devote two hours a week to productive work, although in some cases it may run as high as 12 hours a week. Generally the children leave the school and work in a nearby factory, industrial plant, or collective farm; in some schools labor is done in a school workshop. Since the time spent for vocational training in the general polytechnic secondary schools has been reduced, curriculum changes in this area may also be expected in the junior secondary schools.

THE GENERAL POLYTECHNIC SECONDARY SCHOOL WITH PRODUCTION TRAINING

The 1958 Reform projected three main types of secondary schools: the general polytechnic secondary schools with production training, schools for working or rural youth, and the *tekhnikumi.* The first of these are very similar to the older ten-year schools. Ideally such a school would be attached to an individual industrial plant or to a collective or state farm. All youths who completed the eight-year school could attend such a school full time, and have work experience outside, or could work in factories or on farms and attend school part time. Where a school is not available, correspondence courses might be substituted. A large proportion of the graduates of this type of school hope to enter higher educational institutions. The curriculum for grades nine, ten, and eleven in this school is shown in Table 16–3.

Soviet educators insist that the addition of emphasis on labor in secondary schools does not result in the reduction or dilution of the academic side of the program, but there seems to be no doubt that some academic educators have feared that result. Although academic courses were supposed to receive as many hours of instruction in the eleven-year school as in the older ten-year school, critics of the schools in 1964 maintained that standards in the eleven-year schools were not good.

TABLE 16–3

Curriculum of Urban Secondary Schools with Production Training, in U.S.S.R.

	HOURS PER WEEK			TOTAL HOURS	
SUBJECTS	IX	X	XI	Weekly	Yearly
Literature	3	3	3	9	339
Mathematics	4	4	4	12	452
History	2	3	4	9	335
Constitution of the U.S.S.R.			2	2	70
Economic geography		2	2	4	148
Physics	4	4	2	10	382
Astronomy		1		1	39
Chemistry	2	3	2	7	265
Biology	3			3	117
Technical drawing	2			2	78
Foreign language	2	2	3	7	261
Physical culture	2	2	2	6	226
	24	24	24	72	2,712
General technical subjects: production training (theoretical and practical) and productive work	12	12	12	36	1,356
Optional subjects	2	2	2	6	
Total	36	36	36	108	4,068

SOURCE: *Soviet Education, op. cit.*, p. 30. Reprinted by permission of the International Arts and Sciences Press.

One problem that has appeared is that pupils become more or less tied to the type of occupation represented by the factory or farm nearby. A good deal of emphasis has been placed on the freedom of the child and his parents to select the type of vocation he will enter. But if the only industrial plant in the town is an electrical factory, all children, or at least all boys, will be trained in electrical skills, even though the plant will not be able to employ more than a fraction of the graduates. Rural secondary schools prepare everyone for work in agriculture.

Manual trades are classified in the Soviet Union on the basis of six skill grades, with the sixth the highest. All children are expected to qualify for the first grade rating in some skill, and some may qualify as second grade specialists. This rating facilitates placement in later employment. In some schools children may graduate with two skills, such as in joinery and metalworking.

Public school No. 544, in Moscow, a prolonged day school, has woodworking shops attached to the school, where children are engaged in building furniture for kindergartens, and shops, where girls make work clothing. At the end of each school year the pupils are examined in manual labor as well as in academic subjects. Each pupil must show the examining committee an article he has made, as well as answer questions on production subjects. This school devotes eight hours weekly to productive labor and four hours to production training for the younger students. The amount of time spent in productive labor increases in the upper grades, until in the last two years the pupils are spending two days a week in the shops. They are paid for this work, at the going rate for their skill grade, and this money goes into school funds, which are used to pay for field trips, vacation camps, and other activities. In some schools the money may be paid to the pupils directly. School No. 544 employs about 20 adult workers, who handle techniques too difficult for the pupils in the manufacturing process or who do the final finishing.

Eric Ashby has stated that the secondary curriculum was remarkable for its rigidity and wide scope. He was stationed in Russia as a scientist during World War II; during that period he examined the courses of study in mathematics, physics, chemistry, and biology and reported that they were "full, not to say turgid." The syllabus is prescribed by the Ministry, and every school must follow it in detail. The only way that such an extensive program can be covered in the time allotted is by didactic, ex cathedra statements by the teachers, and much memorization by the pupils.[8]

The Social Studies

The teaching of social studies in any country is affected by the prevailing political, economic, and social opinions within the country. Even though the teacher may be completely free to teach, he does so within the limitations of his own education and background, and also within the limits of what is "socially acceptable" in the country in which he lives and works. Ashby pointed out that such

[8] Ashby, op. cit., p. 50.

subjects as history and geography are taught in British schools in the light of traditional British opinion, and that the British schoolboy is "unlikely when he learns about India, to become familiar with American or Russian opinions of British rule there." [9] Much of this is informal, indirect limitation of the teacher. But in the Russian schools the control of what is taught is direct and intentional. The courses of study are full of explicit directions to the teachers about the way to teach and the point of view to follow. Statements from the syllabus quoted by Ashby show the bias and the emphasis in teaching subject matter:

> In the teaching of Russian, emphasis must be laid on the profound patriotism of Russian literature. . . . The teaching of history of the U.S.S.R. must develop in school children a love for the heroic past of our people which throughout the whole of its history has displayed unexampled bravery. . . . The Russians stopped the Mongols and saved Europe from them. They saved Europe from being enslaved by the French and Napoleon. They have saved the whole world from the most terrible bondage which ever threatened anyone—the bondage of Hitlerite Germany. . . . The teaching of geography of the U.S.S.R. must reveal the innumerable resources of our great country.[10]

Foreign Languages and Religion

From the *Programs for Secondary Schools*, as drawn up by the Ministry of Education of the R.S.F.S.R., Ashby quotes the following from the course of study in foreign languages (English, French, German):

> In the senior classes reading and discussion arising out of the texts must be "utilized to impart a communist education and to inculcate selfless love and devotion to our socialist fatherland, the Communist Party, and the leader of the workers of the whole world—Comrade Stalin. . . . A feeling of solidarity with the workers of the whole world who are fighting to free themselves from the yoke of capitalism must be awakened in the pupils. From the eighth class onwards they should read classical and contemporary authors in the foreign language outside of school hours. In the senior classes, social and political ideas must take an increasingly important place. . . ." [Among the specified subjects

---

[9] Ashby, *op. cit.*, p. 50.

[10] Ashby, *op. cit.*, p. 51. Throughout the Soviet Union, World War II is always referred to as the "Great Patriotic War." Quotations from Ashby appear with his kind permission.

for discussion in foreign languages are the home life of the pupil], "the happy life of children in our country and the hard life of children in capitalist countries [sixth class] . . . life and work in collective farms and in farms before the revolution . . . life of the peasantry in capitalist countries [seventh class] . . . episodes in the revolutionary struggle in capitalist countries [tenth class]." The material necessary for discussion is amply provided in textbooks. For instance the English reader for the eighth class at school [children about 15 to 16] has passages on the slums of Chicago (Upton Sinclair), the East End of London (Jack London), children at work (from the *Underworld*, by Welsh), a General Strike in London (Galsworthy), the story of a Negro being burned to death in Arkansas (Haywood), an extract about Mr. Squeers (Dickens), John Barton, a Chartist delegate from Manchester (Gaskell), Kingsley's poem "Three Fishers" (a vignette of the British fishing industry), and some touching anonymous pieces.[11]

This statement, written in 1947, is probably equally true of the situation today, with the elimination of the reference to Comrade Stalin.

Antireligious propaganda might be expected as an important part of the syllabus, but there is actually less such propaganda than formerly. The tendency now is to show that religious ideas are incompatible with historical and dialectical materialism and science. Ashby quotes a statement that was published in a newspaper in 1944:

"By giving the correct scientific understanding of the essence of the phenomena of nature and human society, the school must dispel the prejudices and superstitions of children who are under the influence of such things. It is no use concealing the fact that among teachers there are people, a small number it is true, who have recently begun to show great tolerance towards religion. Cases of the observation of religious ceremonies by teachers have increased somewhat. Our Party's attitude toward religion is well known and has not changed. Our Party fights religious prejudice because it stands for science, whilst religious prejudices go against science, since all religion is contrary to science." [12]

Russian teachers report to American visitors that the former League of Militant Godless has been disbanded, since it is no longer necessary. One method of circumscribing religion is reported in

[11] Ashby, *op. cit.*, pp. 51–54.
[12] Ashby, *op. cit.*, p. 54.

the Central Asian republics, where most of the population were formerly Muslims. The Arabic language is still taught, but in the Cyrillic script. The Koran and other religious writings are not easily available in this alphabet, with the result that even the Arabic-speaking peoples are effectively cut off from the literature of their religion.

The secondary schools, like the elementary schools, have no elective subjects. Every pupil takes the same pattern of subjects regardless of his vocational objectives. There is some choice of foreign languages (English, French, German) in the larger schools, and it is reported that more pupils study English than the other languages combined. Apart from this choice subject-matter specialization begins in the university or higher institute.

Coeducation

For many years the Soviet Union took great pride in the fact that all schools were coeducational. Coeducation was part of the Party's program of raising the status of women and of increasing the proportion of girls and women in the schools and in the work force. In 1943 the world was surprised to hear that coeducation was being abandoned. In that year separate schools for boys and girls were established in 71 larger cities. Most elementary schools, some rural secondary schools, and some types of vocational schools remained coeducational. Mixed education continued to be general in universities and technical schools.

This change did not come about without much discussion and controversy. When the Moscow Education Authority asked permission in 1940 to experiment with separate schools, the official decision was against the change. However, in 1942 Moscow was permitted to set up a number of experimental schools, and in 1943 this was followed by the decision to extend the program.

Many parents and teachers did not like the change, but the teachers seem to have gone along without much protest. Girls who had spent some time in a coeducational school disliked the change more than the boys. Teachers for both boys' and girls' schools were trained in coeducational training institutions, with the avowed purpose of ensuring that the academic program and methods would be the same for boys and girls. The same curriculum was followed in both, except that the older boys got some military training and the girls some homemaking. The Communists have always insisted that all careers are open on an equal basis to both men and women in the Soviet Union.

Within recent years the trend has been back toward coeducation. All new schools have been made coeducational, and most of the separate schools have been changed back. These changes are an excellent example of the way recurrent changes in the Party line affect educational practices.

Educational Opportunities

At present there are no fees for education, from nursery school through university, in the Soviet Union. This has not always been true. In 1940 school people in other countries were surprised by the introduction of fees for the higher-level schools. Until that date, Soviet educators had boasted that all education was free "from the cradle to the grave" in the workers' republics. In 1940 decrees were promulgated which provided for the collection of fees for the last years of secondary schools, for the technical and professional schools, and for higher education. Several categories of students were exempt from the payment of fees: children of sick or disabled parents; war orphans; children of men in the armed forces; and all adopted children. Students who passed the final school-leaving examinations with honors were also exempt. Many scholarships were provided. The ostensible reason for the change was the rising cost of education and the continued need to increase school facilities to provide for increased enrollments. Another reason, however, was the rising income of the general population and the policy of the government to siphon off as much of the excess earnings as possible.

It was estimated that fee collections in 1941 amounted to less than three percent of the total expenditures for higher education. The annual fees for the eighth, ninth, and tenth grades ranged from 150 to 200 rubles (old valuation). When it is considered that many people were only earning from 250 to 300 rubles a month, it is evident that the fees became a serious bar to further education of a poor child, unless he could earn a scholarship.

There were other forms of discrimination as well. Kulski stated:

The existence of three types of schools—"elementary," "junior high school," and "secondary"—produces further discrimination. Each begins with the first grade, and theoretically the corresponding grades should offer equivalent programs: elementary schools have only four grades, but the fifth, sixth, and seventh grades of the "junior high school" should be interchangeable with the corresponding grades of the "secondary" school. But the pupils at the secondary schools are the favored ones. These are urban schools, and the teachers of the first four grades are certain to be better qualified than the rural teachers of the elementary schools. Moreover, a child lucky enough to be admitted to the first grade of a secondary school has a greater chance of passing through all the grades of the same school. A youngster graduated from the junior high school should be able to transfer to the eighth grade of a secondary school; but the Soviet regulations allot only 15 percent of the vacant places at the eighth grades of the secondary schools for boys and girls who have graduated from the junior high schools; 85 percent of the places are reserved for students already enrolled in the secondary school. Moreover, the compulsory draft of boys and girls to the trade schools (Labor Reserve Schools) does not extend to the students of the upper grades of the secondary schools.[13]

The passage quoted was written before the Reform of 1958, under which the eighth grade would be included in Kulski's "junior high school," and the transfer would be to the ninth grade of the secondary school. Russian educators insist that there are fewer four-year and eight-year schools now, and that the situation described by Kulski is not so common. However, a large proportion of the students still leave full-time education at the age of 15, and are only able to complete the full secondary course by evening and correspondence courses. It is still true that the opportunity to rise to higher positions in the bureaucracy may come at the age of 7 for a Soviet child, depending upon the school he enters, and may be denied to him later. There is no explanation in Russian literature as to the selection of children for the first grade in eleven-year schools. It appears to have depended largely on the proximity of such a school to his home. It is evident, however, that the children of the favored classes have not been refused admission, and this situation will probably continue when the ten-year school has been restored.

Examinations

In addition to the transfer examination at the end of the fourth grade, there are special examinations at the close of the eighth and eleventh grades. These are very similar to the fourth-grade exami-

---

[13] W. W. Kulski, "Class Stratification in the Soviet Union," *Foreign Affairs*, Vol. 32, No. 1 (October, 1953), p. 149.

nation in general organization; except for Russian and mathematics, they are oral and are conducted before a panel which may consist of the class teacher, the school principal, one or two other teachers, and an inspector or other representative of the Education Department. If the student fails in the examination at the end of the school year in June, he has an opportunity to take a second examination in August. If he fails again, he is required to remain in the same grade for another year. If he passes brilliantly, there is a possibility that he may be placed in a higher grade. For the exceptionally able pupil special individual instruction may be arranged, and a professor from a higher school may be asked to come and tutor him.

Ashby reported that the examinations, which are a revival of the old czarist system of testing, are conducted in a surprising spirit of festivity:

In a room decorated with flowers and red cloth there sits the examining commission. . . . On the table there is a pile of cards face downwards with three questions written on each. The examinee selects a card at random and has fifteen or twenty minutes to think over the questions and prepare the answers. A familiar and mild way of cheating is to pick more than one card from the pile, and to select for the examination the card with the easiest questions. In many examinations the results are announced at once, and in the junior classes at any rate, the examination is followed by the presentation of bunches of flowers to the examiners, a happy touch which the Boards of Examiners for British schools might well envy.[14]

The five-point grade system covers not only class work but school behavior. Four times a year pupils are marked on all subjects and on conduct, and passing into the next grade depends on an average of four points throughout the year. Ashby thought that the five-point system had been used to tighten discipline in the schools, since the pupil's mark depends on conduct as well as school work. If the pupil makes a five-point average in all of his subjects he is awarded a gold medal; if he makes a five in the subjects required for matriculation and at least four in three others, he gets a silver medal. For any medal a pupil must not fall below five in conduct, and it has been estimated that not more than 5 percent receive medals. To a foreign observer this may seem like a capitalistic system of rewards.

At the time of the 1964 announcement, a typical large senior sec-

14 Ashby, op. cit., pp. 55–56.

ondary school enrolled about 900 pupils in grades one to eleven, with two or three rooms per grade. The grades averaged about 40 pupils, except in the eleventh, where the desirable maximum was set at 35. Small rural secondary schools have had fewer pupils per room. In the early days of the Bolshevist regime a maximum of 25 pupils was announced as an ideal, but the government has not been able to provide sufficient teachers or classrooms to reach this goal. A secondary school employs a secretary, bookkeeper, business manager, cook, and other kitchen staff.

SCHOOLS FOR URBAN OR RURAL YOUTH

The second type of secondary school is the part-time school for young workers, which they attend while they are employed on farms or in factories. These are three-year schools, organized separately from the preceding eight grades, rather than having them all in the same building. Students are able to attend school because of a shorter working day, or by being granted two or three days off a week. Vocational and general education are included in this part-time program. The curriculum of the rural secondary school is shown in Table 16–4, and of the urban evening school for factory workers in Table 16–5.

"TEKHNIKUMI"

The third type of secondary school is the *tekhnikum*, which is a specialized secondary school intended to train "middle-grade" specialists, in three-, four-, or five-year courses. Approximately one ninth-grader in ten enters one of the *tekhnikumi*, where he is prepared for a single specialized skill. These schools also provide a general and theoretical education. From them the best students may proceed to higher institutes.

Students who enter the *tekhnikumi* have made excellent records in the eight-year school, and so are not required to work full time and pursue their education in part-time schools. In spite of the large amount of determinism inherent in the Soviet system of planned economy, a certain amount of choice is allowed these students. Some pupils who received high enough ratings to permit them to enter the last three grades in the eleven-year school were allowed to enter a *tekhnikum* to prepare for specialized jobs. Now they will probably be given the choice of transferring to the ten-year school. In the larger cities there is always a choice of technical schools. At the end of the

TABLE 16-4

Curriculum of the Rural Secondary School with Production Training, in U.S.S.R.

SUBJECTS	HOURS PER WEEK*			TOTAL HOURS	
	IX	X	XI	Weekly	Yearly
Literature	4	3	4	11	338
Mathematics	4	4/5	5	14.5	445
History	3	4	4	11	338
Constitution of the U.S.S.R.			2	2	64
Economic geography		3/2	2/3	5	155
Physics	5	5	3/2	12.5	380
Astronomy		1		1	30
Chemistry	2/3	3	3	8.5	261
Biology	4			4	120
Technical drawing	3/2			2.5	75
Foreign language	3	3	3	9	276
Physical culture	2	2	3	7	216
	31	28	29	88	2,698
Bases of agricultural production and production instruction (theoretical and practical)	5	8	7	20	614
	36	36	36	108	3,312
Productive work (according to seasons)					
DAYS	54	54	18	126	
HOURS	324	324	108		756
Optional subjects	2	2	2	6	
Total hours					4,068

SOURCE: *Soviet Education*, II: 3, p. 31. Reprinted by permission of the International Arts and Sciences Press.

* Two numbers in the columns indicate hours for the first and second semesters.

school year eighth-grade pupils are faced with placards and advertisements urging them to choose one school or another. Pupils in smaller towns or in rural areas may find their choice restricted to the particular *tekhnikum* available in their area.

Sons of officers and men killed in military service may be educated between the ages of 8 and 18 in special military boarding schools which prepare officers for the army and navy. The army schools are called "Suvarov" schools, after a famous eighteenth-century hero, and the navy schools are called "Nahkimov" schools, after a Crimean War admiral.

Tekhnikumi are the responsibility of the Ministry or industrial trust or other agency which needs trained personnel for positions of medium responsibility. If the Ministry of Mines needs junior personnel, it establishes a mining *tekhnikum*. The State Bank operates a *tekhnikum* for engravers. There are special music, art, ballet, or theatrical *tekhnikumi*. Buildings are erected and equipped, and the cost of operation paid, by the Ministry or trust that established

TABLE 16–5
Curriculum of Evening Secondary Schools, in U.S.S.R.

SUBJECTS	HOURS WEEKLY*			Total weekly hours
	IX	X	XI	
Literature	2	2	2	6
Mathematics	3	3	3	9
History	1	2/1	2	4.5
Constitution of the U.S.S.R.			1	1
Economic geography	2	2/1	1/2	3
Physics	3	3	2	8
Astronomy		0/1		0.5
Chemistry	1/2	2	2/1	5
Biology	2/1			1.5
Technical drawing	1/2			1.5
Foreign language	2/1	1/2	2	5
	15	15	15	45
Optional subjects for improving professional qualifications of pupils	2	2	2	6
Consultations	3	3	3	9
Total hours	20	20	20	60

SOURCE: *Soviet Education*, II: 3, p. 31.   Reprinted by permission of the International Arts and Sciences Press.

* Two numbers in the columns indicate hours for the first and second semesters.

the school. The educational program is supervised and controlled by the Ministry of Higher Education and Specialized Technical Schools.

Each *tekhnikum* trains all pupils in a single occupation or specialty, or in a group of closely related specialties. In addition to the specialized subjects, much of the general education program of the senior secondary school is covered, but the academic subjects are adapted to meet the needs of the specialized field. For instance, the type of science taught in a nursing *tekhnikum* would vary in emphasis from that given in a railway *tekhnikum*. The upper 5 percent of the pupils completing a *tekhnikum* program may apply for admission to a university or higher institute on the same basis as those who have completed the senior secondary school.

In Great Britain secondary education has become more flexible since 1944, giving more children opportunities within the three types of secondary schools. French secondary education has also been liberalized, and more French children have opportunities for advanced education. There is reason to believe that Russian secondary education is becoming more stratified. Although pronouncements of the Ministries of Education state that first choice for all places in higher schools and universities is reserved for children of peasants and workers, the selection has not been carried out in that manner. The young people (mostly from working-class families) who were formerly drafted into the Labor Reserve each year have had little chance to rise above the status of semiskilled workers.

Carter believes that up to 1958 opportunities to rise to positions of management or leadership in business or industry, or in the bureaucracy, were more and more reserved to children of skilled workers and the intelligentsia. Places in higher education institutions were open only to those who had "excellent" records. In spite of a large number of scholarships, the imposition of fees became a bar to children of low-paid, unskilled workers. She says: "Under these circumstances education in the Soviet Union remains equalitarian only in the sense of being nondiscriminatory on the ground of sex or race. Temporarily, at least, a new hierarchy reflecting different functions in the planned society, different grades of skill, and therefore different scales of wages marks both education and the social order." [15]

[15] Carter and others, *Major Foreign Powers*, 2nd ed., 1952, p. 551.

The Reform of 1958 was intended, among other things, to correct some of the advantages given to children of the higher classes in the Soviet "classless" society. It provided that all children, regardless of background, would have experience with labor. In some ways, however, it further restricted the opportunity for full-time secondary education, and it did not change the wide differentials in earning power which depend upon education and occupation. Education remains the only way to preferment in the Soviet Union.

BOARDING SCHOOLS

Boarding schools have been known in Russia since czarist times, but the big expansion in this program has come since the 1958 Reform. Khrushchev proposed the establishment of many more of these schools, which would take children at the age of 3 (or even earlier), and retain them until the completion of the eleven-year (now ten-year) school program. In the boarding school, it is held, in ideal surroundings, where children would be freed from family influences, a new elite of dedicated Communists can be developed. Marx once said, "social education must replace family education." The Party believes that the boarding school is the device by which this can be done. Most Russians seem to prefer the older system of retaining their children at home, and Khrushchev's grandchildren are not in boarding schools.[16]

From a small beginning in 1958, the Soviets were able to announce by 1960 that there were 701 boarding schools with 170,000 students. Plans have been made to increase the number of students enrolled to 1,340,000 by 1965.[17] Some authorities say that eventually one-third of all children will be in these schools. One advantage of the system is that orphanages are being closed or changed into boarding schools by the addition of other children.

A typical boarding school in Alma-Ata, in Kazakhstan, proposes to take children as young as 6 months, and expects to retain them until the age of 18. It has absorbed a former orphanage and enrolls 300 children of 18 different nationalities. The teaching is done in Russian but all children are required to study the Kazakh language as well. Parents apply for admission of their children. Preference is given to children of disabled war veterans, to families with many children, or to children with poor living conditions at home. A uni-

16 "Soviet Boarding Schools," *Time*, January 18, 1960, p. 86.
17 Gerald H. Read, *op. cit.*, p. 79.

form fee schedule has been established throughout the Soviet Union, based on family income and the number of children in the family. For example, of the 300 children in the Alma-Ata schools, the director reported that 5 percent come from well-to-do homes and pay from 30 to 50 rubles a month. Some children from poorer families pay from three to six rubles a month; 43 children are exempt from fees.

Children come to this school from all over Kazakhstan, but it is planned that later schools will be built on a neighborhood basis, and in the future children may attend boarding schools very near their homes. Parents may come to see their children, and the pupils may go home on weekend visits. During the summer all children are in Pioneer camps. The older children get their work experience in nearby factories; the girls in a clothing factory, the boys in a car manufacturing plant. Ninth-graders work eight hours a week—four days a week for two hours each day; tenth-graders spend five hours a day, two days a week in the factories; eleventh-graders work five hours a day five days a week.

A Tadjik boarding school near Dyushambe takes many children from nomad homes and mountain villages, where the parents live under primitive conditions. When the director was asked how the children were expected to adjust to home conditions when they went back, he replied, "We do not expect them to adjust. They will be expected to change conditions at home. This is part of a social program. There is a problem of social education in the school and family education in the home; we don't want these to oppose each other. We encourage the parents to visit the children once or twice a week; they will learn new ways on these visits, and so some changes may start in the villages when the parents return home. We are developing new forms of parent-child relationships and of home-school relationships." He admitted that it was easier to persuade nomadic parents to send their boys away from home than their girls. It is apparent that the purpose of the boarding school program is to accelerate the plan of bringing children into conformity with the social ideals of the regime. The Party believes that the system will hasten the eradication of "prejudices and superstitions" that cling about homes, such as the traditional beliefs and practices and old religious ideas.

A boarding school employs a large staff and includes both teachers and "educators." The educators are trained as teachers, and are in charge of outside-of-classroom activities, such as Pioneer activities, clubs and circles, and recreation. None of the teachers or educators live in the school. At night the pupils are under the supervision of the school nurses.

University and Higher Education

IN THE Soviet Union universities are higher schools for the training of specialists. A principal motto of Communist educational policy above the elementary level is "science for the workers." There is a tendency to call all highly educated persons, whether in chemistry or literature, atomic physics or political science, "scientists." Perhaps, as King suggested, a better description in English might be "active scholars." A higher educational institution with more than one faculty, training for several different specialties, is usually called a university. A single-faculty institution, training "scientists" for a single line of work, or for closely related specialties, is termed a higher institute. Such institutes are on the same academic level as universities and are organized in similar fashion.

Scientists are highly esteemed in Russia and hold a high social and economic position. Whether as research scientists, members of faculties of higher institutions, administrators, or government officials, they have special privileges. Usually they take an active part in the life of the state and have strong social and political interests. Many of them serve on rural or city councils, in regional or republic soviets, or even in the Supreme Soviet.

University education is not a general, liberal education; it is a highly specialized training for a definite occupation or profession. It is possible to make a vocational choice later, but this means a serious loss of time and is discouraged. The student is expected to study the fields open to him while he is in secondary school or while he is employed, and he should have decided upon his specialty before he begins the higher course. Not only must the decision be made in a general field, but in the specialized field within the area before he comes to the university. A student does not select chemistry, but oil chemistry or biochemistry; not literature, but classical, modern, European, or Russian literature. Even in the medical institutes the students must decide on the specialty they wish to follow before they begin the course. Actually the freedom of student choice is somewhat restricted by the requirements of state planning—students express their own choices, but matriculation examinations and university quotas decide how many may be admitted to any field.

In czarist Russia there were no specialized secondary schools or higher institutions in many of the national areas. There were universities before the revolution in the area which is now the R.S.F.S.R., in Georgia, and the Ukraine. There are now 39 universities, with at least one in each republic. In addition to the universities, there are many higher institutes—in 1958 there were 727. Of these, 200 were technical institutes, 200 pedagogical institutes, 100 agricultural institutes, 70 medical institutes, and 30 institutes of railway communications. The remainder were music conservatories, drama schools, physical culture institutes, and a few others.[18]

Kuprianov gives figures showing the increase in specialized secondary schools, scientific institutions, and higher educational institutions in some of the Central Asian nationality areas since the 1917 Revolution. In the Kirgiz S.S.R., which had no higher schools in czarist times, by 1949 there were 33 specialized secondary schools, 6 higher educational institutions, 23 scientific institutions, and a branch of the Academy of Sciences of the U.S.S.R. The Yakutsk Autonomous Republic, which is a part of the R.S.F.S.R., in the same year had 16 specialized secondary schools and 24 scientific research institutions.[19]

Enrollment in higher educational institutions has increased rapidly since World War II. In 1939 it was reported that 1,080,000 persons, or 0.6 percent of the total population, were specialists who had completed higher education courses. By 1952 these figures were given as 1,894,000, or 0.9 percent of the total. The 1959 census reports that 3,778,000, or 1.8 percent of the population, are higher education graduates. In 1960 it was reported that 2,160,000 students were enrolled in universities and higher institutes.

Higher education was originally under a Committee for Higher Education, attached to the Council of Ministers of the Union. In 1946 this committee was replaced by an All-Union Ministry for Higher Education. Later that was reduced to the status of a Main Administration of Higher Educational Institutions and was attached to the All-Union Ministry of Culture. Now each of the fifteen Union republics has its own Ministry of Higher Education and Specialized

18 Bereday and others, The Changing Soviet School, p. 274.
19 Trofim I. Kuprianov, Year Book of Education, 1949, p. 385.

Secondary Schools, and an All-Union Ministry of Higher Education and Culture coordinates curricula and academic standards throughout the Union.

A university is headed by an administrative officer called the "rector," who has two assistants (pro-rectors), one of whom is in charge of the academic program and the other in charge of finance and administration. A university may have from four to eleven or more faculties, each headed by a dean, who has responsibility for the staff, organization, and discipline of his school. Academic departments are called "chairs" and are headed by professors. Academic ranks are those of professor, assistant professor (*dotsent*), assistant, and lecturer. Every professor is expected to carry on some research work in addition to teaching, but he has very little administrative responsibility. A university or higher institute has a senate, or "Learned Council," made up of the rector, the two pro-rectors, the deans, and representatives elected by the students from among their own numbers. This body is consultative to the rector, although it passes on theses for advanced degrees, and may make recommendations on academic matters. There is a faculty committee within each faculty, which considers procedural matters within the particular school. Professors and *dotsenty* are elected for a period of five years; and the final appointments are made by the Minister. At the end of every five-year period a "competition" is advertised for the position. Thus every professor and assistant professor finds himself in competition with other candidates every five years.

MATRICULATION

The 1958 Reform had its impact on higher education as well as on the secondary school, and one of these effects was in respect to matriculation requirements. Graduates are guaranteed, under the Constitution, the right to apply for entrance examinations at any higher institution. Since each of these institutions, university or higher institute, has a quota of new students, usually the number of applicants far exceeds the available places. Each faculty sets its own entrance requirements, but every student has to pass in historical and dialectical materialism. Entrance examinations also generally include Russian, a foreign language, and the special technical field selected for study.

The Reform regulations provided that 80 percent of the new entrants had to have at least two years of practical labor on a farm or

in a factory or industrial enterprise (or in military service) after completing secondary school. Not more than 20 percent (probably the
brightest students in science and mathematics) may proceed directly
from secondary school to university. Some Russian educators admitted
that the examination standards were higher for the 20 percent than
for the 80 percent who have been out of school for at least two years.
One result of the Reform was that those coming from secondary
school were at least 18 rather than 17 years old, and that the remainder
were at least 20 before beginning the five-year university course. The
effect of the 1964 changes on these requirements is not yet clear.
University administrators reported that there were from two to five
times as many applicants as there were places, depending upon the
faculty chosen by the students.

PRODUCTIVE LABOR

The close relationship between labor and education is not forgotten on the university level. All students are expected to do work
around the school, in the dormitories, cafeterias, or in general cleaning and maintenance, on a regularly scheduled basis. University
administrators frequently say something like this: "We have been
able to dispense with 80 cleaning women since the new program
went into effect." This is assigned, unpaid work.

In addition to the above, all students put in a year at some productive work. If their specialty is in a technical field, the work will
probably be in a nearby factory. Students in electrical engineering
or electronics may work for a year (usually the third year) in an
electrical plant or factory. Students in agriculture actually work for a
year on a collective or state farm. Students in fields which are not
closely related to manual labor, such as literature, language, or
librarianship, spend their work year in construction projects, perhaps
building roads or apartment houses. For this year the student works
a regular 42-hour week, is paid at the regular rate, and does not
receive the stipend that a full-time student gets. But all come back
to the institution for 16 hours of evening classes while they are working. University officials insist that there is no dilution of the academic program because of the working schedule.

CURRICULA

Two types of subjects are taken by all students in universities or
higher institutes: those that are compulsory for all and those that are

specialized and connected with the vocational field. The compulsory subjects are those which the Communists call the social sciences: foundations of Marxism-Leninism, political economy, and historical and dialectical materialism. In addition all students continue for at least three years the foreign language they studied in secondary school, and all take physical education.

During the first two years students spend six hours daily, six days a week, in lectures, seminars, and laboratories. The first years are somewhat general, although the historical and scientific courses are integrated with the specialized field. Beginning with the fourth year, the work is highly specialized, with a great amount of time spent in laboratories or in practical work in the selected specialty. More time is allowed for individual work in the laboratories or workshops, or in reading. The last half of the fifth year is devoted almost entirely to the preparation of a thesis and to preparing for the final examinations.

Examinations, still mainly oral, are required in every subject each year. Final examinations cover the specialty and the thesis. At the end of the five-year course the student does not get a degree but a diploma which certifies that he is qualified to hold a position as a specialist in the area for which he has trained.

Student attendance is carefully checked daily; absence from required lectures or laboratory sections brings reprimands, and a poor attendance record may cause a student to lose his stipend, or even to be dismissed. Students are expected to be serious-minded and to avoid such student activities as the "rags" of British universities or the highly-publicized "panty raids" in American colleges. Soviet students are expected to demonstrate what the authorities call "cultured conduct," both in activities and in personal appearance. King reported that it was considered ill-mannered and "uncultured" to come late to class or to appear in class wearing galoshes.[20]

Soviet university students have had experience in all types of school clubs and Young Communist activities throughout their previous schooling, and these activities are continued throughout higher education. They are expected to take an active interest in political matters and in the serious problems facing their country. There are, however, social and athletic activities as well. Music, drama, and student dances are popular, and the annual university ball is a very

[20] Beatrice King, *Russia Goes to School: A Guide to Soviet Education*, p. 91.

important event of the year. There are no organized athletic teams, but there are ski clubs, mountain-climbing clubs, and hiking groups. Students are entitled to reduced fares on the railroads and to tickets at reduced prices for theaters and concerts. There is a student council, elected by the student body, and student committees for each faculty. Much of the responsibility of these groups concerns discipline and attendance problems.

Soviet educators are proud of the fact that higher educational institutions have no fee charges at all and that from 75 to 85 percent of the students receive stipends from the state, the amount depending upon the school or specialty in which they enroll. A large proportion of the students live in dormitories, where costs are low. Stipends may range from 30 to 80 rubles a month and may be increased in the later years of the five-year course. (The Soviet government now sets the value of the ruble at $1.11, although it is not convertible to foreign currencies.) Students may lose their stipends if they are politically inactive, or if their grades drop too low, or if their attendance records are poor. Stipends seem to be used sometimes to direct students into fields where the state planning authorities expect shortages of trained personnel, by increasing the stipends in fields with shortages, and by decreasing or eliminating them in less critical fields.

The new buildings of the Moscow State University (which is officially named for Lomonosov, a great Russian scientist) rise on the low Lenin Hills above the Moscow River. The science faculties are located in these buildings, while the humanities faculties are still in older buildings in the center of the city. The central building rises to a height of 32 stories. The complex of buildings include classrooms, lecture rooms, laboratories, dormitories, auditoriums, club rooms, and a swimming pool. The building is of the ornate Stalin "wedding cake" style of architecture, currently out of favor in the Soviet Union, and is decorated with statues, friezes, and paintings. The university enrolls about 25,000 students, of whom 51 percent are women. Science subjects attract about 60 percent of the student body, Some 2,000 foreign students, from 50 countries, are enrolled.

Staff salaries are probably higher at the Moscow State University than the average for the country. In 1960 the average salaries were reported as follows: professors, 500 rubles per month; *dotsenty*, 230 rubles, and instructors, 170 rubles. The staff ratio was reported as one teacher to every nine students. This figure did not include demonstrators and assistants.

A new Friendship University has been established for foreign students, largely for those from developing countries in Africa and Asia. The projected buildings have not been completed, and the university is still housed in old buildings in the heart of Moscow. Some of the African students have been unhappy about the segregation of foreign students in a separate institution, away from the Russian students. University authorities say that they intend to have at least 10 percent of the student body from the Soviet Union at Friendship University, and that the separation was made because foreign students need to spend at least one year in an intensive study of the Russian language.

GRADUATE WORK

Although students receive diplomas instead of degrees on completion of a university course, there are two postgraduate degrees—candidate and doctor. The main purpose of advanced study is to prepare for a teaching position or for a place in a research institute. Graduate students are known as "aspirants" and are older than the average student, having completed at least two years work in their specialty before returning to the university or higher institute to work for an advanced degree. Applicants for admission to graduate work present an original research paper and take examinations in the Russian language, the history of the Communist Party, and their special field. Aspirants study for three years, and get a stipend of about 100 rubles a month. They take special graduate courses, carry on approved individual study and research, and prepare a dissertation. The dissertation must be approved by the department, published in the press or as a monograph, and defended before a committee of the faculty.

If the aspirant is finally passed by the Learned Council of the institution, he is awarded the title of candidate. A candidate who has worked in an institution for several years, and has published several papers, may be awarded the title of *dotsent*. All of the higher educational institutions are qualified to award the degree of candidate.

Special doctorate institutes (*doctorantura*) have been set up in a few universities and higher institutes which are permitted to award the doctor's degree. Students who hold the degree of candidate must be nominated by their university, and must be approved by a joint commission set up by the Ministry of Higher Education and Culture and the Academy of Sciences of the U.S.S.R. in order to study for the degree. After several years of additional work, writing, publishing, preparing, and defending a doctoral dissertation, the candidate may be awarded the title of doctor. Holders of such degrees may be given positions as professors, or may hold high research positions. (A man with long service and a distinguished publication record may attain the position of professor even without the doctorate.) Predoctoral students are paid higher stipends than precandidate students.

EVENING AND CORRESPONDENCE COURSES

Higher education by evening and correspondence courses has a long history in Russia. Soviet educators say that there were experiments with it even in czarist times. In 1960 there were 2,160,000 students in universities and higher institutes; of these 1,100,000 were in evening and correspondence classes. (In the same year many of the 1,907,000 who were enrolled in specialized secondary schools were not attending full-time day classes.) Practically all of the universities and higher institutes have evening and correspondence faculties. There are 20 institutes where all course work is done by correspondence, and ten with only evening faculties. Over 500 schools have correspondence faculties, and over 300 have evening faculties. These are regular, full-time faculties, which use special methods of teaching but cover the same amount of subject matter and require the same academic standards as the day classes. Subjects such as medicine and complicated technologies are not taught except in full-time day classes.

About 55 percent of those enrolled in evening and correspondence classes are women. More men than women are found in the technical courses and more women than men in the humanities and teacher training. It is reported that about 48 percent of the students come from urban areas, which is proportionate to the total population from these areas.

Soviet educators speak a great deal about the "favors" extended to evening and correspondence students. The courses are free, like the day classes. Students buy their own books, but they may borrow them from a book-loan program set up by the institutes. Evening students are given 15 days' leave without pay for examination periods, plus travel time, and their jobs are held for them. Correspondence students who pass the first two years successfully may get 30 days' leave with pay for examinations; in the higher years this may be 40 days. Evening students in the last years may get 30 days' leave with pay. Travel fares are at half price. All evening and correspondence students are given 30 days' leave with pay for final state examinations. If the course requires the completion of a thesis they are given four months with pay to do the writing.

Evening classes meet four nights a week, 16 hours weekly. This is after the students have worked a 7-hour day on a full-time job. It is estimated that correspondence students spend 20 percent of their time coming to a consultation point, where they hear lectures on complicated subjects, do laboratory work, and consult with their instructors. Laboratory work is approximately the same as for day students. Usually an evening or correspondence student takes a full year longer to complete a course than a day student. A student who enrolls in an evening or correspondence course takes the entire yearly course; there is no provision for enrollment in a single subject as in American extension courses.

Adult Education

DURING the first 20 years of the Soviet regime, great emphasis was given to the organization of schools for adult illiterates. With the increase in general education throughout the country, these gradually disappeared. According to the 1959 census, 98.5 percent of the total population between the ages of 9 and 49 are literate.

An announced aim of the Party has been to raise all adults to the level of completion of the ten-year school and, more recently, of the eleven-year school. This program is far from realization, and under the Reform it will be necessary for a large proportion of the last three years to be part-time schooling. The 1959 census showed that 14,-322,000 people had completed the tenth grade or above, and that 35,386,000 had completed at least the seventh grade. The remainder of the population had less than seven years of schooling.

Cultural agencies are used extensively to provide informal adult education throughout the Union. Instead of museums, theaters, the ballet, concerts, lectures, and the opera being considered of interest only to the upper classes and the intelligentsia, these agencies have been brought within reach of everyone. Museums, art collections, and historical monuments are arranged or designed to direct the attention of the people to the struggle which terminated in the 1917 Revolution, and to the Communist ideas of an unceasing class struggle and the ultimate classless society. Industrial, agricultural, and antireligious museums have been established to continue the political and economic education of the masses. Trained guides are on duty in these places to explain the exhibits and to give lectures. The theater and moving pictures are used exclusively as weapons in the political-indoctrination program. Clubrooms are provided with libraries and with "Red Centers," which are shrines to Marx and Lenin and their works, and which replace the ever-present ikons of prerevolutionary days. The radio constantly carries to the people the opinions of the leaders of Party and government and builds attitudes which the government wishes all citizens to adopt. In recent years television (with 11-inch screens) has been available in the larger cities to reinforce the message of the radio stations.

The development of evening and correspondence courses by secondary schools and universities has been mentioned. Traveling libraries play an important part in the education of adults. Sets of books are available on loan to clubrooms and union meeting halls, and sets of adult books are lent to small schools for the use of parents. The Moscow State Libraries Institute has provided bookmobiles, which can carry up to 5,000 books. They are divided into three compartments: one has catalogs of books available, the second has a librarian's desk and shelves for books, the third has folding tables and chairs and serves as a reading room. These traveling libraries move from one rural center to another, providing a link between the country people and the facilities of the larger towns.

The part played by the Soviet press in adult education cannot be underestimated. All newspapers and periodicals are filled with material which is intended to further the education of readers. In addition to news stories (and the proportion of news carried in Communist papers is much less than in other countries), the newspapers carry articles on Soviet policy, on the industrial development of the nation and the progress of the Seven-Year Plan, reprints of portions of Russian literature, and original poems and short stories. The anniversary of a great man, politician, scientist, writer, musician, or philosopher, is covered by special articles and reports. Changes in government policies or in the direction of the Party line are fully covered in news stories, so that members of the Party and others may always be fully informed. A certain amount of the material published in any paper also appears in all other papers. Since every article in every publication in the Soviet Union follows without deviation the current Party policy, the total impact on the people is very great. Newspapers have wide circulation and are printed in almost every language. For those who cannot afford to buy a copy of the paper, copies are posted as wall newspapers in prominent places.

The Education and Status of Teachers

EVEN though the economy is planned, the supply of qualified teachers has never quite equaled the demand. The expansion of education and the great increase in the number of teachers needed is illustrated by King's statement that the number of pupils in elementary and secondary education increased from 8 million in 1914 to 32 million in 1940. Soviet educators were determined to get everyone into school; they preferred to use large classes with double and triple shifts and with poorly trained teachers rather than to delay the education of children until teachers and facilities might be available. (The same decision is being made in many of the developing countries of Asia and Africa today.) In Russia various expedients, familiar to education authorities in other countries, were used to meet the emergency. Teachers with varying amounts of training were employed, and short courses were set up to secure a quick supply of partially trained teachers. By 1936 it appeared that the supply of teachers would catch up with the demand, and a decree promulgated that year provided that all untrained teachers would have to pass a qualifying examination by 1938, if they wished to remain in the service. But the imminence of war made it impossible to put this decree into effect, and it was never possible to enforce it.[21]

Because qualified teachers were not available to meet the demand, practically all applicants for teaching positions were employed unless they were considered to be politically unreliable. In 1941, before the outbreak of war, 1,022,085 teachers were employed in the Soviet Union. At the beginning of 1943–44 only 774,795 were available, due to losses to the armed forces and to the German occupation.

Local education authorities appoint the teachers in the preschools and the elementary schools. The Ministries of Education appoint secondary school teachers, and teachers in the specialized secondary

[21] King, op. cit., p. 98.

schools and higher schools are appointed by the Ministries of Higher Education.

Under the former system, teachers for the elementary grades were trained in teachers' institutes. Students were required to hold a certificate from the seventh grade in order to be admitted. The course was three years, and consisted of a general scientific and literary education similar to that of the senior secondary schools with the addition of professional training. Students between the ages of 14 and 25 were admitted, and the course was conducted in the native language. Training schools for observation and practice teaching were attached to each institute. The Department of Education of the region, autonomous republic, province, or city was responsible for the establishment, operation, and support of these institutions, which were supervised by the Ministry of Education. Practically all of these schools have now been closed and replaced by newer teacher education programs.

An intermediate type of teacher-education institution, called the Institute of Teaching, formerly provided for the middle grades of the secondary schools. This type of training program, as well as the teachers' institutes, was considered to be a temporary expedient, since it was planned eventually to train all teachers in pedagogical institutes on the university level. Students entering the Institute of Teaching had completed grade ten and passed an entrance examination. Elementary teachers were trained in teachers' institutes to teach all subjects in the first four grades; the Institutes of Teaching made provision for specialization in subject areas, so that one teacher might handle two or more related subjects. The three most usual combinations were Russian and history; physics and mathematics; and geography combined with biology or chemistry. All students took courses in Marxism-Leninism, psychology, pedagogy, school hygiene, and physical education. Practice teaching was done in grades five to seven in a school attached to the institute. Most of these schools have now been closed or combined with pedagogical institutes.

The teacher education institution in general favor in the Soviet Union today is the pedagogical institute, which offers a four-year course (four years for elementary teachers) based on completion of the tenth grade. These schools are on the university level, and the entrance requirements are the same as for universities. The requirement that 80 percent of the entering students must have had at least two years of labor is enforced, as are provisions for productive labor during the course. The types of entrance examinations an individual is required to take depend upon his teaching subjects. A future teacher of mathematics, physics, astronomy, or fundamentals of production takes entrance examinations in Russian, literature, a foreign language, physics, and mathematics. Those who expect to teach foreign languages take examinations in Russian, literature, a foreign language, and history of the U.S.S.R. In selecting future students the institute gives preference to those with the highest grades in their special subjects.

The course of study for each subject is uniform throughout the country. A secondary teacher is prepared to teach two or three related subjects: Russian language, literature, and history; mathematics and technical drawing; geography and biology; or general subjects and production training. Students are required to master the secondary school course of study in their subjects. They must be thoroughly acquainted with the textbooks used, and be able to do all of the laboratory work and the practical work called for in the curriculum.[22]

Second- and third-year students spend 6 hours weekly in practical teaching; in the fourth year they spend 8 weeks; in the fifth year 12 weeks. After graduation from the pedagogical institute the students take the state examinations. They do not get a degree but a certificate and the title "secondary school teacher." When the emphasis was placed on production training in the schools, the pedagogical institutes began to train many teachers for this program. Teachers of physics and mathematics, for example, were also prepared to handle production training courses in the ten- or eleven-year school, and have the double title of "secondary school teacher and engineer." For rural secondary schools, where the training within the school is for productive labor on the farms, the biology and geography teacher may have the double title of "secondary school teacher–agronomist," or "secondary school teacher–animal husbandryman."

The problem of rural teachers who may not be as well trained as urban teachers in the scientific fields has received attention. Special "Institutes for the Perfectability of Skills" have been set up to handle the retraining of these people. These special institutes are also used to retrain teachers who are not considered efficient. In connection with the new production training courses the Lenin

[22] Fyodor Maximenko, "Becoming a Teacher," USSR *Magazine*, October, 1960.

Pedagogical Institute in Moscow is developing plans to send fifth-year students into country schools for half a year, and to bring the rural teachers replaced into the Institute for one-half year of retraining. Efforts are being intensified to require experienced teachers with less than the five-year pedagogical institute course of training to complete the course through evening and correspondence courses. Authorities estimate that between 10 and 20 percent of the teachers employed are in this group.

Training of teachers in the Soviet Union has two main purposes: first, to make certain that they are politically reliable and loyal to the teachings of the Party; and second, to ensure that they are prepared to illustrate in every way the relationship between general education and the economic life and labor of the country. Lenin has been quoted as saying, "We must raise our teacher to a height such as he had not attained and will never attain in a bourgeois society." Soviet propaganda stresses the fact that without teachers there can be no education; without education the standard of living cannot be raised and the people freed from insecurity and poverty. However, this attempt to raise the prestige of teachers has not yet extended to raising their salaries to a level comparable with other members of the intelligentsia.

Teachers are paid for a basic week of 24 hours, with additional amounts for overtime. They may earn from 85 to 120 rubles a month, although a few get as much as 140 rubles. A teacher in the elementary grades who worked eight hours extra per week was paid 116 rubles. A typical teacher of Russian language, with more than ten years' service, teaching a 24-hour week, is paid 113 rubles, plus 8 rubles for correcting homework, plus 7.5 rubles for responsibility for a home room—a monthly wage of 128.5 rubles. A science teacher may be paid from six to fifteen rubles additional for supervising a laboratory. Teachers who work in remote areas—the far north or far east—may receive an additional 20 to 100 percent above the base pay, depending upon remoteness and hardship. In the Irkutsk region this amounts to 20 percent; in the Murmansk region of the far north it is 50 percent; in the Kuril Islands it is 100 percent.[23]

Like all Soviet citizens, teachers are eligible for old-age pensions at the age of 55 for women and 60 for men. Special pensions are

[23] Ivan Grifkov, "Economic Status of Teachers," USSR Magazine, October, 1960.

paid for extra-long service. Grifkov says that teachers who do not wish to retire after 25 years' service may continue to teach and draw 40 percent of the pension, and the full teaching wage besides. When they retire, they get the full pension.[24]

The real income of the teacher is increased by social service grants provided to all Soviet citizens—social insurance payments, grants to widowed mothers, grants to mothers with many children, stipends to university students, free medical and dental care and free higher education. The administration of the social insurance fund was turned over to the trade unions in 1940. The Union of Educational Workers enrolls about 98 percent of the nation's teachers. From this fund are provided sick benefits, old-age and disability pensions, allowances to widows, pensions for those who continue working until they are eligible for full retirement, maternity allowances, summer camps and rest homes, and children's sanitoriums. During two summer months the teachers are on vacation with pay, and may spend much of this time at tourist resorts maintained by the union. Union officials say that members get certain advantages over nonmembers: they get better apartments and additions to the half-pay the government allows for sick leaves.

Teachers who work in the villages (these are almost invariably on collective or state farms) get their houses rent free, with free utilities and heat. Rent charges for city and town teachers (which are uniform throughout the Soviet Union) are based on square meters of living space, not counting kitchens and bathrooms, which are used in common by several families. Soviet teachers estimate that rent and utilities amount to about 8 percent of their monthly budget.

The Work of Communist Party Organizations

UNDER a system of government controlled by a single dominant political party, every aspect of the life of the people has been controlled and directed by Party ideas. The educational system has been found to be the most effective means for developing the kind of political, economic, and social ideas and attitudes that the Party leaders consider to be essential. Education has been devoted to the task of political education, and everything about the school has been permeated with Communist ideology. According to Kandel:

[24] Grifkov, *op. cit.*

At whatever point the vast educational structure of the Soviet state is touched, it is obvious that it is dominated by political activity. Education, according to Communist theory, has no meaning except in the social order in which it takes its being; education cannot be autonomous. . . . Education must be synonymous with indoctrination and propaganda in all its stages and in all its processes, even though instruction must follow the psychological characteristics of the individual. All members of the Communist society must be "conditioned" by education and their environment into an acceptance of the dominant doctrines.[25]

The school system, reinforced by all the informal influences of mass communication and the mobilized forces of the nation, can be expected to educate the masses to be the type of docile citizens the Communists desire. No source of information is ever available except through official channels; no chance is ever given to hear the "other side" of.any question. There is no tradition of political parties contesting for the votes of the people and presenting different arguments and issues. From infancy the Soviet citizen is trained to accept the opinions and orders of the leaders of state and Party as wise. Undoubtedly there is disagreement, but it is almost impossible to criticize official policy in any effective way. There is, however, a good deal of criticism, in Party meetings and in letters to the editor, of the way in which individuals may be administering a policy that has been adopted. This type of criticism seems to be encouraged.

The Communists believe, then, that the mass of the population can be trained and conditioned in the schools and through other media of propaganda. But they realize that it is necessary to develop outstanding leaders who will be intensely loyal to Party doctrines, and also that a training course for new Party members must be provided. As we have pointed out, membership in the Party is a coveted privilege that is granted only to a small minority, at the end of a long and arduous apprenticeship. To reinforce the public schools, and to perform the dual function of preparing leaders and new Party members, the Communists have organized a complex system of youth organizations parallel with the schools and within them. There is no possible difference between the policies of leadership in the schools and in the Communist Youth organizations, for both are directed by the same leaders at the top of the Party hierarchy, and for the same purposes.

[25] Kandel, *op. cit.*, p. 185.

The Young Pioneers were organized in 1922 to take over what was left of the Boy Scout movement in Russia, and were composed of both boys and girls between the ages of 10 and 16. It has been said that this organization has had greater effect on the children of Russia than any other force. In 1923 the Little Octobrists were organized, a loose and informal organization of children in the primary grades. One may become an Octobrist by behaving properly and studying well. There are no particular tasks or rules. Many of these children wear little red stars on their school uniforms.

The Young Pioneers are more highly organized. A child at the age of 10 asks to be admitted. He must be passed upon by the Pioneer group in his class, then by the school council. The initiation ceremony is a solemn affair, where the applicants make a "solemn promise" and line up to kiss the red flag. They are then entitled to wear the triangular red scarf. The organization publishes a newspaper, *Pioneerskaya Pravda*, which has wide circulation and which "hotly suppresses any other type of children's organizations in the schools." [26] Each school may have a Pioneer room, decorated with red cloth and with pictures of Soviet heroes. Until the eighth grade the red scarf is seen on almost every child; above that grade it disappears, for the pupils are now old enough to become Komsomols. Adult leaders, who are usually trained as teachers, are paid on the same basis as teachers. Pioneers serve as leaders of the Little Octobrists.

For young people between the ages of 15 and 23, the Leninist Communist League of Youth, usually called the Komsomols, was organized. The age levels of the three youth groups overlap, thus permitting membership in two of the programs at the same time, and helping to keep all three integrated into one great youth program. At every level Party officials in the local community keep the groups under supervision and provide leadership.

It is considered to be a more serious step to join the Komsomols than to join the earlier groups. The Komsomols are still a mass organization but their organization does not include as high a proportion of the age group as do the Pioneers. Candidates must be recommended by two Komsomol members or by a Party member. The organization is modeled after that of the Communist Party. There are organizations in schools, offices, farms, and factories. At the dis-

[26] Ashby, *op. cit.*, p. 59.

trict and republic levels there are central committees like those in the Party. Each unit has a secretary, who is the powerful officer in Party organization. There is a National Congress of the Komsomol, which elects a central committee and a secretary. On the higher levels the secretaryship is a full-time job, and must be filled by a Party member. Office holders may remain in the organization until age 26.

The Komsomols publish a newspaper, *Komsomolskaya Pravda*, which was founded in 1925. They run special schools, giving "activists" a special one-year course in Party theory. Like the Party, they are organized into cells and committees on farms and in factories and schools. They serve not only as a novitiate and recruiting ground for Party membership, but also as a transmission line that connects the Party apparatus with the masses of youth. They have conducted vigorous purges of their membership, like the Party, to eliminate those who are not enthusiastic about the program or who cannot be happy under its rigorous discipline. They are taught to stand for high ideals of public and private morality, in the Soviet interpretation of the words.

Leaders of Pioneer groups are chosen from the Komsomols, and they have great influence among the children. The Pioneers develop local projects, such as cutting firewood for the schools, and cleaning, repairing and decorating classrooms, helping local authorities register the 7-year-olds for entrance into school, and exerting a strong influence on classroom discipline and regular school attendance. A large proportion of the children go to Pioneer camps each summer.

In earlier years the activities of the Komsomols seemed to interfere with regular school life and procedures, since they attempted to influence, through local committees, the selection of teachers and to check on their political responsibility. They also organized meetings to discuss new policies, such as the elimination of coeducation from the schools. The teachers' unions objected to some of these activities, and in 1944 the general secretary of the Komsomols, Mikhailov, warned that they must not interfere with teachers, or criticize them in Komsomol meetings, or conduct independent investigations of the educational activities of the schools. "This would create a violation of the unity of authority within the school, and would interfere with the strengthening of discipline." Mikhailov also stated that "mass political and cultural work outside of school hours, and physical-education and military-training programs in the school day were to be considered legitimate activities of the Komsomols." [27]

Membership statistics are difficult to obtain, and are usually approximations. It can be assumed that most of the children in the younger grades belong to the Octobrists. It is claimed that 98 percent of the children between 10 and 15 are Pioneers. Membership in these organizations is voluntary, but with such a high proportion of members it is difficult for the boy or girl who chooses to remain outside, or who is rejected for membership. The Komsomols reported 4 million members in 1936; this increased to 9 million in 1939 and to 15 million in 1945. Purges and tightening of membership requirements reduced the total to an announced 10 million in 1951. Recent news stories have claimed a membership of 20 million in 1962.

Problems and Achievements of Soviet Education

THE SOVIET educational system is not without its problems. There has been a shortage of adequately trained teachers, but recent reports indicate that this is being solved. Ashby noted that during the war, when many of the teachers were in military service, about half of the teachers in the seven-year schools, and about 15 percent of the elementary teachers were inadequately trained.[28] The aim now is to have all secondary teachers trained in five-year pedagogical institutes or universities, and all elementary teachers trained in four-year courses.

CLASS STRATIFICATION

The development of new favored classes of children of administrators, Party leaders, intelligentsia, and higher technicians, with advantages in securing entrance to higher schools, before 1958 was tending to develop a stratification which seriously affected the concept of the classless society. The 1958 Reform was intended to correct this development, in part, as well as to increase the work force during a difficult period caused by manpower shortages in the age levels born during war years. Certainly the Communist elite today have advantages that are comparable to those of the upper classes under the czars. The system is marked by wide differences in income levels, based in part on educational attainments. A new hierarchy

[27] Ashby, *op. cit.*, p. 61.
[28] Ashby, *op. cit.*, p. 58.

has arisen in the Soviet Union, and this has had its effect on educational philosophy and practice.

FORMALISM IN TEACHING

Western visitors are always impressed by the extreme rigidity and formalism in teaching practices in Soviet schools. The courses of study are so crammed with requirements that the teachers have to fall back on formalism and rote teaching. Russian educators have from time to time criticized formalism as an evil. Potemkin, an early Commissar of Education, stated: "Its basic symptoms are a purely mechanical assimilation of what is being taught, the learning of words and phrases or formulas which have no concrete meaning; the absence of any link between what is taught and life." [29]

Similar criticism was voiced by Khrushchev in his famous 1958 speech. The eleven-year school was an attempt to strengthen the ties between school and life; between general education and labor; but it does not appear to have decreased the load of subject matter to be mastered or the extreme formalism of teaching procedures. Ashby said:

> The biology syllabus . . . could be interpreted to cover more than first-year university work in Botany and Zoology, beside a good deal of human physiology and genetics. Such a syllabus as this, taught together with no less than ten other subjects, could not be covered except in a slovenly way. It seems as though the Russian education authorities have provided too much of an intellectual feast in their school curriculum; and have accordingly produced in their schools symptoms of mental indigestion.[30]

Much of the research work reported by the Academy of Pedagogical Science and in the pedagogical institutes is concerned with the generalization of successful classroom methods and procedures. If these studies have had any effect upon what is actually being done in the everyday classrooms of the U.S.S.R., they are not apparent to Western observers.

AUTHORITARIANISM IN EDUCATION

Related to the criticisms of formalism is the problem of authoritarianism in education. Much has been written about the way Soviet

[29] Ashby, *op. cit.*, p. 57.
[30] Ashby, *op. cit.*, p. 58.

scientists are circumscribed by the prevailing Party line. The vagaries of Party doctrine have been well illustrated by the Michurin-Lysenko controversy over genetics. Biological research has not been free to search for truth in any direction and wherever it may lead, but has had to conform to orthodox theories. Research in physical sciences seems to be less trammeled, because it is relatively free from political implications. Eugene Varga, Director of the Institute of Economics in Moscow, was disciplined because in a scholarly article he drew conclusions which were not in accord with Party theories, although they may have conformed to facts. Artists, composers, poets, and writers have been forced to make their creative work conform to Marxist-Leninist theories of life and culture. The political influence of the Communist Party stifles free and independent thinking in any academic field. General education everywhere is subordinated to the vocational ideal; the task of preparing specialists for particular jobs comes first. Whether there can be productive scholarship and research or real cultural achievements (except perhaps in the physical sciences) under the heavy hand of the Party is still to be demonstrated.

THE RISING EDUCATIONAL LEVEL

Each year more and more Soviet citizens are being educated to higher levels. Observers sometimes question whether people can really be educated to high levels and still fail to try to think for themselves. The question arises whether the Communists, in raising educational standards for the mass of the people, may not risk developing citizens who may form their own opinions rather than accept unquestioningly the predigested concepts of the Party line.

In any event, the real achievements of Soviet education cannot be discounted. If we consider the aims of education in a Communist society, the schools have been doing what the leaders want done. They have successfully indoctrinated the masses in the theories of Communist society, and have produced technically competent people to carry forward the economic development of the nation. The elimination of illiteracy in forty years in a far-flung empire with dozens of nationality groups has been a tremendous achievement. Although the system of preschools is not yet extensive enough to reach all of the 3-year-olds to 6-year-olds, it has been carefully planned, and has attracted favorable comment from foreign observers. The Communist minority has used the school system to develop a loyalty to the state, and from their point of view, these efforts have been successful. Evidence obtained from refugees from behind the Iron Curtain and from other sources, however, seems to indicate that acceptance of the system is not universal, and a certain amount of skepticism may be justified in any evaluation of the Communist program of indoctrination.

17

West German Schools in Action

EDUCATION in Germany has a long history and traditions that are deeply ingrained. Various periods of government have seen differences of approach and control, as explained in Chapter 9, but except for the interruption of the Nazi period there has been a continuous philosophy of education discernible. Although educational organization is complex and diversified, there has always been some underlying uniformity.

Since German schools are the responsibility of the *Länder*, or state governments, there are various systems in operation. Some conformity of practice, however, has been achieved through the work of the voluntary Conference of State Ministers of Education. All states have laws requiring a pupil to attend for at least eight years; this requirement is nine years in Bremen, Hamburg, Schleswig-Holstein, and West Berlin. Children begin school at the age of 6; if they are permitted to wait until age 7 to enter, they must still fulfill the number of years required by the compulsory attendance legislation. In all states children who leave the full-time school after eight or nine years must continue in a part-time vocational school until they reach the age of 18, or until they have completed an apprenticeship.

The general education schools, elementary, intermediate, and secondary, operate on the "long morning" basis, from 8:30 A.M. to 1:30 P.M. There is some variation of hours among the states and among the different types of school, but most German children attend school six mornings a week and have their afternoons free. Suggestions that the schools remain open one or two afternoons a

17-1 Postwar West German Schools

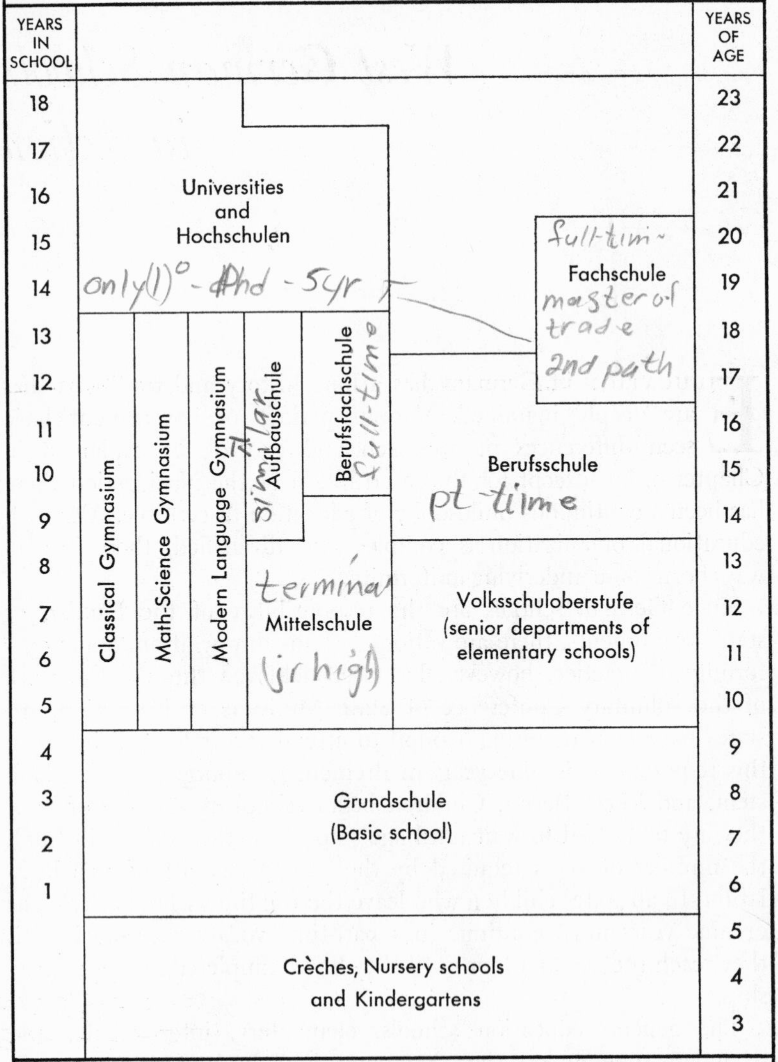
YEARS IN SCHOOL
YEARS OF AGE
18 17 16 15 14 13 12 11 10 9 8 7 6 5 4 3 2 1
23 22 21 20 19 18 17 16 15 14 13 12 11 10 9 8 7 6 5 4 3
Universities and Hochschulen
Fachschule
Classical Gymnasium
Math-Science Gymnasium
Modern Language Gymnasium
Aufbauschule
Berufsfachschule
Berufsschule
Mittelschule
Volksschuloberstufe (senior departments of elementary schools)
Grundschule (Basic school)
Crèches, Nursery schools and Kindergartens

Note: This is a generalized diagram. No attempt is made to show every type of specialized school. There are variations between the states. Teachers are educated in *Hochschulen*.

week and take all day Saturday off have not been favorably received by parents, pupils, or teachers. All of the states except Bavaria open the school year in the spring, although the long vacations come in the summer.

In general the elementary schools are coeducational, and the classical secondary schools are segregated by sex. Other types of schools vary in this regard. It has been said that coeducation is more a matter of expediency than of principle in Germany. The organization of schools in the West German Republic is shown in Figure 17–1.

Preschool Education

SOME of the states have established kindergartens for 6-year-olds who are considered too immature for the first grade. Attendance is not compulsory, and only in West Berlin is it considered a part of the regular school system, and even here all children do not attend. One type of kindergarten, for children of working mothers, provides for 3- to 6-year-olds. These kindergartens are not connected with the elementary schools and may be established by the industrial concern that employs the mothers, by labor or religious groups, or by the local community. In 1955 there were only 176,048 children under the age of 6 in any type of school in West Germany, but there were 673,970 children aged 6.[1] Enrollment statistics are shown in Table 17–1.

Elementary Education

IN ALL of the states the elementary school (*Volksschule*) covers the first eight or nine grades, depending upon the compulsory education law of the state concerned. The first four grades are usually called the basic school (*Grundschule*). In the city states of Bremen, Hamburg, and West Berlin the basic school includes the first six grades. Above the basic school is the upper level (*Volksschuleoberstufe*), which may be three or four years depending upon the state. In the city states this is called the practical branch of the upper school.[2] The successful completion of the basic school is required for entrance into intermediate or secondary schools, which may come at the end of the fourth or sixth grade. The vast majority of German

[1] UNESCO, *World Survey of Education*, Vol. 1, 1955, p. 303.
[2] *Education in Germany*, 1954, p. 14.

TABLE 17–1

Enrollment Statistics in West German Schools, 1959

TYPE OF SCHOOL	NUMBER OF PUPILS	NUMBER OF SCHOOLS
Elementary schools	4,914,000	31,412
Intermediate schools	317,000	911
Secondary schools	784,000	1,647
Schools with special character and schools in West Berlin	469,000	956
Vocational schools	2,145,000	6,301
Totals	8,629,000	41,227

SOURCE: Helmut Arntz, *Facts About Germany*, Wiesbaden: Press and Information Office, German Federal Republic, 1962, p. 273. The same source gives the total number of teachers as 247,000.

children fulfill the compulsory attendance requirement in the *Volksschule*. About 80 percent of them complete their education in this school, which is supposed to be the equivalent of the early years in intermediate and secondary schools.

No fees are charged for the period of compulsory attendance, and the moderate fees charged in some secondary schools are rapidly being eliminated. In one state, Hesse, even the higher institutions are free. A policy of providing free textbooks and school supplies has been generally adopted but has not been universally implemented because of a shortage of funds. The Weimar Republic had provided grants-in-aid to children from poor families; present state constitutions provide for these, but they are not frequently awarded. Some additional grants-in-aid have been made available for children from refugee families.

Some states permit children to remain in the elementary school after completion of the compulsory period, if they have not completed the course. This also applies to some older pupils who find it difficult to find employment or to get placed in an apprenticeship.

Efforts are being made to improve the quality of rural education. Consolidation of schools has been encouraged, and an attempt has been made to provide continuation schools for rural youth who live too far from town and city schools. Figures published in 1952 indicated that 46.6 percent of all elementary schools in West Germany had only one or two classrooms; and that 14.9 percent of the elementary pupils were in these schools.[3]

One of the agreements reached by the Ministers of Education provided for the elective study of one foreign language in the elementary schools. The city states provide for the compulsory study of a foreign language beginning with the fifth grade. On the upper level one foreign language is generally required.

Secondary Education

GERMAN usage defines a "secondary school" as one that provides a course leading to the Certificate of Maturity (usually at the end of the thirteenth grade), which entitles its holder to admission to an institution of higher learning. Also included as secondary schools are some schools which are specialized but do not provide unqualified admission to universities. Under this definition the intermediate schools could not be considered secondary, but for the purposes of this discussion they are so classified.

It is characteristic of German secondary education that a subject introduced at any grade level is never dropped, but is continued to the end of the course and considered a possible subject for the final comprehensive examination. There is no promotion by single subjects; a student who fails in two or more subjects will repeat the work of the entire grade, even in those courses in which he passed. Except in the final years, there are no electives; all students take all of the subjects in the courses they are following.

INTERMEDIATE SCHOOLS ("MITTELSCHULEN")

In most of the states entrance to the intermediate school comes at the end of the fourth grade; in the city states, at the end of the sixth grade. The school continues to the end of the tenth grade. It is a terminal type of school program, with a character of its own, and is not intended to prepare for the upper levels of the secondary schools. Except for its terminal character, the intermediate school has some similarities to an American junior high school, but it is probably closer to the English modern school, which is terminal for most of its pupils. The intermediate school prepares pupils for medium-level positions in business, technology, or the government services. In the city states it is called the practical or technical branch of

[3] *Ibid.*, p. 31.

the upper school (*Oberschule*). In a few of the states transfer to a secondary school is possible.

THE "EINHEITSSCHULE"

The unified school system (*Einheitsschule*) has been widely discussed by German educational leaders, and can be compared with the idea of the *école unique* in France. The city states of Bremen, Hamburg, and West Berlin have introduced this type of organization, which is based on a common six-grade elementary school for all pupils, and a differentiated upper level. In these schools children of the same age are kept together as much as possible, in common activities. Some of the problems of "parity of esteem" are alleviated by teaching all students in the same buildings. The vocational schools in Bremen and West Berlin are entirely separate from the unified schools, but in Hamburg they are included in the same system.

This type of organization facilitates transfer from one upper-school course to another. The innovation represented by the *Einheitsschulen* is more one of organization than of subject matter. Conservative educators tend to criticize it as tending to lower subject matter standards in the classical disciplines. The experiment has suffered from being involved in partisan politics, since one party favors it and another opposes it, regardless of its virtues or faults. The further development of this plan will be interesting to watch.

Academic Secondary Schools

THE TRADITIONAL secondary school in Germany has been the classical (ancient language) *Gymnasium*. Modifications in curriculum have usually been achieved by establishing a new type of school, not by changing the classical school. Germany, like other European countries, has believed strongly in a long period of secondary education, extending over seven to nine years, and more modern types of secondary schools have tended to follow this pattern.

Admission to a secondary school has always been a selective process, formerly based entirely on an entrance examination conducted by the school the student wished to enter. In recent years much attention has been given to improving the selection procedures. Objective tests, intelligence test results, school records, and recommendations of principals have all been used. In many cases a one- or two-week trial period has been set up, where the children are observed in action. Sometimes the first year is considered to be a probationary period.

Today there are three types of secondary school called *Gymnasien:* the classical school, the modern language school, and the mathematics-science school. The classical *Gymnasium* is still considered to be the high-prestige school, like the English grammar school. Until late in the nineteenth century it was the only path leading to the university. Accurate knowledge of factual material and mental discipline were stressed, as objectives which could be measured, and subjects were esteemed for their disciplinary value. Much concern was devoted to the integration of knowledge. Today the classical *Gymnasium* offers a rigorous course of studies, based on Latin and Greek, but the curriculum now also includes German, history, mathematics, one modern language, physical education, and some science. At the end of the course students take a comprehensive examination over all work they have done, to determine if they are ready for work at the university level. In this century the number of schools of this type has been decreasing, as other types of secondary schools have been developed.

The most popular type of secondary school in Germany today is the modern language *Gymnasium,* which emphasizes the study of two modern languages and Latin. This school offers more science and mathematics than the classical *Gymnasium,* with which it favorably competes.

A third type of *Gymnasium* places special stress on science and mathematics, and offers two modern languages. This school is more numerous than the classical type, but the modern-language schools exceed the enrollments of the mathematics-natural science *Gymnasien* by one-third. As the technological development of the country continues, however, the mathematics-science *Gymnasien* may become more important than they now are.

There are several forms of a special secondary school called the *Aufbauschule,* which means "build-up school." This school provides opportunities for the secondary education of children who develop late and who may be admitted at the end of the sixth instead of the fourth grade. After World War II it became popular among rural children, who were thus able to start a secondary course at a later age than their somewhat more privileged urban contemporaries. This type of school usually offers a seven-year course, somewhat similar to that of the modern-language *Gymnasium,* with English as the first foreign language. Since 1950 Bavaria has developed *Aufbauschulen* which represent all types of the nine-year secondary schools: ancient language, modern language, or science-mathematics. There are not many of these schools in the country, but they are popular and their number is increasing.

SPECIAL SECONDARY SCHOOLS

The *Frauenschule* (girls' high school) covers grades eleven to thirteen, which follow a ten-year course in an advanced girls' school (*Lyzeum*). Courses in domestic sciences predominate, but these are combined with academic, artistic, and some scientific courses. Graduates of this school may enter institutions for training elementary teachers, but their certificates of maturity do not admit them to the university.

The *Wirtschaftoberschule* (economics high school) also offers a three-year program, grades eleven to thirteen. It admits pupils from the secondary and intermediate schools at the completion of the tenth grade. These schools are comparatively new and are not always recognized as secondary schools. They offer a general course with emphasis on business subjects and economics. Their graduates may enter university-level schools of business administration or economics departments in the universities.

Vocational Education

ABOUT 80 percent of German children, after having met the legal requirements for full-time attendance (eight or nine years), take up an apprenticeship or go into full-time employment. However, under the law they must attend a part-time vocational school until age 18. About five percent of these pupils continue in full-time vocational schools. The remainder are supposed to be in continuation schools called *Berufsschulen*. These have been developed from continuation schools which started as early as 1870 in Munich, under der Georg Kerschensteiner. Germany made part-time continuation schools compulsory for young workers and apprentices in the Weimar constitution of 1919 and was the first nation to do so. It has not been possible to make enforcement universal, particularly in the rural districts, and sometimes not for girls.

Berufsschulen are intended to provide fundamental theoretical information and some practical work in skills required for a trade or occupation, combined with a continuation of general education. There are part-time vocational schools in such fields as agriculture, domestic science, and trades and industries. No entrance examinations are required.

The full-time vocational schools (*Berufsfachschulen*) may be one-, two-, or three-year schools. Completion of one of these courses fulfills the requirement of compulsory attendance. *Berufsfachschulen* may be organized by the community, by an industrial organization, or by a private person. Most of them require the completion of the elementary school or intermediate school for entrance. There are many more than twice as many girls' schools as boys' schools of this type. They prepare the students to take the journeyman's examination in a trade.

The *Fachschulen* are advanced vocational schools, operated on a full-time basis. Courses of varying length up to four years are offered. They are open to students who have completed their apprenticeship, and lead to an examination for a "master of trade" certificate. These schools are intended for students who are beyond the compulsory education age, but they do not rank as university-level institutions. Students who have earned high grades may be admitted to some university faculties. This is the so-called "second path" to university entrance.

University Education

INSTITUTIONS of higher learning in Germany are called *Hochschulen* (higher schools). These include the traditional universities, as well as a variety of institutes of technology, academies of mining, institutes of business and finance, and other professional schools. The *Hochschulen* are almost all supported by public funds, and the professors have civil-service status and old-age pensions. The universities are interested in specialized higher learning and research and leave applied sciences and professional training to the higher institutes. Measured by American standards, the German *Hochschulen* are comparable to graduate schools. The requirement for admission is uniform in all of them, the certificate of maturity or its equivalent.

German universities give only one degree, the doctorate, after a five-year course. In certain fields diplomas are granted, some of them at the end of four years. The doctor's degree demands a thesis and a comprehensive examination. There are also comprehensive written or oral examinations for diplomas, and often a thesis. Diplomas or degrees, although they may be prerequisites for certain types of positions, do not entitle the holder to such careers. Most upper-level positions depend upon passing a state examination; there are examinations for doctors, lawyers, administrators, teachers, and others. Only in the case of university professors is the doctor's degree indispensable.

Those who plan to be secondary teachers usually do not take the final examinations at the university but prepare for the state examination. In some cases secondary teachers eventually take the doctorate too. Some individuals may pass one of these examinations and fail in the other.

Although the German universities might be called state universities in the American sense of that term, they enjoy almost complete freedom and autonomy. Financial support from the government, aside from a minimum amount of supervision in financial matters, does not mean interference in internal affairs. The academic freedom of professors in matters of teaching and research is complete.

This is matched by an almost equivalent freedom of learning on the part of the students. German students plan their programs and decide when, how, and where they will prepare themselves for the examinations leading to degrees or diplomas in their chosen fields. They may choose to attend or not to attend lectures outside of their fields. They may choose to take or not to take the examinations at the end of each course. Students who apply for scholarships or grants-in-aid customarily take the course examinations, to show that they are proceeding normally and that the standard of their work merits aid. To sit for the state examinations, students usually are required to show that they have attended courses for at least eight semesters or four years. Each student has a *Studiumbuch*, in which registration, attendance, and seminar papers are recorded. Registration is necessary each term, because students may wander from university to university, in order to choose the professors under whom they wish to work. It is common for students to spend two years at each of two universities; others may attend an even greater number of schools. Statistics on enrollment by faculties is shown in Table 17–2.

Academic standards are high, particularly with regard to knowledge of the factual, encyclopedic type. Courses provide outlines of

TABLE 17-2

Enrollment in Higher Education, West Germany and West Berlin, 1960–61

FACULTY	TOTAL NUMBER OF STUDENTS	NUMBER OF FOREIGN STUDENTS
Theology	7,330	408
Medicine, dentistry, pharmacy, veterinary science	35,436	6,292
Law and economics	44,735	1,762
Cultural studies	49,882	2,590
Sciences	31,528	2,120
Agriculture, forestry	2,743	627
Technical studies	40,346	5,944
Totals	212,020	19,743

SOURCE: Helmut Arntz, *Facts About Germany*, p. 292.

the subject in its entirety—the study of English literature begins with *Beowulf* and extends to contemporary writers; there are lengthy reading lists instead of prescribed textbooks. Lectures deal with factual data in an omnibus fashion and are usually circulated afterwards in typewritten scripts which are available for purchase. In some faculties a system of *Repetituren* is common: enterprising tutors obtain copies of reading lists and lectures and hold cramming sessions with small groups for moderate fees. It has been said that standards are set by these "crammed" groups.

Since students may or may not attend lectures as they please or may attend lectures in faculties other than their own, freedom creates problems for the lazy student, and for the student with a wide range of interests who neglects preparation in his own field. There is a low faculty-student ratio—only one professor to each 54 students. Lectures may be crowded by 500 students or more, and seminars, which should provide opportunities for individual work, may enroll as many as 100 students. There is little counseling, and professors have very little time for each student.

Fees are generally low, and each course is paid for pro rata. Most students attend 20 to 30 lectures a week, depending upon their economic status. Less than 10 percent of the students may hope to secure scholarship aid. There are very few university dormitories;

most students seek lodgings in the town. Student activities have become more numerous since the war—film societies, international clubs, ski clubs, and the like. German men have always congregated in fraternal groups with others of the same tastes. Interest in the old prewar dueling and drinking fraternities died down after the war, but there has been an enthusiastic revival in recent years. Women students are largely unorganized and enjoy much less social life than do the men.

It is a long and arduous path that leads to appointment as a university professor. The applicant must first pass his doctoral examination with high standing. Then he continues to work at a university for from two to five years, during which time he must publish several scholarly articles and prepare a more mature thesis than the one submitted for his doctorate. If this thesis is approved, he is subject to a rigorous examination before the entire university faculty in his field. He then has to prepare and deliver several lectures to the satisfaction of this faculty. If he passes all of this, his "habilitation" is announced, and he is qualified to teach at his own institution or any other that might call him. He gets the status of *"privat-docent,"* which means that he may lecture in his field but is compensated by the fees paid by his students and not by a set salary. He may have to wait many years before he is called, if at all, as a professor (there are several ranks of professors) and enters the civil service at a regular salary. It is evident that few individuals have the financial resources to support themselves through this long period.

When a vacancy occurs in a professorial position, the faculty and senate nominate three qualified candidates to the Ministry of Education, which makes the appointment. The Ministry may not appoint professors without faculty endorsement, but they may reject nominations made to them.

The Education and Status of Teachers

ONE OF the agreements reached by the Conference of Ministers of Education was to raise the status of elementary teacher training institutions to university level in all states. Elementary teachers are trained in special institutions that have different names, such as Pedagogical Institute, in the different states. In Hamburg the pedagogical institute is closely related to the university. The four-year

curriculum covers a thorough training in the subject matter taught
in the elementary school, plus work in educational psychology, methods of teaching, observation in the schools and student teaching
experiences. Most of these institutions are coeducational although
there are some separate schools for men and for women. Some training institutions are for Catholics and some for Protestants, but most
are interconfessional.

About two-thirds of German teachers are men. Boys' schools are
usually staffed by men teachers, although men are often employed
in girls' schools. The principals of girls' schools are usually women.

At the end of his training-college course the student takes a state
examination, and is then assigned to a school where he teaches full
time on a probationary basis. During his probationary period he is
under special supervision, and carries on in-service training under the
direction of his superintendent (Schulrat). At the end of two or
three years (depending upon the state) he takes a second examination. This includes the submission of a thesis on some phase of
educational practice, a report on his experiences during the in-service
period, and the teaching of two trial lessons. One of these may be
chosen by the candidate, the other is selected by the examiners. Following this is an oral examination which covers the thesis, the report,
the trial lessons, and the practical aspects of teaching. If he passes
this second test, he is given a certificate of qualification and is eligible
for permanent appointment in the state service.

Teachers in intermediate schools may be regularly certificated elementary school teachers, or university-trained teachers with preparation in school subjects and education who take a special examination to qualify them for this level of teaching. Since the education of elementary teachers has been raised to university level there
is a tendency in some states to permit elementary teachers who have
passed the second state examination to teach in intermediate schools.

Secondary school teachers must spend at least eight semesters at
a university before they take the first state examination. In some
subjects, such as science or mathematics, these eight semesters may
be spent in an institute of technology. The first examination covers
the subject matter which the student proposes to teach in a secondary school. In some universities, but not all, these students have also
had some education courses and observation of teaching.

The first examination covers the submission of a thesis in the
teaching field, and a written and oral examination. Having passed

this, the student becomes a *Studienreferendar* and is assigned to a secondary school as a teacher. The second year he is assigned to another school. For the duration of the two-year period he is on probation and attends weekly seminar sessions to discuss problems of practical teaching. At the end of this period he must submit another thesis and pass another examination on educational theory and practice. He teaches two demonstration lessons before the examining committee. If he passes this examination he becomes a *Studien-assessor*, and is eligible for a permanent position in a secondary school.

Departments of education in German universities are mainly interested in the history and philosophy of education, and the close relationships between teacher-education institutions and public schools, which are characteristic of the United States, have not been developed yet. University professors are not interested in helping to solve the everyday problems of the schools. Since the increase in status of the elementary teacher-training institutions, the professors in these schools are now beginning to show more interest in the problems of the schools.[4]

Salary and promotion schedules for teachers are established by the state, and are uniform state-wide. Usually the basic salary schedule applies to single teachers, with allowances for dependents, as in France. Permanent teachers, with civil service status, may be transferred from one position to another by the state authorities. Appointment to permanent positions is made by the Ministry. Salary schedules compare with those in effect in England, although they may vary from state to state. There are separate schedules for elementary and secondary teachers. Anthony Kerr says that German teachers are relatively better off than English teachers because of relatively lower living costs.[5]

Suggestions for Reorganization

THE "RAHMENPLAN"

In 1953 the Federal Ministry of the Interior and the Conference of Ministers of Education appointed a committee to study the development of the German school system as a whole. An example of cooperation between the federal government and the state minis-

[4] *Ibid.*, p. 68.
[5] Anthony Kerr, *Schools of Europe*, p. 80.

tries, carried out by an appointed group of citizens, the committee consisted of seven professors, five heads of training institutions, four administrators, two theologians, and one radio executive. Its aim was to explore the possibility of unifying the many diverse patterns of school organization and practices among the 11 *Länder*. It attempted to find a solution to the problem of meeting the needs of an advancing technological society while at the same time preserving cultural traditions.[6] In 1959 the committee's report appeared, offering the outlines for a generally new system of public education below the university level but excluding vocational education. This has been called the *Rahmenplan* (master plan).

The plan is not revolutionary, but it has suggested some administrative and organizational changes, devoting most of its attention to the upper elementary and secondary levels. The committee recognized the increasing pressure of parents who are ambitious to see their children admitted to secondary education. Helmut Schelsky, a sociologist, recognized that the school today is "the primary, decisive, and almost exclusive distributor of chances for future rank, position, and living standards." [7]

The report leaves the first four years of the *Grundschule* unchanged, but the next two, the fifth and sixth grades, are proposed as a differentiating stage (*Forderstufe*), suggestive of the French *cycle d'orientation*. This would keep all fifth- and sixth-grade pupils together in most subjects but make some elective work available for brighter pupils. The two years would be a diagnostic or "try-out" period to determine the course of future education, which would still be on a tripartite system of organization.

The main school (*Hauptschule*) would run from the seventh to the ninth or tenth year, and would provide for about 60 percent of the children a terminal course like the English secondary modern school. The upper level of the former elementary school would thus be replaced.

After the *Forderstufe* about 20 percent of the children would enter the *Realschule* for the seventh to tenth or eleventh grade. This would provide terminal education for the children who plan to go into lower-grade white collar occupations in business and industry. At the present time many of these children take a few years of

[6] Ursula Kirkpatrick, "The *Rahmenplan* for West German School Reform," *Comparative Education Review*, Vol. 4, No. 1 (June, 1960), p. 18.

[7] Helmut Schelsky, *Schule und Erziehung in der Industriellen Gesellschaft*, Werkbund-Verlag Wurzburg, 1959, p. 18.

schooling in the *Gymnasium*, because of its prestige, but do not intend to complete the course.

The *Gymnasium*, including the seventh through the thirteenth grades, would take about 20 percent of those who complete the *Forderstufe*. This school would retain its classical character but provide opportunities for students to specialize either in language or science. It would be expected that most of the students complete the thirteenth grade and obtain the *Abitur*, which would admit them to a university. However, some students might leave at the end of the eleventh grade and take an examination for an intermediate certificate, the *Mittlere Reife*. The last two years of the *Gymnasium* would offer some electives and directly prepare students for university courses.

In addition to these types of schools, which would provide for the education of 95 percent or more of all pupils, the plan proposes another type of school, the *Studienschule*, for exceptionally gifted children. These pupils would not attend the *Forderstufe* but would be separated at the end of the fourth grade and start a program including the fifth through the thirteenth grades. This would be a highly classical, humanistic school like the older *Gymnasium*, with emphasis on Latin, Greek, and French. It would prepare able students for university work.

As of 1964, the plan has not been adopted in any of the states, although Lower Saxony has experimented for several years with a plan something like the *Forderstufe*. The *Rahmenplan* has been bitterly attacked by many critics, particularly the secondary school teachers and the professions, who fear the lowering of academic standards, and probably also fear encroachment on their vested interests in subject areas. Groups and organizations who might be expected to be in favor of the plan have been less vocal in their expression of opinions.

Since the Occupation, West German education has shown a great deal of vitality and activity. Although the completely democratic organization which the occupation powers hoped for has not been attained, still the decentralized control within the states has allowed for diversity while attaining a certain amount of conformity in practices. German educators are still trying to find an organizational plan that will conserve the traditional cultural influences of the historical German school system and yet be adaptable to a technological civilization.

Part IV

Educational Developments in Some Asian Countries

Introductory Note

Education seems to be on the march all over the world. There are plans for reorganization and modernization in many countries. New concepts of secondary education raise questions in the minds of educators and citizens alike. Problems of the education of minority groups are receiving greater attention than ever before. The education of girls and women is being liberalized and extended in countries where these opportunities were formerly restricted. New attention is being devoted to vocational and technical education. The problem of coeducation is being debated in school systems where boys and girls have always attended separate schools.

In many parts of the world a new spirit of intense nationalism is making itself felt. In some cases this occurs in new nations which have recently achieved independence; in others it is in old countries which are trying to modernize their entire outlook on the modern world. In each case the educational system is accepted as one of the most important factors in achieving the desired results.

The rise of new nations has drawn attention to the problem of mass education. In the developing nations of Asia, Africa, and Latin America all of the problems of education are in sharp focus. How to find enough school rooms, enough books, enough teachers, and enough money concerns all of the newer governments. Expanding birthrates are a problem in every country. In nations where illiteracy rates have been high, the extension of educational opportunities to all is among the first concerns of the leaders.

One of the problems faced in such a book as this is to decide what items to include and what to omit. Space does not permit coverage of every country in the world or even of every continent, and thus the treatment must be selective. The fact that space does not permit the inclusion of African and Latin American nations does not mean that these countries are not important or interesting.

The authors have selected three Asian nations for further coverage.

Japan is a highly developed country, with a long history of almost complete literacy. Like West Germany, it went through a period of war, occupation, and reconstruction, with some years of tutelage by the Occupying Powers. The post-occupation development of Japan, combining a return to traditional Japanese ideas and methods with modern Western procedures, is covered in Chapter 18.

China is proud of its old civilization and of its highly developed educational system for the scholarly elite of the country. It was influenced by Western ideas of education for half a century. Now China is engaged in an energetic program which seeks to discard most of its traditional philosophies, to develop universal literacy, and at the same time to create a new type of Communist citizen. Modern Chinese schools have been greatly influenced by Soviet ideas, but they have developed along Chinese lines. This development is treated in Chapter 19.

Great developments are also stirring in the Republic of India. This ancient nation, second largest in the world in terms of population, faces serious problems—those created by a huge, illiterate or semi-literate population which is increasing rapidly, by many languages and dialects, and by great poverty. While historically it is not a new country, it is new among modern independent states. Indian education was greatly influenced by the long British occupation; British influences cannot be wholly discarded, and English is still an important lingua franca among the various peoples of the country who speak different languages. But the idea that anything British or European smacks of "colonialism" still perturbs the Indians. The active attempts to meet these problems are presented in Chapter 20.

In an age when every nation spends more money for defense than for schools, all the peoples of the world are eager for peace. The part which the schools may play in developing an understanding of other peoples, of their cultures, interests, ideals, and ambitions, is receiving more attention in many school systems. But in some countries this runs counter to the strong winds of nationalism which blow across them.

No two countries will agree on the objectives of education for their people. Each country, however, uses its school system to achieve the results it seeks for its own development. The importance of education, reaching far beyond training in the basic subjects and skills, is increasingly recognized everywhere. In no part of the globe is education more important than it is in Asia.

18

The Schools of Japan

THIS chapter should be of distinct interest to the student of comparative education for the following unusual reasons: Twenty years or so ago we were at war with Japan, which was under militaristic control with much glorification of war in the schools. Today that is all changed. We are now friendly with Japan, a firm democracy possessing one of the most democratic and effective systems of education in the world. (Japan has hardly any illiteracy in a nation of 96 million.) Since World War II educational administration has been changed from centralization to decentralization, girls and women have been given educational opportunities equal to those of boys and men, and coeducation is the general rule of the schools. This chapter will relate the course of this Japanese revolution in education.

Japan consists of four main islands, the total area of which is roughly equal to that of Montana. In these islands live more than 96 million people, but the birthrate is being steadied, and it is hoped to stabilize the total at a figure between 96 and 100 million. Only one-fifth of the land area is arable. The Japanese have lost all their overseas dependencies and spheres of control, and it is hard for them to produce enough food for this huge population. The Japanese islands are extremely beautiful, with mountains, landlocked seas, hundreds of picturesque islands, and many harbors. The soil is volcanic and rich, and every foot of suitable land must be made productive. There is abundant timber of good quality, a reasonable amount of coal and copper, but there is neither oil nor iron ore, and raw materials for heavy industries must be maintained by extensive imports. The islands lie along one of the earth's geological lines of weakness, with the result that the country is subject to serious earthquakes and has nearly fifty active volcanoes. The climate suffers from extremes: autumn and spring are delightful, but there is a hot, moist summer and a very cold winter.

Few cattle, horses, or sheep are to be seen; there is little room for them except in the northern island of Hokkaido. Rice and vegetables form the staple items of diet, together with fish. During the last five years the rice crop was abundant. The rich daily catch of fish makes the harvest of the sea as important to the Japanese as the harvest of the land.

Although the beauty of their country has made the Japanese a people passionately devoted to their homeland, it is obvious that one of their main problems is to maintain an adequate food supply from home and external sources. Some years ago there was a need to find places for their surplus population, but in the years prior to 1964 Japan has been suffering from a lack of laboring people as well as of scientists and technicians.

It speaks well for the quality and determination of the Japanese people that in addition to the manufacture of silk goods, lacquer ware, and beautiful pottery, they had built up industries before World War II until they had become one of the leading industrial nations of the world, able to make almost anything—from an electric light bulb to a battleship.

In many ways, in the years immediately following defeat, Japan presented a very different picture from that of Germany. The occupation took a different form. There were no zones with conflicting political ideas. Japan remained a national unit, with the Emperor retaining the technical headship of the nation. The occupation was accepted in good spirit, and the directions of the occupying powers were followed in a spirit of promptness and willingness. In defeat Japan suffered a terrible blow to her prestige and pride, but the Japanese were inured to natural disaster, and seemed, to the end, to view the situation with philosophic calm.

From the beginning the aim of S.C.A.P.[1] was to help Japan to regain its position in the world and to become a friendly democratic nation. As a result the country lived not in constant perplexity and division, but in an atmosphere of hope for the future. Industries and commerce began to reestablish themselves. While the future of

[1] S.C.A.P. was the name given to the general administration carried out by the occupying powers in Japan. The letters were an abbreviation for "Supreme Commander of the Allied Powers."

Germany remained uncertain, a peace treaty was signed with Japan in September, 1951, with 48 nations signing the document.

Throughout the occupation the Allied authorities worked insofar as possible with the cooperation of the Japanese. After certain necessary directives, aimed at preventing the resurgence of militarism, had been carried out, the role adopted was one of suggestion and recommendation rather than direct order. This was particularly true of education, where the approval and initiative of the Japanese Ministry of Education (known as Mombusho) was sought in connection with every move.

Rarely if ever before in the history of education has such a momentous problem confronted any group of educational reformers. The task involved an attempt to change a whole people's habits of thought, to turn a totalitarian nation into a democratic nation through the medium of its schools. Moreover, the nation concerned was a literate and capable one with centuries of culture and tradition in its background. After six years of hard and persistent efforts by American educational specialists, there came the peace treaty; from that date on, educational developments lay in the hands of the Japanese themselves. In order to evaluate the democratic trend in Japanese education, it will be helpful to examine Japanese national characteristics and traditions and the nature of the prewar educational system.

Landmarks in Japanese History

JAPANESE mythology sets 600 B.C. as the date when the Japanese Empire was founded, and alleges the first Emperor to have been the direct descendant of the Sun Goddess. The Japanese claimed that the present Emperor could trace his ancestry back to this date in a dynastic line "unbroken for ages eternal." Today this mythology is not believed, nor is it taught in the schools.

During the seven centuries that followed, the Japanese were greatly influenced by Chinese learning and art. From the Chinese came the system of writing, the Buddhist religion, and Chinese methods of painting and craftwork. To the Japanese, the Chinese classics stand in the same position as do Latin and Greek classics to the Western nations.

Japan began to have relations with the continent of Asia in the third century. Chinese learning and Buddhism were introduced in the sixth century. In the sixteenth century traders and missionaries from Europe began to enter Japan, but after a little experience with them the rulers of the country in 1635 ordered all foreigners to depart, and the Japanese withdrew from any further contact with Western nations. This isolation lasted for 220 years, Japan slumbering quietly amid her cherry blossoms while Europe established colonies, fought great wars, and experienced the changes of the Industrial Revolution.

In the early part of the nineteenth century, attempts of the West to establish trade with Japan were stubbornly opposed and foreign ships were turned away from the Japanese coast. But social and political changes were under way within Japan itself. The feudal lords were losing their power, a new commercial class was rising, and the Emperor was soon to triumph by establishing his authority over his chief feudal rival, the Shogun.

In 1853 and 1854 Commodore Perry "persuaded," or rather forced, the Japanese to open certain treaty ports and admit foreigners. Once the die had been cast, Japan decided to change as quickly as possible from a medieval nation to a modern industrial power. One of the strongest supporters of this policy was the new Emperor Meiji (1867–1912) whose reign is termed "the period of enlightened government." He sent missions all over the world to examine modern institutions, transferred the capital to Tokyo, built up an army under German instructors, and with the help of British shipwrights and sea captains, established a Japanese navy and merchant marine.

From that time on Japanese progress was remarkably swift. The Japanese proved to be very apt pupils and soon began to outdo the West. Japanese banks and warehouses extended from India around the rim of the Pacific Ocean to South America, and cheap but efficient labor enabled Japanese industries to outproduce and outsell many of the Western countries.

In the military and territorial spheres the Japanese successes were sensational. China and Russia were defeated, and gradually Formosa, Korea, Sakhalin, and the Marshall and Caroline islands were added to the empire. In addition, Japan gained control over many railways and industrial enterprises in Manchuria and China. Inevitably, the Japanese began to see themselves as the future leaders of all East Asia.

From 1928 on the imperialistic military group began to control the government, forming an alliance with the Zaibatsu (rich and powerful commercial families), with the result that the country's whole energies were turned toward military aggrandizement. In 1931 Japanese armies invaded Manchuria and soon had that rich province under control, in spite of the protests of the Western powers and the League of Nations. In 1937, after a series of incidents in China, Japanese forces invaded that nation by land and sea. For the next five years Japan waged an undeclared war in China. The Chinese lost a great deal of their territory but never gave up the struggle and never allowed the Japanese to reach a victorious conclusion. Meanwhile World War II had begun, and the watchful militarists under Prime Minister Tojo gained even more power. Nothing was allowed to interfere with Japan's dream of domination over Asia, and the climax came on December 7, 1941, when the Japanese struck at Pearl Harbor.

During the following four months, Japan achieved victory after victory. Her forces moved south into the Pacific and rapidly overran the Philippines, Indochina, Hong Kong, Thailand, Burma, Malaya, Borneo, Indonesia, many Pacific islands, and part of New Guinea. The Japanese gambled on the fact that the United States and the European nations were so heavily engaged in Europe that they would be able to give little attention to affairs in the Pacific. But the triumph was not to endure. As the Allies strengthened their forces in the Pacific, the Japanese advance, after fierce fighting, was first checked and then turned. The rest of the story was one of forced withdrawal, until in August, 1945, Japan's dream ended, and she was forced to acknowledge defeat.

Traditional and Institutional Influences

ALTHOUGH Japan had clearly attained great power status by the outbreak of World War II, in a sense she had only partially entered the modern world. Her industrial efficiency was combined with an anachronistic semifeudal philosophy. The ideas of Confucianism still influenced her thinking, but the calm mask of Nippon concealed a fanatical belief in her destiny to rule the world. The first step in this mission was to liberate East Asia from the overlordship of white imperialism. Associated with this belief was the unique position of the Emperor, who was considered to be divine; the Emperor *was* the state, and every Japanese individual regarded it as his duty to serve, guard, and maintain his prestige. From this stemmed a system of conditioned obedience associated with Emperor-worship, ancestor-worship, and reverence for one's elders and superiors. For instance, every Japanese woman in her life owed three obediences—as a girl, to her father; as a wife, to her husband; in her old age, to her eldest son. This virtue was observed during the Shogunate period, and had no relation to such virtues as Emperor-worship, ancestor-worship, and reverence for elders and superiors; these were still observed by all people after the Meiji Restoration. During the war one of the Ministry of Education's publications to the schools included the following: "To give up one's life for the Emperor cannot be called self-sacrifice. Rather, it is a discarding of one's lesser self to live in the great Imperial Virtue."

From the days of the samurai, the powerful military retainers of feudal times, came the code of *Bushido,* the Way of the Warrior. This developed through the centuries into a nation-wide creed of loyalty, heroism, endurance, and self-sacrifice. This was linked to, and strengthened by, the national religious cult of State Shinto, the Way of the Gods. Shinto involved a ceremonial worship of the Emperor and of ancestors; it enjoined upon all Japanese the virtues of obedience, loyalty, filial piety, pride in ancestry, pride in the nation, belief in the divinity of the Emperor, and willingness to die for him. It had many beautiful shrines throughout the country and there was a strong religious fervor associated with it, but it was considered by the Japanese as an expression of national devotion and loyalty rather than as a religion. Buddhism, with 46 million adherents immediately before the war, was the principal religion, but it could be combined with State Shinto.

Thus we find the Japanese, as the war in the Pacific progressed, convinced of a divine mission, united in adoration of their Emperor, and ready for any type of sacrifice for the future glory of Nippon. They were fatalistic in attitude and would often face suicide rather than any form of disgrace. Their system of education was thorough and effective, although formal and militaristic in character, and the percentage of illiteracy was low. Newspapers, drama, literature, radio, and films were all of high quality but often reflected the militaristic and ultranationalist feeling of the times.

Keeping in mind Japan's eventful history since 1853, the strength of the basic influences, and the way the whole nation was disciplined by centuries of obedience to authority, let us see what kind of educational system had developed between 1853 and 1941.

One of the later results of this conditioned obedience, incidentally, was evident at the beginning of the occupation, when the Emperor told the Japanese that they must respect and obey the orders of General MacArthur and his staff. The whole nation listened and then obeyed like a disciplined battalion.

Prewar Japanese Education

AFTER Japan had emerged from 220 years of self-imposed seclusion and had decided to become a modern nation, missions were sent abroad to examine the education systems of other countries. The model chosen for further development of education was France, in the belief that a centralized system of education could be so organized that it would be an effective instrument for the control of the people by the government. The basic education law was laid down in 1872, and the system developed rapidly. It had its model in the French educational system, and its general spirit was progressive and pragmatic. It was abolished in 1879 to be replaced by another law based on the American model. After a few years nationalistic tendencies developed, these tendencies being expressed in the Imperial Rescript issued by the Emperor Meiji in 1890. It showed a nationalistic and feudalistic spirit. Copies of this edict were displayed in each school, and the text was regularly recited by pupils. Many of the textbooks had the Imperial Rescript, printed on superior paper, inserted as a supplementary page. Coming from the Emperor, the Rescript had the force of a divine pronouncement. It was couched in beautiful language which loses little in the English translation:

Know ye, Our subjects:
Our Imperial Ancestors have founded Our Empire on a basis broad and everlasting and have deeply and firmly implanted virtue; Our subjects ever united in loyalty and filial piety have from generation to generation illustrated the beauty thereof. This is the glory of the fundamental character of Our Empire, and herein lies the source of Our education. Ye, Our subjects, be filial to your parents, affectionate to your brothers and sisters, as husbands and wives be harmonious, as friends true; bear yourselves in modesty and moderation; extend your benevolence to all; pursue learning and cultivate arts; and thereby develop intellectual faculties and perfect moral powers; furthermore advance public good and promote common interests; always respect the Constitution and observe

the laws; should emergency arise, offer yourselves courageously to the State; and thus guard and maintain the prosperity of Our Imperial Throne coeval with heaven and earth. So shall ye not only be good and faithful subjects, but render illustrious the best traditions of your fore-fathers.

The Way set forth here is indeed the teaching bequeathed by Our Imperial Ancestors, to be observed alike by their Descendants and the subjects, infallible for all ages and true in all places. It is Our wish to lay it to heart in all reverence in common with you, Our subjects, that we may all thus attain the same virtue.

The 30th day of the 10th month of the 23rd year of Meiji

NATIONAL CONTROL OF EDUCATION

It should be noted, however, that in 1886 a new system of educa-tion was established by Mori, the greatest Minister of Education ever born in Japan. It was largely responsible for the thoroughness and high literacy of Japanese education and lasted until World War II. The National Ministry of Education (Mombusho) was very powerful. It was the organization through which the government controlled what the people should learn, read, and believe. In addi-tion to supervising the schools and universities, it controlled art, science, literature, and religion. The Minister was appointed by the Emperor from the party in power, on the advice of the Premier. The Ministry itself, which had an imposing building in Tokyo, worked through a Secretariat and eight bureaus. Figure 18–1 illus-trates the general organization.

The five sections of the Secretariat had important, and in some cases unusual, duties. For instance, the Personnel Section controlled the classification and promotion of teachers, distributed Imperial portraits and Imperial Rescripts, and supervised all national festi-vals. The Bureau of Thought Supervision, established in 1929, was strengthened in 1937. It sought to combat "leftist" movements among students. Students suspected of having "dangerous thoughts" were drafted into special corrective classes or even imprisoned until they were deemed to have been cured.

There were three types of schools: (a) government schools, es-tablished by the Mombusho, relatively few in number; (b) public schools, established by the prefectures,[2] towns, and villages; and (c)

[2] There are 46 prefectures in Japan. They correspond roughly to states in the United States or counties in England.

Fig. 18–1   Organization of Ministry of Education in Prewar Japan

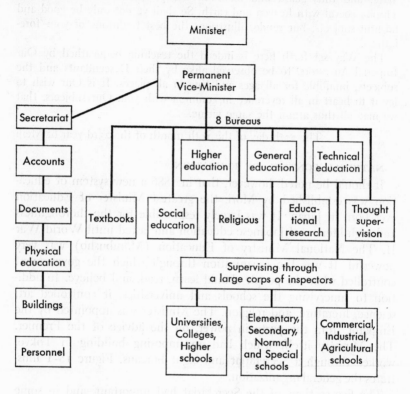

private schools, with a certain degree of independence, but subject to regulation by the Mombusho. The great majority of the schools came under the second heading.

There were three sources from which funds were obtained to support prewar Japanese schools. The National Treasury provided about 30 percent of the total, the prefectures approximately 20 percent, and the local cities, towns, and villages raised the remaining 50 percent.

No fees have been charged in elementary schools since 1900. For the schools above this stage the average fee was 6 yen (about $1.70) a year. The amount thus obtained provided less than 2 percent of the total expenditure for education. Numerous funds existed for helping students who were in financial straits and showed marked ability.

As late as 1939 the Japanese expenditure for education (592 million yen) exceeded the combined total for the army and navy (443 million yen). At that time there were 3.57 yen to an American dollar, so that the educational expenditure in 1930 in Japan amounted to 165 million dollars. Later, military expenditures mounted rapidly and far exceeded the amount spent on education.

LOCAL PARTICIPATION IN CONTROL

Although control of curriculum, textbooks, and methods of teaching was completely in the hands of the central authority, there was a certain amount of local participation in the building, equipping, and maintenance of schools. Local prefects, mayors, and headmen organized these functions in accordance with the regulations of the Ministry, and they also had a voice in the selection of teachers. In the schools themselves neither headmaster nor teachers had much opportunity for initiative. They simply obeyed the rules. Inspectors were regarded with the greatest respect and their word was law.

FEATURES OF PREWAR JAPANESE SCHOOLS

Prewar schools in Japan had many excellent characteristics. Although there were many ultranationalist and militaristic elements in the curriculum, and although the system of centralized control made for rigidity and conformity in many directions, the schools were in many ways pleasant places for children and reflected the general Japanese interest in art, music, codes of courtesy, and national festivals. The percentage of illiteracy in the country was very low. Figure 18–2 shows the prewar organization of the schools; some brief comments on the principal types are given below.

Kindergartens

Prewar kindergartens were interested in the physical health of the children and the cultivation of good manners. Care was taken to cultivate character training in the Japanese fashion, associated with affection, piety, obedience, orderliness, and familiarity with noble deeds. The greater proportion of the kindergartens were established by private groups or associations. Attendance was not compulsory, and only a small proportion of Japanese 3- to 5-year-olds attended.

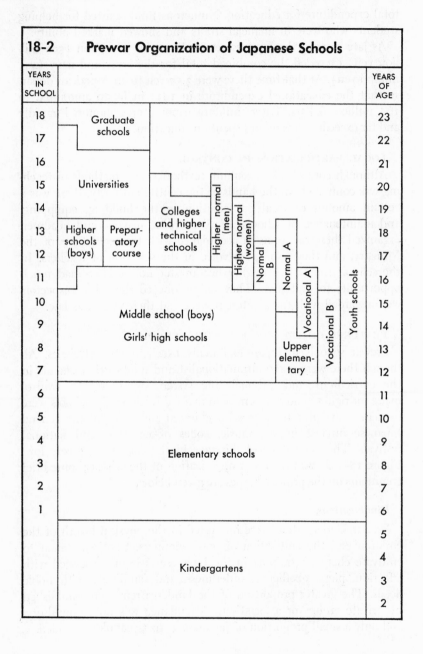

18-2 Prewar Organization of Japanese Schools

YEARS IN SCHOOL		YEARS OF AGE
18	Graduate schools	23
17		22
16		21
15	Universities	20
14	Colleges and higher technical schools	19
13	Higher schools (boys) / Preparatory course / Higher normal (men) / Higher normal (women)	18
12	Normal B	17
11	Normal A	16
10	Vocational A	15
9	Middle school (boys) / Vocational B	14
8	Girls' high schools / Upper elementary / Youth schools	13
7		12
6		11
5		10
4		9
3	Elementary schools	8
2		7
1		6
		5
		4
	Kindergartens	3
		2

Elementary Schools

The elementary schools were the kernel of the prewar system and accounted for two-thirds of the total enrollment. The usual elementary subjects were taught, with stress on mathematics, Japanese history and language, physical education, and morals. Morals, history, geography, mathematics, and English were important, though English was dropped during the war. There was direct teaching of morals, using such topics as the Emperor's Birthday, Obedience, Determination, Truthfulness, Loyalty, and National Festivals. History and geography emphasized Japan's growing power and future place as the leader of the world. Classes were often large and the teaching was formal in character. Some students remained in the higher elementary school until age 14, but most went to work after their twelfth birthday.

Secondary Schools

The prewar middle school gave an education similar to that in a junior high school, general in character, with preparation, where necessary, for entrance into a higher school. It was open to boys only. Some pre-vocational training was offered in commercial subjects. Morals, history, and geography were important parts of the curriculum. In the years immediately before the war, military instructors gave the boys strenuous training in sword-fighting and other warlike exercises.

The girls' high schools prepared girls for what the Japanese thought was the proper place of women in society. Great importance was placed on homemaking, child welfare, and decorative arts. These schools were pleasant places, less troubled by strenuous examinations than the boys' secondary schools. There were some unusual extracurricular subjects such as tea ceremony, flower arrangement, etiquette, ceremonial dancing, and participation in festivals. The Japanese did not believe in coeducation, thinking it unwise on both national and moral grounds. One result of the program of the girls' high schools was that so much stress was placed on homemaking subjects that very few girls were able to obtain the training in science, mathematics, and classics that would take them eventually to the university. Moreover, as there were no higher schools for girls, the great majority of girls could not hope to proceed to a university.

The higher schools, some of which were boarding schools, were also for boys only. The Japanese name for them was *koto gakko*, and many of these schools were famous throughout the land. They provided an advanced education for boys who wished to proceed to universities. The main subjects were Chinese and Japanese literature, science, mathematics, economics, philosophy, and sociology. There were 32 of these schools in Japan and a government ordinance issued in 1918 enjoined upon them the cultivation of "national morality." They were really preparatory schools for the Imperial Universities, and a successful graduate was entitled to enter an Imperial University without examination. Actually the number of applicants for these schools was so great that for many years a severe and selective entrance test had been necessary.

Youth Schools

The youth schools offered part-time courses ranging over seven years. They were instituted in 1935 as a part of the nationalistic program which was then growing in intensity. The aim was to increase productivity and to make better citizens of those who had left school at a relatively early age. As war grew nearer, these schools were used as centers of ultranationalist and militaristic propaganda. Boys and young men made up 70 percent of the enrollment; there were separate schools for girls. In 1939 attendance was made compulsory for boys under 19 who had not attended middle school, but even six years earlier, in 1933, there were 2,300,000 in attendance at youth schools. Subjects taught represented an extension of elementary school courses, with great emphasis on morals and physical exercises. Vocational subjects were added, particularly those dealing with agriculture and fisheries. In most cases the buildings were poor: temples, warehouses, and elementary schools were frequently used to house the youth schools. In the end, they were utilized to give boys and some of the girls intensive military training.

Special Schools (Semmo Gakko)

With the development of secondary education in the latter part of the nineteenth century, a variety of vocational special schools were set up for young people graduating from the middle schools and girls' high schools. In 1903 the government issued the "Special Schools Ordinance" in order to systematize these *semmo gakko* and to further their development. The length of the course was fixed at three years, and in that year 17 national schools and 31 local and private schools were established.

Universities

In prewar Japan there were 48 universities at the apex of the educational pyramid. About 1 percent of the pupils who entered elementary school might hope to secure a university degree. There were three kinds of institutions: government, those organized by the prefectures, which were called public, and private. Seven of the government universities were named Imperial Universities and these had great prestige. To be a graduate of the Imperial University of Tokyo or Kyoto carried such social and intellectual standing that graduates from other universities often found themselves debarred from important positions. The Ministry of Education exercised considerable control over the universities, and changes in numbers and types of faculty required the Ministry's consent. There were 26 private universities, the best known being Keio in Tokyo, Waseda, also in Tokyo, and Doshisha, a Christian university in Kyoto.

The instruction was very formal; lectures were taken down verbatim and memorized by the students. Students could read in libraries, but the accommodation was very crowded. Examinations were very severe. Between 1935 and 1945 the Ministry of Education instituted a strict totalitarian control over student thought and activities. There were almost no opportunities comparable to those in American or British universities for discussion, student government, radical clubs, or widespread student social activities.

The Machinery of Change

AS THE war situation changed in 1944 and 1945 and the dreams of victory began to fade, almost all of the schools above the elementary level were closed and their students diverted to productive work in factories and on farms. When defeat actually came, the educational system was prostrate. Hardly any schools were operating. Nearly 20 percent of the existing floor space in schools was damaged. Over 2,000 elementary schools, 38 professional colleges, over 100 colleges and universities, and 64 normal schools were heaps of rubble. Many of the remainder were in a neglected condition, having suffered badly from a lack of maintenance and repair while the nation's whole energy was being directed toward the war effort.

Immediately before the occupation, the Japanese Ministry of Education took certain remedial steps. It made a survey of the damage through bombing, canceled all regulations and instructions calculated to promote militarism, and began to bring pupils back to school. Early in September, 1945, the occupation commenced, and S.C.A.P. began to build up its organization. One of the special sections of the Administrative and Executive Group of S.C.A.P. was called Civil Information and Education (C.I. and E.), which was staffed entirely by education and military officials from the United States. It was divided into six divisions, the first of which was called the Education Division. The tasks assigned to the Education Division were to remove all militarism and ultranationalism from the school system and gradually to introduce new educational patterns to ensure the training of young people and teachers for a democratic Japan.

Four fundamental objectives, aimed at clearing the way for the introduction of democratic procedures in schools, were stated at an early stage by S.C.A.P. These were: (a) formulation of new objectives in education (October, 1945); (b) screening of teachers to remove all ultranationalists and militarists (October, 1945); (c) banning of State Shinto from the schools (December, 1945); (d) suspension of the teaching of morals, history, and geography until new textbooks were prepared (December, 1945).

C.I. and E. decided on a wise procedure in putting into operation the progressive educational policy which was to follow. The principle adopted was that the reforms were to be carried out by the Japanese themselves, if and when they were convinced that the suggested plans were sound. Naturally there was eloquent American persuasion in the background, but from the beginning the American schoolmen and the Mombusho worked in cordial cooperation, with their offices in adjacent buildings. Conferences took place every day, and the instructions to prefectures, schools, and teachers were issued by the Japanese themselves.

An interesting example of this method of procedure occurred when, in March, 1946, an American commission of 27 prominent educators visited Japan, stayed for a month, conferred with many Japanese educators and officials, and produced a report containing a number of interesting and valuable recommendations. C.I. and E., however, referred the report to a representative Japanese committee, the Japanese Educational Reform Council. This council drew up a report similar in spirit to the American report, and this was accepted by the Mombusho as the basic document for reform.

A statement of new objectives for education was circulated to the schools before the Diet formulated a new Constitution for Japan. When the Constitution was accepted by the Diet in October, 1946, it contained the following articles pertinent to education in the country.

Art. 13. All the people shall be respected as individuals. Their right to life, liberty and the pursuit of happiness shall, to the extent that it does not interfere with the public welfare, be the supreme consideration in legislation and other governmental affairs.

Art. 14. All of the people are equal under the law, and there shall be no discrimination in political, economic or social relations because of race, creed, sex, social status or family origin.

Art. 19. Freedom of thought and conscience shall be held inviolate.

Art. 20. Freedom of religion is guaranteed to all. No person shall be compelled to take part in any religious act, celebration, rite or practice. The State shall refrain from religious education or any other religious activity.

Art. 23. Academic freedom is guaranteed.

Art. 26. All people shall have the right to receive an equal education correspondent to their ability. All people shall be obligated to have all boys and girls under their protection receive ordinary education as provided in the law. Such compulsory education shall be free.

These articles in the Constitution were expanded in a Fundamental Law of Education passed by the Diet in March, 1947. This law gave the same points in more detail, set down compulsory education as of nine years' duration, made coeducation compulsory, abolished all school fees, and ordered local boards to establish libraries and community halls for the furtherance of social education for adults.

The screening of teachers was a difficult task. All teachers found to be antagonistic to the policies and objectives of the occupation were to be removed. Obviously the C.I. and E. officers could not interrogate half a million teachers in a language not their own and find out what the teachers were really thinking. However, the Japanese prefectures cooperated and formed screening committees which were partially effective. The Ministry of Education announced that it would suspend the pension rights of any teacher who had to be dismissed after a certain date, and this measure caused thousands to resign before the date announced. Between August, 1945, and May, 1947, out of a teaching force of approximately half a million, 119,700 resigned or were dismissed. It was felt that the remainder were friendly to the new regime. The loss of one-quarter of the teaching force was a severe blow, but the authorities believed it was impossible to follow any other line of action. Young teachers were recruited as fast as possible to fill the gap, but it took several years to restore the teaching force to anything like its proper strength.

Banning of State Shinto meant the cessation of ultranationalist ceremonies in the schools and provided no great difficulty. Personal Shinto was not interfered with.

The textbooks used in prewar courses in morals, history, and geography were so permeated with militaristic ideas and maps showing Japan's future role in the Pacific that some action about them had to be taken. An attempt was first made to excise the objectionable statements and diagrams, or to black them out with ink, but this proved ineffective, and the books were suspended and abolished. New textbooks then had to be written, and until these were ready, the teaching of these subjects was suspended. The new books were compiled by Japanese writers under the guidance of C.I. and E. Millions of copies were required, and the Ministry soon ran out of paper. At that point several of the leading Japanese newspapers— some with a circulation of more than a million—offered to cut their editions to tabloid size twice weekly for three months in order to provide the necessary paper. This released more than 6 million pounds of paper. Interim textbooks of a few pages had been hastily prepared and issued, but this action of the newspapers meant that new textbooks were ready for all pupils by the beginning of the 1947–48 school year.

Meanwhile the whole educational system was being reorganized. Many conferences were held, and, one by one, new measures were set in operation through the Ministry of Education. These are discussed below.

It was strongly recommended by the American Education Mission that an attempt be made to break down the centralized system of educational administration whereby the Mombusho dictated curricula and procedures of schools and insured conformity through the zealous activities of its inspectors. It was felt that this system was definitely undemocratic. There was much discussion on this subject, for centralization was the only system the Japanese knew. From

April, 1947, however, measures of decentralization were gradually introduced. Each prefecture was to have its own board of education, preparing its own budget, training and certifying its own teachers, and working out its own building program. Moreover, there were to be boards of education in each city and in each town and village. The rural areas were to be cared for by the prefectures, but districts were to be consolidated for efficiency and each district was to have its own elected committee.

Changes were made in the functions of the Mombusho, which was ultimately to be an advisory body exercising the functions of leadership, stimulation, and encouragement. These changes had to be gradual, but the Mombusho, like the Ministry of Education in England, was to become the national planning agency for Japanese education, free from a mass of administrative detail.

Mounting costs made the reorganization of the financial system essential but difficult. For example, in 1929 the average salary of an elementary teacher was 57 yen a month; by 1947 this had risen to 1,487 yen a month. This seemed an enormous increase, but the cost of living had multiplied during that period and the price of commodities rose faster than teachers' salaries. All felt that the national contribution to education had to be increased. It was suggested that the National Treasury provide half of the operating costs and one-third of the cost of buildings and equipment, the remainder to be shared by prefectural and local budgets. The total amounts raised were to be redistributed by the national government in such a way that the prefectures would be able to provide equal educational facilities. The problem of how to provide for the reconstruction of war-damaged buildings and also how to build the new schools which were urgently needed was a knotty one. General opinion was that the national budget should provide the entire cost of rebuilding war-damaged schools, and that local authorities should issue bonds to provide their share of building costs, instead of trying to pay these out of current taxation.

The situation in 1947 was vividly revealed by an article in the *Nippon Times,* an English-language newspaper published in Tokyo:

The draft of the new Basic Education Law, reviewed by the press last week in anticipation of its early presentation to the Diet, has met with a most favorable response. This favorable reaction, however, should not blind one to the fact that a law of this sort can have but little meaning without adequate means for practical implementation. For instance, as long as one harassed teacher has to ride herd over eighty or one hundred squirming youngsters instead of the twenty or twenty-five which should be the limit for any one class, she is not going to be able to worry too much about bringing out the individual personality of each of her dear little pupils. To protect her own sanity of mind, the teacher will have no choice but to resort to regimentation and drill-sergeant discipline. As long as the pay is so poor as to attract teachers' candidates from only the lowest social strata, and as long as these teachers have to be constantly threatening to strike, or to be marching in demonstrations waving red flags, or to be engaging in black-market business after school hours in order to wangle enough to eat, civic education for responsible citizenship is bound to remain pretty much of a farce. As long as there is no glass in the schoolhouse windows, no heat in classroom stoves, no shoes for the children to wear, paper enough for only one textbook for every two pupils, and note-books cost a small fortune when occasionally there are any to be had at all, and schools have to solicit donations of discarded pencil stubs from business offices and foreign sources, it is pretty far-fetched to be talking about democratic and enlightened education.[3]

In view of the long-standing Japanese tradition of centralized control, the changeover to decentralization was not easy. It was difficult to secure responsible leaders in all local centers, and at the beginning it was not possible to form boards of education in all villages and small towns. But as the early years went by, there was a growing local interest, partly due to the fact that since the end of the war the number of landholders had increased from 30 to 90 percent as a result of the government policy of land reform. This policy has meant, for many, a stake in the country and more interest in local affairs. Parent-teacher associations became stronger and stronger—in 1953 there were 35,000 local groups with a membership of 15 million— and other signs began to appear of the disappearance of the old attitude of looking to the central government for everything. The Central Council studied methods of giving more responsibility to the local boards and drafted legislation to this effect. Nevertheless, owing to a background of centuries of centralized administration, it was a slow process to induce local citizens to shoulder more responsibility in a decentralized system.

These, then, represent the main changes that were taking place. It should be emphasized again that although the main driving force

[3] *Nippon Times,* March 13, 1947.

in almost all cases was the advice tendered by C.I. and E., the actual changes were made by the Ministry of Education with the backing of the Japanese Education Reform Council.

Operation of the Educational System After Reorganization

IT REMAINS to show how the new educational system in Japan has worked from about 1949 onward, and particularly what changes were made after the peace treaty in 1952. Some pessimists predicted that after 1952 the Japanese would discard many of the new democratic features and swing back toward their old authoritarian centralized system. No sign of this has yet appeared. That there would be some changes was inevitable, but so far these have been minor ones and the democratic framework remains untouched. A forecast of certain alterations was contained in the first free report of the Japanese Ministry of Education, for the year 1952–53, which opens with the following interesting paragraphs:

Nineteen fifty-two was a year of great significance in the history of Japan's new education in that the system, which had been under the Occupation of the Allied Forces since September, 1945, began to make its way with complete independence.

The Civil Information and Education Section of S.C.A.P.'s General Headquarters, which had had a powerful leadership in education in postwar Japan, was entirely dissolved on April 28, 1952 with the coming into force of the Peace Treaty. Thus education in Japan took a step toward a new development, by furthering the merits and examining the demerits of the educational plan which had been under the influence of the Occupation Authorities for the past six years, from the standpoint of establishing an educational policy better suited to the national circumstances.[4]

In 1953 the Japanese Ministry of Education issued an illustrated booklet entitled *Education in Japan—A Graphic Presentation.* The object was to give educational administrators in Japan and the public generally a basic understanding of the reformed system. This booklet, illustrated with many diagrams and charts, was widely read and many requests were received for the English edition. The latest edition was published in 1961, and gives a picture of a system of education thoroughly democratic in all its aspects, although certain

[4] *Annual Report for 1952–53,* Ministry of Education, Tokyo, 1953.

small changes suitable to the Japanese background have been made since 1952. Let us examine, in some detail, the working of the new system in 1960.

ADMINISTRATION AND FINANCE

In the reforms after the war the Ministry of Education was removed from its role as a centralized, controlling organization of authoritarian type. It has become instead an agency to give professional and technical assistance and advice to school boards, universities, and schools, issuing drafts of laws and reports, watching national standards, and carrying out investigations and research. It has a Ministerial Secretariat and six bureaus: Elementary and Secondary Education, Higher Education and Science, Social Education, Physical Education, Research, and Administration. There are 19 Councils assisting the Ministry on such subjects as health and physical education and Japanese language. The most important of these is the Central Council for Education, which is an expert consultative body to advise the Ministry on general policy.

The Ministry provides financial aid to the boards of education and requires reports on their educational activities. The Ministry also approves the establishment of new universities, both public and private, and offers them administrative supervision and advice.

In the sphere of local educational administration there are 46 prefectural boards of education and 3,770 local boards. The number of boards has decreased yearly since 1953, when there were 8,700. The decrease has resulted from the unification of municipalities in the intervening years. The prefectural and local boards do not conflict, each having its own area of jurisdiction. The Ministry of Education may offer guidance and advice to prefectural and local boards of education, and the prefectural boards carry out a similar function in relation to the municipal boards. Prefectural boards of education administer public upper secondary schools and cultural and social educational institutions established by the prefectures. Local boards of education administer public elementary and lower secondary schools, and cultural and social educational institutions established by municipalities. Prefectural boards of education appoint public elementary and junior secondary school teachers and handle the certification of teachers. Salaries are paid half by the national government and half by the prefectural board concerned. Private schools, except private universities and colleges, are under the direct supervision of the prefectural governors.

The responsibility for finance is three-tiered—national, prefectural, and local. Each level finances the schools established by it—colleges and universities by the national government, upper secondary schools by the prefectures, and lower secondary schools, elementary schools, and kindergartens by the municipalities. National subsidies are granted by the Ministry to assist prefectures and municipalities in their educational expenditure. Municipalities receive prefectural as well as national subsidies. No special school tax is levied, but the funds are drawn from general revenues.

In 1960–61 the total national and local expenditure on education amounted to 612,492,000,000 yen (360 yen equal one dollar), which amounted to 5.15 percent of the national income for the year. Of the total educational cost the national government met 47.9 percent, and the local governments met 52.1 percent. This total was supplemented to a minor extent by donations from benefactors and from fees paid by students and parents.

INCREASE IN ENROLLMENTS

Compulsory education, covering six years of elementary school and three years in a lower secondary school, is now well established, and 99.8 percent of all school-age children are enrolled. There are still many problems to be solved in connection with shortage of well-equipped buildings, but all school buildings and equipment damaged during the war have now been completely replaced. Changes that have taken place in numbers of schools, teachers, and enrollments are shown in Table 18–1. This table compares the year of 1937 with the treaty year of 1952, and with 1960, 15 years after the end of the war. It is not always easy to make comparisons, because the adoption of a 6-3-3-4 plan of organization has changed the names of many of the schools. For this reason the table includes both the old and the new names in some sections.

The population of Japan in 1937 was 70 million; in 1952, 85 million; and by 1960 this had risen to 95 million. The steadily increasing population accounts for part of the increased enrollments. The percentage of lower secondary school graduates who advanced in 1960 to upper secondary schools reached 62 percent. There appear to be fewer pupils in the elementary schools than formerly, but this

TABLE 18–1 Education in Japan, 1937–1960

TYPE OF SCHOOL	NUMBER OF SCHOOLS			NUMBER OF TEACHERS			ENROLLMENT		
	1937	1952	1960	1937	1952	1960	1937	1952	1960
Kindergartens									
Public	601	1,115	2,580	2,047	5,033	8,360	71,745	157,851	241,418
Private	1,399	1,720	4,638	4,184	9,125	24,430	90,582	212,402	557,667
Elementary									
Public	20,832	21,415	26,580	276,762	321,410	346,942	11,764,000	11,118,000	11,763,000
Private	97	113	161	923	1,490	1,934	28,000	30,200	48,300
Secondary									
Old types									
Public	2,210	—	—	35,918	—	—	941,500	—	—
Private	695	—	—	11,103	—	—	347,300	—	—
Lower secondary									
Public	—	11,673	12,200	—	180,700	223,843	—	4,885,000	6,678,365
Private	—	709	611	—	14,700	7,750	—	191,300	246,328
Upper secondary									
Public	—	2,160	3,550	—	108,300	103,459	—	1,929,000	2,245,448
Private	—	875	1,051	—	25,700	30,919	—	412,700	873,448
Special schools (for blind, deaf, handicapped)	140	152	243	1,386	4,790	6,325	11,030	22,091	37,130
Higher education									
Higher schools (old style)	32	2	—	1,438	17	—	17,017	72	—
Technical schools (old style)	179	330	—	8,467	11,060	—	99,700	62,500	—
Normal Schools (old style)	158	127	—	2,746	4,290	—	35,300	32,000	—
Junior colleges	—	205	290	—	*	4,337	—	*	93,361
Universities (old type)	45	20	—	5,130	45,306	—	52,500	452,743	—
Universities (new type)	—	201	250	—	*	42,545	—	*	670,192
Totals	26,388	40,817	52,154	341,104	731,921	800,844	13,458,374	19,505,859	23,454,657

SOURCE: Figures furnished by the Ministry of Education, Tokyo.   * Figures included in Universities (old type).

is because some of the 13- and 14-year-olds who were previously in the upper elementary schools are now included in secondary school figures. Similarly many who would formerly have been enrolled in technical schools are now listed in junior colleges which offer vocational courses with a cultural background.

The Reorganized School System

IN THE Fundamental Law of Education it was stated that education was to be free and compulsory for nine years, from age 6 to 15. This requirement had to be introduced gradually, depending upon school facilities and the number of available teachers. In 1947 the top was set at the seventh grade (age 13); in 1948 it was raised to the eighth grade (age 14); and in 1949 to the ninth grade (age 15). By 1950 it was announced that more than 99.5 percent of all children from 6 to 15 were actually in attendance.

After long deliberations, the Japanese Education Reform Council had recommended that the nation's educational system should be reorganized on the 6-3-3-4 plan. This meant a six-year elementary school, to be followed by a three-year lower secondary school, then a three-year upper secondary school, and finally a four-year college or university. The middle schools, higher elementary schools, girls' high schools, and youth schools were merged into the standard types of either lower or upper secondary school; while the higher schools, preparatory schools, and special technical schools became a type of college or university department. This can best be shown by comparing the complicated diagram of prewar schools in Figure 18–2, on page 500, with the much simpler chart in Figure 18–3, showing the arrangement of schools under the postwar system. There are many marked changes in the schools themselves as the following brief survey will show.

KINDERGARTENS

Under the reorganization the number of public kindergartens has increased, and so has the number of private kindergartens. Approximately 800,000 children are now enrolled, but the number is still proportionately small. Modern methods of kindergarten organization and procedures are being adopted, largely as a result of the special training courses and demonstrations arranged by specialist members of C.I. and E. There has been a distinct improvement in

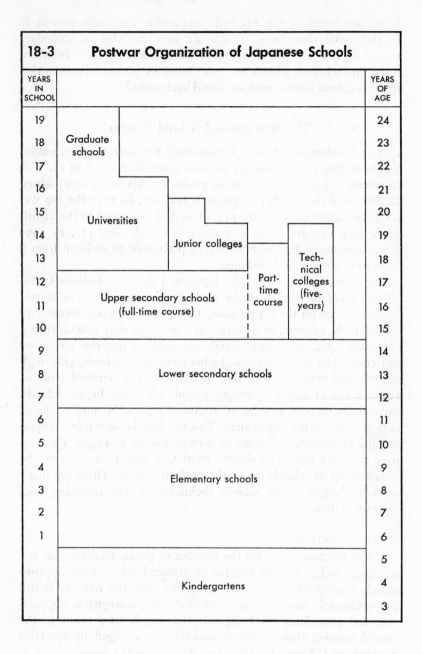

18-3   Postwar Organization of Japanese Schools

YEARS IN SCHOOL		YEARS OF AGE
19	Graduate schools	24
18		23
17		22
16		21
15	Universities	20
14	Junior colleges	19
13	Technical colleges (five-years)	18
12	Upper secondary schools (full-time course) Part-time course	17
11		16
10		15
9	Lower secondary schools	14
8		13
7		12
6	Elementary schools	11
5		10
4		9
3		8
2		7
1		6
	Kindergartens	5
		4
		3

publicly supported kindergartens since the organization and equipment of these schools has been made a responsibility of the local boards.

ELEMENTARY SCHOOLS

The new type of elementary school remains a six-year school, as it was in prewar days, for the 6- to 11-year-olds. Japanese language and social studies are the key subjects, with arithmetic, morals, health and physical education, nature study, and art also prominent. Subjects that are peculiarly Japanese are courtesy, flower arrangement, tea ceremony, and participation in festivals. These add a picturesque quality to the work of the schools. Art is very well taught and the standard of general achievement in this subject is high.

In prewar days teachers' guides were issued, both for elementary and secondary schools, which laid down the exact procedure for almost every lesson and gave the teacher no chance of exercising any initiative or using any opportunity to experiment. These guides were abolished by the Mombusho and have been replaced by courses of study that permit modern methods of teaching the various subjects. Discussion, activities, free study periods, and the effective use of libraries are all stressed.

With the introduction of the new system, health and physical education became important educational subjects. Much material concerning the teaching of health has been published and circulated. Most of the schools set up health committees and tried to obtain more school nurses. There were 12,000 of these nurses in 1962, and medical and dental staffs included 66,400 persons. Wherever possible traveling units have been organized and sent around the rural districts.

The campaign against tuberculosis, which had been a scourge among underfed pupils, met with some striking early successes. In 1943, during the war, deaths from tuberculosis were 329 per 100,000; by 1960 this had dropped to 34.1 per 100,000.

An important role in health improvement is played by the school lunch program. This was introduced by C.I. and E. and the occupation forces, with generous American aid in supplying foods. By 1951, 8 million children were partaking of a hot midday meal. It was difficult to continue this after the occupation ended, but the Japanese government has made strenuous efforts to keep the program going. They decided to pay half the cost of the raw wheat which is the chief material for the lunches, and to ask the local authorities and the parents to supply the balance of the money needed. In 1960 school lunches were served daily to 9,700,000 pupils in 18,600 schools; 8,450,000 of these were in the elementary grades. Some part-time secondary schools are also offering school meals; these have proved to be a great boon where students generally come straight from their work to school.

The new program in physical education is proceeding satisfactorily. The original shortage of equipment is being steadily overcome. Handbooks and guidebooks have been issued, and tables of age standards for athletic achievement circulated. In 1952 there were 27,000 instructors of physical education; in 1960, 48,000. Besides calisthenics and mimetic dancing, Western games such as baseball, softball, soccer, tennis, and basketball are popular. Swimming is taught in most of the schools. In all sports, emphasis is placed on general participation rather than on the development of specialized teams. Local boards of education have become interested in providing equipment.

The provision of textbooks for such an immense number of pupils is a serious undertaking. Since 1945 many million copies have been printed. Originally all textbooks were compiled and printed by the Ministry of Education, but one of the most popular postwar changes has been to allow private individuals or publishers to submit manuscripts to the Ministry of Education for authorization. The Ministry consults with a newly formed Textbook Authorization and research Council. In 1960, approximately 229 million textbooks approved by the Ministry were published by 163 individual publishers. There has been a steady improvement in the quality of textbooks, with a return to something like prewar standards of illustration and binding. Many of the books suggest activities and unit assignments. Beginning in 1963 all newly enrolled children in the elementary schools are to be supplied by the state with free textbooks in all subjects, for the nine years of compulsory education. School libraries in the past were almost nonexistent. The system of authoritative class teaching and the use of prescribed texts hindered the development or use of libraries in the schools, but now these are being widely developed.

Probably the greatest change in the elementary school has been in the general atmosphere of the school. In the past the teaching had been stereotyped and formal, with poor instructional equipment.

Head teachers were autocrats within their schools, and 450 inspectors (averaging ten to a prefecture) supervised school work in such a fashion that almost complete uniformity resulted.

This authoritarian attitude had to be broken down. In 1946 a beginning was made by organizing regional conferences for inspectors, with demonstrations of modern methods followed by discussions. In 1947 a *Handbook of Suggestions* was published for head teachers. The next step was a widespread series of conferences and workshops for teachers, with demonstrations of activity methods.

An interesting document issued to Japanese teachers contrasted old and new procedures in the elementary grades. Some of the points made were as follows:

"In the old system the teacher is the taskmaster and main figure: in the new system he is a guide and counselor giving good lessons, but also helping to organize activity programs. . . . Silence used to be the part of the pupils except when asked questions. Listening was their main role. But the schoolroom should be a place where the pupils are free to move about and consult with each other while engaging in worth-while tasks. . . . The old classrooms had formal desks set in fixed rows; the newer ones have tables and chairs arranged informally for group activity."

All Japanese schools moved quickly to adopt new methods. The teachers were reeducated and persuaded that the new ideas were sound. A spearhead of the attack is the new social studies course which combines history, geography, and civics. It puzzled teachers at first, but is now well done throughout Japan. A handbook has been issued for this subject, giving suggested headings only and many instances of suitable activities. One promising feature of this program is that Japanese school children, always lively and full of energy, respond quickly to activity methods and become very much interested in them.

SECONDARY SCHOOLS

The prewar secondary schools of Japan were of many complicated types. Under the new plan all of these schools were changed into two kinds of secondary schools. The lower secondary school, for ages 12 through 14, became very important in the program. A familiar sight in all parts of Japan in the years 1947 through 1950 was the building of new schools for this group. There are now 12,000 of them, and they enroll nearly 7 million pupils.

In the lower secondary schools there are 32 class hours per week, of which required subjects take up about 26 hours. These required subjects include Japanese language, social studies, physical education, mathematics, science, music, art, workshop practice or homemaking. The remaining six hours are devoted to elective subjects such as foreign language or vocational subjects, or to free study. Courtesy, flower arrangement, tea ceremony, and festivals are brought in regularly as special activities.

Free and compulsory education ceases at age 15, but 1962 figures showed that 62 percent of the pupils finishing the lower secondary school went on to the upper secondary school, either full time or part time. The sexes were fairly evenly distributed in this 62 percent, although more girls than boys elect to take the full-time course.

The upper secondary school, for the group aged 15 through 17, was established, after the reorganization of many schools, in 1948. The tuition fee charged for upper secondary education varies greatly among national and private schools. The fee of ¥3,600 (U.S. $10) is uniform in national schools throughout the country, but fees in prefectural and municipal public schools are determined by the local authorities and may vary from ¥7,200 to ¥8,400 ($20 to $23.33). In private schools the tuition has a wider range, from ¥6,000 to ¥37,500 ($16.66 to $104). The upper secondary school works under a "unit" plan similar to the Carnegie units in an American high school. A Japanese unit, however, consists of thirty-five 50-minute periods per year. Successful completion of more than 85 units from the general course of the upper secondary schools is needed for graduation, and most schools offer a choice of about 160 units. Compulsory units account for at least 85 of the total for boys and 70 for girls—Japanese language, 17; social studies, 15; mathematics, 10; science, 15; physical education, 9; and foreign language, 9. Upper secondary schools offer a college preparatory course and a variety of vocational courses.

The youth schools have ceased to function and technical schools have lost many of their pupils, due to the fact that vocational education is now included in the upper secondary school courses, in independent vocational high schools or in comprehensive high schools. Correspondence courses in vocational subjects have been organized to help those who cannot attend classes.

Something had to be done for those pupils who were financially unable to attend upper secondary schools, but wished to continue their education. Part-time courses were arranged in 2,100 upper secondary schools and centers, which in 1962 enrolled 510,000 young workers attending school after working hours.

Physical education is still very important, but games and sports are much more popular than before the war. At youth and young adult levels two national bodies have been formed: the Japan Physical Education Association and the Japan Recreation Association. These organizations help in the formation of physical education groups and athletic teams, and hold national physical education rallies every year. Teams from Japanese universities have visited Los Angeles, Honolulu, and other places for friendly contests, and Japan was the host country for the 1964 Olympic Games.

VOCATIONAL SCHOOLS

In 1960, 33 percent of the Japanese people were engaged in agriculture and fisheries, and 62 percent in industry and commerce. It was clear that any reorganization had to give emphasis to vocational training. All lower secondary schools offer exploratory courses in industrial arts or homemaking as required subjects covering three hours a week, and any one of five elective subjects, such as agriculture, industry, commerce, fisheries, or homemaking for three hours a week. Vocational guidance has been introduced and a study made in each district of the absorptive capacity of each branch of occupation. Upper secondary schools have more specific vocational departments, such as agriculture, fisheries, commerce, industry, and home economics. Each of the vocational departments is divided into various courses. For example, the agricultural department offers such courses as general agriculture, horticulture, livestock farming, sericulture, processing of agricultural products, agricultural civil engineering, forestry, and gardening. Junior colleges provide upper secondary graduates with two or three years of practical professional courses such as home economics or accountancy. Plans have been made for the eventual establishment of institutes of technology or of teacher training. Special allowance is given to teachers in charge of vocational subjects in the upper secondary schools.

TECHNICAL COLLEGES

In compliance with recent developments in the technical field, technical colleges were established in 1962, to secure middle-level technicians who could be deeply grounded in science to meet present day needs of the country. The prerequisite for admission to a technical college is graduation from the lower secondary school. The course in a technical college covers five years, and by 1962, 32 of these colleges had been established.

UNIVERSITIES

Big changes have taken place in the Japanese university system, and now Japan is second only to the United States in ratio of colleges and universities to population. The new organization began in 1949 and was completed in 1952 when the universities became the apex of the new 6-3-3-4 pyramid. The aim was to give as much opportunity as possible to young men and women in order that they might have access to the higher divisions of culture and professional skills.

The number of colleges and universities was increased greatly by the conversion of many *semmo gakko* (higher technical schools) and *koto gakko* (higher schools) into four-year institutions of higher learning. In 1963 there were 270 universities and colleges, 88 of which are located in Tokyo. They are classified as follows: (a) those with graduate schools, doing work of advanced level; (b) undergraduate institutions, providing both professional and vocational education; and (c) those whose main purpose is the training of teachers. In addition there are 321 junior colleges, 78 of which are in Tokyo. These offer two- and sometimes three-year courses giving professional and vocational training with a cultural background.

The Imperial Universities were renamed National Universities and the special privileges of Tokyo and Kyoto were eliminated. As a rule one university in each prefecture has been designated a National University. The former entrance examinations had been very severe, relying largely on rote memorization. Even in 1947 only 62 percent of the applicants for admission were accepted. A new entrance test was devised, consisting of a scholastic aptitude test, an achievement test in special fields, and an examination of the school record.

There are still three vital problems facing Japanese universities— finance, equipment, and qualified staff. Professors are expected to teach 6 to 8 hours a week and are given time for research. Although their salaries have been revised upward year by year, some have to undertake part-time teaching in other universities to make ends meet. A lecture course of one hour per week for 15 weeks gives one credit. A nonlecture course meets two hours a week for one credit. University students take 36 credits in general education and 76 in professional subjects in courses other than medicine or dentistry.

Student life is very difficult and there is need for much financial assistance. Many scholarships are given by public bodies to graduate students, and by religious groups, by schools, and by individual donors to students in upper secondary schools. In 1962 there were 79,000 of these scholarships from 685 different donors. In addition there is the Japan Scholarship Society, supervised by the Ministry of Education, which gives loans to students at no interest. In 1962 there were 241,000 beneficiaries from this loan fund. A student in a graduate course received ¥8,000 to ¥15,000 (about $22 to $42) and an undergraduate ¥2,000 to ¥7,500 (about $5 to $20) per month. There were 104,000 students in upper secondary schools who received from ¥1,000 to ¥3,000 (about $3 to $9) per month.

The International Christian University, an interdenominational institution of higher learning, was founded in 1949 on a 350-acre site in a suburb of Tokyo. The site was purchased with a fund of 150 million yen ($416,000) raised in Japan by public subscription. In New York the Japan International Christian University Foundation provides operating support. The university has a Japanese president and two American vice-presidents. One-half of the students are Japanese and the other half come from other nations.

One of the most significant facts is that while in prewar days there were 52,000 students in Japanese universities with only a handful of women, in 1961 there were 765,000 students of whom 160,000 were women. Moreover, in 1937 only one university teacher was a woman; in 1961 5,300 members of the total faculty were women.

PRIVATE SCHOOLS

Private schools in Japan have had a long history. In the present century from about 1910 to 1925 they were regarded with favor, since they relieved the pressure on the rapidly growing system. From 1930 onward, however, when the national schools were being used to inculcate fierce patriotism, private schools found themselves being treated rather coldly. Many of them were secondary schools associated with particular religious groups such as Buddhism and Christianity, and it was felt that they might be a little too independent in their attitude to suit government purposes. In consequence, limitations were placed on their privileges and their diplomas were not given the same credit as those from national schools.

Private schools have now regained their importance and prestige. Their contribution to Japanese education has been valuable, and at present they provide more than half of the kindergartens and half of the institutions of higher learning. Religious education is prohibited in the public schools, but the private schools may, under certain circumstances, teach religion. As a result there have been, and still are, numerous Buddhist and Christian schools, many of them with long traditions and creditable records.

An example of a good private school is Jiyu Gakuen, or "Freedom School," located a few miles out of Tokyo under the management of Mr. and Mrs. Hani. This school, which has acquired an international reputation, is a coeducational boarding school with attractive buildings. For years it has used modern methods of teaching, with activity units and discussion seminars. Its effective treatment of music and art has attracted visitors from far and wide.

The private schools follow the same pattern of organization as the public schools. In 1949 a Private School Law laid down conditions for efficient operation and placed private schools below the upper secondary level under the control of the prefects. Higher schools and universities and colleges are under the jurisdiction of the Minister of Education. The establishment of private schools may be authorized by an appropriate official, but if a school violates standards of health, staffing, or achievement it may be closed.

Many of the private schools were severely damaged by bombing during the war, and subsequently had such a struggle to reestablish themselves and secure adequate equipment that in 1946 the government tried to give loans to some of them. In 1952 this program was placed on a sounder basis by an act establishing an Association for Promotion of Private Schools, under the supervision of the Minister of Education. This association was given a capital of 2,100,000,000 yen and authorized, after making a survey of the situation, to grant loans at a low rate of interest to private schools for buildings and equipment.

ADULT EDUCATION

A general framework of adult education had existed in Japan for some years, but in the immediate prewar period it had been used for militaristic propaganda, and anything in the nature of free discussion was impossible. C.I. and E. planned to use this frame-work for the inculcation of democratic citizenship and encouraged the continuance and formation of many adult groups. The Japanese now have an ambitious plan to serve as many as 50 million adults. There is little need for anything in the nature of fundamental edu-cation, for the nation has been 99 percent literate since 1920.

In 1947 a number of four-day schools were held for adult leaders, at two schools in each prefecture, and these were attended by 40,000 people. In 1949, the Social Education Law was enacted in order to give systematic educational activities for youth and adults outside the formal school curriculum. According to this law 8,000 Public Citizens' Halls had been established all over Japan by 1960. Various courses are open to youth and adults to provide working people with knowledge and techniques necessary to their vocations or household affairs and to encourage intellectual and cultural life.

Radio and television are powerful influences in adult education in Japan. More than 23 million radio and TV sets are installed throughout the country, and the Japan Broadcasting Corporation and many commercial stations provide many educational programs for adults.

The Ministry of Education keeps an eye on all adult education ventures. It no longer controls them with an objective of general conformity, but it issues pamphlets and leaflets, makes suggestions, arranges conferences, and encourages the formation of new activi-ties.

As far as youth groups are concerned, the elimination of the youth schools left a gap which has been filled by youth study classes which number about 2,000. The Japanese Council of Youth Associa-tions has been active, fostering organization of youth groups all over the islands. A new feature has made an appearance: in the past these groups were led by village headmen, school principals, or prom-inent adults, but now the management is in the hands of the young people themselves. On a national scale there have been 22 organi-zations established, the membership of which has now reached four million. Youth groups were formerly single-sex, but are now mostly open to membership by both sexes. The Japanese are very fond of drama and dancing, and Drama Leagues, of which most of the members are young people, are found in many towns and villages— a possible counteracting influence to the growing popularity of ballroom dancing and the so-called "taxi-dances" which have alarmed parents who originally were wary about allowing their daughters out in the evenings at all.

As is the case with many new education ventures in Japan, the youth and adult movements in the beginning were hampered in many cases by lack of adequate finances and suitable meeting places, but the Ministry of Education has given active help in developing such activities.

Education and Status of Teachers

EARLIER in this chapter a statement was quoted from the *Nippon Times* showing the unhappy lot of the Japanese teacher in the early years of the occupation. The reader will wonder whether any improvement has been effected in this situation, which was caused by the shortage of teachers, low salaries, and large classes in damaged schools. There has been a distinct improvement, but much remains to be done. The Ministry of Education, referring to the inadequate number of teachers and the low qualifications of many of them, declared in 1952 that "the whole foundation of education in the New Japan is endangered."

The standard of training has been raised considerably since the war. Instead of entering the older normal schools, students who plan to teach attend a university or college that offers courses in education. The national universities in each prefecture now have departments of education. The better normal schools have been raised to university rank as four-year colleges. Elementary teachers are trained for two years or longer, secondary teachers for four years. There are many in-service training programs for the reeducation of older teachers, and these can lead to higher certificates.

In 1949 a new system of national certification of teachers was adopted. Certificates are now classified as regular and emergency, both recognized in any part of the country. Emergency certificates are valid for three years. Teachers are now recognized as government officials, whether they are employed by the Ministry, by the prefectures, or by the towns. This has improved their status, and their salaries have been raised to a level a little higher than the salaries of most civil servants. In 1962 the average salaries for teachers were: elementary schools, $62 per month; lower secondary schools,

$63 per month; and upper secondary schools, $78 per month.[5] All teachers are eligible for a pension after 20 years of service. But if a teacher retires at 60, the general retirement age, he finds that his pension is inadequate and he has to find work on a farm or in some other occupation to maintain his household.

Teachers seem to suffer more from tuberculosis than do workers in other occupations. It has been estimated that 12 percent of the teachers are affected, and sanatoriums are provided for them in each prefecture. The Mutual Aid Association for Local Public Servants, aided by the Ministry and enrolling 750,000 teachers and board of education officials, attempts to provide houses for them and to help married women teachers during childbirth; prefectures allow 12 weeks' leave, with full salaries and a small subsidy, during pregnancy and immediately after childbirth.

Promotion is usually attained by becoming a headmaster or a specialist consultant, but not many women are appointed to these positions. In 1959 the average age of teachers in the upper secondary schools was 34, and in the lower secondary schools and elementary schools 33. The number of women teachers is about the same as that of men in the elementary schools, but in the secondary schools they provide only about 22 percent of the total.

There are three important professional organizations, the Japan Teachers' Union, the Japan Upper Secondary School Teachers' Union, and the Federation of Teachers' Associations. The Japan Teachers' Union consists of organizations generally referred to as welfare groups and the other two are professional associations. As of June, 1962, the Japan Teachers' Union had a membership of 565,700 (74 percent of the elementary and secondary teachers). The Japan Upper Secondary Teachers' Union had 47,000 members (62 percent of the upper secondary teachers). The Federation of Teachers' Associations was formed in 1962 by 11,000 elementary and secondary teachers who seceded from the Japan Teachers' Union. Numerous organizations for research and study have been formed since the end of the war. The results of their research are contributing to the development of education in Japan.

A brighter side of the picture is seen in the opportunities now available for Japanese educators to have cultural experiences in

[5] Salaries in United States dollars are based on the official rate of exchange between dollars and yen at the time. It is unwise to compare them, however, with American salaries, for living costs are much different.

countries abroad. In 1949–50 an invitation was extended for 50 Japanese professors and lecturers in education to spend a year at various American universities. In 1950–51, 283 Japanese teachers, including 56 women, were sent for 12 months' study in 97 American colleges. In 1951–52 a similar experience was given to 500 Japanese teachers, including 80 women. The visitors were popular in the schools they attended, and the authorities reported that there were no unpleasant incidents during their stay in the United States. In addition, other foreign governments offered fellowships and scholarships, 18 in 1961 and 15 in 1962, to Japanese professors. On the other hand, the Japanese Ministry of Education every year sends about 200 research scholars abroad for study, and about 50 principals and teachers for firsthand observation of educational situations in various countries. These trips are usually for two months.

Japanese teachers have better opportunities for gaining improved training than ever before. Their status has risen, although there is still room for improvement. The Ministry and the prefectures are combining their efforts to attract many more capable young people into the teaching service.

Problems of Japanese Education

MANY of the problems facing Japanese education arise from the lack of sufficient financial resources. This is reflected in the difficulty of providing the increasing school population with sufficient equipment.

Provision of School Facilities

Various factors have interfered with the program of building new schools. During the war 80,000 classrooms were destroyed, but by 1950 36 percent of these had been restored. Schools were not the only sufferers during the war. Railways, hydroelectric plants, and industrial plants all presented heavy reconstruction demands. Schools in reasonable condition had to be used, and in many cases were forced to operate in two shifts. Thousands of new heating systems were required for the intensely cold Japanese winters.

The Ministry issued a booklet entitled *Bricks Without Straw*, describing for local authorities various makeshift devices which could be used, and in 1953 7,400,000,000 yen was voted in special grants to aid local programs of rehabilitation and improvement of school facilities. To assist local authorities in planning modern buildings, the Ministry in 1950, 1951, and 1952 issued lists of commended new school buildings. In 1953 there were 140 schools listed as models.

The bulge in school enrollment produced by the sharp increase in the birthrate in the years immediately following the war has now approached the upper secondary level. The percentage of lower secondary students advancing to upper secondary schools has now reached 64 percent and will reach 70 percent in 1965, when it is expected that there will be 1.1 million more students in the upper secondary level.

To solve the problem of expanding upper secondary education in conformance with the government's overall plan for doubling the national income by 1970, the Ministry of Education adopted special measures in 1961 to create a considerable number of new, industrial upper secondary schools. This was accompanied by an emergency program to train teachers of technical subjects in order to staff these new schools.

At present, although almost all the school buildings have been rehabilitated, a great number of new buildings are still required. In addition, wooden buildings represent 84.4 percent of all public schools, and the Ministry of Education is strongly encouraging the construction of reinforced concrete or mass-produced prefabricated buildings that are designed to resist the stresses of earthquakes and typhoons and to be fire-resistant.

Japanese schools are often attractive and unusual in appearance. The majority of them are of wood, with concrete supports and curved roofs of gray tiles. The grounds are well kept and are sometimes adorned with statues of Diligence and Courtesy. Special rooms for Japanese ceremonies have thick *tatami* matting, made of rice straw, as a flooring—all pupils must take off their shoes before entering these rooms. There is no doubt that Japan could make an interesting contribution to school architecture if the necessary funds were available, particularly since schools are now being designed and built for a progressive form of education.

Language Reform

This is a subject which has been long discussed in Japan. S.C.A.P. was reluctant to make a pronouncement about it, feeling that it was a matter for the Japanese people to decide for themselves. There are four systems of writing the Japanese language.

1. *Kanji.* This is made up of Chinese characters or ideographs that were borrowed in the seventh century. In the nine-year period of compulsory education a pupil should learn 1,850 of these Chinese characters; 881 of them are taught in the elementary schools.

2. *Kana.* This employs syllabic letters made by simplifying the ideographs. It is phonetic and is made up of an alphabet of 48 characters, which are also taught in the elementary schools. There are both cursive and print forms.

3. *Kanamajiri.* This is a mixture of *Kanji* and *Kana,* and is widely used for writing. The newspapers commonly use 1,850 *Kanji* characters and 881 *Kana* letters.

4. *Romaji.* This consists of Roman letters and attempts to express the Japanese language in Western form. There are two rival systems, both invented about 1870. One is the Hepburn system devised by an American medical missionary; the other is called *Kunreisiki* and was worked out by Japanese scholars.

The United States Educational Mission in 1946, after some hesitation, recommended the adoption of *Romaji* in the schools. Some of the mission's comments were as follows:

Clearly the matter of language reform is basic and urgent. . . . The Japanese language in its written form constitutes a formidable obstacle to learning. The memorizing of *Kanji* places an excessive burden on the pupils. They are required to give a very large part of their study time to the sheer task of learning to recognize and write the language characters. The need for linguistic reform has long been recognized in Japan and distinguished scholars have devoted much attention to the question.

The mission was of the opinion that *Kanji* should be wholly abandoned. The members felt that the adoption of *Romaji* would constitute "a major contribution to the transmission of knowledge and ideas across national boundaries." This statement and recommendations by the mission revived interest in the whole question of language simplification, particularly as the occupation authorities thought that the whole matter should be left to Japanese initiative. Much activity resulted, both on the part of the Ministry of Education and linguistic scholars generally. In 1946 a simplification of *Kanji* spelling was completed, and the thousands of Chinese characters were reduced to 1,850 for daily use. Students in the upper secondary level and above are supposed to learn many more in order to pursue advanced studies.

The Ministry of Education sponsored a trial of *Romaji* in the schools, on a voluntary basis. After the war a questionnaire was sent out to all elementary schools asking whether they would be willing to try it. As a result of affirmative replies from more than 80 percent of the schools, *Romaji* is now to be taught in the fourth grade of all elementary schools.

There is still much difference of opinion on the whole question, and none of the new systems has gained extensive support. The experiment that is now running in the schools should throw light on this intricate problem. Meanwhile the experiment is being closely and sympathetically watched by the Japanese Institute for Language Research.

Psychological Problems

The greatest difficulties, in a way, are more subtle ones. The school influences its pupils for only a few hours a day, and a child's ideas and sentiments are mainly formed in the family circle. Japanese family life, even in the small temporary shacks that in many cases have replaced comfortable homes, is permeated with centuries-old beliefs and customs that are very different from the Western attitudes which lay behind C.I. and E.'s social studies program. Under the new Constitution, these customs are changing, but a nation's habits of thought cannot easily be altered.

The Future: Advance or Regression?

THE ACCOUNT given in the latter part of this chapter has shown that in the years immediately following the signing of the peace treaty in 1952 progressive and democratic educational procedures have held their own, with the apparent approval of the Japanese. It was said by some observers that with no C.I. and E. in the background, the old basic influences would begin to prevail again, and a return would be made to some of the old procedures. No sign of this has appeared. Does this mean that a new Japan is emerging? Only the years can tell.

Some indication of the Japanese attitude toward the new system of education can be gathered from the 1952–53 Report of the Japanese

Ministry of Education, published after the peace treaty. This report definitely favored the new measures, but stated that certain parts of the postwar structure have been objects of criticism and that a reexamination would have to take place to ensure that Japanese education fits in more exactly with the national temperament and economic circumstances.

These appear to be relatively small matters, and have not affected the basic reorganization of Japanese education. So much depends on the economic future of the country. There is no doubt that this attempt to plant democratic and liberal educational ideas in a country formerly hostile to them is one of the most interesting and significant experiments in modern times. A generation may have to pass before the real results emerge, but at the present time there appears to be no sign of a departure from the principle expressed in the opening paragraph of the Fundamental Law of Education promulgated in 1947: "having established the Constitution of Japan, we have shown our resolution to contribute to the peace of the world and the welfare of humanity by building a democratic and cultural State. The realization of this ideal shall rest fundamentally on the power of education."

19

The Schools of Communist China

THE People's Republic of China occupies the second largest continuous land area on the globe today, second only to the Soviet Union. Two thousand five hundred miles separate the Manchurian border from the border of Indochina; the province of Sinkiang, on the far western frontier, is three thousand miles from the coast. The area of China is larger than Europe without Russia. It includes steamy tropical jungles on the borders of North Vietnam, tremendous ice-clad mountains and deep gorges on the Indian frontiers, the wide Gobi desert on the west and north, and a long common border with the Soviet Union. China has great rivers, wide fertile plains, and waterless deserts.

More striking than the size of the country is the fact that it has the largest population of any nation on earth. Estimates of present population vary from 650 million to 700 million. The Chinese claim a net annual increase of about 2.5 percent. Demographers have said that there will be one billion Chinese by the end of this century.

About 94 percent of the population belong to the Chinese, or Han, people. As in the Soviet Union, there are many minority national groups, among them the Miao, Yao, and Chuang. These peoples are usually classified as falling into three distinct linguistic groups: Mon-Khmer, Shan, and Tibeto-Burman. The recent reestablishment of effective control over Tibet has added many Tibetans. Some of the minority groups are closely related ethnically and linguistically to the peoples of Thailand, Burma, or Indochina. In the north and northwest are other peoples: Mongols and Tungus near the Siberian border; Arabs, Turks, Uighurs, and Kazakhs in Sinkiang (formerly called Chinese Turkestan).

The several minority groups speak their own languages. They wear distinctive dress, eat their own types of food, and do not think of themselves as Han people. The Chinese Communists, like the Russians, believe that minority peoples should be given full cultural autonomy, as a means of securing loyalty to the regime. Since some of the groups had no written language, this has meant providing them with alphabets and books and establishing schools in the native tongues.

Even among the Chinese people there are many local dialects. These dialects differ among themselves so much that a Cantonese cannot understand a man from Peking, or one from Fukien. Although different enough to be called languages, they are usually listed as dialects, because all who speak them can read the same written characters.

China has had a long and turbulent history of wars and conquests, of the rise and fall of empires and dynasties. From time to time it has been ruled by foreign dynasties, but these have always eventually been absorbed into Chinese culture. Throughout this history the city of Peking, although it has not always been the political capital, has been one of the major cultural and educational centers of the country.

In this century China has had a difficult time trying to establish a strong central government and to bring unity to its people. The old Manchu dynasty was overthrown in 1911 by the Nationalists under Sun Yat-sen, who attempted to establish a republican government. The country was torn by internal dissension for years, until Chiang Kai-shek, leader of the Kuomintang, consolidated his hold over most of the country. Japanese aggression and an undeclared war kept the country in turmoil until the opening of World War II, in which China was deeply engaged. The Communists, led by Mao Tse-tung, had concentrated in the north, and they carried on a rebellion against the Kuomintang until Chiang Kai-Shek was finally expelled from the mainland in December, 1949. Chiang, with the remainder of his army, fled to Taiwan, where he governs as President of the Republic of China. The Communist People's Republic of China was inaugurated in October, 1949.

After seizing power the Communists moved rapidly to reform the educational system. The leaders realized that China was a backward nation and that to transform it into a major world power required the development of a mass education system. Conferences were called to discuss necessary changes. The early aims developed from these meetings were to provide equal educational opportunities for girls and women and to establish more coeducational schools, to increase the emphasis on modern scientific education, and to organize a mass education system that could eliminate illiteracy.

As in the Soviet Union, which was taken as a model in education as well as in ideology and economic development, the aims of the school system soon crystallized in two directions: (1) the emphasis on Marxist-Leninist ideology in every part of school and life, with the rewriting of all courses and textbooks in terms of this point of view (the purpose of this practice being to develop the new type of Chinese Communist citizen); (2) the training of specialists and technicians required to bring about the rapid development of the economy and to create a modern and technologically competent nation.

Some of the best of the pre-Communist schools and universities had been supported by foreign funds and operated by missionary groups or through relations with foreign universities and foundations. The Communists moved quickly to sever all foreign ties and to close or take over all of these schools. New types of schools were opened quickly to meet the problems of illiteracy and the shortage of regular schools. Among these were the so-called "Red and Expert Universities" (which were not on the university level), short-course schools, spare-time schools, and winter schools. The programs in these schools were directed toward the great mass of uneduated peasants, upon whom Mao had relied for support. Little attention heretofore had been paid to this large proportion of the population, and there were few facilities for them.

An intensive campaign to eliminate illiteracy has been carried on, with the announced goal of complete literacy by 1965. In 1960 the Ministry of Education claimed that 130 million adults had already passed literacy tests, but the possibility of achieving universal literacy is probably to be determined by the course of economic and political conditions. Since a vast number of characters must be mastered for the writing of Chinese, the literacy problem is particularly complicated. Children in the elementary schools may learn as many as

TABLE 19-1
Higher Education in China, 1922

TYPES OF SCHOOLS	NUMBER OF SCHOOLS	NUMBER OF TEACHERS	NUMBER OF STUDENTS
Universities	33	2,092	13,098
Agricultural academies	7	300	1,271
Higher normal schools	8	731	3,093
Industrial academies	13	429	2,026
Commercial academies	8	280	1,890
Medical academies	7	219	832
Law academies	33	1,084	10,864
Other academies	14	478	1,806
Totals	125	5,613	34,880

SOURCE: *China Educational Dictionary*, China Book Company, 1929, p. 551.

4,000 characters. In the cities, the literacy test is based on knowledge of 2,000 characters; in the country it may be as few as 1,200, which is said to be the minimum requirement for the reading of a simple newspaper.

Mandarin, the spoken language of the capital, Peking, has been made the official language of the country. For many years the authorities considered the use of a phonetic alphabet that would replace the thousands of ideographs which have been used for centuries. An official version, based on the Roman script, has recently been adopted. If this alphabet is pushed vigorously, it will probably help to decrease illiteracy, shorten the time required to learn to read, and help the non-Chinese minorities to learn the Mandarin language.

Higher educational institutions of the Western type in China are almost entirely a development of the twentieth century. Peking University, the first national university, was established in 1898. By 1912 there were four universities in the entire country, and 111 independent colleges and specialized higher institutes. The total enrollment in these institutions was 40,114, about one student in every 10,000 of the total population.[1]

During the ten years following 1912 there was little progress, and

[1] Chung Shih, *Education in Communist China*, Union Research Institute, Hong Kong, 1958, p. 2.

the total enrollment actually declined. A study made by the China Reform Society in 1922 showed the statistics given in Table 19-1. By 1936 the number of higher institutions had dropped to 108, and during the undeclared war with Japan 77 of these schools moved back into the interior and 17 had to close. In 1937 there were only 91 schools remaining with 31,388 students.[2]

The Communist Philosophy of Education

IT IS evident that the Communist plan for education is modeled after that of the Soviet Union and must serve revolutionary purposes—to rid the people of traditional attitudes and ideas and to prepare them for participation in the "New Democracy." The plan follows the Marxist-Leninist ideas on combining education with productive labor. Many of the textbooks used in Chinese schools are translations of standard Russian texts.

If a government wishes to mold the thinking of all of the people, its most powerful weapon is the educational system. Control of that system, combined with control of all means of mass communication, makes it possible to reiterate the same ideas constantly to all of the people all of the time. This fact has been well understood in all totalitarian countries, such as Hitler's Germany, Tojo's Japan, and Stalin's Russia. The Chinese national plan of social reconstruction is clear and definite, and the total resources of mass communication and education are mobilized to carry it out.

One of the slogans of Communist education is "Let politics take command." This slogan means that the life and character of every Chinese, young and old, is to be molded into the pattern of Communist citizenship and morality. Much attention is paid in the schools to the study of Marxism-Leninism-Maoism, and in every school the Communist Party has a representative to whom the teachers must report. If he designates a pupil as being "good political material," that pupil is promoted, regardless of scholastic achievement.[3]

Under the new government the curriculum has been drastically

[2] *National Defense Almanac*, Part V, Vol. I, Section 1 (quoted in Chung Shih, *op. cit.*, p. 5).

[3] Theodore Chen, "Primary Education in Communist China," *Newsnotes on Education Around the World*, U.S. Office of Education, Washington, June, 1952, p. 5.

revised to eliminate all "politically reactionary courses." It is interesting to note that among the courses considered reactionary were
ethics, introduction to philosophy, psychology, and pedagogy.[4]

Chinese Communists are also showing a great interest in the education of overseas Chinese, mainly those who live in various countries of Southeast Asia. Special schools have been set up for these
students, and considerable financial aid provided. The purpose of
this program seems to be to extend the influence of the Communist
regime among Chinese living abroad.

Three basic principles have been announced as governing all education in China today. These are:

1. Education must be led by the Communist Party. Every part of
the educational process must be controlled by Party machinery.

2. Education must serve political ends. Political ideology must
take up a great part of the educational program at any level.

3. Education must be combined with labor. An attempt must be
made to bridge the historical gap between the illiterate mass of
peasants and the highly educated intellectual elite.

The Role of the National Government in Education

ACCORDING to the Constitution of 1954, the real source of power
in the People's Republic of China is the National People's Congress,
which is elected by the provincial and local governing bodies. While
this body is not in session decisions are made by a Standing Committee. A powerful executive committee, the Presidium, is chosen
from the Standing Committee. The National People's Congress de-
cides on the establishment of national ministries or commissions.
When the Communist government was established in 1949 it included a national Ministry of Education that was under the general
supervision of a Committee on Education and Cultural Affairs. This
Committee was not continued by the 1954 Constitution. The heads
of ministries and commissions are members of the State Council,
which is similar to the ministry or cabinet in other countries. This
Council may establish other agencies, such as the Committee on Ed-

---

[4] *Star Island Daily*, Hong Kong, November 2, 1950. Educational statistics from
China are obtained from news releases, usually translated in Hong Kong, or from
translated reports of speeches given by high officials. Most of these lack precision,
and are at times contradictory.

ucation and Cultural Affairs, and these agencies may have some control over programs. Seldom, if ever, is a matter as important as national education left to the complete charge of a single ministry.

In the early days of the Communist regime the work of the Ministry of Education was carried on by five major departments: Elementary Education, Secondary Education, Higher Education, Social Education, and Supervision. In 1952 the administration of higher education was taken from the Ministry of Education and a separate Ministry of Higher Education was established. However, as in the Soviet Union, some specialized higher institutes were left under the supervision of industrial ministries; for example, a mining institute might be under the Ministry of Mines. The Institute of the Petroleum Industry is under the joint control and supervision of three ministries—Higher Education, Geology, and Fuel.

At the outset almost all schools were national schools, supported from the national budget. Under a decentralization policy more and more schools have been placed under the control of provinces, communes, or industrial enterprises, and these bodies have, in varying degrees, assumed responsibility for finance.

In the fields of textbooks, curricula, and teaching methods, uniformity and conformity have been secured through national prescriptions. An ambitious plan, called the "Great Leap Forward," was introduced in 1958 for the purpose of national development. But the program strained the resources of the country and attempted much more than could be achieved. National standards in academic work have become increasingly difficult to maintain.

The Role of the Communist Party

AS IN the U.S.S.R., there is an appearance of great decentralization of government functions and control, with an actual complete centralization of authority in the monolithic Communist party. The multifarious government agencies are the machinery of government: beside them at every level is the apparatus of the Party, which actually makes the important decisions and sets the policies. The organization of the Party reflects that of the government at every level.

At the top, there is the National Party Congress, which is parallel to the National People's Congress. Beside the Standing Committee of the National People's Congress, there is the Central Committee of the Party, with 170 members. Because of overlapping memberships, high Party officials hold important government positions, and government officials hold high Party positions. The highest administrative agency is the Presidium, a select group from the Standing Committee. Parallel with this group is the Politburo, which is the highest authority in the Party.

Party committees are set up at all levels, paralleling the government congresses, committees, and commissions. Each local education committee must have at least one active member of the Party in its membership. Most of the Party organizations exert direct influence upon the daily work of all educational institutions. The General Propaganda Department of the Party probably has more influence on the educational life of the country than the Ministry of Education.

It is reported that there are 14 million Party members in China, which would mean about 2 percent of the total population. Most of these Party members are active in some phase of government or industry. The law provides for the organization of a Party branch (similar to the Soviet cell) in any factory, mine, village, industrial enterprise, city street, army company, office, or school where there are three or more Party members. These make up the active "cadres" so often discussed in Chinese literature. The major responsibility of all such groups and individuals is to ensure that the Party line is followed implicitly in every phase of life and that education is Communist first and academic or technical second.

The Role of Regional Subdivisions

IN THE first years of the Communist regime, the historical provinces of China were grouped into six "Greater Administrative Regions." These were abolished in 1954, and the province remains the sole intermediate unit between the local subdivisions and the national government. The provinces have some responsibilities in higher education and in specialized vocational education, but most of the responsibility now rests with local agencies.

The Role of Local Agencies

UNDER the organic law of the People's Republic, local congresses are established at each level of administration. Smaller municipalities, municipal districts in the larger cities, towns, counties, and minority areas all elect members of these congresses by direct vote of the people. Larger cities and provinces have congresses, elected by the subdistrict congresses. In addition, communes, factories, and other enterprises have elected councils. According to Article 31 of the Constitution the people's congresses at all levels have responsibility for education. Each local congress is required to carry out the decisions of the next higher level, and so on up the scale. The final decisions are made at the top.

Each congress has a People's Council as its executive body. As in the Soviet Union, there is a double responsibility, that of supervising the work of congresses at the next lower level, and that of carrying out the dictates of the next higher congress. The rights of minority groups are protected by a provision for representation in all of the various governing bodies. Provincial and larger municipal Councils have legal authority to establish boards, bureaus, divisions, committees, or commissions to assume direct responsibility for education.[5]

The People's Councils, which are executive agencies, set up subordinate committees or boards to control schools. These committees are parallel with other similar committees of comparable organization that carry out other functions of government. Here again, the educational committees receive directives from higher levels and issue them to lower levels of organization. Important changes in educational organization and procedures may come almost overnight under such a system, when once the highest authority makes a decision. Since the Communists do not subscribe to historical and traditional points of view, they are free to change speedily every part of the program at will, as conditions permit.

Finance

IN THE early years of the revolutionary regime nearly 90 percent of the financial support of education came from the central government. Earlier governments derived most of their income from customs duties, land taxes, and salt taxes. The Communist government has the profits from all government-owned farms and business enterprises, and collects taxes on grain and business profits directly. The government also raises funds from the sale of bonds, and during the first years of the regime large sums were derived from the confiscation of private wealth. There were also large credits granted

[5] Reller and Morphet, *Comparative Educational Administration*, p. 278.

by the Soviet government, but these have not been important since 1958, and the Chinese are being forced to repay them.

With the emphasis on the "Great Leap Forward" and the accelerated development of the industrial capacity of the country, the central government has found itself unable to continue to support the schools. Increasingly the responsibility for support has been thrown back upon local governmental bodies, communes, and factories that operate the schools. Out of this has developed a new type of "self-supporting" school, in which the students work half time and go to school half time, often on farms or in factories operated by the schools themselves.

Local authorities have the right to levy taxes on any private property remaining and to add a surtax to the national grain levy. In theory, education is free, but many schools charge fees, and students pay for their own books and supplies. Promising students are given government subsidies. Many schools are maintained by industrial enterprises or communes, which pay the costs of operation.

The Organization of Chinese Schools

THE TRADITIONAL Chinese educational system was devoted to the old classics and aimed at producing highly trained scholars to become teachers or government officials. Usually a two-year kindergarten was followed by a six-year elementary school, divided into a three-year lower school and a three-year upper school. Elementary school was followed by a six-year middle school, which was also divided into a three-year lower middle school and a three-year upper middle school. Much vocational work was often included in the upper middle school. After this secondary school came a four-year university course. A huge proportion of the population received no schooling at all, and illiteracy was high.

The general organization of schools in Communist China looks very much like the outline that might have been drawn up in prerevolutionary days. Various types of "proletarian" schools have been added, as illustrated in Figure 19-1.

Preschool Education

KINDERGARTEN programs in present-day China seem to be attuned to the need to provide day care for children while their mothers

19-1 The Educational System of Communist China

YEARS IN SCHOOL					YEARS OF AGE
16	Universities		Research departments		22
15			Independent colleges		21
14					20
13		Specialized institutes			19
12					18
11	Upper middle schools	Upper secondary technical schools	Proletarian short-course middle schools (3-4 years)	Vocational upper middle schools	17
10					16
9					15
8	Lower middle schools			Vocational lower middle schools	14
7					13
6					12
5	Elementary schools		Proletarian short-course elementary schools (2-3 years)	Vocational elementary schools	11
4					10
3					9
2					8
1					7
	Kindergartens				6
					5
					4
					3

SOURCE: *Jen Min Jih Pao*, Oct. 2, 1951 (quoted in Chung Shih, *op. cit.*, p. 13).

work. In a society where all manpower and womanpower is required to provide enough food for an increasing population and to improve the industrial potential of the nation, practically all women are employed outside the home. Having small children below school age is no excuse for staying at home. Very little information is available about Chinese kindergartens. It is probable that some are well organized and provide educational programs; it is equally probable that the majority of them provide "checkrooms" for little ones, in charge of women too old to work in fields or factories.

Chandra-sekhar reported visiting crèches and kindergartens and being greeted by joyous clapping of hands and singing of songs extolling Chairman Mao and the commune system. Like all Communists the Chinese believe in starting to teach Communist doctrines early and in indoctrinating the little ones with "collectivist" spirit. Most factories, farms, communes, and mills provide such crèches and kindergartens.[6]

Elementary Education

IT WAS reported in 1955 that there were 53 million children in elementary schools. By the end of 1956 this number had risen to 62 million, and in October, 1958, an official of the Chinese Communist government stated that there were 1,470,000 elementary schools with 118 million pupils. If these figures are reliable, they indicate that practically all children of elementary age were then in school. This would of course include all types of regular schools, part-time schools, factory schools, and farm schools.[7]

In 1961 the Red Flag Commune at Shenyang was said to be operating nine elementary schools for children aged 7 to 12, as well as 32 regular kindergartens and 130 small nurseries. They also had four secondary schools. In all, this one commune provided education for 17,000 school age children.[8]

The elementary school program attempts to get all children of school age into some sort of school program. The three R's are stressed, as in every country, but with one significant difference. Read-

[6] Sripati Chandra-sekhar, *Red China: An Asian View*, p. 79.

[7] O. Fisher, "Education in Communist China," *School and Society*, Vol. 87, No. 2156 (June 20, 1959), p. 302.

[8] Felix Greene, *China, The Country Americans Are Not Allowed to Know*, p. 249.

ing and writing are much more difficult in a language made up of thousands of characters. It is claimed that no less than six years, over 5,000 hours of classroom time, are necessary to teach the Chinese script. If acceptance of the new Roman script becomes general, the process should be greatly simplified.

Class work in Communist China tends to be centered upon instruction by the teacher, with much drill through oral recitations. In all Communist countries there is great faith in the value of literacy and in the ability to read newspapers and Party documents. But at the same time, the strained economic situation of the country, as well as Communist ideology, requires that academic education be combined with labor, even in the elementary years. Elementary pupils are not spared from work in factories and in the fields, although more attention is given to inculcation of the right attitude toward labor than to productive labor itself.

Increasing numbers of elementary schools are attaching themselves to factories, farms, or gardens for work hours, or are establishing small factories or gardens which they operate themselves. Some foreign observers have felt that these programs exploit the children to the detriment of the academic program.

Secondary Education

SECONDARY schools are usually called "middle schools" in China, and are divided into two three-year cycles—the lower middle school and the upper middle school. Successful completion of the elementary school is officially the standard for entrance. However, under the emphasis of getting more children into school it appears that academic standards have suffered and that some children are in the middle schools because they are in the secondary age group.

General middle schools have an academic curriculum, with emphasis on political indoctrination. Public opinion seems to favor the academic type of middle school as a door opening to business or governmental occupations. The general middle school spends 26 weeks a year, six days a week, in regular class work, four weeks for reviews and examinations, and three weeks on a special work project. The students are also expected to work during school vacations. The daily time schedule is divided into six or seven 50-minute periods.[9] Military drill is required for boys.

[9] Felix Greene, op. cit., p. 220.

Specialized or vocational middle schools are somewhat like the Russian *tekhnikumi*. They prepare students for semiskilled positions in industry or agriculture. Some of these schools are attached to and supported by industrial ministries or specific business enterprises.

University and Higher Education

THE PRESENT century has seen the development of Chinese university education. Peking had four important universities before the revolution. National University of Peking (usually called "Peita") was truly Chinese. Here the traditional Chinese classics were taught by some of the nation's best scholars. Many leaders of the government and of the life of the country were graduates of this school. Yenching University was supported by American funds and had close relations with "Harvard-in-China." It offered a more Western type of education, and also had an important effect on the life of the country. Tsinghua University was also Western and was supported by funds from the Boxer Indemnity. The fourth school was a Catholic university, Fu Jen.

A radical reduction in the number of universities and colleges followed the reorganization made by the China Reform Society in 1922, which also increased the number of higher technical schools. Under the Communists all schools with foreign connections or support were closed or reorganized under new administrations. Great progress has been made in establishing higher schools and in increasing the number of students enrolled. This progress is shown in Table 19–2. Under the new regime, higher educational institutions may be classified in three groups: (1) those under the Ministry of Education or associated ministries; (2) those under the provincial governments; and (3) those established by local agencies. Under the program of decentralization many institutions have been transferred to provincial or local control. This has been a logical development of the policy of reducing the burden on the national budget. If the figure of 810,000 students is accepted, one Chinese in 800 gets some sort of higher educational opportunity, compared with one in 9,000 fifteen years ago.[10]

Under the last Five-Year Plan student enrollment was to be in-

[10] Felix Greene. *ob. cit.*, p. 219.

TABLE 19-2
Chinese Higher Education

YEAR	NUMBER OF COLLEGES AND UNIVERSITIES	NUMBER OF STUDENTS (IN THOUSANDS)
1947	207	155
1949	205	117
1952	201	194
1957	229	444
1958	1,408	790
1959*	—	810

SOURCE : *Peking Review*, No. 40, December 2, 1958.

* Figures for 1959 (which do not list the number of institutions) are from *Ten Great Years*, Peking: People's Publishing House, 1959.

creased to 850,000 by 1962. The Plan proposed to graduate 250,000 students annually from the five-year course, a total that would be comparable to Soviet or American graduating classes.[11]

Much of the increase in number of institutions and in student enrollment came during the time of the "Great Leap Forward," and much of it is in spare-time colleges and in the so-called "Red and Expert Universities." Most of these would not qualify as universities under Western standards.

In many respects Chinese universities do not resemble Western universities. The program of indoctrination has assumed a place of central importance. An announcement in the press on December 30, 1959, concerning the University of Peking, expressed the official point of view:

In 1958, the University launched a vigorous revolutionary campaign to criticize bourgeois ideas of conducting education simply for education's sake, or detaching mental labor from manual labor, and of allowing only experts to direct education. As a result, the Party's policy, of making education serve the political purposes of the proletariat and integrating education with productive labor, was implemented in an overall manner, and Party leadership over all phases of school work was further consolidated. By holding red and expert debates and starting a revolution to

[11] O. Fisher, *op. cit.*, p. 304.

raise self-consciousness, all the teachers, students, and workers of the university made a great change in their ideological look, set their courses in the red and expert directions and resolved to train themselves to be intellectuals of the working class.[12]

The curriculum of the modern Chinese university includes very little that would be called "liberal arts." The only such course taught in many institutions is linguistics and phonetics, the inclusion of which is understandable in a country that has the problem of making an official dialect standard for the whole nation. Courses in history, political science, anthropology, sociology, and world literature are taught only in comprehensive universities. All students are required to take the four so-called social science courses: foundations of Marxism-Leninism; political economy; history of the Chinese Revolution; and historical and dialectical materialism. Most of the student's time, in addition to the required subjects, is spent in the field of his specialization. It is not only in institutions that are called "red and expert" that the students are expected to be red first and expert second.

Lauerys has reported that in spite of the emphasis on proletarian education over 80 percent of the students come from the middle classes.[13] The average age of entrance is about 18 years. Arts students take a five-year course; science students may spend six years. In some of the higher technical institutes there are shorter courses. About 20 percent of the students are women. There are several hundred foreign students in Chinese universities from other Iron Curtain countries and from some African and Asian countries.

No charges are made for tuition, books, housing, or medical care. If a student is able to pay, he is charged 12 yuan (about $4.80) per month for his food. Poorer students may receive grants to cover costs of food and clothing. Under the half-work, half-study plan students are paid at regular rates for their labor and receive no subsidies.

Comprehensive universities require completion of the middle school for entrance, but some of the spare-time and "red and expert universities" have no academic requirements for entrance. One of the technological universities listed its entrance requirements, in order of priority, as follows: (1) a thorough orientation to the

---

[12] Reller and Morphet, *op. cit.*, p. 291.

[13] J. A. Lauerys, "Problems of Education in Communist China," *Comparative Education Review*, Vol. 1, No. 2 (October, 1957), p. 6.

Marxist approach to all problems; (2) excellent health; and (3) requisite mental ability to do the work.[14]

The Ministry of Higher Education controls schools through a carefully planned system of unified enrollments. A uniform examination is given at many local centers throughout the country in August. Those who take this examination list on their applications their preferences for fields of specialization and for schools they would like to attend. They may apply for any institution in the country. A National Enrollment Committee for Institutes of Higher Education allocates the students to subject fields and to institutions—the student, if he enters higher education, must accept the assignment. When he graduates, he may express a preference for the type of job and the area of the country to which he wishes to be assigned, but assignment is also on a national basis, and he must accept the assignment given to him. Since practically everyone works for the government, to refuse a government assignment is to remain unemployed. There is some criticism of the system, and students are not too happy with it, but to speak out too loudly is to run the risk of being classified as "counter-revolutionary."

Even in the faculties it has been more important to be reliable politically than it is to be qualified academically. The policy of the government has been to assign military men or long-time revolutionaries to administrative positions as presidents and deans of universities. There has been some notable change in this policy, and expertness is now being stressed as well as "redness." The policy has seemed to be that education is too important to be left in the hands of educationists. Some professors have little academic background, but may have long experience and skill in a particular activity; for example, a successful sheep raiser may be assigned as a professor of animal husbandry.

Postgraduate work in China is a recent development and has not progressed very far. Some work is done in a few universities and in the Chinese Academy of Sciences. It is estimated that about 2,000 Chinese graduate students are studying in the Soviet Union or in the European satellites. When they return these people are usually employed as professors or in research work. There has been a determined effort to persuade Chinese who did graduate work in the United States to return and help in the development of their country.

[14] Chandra-sekhar, *op. cit.*, p. 95.

Education and Status of Teachers

ALTHOUGH the regular university course is five years, the shortage of secondary teachers has driven the universities to reduce the training course for them to two or three years. Elementary teachers are trained in specialized middle schools, which cover the last three years of the secondary school course, with some courses in teacher preparation. In the first years of the regime teachers in part-time schools were often trained, if at all, in special short courses set up by the factory, farm, or commune that operated the schools. Some of these courses have been as short as two weeks.[15]

Teachers are not well paid, and in some cases must take part or all of their pay in food. In spare-time schools the teachers usually work on full-time jobs and teach in their spare time, a practice which cuts down on teaching efficiency, because working hours on the regular job are long and the work is often exhausting. Spare-time teachers have been paid 2 catties (2⅔th pounds) of rice for every three hours taught.[16]

All teachers must belong to the Teachers' Union which is organized by the Party rather than by the teachers. Its purpose is not to improve salaries or working conditions but to ensure that government policies are carried out faithfully and that political education is extended.

Productive Labor

IN September, 1958, even before the Soviet Union proclaimed its educational reform of 1958, the Central Committee of the Party in China issued a directive that provided a close integration of schools and work, required schools to set up farms and factories, and required farms and factories to establish schools. By November it was reported that over 150,000 small factories and 100,000 farms and gardens had been put into operation by over 20,000 educational institutions.[17]

[15] Chi Tung-wei, "Education for the Proletariat in Communist China," Union Research Institute, Hong Kong, 1956, p. 36.

[16] Ibid., p. 40.

[17] Survey of the Chinese Mainland Press, Hong Kong: Vol. 1829 (November 5, 1958), p. 13.

Following the Party directive, on every Chinese college and university campus, and in many lower schools, banners appeared with one of the inevitable Communist slogans, such as "Education Must be Combined with Productive Labor." School gardens and workshops were set up in every part of the country. Where the Russian worker is exhorted to work harder to "catch up with the United States" in production, in China the slogan seems to be to "catch up with Great Britain in fifteen years." Older students in middle schools and universities are sent out into the fields and factories for two months "putting theory into practice." Even teachers and professors are included in this program.

One interesting development coming out of this program is the "self-supporting" school. This type of school, which is for older students, engages in work half of the time and in study half time, and the earnings of the students are used to support the school. Evidence seems to indicate that, although some of these schools have been called "people's universities," they are not on the university level but are narrowly vocational, at the secondary level. This type of school (which was also attempted in India) offers possibilities for expansion under the present conditions of Chinese financial stringency and the drive for economic development.[18]

Chandra-sekhar believes that this movement will lead to the dissolution of schools as the Western world ordinarily understands them.[19] The program is nothing like the well-established American one of "working one's way through college." While it stresses the Marxist-Leninist idea of a combination of education with labor, its major purpose seems to differ from that of the Soviets. The Russians are interested in making sure that every citizen has had experience with labor and in placing emphasis on the dignity of manual work. The Chinese, on the other hand, actually stress getting manual work done for the immediate development of the country and adding to the work force. This motive is not lacking in Russian thinking, but the Chinese emphasis indicates that the development of China is at a much lower level than that of the U.S.S.R.

---

[18] Robert D. Barensen, "Half-Work, Half-Study Universities," *Newsnotes on Education Around the World*, Washington: U.S. Office of Education, June, 1962, p. 5.

[19] Chandra-sekhar, *op. cit.*, p. 99.

Boarding Schools

LIKE the Russians, the Chinese have been experimenting with the operation of boarding schools. These are usually on the elementary level and provide places for young children to attend school, work, eat, and sleep. As in the Soviet Union, the Chinese believe that these schools will help the children to "rid themselves at an early age of their mental development of the influences of backward and self-ish concepts born with the old family institution." In other words, it will be easier to develop dedicated Communists. But in addition to this, the mothers are needed in the fields and factories, and such schools free them from family responsibilities. Family traditions are strong in China, and the peasants have not been happy with the boarding schools.[20]

Youth Organizations

FOLLOWING the pattern set by their Soviet mentors, the Chinese Communists have established a comprehensive program of Young Communist organizations. For children between the ages of 9 and 15 there is the Young Pioneers, with the red scarf as the badge of membership. Much of the political education of children is carried on in these groups, which also provide activities for the spare time that is left after school and work. The activities of these groups are very similar to those of the Russian Pioneers. Teachers are used as adult leaders. It was estimated that there were 60 million members in 1960.

For older students, between the ages of 14 and 25, there is the Communist Youth League. If there are five members in any school, an official branch is established. This organization carries on projects and activities similar to those of the Russian Komsomols. It has the responsibility of impressing the Party line and Communist ideology on the mass mind of the youth of the country. The organization is also considered to be the novitiate which trains new members for the Party.

Problems of Chinese Education

THE ATTEMPT to carry out a crash program of providing a mass education system for 700 million people, from a low base, cannot

[20] "Collective Life for School Children in Communist China," Current Background, Vol. 45 (December 18, 1958), p. 10.

be done without many strains, dislocations, and problems. Many of these are apparent in the reports which come out of mainland China and are monitored in Hong Kong or Taipei. A few of the problems are indicated below.

The Establishment of an Efficient System of Mass Education

To establish a system of universal education for such a huge population is a tremendous task. To do this when all of the financial and physical resources of the nation are being devoted to making a "Great Leap Forward" economically, from an almost primitive economic structure to that of a modern technological power, makes the task even more difficult. Recent measures of decentralization, which throw the burden of educational support back on the local subdivisions or even on the schools themselves, indicate that the national government is unable to finance the program. Results have been part-time education, unqualified teachers, poor buildings and equipment, and lowered educational standards.

It must be admitted that there are some "point of emphasis" schools where academic standards are high, teachers are good, and facilities adequate. The number of such "good" schools is still small but probably no smaller than in pre-Communist days. The educational level of the people is undoubtedly rising, even though standards are still below those acceptable in Western countries. The effort at mass education is nation-wide in scope and will have its effects upon economic development as the literary and technical skills of the people improve.

A Bridge Between the Uneducated Proletariat and the
Highly Educated Intelligentsia

The Chinese Communist movement was based upon the support of peasants and workers. Great efforts are being made to make "every worker an educated, cultured Communist citizen, and every intellectual a worker." But in 1956, 80 percent of the college students came from the middle classes. They were the children of teachers, government officials and servants, and professional men. Later figures are not available, but the leaders would like to see a higher percentage of the students coming from the proletariat. The problem seems to be how to get more good quality students from the homes of peasants and workers.

Traditional Attitudes

The Chinese people have a cultural tradition that has unified them for over a thousand years. Alien conquerors have ruled them many times during their long history, but the Chinese have always been able to assimilate even the most oppressive of the foreign groups and have effectively made them essentially Chinese. This is the first time that an alien philosophy of life and government (Marxism) has been forced on them, not by foreigners, but by a wholly Chinese government. The new regime is pledged to wipe out the old, traditional Chinese loyalties and beliefs. In the beginning this was done by coercive means, but now the government is relying more on indoctrination and control of mass communications. The communes have broken up the little family farms; the families are being weakened by communal living and boarding schools; the old religions are held up to ridicule. But old ideas die hard. Although the new leaders are ruthless and single-minded, it has not yet been proven that they can develop the ideal of an all-around New Man in a Communist society. According to reports in the Communist press, there are still rebellious young people in China, who object to long hours of work and constant indoctrination and rigorous assignment of jobs. These individuals are powerless under the present regime, but they indicate the existence of dissatisfaction.

Through their knowledge of the Russian experience, the Chinese are attempting to develop a monolithic state and an educational system that will create the "New Communist Man." In statistical terms—number of roads, schools, factories, and steel mills built—they can show impressive progress, but much of this has been achieved at the expense of quality. They do, however, seem to prefer a little education for everyone to a high quality of education for a few favored individuals.

20

Education in India

SOUTH of the great Himalayan mountain range, and geographically isolated from the rest of Asia, lies what modern geographers call the subcontinent of India. At one time it was entirely under British rule, but since 1947 it has been divided into two independent countries, India and Pakistan. The Republic of India covers an area of 1,266,000 square miles and in 1963 had a population of 446 million people, a population density of 352.2 per square mile. Although Europeans for many years thought of all of the people of India as Indians, the population includes peoples of many different races, who speak over 200 different languages. Many of these languages might properly be called dialects, since there is little difference between them, but there are 14 different linguistic groups.

India has been overrun in the last 4,000 years by waves of conquerors, all of whom have left their mark on the racial composition and culture of the people. The early Aryans came into the area thousands of years ago and effectively submerged the original inhabitants. Muslim invaders conquered large parts of the country in the twelfth century and converted many of the people to Islam. India has made great contributions to the world's store of learning, particularly in mathematics, philosophy, religion, and art, but these activities were restricted to a small portion of the people. Some education was provided by religious groups and private enterprise, and most of the people, except the untouchables, came more or less in contact with it. Apparently schools were more widespread three centuries ago than immediately before the period of the two world wars.

In 1600 the British East India Company was established by Parliamentary Charter, and in the next 150 years the power of the Company was extended over most of India. In 1773, Parliament took over political responsibility from the East India Company and set up a governor-general appointed by the Crown. The British government gradually increased its control, restricting and finally abolishing the Company's commercial monopoly and extending the power of the governor-general. The rule of the company was finally removed in 1858, and Parliament assumed the remainder of the duties that had been in the Company's hands and replaced the governor-general with a viceroy. England began to direct development toward native participation in government, and agitation from India's rising middle class resulted eventually in concessions of representative government.

A revised Charter in 1813 had placed responsibility for education upon the Company. It took a number of years and much debate to decide whether to continue the traditional type of Indian education, based on the classical Sanskrit, or to develop a modern, Western-oriented school program with English as the medium of instruction. Influenced by the recommendations of the historian Macaulay, who was adviser to the governor-general, the British government encouraged the organization of schools which would teach the English curriculum. Such a program was offered as a means of permitting the intellectual elite to take over minor administrative positions, and it was hoped that its influence would work from the top downwards. The result was the training, in English, of many capable clerks and aspirants for government positions, but the mass of the people were left unschooled. The system of education concentrated on the aim of public employment rather than on knowledge for its own sake and ignored the vernacular languages.

It might be thought that the British had a wonderful opportunity of instituting a nation-wide system of education. However, in the early days of British rule trade was the main objective, and even in England there was no system of national education. Later, when mass education became popular, the difficulties and the enormous cost of any such plan for India prevented the British from embarking on anything of the sort, although they did do a great deal for India in the fields of health, transportation, industrial development, the prevention of famine, and the gradual development of self-government.

India attained independence in August, 1947, as a Dominion of the British Commonwealth of Nations. It was the first major addition to the postwar world community of free nations. In 1950 the country elected to become an independent republic. The educational task ahead of the new nation was colossal. In 1951, of a population of

360 million [1] the census estimated that 72 million were in the age group of 6 to 14 years; of these, only 12,777,000 boys and 4,617,000 girls were in school; that is, only one child in four was receiving any schooling. Facilities varied startlingly between the states. Bombay and Travancore had well-attended systems of elementary education; in Rajasthan and Bhopal hardly any children were in school. Illiteracy was estimated at about 85 percent for the whole country.

The task of providing a universal school system for a huge population in a country with undeveloped resources, many languages, and many religions is tremendous. The national and state governments have applied themselves to these problems and are slowly making headway. Although India has an immense population, the distribution of these large numbers is such that the establishment of schools is not easy. About 70 percent of the people live in small villages, the majority of which have fewer than 800 people. Except in the very fertile areas such as the Indo-Gangetic plain, the population is thinly dispersed and the roads very poor. Villages need to be grouped, with a school centrally located, but the children cannot walk very far in the scorching heat and torrential rains which are characteristic of Indian seasons. The cost of bus transportation continues to be prohibitive. On the Himalayan slopes and in Kashmir the hamlets are miles apart and the mountain paths blocked by snow.

When the Indian people gained their independence and drew up, in 1947, a new Constitution, Article 45 read as follows:

"The State shall endeavor to provide within a period of ten years from the commencement of this Constitution for free and compulsory primary education for all children until they reach the age of 14 years."

So far the results are disappointing. The difficulties facing the implementation of this objective were enough to daunt the government and cause it to go slowly. That a system of general education was badly needed was shown in the first general elections when 90 million voted. Many of these voters were illiterate and could not read the directions or the names of candidates. Oral instructions were given by the polling officers, and symbols and pictures were placed on the ballots. Actually the unlettered voters did very well, but there were some cases of misunderstanding and misrepresentation

[1] In the partition (1947) of the former British territories on the Indian subcontinent, about 23 percent of the area went to Pakistan.

and some were tricked into voting for opponents of their party. It was clearly shown that illiteracy of the electorate might easily be a serious danger to the development of Indian democracy.

Social, political, and economic life in India have always been conditioned by religious beliefs. Religions serve both to unite and to divide the people. Of every 100 Indians, 85 are Hindus, 10 are Muslims, 2 are Christians, and 1 or 2 are Sikhs. There are smaller groups of Jains, Buddhists, Parsees, animists, and others. Hinduism divides its own people into the four castes of Brahmins, warriors, merchants, and farmers, with an additional army of untouchables. These divisions have been weakened by recent social legislation, and the appellation "untouchable" has been outlawed. But caste differences still exist and hamper reforms. In schools, for example, people of higher castes disapprove of their children mixing with those of lower castes, particularly with the former untouchables. Religion means a great deal in the lives of the Indian people: it was the religious atmosphere of Gandhi's great crusade—the religion of love, sacrifice, and suffering—that made it a success.

Muslims, Hindus, and Christians all favor general education but would prefer to have it tied to their own religious beliefs. They have all supported the idea of separate schools for each religious community, but this would enormously increase the expense and defeat the aim of national unity through education. Moreover, the new Constitution adopted in 1950 declares India a secular state, so that no religious instruction can be given in schools which receive tax support.

Child marriage, still practiced in spite of legal prohibitions, draws girls away from school. Muslim groups object to their girls going to coeducational schools, and separate elementary schools for boys and girls are a financial impossibility. One of the most serious obstacles to the education of children is the illiteracy of adults. When a child lives in an atmosphere of ignorance at home, there is the chance that he will lapse into illiteracy through the lack of anything to read. It is evident that the campaign for the education of adults must accompany the plan for the education of their children.

The 14 major languages of India are not all confined to their own regions, and there are linguistic minorities in almost every area. Hindi has been declared the official national language and is spoken by more people than any other, but millions speak Tamil, Bengali, Urdu, Teluga, Bihari, Punjabi, and Marathi. Some of the hill tribes have spoken but no written languages. Recent reorganizations of boundaries have attempted to make the states more homogeneous linguistically. The script of Hindi (Devanagari) makes it a difficult language, and the general adoption of a Roman script has been suggested in its place. Such a change might be ideal for the general extension of elementary education, but Indian tradition and opinion suspect "colonialism" and anything that suggests Western superiority. Provision, then, has to be made for instruction to be carried out in the native language, with Hindi added if it is not already spoken as the regional language.

The 1950 Constitution provides that while Hindi "in the Devanagari script" is the official language, English may be used until 1965 "for all official purposes of the Union for which it was being used" when the Constitution was adopted. Some of the states where Hindi is not spoken have shown resentment at attempts to enforce Hindi as the official language. The increased use of regional languages in higher education has brought about some deterioration in academic standards, according to some Indian educators.[2]

The Conference of State Education Ministers decided, in 1949, that separate schools would be set up for children whose mother tongue was a language other than the regional or state language, if the numbers justified. These children would also study the state language as a second compulsory subject in the elementary grades. In the secondary schools, the medium of instruction would be in the mother tongue of the pupils, but they would also be required to study the regional language, if it was different, and Hindi as the official language. Kanungo reported that some Indians might find it necessary to study five languages if they wished to complete higher education: the mother tongue, the regional language, the official language (Hindi), the classical language (Sanskrit), and the cultural language (English) as a vehicle of modern knowledge and science.[3] The lack of scientific and technical terms in many of the languages is a real drawback in university education. Many Indian students are eager to study in the United Kingdom or in the United States, for which facility in English is essential.

All of these problems fade into insignificance compared with the difficulties presented by the poverty of the people. When the average

[2] Gostha Behari Kanungo, *The Language Controversy in Indian Education,* Comparative Education Center, University of Chicago, Chicago, 1962, p. 64.
[3] *Ibid.,* p. 76

Indian worker has an income of $54 a year (with which he has to support himself, his wife and children, and sometimes several dependent relatives), it is a drastic measure to take from him the labor of his child, who could be working on the little family farm or as a domestic servant elsewhere, in order to send that child to school.

The expense of the planned program on a nation-wide scale is beyond the financial resources of the national and state governments combined. Moreover, the national government has increasingly heavy and costly defense commitments and the expense of undertaking many important developmental programs, such as the construction of huge hydroelectric plants and irrigation schemes. But the government does feel that economic development and the expansion of educational facilities must go hand in hand. So far the increase in agricultural production due to improved methods of farming and new irrigation projects has barely kept up with the increase in population.

The Role of the National Government in Education

THE Republic of India is a Union of States, with a federal form of government. There is a President, a Prime Minister, and a bicameral legislature divided into a Council of States and a House of the People. Three categories of powers are distributed between the Union and the state governments by the Constitution: those powers exclusively allotted to the Union; those reserved to the states; and those in which state and nation have concurrent jurisdiction. Education is considered to be almost entirely a state function. In the Union government there is a Ministry of Education, whose head, the Minister of Education, is a member of Parliament and of the Council of Ministers of the Union. The function of the Union Ministry is considered to be that of an "advising, coordinating, and serving agency." It is interested in some of the specialized aspects of the educational system. As such, it has established certain specialized agencies, such as the National Institute of Audio-visual Education, the National Institute of Basic Education, and the Central Institute of Education. It creates advisory bodies to assist the state governments.

Some other federal ministries have educational functions. The Ministry of Agriculture established a college for higher training in agricultural subjects; the Ministry of National Defense established and controls the officer training college; and the Ministry of Scientific Research and Culture awards scholarships and aids in scientific research.

The Ministry of Education (1) works with advisory bodies to draft educational policy and related programs and to plan for the financing of projects; (2) has responsibility for general supervision over educational aspects of the Five-Year Plans and the annual Educational Development Programs; (3) renders financial assistance (in keeping with parliamentary appropriations at various levels) and controls the utilization of such funds; (4) grants scholarships for specialized study in India and abroad in many fields; (5) maintains certain Union institutions and has control of, without operating, educational programs and institutions for backward classes and schools in Union Territories (Amindivi, Andaman, Laccadive, and Nicobar Islands; Minicoy in Assam; and the states of Delhi, Himachal Pradesh, Manipur, and Tripura); (6) develops textbooks and prepares and encourages the preparation of educational materials in general; (7) organizes educational conferences, seminars, and workshops; (8) has some responsibility for the propagation of Hindi; and (9) has certain responsibilities for higher education.[4]

The federal government has established a University Grants Commission, similar to that of the United Kingdom. It allocates national funds for the support of universities that are centrally controlled and makes grants to development schemes of state controlled universities.

The Role of the State in Education

THE REAL administrative units for education are the states. Four different groups of states organize their educational systems in different ways according to the nature of their population and their economic strength. Group A consists of former provinces of British India. Group B is made up of states constructed from the former princely states. States in groups A and B have complete responsibility for providing the necessary educational facilities and delegate the management of elementary schools to local governmental bodies. Each state has a Minister of Education who is responsible to his state legislature and has a directorate of administrative officials. The

4 Kathryn G. Heath, *Ministries of Education*, p. 333.

great majority of the people live in group A and B states. Only about 10 million people live in groups C and D, and their educational affairs are administered by the National Ministry of Education.

With the phenomenal increase in enrollments at all levels of the school system, and the corresponding expansion of the teaching force, has developed the problem of lowered standards, which has been growing increasingly acute. Both elementary and secondary schools have been affected but, because they provide preparation for the universities and for new teachers, the improvement of secondary schools is the crux of this problem, and Indian educators have been much concerned about finding a solution.

The national and state ministries have been dealing steadily with the problem of expanding all educational services. The changes that have taken place since India gained independence are indicated in some measure in Table 20–1, which shows the number of institutions in operation, with their enrollments, in various years. It should be noted that the figures for 1936–37 include Pakistan as well as India but do not include the former princely states, for which figures were not available. Figures for the last periods are for the Republic of India and include all groups of states.

Many new institutions have been established by the different states, most of them technical or vocational schools, but there are some new universities. A high proportion of the secondary schools and

TABLE 20–1
Education in India, 1936–59

LEVEL OF EDUCATION	BRITISH INDIA 1936–37		REPUBLIC OF INDIA 1949–50		REPUBLIC OF INDIA 1958–59	
	Institutions	Enrollment	Institutions	Enrollment	Institutions	Enrollment
Elementary	197,227	10,538,000	206,898	17,402,000	410,999	30,665,815
Secondary	14,414	2,495,000	19,926	4,709,000	39,597	8,515,499
Vocational	1,542	82,000	1,850	151,000	3,563	342,448
Teacher training	—	—	—	—	974	89,514
Universities	16	9,500	28	17,000	40	67,104
Colleges	363	118,000	732	1,046,000	1,497	876,314
Totals	213,562	13,342,000	239,434	33,325,000	456,670	40,556,694

SOURCES: Table 20–1 was constructed from figures in the *UNESCO World Handbook*, I, 1951, and III, 1961; *The Statesman's Yearbook, 1952*, London: Macmillan & Co., Ltd., 1952; and *Education in India, 1958–59*, New Delhi: Ministry of Education, 1962.

colleges are run by private groups. The states control the salary schedules and working conditions of teachers and set the maximum amounts that may be charged as fees. Detailed curricula are prescribed and official textbooks adopted. Most schools, whether public or private, receive aid from state funds. For the private schools this amounts to from 25 to 30 percent of the total approved budget.[5] Centralization of school administration is a heritage from the days of British rule, but it has been increased under the state governments in the field of secondary education.

The Role of Local Subdivisions in Education

ALTHOUGH the state ministries of education have almost complete control over elementary and secondary education, they have chosen to delegate responsibility for elementary schools to the local subdivisions of government. Provision for elementary education is in the hands of the municipalities in the cities and towns, and in local district boards in the rural areas. The local governing authority sets up a school board, made up of members from the governing council and others appointed from the community. Usually these appointed members are experts in education; one must be a woman, and at least one must represent the backward groups in the community. In a minor way, and with less authority, these school boards resemble the local education authorities in Great Britain. The school board appoints an education officer as a sort of local superintendent of schools. He is in charge of the operation of schools and is responsible for seeing that ministerial regulations are followed. Since regulations governing matters such as courses of study, textbooks, salaries of teachers, length of school term, vacations, and examinations are set by state authorities, the local boards have little responsibility and, unfortunately, in many cases these local groups have proved neither efficient nor enthusiastic; nor have they sufficient money.

Finance

DURING the last years of British rule, figures indicate that about 60 percent of the financial support of education came from state funds, 18 percent from rural local units, 13 percent from municipal funds,

[5] Reller and Morphet, *Comparative School Administration*, p. 240.

TABLE 20–2

Indian Expenditures on Education, 1957 (in millions of rupees)

SOURCE	EXPENDITURES	PERCENTAGE
Central government	141.8	6.9
State governments	1,154.0	55.9
Local governments	176.1	8.5
Fees	401.0	19.5
Endowments and gifts	64.4	3.1
Other sources		
(not specified)	125.8	6.1
Total	2,063.1	100.0

SOURCE: *UNESCO World Survey of Education*, III, 1961, p. 660. Reprinted by permission of UNESCO.

3.5 percent from fees, and 5.5 percent from all other sources. In the past, grants had been made by the central government to assist the provinces in their educational expenditure, but these had disappeared by about 1921. Very large increases in educational expenditures have been made, but some of the states have been unable to meet the required increases. Table 20–2 shows sources of funds for 1957.

Organization of Education

ACCORDING to the Constitution, education shall be secular (in tax-supported schools), free, and compulsory between the ages of 6 and 14. It is expected that the goal of having all children within this age group actually in school may be reached by 1976. In the meantime, efforts are being intensified to get all children into school at least until age 11.

Four levels of teaching are recognized in the Indian school pattern: elementary, four or five years for 6- to 10-year-olds; middle, three years for the 11- to 13-year-olds; secondary, four years for the 14- to 17-year-olds; and higher education, three to five years of specialized training. There are some variations between the states. When universal free and compulsory education for all children up to the age of 14 has been achieved, the secondary stage will be set at three years, as will the college course for the bachelor's degree. Figure

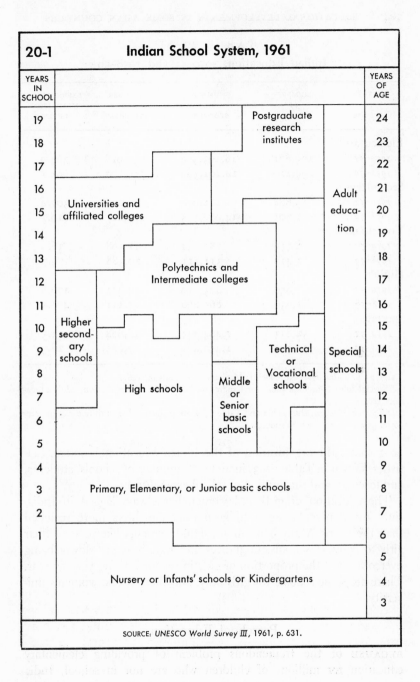

20-1   **Indian School System, 1961**

YEARS IN SCHOOL		YEARS OF AGE

Postgraduate research institutes

Universities and affiliated colleges

Polytechnics and Intermediate colleges

Higher secondary schools

High schools

Middle or Senior basic schools

Technical or Vocational schools

Adult education

Special schools

Primary, Elementary, or Junior basic schools

Nursery or Infants' schools or Kindergartens

SOURCE: *UNESCO World Survey III*, 1961, p. 631.

TABLE 20-3
Indian Education, 1950–51 and 1958–59

TYPE OF SCHOOL	NUMBER OF SCHOOLS	NUMBER OF STUDENTS	NUMBER OF TEACHERS	EXPENDITURE IN MILLION RUPEES
Elementary				
1950–51	209,671	18,293,976	537,918	364.9
1958–59	299,220	24,101,399	715,177	662.1
Secondary				
1950–51	29,884	5,232,009	212,000	307.4
1958–59	53,302	14,078,334	471,207	819.3
Vocational				
1950–51	2,339	187,194	11,598	36.9
1958–59	3,410	311,313	20,388	79.7
Higher				
1950–51	850	403,519	24,453	176.8
1958–59	1,650	865,696	45,531	428.5
Special*				
1950–51	52,813	1,404,443	16,684	23.3
1958–59	51,300	1,450,474	27,005	28.9

SOURCE: *India, 1961*, New Delhi: Ministry of Education, 1961.

* Special schools include those for handicapped children, art instruction, adult education, etc.

Differences between this Table and Table 20-1 are probably due to differences in categorizing schools in the two sources.

20-1 shows the organization of the Indian educational system. Statistics, shown in Table 20-3, include the number of schools, students, and teachers, and the amount of school expenditures.

The education of girls and women has always lagged in India, since many parents prefer to keep their daughters more secluded than their sons. Many Muslim and Hindu parents like to send their girls to convent schools. Prejudices and traditions are slowly being overcome, and the proportion of girls in school is rising year by year. There are some schools for girls only, and there is one women's university.

Preschool Education

BECAUSE of the tremendous problem of providing elementary education for millions of children who are not in school, India has not been able to devote much attention to preschool programs. Facilities are inadequate, and there are only a few nursery schools or kindergartens scattered through urban areas. In 1959 the government reported 1,190 schools enrolling 111,391 children.

Elementary Education

WHILE the elementary schools are mainly supported by the state, they are operated and maintained by the local government units. Depending upon the economic and social development of the particular state, these schools may cover four, five, or six years. The curriculum is based upon the mother tongue, but, depending upon the state, the children may also need to learn the regional language. Elementary arithmetic and weights and measures, history and geography are taught. There is much variation between the states in these social studies. Most schools place strong emphasis on health habits and physical fitness. Science may or may not be included; it is usually not a part of the prescribed curriculum. There is no course in religion in the public schools, but there is some stress on moral and spiritual values. Most elementary schools offer instruction in handicrafts: spinning, weaving, clay modeling, leather work, and so on. This varies according to the regional occupations. Some schools maintain school gardens.

Auxiliary services such as health surveys and medical inspection are relatively undeveloped but are improving. Some schools for the blind and deaf are operating, but schools for the mentally handicapped are rare. Physical training camps have been established in some states. An audio-visual center under the Union Ministry has been doing good work and is trying to extend its activities.

Basic Education

MAHATMA Gandhi believed that all education should be craft-centered. His teaching placed particular stress on spinning and weaving. Some of his disciples felt that the craft school was the answer to the problems of India after independence. They proposed a school program based equally on literacy and the three R's on the one hand, and practical crafts on the other. Some of the more extreme advocates of this policy believed that a school could support itself through the sale of articles or materials produced by the students, and that no tax support would be necessary. This idea is similar to that of the self-supporting schools of Communist China. It was soon abandoned, but the idea of a basic school, teaching elementary subjects and crafts, has been widely accepted. In some ways it was a reaction against the bookish education prevalent under the British rulers.

Basic schools may offer from four to eight years of courses, with elementary subjects and cottage crafts and agriculture emphasized. They look at the school as a community, where children learn democracy by living in its atmosphere. Basic schools are inclined to consider the curriculum as an integrated whole, rather than as a collection of separate subjects.

Children, and adults, enrolled in basic schools take great interest in community activities and improvements. Programs of sanitation and cleaning, improved water services, and the like are frequently a part of the school program. One might say that the distinction between school and community is less evident than in more formal school programs. The national programs of providing agricultural and homemaking extension services and community development programs have increased interest in the basic school. Basic schools and more formalized elementary schools (which also offer craft work) may be found throughout the country.

The middle schools, which may be two or three years, ought probably to be classed as elementary in level. Their avowed purpose is to prepare pupils for high school work, and in future plans it is intended to consider the elementary level as extending for eight years, from ages 6 to 14. The middle school is sometimes joined to an elementary school, or in some places to a high school.

Secondary Education

HIGH school programs are two to four years in length. By 1976 it is proposed that all high schools be three-year programs, followed by the three-year college course. Traditionally the only purpose of a high school education has been to prepare for university entrance examinations. Under the British most secondary education was conducted in English; since independence most of the high schools teach in the regional language and offer English as an elective subject. The development of secondary education in India is indicated in Table 20–4.

TABLE 20–4
Trends in Secondary Education in India

YEAR	GENERAL SECONDARY		VOCATIONAL		TEACHER TRAINING	
	Enroll-ment	Percentage female	Enroll-ment	Percentage female	Enroll-ment	Percentage female
1930	1,122,420	5	44,786	12	32,163	22
1935	1,456,420	9	52,678	14	27,133	27
1940	1,820,355	12	64,467	17	31,331	29
1945	2,719,985	13	59,065	20	31,411	30
1950	4,817,011	17	120,505	19	70,063	26
1955	6,826,605	20	159,101	*	90,914	28
1959	8,515,499	19	342,448	25	89,514	28

sources: Table 20–4 was constructed from *UNESCO World Handbook*, III, 1961, p. 661, and *Education in India, 1958–59*, Ministry of Education, Republic of India, New Delhi, 1962.
* Figure not available.

The curriculum of the average secondary school in India is still pedantic and dominated by examinations. Languages are very important; Hindi is a compulsory subject for all, and where it is not the regional tongue it is taught as a second language. Pupils who expect to go on to college or university usually need to take English, which is still the best door to higher education. Crafts are taught in the middle schools, but less often in the high schools. In addition to the required languages, in the better schools an Indian student may choose three other fields from the following areas: humanities, science, technology, commerce, agriculture, fine arts, or home science.

A Ford Foundation report described secondary education as "one of the weakest links in the chain of Indian education." Yet it holds a pivotal position in the whole system. Criticisms of academic standards in the colleges reflect on high school preparation. Since the secondary schools are the main source of supply for elementary teachers, the improvement of elementary education depends on improving the high schools.[6]

Although secondary teachers are paid better than those in the elementary schools, the salaries are still inadequate, conditions of serv-

[6] *The Ford Foundation and Foundation-supported Activities in India*, Ford Foundation, 32 Ferozshah Road, New Delhi, 1962, p. 72.

ice poor, and status in society comparatively low. University teachers have high status, but secondary teachers do not rank well, and elementary teachers are even lower. Standards in secondary schools cannot be raised until the quality of teachers and teaching are improved.

A secondary Education Commission appointed by the central government has made a number of recommendations for the improvement of high schools. At present, undergraduate programs in the colleges and universities provide for a two-year intermediate program leading to the Intermediate Examination. This is followed by another two years of instruction before the final examination for the degree. The Commission recommended that the first year of the present intermediate stage be added to the high school course and the second year be added to the regular college degree course. They also recommended that the traditional, university-preparatory high schools be modified to become "multi-purpose" schools, in some ways like the American comprehensive high school. They felt that a variety of courses in science, technology, commerce, agriculture, homemaking, and the fine arts should be available, according to the aptitudes and interests of the pupils. Indian pupils are still accustomed to regard the high school as a path leading to the university and a white collar job. Efforts are being made to change this attitude and to direct more secondary students into practical fields, with a view of providing more trained personnel required by the rapid industrialization of the country. Some financial support is being offered to high schools if they will add one or more technical or vocational areas to their classical curricula. This gives more choice to students and frees the secondary schools a little from the restrictions of university examinations and university prescriptions.

EXAMINATIONS

External examinations are very important in Indian education. The system was inherited from the British, but it has been extended and now grips the entire educational program. For a hundred years the system of public examinations, dominated by the universities, has largely controlled the high school curriculum. It has determined who would successfully complete the secondary course and proceed to higher education. Since the majority of Indian secondary students aim at the university, this has meant a whole course permeated by the necessity of passing the all-important School Leaving Certificate

Examination. The attempt to make secondary schools more "multi-purpose" and provide other incentives for secondary work than college entrance will succeed or fail depending very much on loosening the grip of university examinations on school leaving.

In the universities, examinations are widely criticized as an evil. It has been asserted that students direct their study entirely toward passing the end-of-year examinations. They may neglect to study for eight months and then cram intensively during the last month on notes, guides, and questions asked in previous examinations. Practically no check is made on daily assignments, and large classes make it difficult or impossible to administer periodic tests during the year. Usually the students identify their test papers by number rather than by name, to avoid favoritism on the part of examiners. Because of the tremendous number of papers to be graded, there must be a great number of examiners marking papers, and it is difficult to achieve consistency in grading standards.

The magnitude of the examination process can be illustrated by the fact that the Examination Board for a portion of the former Bombay state in one year examined more than 100,000 secondary school students, in 70 different subjects and in 40 cities. The same bulk of examination papers confronts the examiners for the universities, with their many affiliated colleges.[7]

Students pay fees to take examinations, and the income from these fees amounts to a considerable part of the budget of the universities. The University of Rajasthan has received about one-half of its total income from such fees; the University of Calcutta over 35 percent. The University of Agra has received fifteen times as much from examination fees as from government grants.[8]

Private Schools

ONE result of the long British rule in India was the development of private schools organized on the plan of the public schools of England. Although the public schools have been much discussed and criticized in Great Britain in recent years, their copies in India still seem to be popular, and enrollments are high. India has an Indian Public Schools Conference, patterned after the Headmasters'

---

[7] Reller and Morphet, *op. cit.*, p. 248.

[8] Oliver C. Carmichael, *Universities, Commonwealth and American*, 1959, p. 123.

Conference in Britain. Not all of the private schools belong to the I.P.S.C., but all are affected by the standards of these schools.

Before independence the sons of rajahs and other princes were sent to the private boarding schools, and much of the financial support for these schools came from the Indian princes. It is reported that one young aristocrat arrived at school on an elephant, and that another was accompanied by a retinue of 300 servants. Some of the noble students had servants to cook their meals and lay out their books on their desks.[9] Since independence there have not been such spectacular deviations from normal school procedures, but many upper-class Indians prefer to send their children to such private schools. Leading people want their children to have a good education in English—Nehru's sister recently called English "our window on the world"—and often the standard of English teaching is higher in private than in state schools.

Technical Education

TECHNICAL and vocational schools are making reasonable progress in India. Most of the states have been more interested in establishing new state-supported technical schools and colleges than they have been in increasing the number of state high schools. In the larger cities courses are available in a number of fields, particularly in textiles, metallurgy, aeronautical engineering, and chemical technology. Special grants have been made by the Central Ministry to technical and engineering schools to improve facilities and equipment. An All-India Council for Technical Education has been established in order to study the best methods of developing technical and commercial education.

University Education

IN 1900 there were four universities in India, patterned after British traditions. Fifteen more were established between 1900 and 1947, and fourteen others since independence, making a total of 33 today. In addition, there are about 650 affiliated colleges, of two types: liberal arts colleges that offer courses in arts or sciences, and professional colleges that generally offer instruction in one specialized

[9] "India's Public Schools," *The Times Educational Supplement*, London, December 28, 1962, p. 389.

field, such as commerce, teacher training, agriculture, forestry, art, or medicine. Most of the colleges are maintained by missionary or other religious groups, or by private foundations. Affiliation means that the complete teaching program is offered by the college, but the students take examinations prepared and administered by the university, and the university awards the degrees. These colleges would probably be called "university colleges" in England.

There has been a phenomenal rise in student enrollments in the colleges and universities. Much of this is due to the desire of students to improve themselves educationally and culturally; much more is due to the fact that many high school graduates cannot find suitable employment and hope that a college degree will improve their opportunities. It is not necessarily true that a university course assures a good position. There has been some concern about the number of college graduates who do not find suitable positions, and this has meant a certain amount of unrest and dissatisfaction. Too many university students choose courses leading to managerial and governmental positions; too few prepare for industrial and technological work. Observers have noted the attitude that holders of degrees expect to find white collar jobs and refuse to take lower-level positions. An Indian engineer trained in the United Kingdom or in the United States may feel that he should sit at a desk and direct others instead of going out into the field to construct irrigation ditches.

As mentioned before, undergraduate programs provide for a two-year intermediate course. There have been recommendations that the first year of the intermediate course be returned to the high school and that the university course be three years, as in Britain. This change will probably depend upon an improvement being made in secondary academic standards, or it will result in still further lowering the standards of the colleges.

Many observers, Indian and foreign, have commented upon the low standards of achievement in many Indian universities. This is due in part to inadequate secondary preparation, and also to the fact that many students of borderline ability seek university training in order to get better positions. It is also due to the large size of classes, with no opportunities for individual attention from the teachers. The situation has been intensified by the policy of changing from English to the regional language as the medium of instruction. There are not a sufficient number of adequately trained university-level lecturers in all of these languages, nor are there adequate textbooks.

Most of the languages lack a rich vocabulary of scientific and technological terms. The system of affiliation with a university of a large number of small colleges and institutes, of varying quality, results in a high rate of failure in both the intermediate and degree examinations. The University of Calcutta, which is one of the academically strong schools, has 111 affiliated institutions and an enrollment of potential candidates for examination that totals over 100,000 students. Most of the teaching has to be coaching to prepare for examinations.

There are no privately supported universities in India. Four of the universities are totally supported by the federal government. The others are state-supported, but receive some federal grants. Funds from the central government are administered by the University Grants Commission, made up of a permanent chairman and eight part-time members. It is called upon to advise the government on all matters pertaining to higher education and to allocate funds appropriated by Parliament. Funds distributed to state universities usually support graduate work and research activity. A large part of the funds available are used to help build and equip new university buildings for science and technology.

More and more women are attending universities in India. The only university for women in the British Commonwealth is the Shreemati Nathibai Damodar Thackserset Women's University, which stresses training in homemaking and nursing. Many other universities offer courses in these fields.

Graduate work began in the three original Indian universities in 1927. By 1951 some of the affiliated colleges were permitted to offer graduate work. The program of advanced study has developed rapidly since independence. The University of Calcutta offers graduate work in 32 subjects.[10]

The complete elementary and secondary course takes eleven years in most states, and in some it takes only ten. This means that Indian students come to the university younger than would be the case in other countries. It is reported that it is not uncommon to find 14-year-old boys and girls in the first-year classes.[11] The immaturity of the students and the low academic standards in the secondary schools force the university teachers to "teach down" to the level of the

[10] Carmichael, op. cit., p. 32.

[11] A. R. Dawood and K. G. Saiyidian, "Relationship Between Secondary Schools and Universities—India," Year Book of Education, 1959, p. 489.

students, thus lowering university standards. "It is not surprising, therefore, that the standard of the average Indian undergraduate is generally inferior to that of a graduate of a European or American University." [12] Another result of the admissions policy has been the high rate of failure in the colleges and universities. It has been estimated that of every 1,000 students who matriculate not more than 100 graduate.[13] There has also been much discussion about the poor student discipline in India. Riots and strikes are not uncommon, and defiance of rules and ignoring of university regulations are other forms of indiscipline. One university, Banaras, was closed by its Executive Committee in 1956 because of "acts of grave indiscipline and defiance of law, committed systematically and in an organized manner." Humayun Kabir, a former secretary of the Central Ministry of Education, made a report on the situation. He believed that the causes of student unrest and indiscipline were lack of leadership by the teachers; economic difficulties of the students; loss of idealism; and general defects of the educational system.[14]

Adult Education

EDUCATION of adults is very important in a developing country such as India. There is a great need to raise standards in literacy, health, sanitation, and handicrafts. A basic aim has been the reduction of illiteracy. At the time of independence it was estimated that more than 85 percent of the population was illiterate. The improvement attained in recent years is shown in Table 20–5. It has been announced that the aim of the government is to reduce illiteracy by 50 percent in the next five years. Indian educators prefer to call the program "social education" rather than adult education, because in addition to literacy the aims include training in crafts, health, and sanitation.

A number of social education centers have been opened in the various states. Delhi has experimented with a Social Caravan consisting of four large trailers which contain a mobile theater, moving picture projector, a library, and a lecture and demonstration room. The caravan camps in a village for three or four days and then moves on. This venture was so successful that several more Caravans were

[12] *Ibid.*, p. 489.
[13] Carmichael, *op. cit.*, p. 314.
[14] *Ibid.*, p. 313.

TABLE 20-5

Literacy in India (percentages of population)

YEAR	MALES	FEMALES	TOTAL
1951	24.8	7.87	16.5
1961	33.9	12.8	23.7

SOURCE: *India, 1961,* New Delhi: Ministry of Education, 1961.

organized. Mobile cultural squads follow the Caravans to continue the work begun. UNESCO is giving valuable assistance to these activities.

Kabir believes that the presence of hundreds of thousands of European and American troops in India during the war demonstrated to the Indians the higher living standards of the West. This contrast is used to emphasize the advantages to be gained from freedom and education and to stimulate programs for local improvement in Indian communities.[15]

A variety of extension courses in many fields are being developed by the colleges and universities. The University Grants Commission provides financial assistance to those institutions which establish such programs. Various extension and home demonstration services are working in the field of community improvement, and providing valuable adult education programs.

The Training and Status of Teachers

AS IN all rapidly developing nations, the problem of recruiting and training an adequate supply of qualified teachers is a very difficult one. The central government has set up an advisory body to assist in these matters. It is called the National Council of Educational Research and Training, and helps in the training of upper-level administrative officers, conducts research, and provides extension services for in-service training. But the major responsibility in the area of teacher training remains with the states.

Although the minimum training for elementary teachers has

---

[15] Humayun Kabir, "Education for Village Improvement in India," *Education for Better Living* (Yearbook on Better Living Around the World, 1957), U.S. Office of Education, Bulletin No. 9, Washington, 1956, p. 296.

been set at two years of teacher education in addition to completion of the middle school, at least one-third of the teachers employed have had no professional training. Some of them have had one year or less. Although there are nearly 1,000 teacher training schools in the country, most of them are very small. A few of the more advanced states are trying to require passing of the university matriculation examination plus two years of professional training. The increase of enrollments and shortage of teachers has forced the states to resort to temporary expedients, such as emergency training schools and special short courses. Elementary teachers are appointed by inspectors of schools.

For secondary teachers the ideal sought is a university degree in arts or science plus one year of additional professional training. Many of the universities have teacher training colleges among their affiliated institutions, and all of the universities except three have schools or departments of education. Usually a second bachelor's degree, Bachelor of Teaching or Bachelor of Education, is awarded after one year of postgraduate work. Some universities give a master's degree in teaching, and a few the Ph.D. degree. High school teachers are appointed by the state director of public instruction from university graduates, or, in many cases, are promoted from the lower schools. In the latter case they may lack the training requirements expected.

Salary schedules vary between the states, but are generally very low, and below those for other professions. Secondary school teachers generally may expect higher pay scales than elementary teachers. Many of them tutor private students to supplement their salaries. Since most of the secondary schools are in towns and cities, working and living conditions are usually better for the secondary teachers than for those in elementary schools. Teachers working for state or local governments usually receive higher rates of pay than teachers in private schools.

The training curriculum for the elementary teacher includes methods in the subjects to be taught, psychology, and special preparation to teach crafts. Health and hygiene are stressed. Since secondary teachers usually specialize in one or two subjects, they take work in these fields and additional courses in methods and psychology. However, it is possible to select a teaching field in which one has had no work in college, but only the methods courses.

Plans and programs for the improvement of teacher education are being developed, both nationally and in the states. Regular meetings of representatives of the teachers' colleges are held to consult on common problems. Special attention has been given to improving the qualifications of headmasters of secondary schools. The Ford Foundation has assisted the Ministry of Education in setting up an extension service for secondary school teachers, and a variety of experiments and research projects are being undertaken.

India's Educational Plans

IT HAS become evident that the implementation of ambitious educational plans must proceed more slowly than it was originally hoped. The Kher Committee (headed by the late B. G. Kher, former Chief Minister of Bombay) appointed by the Central Advisory Board of Education, recommended in 1950 that compulsory education be introduced by two stages, composed of two five-year plans and one six-year plan. This proposal found favor and was intended to operate as follows:

1. The first five-year plan was to attempt to provide as much education as possible for the group aged 6 to 11 and to lay the foundations for further expansion.

2. The second five-year plan was to make education from 6 to 11 compulsory for all children.

3. The six-year plan was intended to raise the compulsory school age to 14, so that at the end of 16 years the whole scheme of compulsory education for all children to the age of 14 would be realized.

The Central Advisory Board recognized that certain objectives had to be kept in view, namely:

1. The early liquidation of illiteracy through the provision of universal, free, and compulsory *basic* education for all children of school age.

2. Provision of fundamental *social* education for adults which would not only make them literate, but endeavor to raise their material and cultural standards and widen their interests and outlook.

3. Provision for *technical* education so as to provide fully trained personnel for the industrial and technological projects which are directed toward raising the productivity and national wealth of the country.

4. Reorganization of *university* education in the light of new na-

tional needs and aspirations so as to provide effective leadership in the various fields.[16]

A reasonable beginning on a program of this nature was estimated to cost, during the first five years of the 16-year plan, about $500,000,-000 a year in addition to the going expenditures of about $65,000,-000. The Indian government was determined to go ahead, but realized that the rate of progress had to be geared to the general financial condition of the country.

The first five-year plan also stressed needs in building and in agriculture. The planners decided that education should not be entirely bookish and academic but should meet the immediate needs of the majority of the people, who live in rural areas and depend upon primitive agriculture and handicrafts for their livelihood.[17] The second five-year plan added concern for problems of industrial development. As a matter of fact, the great investment on new industrial plants creates a difficulty in finding funds to carry on the educational plans as rapidly as the planners had hoped. The third plan developed all of the previous activities, and increased stress on agriculture, communications, and transportation. By this time it was evident that the ideal of compulsory education could not be realized in sixteen years, but the planners still aimed at getting all children in school until age 14. Each year the government draws up an Educational Development Program, which is part of the overall national plan. New plans will follow from time to time, with new goals, and with new dates set for achieving original goals.

Like all of the newer, developing nations, India's educational system has been suffering from growing pains. But a good deal of solid progress has been made. Encouraged by the Central Ministry of Education, the states have accomplished many things. There have been many commissions, surveys, and committees of inquiry, and a number of excellent plans have been worked out and parts of them have been put into effect. Lack of finance has been a drag on rapid expansion; there must be a considerable increase in total national wealth before spectacular improvements can be expected. Although it is difficult to predict precisely the outcome of all this planning, it is evident that India is determined to press forward.

[16] *International Yearbook of Education, 1951*, pp. 143–44.
[17] Samuel Mather, "Education in India," *Current History*, February, 1956, p. 87.

Bibliography

General References

Belding, Robert E., *Students Speak Around the World*, Iowa City: privately printed, 1959.

Carmichael, Oliver C., *Universities, Commonwealth and American*, New York: Harper & Row, 1959.

Carter, Gwendolen M., Ranney, John C., and Herz, John H., *Major Foreign Powers*, New York: Harcourt, Brace & World, 1952.

Carter, Gwendolen M., and Herz, John H., *Major Foreign Powers*, Harcourt, Brace & World, 4th ed., 1962.

Educational Yearbook, International Institute of Teachers College, New York: Teachers College, Columbia University, annual volumes 1924–43.

Hans, N., *Comparative Education*, London: Routledge and Kegan Paul, 1949.

Heath, Kathryn G., *Ministries of Education: Their Functions and Organization*, Washington: U.S. Office of Education (Bulletin No. 21, 1961), 1962.

International Yearbook of Education, Paris and Geneva: UNESCO and International Bureau of Education, annual volumes.

Kandel, I. L., *Comparative Education*, Boston: Houghton Mifflin, 1933.

————, *The New Era in Education*, Boston: Houghton Mifflin, 1955.

————, *Types of Administration, with Particular Reference to the Educational Systems of New Zealand and Australia*, London: Oxford, 1938.

Kerr, Anthony, *Schools of Europe*, London: Bowes and Bowes, 1960.

King, Edmund J., *Other Schools and Ours*, New York: Holt, Rinehart and Winston, 1963.

————, *World Perspectives in Education*, New York: Macmillan, 1962.

Mallinson, Vernon, *An Introduction to the Study of Comparative Education*, New York: Macmillan, 1960.

Meyer, Adolphe, *Development of Education in the 20th Century*, Englewood Cliffs, N.J.: Prentice-Hall, 1949.

Moehlman, A. H., and Roucek, J. S. (editors), *Comparative Education*, New York: Dryden, 1951.

Reisner, Edward J., Nationalism and Education Since 1789, New York: Macmillan, 1929.
Reller, Theodore L., and Morphet, Edgar L. (editors), Comparative Educational Administration, Englewood Cliffs, N.J.: Prentice-Hall, 1962.
Sasnett, Martena T., Educational Systems of the World, Los Angeles: University of Southern California Press, 1952.
Scanlon, David G., International Education: A Documentary History, New York: Teachers College, Columbia University, 1960.
The Statesman's Yearbook, London: Macmillan, annual volumes.
Ulich, Robert, The Education of Nations, Cambridge: Harvard University Press, 1961.
World Handbook of Educational Organization and Statistics, Paris: UNESCO, 1952.
World Survey of Education, Paris: UNESCO, Vol. II, 1958, Vol. III, 1962.
Year Book of Education, London: Evans Bros. Ltd., annual volumes 1935–1952.
Year Book of Education, New York: Harcourt, Brace & World, annual American editions published since 1953.

United States

Bereday, George Z. F., and Volpicelli, L. (editors), Public Education in America, New York: Harper & Row, 1959.
Biennial Survey of Education in the United States, Washington: U.S. Office of Education (issued biennially, several years late).
Bogue, Jesse P., The Community College, New York: McGraw-Hill, 1950.
Callahan, Raymond E., An Introduction to Education in American Society, New York: Knopf, 1960.
Conant, James Bryant, Education and Liberty, Cambridge: Harvard University Press, 1953.
————, The American High School Today, New York: McGraw-Hill, 1959.
Cressman, George B., and Benda, Harold W., Public Education in America, New York: Appleton-Century-Crofts, 1961.
Educational Policies Commission, The Structure and Administration of Education in American Democracy, Washington: National Education Association, 1938.
————, The Unique Function of Education in American Democracy, Washington: National Educational Association, 1937.
Hansen, Kenneth M., Public Education in American Society, New York: Dodd, Mead, 1960.
Hillway, Tyrus, Education in America Society, Boston: Houghton Mifflin, 1961.

Hughes, James, *Education in America*, New York and Evanston: Harper & Row, 1960.

Johns, Roe L., and Morphet, Edgar L., *Financing the Public Schools*, Englewood Cliffs, N.J.: Prentice-Hall, 1956.

Lee, Gordon C., *An Introduction to Education in Modern America*, New York: Holt, 1957.

Miller, Van, and Spalding, Willard B., *The Public Administration of American Schools*, New York: Harcourt, Brace & World, 1952.

National Education Association, *Fiscal Authority of City School Boards*, Washington: National Education Association (Research Bulletin No. 28), 1950.

————, *The American Public School Teacher*, Washington: National Education Association, 1963.

Pounds, Ralph L., and Bryner, James R., *The School in American Society*, New York: Macmillan, 1959.

Statistical Abstract of the United States, 1962, Washington: Bureau of the Census, U.S. Department of Commerce, 1962.

Thayer, V. T., *The Role of the School in American Society*, New York: Dodd, Mead, 1960.

Great Britain

Adamson, J. W., *English Education 1789–1902*, London: Cambridge University Press, 1930.

Central Advisory Council for Education in England, *School and Life*, London: H.M.S.O., 1947.

Dent, H. C., *Education in Transition*, London: Routledge and Kegan Paul, 1945.

————, *Secondary Education for All*, London: Routledge and Kegan Paul, 1949.

————, *The Educational System of England and Wales*, London: University of London Press, 1961.

Education Act, 1944, London: H.M.S.O., 1944.

Educational Reconstruction (White Paper), London: H.M.S.O., 1943.

Education in 1963 (The Annual Report of the Ministry of Education), London: H.M.S.O., 1964.

Education in Scotland in 1963 (The Annual Report of the Secretary of State for Scotland), Edinburgh: H.M.S.O., 1964.

Everett, Samuel, *Growing Up in English Secondary Schools*, Pittsburgh: University of Pittsburgh Press, 1959.

Higher Education in the United Kingdom, A Handbook for Students from Overseas and Their Advisers, London: Longmans, Green and Co., Ltd. (issued biennially).

Kneebone, R. M. J., *I Work in a Secondary Modern School*, London: Routledge and Kegan Paul, 1957.

Lowndes, G. A. N., *The English Educational System*, London: Hutchinson, 1960.
Ministry of Education, *The Public Schools and the General Education System* (The Fleming Report), London: H.M.S.O., 1944.
————, *Statistics of Education, 1963, Parts I and II*, London: H.M.S.O., 1964.
————, *Ministry of Education Pamphlets*, London: H.M.S.O.
    No. 2. *A Guide to the Educational System of England and Wales*, 1945
    No. 3. *Youth's Opportunity (County Colleges)*, 1945
    No. 8. *Further Education*, 1947
    No. 9. *The New Secondary Education*, 1947
    No. 15. *Seven to Eleven*, 1949
    No. 17. *Challenge and Response (Emergency Training Colleges)*, 1950
    No. 28. *Evening Institutes*, 1956
    No. 30. *Education of the Handicapped Pupil*, 1955
    No. 31. *Health Education*, 1955
    No. 33. *Post-War School Buildings*, 1957
————, *The Future Pattern of the Education and Training of Teachers*, London: H.M.S.O., 1962.
Norwood, Cyril, *The English Tradition of Education*, London: John Murray, 1929.
Sharp, John, *Educating One Nation*, London: Max Parrish, 1959.
United Kingdom Information Service, *Technological Education in Britain*, London: H.M.S.O., 1959.
University Grants Committee, Various reports on British universities, London: H.M.S.O.

France

Berger, Ina, "Professional Uneasiness Amongst Elementary Teachers in France," *International Review of Education*, Vol. 3, No. 3, 1957, pp. 343–44.
Comité France Actuelle, "Education in France Today," *France Actuelle*, Vol. 7, No. 15 (August 1, 1959), entire issue.
Dobinson, Charles H., "French Educational Reform," *Comparative Education Review*, Vol. 3, No. 1 (June, 1959), pp. 5–14.
Education in France: French System of Education, New York: Cultural Service of the French Embassy (no date).
Forestier, Denis, "Educational Reform in France," *Panorama*, Vol. 1, No. 3 (Autumn, 1959), pp. 6–7.
Gal, Roger, "The Development of Education in France, 1945 to 1961," *Phi Delta Kappan*, Vol. 43, No. 2 (November, 1961), pp. 60–63.
Hans, N., "Church and State in Education in Italy and France," *Com-*

parative Education Review, Vol. 2, No. 3 (February, 1959), pp. 10–12.

Hoyt, Deming N., "Educational Reform in France," *Harvard Educational Review*, Vol. 18 (October, 1948), pp. 220–27.

Jolly, Robert, "Regional Training Centers for Secondary Teachers in France," *Comparative Education Review*, Vol. 2, No. 3 (February, 1959), pp. 14–17.

Miles, Donald W., *Recent Reforms in French Secondary Education*, New York: Teachers College, Columbia University, 1953.

Richardson, C. A., Brule, Helene, and Snyder, Harold H., *The Education of Teachers in England, France, and the U.S.A.*, Paris: UNESCO, 1953.

Yale French Studies, No. 22 (Winter–Spring, 1958–59). (The entire issue is on French education.)

Australia

Annual Reports of State Departments of Education, Adelaide, Brisbane, Hobart, Melbourne, Perth, Sydney: Government Printer.

Australian College of Education, *The Challenge to Australian Education*, Melbourne: Cheshire, Ltd., 1961.

Australian Council for Educational Research, *Review of Education in Australia*, Melbourne: University of Melbourne Press.
Vol.   I. Cunningham, Kenneth S., and others, 1938
Vol.   II. Cunningham, Kenneth S., and Pratt, J. J., 1939
Vol. III. Waddington, D. M., and others, 1940–48
Vol. IV. In press.

"Australian Education: Cultural Activities and Research," *Official Yearbook of the Commonwealth of Australia*, 1963, Canberra: Government Printer, 1963, Chapter XVII.

Australian Journal of Education, Melbourne: Australian Council for Educational Research (published three times a year).

Butts, Freeman R., *Assumptions Underlying Australian Education*, Melbourne: Australian Council for Educational Research, 1955.

Cramer, J. F., *Australian Schools Through American Eyes*, Melbourne: University of Melbourne Press, 1936.

Jackson, R. W. B., *Emergent Needs in Australian Education*, Melbourne: Australian Council for Educational Research, 1962.

Kandel, I. L., *Types of Administration, with Particular Reference to the Educational Systems of New Zealand and Australia*, Wellington: New Zealand Council for Educational Research, and London: Oxford University Press, 1938 (reprinted 1961).

Webb, Leicester, *The Control of Education in New Zealand*, Wellington: New Zealand Council for Educational Research, 1937.

Canada

Althouse, J. G., *Structure and Aims of Canadian Education* (The 1949 Quance Lectures in Canadian Education), Toronto: W. J. Gage, Ltd., 1949.

Bissell, C. T. (ed.), *Canada's Crisis in Higher Education* (The Proceedings of the National Conference of Canadian Universities), Toronto: University of Toronto Press, 1957.

Campbell, H. L., *Curriculum Trends in Canadian Education* (The 1952 Quance Lectures in Canadian Education), Toronto: W. J. Gage, Ltd., 1952.

Chamberlin, William Henry, *Canada, Today and Tomorrow*, Boston: Little, Brown, 1942.

Dominion Bureau of Statistics, *The Organization and Administration of Public Schools in Canada*, Ottawa: Dominion Bureau of Statistics, 1960.

Education in Quebec (An Explanation of the System of Education in the Province of Quebec), Quebec: no date, no author, no publisher listed.

Frecker, G. A., *Education in the Atlantic Provinces* (The 1956 Quance Lectures in Canadian Education), Toronto: W. J. Gage, Ltd., 1956.

Gilmour, C. P., *The Canadian University and Its Neighbors* (The 1954 Quance Lectures in Canadian Education), Toronto: W. J. Gage, Ltd., 1954.

Jackson, R. W. B., *Educational Research in Canada Today and Tomorrow* (The 1961 Quance Lectures in Canadian Education), Toronto: W. J. Gage, Ltd., 1961.

Katz, Joseph (ed.), *Canadian Education Today*, Toronto: McGraw-Hill, 1956.

LaZerte, M. E., *Teacher Education in Canada* (The 1950 Quance Lectures in Canadian Education), Toronto: W. J. Gage, Ltd., 1950.

Lloyd, Woodrow S., *The Role of Government in Canadian Education* (The 1959 Quance Lectures in Canadian Education), Toronto: W. J. Gage, Ltd., 1959.

Lussier, Irénée, *L'Education Catholique et la Canada Français* (The 1960 Quance Lectures in Canadian Education), Toronto: W. J. Gage, Ltd., 1960.

MacKinnon, Frank, *The Politics of Education*, Toronto: University of Toronto Press, 1962.

McIlhone, J. T., "Catholic High School Education in Quebec," *Canadian Education*, Vol. 7, No. 4 (September, 1952), pp. 37–42.

Miller, James C., *National Government and Education in Federated Democracies, Dominion of Canada*, Philadelphia: Science Press, 1940.

Moffatt, H. P., *Educational Finance in Canada* (The 1957 Quance Lectures in Canadian Education), Toronto: W. J. Gage, Ltd., 1957.

Paton, J. M., *The Role of Teachers' Organizations in Canadian Education* (The 1962 Quance Lectures in Canadian Education), Toronto: W. J. Gage, Ltd., 1962.
Percival, W. P., *Across the Years*, Montreal: Gazette Printing Co., 1946.
———, *Life in School*, Montreal: Herald Press, 1946.
———, *Should We All Think Alike?* (The 1951 Quance Lectures in Canadian Education), Toronto: W. J. Gage, Ltd., 1951.
Phillips, C. E., *The Development of Education in Canada*, Toronto: W. J. Gage, Ltd., 1957.
———, *Public Secondary Education in Canada* (The 1955 Quance Lectures in Canadian Education), Toronto: W. J. Gage, Ltd., 1955.
Russell, David H., *Implications of Research for Canadian Classroom Practices* (The 1953 Quance Lectures in Canadian Education), Toronto: W. J. Gage, Ltd., 1953.
Swift, W. H., *Trends in Canadian Education* (The 1958 Quance Lectures in Canadian Education), Toronto: W. J. Gage, Ltd., 1958.

The Soviet Union

Ashby, Eric, *Scientist in Russia*, Harmondsworth: Penguin Books, 1946.
Bauer, R. A., *The New Man in Soviet Psychology*, Cambridge: Harvard University Press, 1952.
Bereday, George Z. F., Brickman, W. W., and Read, Gerald H., *The Changing Soviet School*, Boston: Houghton Mifflin, 1960.
Bereday, George Z. F., and Pennar, Jan, *The Politics of Soviet Education*, New York, Praeger, 1960.
Counts, George S., *The Challenge of Soviet Education*, New York: McGraw-Hill, 1959.
———, *Khrushchev and the Central Committee Speak on Education*, Pittsburgh: University of Pittsburgh Press, 1959.
DeWitt, Nicholas, *Soviet Professional Manpower*, Washington: National Science Foundation, 1955.
———, *Education and Professional Employment in the U.S.S.R.*, Washington: National Science Foundation, 1961.
Galkin, K., *The Training of Scientists in the Soviet Union*, Moscow: Foreign Languages Publishing House, 1954.
Johnson, William H. E., *Russia's Educational Heritage*, Pittsburgh: Carnegie Press, 1950.
King, Beatrice, *Changing Man: The Education System of the U.S.S.R.*, New York: John Day, 1937.
———, *Russia Goes to School*, London: William Heineman, Ltd., 1948.
King, Edmund J., *Communist Education*, New York: Bobbs-Merrill, 1963.
Korol, A. C., *Soviet Education for Science and Technology*, New York: Wiley, 1957.
Kulski, W. W., "Class Stratification in the Soviet Union," *Foreign Affairs*, Vol. 32, No. 1 (October, 1953), pp. 145–53.

Levin, Deanna, *Soviet Education Today*, London: Staples Press, 1959.
Medlin, William K., Lindquist, Clarence B., and Schmitt, Marshall L., *Soviet Education Programs*, Washington: U.S. Office of Education, Bulletin No. 17, 1960.
Read, Gerald H., "Trends and Problems in Soviet Education," *Phi Delta Kappan*, Vol. 42, No. 2 (November, 1960), pp. 49–51; 76–82.
Vigdarova, F., *Diary of a School Teacher*, Moscow: Foreign Languages Publishing House, 1954.
U.S. Office of Education, *Education in the U.S.S.R.*, Washington: U.S. Office of Education, Bulletin No. 14, 1957.
————, *Soviet Commitment to Education*, Washington: U.S. Office of Education, Bulletin No. 16, 1959.
————, *Bibliography of Published Materials on Russian and Soviet Education*, Washington: U.S. Office of Education (Studies in Comparative Education, OE–14033–3), 1960.
————, *Textbooks for Russian Schools*, Washington: U.S. Office of Education (Studies in Comparative Education, OE–14034–3), 1960.

There have been innumerable articles in current journals about Soviet education. For Russian articles on the subject see *Soviet Education*, a monthly journal in English giving translations of articles from many Soviet pedagogical journals.

West Germany

Bodenham, P. S., *Education in the Soviet Zone of Germany*, Washington: U.S. Office of Education, Bulletin No. 28, 1958.
British Foreign Office, *University Reform in Berlin*, London: H.M.S.O., 1949.
Education in Germany: An Introduction for Foreigners, Frankfort on the Main: Hochschule fur Internationale Pädagogische Forschung, 1954.
Huebner, Theodore, *The Schools of West Germany*, New York: New York University Press, 1963.
Kirkpatrick, Ursula, "The *Rahmenplan* for West German School Reform," *Comparative Education Review*, Vol. 4, No. 1 (June, 1960), pp. 18–25.
Lindegren, Alina M., *Germany Revisited: Education in the Federal Republic*, Washington: U.S. Office of Education, Bulletin No. 12, 1957.
Mann, Erika, *School for Barbarians*, London: Drummond, 1939.
Post-War Changes in German Education, Frankfurt: Office of the High Commissioner for Germany, U.S. Education and Cultural Division, 1951.
Schultze, Walter, "Recent Changes in Secondary Schools, Federal Republic of West Germany," *Phi Delta Kappan*, Vol. 43, No. 3 (November, 1961), pp. 64–68.

Japan

Alden, Jane, "Japanese Education in Review," *Department of State Bulletin*, Washington: Office of Public Affairs, Department of State, October 27, 1952.

Anderson, Ronald S., *Japan—Three Epochs of Modern Education*, Washington: U.S. Office of Education, Bulletin No. 11, 1959.

Gibney, Frank, *Five Gentlemen of Japan*, New York: Farrar, Straus, 1953.

Japanese Reform Council, *Education Reform in Japan*, Tokyo: Ministry of Education, 1950.

Ministry of Education, Tokyo. The following publications are printed in English:

Annual Report of the Japanese Ministry of Education (issued annually)

Local Expenditures on Education (issued annually)

Education in Japan—A Graphic Presentation (revised biennially)

School Lunch Programs in Japan with Statistics—A Graphic Presentation, 1955

Social Education in Japan, 1958

Science Achievement in Japan, 1959

Demand and Supply for University Graduates, 1958

Revised Curriculum in Japan for Elementary and Secondary Schools, 1960

The School Education Law, 1960

Youth Education in a Changing Society, 1961

A Survey of Japanese Education in 1960–61, with Statistics, 1961

Oshiba, Mamoru, *Four Articles on Japanese Education* (pamphlet), Tokyo: Maruzen Co., 1963:

1. "Education in Japan Before and After the Meiji Restoration"
2. "Japanese Education—After the Americans Left"
3. "Moral Education in Japan"
4. "Japanese Education Today"

Sansome, G. B., *Japan, A Cultural History*, New York: Century, 1931.

China

Barendsen, R. D., "Educational Changes in Chinese Areas," *School Life*, Vol. 43, No. 1 (September, 1960), pp. 19–21; 30.

———, "Learning, Labor and Life in Communist Chinese Schools," *School and Society*, Vol. 89, No. 2194 (Summer), pp. 274–76.

Chandra-sekhar, Sripati, *Red China: An Asian View*, New York: Praeger, 1961.

Cheng, J. C., "Half-Work and Half-Study in Communist China," *Pacific Affairs*, 32 (June, 1959), pp. 183–87.

Chi Tung-wei, *Education for the Proletariat in Communist China*, Hong Kong: Union Research Institute, 1956.

Chu, Don Chean, "Educational, Cultural, and Scientific Plans of Communist China," *School and Society*, Vol. 89, No. 2186 (February 11, 1961), pp. 58–59.

Chung Shih, *Education in Communist China*, Hong Kong: Union Research Institute, 1958.

Fisher, O., "Education in Communist China," *School and Society*, Vol. 87, No. 2156 (June 20, 1959), pp. 302–05.

Fraser, S., "Recent Educational Reforms in China," *School Review*, Vol. 69, No. 3 (Autumn, 1961), pp. 300–10.

Greene, Felix, *China, The Country Americans Are Not Allowed To Know*, New York: Ballantine Books, 1961.

Hu, C. T., *Chinese Education Under Communism*, New York: Teachers College, Columbia University, 1962.

Orleans, Leo A., *Professional Manpower and Education in Communist China*, Washington: National Science Foundation, 1960.

Yang, H. F., "Educational Revolution and Progress, 1949–1959," *School and Society*, Vol. 89, No. 2198 (November 4, 1961), pp. 378–81.

India

Eels, Walter Crosby, *Communism in Education in Asia, Africa, and the Far Pacific*, Washington: American Council on Education, 1954.

Kabir, Humayun, *Education in the New India*, London: George Allen & Unwin, Ltd., 1956.

Kanungo, Gostha Behari, *The Language Controversy in Indian Education*, Chicago: Comparative Education Center, University of Chicago, 1962.

Kaul, N., *A New Basis for Indian Educational Thought*, Baroda: N. K. Kate Publishing Co., 1953.

Ministry of Education, *Education in India*, 1958–59 (The 1958–59 Annual Report of the Ministry of Education, Government of India), New Delhi: Publications Civil Lines, 1962.

Nurullah, S., and Maik, J. P., *A History of Education in India*, London: Macmillan, 1951.

Planning Commission, Government of India, *Third Five Year Plan*, New Delhi: Planning Commission, 1960.

Woytinski, W. S., *India, the Awakening Giant*, New York: Harper & Row, 1957.

Zellner, Aubrey A., *Education in India*, New York: Bookman Associates, 1951.

Index

Boldface numbers indicate figures and tables.

A 4
B 5
C 6
D 7
E 8
F 9
G 0
H 1
I 2
J 3